MW00325442

Shakespeare's QUOTATIONS

A PLAYERS PRESS GUIDE

Trevor R. Griffiths
Trevor A. Joscelyn

PLAYERS PRESS

SHAKESPEARE'S QUOTATIONS
ISBN 0-88734-620-0
Library of Congress Catalog Number: 92-54180

PLAYERS PRESS, Inc.
P. O. Box 1132
Studio City, CA 91614-0132

This edition is published by arrangement with Longman Group U.K. Limited, London.

First published in the United Kingdom, 1985.

Simultaneously Published
U.S.A, U.K., Canada and Australia

Printed in the U.S.A.

Library of Congress Cataloging-in-Publication Data

Shakespeare, William, 1564-1616.
Shakespeare's quotations : a Players Press guide / (compiled by) Trevor R. Griffiths, Trevor A. Joscelyn.
p. cm.
Includes index.
ISBN 0-88734-620-0
1. Shakespeare, William, 1564-1616--Quotations. 2. Quotations. English. I. Griffiths, Trevor R. II. Joscelyn, Trevor A. III. Title.
PR2892.G68 1992 92-54180
822.3'3--dc20 CIP

Contents

In memory of Adrian Gunn and Joseph Lederer, *colleagues and friends.*

INTRODUCTION

Shakespeare has been quoted - and misquoted - for nearly 400 years; since at least 1592, when another writer, Robert Greene, laced an attack on him with a parody of a line from *Henry VI Part 2*. Since then, Shakespeare's lines have been enlisted by politicians spurred on by praises of English virtues, by lovers seeking to impress their loved ones with their borrowed eloquence, by ordinary people who see in his words a crystallization of their own hopes and fears.

Quotation always involves removing the lines quoted from their context and can lead to serious falsification if it is assumed that, for example, Hamlet's meditation on suicide or Jacque's Seven Ages of Man speech represents Shakespeare's own thoughts. In this book we have selected over 2000 quotations from Shakespeare's works - many of them familiar, some less so - and replaced them in a context. In the case of lines from the plays, this usually involves stating who says the lines to whom, in what context, and commenting on any other features which contribute to the words being particularly memorable; perhaps the quality of the expression, perhaps their subsequent use by others.

In our choice of quotations we have naturally included many old favourites, but the increased representation of the comedies and histories reflects their growing reputation since the established selections of Shakespearean quotations were made. As well as all the plays and poems substantially attributed to Shakespeare (including *The Two Noble Kinsmen*), we have included the will and epitaph. We have interpreted context in a wide sense to mean anything that is helpful to understanding the quoted lines. In our comments we sometimes give an approximate 'meaning' for an obscure word or phrase, but that 'meaning' is often only one of a number of possible readings. In a work of this kind the editors must rely heavily on the labours of many editors, scholars, and critics who have established reliable texts, elucidated difficult passages, and enhanced our knowledge of Shakespeare's period, life, and works. Our gratitude is great but our errors are our own. We are particularly grateful to Penguin Books Ltd for permission to use the texts of those volumes of the New Penguin Shakespeare that have so far been published; in the case of works not yet available in that series we have returned to the earliest authoritative editions and modernized spelling and punctuation.

The most important thing to remember about a quotation is that, however well-phrased or 'true' it may seem, it is best appreciated in the context of the work in which it appears. No quotation is an island of meaning itself - its meaning depends first on its place in the greater whole of which it is part. Shakespeare wrote poems and plays within certain conventions and we can never assume, except perhaps in the will, that he was writing in the first person - even the ' I ' of the sonnets does not necessarily correspond exactly with William Shakespeare, the man. In the plays a character's words may be undercut or disputed by the next character, or by the context, or by the action of the play. We hope that this collection will make it a little easier to appreciate this fact.

In preparing this work we have benefited not only from the work of all those scholars we have already acknowledged, but also from the material support and help of Caroline Thorley, Karen Swinden, and Craig Thomson.

To Kathy Rooney we owe our grateful thanks for her encouragement, help, guidance, and forebearance during the gestation of this book.

Trevor R. Griffiths *Trevor R. Joscelyne*

All's Well That Ends Well

1 'Twere all one
That I should love a bright particular star
And think to wed it, he is so above me.
In his bright radiance and collateral light
Must I be comforted, not in his sphere.
(I.1.84–8)

Helena, brought up in the household of the Countess of Rossillion, has fallen in love with the Countess's son, Bertram, who is, as she says, of a higher social class. She uses imagery drawn from Ptolemaic astronomy to make the contrast between their status, seeing them as confined to separate spheres.

2 The hind that would be mated by the lion
Must die for love.
(I.1.90–1)

Helena sees herself as a deer whose love for Bertram ('the lion') is inevitably doomed.

3 It is not politic in the commonwealth of nature to preserve virginity. Loss of virginity is rational increase, and there was never virgin got till virginity was first lost. That you were made of is mettle to make virgins. Virginity, by being once lost, may be ten times found; by being ever kept it is ever lost. 'Tis too cold a companion. Away with't!
(I.1.124–31)

Parolles, a braggart soldier and follower of Bertram, is talking to Helena about virginity, using sophistry to argue against the preservation of virginity. 'Got' means begotten.

4 Your virginity, your old virginity, is like one of our French withered pears: it looks ill, it eats drily.
(I.1.157–9)

Parolles continues to decry virginity to Helena.

5 Our remedies oft in ourselves do lie,
Which we ascribe to heaven. The fated sky
Gives us free scope, only doth backward pull
Our slow designs when we ourselves are dull.
(I.1.212–15)

Helena decides that her former view that she could do nothing about her love for Bertram was misguided, drawing ideas from astrology and theology to stress the importance of free will.

6 Was this fair face the cause, quoth she,
Why the Grecians sackèd Troy?
(I.3.68–9)
Lavatch, the Countess's Clown, sings this song to her while they await the arrival of Helena. The song is presumably occasioned by Helena's name, since the 'fair face' is that of Helen of Troy, whose abduction led the Greeks to besiege and sack the town of Troy.

7 That man should be at woman's command, and yet no hurt done!
(I.3.89–90)
Lavatch the Clown comments on his being a woman's servant, probably with a sexual innuendo.

8 This thorn
Doth to our rose of youth rightly belong.
(I.3.124–5)
The Countess muses on Helena's love for Bertram, seeing the pain it causes her as the thorn which goes together naturally with youth.

9 Mars dote on you for his novices!
(II.1.47)
Parolles, who has gone to the court with Bertram, bids farewell to some lords who are going off to the wars in Italy. He asks the god of war to take good care of them as his pupils.

10 Now, Dian, from thy altar do I fly,
And to imperial Love, that god most high,
Do my sighs stream.
(II.3.73–5)
Helena as a virgin has previously devoted herself to Diana, the chaste goddess, but she is now choosing a husband as her reward for curing the King of France. She therefore abjures her former goddess in favour of love.

11 From lowest place when virtuous things proceed,
The place is dignified by th'doer's deed.
Where great additions swell's and virtue none,
It is a dropsied honour . . .
Honours thrive

When rather from our acts we them derive
Than our foregoers.
(II.3.124–7, 134–6)

As her reward for curing the King of France, Helena has chosen Bertram as her husband; but Bertram has objected to the marriage, partly on the ground of their different social status. In this speech the King counters that Bertram's view is based on a mistaken reverence for inherited honour and on too little regard for the individual's innate honour. Similar conflicts of views run through much of the play in the form of arguments about male and female values, war and love, and inherited and achieved honour. 'Additions' means titles or honours; 'swell's' is short for swell us.

12 He wears his honour in a box unseen
That hugs his kicky-wicky here at home.
(II.3.277–8)

Bertram, appalled at being married off to Helena, has decided to go to the Italian wars before the marriage can be consummated. Parolles encourages him to do so with this dismissive view of domestic bliss. Although 'kicky-wicky' does not appear elsewhere, it is clearly a term of endearment or a pet name, meaning darling or lover.

13 Wars is no strife
To the dark house and the detested wife.
(II.3.289–90)

Bertram sees going to war as preferable to ('To') the available alternatives. The 'dark house' probably refers to the gloomy marital home but there may also be a reference to the madhouse, since madmen were often kept in darkness in this period.

14 A young man married is a man that's marred.
(II.3.296)

Parolles adopts a proverbial phrase to the context of Bertram's forced marriage. Once again the idea of honour is prominent.

15 The soul of this man is his clothes.
(II.5.43–4)

Lafeu, an old courtier, comments on Parolles to Bertram. He, unlike Bertram, has spotted Parolles's essential worthlessness.

16 Here comes my clog.
(II.5.53)

Bertram, unhappy at being forced to marry Helena, comments on her arrival, seeing her as being like a clog, a block of wood tied to an animal to stop it from straying which thus prevents it from following its own inclinations.

17 Strangers and foes do sunder and not kiss.
(II.5.86)
Helena, instructed by Bertram to leave for Rossillion before they have consummated their marriage, attempts unsuccessfully to beg at least a farewell kiss.

18 I knew a man that had this trick of melancholy hold a goodly manor for a song.
(III.2.8–9)
Lavatch, the Countess's Clown, is telling her that he thinks Bertram is a melancholy man because of the way that he sings while doing other things. In this remark he refers to the use of 'going for a song' to mean selling at a very low price – the melancholy man sold the manor very cheap, or he was so pleased by a song that he was willing to accept it as payment for the manor.

19 *When thou canst get the ring upon my finger, which never shall come off, and show me a child begotten of thy body that I am father to, then call me husband; but in such a 'then' I write a 'never'.*
(III.2.56–9)
Bertram's letter rejecting Helena, here read by Helena, is presumably meant to be no more than a hyperbolic rejection of her, but she eventually chooses to regard it as a set of folk-tale tasks which she sets about fulfilling in the rest of the play.

20 Let us assay our plot, which, if it speed,
Is wicked meaning in a lawful deed,
And lawful meaning in a lawful act,
Where both not sin, and yet a sinful fact.
But let's about it.
(III.7.44–8)
Helena has arrived in Florence, where she has met Diana who is being sexually pursued by Bertram. She has formulated a plot to fulfil Bertram's demands on her by persuading Diana to get his ring as a love token and to arrange a night-time assignation. Helena plans to substitute herself for Diana at this assignation in the hope that she will become pregnant as the result of their lovemaking. The result of the plot, as Helena's speech makes clear, will be paradoxical: Bertram intends to commit adultery ('wicked meaning'), but will actually make love to his wife ('a lawful deed'), and Helena will be sleeping with her husband ('a

lawful act'), which is what she intends ('lawful meaning'), so that what might appear sinful is in fact legitimate ('both not sin, and yet a sinful fact'). The final line reflects Helena's businesslike approach to getting things done. 'Speed' means succeed; 'meaning' means intention.

21 So you serve us
Till we serve you; but when you have our roses,
You barely leave our thorns to prick ourselves,
And mock us with our bareness.
(IV.2.17–20)
Diana distrusts Bertram's vows of undying love, complaining that men always make such vows ('so you serve us') until women agree to have sex with them ('we serve you'). According to Diana, using the familiar associations of flowers and love, when men have had sex they leave women exposed to the pricks of remorse.

22 The web of our life is of a mingled yarn, good and ill together. Our virtues would be proud if our faults whipped them not, and our crimes would despair if they were not cherished by our virtues.
(IV.3.70–3)
The First Lord, one of the brothers Dumaine, speaks these lines which many critics see as a key to the play in which 'realistic' and folk-tale elements coexist in an unstable mixture. The immediate occasion of the speech is the (false) news that Helena is dead and the nobles' anticipation of Bertram's reaction.

23 A whale to virginity.
(IV.3.215–16)
Parolles, believing that he has been captured by the enemy, is busy telling his captors – who are actually the Dumaine brothers demonstrating his falsity to Bertram – the secrets of the army. Here he is describing Bertram's attitude to virgins: he is like a whale swallowing all the small fish that come within reach.

24 Who cannot be crushed with a plot?
(IV.3.315)
Parolles has had his deficiencies exposed to Bertram but, as this line indicates, he remains resilient.

25 Simply the thing I am
Shall make me live.
(IV.3.323–4)

Parolles, his pretensions deflated and his hollowness exposed, decides that he will have to find another, more honest, means of getting his livelihood.

26 I am for the house with the narrow gate, which I take to be too little for pomp to enter; some that humble themselves may, but the many will be too chill and tender, and they'll be for the flowery way that leads to the broad gate and the great fire.

(IV.5.48–53)

Lavatch, the Countess's Clown, in joking with Lafeu, the old courtier, hopes for salvation, drawing on the biblical imagery of the narrow and difficult path to heaven and the broad path to hell. Shakespeare uses the idea of the flowery path to hell in *Hamlet* (see 35) and *Macbeth* (see 53) as well, though there is no biblical justification for it.

27 Natural rebellion done i'th'blade of youth.

(V.3.6)

The Countess asks the King to forgive Bertram for his folly in rejecting Helena, on the grounds that youth is naturally rebellious. 'Blade' means a plant's shoot.

28 Praising what is lost
Makes the remembrance dear.

(V.3.19–20)

The King comments on Lafeu's praise of Helena ('what is lost').

29 For we are old, and on our quickest decrees
Th'inaudible and noiseless foot of time
Steals ere we can effect them.

(V.3.39–41)

The King has decided that Bertram should marry Lafeu's daughter and wants to move quickly because of his age, at which time creeps up silently before things can be done.

30 'Tis but the shadow of a wife you see,
The name and not the thing.

(V.3.305–6)

The pregnant Helena has reappeared to claim Bertram. She is the ghost of a wife, an actor in the role of wife, an imitation of a wife (all conveyed by 'shadow'); she has the title ('name') but not the substance of a wife.

31 If she, my liege, can make me know this clearly
I'll love her dearly, ever, ever dearly.
(V.3.313–14)
Bertram, baffled to find Helena alive and pregnant by him, tells the King ('my liege') that if Helena ('she') can explain things to him he will love her. Some critics and audiences find his conditional response ungenerous, but those who see the play as testing the values of the Romance genre against those of the everyday world tend to view this as another example of Bertram's prosaic nature.

32 Mine eyes smell onions, I shall weep anon.
(V.3.318)
Lafeu, the old courtier, protests that the cause of his weeping is an external stimulus ('onions') rather than a sentimental reaction to the reunion of Bertram, Helena, and the Countess.

33 All yet seems well, and if it end so meet,
The bitter past, more welcome is the sweet.
(V.3.330–1)
The King ends the action of the play with a summing-up couplet which stresses the play's characteristic mixture of bitter and sweet and the conditional nature of the final reconciliation. 'Meet' means appropriately.

34 The King's a beggar, now the play is done.
(Epilogue 1)
The King speaks the epilogue, using the disparity between his commanding role in the play and his dependence, as an actor, on the audience's generosity to beg their applause.

Antony and Cleopatra

1 His captain's heart,
Which in the scuffles of great fights hath burst
The buckles on his breast, reneges all temper,
And is become the bellows and the fan
To cool a gypsy's lust.
(I.1.6–10)
In the opening speech of the play, Philo, a follower of Antony, is explaining to a companion, Demetrius, how Antony's martial values have been debased by his infatuation with Cleopatra. 'Reneges all temper' means renounces moderation. The pejorative use of 'gypsy' to indicate Cleopatra combines the

Renaissance belief that gypsies were of Egyptian origin with the early seventeenth-century cant use of the term to mean a woman.

2 Take but good note, and you shall see in him
The triple pillar of the world transformed
Into a strumpet's fool.
(I.1.11–13)

Philo's denunciation of Antony opposes his desertion of Roman military values to his embrace of Egyptian sensuality. Antony's designation as 'the triple pillar of the world' refers to his being one of the triumvirs (Lepidus and Octavius Caesar being the other two) who ruled the Roman world between them.

3 CLEOPATRA
If it be love indeed, tell me how much.
ANTONY
There's beggary in the love that can be reckoned.
CLEOPATRA
I'll set a bourn how far to be beloved.
ANTONY
Then must thou needs find out new heaven, new earth.
(I.1.14–17)

In the first exchange of Antony and Cleopatra, the vastness of their love is expressed in terms of wealth and distance that transcend the limits of the Roman Empire and comprehend the spiritual realm. 'Beggary' here signifies meanness and 'bourn' a boundary.

4 Let Rome in Tiber melt, and the wide arch
Of the ranged empire fall! Here is my space.
Kingdoms are clay.
(I.1.33–5)

Cleopatra has mocked Antony for being at the beck and call of Fulvia, his wife, and of Octavius Caesar, because a messenger has arrived from Rome. Antony's response is anarchic in its image of the destruction of empire. His elevation of his mistress ('my space') above 'kingdoms' is a commonplace of the love poetry of the period. 'Ranged' has given rise to much editorial comment, but the weight of philological evidence would suggest that it combines the sense of extent with a term from masonry indicating course or foundation, and so following the architectural image of 'arch'.

5 There's not a minute of our lives should stretch
Without some pleasure now. What sport tonight?
(I.1.46–7)
Antony's line indicates his enslavement to the sensual pleasures of Egypt and his rejection of the demands of Roman public life.

6 In Nature's infinite book of secrecy
A little I can read.
(I.2.10–11)
The soothsayer is speaking to Charmian and Iras, attendant women of Cleopatra, and to Alexas, the eunuch. Egypt is associated in the play with intuitive modes of perception in contrast to Rome's cool rationality. It was a medieval and Renaissance commonplace to conceive the world, or realm of nature, as a book to be read.

7 O, excellent! I love long life better than figs.
(I.2.33)
Charmian has just been told by the soothsayer that she will outlive Cleopatra. Her response is flippant, but the soothsayer's predictions in this scene are significant. Charmian does outlive her mistress, but only by a tragically brief span.

8 Mine, and most of our fortunes, tonight shall be drunk to bed.
(I.2.46–7)
Enobarbus is present at the fortune-telling session of the soothsayer with Charmian, Iras, and Alexas. He has on his entrance called for the preparation of a banquet with 'wine enough / Cleopatra's health to drink'. He therefore knows that the evening is to end in revelry and drunkenness.

9 He was disposed to mirth; but on the sudden
A Roman thought hath struck him.
(I.2.82–3)
Cleopatra is describing the changed disposition of Antony, who was last seen dedicating himself and the night to revelry. Antony's mind has turned to the news brought by the messenger from Rome. Immediately after these lines, Antony enters listening to the messenger's narrative. The essence of the statement contrasts the Roman world of public duty with the private world of the senses represented by Egypt.

10 These strong Egyptian fetters I must break,
Or lose myself in dotage.
(I.2.117–18)

These lines are delivered by Antony in an aside on learning of Rome's military setbacks from the messengers arrived from various parts of the Empire. The image of 'fetters' implies enslavement, while the term 'dotage', signifying feebleness of mind, had been applied to Antony by Philo in the first line of the play.

11 ANTONY She is cunning past man's thought.
ENOBARBUS Alack, sir, no; her passions are made of nothing but the finest part of pure love. We cannot call her winds and waters sighs and tears; they are greater storms and tempests than almanacs can report. This cannot be cunning in her; if it be, she makes a shower of rain as well as Jove.
(I.2.146–52)
Antony has decided to leave Egypt to see to affairs of state in the Empire. The hard-bitten Enobarbus, who has been entranced by Cleopatra, is pointing out the effect the news of Antony's departure will have upon the Queen. A dual perspective is given of Cleopatra through Antony's picture of a cunning enchantress and Enobarbus' vision of 'pure love' which rivals the forces of nature.

12 O, sir, you had then left unseen a wonderful piece of work, which not to have been blessed withal would have discredited your travel.
(I.2.154–6)
Enobarbus is responding to Antony's wish that he had never seen Cleopatra. Cleopatra is pictured by Enobarbus almost as if she were one of the wonders of the world. To depict the beauty of mankind's form as the masterpiece of nature's handiwork was a Renaissance commonplace.

13 This grief is crowned with consolation: your old smock brings forth a new petticoat; and indeed the tears live in an onion that should water this sorrow.
(I.2.168–71)
Although Enobarbus is smitten with Cleopatra's charms, he remains cynical about relations with women in general. His response to Antony's news of the death of his wife, Fulvia, is an example of this cynicism.

14 If you find him sad,
Say I am dancing; if in mirth, report
That I am sudden sick.
(I.3.3–5)
Cleopatra's instructions for the message that Alexas, the eunuch, is to bear to Antony are a demonstration of the wiles by which

she enslaves him. Variety of mood is the essence of her attraction.

15 CHARMIAN
In each thing give him way. Cross him in nothing.
CLEOPATRA
Thou teachest like a fool: the way to lose him.
(I.3.9–10)

The exchange of Charmian and Cleopatra opposes two contrasted views of how to keep a man. Of these two, the play seems to endorse Cleopatra's, provided you have her attractions and wiles. Ultimately though, the play suggests that only death ensures eternal fidelity and inseparability.

16 Eternity was in our lips and eyes,
Bliss in our brows' bent; none our parts so poor
But was a race of heaven.
(I.3.35–7)

Cleopatra is feigning illness and displeasure, fearing news of Antony's departure. Whilst not allowing him to speak, she is contrasting the high point of their union, which merited words ('Then was a time for words', line 34), with this separation, for which none are fitting. Her depiction of their love in spiritual absolutes ('eternity', 'bliss', 'heaven') reinforces the sense of deities: she as a Venus, he as a Mars. 'Bent' means arch.

17 This is the news: he fishes, drinks, and wastes
The lamps of night in revel.
(I.4.4–5)

This is Octavius Caesar's summary of the news from Egypt concerning Antony. The accusation derives from Sir Thomas North's translation of Plutarch's *The Lives of the Noble Grecians and Romanes* (1579), the main source of Shakespeare's play.

18 Give me to drink mandragora...
That I might sleep out this great gap of time
My Antony is away.
(I.5.4–6)

Cleopatra is speaking to Charmian. Mandragora, the juice of the mandragora or mandrake plant, was credited with strong narcotic powers in the Renaissance. Amongst other things, it was thought to be an aphrodisiac.

19 Where think'st thou he is now? Stands he, or sits he?
Or does he walk? Or is he on his horse?
O happy horse, to bear the weight of Antony!

Do bravely, horse, for wot'st thou whom thou mov'st?
The demi-Atlas of this earth, the arm
And burgonet of men.
(I.5.19–24)

Ostensibly, Cleopatra is speaking to Charmian; but this passage, in which she is evoking to her mind's eye an image of the absent Antony, is more akin to stream of consciousness than dialogue. It demonstrates the remarkably colloquial flexibility of Shakespeare's blank verse in his later work. A 'burgonet' was a form of helmet but appears, by metonymy, to stand for the perfect soldier. Antony is depicted verbally as a semi-divine hero, even though his military prowess only exists in the play in the form of memory.

20 He's speaking now,
Or murmuring 'Where's my serpent of old Nile?'
For so he calls me. Now I feed myself
With most delicious poison. Think on me,
That am with Phoebus' amorous pinches black
And wrinkled deep in time.
(I.5.24–9)

Cleopatra's reverie on the theme of Antony moves from visualizing him to hearing him speak, and ultimately to penetrating and attempting to control his mind. Cleopatra is proud of her ability to win the love of one of the great leaders of her time despite her age and her swarthy complexion, two factors contradicting the Renaissance stereotype of beauty. Her swarthiness she ennobles by attributing it to the 'amorous pinches' of the sun-god, Phoebus.

21 My salad days,
When I was green in judgement, cold in blood.
(I.5.73–4)

Cleopatra is asserting that she loves Antony more than she ever loved Julius Caesar, one of his notable predecessors. Charmian has a lingering admiration for Caesar which prompts Cleopatra's angry response that only her ignorant youth (her 'salad days') was given to Caesar. Most editors have followed the eighteenth-century editor Warburton in taking 'cold in blood' to be a rebuke to Charmian. It appears, though, to be a phrase in apposition to 'green in judgement' and seems to suggest that the love she gave as a young woman had not the intensity of passion she gives in maturity. The phrase 'salad days' has given the title to a musical of 1954 by Julian Slade, peopled by the vivacious youth of the 1950s.

22 But all the charms of love,
Salt Cleopatra, soften thy waned lip!
Let witchcraft join with beauty, lust with both!
(II.1.20–2)

Sextus Pompey, who is in rebellion against the triumvirate of Rome, is in conversation with the pirates, Menas and Menecrates, with whom he has allied himself to form a great marine force. Pompey is hoping that division continues amongst the triumvirate and that, above all, Antony remains in Egypt with Cleopatra. 'Salt' indicates 'lustful' and 'waned lip' refers to a lip past its fullness and perfection.

23 As for my wife,
I would you had her spirit in such another;
The third o'th'world is yours, which with a snaffle
You may pace easy, but not such a wife.
(II.2.65–8)

Antony, the speaker, has come to Rome to make peace with his fellow triumvirs, Octavius Caesar and Lepidus, and to cement the alliance against Pompey. Caesar is complaining of the rebellious activity of Fulvia, Antony's late wife, and her brother, with whom Antony is protesting that he was not in league. The spirit of Fulvia was commented upon by Antony when he received news of her death ('There's a great spirit gone!', I.2.123). The terms 'snaffle' and 'pace' are drawn from horsemanship: a 'snaffle' is a simple form of bridle.

24 A sister I bequeath you whom no brother
Did ever love so dearly. Let her live
To join our kingdoms and our hearts.
(II.2.155–7)

Octavius Caesar gives his approval to the marriage of Antony to Octavia, his sister, that has been proposed by Agrippa as a means of reconciling their differences and ensuring their future amity.

25 The barge she sat in, like a burnished throne,
Burned on the water. The poop was beaten gold;
Purple the sails, and so perfumèd that
The winds were lovesick with them. The oars were silver,
Which to the tune of flutes kept stroke and made
The water which they beat to follow faster,
As amorous of their strokes. For her own person,
It beggared all description. She did lie
In her pavilion, cloth-of-gold of tissue,
O'erpicturing that Venus where we see
The fancy outwork nature. On each side her

Stood pretty dimpled boys, like smiling cupids,
With divers-coloured fans, whose wind did seem
To glow the delicate cheeks which they did cool,
And what they undid did.
(II.2.196–210)

Enobarbus' famous panegyric of Cleopatra at her first meeting with Antony is based on the account available to Shakespeare in Sir Thomas North's translation of Plutarch's *The Lives of the Noble Grecians and Romanes* (1579). The incident refers not to the Nile but to the river Cydnus in Cilicia. The description borders on erotic fantasy in its appeal to the senses of sight, smell, sound, and touch. Cleopatra (as in Plutarch) is presented as a Venus, a goddess of love, complete with attendant cupids. Enobarbus is speaking to Agrippa. T. S. Eliot gave a pastiche of this famous speech in the section of *The Waste Land* called 'A Game of Chess'.

26 Her gentlewomen, like the Nereides,
So many mermaids, tended her i'th'eyes,
And made their bends adornings. At the helm
A seeming mermaid steers. The silken tackle
Swell with the touches of those flower-soft hands,
That yarely frame the office. From the barge
A strange invisible perfume hits the sense
Of the adjacent wharfs. The city cast
Her people out upon her; and Antony,
Enthroned i'th'market-place, did sit alone,
Whistling to th'air; which, but for vacancy,
Had gone to gaze on Cleopatra too,
And made a gap in nature.
(II.2.211–23)

In the second section of Enobarbus' eulogy of Cleopatra (separated from the first by an ecstatic interjection of Agrippa), the emphasis is now placed on her being a goddess of the sea. Cleopatra is presented as the epitome of femininity and as belonging to the element of water, while Antony's masculinity is land-locked ('enthroned i'th'market-place'). The speech continues to make extensive appeal to the senses, while the final hyperbole (the idea that the element of air would depart to gaze on Cleopatra) further projects Cleopatra as a divine being transcending nature.

27 I saw her once
Hop forty paces through the public street;
And, having lost her breath, she spoke, and panted,
That she did make defect perfection,

And, breathless, power breathe forth.
(II.2.233–7)

Enobarbus narrates to Agrippa an incident concerning Cleopatra. Her fascination is a combination of regal, even divine, qualities with hoydenish, even sluttish, ones. The point is made explicit by Enobarbus in the quotation that follows.

28 Age cannot wither her, nor custom stale
Her infinite variety. Other women cloy
The appetites they feed, but she makes hungry
Where most she satisfies; for vilest things
Become themselves in her, that the holy priests
Bless her when she is riggish.
(II.2.240–5)

Enobarbus' eulogy of Cleopatra to Agrippa culminates in the paradoxes of her fascination. The juxtaposition of the sacred and the profane in her composition is evident. 'Custom' indicates habit and 'riggish' wanton.

29 I'th'East my pleasure lies.
(II.3.41)

Despite his marriage to Octavia, Antony has decided to return to Egypt. His decision has been prompted by the counsel of the Egyptian soothsayer, who has warned him that his guardian spirit or daemon cannot thrive in Octavius Caesar's company. In fact, the soothsayer has rightly predicted that Caesar's fortunes will rise above Antony's.

30 Give me some music – music, moody food
Of us that trade in love.
(II.5.1–2)

Cleopatra's call for music to assuage the melancholy caused by her separation from Antony is reminiscent of Orsino's similar demand at the beginning of *Twelfth Night*. 'Moody' signifies melancholy here. 'Trade in' (have dealings in) is not necessarily commercial in association, though it could retain that connotation.

31 I will betray
Tawny-finned fishes. My bended hook shall pierce
Their slimy jaws; and as I draw them up,
I'll think them every one an Antony,
And say 'Ah, ha! Y'are caught!
(II.5.11–16)

Ostensibly Cleopatra is devising pastimes with Charmian, Iras, and Alexas, to help forget the absence of Antony. As the quotation indicates, even the sports devised remind her of her absent lover and her desire to retain him.

32 I laughed him out of patience; and that night
I laughed him into patience; and next morn,
Ere the ninth hour, I drunk him to his bed;
Then put my tires and mantles on him, whilst
I wore his sword Philippan.
(II.5.19–23)
Charmian has reminded Cleopatra of a trick she once had played upon Antony when they went fishing together, getting a diver to attach a salt-fish to his line. Cleopatra's account of Antony's changes of mood, his revelry, and even his loss of sexual identity constitutes the behaviour for which at Rome he is taxed with having been emasculated by Cleopatra. 'Tires' usually indicates headdress, but it could suggest a complete costume. Antony's sword derived its name from the battle of Philippi, where he had triumphed over Brutus and Cassius.

33 There is gold and here
My bluest veins to kiss, a hand that kings
Have lipped, and trembled kissing.
(II.5.28–30)
This is the promise made by Cleopatra to the messenger, if he should bear news that Antony is 'well and free'. Cleopatra cannot anticipate the sense in which Antony is no longer 'free' (he is now married to Octavia), but her fluctuating moods towards the messenger will be an illustration of her 'infinite variety'.

34 Thou shalt be whipped with wire and stewed in brine,
Smarting in lingering pickle!
(II.5.65–6)
The torment proposed for the messenger by Cleopatra on learning of Antony's marriage to Octavia illustrates the sadistic ingenuity of her violent temperament.

35 Melt Egypt into Nile, and kindly creatures
Turn all to serpents!
(II.5.78–9)
Despite the messenger's protestations that he is not responsible for the news he brings of Antony's marriage to Octavia, Cleopatra has threatened to kill him and he has fled. Her fury and despair give vent to an image of anarchy and destruction which parallels Antony's 'Let Rome in Tiber melt' (see 4). Antony's utterance was a rejection of public duty, Cleopatra's an outburst of private passion.

36 Though it be honest, it is never good
To bring bad news. Give to a gracious message
An host of tongues, but let ill tidings tell
Themselves when they be felt.
(II.5.85–8)
Cleopatra has regained some control over herself, after learning of Antony's marriage to Octavia, and has recalled the messenger. She acknowledges the messenger's point that it is a luckless task to bear ill news (a point also made by the messenger at I.2.95, when informing Antony of the military setbacks to the triumvirate: 'The nature of the news infects the teller').

37 Hadst thou Narcissus in thy face, to me
Thou wouldst appear most ugly.
(II.5.96–7)
Cleopatra has recalled the messenger (whom she is addressing here), but has only received confirmation of Antony's marriage to Octavia. Narcissus was the youth of Greek myth so beautiful that he fell in love with his own reflection in a pool.

38 ENOBARBUS But you shall find the band that seems to tie their friendship together will be the very strangler of their amity. Octavia is of a holy, cold, and still conversation.
MENAS Who would not have his wife so?
ENOBARBUS Not he that himself is not so; which is Mark Antony. He will to his Egyptian dish again.
(II.6.118–24)
Enobarbus is talking with Menas, a follower of Pompey, following Pompey's reconciliation with the triumvirate. Enobarbus rightly predicts the future of Antony's marriage to Octavia and his friendship with her brother. Octavia's character contrasts markedly with Cleopatra's, for her cold piety and sense of public duty show her very much the sister of Octavius. 'Still conversation' means sober behaviour.

39 LEPIDUS What manner o'thing is your crocodile?
ANTONY It is shaped, sir, like itself, and it is as broad as it has breadth. It is just so high as it is, and moves with its own organs. It lives by that which nourisheth it, and the elements once out of it, it transmigrates.
LEPIDUS What colour is it of?
ANTONY Of it own colour too.
LEPIDUS 'Tis a strange serpent.
ANTONY 'Tis so; and the tears of it are wet.
(II.7.41–9)

This conversation takes place at the drunken banquet aboard Pompey's galley. Lepidus is already the worse for drink, but his questions illustrate his stupidity more than his inebriation.

40 Ah, this thou shouldst have done,
And not have spoke on't. In me 'tis villainy;
In thee't had been good service.
(II.7.73–5)

Menas, a follower of Pompey, has just proposed to his master that he could make himself ruler of the world. The proposal takes place at the banquet aboard Pompey's galley, when he could slip anchor and then murder the triumvirate. Pompey's reply indicates a cynical insight into political acts.

41 O noble emperor, do not fight by sea.
Trust not to rotten planks. Do you misdoubt
This sword and these my wounds? Let th'Egyptians
And the Phoenicians go a-ducking; we
Have used to conquer standing on the earth
And fighting foot to foot.
(III.7.61–6)

Antony and Caesar have fallen into dispute. Caesar has first destroyed the power of Sextus Pompey with the support of Lepidus and then dismissed this ally from the triumvirate, so becoming sole master at Rome, while Antony in Egypt has assigned kingdoms to Cleopatra and their progeny. The Empire is thus divided between the two men and Caesar is leading a maritime power against the forces of Antony and Cleopatra, which are located at Actium in Macedonia. Antony has rashly decided to fight at sea, contrary to his strategic advantage on land and his association as a soldier with the element of earth. Cleopatra, who is associated in the play with the element of water, has promised the assistance of her navy and has just been addressed by Antony as Thetis, a sea-nymph, when the unnamed soldier makes this plea to him. Enobarbus had given the same advice more soberly at 41–2: 'you therein throw away / The absolute soldiership you have by land'.

42 Antony,
Claps on his sea wing and, like a doting mallard,
Leaving the fight in height, flies after her.
I never saw an action of such shame.
(III.10.18–21)

During this scene, the sounds of the sea-battle of Actium are heard off-stage, while Scarus gives to Enobarbus an account of the action. He has just described in unflattering terms how at the height of the battle, just when the advantage seemed to be Antony's, Cleopatra's ships had taken flight. He here provides the culminating dishonour, that Antony followed, like an amorous drake, his duck.

43 I found you as a morsel cold upon
Dead Caesar's trencher.
(III.13.116–17)
Antony has caught the ambassador of Caesar, Thidias, kissing the hand of Cleopatra and fears treachery. Thidias has, in fact, been instructed by Caesar to win Cleopatra's fidelity from Antony. Having ordered the ambassador to be whipped, Antony turns on Cleopatra. Imagery of food and appetite is used throughout the play to suggest sexual appetite. Antony refers to the liaison between Cleopatra and Julius Caesar, wrongly identified in the play as Octavius Caesar's father.

44 He makes me angry,
And at this time most easy 'tis to do't,
When my good stars that were my former guides
Have empty left their orbs and shot their fires
Into th'abysm of hell.
(III.13.143–7)
Antony is speaking to Thidias, the ambassador of Octavius Caesar whom he has had whipped (ostensibly for the presumption of kissing Cleopatra's hand), about his master's conduct. There co-exists with Antony's anger an awareness that his fortunes are in decline, imaged by the eclipse of his 'good stars'.

45 Let's have one other gaudy night. Call to me
All my sad captains. Fill our bowls once more.
Let's mock the midnight bell.
(III.13.182–4)
Antony's exhortation to Cleopatra to share one final Egyptian revel is an act of defiance in the face of (and realization of) defeat. The dishonour of defeat by Caesar at Actium is the reason for the captains' sadness. 'Gaudy' means festive. Thom Gunn employed the phrase 'my sad captains' as the title of a poem and a collection of poems of 1961.

46 'Tis one of those odd tricks which sorrow shoots
Out of the mind.
(IV.2.14–15)
Before the final Alexandrian revel, Antony takes a formal and lacrimose farewell of his followers and servants, so transforming

it into a kind of last supper. Enobarbus in an aside to Cleopatra observes that the action is prompted by Antony's own sorrow.

47 'Tis the god Hercules, whom Antony loved,
Now leaves him.
(IV.3.17–18)

In this curious atmospheric scene, a company of soldiers is passing an uneasy watch on the eve of the battle at Alexandria. They hear ethereal music in the air and under the earth. The stage direction indicates that oboes (hautboys) should be played under the stage. The interpretation is provided by the second soldier. Throughout the play, Antony has been identified with the martial gods, Mars and Hercules.

48 To business that we love we rise betime
And go to't with delight.
(IV.4.20–1)

The action of the scene is the arming of Antony for battle by Eros and Cleopatra. The arming of the hero was a theme of classical epic and Antony, back in the context of a military leader, seems to have recovered from the defeat and dishonour of Actium. His comment is made to a soldier already armed for - battle. 'Betime' means early or in good time.

49 O, my fortunes have
Corrupted honest men!
(IV.5.16–17)

Antony has just been informed by a soldier that Enobarbus has deserted him for Octavius Caesar. Antony magnanimously sends Enobarbus' treasure after him, together with 'gentle adieus and greetings'. His reproach is reserved for himself.

50 I am alone the villain of the earth,
And feel I am so most...
... I will go seek
Some ditch wherein to die; the foul'st best fits
My latter part of life.
(IV.6.30–1, 37–9)

Enobarbus, on learning from the soldier that Antony has forwarded his treasure to him in magnanimous fashion, is smitten with remorse. He decides that suicide offers the only release from his dishonour. The action takes place before the battle at Alexandria.

51 We have beat them to their beds.
(IV.8.19)

Antony is initially successful in the land battle at Alexandria, driving Octavius Caesar back to his camp. This is the jovial manner of Antony's giving the news to Cleopatra.

52 Fortune and Antony part here; even here
Do we shake hands. All come to this? The hearts
That spanieled me at heels, to whom I gave
Their wishes, do discandy, melt their sweets
On blossoming Caesar; and this pine is barked
That overtopped them all. Betrayed I am.
O this false soul of Egypt! This grave charm,
Whose eye becked forth my wars, and called them home,
Whose bosom was my crownet, my chief end,
Like a right gypsy hath at fast and loose
Beguiled me to the very heart of loss.
(IV.12.19–29)

Following his defeat on land at Alexandria, Caesar has trusted to battle at sea again. The sea proves fatal to Antony a second time, since his fleet goes over to the enemy. Antony's theme is the ingratitude of friends who desert to follow a rising star and, above all, the treachery of Cleopatra, whose love has been his downfall and whom he suspects of complicity with Caesar. The passage is dense in metaphor, moving rapidly from an image of a fawning spaniel, to one of melting perfumes, to one of the stripping of a pine's bark.

53 Sometime we see a cloud that's dragonish,
A vapour sometime like a bear or lion,
A towered citadel, a pendent rock,
A forkèd mountain, or blue promontory
With trees upon't that nod unto the world
And mock our eyes with air. Thou hast seen these signs;
They are black vesper's pageants.
(IV.14.2–8)

Antony is speaking to Eros following his defeat at Alexandria where, after initial victory on land, he has been betrayed by the Egyptian fleet. The passage expounds how the intellect and imagination give form and meaning to nature. More specifically, through these images Antony is analysing how the psyche gives apparent meaning to identity, which he can no longer grasp: 'Here I am Antony, / Yet cannot hold this visible shape' (lines 13–14). 'Vesper' means evening. 'Pageants' here are illusory spectacles. Antony's imagery is drawn from the visual arts of drawing and stage design.

54 Unarm, Eros. The long day's task is done,
And we must sleep.
(IV.14.35–6)
Following the defeat at Alexandria, Cleopatra has withdrawn to her monument. She has sent Mardian to Antony with the false report that Cleopatra has killed herself. The news completes Antony's sense of life-weariness and the act of unarming, which follows, conveys the sense of his disintegration. The phrase 'the long day' has become synonymous with a day of battle, although its meaning here seems to extend to life itself.

55 I will o'ertake thee, Cleopatra, and
Weep for my pardon. So it must be, for now
All length is torture; since the torch is out,
Lie down, and stray no farther. Now all labour
Mars what it does; yea, very force entangles
Itself with strength. Seal then, and all is done.
Eros! – I come, my queen – Eros! Stay for me.
Where souls do couch on flowers, we'll hand in hand,
And with our sprightly port make the ghosts gaze:
Dido and her Aeneas shall want troops,
And all the haunt be ours.
(IV.14.44–54)
Antony, believing Cleopatra's false report that she is dead, decides to join her in death. He finds existence a torment now that his 'torch' (Cleopatra's love and vitality) is extinguished. The very exercise of might and will ('force') merely exhausts him. He visualizes himself with Cleopatra in the Elysian fields eclipsing the splendour of the great lovers of legend. His vision is punctuated by his summoning his servant Eros, aptly named after the god of love, to perform the act of his dispatch.

56 I will be
A bridegroom in my death, and run into't
As to a lover's bed.
(IV.14.99–101)
Eros, Antony's servant, has just killed himself rather than fulfil his master's wishes to dispatch him. Antony wants to escape the dishonour of defeat by Octavius Caesar and to join Cleopatra, whom he believes to be dead. He envisages death as a bridal bed where his union with Cleopatra will be complete. In fact, he botches the act of suicide.

57 All strange and terrible events are welcome,
But comforts we despise.
(IV.15.3–4)

Cleopatra has withdrawn to her monument, for which the upper stage of Shakespeare's theatre was undoubtedly used, since the stage direction indicates that she appears 'aloft'. She foresees she will never leave that place and rejects Charmian's comfort with these lines.

58 I am dying, Egypt, dying; only
I here importune death awhile, until
Of many thousand kisses the poor last
I lay upon thy lips.
(IV.15.18–21)

Antony has been brought to the base of Cleopatra's monument, fatally wounded after his unsuccessful attempt at suicide. 'Egypt' refers, of course, to Cleopatra: it was customary for monarchs to be addressed by the name of their realm. The use of 'importune' is not easily explained, though the sense that Antony begs death to delay is clear.

59 The miserable change now at my end
Lament nor sorrow at, but please your thoughts
In feeding them with those my former fortunes,
Wherein I lived; the greatest prince o'th'world,
The noblest; and do now not basely die,
Not cowardly put off my helmet to
My countryman; a Roman, by a Roman
Valiantly vanquished.
(IV.15.51–8)

In his last speech before death, Antony revives the image of the great soldier and magnanimous prince that he was at the zenith of his fortunes. The description does not really tally with the botched attempt at suicide that the spectator has witnessed.

60 Shall I abide
In this dull world, which in thy absence is
No better than a sty? O, see, my women,
Antony dies
The crown o'th'earth doth melt. My lord!
O, withered is the garland of the war,
The soldier's pole is fall'n; young boys and girls
Are level now with men. The odds is gone,
And there is nothing left remarkable
Beneath the visiting moon.
She faints
(IV.15.60–8)

Cleopatra's reaction to Antony's death is to find the world a place of mediocrity, darkness, and desolation. The imagery and the bases of the analogies to Antony's death mark him out as a demi-god among men. The phrase 'soldier's pole' is open to interpretation either as the soldier's standard or as the pole star of soldiers. The latter interpretation moves more naturally to the desolation of the sublunary world in which men live subject to flux and decay. The phrase may also carry phallic implications.

61 No more but e'en a woman, and commanded
By such poor passion as the maid that milks
And does the meanest chares. It were for me
To throw my sceptre at the injurious gods,
To tell them that this world did equal theirs
Till they had stolen our jewel. All's but naught.
Patience is sottish, and impatience does
Become a dog that's mad; then is it sin
To rush into the secret house of death
Ere death dare come to us?
(IV.15.72–81)

Paradoxically, in her desolation at Antony's death, Cleopatra becomes both more human and more regal. She is ennobled both as woman and queen. Her resolve that death is not simply the only possible course of action, but the right one, strengthens. 'Chares' are tasks or chores. Cleopatra is locked within her monument to escape capture by Octavius Caesar.

62 What's brave, what's noble,
Let's do't after the high Roman fashion,
And make death proud to take us.
(IV.15.85–7)

Cleopatra is locked within her monument to escape capture by Octavius Caesar. She has just witnessed the death of Antony and is resolved to die herself. It is a paradox that in death she attains a Roman stoicism, while in life her Egyptian values were so opposed to those of Rome.

63 The breaking of so great a thing should make
A greater crack.
(V.1.14–15)

Dercetas has taken the sword of Antony to Octavius Caesar with the news of Antony's death and in the hope to be accepted into Caesar's good will. Antony's death is recounted by Dercetas in a matter-of-fact manner, but Caesar's response to the news shows the value he placed on Antony's worth.

64 A rarer spirit never
Did steer humanity. But you gods will give us

Some faults to make us men.
(V.1.31–3)
Agrippa's evaluation of Antony, when the Roman camp learns of his death from Dercetas, balances the greatness of Antony's qualities with his human weaknesses and implies that all men, even the greatest, are flawed.

65 My desolation does begin to make
A better life. 'Tis paltry to be Caesar:
Not being Fortune, he's but Fortune's knave,
A minister of her will. And it is great
To do that thing that ends all other deeds,
Which shackles accidents and bolts up change;
Which sleeps, and never palates more the dung,
The beggar's nurse and Caesar's.
(V.2.1–8)
Following the death of Antony, Cleopatra is locked in her monument with Charmian, Iras, and Mardian, awaiting the approach of her victor, Octavius Caesar, and contemplating suicide, her only escape from him. Her material and emotional desolation permit her to see beyond the favours of Fortune and suicide is contemplated as the act which scorns Fortune and places the individual beyond her reach. As Dr Johnson pointed out, Cleopatra's contemplation conflates the act of suicide and the state of death.

66 This mortal house I'll ruin,
Do Caesar what he can. Know, sir, that I
Will not wait pinioned at your master's court,
Nor once be chastised with the sober eye
Of dull Octavia. Shall they hoist me up
And show me to the shouting varletry
Of censuring Rome? Rather a ditch in Egypt
Be gentle grave unto me! Rather on Nilus' mud
Lay me stark nak'd and let the waterflies
Blow me into abhorring!
(V.2.51–60)
Proculeius, the ambassador of Caesar, has tricked Cleopatra into allowing him entry into the monument. Antony had told Cleopatra that he was trustworthy. The Queen has consequently been taken captive. 'This mortal house' is Cleopatra's body or physical existence which, she threatens Proculeius, she will destroy rather than allow the Romans their triumph over her. The comparison of the human form to an architectural construct derives from the Vitruvian tradition of Renaissance architecture. Cleopatra's language expresses the extremity of her situation in

hyperbolic images of death which add sexual overtones to their physical violence.

67 I dreamt there was an emperor Antony.
O, such another sleep, that I might see
But such another man!
(V.2.76–8)

Cleopatra is addressing Dolabella, who has replaced Proculeius in guarding the Queen in her monument. She has observed that he is known to be sceptical of the significance of dreams. What follows is Cleopatra's subjective image of Antony, what he represented to her, which she refuses to allow to be qualified by contact with reality.

68 His legs bestrid the ocean; his reared arm
Crested the world; his voice was propertied
As all the tunèd spheres, and that to friends;
But when he meant to quail and shake the orb,
He was as rattling thunder. For his bounty,
There was no winter in't; an Antony it was
That grew the more by reaping. His delights
Were dolphin-like; they showed his back above
The element they lived in. In his livery
Walked crowns and crownets; realms and islands were
As plates dropped from his pocket.
(V.2.82–92)

Cleopatra's 'dream' of Antony depicts him as a colossus, a semi-divine figure, boundless in his magnanimity and pleasures. Cleopatra's eulogy amounts to a funeral oration and, in fact, this speech corresponds in the narrative to the funeral oration made by Cleopatra at the tomb of Antony found in Plutarch's *Lives of the Noble Grecians and Romanes* (Sir Thomas North's translation of 1579). It was in this section of Plutarch that Shakespeare found the name Dolabella. Here in the play, as elsewhere, Roman pragmatism blunts Egyptian imagination. When Cleopatra asks, 'Think you there was or might be such a man / As this I dreamt of?', Dolabella replies, 'Gentle madam, no' (93–4).

69 CLEOPATRA
He words me, girls, he words me, that I should not
Be noble to myself. But hark thee, Charmian.
She whispers to Charmian
IRAS
Finish, good lady; the bright day is done,
And we are for the dark.
(V.2.191–4)

Octavius Caesar has sought to obtain Cleopatra's compliance with his wishes by flattery and pretence of generous terms. Cleopatra, who is held captive within her monument, is not to be deceived but remains bent on suicide to escape Caesar's Roman triumph. The whispered message to Charmian obviously refers to the plan to have asps brought to her. Cleopatra's attendants clearly share her view of the inescapability of death.

70 Saucy lictors
Will catch at us like strumpets, and scald rhymers
Ballad us out o'tune. The quick comedians
Extemporally will stage us, and present
Our Alexandrian revels. Antony
Shall be brought drunken forth, and I shall see
Some squeaking Cleopatra boy my greatness
I'th'posture of a whore.
(V.2.214–21)

Cleopatra is strengthening her own resolve and that of her attendant, Iras, for death by imagining their presentation in the Roman triumph. Two ideas are, in fact, conflated: that they themselves will be exhibited and that they will be impersonated in various forms of theatrical entertainment. The forms of presentation that Shakespeare has Cleopatra imagine reflect his own theatrical world, not ancient Rome, and there is an ironical reference to features of his own play. Until 1663 it was English stage practice for female roles to be played by young males. Indeed, Shakespeare's presentation of the narrative was considered too undignified for many generations of spectators and Dryden's neoclassical adaptation, *All for Love* (1677), held the stage from the Restoration period until the late nineteenth century.

71 Show me, my women, like a queen. Go fetch
My best attires. I am again for Cydnus,
To meet Mark Antony.
(V.2.227–9)

Cleopatra is determined that her last act (of suicide) shall be a regal one and dresses for the occasion. Her statement that she is to meet Antony again at Cydnus recalls both the lyrical description of Cleopatra's meeting with Antony given by Enobarbus in II.2. (see 25–8 above) and the speeches of Antony (see 55–6 above), in which he imagines death as the consummation of their union.

72 What poor an instrument
May do a noble deed! He brings me liberty.
My resolution's placed, and I have nothing

Of woman in me. Now from head to foot
I am marble-constant; now the fleeting moon
No planet is of mine.
(V.2.236–41)

The Guard has announced the arrival of a rustic, ostensibly bringing figs for Cleopatra but in fact bearing the asps in a basket. Cleopatra orders his entrance. The first line and a half refers to the rustic (and perhaps by extension to the asp). In her final act, Cleopatra is elevated to a regal stoicism matching Antony's. In fact, she divests herself of all those qualities and associations that were initially opposed to Antony's Roman values: femininity, inconstancy, association with the moon (and thereby water). In rejecting the moon, she is not only rejecting inconstancy and fluctuation, but indicating that, by embracing death, she no longer belongs to the sublunary world of change.

73 But I would not be the party that should desire you to touch him, for his biting is immortal. Those that do die of it do seldom or never recover.
(V.2.245–8)

The Clown is referring to the asp that he has brought to Cleopatra concealed in a basket of figs. Clown, in this context, means a rustic or peasant. The comic tautology and malapropism are conventional to this character stereotype. It is also characteristic of Shakespearian tragedy, and indeed of much tragedy of the period, that even the climax of the tragedy is juxtaposed with touches of comedy.

74 I wish you all joy of the worm.
(V.2.259)

The Clown's line is based on a bawdy pun, since in his dialogue 'worm' signifies both snake/asp and the male sexual organ. In a comic vein, his utterings therefore reinforce the thematic identification of death with sexual union that Cleopatra is also pursuing at a more exalted level. The line is repeated to Cleopatra (with the omission of 'all') at line 278. The Clown is a rustic or peasant who has brought the asp to Cleopatra concealed in a basket of figs.

75 Give me my robe; put on my c Immortal longings in me.
(V.2.279–80)

Cleopatra is addressing her waiting-women, in particular Iras who has just entered with the royal regalia. She dresses as a queen for her appointment with death and with Antony. It is also an appointment with Octavius Caesar, for in this way she will triumph over him by leaving for him and for posterity a regal image of herself. 'Immortal longings' are longings for immortality, but there is an ambiguity in the phrase, since immortality has been substituted for mortality or death. Her usage picks up the Clown's malapropism (see 73 above). Cleopatra's final act is to be a triumph over death, as well as over Caesar.

76 Methinks I hear
Antony call. I see him rouse himself
To praise my noble act. I hear him mock
The luck of Caesar, which the gods give men
To excuse their after wrath. Husband, I come.
Now to that name my courage prove my title!
I am fire and air; my other elements
I give to baser life.
(V.2.282–9)

Cleopatra's resolve to take her own life is strengthened by evoking a strong visual image of Antony. The perspective is a dual one: he is envisaged beyond the grave both as a husband urging on Cleopatra to join him and as a scoffer at Caesar's earthly fortunes. Octavius Caesar was noted in the ancient world for his good luck, but it was believed that felicity on earth would be punished in the afterlife. Cleopatra separates herself from the material success of Caesar; she rejects the lower elements in the human composition, earth and water, and aspires to the higher, spiritual elements, fire and air.

77 If thou and nature can so gently part,
The stroke of death is as a lover's pinch,
Which hurts, and is desired. Dost thou lie still?
If thus thou vanishest, thou tell'st the world
It is not worth leave-taking.
(V.2.293–7)

Cleopatra is commenting upon the death of her waiting-woman, Iras, who has preceded her in death. The death of Iras is not made plain in the text, perhaps because of a missing stage direction. Cleopatra has just kissed Iras farewell and asks at line 292, 'Have I the aspic in my lips?'. Since it would not appear, however, that Cleopatra applies an asp to herself till line 302, it must be assumed that Iras has secretly applied an asp to herself. Cleopatra's comment on Iras's death pursues her twin themes of death as sexual union and the vanity of the world which makes departure from it easy.

78 This proves me base;
If she first meet the curlèd Antony,

He'll make demand of her, and spend that kiss
Which is my heaven to have. (*To an asp*) Come, thou mortal wretch,
With thy sharp teeth this knot intrinsicate
Of life at once untie. Poor venomous fool,
Be angry, and dispatch.
(V.2.299–305)

Cleopatra's resolve for suicide is finally confirmed by Iras's death. In a characteristic feeling of jealousy, she fancifully imagines that Iras will be the first to meet Antony in the afterlife and so receive his kiss. She therefore applies the asp, the 'mortal wretch' (deadly creature), to her bosom. The notion that the essence of life is constituted of knots or bonds too intricate for human comprehension is expressed elsewhere in Shakespeare (see *King Lear* 24). Antony is perhaps termed 'curlèd' in keeping with contemporary male fashion.

79 Dost thou not see my baby at my breast,
That sucks the nurse asleep?
(V.2.308–9)

Cleopatra is calming her waiting woman, Charmian, who is distraught at the sight of her mistress's suicide. Cleopatra inverts the image of the child at the nurse's breast in order to depict death as a sleep. Plutarch, in *The Lives of the Noble Grecians and Romanes* (translated by Sir Thomas North, 1579), had stated that after Actium Cleopatra had sought painless poisons and discovered that aspic brings only a desire for sleep and induces loss of the vital powers without apparent sense of pain. Caesar refers to her search in the last speech of the play.

80 Now boast thee, death, in thy possession lies
A lass unparalleled. Downy windows, close;
And golden Phoebus never be beheld
Of eyes again so royal! Your crown's awry;
I'll mend it.
(V.2.314–18)

Charmian performs the last rites for Cleopatra, closing her eyes ('downy windows') and speaking the briefest of funeral orations before the guard enters. She then takes her own life. It is characteristic of Cleopatra that even in her finest moment there remains the imperfection of her crown being 'awry'. It is only beyond the grave that perfection is projected.

81 No grave upon the earth shall clip in it
A pair so famous.
(V.2.357–8)

Octavius Caesar's comment in the last speech of the play acknowledges the greatness of Antony and Cleopatra despite his opposition to their values. 'Clip' appropriately means embrace, thus leaving the audience with the notion of death as the lovers' complete and perfect union.

As You Like It

1 As I remember, Adam, it was upon this fashion bequeathed me by will, but poor a thousand crowns, and, as thou sayest, charged my brother on his blessing to breed me well; and there begins my sadness.
(I.1.1–4)
Shakespeare begins the play with a splendidly unrealistic exposition, using Orlando's opening speech to the aged servant Adam as an economical way of presenting a great deal of information to the audience. 'But poor' means merely; 'charged my brother on his blessing to breed me well' means my brother was instructed to educate me properly if he wanted to keep father's blessing.

2 They say he is already in the Forest of Arden, and a many merry men with him; and there they live like the old Robin Hood of England: they say many young gentlemen flock to him every day, and fleet the time carelessly as they did in the golden world.
(I.1.108–12)
Charles, wrestler to the usurping Duke Frederick, explains to Oliver, Orlando's elder brother, that the banished Duke (Duke Senior) is believed to be in the Forest of Arden. Charles sees Arden as the ideal pastoral world, resembling the mythical golden age, in which men pass ('fleet') the time without cares. As with Arden, which is presumably the Ardennes but may also be the Warwickshire Arden, Charles's mention of 'the old Robin Hood of England' serves to bring events into a dual focus for an audience whose original frame of reference is England.

3 Let us sit and mock the good housewife Fortune from her wheel, that her gifts may henceforth be bestowed equally.
(I.2.30–2)
Celia, daughter of Duke Frederick, is proposing a pastime to Rosalind, daughter of the banished Duke Senior. Fortune's wheel was a familiar Renaissance device symbolizing the fickleness of fate. Celia is being ironically disrespectful in comparing the goddess Fortune to a housewife using a spinning wheel.

4 Those that she makes fair she scarce makes honest, and those that she makes honest she makes very ill-favouredly.
(I.2.36–8)
Celia continues to expatiate on the inequality of Fortune's distribution of gifts to women. The idea expressed here is a mildly misogynistic commonplace. 'Honest' means chaste.

5 How now, wit, whither wander you?
(I.2.53–4)
Celia greets Touchstone, the Court Clown, who because he is a 'fool' may be supposed to have a wandering intelligence.

6 It is the first time that ever I heard breaking of ribs was sport for ladies.
(I.2.127–9)
Touchstone mocks the courtier Le Beau who has brought Celia and Rosalind news that Charles the wrestler has defeated and severely injured his challengers, calling it 'good sport'.

7 Only in the world I fill up a place which may be better supplied when I have made it empty.
(I.2.178–80)
Orlando has come to court to try his luck at wrestling with Charles. Here he explains himself to Celia and Rosalind, who are attempting to dissuade him from such a hazardous enterprise.

8 Wear this for me – one out of suits with fortune,
That could give more but that her hand lacks means.
(I.2.234–5)
Rosalind, who has fallen in love with Orlando, gives him a love token – a chain from her neck – following his defeat of Charles the wrestler.

9 Sir, you have wrestled well, and overthrown
More than your enemies.
(I.2.243–4)
Rosalind finds a way of expressing her feelings to Orlando.

10 Hereafter, in a better world than this,
I shall desire more love and knowledge of you.
(I.2.273–4)
The courtier Le Beau has warned Orlando that Duke Frederick has taken an intense dislike to him on finding out his identity. 'In a better world than this' means in better circumstances than these, though there may well be an implicit reference to the better world of Arden.

11 Thus must I from the smoke into the smother,
From tyrant Duke unto a tyrant brother.
But heavenly Rosalind!
(I.2.276–8)

Orlando ends the scene with a comment on his situation: in fleeing the Duke he has to go back to his brother Oliver, out of the frying pan into the fire ('from the smoke into the smother'), but Rosalind is his great preoccupation. 'Smother' is the suffocating smoke of a smouldering fire.

12 CELIA But is all this for your father?
ROSALIND No, some of it is for my child's father. – O, how full of briars is this working-day world!
(I.3.10–12)

Celia attempts to find the cause of Rosalind's distraction; Rosalind gives the riddling reply which suggests that her state is the result of love as well as grief for her father – she is distracted by the man who she hopes will be the father of her child, and the everyday world seems full of thorns. Although there is no reason to doubt the reading reproduced here, many eighteenth- and nineteenth-century editors from Nicholas Rowe (1709) onwards changed Rosalind's remark to read 'for my father's child'. Coleridge found this a sensible emendation, arguing that the Folio reading put 'a very indelicate anticipation in the mouth of Rosalind, without reason'. Most modern readers and audiences find no difficulties with the phrase, which seems characteristic of an open and aware heroine.

13 CELIA Come, come, wrestle with thy affections.
ROSALIND O, they take the part of a better wrestler than myself.
(I.3.21–3)

Celia is provoking Rosalind by deliberately using terms that will exacerbate her condition by reminding her of its cause, Orlando.

14 A gallant curtle-axe upon my thigh,
A boar-spear in my hand, and in my heart
Lie there what hidden woman's fear there will,
We'll have a swashing and a martial outside,
As many other mannish cowards have
That do outface it with their semblances.
(I.3.115–20)

Rosalind, banished by Duke Frederick, is planning to travel to the Forest of Arden with Celia, disguising herself as a man, under the name of Ganymede, in order to ward off possible attackers. A 'curtle-axe' is a cutlass; 'swashing' means swaggering; 'outface it with their semblances' means use their appearance to bluff it out.

15 Now my co-mates and brothers in exile,
Hath not old custom made this life more sweet
Than that of painted pomp? Are not these woods
More free from peril than the envious court?
Here feel we not the penalty of Adam,
The seasons' difference, as the icy fang
And churlish chiding of the winter's wind,
Which when it bites and blows upon my body
Even till I shrink with cold, I smile and say
'This is no flattery; these are counsellors
That feelingly persuade me what I am'?
Sweet are the uses of adversity,
Which, like the toad, ugly and venomous,
Wears yet a precious jewel in his head;
And this our life, exempt from public haunt,
Finds tongues in trees, books in the running brooks,
Sermons in stones, and good in everything.
(II.1.1–17)

Duke Senior addresses his fellow exiles in traditional pastoral terms, contrasting the true life of the country with the false ('painted') life of the court. In Eden it was perpetual spring, so the 'penalty of Adam' is the fact that the seasons change, bringing in winter after summer. The toad was popularly supposed to be poisonous but to have a stone in its head which was an antidote.

16 The big round tears
Coursed one another down his innocent nose
In piteous chase.
(II.1.38–40)

The First Lord is describing a wounded deer to Duke Senior.

17 Sweep on, you fat and greasy citizens.
(II.1.55)

The First Lord describes the reactions of the melancholy lord Jaques to a herd of deer which went past the wounded deer without stopping. Jaques compares their indifference to that of people (particularly perhaps the merchants of London) who are too busy growing fat to care for others.

18 I love to cope him in these sullen fits,
For then he's full of matter.
(II.1.67–8)

Duke Senior plans to meet and engage Jaques in debate ('cope him').

19 Unregarded age in corners thrown.
(II.3.42)
Adam is describing the fate of servants who end up discarded when they are no longer any use to their masters.

20 Though I look old, yet I am strong and lusty,
For in my youth I never did apply
Hot and rebellious liquors in my blood,
Nor did not with unbashful forehead woo
The means of weakness and debility;
Therefore my age is as a lusty winter,
Frosty, but kindly.
(II.3.47–53)
Adam wants to leave with Orlando, whose brother Oliver is now plotting to kill him. He describes his formula for a long and vigorous life. 'Lusty' means vigorous.

21 O good old man, how well in thee appears
The constant service of the antique world,
When service sweat for duty, not for meed!
Thou art not for the fashion of these times,
Where none will sweat but for promotion,
And having that do choke their service up
Even with the having.
(II.3.56–62)
Orlando responds to Adam's offer to go with him with this praise of his old-fashioned virtues. 'Antique' means ancient; 'meed' means reward; 'And having that do choke their service up/Even with the having' means and when they do get promotion they stop performing the services they did in order to get that promotion.

22 At seventeen years many their fortunes seek,
But at fourscore it is too late a week.
(II.3.73–4)
Adam comments at the end of the scene on his changing fortunes. 'It is too late a week' means it is too late in the day.

23 ROSALIND Well, this is the Forest of Arden.
TOUCHSTONE Ay, now am I in Arden, the more fool I. When I was at home I was in a better place, but travellers must be content.
(II.4.12–15)

Rosalind, Celia, and Touchstone have arrived in Arden, which appears not to be living up to previous descriptions of its charms. Touchstone refers to his lack of wisdom in joining Celia and Rosalind as well as to his professional status.

24 Corin, being old thou canst not guess,
Though in thy youth thou wast as true a lover
As ever sighed upon a midnight pillow.
(II.4.21–3)

Silvius, a conventional pastoral shepherd, is conventionally in love with Phebe, who equally conventionally disdains him. Corin, an older and more realistic shepherd, has claimed to have some inkling of Silvius's feelings. Lovers were supposed to be so distracted by thoughts of the beloved that they could not sleep.

25 If thou rememberest not the slightest folly
That ever love did make thee run into,
Thou hast not loved.
. . .
Or if thou has not broke from company
Abruptly, as my passion now makes me,
Thou hast not loved.
O Phebe, Phebe, Phebe!
(II.4.30–2, 36–9)

Silvius continues to behave in the absurd manner of a conventional lover, leaving Corin abruptly with his beloved's name on his lips.

26 We that are true lovers run into strange capers.
(II.4.49–50)

Touchstone, having observed Silvius's ridiculous behaviour and described his own parodistic wooing of a milkmaid, comments in mock-moralistic style.

27 Thou speakest wiser than thou art ware of.
(II.4.52)

Rosalind comments on Touchstone's remarks about the nature of love.

28 Under the greenwood tree,
Who loves to lie with me,
And turn his merry note
Unto the sweet bird's throat:
Come hither, come hither, come hither.
Here shall he see
No enemy

But winter and rough weather.
(II.5.1–8)
Amiens, one of Duke Senior's lords, functions in the play mainly as a singer. This is the first stanza of a typical pastoral song stressing the virtues of the country which he sings to Jaques and other lords.

29 I can suck melancholy out of a song, as a weasel sucks eggs.
(II.5.11–12)
Jaques responds to Amiens's song with a declaration of his talent for melancholy.

30 Who doth ambition shun,
And loves to live i'th'sun,
Seeking the food he eats,
And pleased with what he gets:
Come hither, come hither, come hither.
Here shall he see
No enemy
But winter and rough weather.
(II.5.35–42)
This is the second stanza of Amiens's pastoral song, continuing to stress the superiority of the country to the strife of the court. For the first stanza see 28.

31 AMIENS What's that 'ducdame'?
JAQUES 'Tis a Greek invocation, to call fools into a circle. I'll go sleep, if I can; if I cannot, I'll rail against all the first-born of Egypt.
(II.5.55–8)
Jaques has used the word 'ducdame' as a refrain in his improvised third stanza for Amiens's song. The meaning of 'ducdame' is obscure but, as Jaques comments, its function is clear. The reference to the 'first-born of Egypt', slain by God according to Exodus, is also obscure.

32 If he, compact of jars, grow musical,
We shall have shortly discord in the spheres.
(II.7.5–6)
Duke Senior, informed that Jaques has enjoyed a song, remarks that if he, made of discords ('compact of jars'), becomes musical, the whole organization of the universe will have to alter. The Duke is using the Ptolemaic idea of the universe being made up of spheres which form a heavenly harmony.

33 A fool, a fool I met a fool i'th'forest,
A motley fool – a miserable world! –
As I do live by food, I met a fool,
Who laid him down, and basked him in the sun,
And railed on Lady Fortune in good terms,
In good set terms, and yet a motley fool.
'Good morrow, fool,' quoth I. 'No, Sir,' quoth he,
'Call me not fool till heaven hath sent me fortune.'
(II.7.12–19)

Jaques enters to Duke Senior after having met Touchstone. The professional fool is wearing the traditional motley garment of the fool, usually interpreted as being quartered in primary colours, though there is some evidence that the cloth was actually woven from different coloured threads.

34 ''Tis but an hour ago since it was nine,
And after one hour more 'twill be eleven,
And so from hour to hour we ripe, and ripe,
And then from hour to hour we rot, and rot,
And thereby hangs a tale.' When I did hear
The motley fool thus moral on the time,
My lungs began to crow like Chanticleer
That fools should be so deep-contemplative;
And I did laugh, sans intermission,
An hour by his dial. O noble fool!
A worthy fool: motley's the only wear!
(II.7.24–34)

Jaques quotes Touchstone's parodistic moralizing on the passage of time. There is probably a pun on 'hour', which was pronounced like whore, and on the sexual sense of tail. Chanticleer is a traditional name for a cock; 'sans' means without; 'dial' means watch.

35 A worthy fool: one that hath been a courtier,
And says, if ladies be but young and fair,
They have the gift to know it: and in his brain,
Which is as dry as the remainder biscuit
After a voyage, he hath strange places crammed
With observation, the which he vents
In mangled forms. O that I were a fool!
I am ambitious for a motley coat.
(II.7.36–43)

Jaques continues his description of Touchstone. The supposedly hard dry brain of the idiot is compared to the very hard seaman's biscuit left over at the end of a long voyage; 'places crammed / With observation' probably has the secondary sense of quotations full of maxims; 'vents' means speaks, probably also with the sense of breaking wind.

36 I must have liberty
Withal, as large a charter as the wind,
To blow on whom I please, for so fools have;
And they that are most galled with my folly
They most must laugh.
(II.7.47–51)

Jaques demands the fool's traditional liberty to make his satirical attacks wherever he pleases.

37 Invest me in my motley; give me leave
To speak my mind, and I will through and through
Cleanse the foul body of th'infected world,
If they will patiently receive my medicine.
(II.7.58–61)

Jaques promises that if he dons the fool's coat he will use his liberty to be witty as a medicine to purge the world's ills. This view of the function of comedy has many classical precedents and was held by many of Shakespeare's contemporaries, notably Ben Jonson.

38 ORLANDO Forbear, and eat no more.
JAQUES Why, I have eat none yet.
ORLANDO
Nor shalt not, till necessity be served.
(II.7.88–90)

Orlando interrupts Duke Senior's banquet, seeking food for himself and Adam, both of them faint for lack of food. Jaques reacts in typical fashion.

39 But whate'er you are
That in this desert inaccessible,
Under the shade of melancholy boughs,
Lose and neglect the creeping hours of time:
If ever you have looked on better days;
If ever been where bells have knolled to church;
If ever sat at any good man's feast;
If ever from your eyelids wiped a tear,
And know what 'tis to pity and be pitied,
Let gentleness my strong enforcement be,
In the which hope I blush, and hide my sword.
(II.7.110–20)

Orlando moderates his rough demand for food from Duke Senior into this eloquent evocation of civilized values. His picture of the pastoral world varies considerably from the idealized one painted by other characters earlier in the play. 'Desert' means wild place.

40 DUKE

Thou seest we are not all alone unhappy.
This wide and universal theatre
Presents more woeful pageants than the scene
Wherein we play in.

JAQUES All the world's a stage,

And all the men and women merely players;
They have their exits and their entrances,
And one man in his time plays many parts,
His Acts being seven ages. At first the infant,
Mewling and puking in the nurse's arms;
Then, the whining schoolboy, with his satchel
And shining morning face, creeping like snail
Unwillingly to school; and then the lover,
Sighing like furnace, with a woeful ballad
Made to his mistress' eyebrow; then, a soldier,
Full of strange oaths, and bearded like the pard,
Jealous in honour, sudden and quick in quarrel,
Seeking the bubble reputation
Even in the cannon's mouth; and then, the justice,
In fair round belly, with good capon lined,
With eyes severe, and beard of formal cut,
Full of wise saws and modern instances,
And so he plays his part; the sixth age shifts
Into the lean and slippered pantaloon,
With spectacles on nose and pouch on side,
His youthful hose, well saved, a world too wide
For his shrunk shank, and his big manly voice,
Turning again toward childish treble, pipes
And whistles in his sound; last Scene of all,
That ends this strange eventful history,
Is second childishness, and mere oblivion,
Sans teeth, sans eyes, sans taste, sans everything.

(II.7.137–67)

As Orlando departs to fetch the distressed Adam, Duke Senior cues in Jaques's famous set piece on the seven ages of man. The idea of the world as a stage was a Renaissance commonplace which Shakespeare uses throughout his work in a variety of ways. It is not surprising that Jaques's lines have taken on an independent life of their own as an anthology or recitation piece, but there is absolutely no reason to regard them as representing Shakespeare's philosophy of life. They are simply lines spoken by a melancholy character whose voice is only one of many in the play, and one of their functions is to fill up time to give us an impression that Orlando has gone some way to fetch Adam; indeed, Adam's entrance at the end of the speech undercuts it by offering another version of old age. 'Mewling' means both whimpering and mewing like a cat; 'pard' means leopard; the justice has a large stomach lined with chicken ('capon'); 'wise saws and modern instances' are wise sayings and trite maxims; the pantaloon is the old man in Italian comedy.

41 Blow, blow, thou winter wind,
Thou art not so unkind
As man's ingratitude.
Thy tooth is not so keen,
Because thou art not seen,
Although thy breath be rude.
Hey-ho, sing hey-ho, unto the green holly,
Most friendship is feigning, most loving mere folly;
Then hey-ho, the holly,
This life is most jolly.
Freeze, freeze, thou bitter sky
That dost not bite so nigh
As benefits forgot.
Though thou the waters warp,
Thy sting is not so sharp
As friend remembered not.

(II.7.175–90)

While Duke Senior, Orlando, Adam, and the nobles eat, Amiens sings a song in praise of the pastoral life which comments implicitly on the unkind behaviour of Duke Frederick and Oliver to their relatives Duke Senior and Orlando. 'Rude' means rough.

42 Run, run, Orlando, carve on every tree
The fair, the chaste, and unexpressive she.

(III.2.9–10)

Orlando, who has been hanging love poems to Rosalind on the trees, is going to adopt another conventional lover's ploy by carving his beloved's name on tree trunks. 'Unexpressive' means inexpressible.

43 I know the more one sickens, the worse at ease he is, and that he that wants money, means, and content is without three good friends; that the property of rain is to wet and fire to burn; that good pasture makes fat sheep; and that a great cause of the night is lack of the sun; that he that hath learned

no wit by nature nor art may complain of good breeding, or comes of a very dull kindred.
(III.2.22–9)
Corin replies to Touchstone's question as to whether he has any philosophy in him. Corin, as befits an old shepherd in a pastoral play, is full of homely wisdom. 'Complain of good breeding' means complain of lack of good breeding.

44 I earn that I eat, get that I wear, owe no man hate, envy no man's happiness, glad of other men's good, content with my harm; and the greatest of my pride is to see my ewes graze and my lambs suck.
(III.2.69–73)
Corin explains more of his philosophy to Touchstone. 'Content with my harm' means accepting ill fortune as it comes.

45 *From the east to western Ind,*
No jewel is like Rosalind.
(III.2.84–5)
Rosalind is reading one of Orlando's verses which she has discovered on a tree. '*Ind*' is the Indies or India.

46 I'll rhyme you so eight years together, dinners and suppers and sleeping-hours excepted.
(III.2. 92–3)
Touchstone tells Rosalind he is unimpressed by Orlando's powers of versification, which appear to consist mainly of finding four rhymes for Rosalind.

47 Come, shepherd, let us make an honourable retreat, though not with bag and baggage, yet with scrip and scrippage.
(III.2.156–8)
Celia has told Corin and Touchstone to leave so that she can tell Rosalind that Orlando is in the forest. Touchstone refers to the practice of allowing a defeated army to make its retreat with its baggage; he and Corin have no bags but they do have the shepherd's pouch ('scrip'). 'Scrippage' is an invented word meaning the contents of a scrip, formed by analogy with baggage which means the contents of a bag.

48 O wonderful, wonderful, and most wonderful wonderful, and yet again wonderful, and after that out of all whooping!
(III.2.185–7)
Celia is tantalizing Rosalind by stressing the wonderful fact of Orlando's arrival in the forest without openly stating that it is

Orlando she is talking about. 'Out of all whooping' means beyond all cries of amazement.

49 One inch of delay more is a South Sea of discovery.
(III.2.190–1)
Rosalind, still being teased by Celia, demands that she confirms that she has met Orlando. The phrase means a second's delay is like an eternity, by analogy between a tiny measurement of space and the vast area of the South Seas.

50 It is as easy to count atomies as to resolve the propositions of a lover; but take a taste of my finding him, and relish it with good observance. I found him under a tree like a dropped acorn.
(III.2.225–8)
Celia, frenziedly questioned by Rosalind about Orlando, complains that it is as easy to count the specks in the air ('atomies') as it is answer the questions ('resolve the propositions') of a lover.

51 Do you not know I am a woman? When I think, I must speak.
(III.2.242–3)
Rosalind answers Celia's complaints about her interruptions with a typical misogynist charge against women. Presumably this gains something from Rosalind being dressed as a man and, in the original production, from the part being played by a boy.

52 JAQUES God buy you, let's meet as little as we can.
ORLANDO I do desire we may be better strangers.
(III.2.250–1)
Jaques and Orlando, disagreeing about Orlando's versification and his maltreatment of trees, agree to part, using polite forms to convey impolite messages. 'God buy you' means goodbye.

53 JAQUES I do not like her name.
ORLANDO There was no thought of pleasing you when she was christened.
(III.2.258–60)
Jaques complains about Rosalind's name, perhaps because it leads to Orlando's bad rhymes.

54 You have a nimble wit; I think 'twas made of Atalanta's heels.
(III.2.268–9)

Jaques compliments Orlando. In classical mythology Atalanta was a famous female runner.

55 There's no clock in the forest.
(III.2.292–3)
Orlando tells Ganymede (the disguised Rosalind), whom he has just met, that time in the forest is measured by the cycle of the seasons rather than by clocks.

56 The lazy foot of Time.
(III.2.296)
Ganymede (Rosalind) describes one of the properties of time to Orlando, setting up her subsequent dissertation on its different paces (see 57).

57 ROSALIND By no means, sir: Time travels in divers paces with divers persons. . . . He trots hard with a young maid between the contract of her marriage and the day it is solemnized. If the interim be but a se'nnight, Time's pace is so hard that it seems the length of seven year.
ORLANDO Who ambles Time withal?
ROSALIND With a priest that lacks Latin, and a rich man that hath not the gout: for the one sleeps easily because he cannot study, and the other lives merrily because he feels no pain, the one lacking the burden of lean and wasteful learning, the other knowing no burden of heavy tedious penury. These Time ambles withal.
ORLANDO Who doth he gallop withal?
ROSALIND With a thief to the gallows: for though he go as softly as foot can fall, he thinks himself too soon there.
ORLANDO Who stays it still withal?
ROSALIND With lawyers in the vacation: for they sleep between term and term, and then they perceive not how Time moves.
(III.2.299–300, 304–22)
Ganymede (Rosalind) gives Orlando examples of the varying paces of time. 'Trots hard' means goes at an uncomfortable pace; 'se'nnight' means week; 'softly' means slowly.

58 ORLANDO Can you remember any of the principal evils that he laid to the charge of women?
ROSALIND There were none principal, they were all like one another as halfpence are, every one fault seeming monstrous till his fellow-fault came to match it.
(III.2.338–42)

Ganymede (Rosalind) claims to have been warned against love and women by an old religious uncle. Such misogynist attacks were common in medieval and Renaissance literature.

59 ROSALIND But are you so much in love as your rhymes speak?
ORLANDO Neither rhyme nor reason can express how much.
(III.2.379–82)
Ganymede (Rosalind) questions Orlando about the sincerity of his love.

60 I drave my suitor from his mad humour of love to a living humour of madness – which was, to forswear the full stream of the world and to live in a nook merely monastic.
(III.2.399–402)
Ganymede (Rosalind) claims to Orlando that s/he cured a man of being in love by pretending to be a woman and behaving in such a way that he went truly mad. 'Drave' means drove; 'humour of' means inclination to; 'the full stream of the world' is the full life of the world; 'a nook merely monastic' is a monastic retreat.

61 TOUCHSTONE When a man's verses cannot be understood, nor a man's good wit seconded with the forward child Understanding, it strikes a man more dead than a great reckoning in a little room. Truly, I would the gods had made thee poetical.
AUDREY I do not know what 'poetical' is. Is it honest in deed and word? Is it a true thing?
TOUCHSTONE No, truly: for the truest poetry is the most feigning; and lovers are given to poetry; and what they swear in poetry may be said as lovers they do feign.
(III.3.10–19)
Touchstone is dazzling Audrey, a country woman, with his courtly language, playing on the idea that the best poetry, being the most skilfully contrived, is not spontaneous or truthful. The lines 'it strikes a man more dead than a great reckoning in a little room', which probably mean it stops a man short more than getting a large bill for a private room in an inn, are widely regarded as a reference to the dramatist Christopher Marlowe. Marlowe uses the phrase 'infinite riches in a little room' in *The Jew of Malta* and he was fatally stabbed in a private room of an inn, allegedly in a dispute over the bill.

62 AUDREY I am not a slut, though I thank the gods I am foul.
TOUCHSTONE Well, praised be the gods for thy foulness; sluttishness may come hereafter.
(III.3.34–7)

Audrey, being wooed by Touchstone, presumably sees herself as plain rather than foul.

63 As the ox hath his bow, sir, the horse his curb, and the falcon her bells, so man hath his desires; and as pigeons bill, so wedlock would be nibbling.
(III.3.72–4)
Touchstone explains his reasons for wanting to marry Audrey to Jaques. 'Bow' means yoke.

64 Ne'er a fantastical knave of them all shall flout me out of my calling.
(III.3.96–7)
Jaques has prevented Touchstone and Audrey from being married by the local vicar, Sir Oliver Martext, on the grounds of his incompetence. In his final lines Sir Oliver, a minor character, is given the opportunity to make an impression on the audience.

65 But, mistress, know yourself; down on your knees
And thank heaven, fasting, for a good man's love!
For I must tell you friendly in your ear,
Sell when you can, you are not for all markets.
(III.5.57–60)
Phebe, the disdainful shepherdess, has fallen in love with Ganymede (Rosalind), who urges her to love the devoted Silvius in return for his love. Phebe is the 'mistress' and Silvius is the good man.

66 I pray you, do not fall in love with me,
For I am falser than vows made in wine.
(III.5.72–3)
Ganymede (Rosalind) begs Phebe not to fall in love with him (her). Her claim to be less true than a drunken vow is based on her false identity rather than on her inconstancy, though that is the public meaning of her statement.

67 Dead Shepherd, now I find thy saw of might,
'Who ever loved that loved not at first sight?'
(III.5.81–2)
Phebe, who has fallen in love with Ganymede (Rosalind) at first sight, quotes an apt line from the poem *Hero and Leander* by Marlowe, the 'dead Shepherd'. For another reference to Marlowe in the play, see 61. 'Saw' means maxim.

68 JAQUES Nay then, God buy you, an you talk in blank verse. (*Going*)

ROSALIND (*as he goes*) Farewell, Monsieur Traveller. Look you lisp and wear strange suits; disable all the benefits of your own country; be out of love with your nativity, and almost chide God for making you that countenance you are; or I will scarce think you have swam in a gondola.
(*IV.1.28–34*)
Jaques has told Ganymede (Rosalind) that his melancholy partly stems from the observations he has made on his travels. He departs as Orlando, arriving late for his appointment with Ganymede (who is pretending to be Rosalind), greets her with a line of blank verse. Rosalind, delaying noticing Orlando, complains about the affectations of travellers, using charges often levelled in Elizabethan and Jacobean literature. 'God buy you' means good-bye; 'lisp' means affect a foreign accent; 'disable' means decry; 'swam' means floated. As the reference to the gondola indicates, English travellers often went to Venice – Ben Jonson offers a memorable portrait of one in *Volpone*.

69 ORLANDO My fair Rosalind, I come within an hour of my promise.
ROSALIND Break an hour's promise in love? He that will divide a minute into a thousand parts, and break but a part of the thousandth part of a minute in the affairs of love, it may be said of him that Cupid hath clapped him o'th'shoulder, but I'll warrant him heart-whole.
(*IV.1.37–43*)
Ganymede (Rosalind) has agreed to pretend for Orlando's benefit that s/he is Rosalind. S/he accuses him of not being truly in love. 'Clapped him o'th'shoulder' means arrested or claimed him.

70 Come, woo me, woo me: for now I am in a holiday humour, and like enough to consent.
(*IV.1.61–2*)
Ganymede (Rosalind), continuing the pretence of being Rosalind, decides to stop being angry with Orlando for his lateness, presumably demonstrating the supposed fickleness of the lover.

71 Nay, you were better speak first, and when you were gravelled for lack of matter, you might take occasion to kiss.
(*IV.1.66–8*)
Orlando has told Ganymede (Rosalind), who is at this point in the play pretending to be herself, that the first thing he would do if he were to meet the real Rosalind would be to kiss her. Ganymede suggests a different course of action. 'Were gravelled for lack of matter' means run out of things to say.

72 No, faith, die by attorney. The poor world is almost six thousand years old, and in all this time there was not any man died in his own person, videlicet, in a love-cause. Troilus had his brains dashed out with a Grecian club, yet he did what he could to die before, and he is one of the patterns of love. Leander, he would have lived many a fair year though Hero had turned nun, if it had not been for a hot midsummer night: for, good youth, he went but forth to wash him in the Hellespont and being taken with the cramp was drowned, and the foolish chroniclers of that age found it was 'Hero of Sestos'. But these are all lies; men have died from time to time and worms have eaten them, but not for love.
(IV.1.85–98)
Rosalind, maintaining her disguise as Ganymede, but pretending to be herself at this moment, responds to Orlando's threat to die if the real Rosalind will not marry him by telling him with gentle irony to die by proxy ('attorney'). The world was six thousand years old by Christian chronology; 'videlicet', continuing the legal language, is a Latin word meaning namely. Troilus, the Trojan hero and prototypical true lover, who figures in Shakespeare's play *Troilus and Cressida*, attempted to die when he discovered that Cressida was unfaithful to him. The accepted version of the story of Leander is that he swam the Hellespont every night to visit his beloved Hero of Sestos and was drowned; Rosalind compares the chroniclers to coroners who bring in the verdict that Leander's love for Hero was the cause of death.

73 Men are April when they woo, December when they wed; maids are May when they are maids, but the sky changes when they are wives.
(IV.1.136–8)
Ganymede (Rosalind) uses a commonplace comparison to dispute Orlando's claims to everlasting love.

74 O coz, coz, coz, my pretty little coz, that thou didst know how many fathom deep I am in love!
(IV.1.190–1)
Rosalind confesses to Celia the depths of her love for Orlando. 'Coz' is an affectionate abbreviation of cousin, a term used by Shakespeare and his contemporaries to refer to any relative.

75 The horn, the horn, the lusty horn,
Is not a thing to laugh to scorn.
(IV.2.18–19)

This refrain is part of a song sung by a hunting party who have just killed a deer. The deer's antlers recall the cuckold's horn, which is presumably lusty because it marks the wife's lust which has given the husband the horn.

76 Her love is not the hare that I do hunt!
(IV.3.19)
Ganymede (Rosalind) is surprised to have received a love letter from Phebe.

77 Chewing the food of sweet and bitter fancy.
(IV.3.102)
Orlando's brother Oliver, who has arrived in the forest and been reconciled with him, describes to Celia and Rosalind how Orlando had been preoccupied with love ('fancy') when he came across him.

78 Nay, 'tis true; there was never anything so sudden but the fight of two rams, and Caesar's thrasonical brag of 'I came, saw, and overcame'. For your brother and my sister no sooner met but they looked; no sooner looked but they loved; no sooner loved but they sighed; no sooner sighed but they asked one another the reason; no sooner knew the reason but they sought the remedy: and in these degrees have they made a pair of stairs to marriage which they will climb incontinent or else be incontinent before marriage. They are in the very wrath of love and they will together; clubs cannot part them.
(V.2.28–39)
Ganymede (Rosalind) tells Orlando how Oliver and Celia fell in love at first sight. 'Thrasonical', which means bragging, is derived from the style of a soldier called Thraso in the Roman dramatist Terence's *Eunuch*. Julius Caesar made his claim – *veni, vidi, vici* – after defeating Pharnaces in 47 BC; 'degrees' means steps; the first 'incontinent' means rapidly and the second unchaste. There may be a reference in the last line to the practice of calling 'clubs' to summon the watch to deal with a disturbance.

79 O, how bitter a thing it is to look into happiness through another man's eyes!
(V.2.41–2)
Orlando complains to Ganymede (Rosalind) that his brother's happiness reminds him of his own unhappiness.

80 PHEBE
Good shepherd, tell this youth what 'tis to love.

SILVIUS

It is to be all made of sighs and tears,
And so am I for Phebe.

PHEBE

And I for Ganymede.

ORLANDO

And I for Rosalind.

ROSALIND

And I for no woman.

SILVIUS

It is to be all made of faith and service,
And so am I for Phebe.

(V.2.78–85)

The various lovers with unresolved problems voice their frustrated desires as Phebe asks Silvius to explain the nature of love. The chorus begins again with Silvius's last line.

81 It is to be all made of fantasy,
All made of passion, and all made of wishes,
All adoration, duty and observance,
All humbleness, all patience, and impatience,
All purity, all trial, all observance;
And so am I for Phebe.

(V.2.89–94)

Silvius continues to expound his view of love and initiates another chorus of lovers. 'Fantasy' means unbridled emotion; 'observance' means attention.

82 Pray you no more of this, 'tis like the howling of Irish wolves against the moon.

(V.2.104–5)

Ganymede (Rosalind) ends the chorus of lovers' complaints.

83 It was a lover and his lass,
   With a hey, and a ho, and a hey nonino,
That o'er the green corn field did pass,
   In the spring time, the only pretty ring time,
When birds do sing, hey ding a ding, ding,
Sweet lovers love the spring.
Between the acres of the rye,
   With a hey, and a ho, and a hey nonino,
These pretty country folks would lie,
   In spring time, the only pretty ring time,
When birds do sing, hey ding a ding, ding,
Sweet lovers love the spring.
This carol they began that hour,

With a hey, and a ho, and a hey nonino,
How that a life was but a flower,
In spring time, the only pretty ring time,
When birds do sing, hey ding a ding, ding,
Sweet lovers love the spring.
And therefore take the present time,
With a hey, and a ho, and a hey nonino,
For love is crownèd with the prime,
In spring time, the only pretty ring time,
When birds do sing, hey ding a ding, ding,
Sweet lovers love the spring.

(V.3.15–38)

Two of Duke Senior's pages appear for the only time in the play in order to sing this song to Audrey and Touchstone. Once again the stress is on the joys of pastoral love. 'Ring time' is the time for exchanging rings; 'prime' means both perfection and spring.

84 DUKE
I do remember in this shepherd boy
Some lively touches of my daughter's favour.
ORLANDO
My lord, the first time that I ever saw him
Methought he was a brother to your daughter.

(V.4.26–9)

Shakespeare delights in the convention of disguise, drawing the audience into complicity with his stagecraft by making characters draw attention to their own lack of perspicacity and knowledge of what the audience knows.

85 There is sure another flood toward, and these couples are coming to the ark. Here comes a pair of very strange beasts, which in all tongues are called fools.

(V.4.35–7)

Shakespeare gives Jaques a speech which, by acknowledging the absurdity of a situation in which four couples are to be married, pre-empts a possible audience reaction of incredulity. Jaques is referring to the pairs of animals which Noah took into the ark; the 'pair of very strange beasts' are Audrey and Touchstone.

86 I press in here, sir, amongst the rest of the country copulatives, to swear and to forswear, according as marriage binds and blood breaks. A poor virgin, sir, an ill-favoured thing, sir, but mine own, a poor humour of mine, sir, to take that that no man else will. Rich honesty dwells like a miser, sir, in a poor house, as your pearl in your foul oyster.

(V.4.53–60)

Touchstone explains himself and Audrey to Duke Senior in sonorous terms. 'Country copulatives' means those who are about to be married in the country, with various sexual undertones. The marriage vows bind people together but passion ('blood') may lead to the breaking of those vows; 'honesty' means chastity. The description of Audrey is commonly misquoted as 'A poor thing, sir, but mine own'.

87 We quarrel in print, by the book, as you have books for good manners. I will name you the degrees. The first, the Retort Courteous; the second, the Quip Modest; the third, the Reply Churlish; the fourth, the Reproof Valiant; the fifth, the Countercheck Quarrelsome; the sixth, the Lie with Circumstance; the seventh, the Lie Direct. All these you may avoid but the Lie Direct; and you may avoid that too, with an 'If' ... Your 'If' is the only peace-maker; much virtue in 'If'.
(V.4.87–95, 99–100)
Touchstone gives a set-piece performance demonstrating the seven degrees of the lie before concluding with this list. 'In print' and 'by the book' both mean precisely, according to a book of rules, as well as through publication. 'If' is a peacemaker because it allows the parties to a quarrel to avoid the Lie Direct.

88 He uses his folly like a stalking-horse, and under the presentation of that he shoots his wit.
(V.4.103–4)
Duke Senior comments to Jaques that Touchstone uses his apparent foolishness like a decoy which allows him to make his witty points from cover.

89 Let me have audience for a word or two.
I am the second son of old Sir Rowland
That bring these tidings to this fair assembly.
(V.4.148–50)
This frankly theatrical play draws to a close with the sudden appearance of Jaques de Boys, the brother of Orlando and Oliver, who appears in order to bring news to the assembled inhabitants of Arden of the miraculous conversion of Duke Frederick.

90 If it be true that good wine needs no bush, 'tis true that a good play needs no epilogue.
(V.4.198–9)
The actor who plays Rosalind speaks the epilogue, referring to the idea that a good wine needs no advertisement – wine merchants hung 'bushes' outside their shops.

91 If I were a woman, I would kiss as many of you as had beards that pleased me, complexions that liked me, and breaths that I defied not; and, I am sure, as many as have good beards, or good faces, or sweet breaths, will, for my kind offer, when I make curtsy, bid me farewell.
(V.4.211–16)
Shakespeare uses the fact that Rosalind would have been played by a male actor in his theatre as part of the appeal for applause.

The Comedy of Errors

1 I to the world am like a drop of water
That in the ocean seeks another drop.
Who, falling there to find his fellow forth,
Unseen, inquisitive, confounds himself.
(I.2.35–8)
Antipholus of Syracuse's image of himself as a drop of water in search of another within an ocean anticipates the play's narrative, the quest of others, and its concern with identity and mistaken identity. Antipholus of Syracuse, accompanied by his servant Dromio of Syracuse, has arrived at Ephesus in search of his twin brother (Antipholus of Ephesus, who has as servant the twin of Dromio of Syracuse) and his mother (later revealed as Emilia, now abbess at Ephesus). The water imagery is significant because the family (and the servant twins) has been separated by shipwreck, as recounted in the first scene of the play by Egeon, the father of the two Antipholuses, who as a Syracusan merchant arrested in Ephesus has been condemned to die by that city's laws. Antipholus' speech significantly precedes the first example of mistaken identity in the play when Antipholus takes Dromio of Ephesus for his own servant.

2 They say this town is full of cozenage,
As nimble jugglers that deceive the eye,
Dark-working sorcerers that change the mind,
Soul-killing witches that deform the body,
Disguisèd cheaters, prating mountebanks,
And many suchlike liberties of sin.
(I.2.97–102)
In this description of the magical atmosphere of Ephesus, given by Antipholus of Syracuse and so important to the play, Shakespeare is blending the description of Epidamnum given by Messenio at the beginning of *Menaechmi* by the Roman dramatist Plautus,

which is the major plot source of *The Comedy of Errors*, with the account of St Paul's visit to Ephesus contained in Acts 19.

3 A man is master of his liberty.
Time is their master, and when they see time
They'll go or come.
(II.1.7–9)

In response to the lamentations and railings against the freedom of men by Adriana, wife of Antipholus of Ephesus, her sister Luciana is offering the accepted wisdom of Shakespeare's age on male superiority and female obedience. Adriana's desperation is aggravated in the later section of this scene when her servant, Dromio, returns from Antipholus of Syracuse claiming that his master denies all knowledge of a wife. The emphasis that Shakespeare places on emotion in such situations is an interesting development of Plautine farce.

4 For know, my love, as easy mayst thou fall
A drop of water in the breaking gulf,
And take unmingled thence that drop again
Without addition or diminishing,
As take from me thyself, and not me too.
How dearly would it touch thee to the quick
Shouldst thou but hear I were licentious,
And that this body consecrate to thee
By ruffian lust should be contaminate?
(II.2.134–42)

Adriana is mistakenly addressing Antipholus of Syracuse as her husband who, she believes, is being unfaithful to her. She is using the sacramental idea of man and wife being one flesh as the basis of her inversion of the double ethic by which male infidelity was considered acceptable, but female unchastity intolerable. Her image of the water-drop recalls the quest for reunion undertaken by Antipholus of Syracuse who, as the addressee of this speech, is totally mystified.

5 Are you a god? Would you create me new?
  Transform me, then, and to your power I'll yield.
But if that I am I, then well I know
  Your weeping sister is no wife of mine,
Nor to her bed no homage do I owe.
  Far more, far more to you do I decline.
O, train me not, sweet mermaid, with thy note
  To drown me in thy sister's flood of tears.
Sing, siren, for thyself, and I will dote.
  Spread o'er the silver waves thy golden hairs

And as a bed I'll take thee, and there lie,
  And in that glorious supposition think
He gains by death that hath such means to die.
  Let love, being light, be drownèd if she sink.
(III.2.39–52)

Antipholus of Syracuse is pleading for the love of Luciana who, believing him to be Antipholus of Ephesus, her sister Adriana's husband, is outraged. What Antipholus took to be the magical atmosphere of Ephesus is now transformed into the magic of love. His quest for identity is again evident in the images of the sea-voyager, recalling the background narrative of the play given in I.1., as he conceives Luciana simultaneously as a goddess capable of transforming him and as a mermaid or siren, both sea creatures believed to lure sailors to destruction. Luciana considers what she takes to be Antipholus' almost incestuous passion for her as another manifestation of love's madness.

6 Marry, sir, she's the kitchen wench, and all grease; and I know not what use to put her to but to make a lamp of her and run from her by her own light. I warrant her rags and the tallow in them will burn a Poland winter. If she lives till doomsday she'll burn a week longer than the whole world.
(III.2.98–103)

The pursuit of Dromio of Syracuse by the kitchen wench parodies the mistaken pursuit of his master by Adriana. The earthy and physical parody by servants of the elevated notions of love indulged by their masters is a recurrent feature of Shakespearian comedy. Dromio's allusion to Poland gives rise to an extended geographical, and somewhat scatological, description of the wench's obese body. The last sentence confirms the diabolical nature of her lust, since Dromio associates her kitchen-fire with hell-fire. The wench is named as Nell (line 114) for the sake of a pun, though she appears to be the same figure as the Luce of III.1.

7 I think you all have drunk of Circe's cup.
(V.1.271)

The allusion by Solinus, Duke of Ephesus, to the witch Circe in Book X of Homer's *Odyssey*, who transformed Ulysses' companions into swine, is the play's final image of magic and metamorphosis. It follows the account given by Antipholus of Ephesus of his ill-treatment by his wife Adriana, culminating in his arrest and the exorcism of his 'madness' by Doctor Pinch, and Adriana's counter-claims of her husband's infidelities. Adriana is seeking restitution of her 'husband' from the Abbess Emilia, with whom Antipholus of Syracuse has taken refuge. Since 'behind the ditches of the abbey' is the place appointed for the death of Egeon, the long-lost husband of Emilia and father of the twin Antipholuses, the reappearance of the Abbess prompts a complete dénouement of the complex narrative.

Coriolanus

1 He's a very dog to the commonalty.
(I.1.26–7)
The comment is made of Caius Martius, later Coriolanus, by the first citizen. In the opening scene of the play, the social and political protest of the first citizen, who leads the mutinous plebeians, is presented in class terms, for he opposes patrician luxury and surfeit to plebeian poverty and starvation. Martius is depicted as the embodiment of the ruling class's military ethic. Despite the historical setting of ancient Rome, the plebeians are portrayed as a mob of London citizens.

2 What he cannot help in his nature you account a vice in him.
(I.1.39–40)
The defence of Caius Martius is argued by the second citizen, who is the antagonist in the opening discussion of the play. The vice, or innate weakness, referred to is the pride of Martius (later Coriolanus), which is both personal and social.

3 You may as well
Strike at the heaven with your staves as lift them
Against the Roman state.
(I.1.65–7)
Menenius (Agrippa) portrays the immutable and remorseless power of the Roman state by means of a comparison to heaven. Menenius has been received by the plebeians as an honest and benign patrician, but his disarmingly sympathetic greetings quickly give way to forceful warnings of this kind, just as his relaxed prose gives way to formal verse.

4 The kingly crownèd head, the vigilant eye,
The counsellor heart, the arm our soldier,
Our steed the leg, the tongue our trumpeter.
(I.1.113–15)
The first citizen is pursuing Menenius' parable of the rebellion of the parts of the body against the belly. The analogy of the structure of the body to the state (or to what the Elizabethans aptly termed 'the body politic') was a commonplace of Renaissance

thought, which derived ultimately from classical antiquity. The specific association of this fable with Menenius and with this incident in the Coriolanus legend derives from Livy's *History of Rome* and from Plutarch's *The Lives of the Noble Grecians and Romanes* (translated by Sir Thomas North, 1579). There are also references in William Camden's *Remaines of a Greater Worke, Concerning Britaine* of 1605, where the author is following a medieval work, John of Salisbury's *Policraticus*.

5 The senators of Rome are this good belly,
And you the mutinous members. For examine
Their counsels and their cares, digest things rightly
Touching the weal o'th'common, you shall find
No public benefit which you receive
But it proceeds or comes from them to you,
And no way from yourselves.
(I.1.146–52)

The culmination of Menenius' parable of the rebellion of the parts of the body against the belly is its application to the relationship between the plebeians and the patrician class, between the ruled and the rulers in Roman society. The bonhomie of Menenius' presentation does not entirely conceal the severity of his reactionary political lesson.

6 What's the matter, you dissentious rogues,
That rubbing the poor itch of your opinion
Make yourselves scabs?
(I.1.162–4)

The first lines of Caius Martius (later Coriolanus) reveal his contempt for the plebeians and an almost physical revulsion at their condition. The image of disease relating to political dissension from this class, with the movement of the pun from 'matter' to 'scabs', is indicative of a class hatred which is almost pathological. 'Opinion' appears pejorative, opinion as opposed to knowledge, although the citizens clearly have and can articulate political views.

7 He that will give good words to thee will flatter
Beneath abhorring. What would you have, you curs,
That like nor peace nor war? The one affrights you,
The other makes you proud. He that trusts to you,
Where he should find you lions, finds you hares;
Where foxes, geese.
(I.1.165–70)

These words of Caius Martius (later Coriolanus) are a rebuff to the sarcastic observation of the first citizen that they have his 'good word'. The comment merely brings forth more venom from Martius' tongue. This time his contempt takes the form of derogatory animal images: the plebeians are likened to hares not lions, because they are not courageous but run away; and to geese not foxes, because they are stupid and lack the fox's cunning and intelligence.

8 They threw their caps
As they would hang them on the horns o'th'moon,
Shouting their emulation.
(I.1.210–12)
Caius Martius (later Coriolanus) is describing the conduct of the second band of mutinous citizens, which is heard off-stage during the first scene of the play. Martius recounts how they disbanded after being granted a petition which, in Martius' view, is the final blow against patrician authority. The last phrase quoted requires exegesis, since it is not clear whether the emulation refers to the plebeians rivalling the patricians, to their rivalling one another in their cries, or to the height of the plebeians' cries rivalling that of their caps flung in the air. In fact, it would appear that Shakespeare is condensing multiple meanings in a single phrase, and in the theatre there is no problem of comprehension.

9 Then we shall ha' means to vent
Our musty superfluity.
(I.1.223–4)
Caius Martius (later Coriolanus) has just learned that the Volsces have taken up arms against Rome. His contemptuous reference to the plebeians as 'cannon fodder' neatly encapsulates the cynical political insight that foreign wars distract the masses from domestic insurrection. It was an Elizabethan belief that war was wholesome for society.

10 I sin in envying his nobility,
And were I anything but what I am,
I would wish me only he.
(I.1.227–9)
This is the first reference by Caius Martius (later Coriolanus) to Tullus Aufidius, the warrior leader of the Volsces, who have just declared war on Rome. Martius and Aufidius, who share so many military values, are to be paralleled throughout the play. Envy was, of course, one of the seven deadly sins in Shakespeare's Christian culture and this explains the formula in which Martius expresses his paradoxical sense of rivalry and camaraderie with Aufidius. Shortly afterwards, Martius observes of Aufidius: 'He is a lion / That I am proud to hunt' (233–4).

11 VOLUMNIA To a cruel war I sent him, from whence he returned his brows bound with oak. I tell thee, daughter, I sprang not more in joy at first hearing he was a man-child than now in first seeing he had proved himself a man.
VIRGILIA But had he died in the business, madam, how then?
VOLUMNIA Then his good report should have been my son; I therein would have found issue. Hear me profess sincerely, had I a dozen sons, each in my love alike, and none less dear than thine and my good Martius, I had rather had eleven die nobly for their country than one voluptuously surfeit out of action.
(I.3.13–25)
This exchange establishes the contrast between the martial qualities of the Roman matron, Volumnia, Martius' mother, and the loving fears of her daughter-in-law, Virgilia. Volumnia is referring to her son's participation in earlier wars against the Latins. Shakespeare derived the idea of Martius being crowned with sprays of oak for a brave action from Plutarch. Martius appears crowned with the oaken garland in II.1. after his victory at Corioles. Shakespeare has made the phrase 'cruel war', which he found in Sir Thomas North's translation of Plutarch, part of the English language.

12 It [blood] more becomes a man
Than gilt his trophy.
(I.3.40–1)
The statement is an example of the militaristic attitudes of Volumnia, Martius' mother. It arises from her imagining Martius bloody yet triumphant in battle against the Volsces, much to the consternation of Virgilia, Martius' wife. Blood on the hero's brow is conceived as a symbol of triumph by comparing it to the gilding of monuments which was both a Roman and an Elizabethan practice. Shakespeare could have read of the Roman practice in Sir Thomas North's 1579 translation of Plutarch.

13 I saw him run after a gilded butterfly, and when he caught it, he let it go again, and after it again, and over and over he comes and up again, catched it again; or whether his fall enraged him, or how 'twas, he did so set his teeth and tear it. O, I warrant, how he mammocked it!
(I.3.61–6)
The incident is recounted of young Martius, Caius Martius' son, by Valeria, a Roman noblewoman. The violence of the action

proves the son to be a chip off the old block. Indeed, Volumnia comments: 'One on's father's moods' (67). At the same time, the merciless aggression of the action committed against an innocent and beautiful creature counterbalances the heroic picture of warfare given by Volumnia. 'Gilded' here means golden-coloured and 'mammocked' means tore to pieces.

14 You would be another Penelope. Yet they say all the yarn she spun in Ulysses' absence did but fill Ithaca full of moths.
(I.3.83–5)
Valeria's witty abuse of the story of Penelope as a type of wifely fidelity is used to urge Virgilia to leave the home to which she has confined herself in Martius' absence at the wars against the Volsces. The ironical attitude to classical legend which is manifest here may be used to direct the audience's attention to Shakespeare's own equivocal treatment of the Coriolanus story. In Homer's *Odyssey*, Penelope patiently awaits the return of her husband, Ulysses, from the Trojan war. She parries the advances of suitors by insisting that first she completes her weaving, which she secretly unpicks by night. Ulysses was Prince of Ithaca.

15 You shall not be
The grave of your deserving. Rome must know
The value of her own. 'Twere a concealment
Worse than a theft, no less than a traducement,
To hide your doings and to silence that
Which, to the spire and top of praises vouched,
Would seem but modest.
(I.9.19–25)
The statement of Cominius, one of the Roman generals in the war against the Volsces, on the social importance of heroic actions is made in response to Martius' demurring at praise of his conduct. It shows Martius more confident in military values than social ones. Martius is given the title of Coriolanus in recognition of his valour at the Volscian town of Corioles.

16 I am known to be a humorous patrician, and one that loves a cup of hot wine with not a drop of allaying Tiber in't.
(II.1.44–6)
Menenius' description of himself is a retort to the innuendo of Sicinius, one of the Tribunes of the People, that he is known to be autocratic and hostile to the plebeians. Menenius' response encapsulates his self-confidence and sense of patrician values. The Tiber is the river of Rome. Menenius is therefore saying that he never waters his wine.

17 My gracious silence, hail!
(II.1.168)
Martius' greeting for his wife, Virgilia, after his victorious return from the war against the Volsces is tenderly mocking. Unlike the proud and articulate Volumnia, Virgilia can only welcome home her husband in silence and tears. Martius, now dubbed Coriolanus in recognition of his victory at Corioles, reproves her, suggesting that tears more befit the mothers and widows of that city.

18 All tongues speak of him and the bleared sights
Are spectacled to see him. Your prattling nurse
Into a rapture lets her baby cry
While she chats him. The kitchen malkin pins
Her richest lockram 'bout her reechy neck,
Clambering the walls to eye him. Stalls, bulks, windows
Are smothered up, leads filled, and ridges horsed
With variable complexions, all agreeing
In earnestness to see him.
(II.1.197–205)
The envious description of Rome's adulation of the returning hero, Coriolanus, belongs to Brutus, the second Tribune of the People. The presentation of a compressed yet animated visual image of the crowd's response to Martius' triumph is a fine example of Shakespeare's mature verse. The details of the vignette, most noticeably the architectural details, are drawn anachronistically from Jacobean London and not from ancient Rome. The vocabulary of the passage poses problems to the modern auditor/reader. The following list of difficult terms gives the modern equivalent in brackets: 'sights' (eyes), 'chats' (gossips about), 'malkin' (slattern), 'lockram' (linen fabric), 'reechy' (dirty), 'bulks' (shop-fronts). 'Leads' could refer to either roofs or windows. 'Ridges horsed' indicates people sitting astride roof-ridges as if on horseback, and 'variable complexions' means all sorts of people.

19 Bid them wash their faces
And keep their teeth clean.
(II.3.59–60)
Coriolanus is speaking contemptuously of the plebeians to Menenius after he has been brought into the 'market-place', wearing the gown of humility, in order to beg the 'voices' of the people for his consulship. Like many other phrases in the play, this statement displays Coriolanus' almost pathological disgust of the plebs' physical condition.

20 Better it is to die, better to starve,
Than crave the hire which first we do deserve.
(II.3.112–13)

Coriolanus' maxim is taken from the scene in which he is obliged to beg the people's 'voices', or approval, for his consulship. The maxim displays his belief that actions should speak for themselves: his patrician pride is offended at having to display his wounds and beg approval. His conduct in this situation illustrates his discomfort in the world of politics as opposed to the arena of war.

21 Custom calls me to't.
What custom wills, in all things should we do't,
The dust on antique time would lie unswept
And mountainous error be too highly heaped
For truth to o'erpeer.
(II.3.116–20)

Coriolanus is unwillingly performing the ritual act of begging the people's 'voices' for his consulship. His resentment at the demand of tradition that he appear in the market place, dressed in the gown of humility, to beg public approval is evident in the form as well as the content of Coriolanus' soliloquy. Shakespeare here employs rhymed couplets, the vehicle of satire. Line 117 means: if we should observe every demand of tradition.

22 For
The mutable, rank-scented meiny, let them
Regard me as I do not flatter, and
Therein behold themselves.
(III.1.65–8)

Coriolanus' outburst against the plebeians, made to their Tribunes, asserts that, as he is no flatterer, he will act as a mirror to the common people, wherein they may see a true image of themselves. 'Meiny' indicates a multitude, while 'mutable' stresses the fickleness of the plebs' allegiance.

23 Hear you this Triton of the minnows? Mark you
His absolute 'shall'?
(III.1.89–90)

Coriolanus' sarcasm is directed at Sicinius, one of the Tribunes of the People. Coriolanus is accusing Sicinius of playing the big fish in a small pool – to adapt the image slightly into modern terms. Triton was a Graeco-Roman sea-deity; but the term could also signify one of a race of inferior sea-deities, which may be more appropriate here. The fact that a Triton was conventionally depicted with a shell-trumpet may have suggested the allusion, since Coriolanus is accusing Sicinius of noisy and vain trumpeting.

24 On both sides more respect.
(III.1.180)
These words, so apt an intervention in a heated argument, belong to Menenius, the arch-politician and diplomat. He is seeking to calm the quarrel between Coriolanus and the Tribunes of the People caused by the former's comments on the nature of the plebeians (and their leaders) when he is required to beg their 'voices', or approval, a second time.

25 PATRICIAN
This man has marred his fortune.
MENENIUS
His nature is too noble for the world.
He would not flatter Neptune for his trident,
Or Jove for's power to thunder. His heart's his mouth.
What his breast forges, that his tongue must vent,
And, being angry, does forget that ever
He heard the name of death.
(III.1.253–9)
This exchange between the unnamed patrician and Menenius recognizes the political folly and self-destructiveness of Coriolanus' act in drawing his sword and turning on the plebeians in violent abuse. Menenius, Coriolanus' political mentor, locates the cause of such action in the temperament of Coriolanus, which he describes in terms akin to Aristotle's notion of the magnanimous or great-souled hero. 'His heart's his mouth', meaning he utters directly what he feels, may allude to Ecclesiasticus 21:26: 'The heart of fools is in their mouth; but the mouth of the wise is in his heart.'

26 You common cry of curs, whose breath I hate
As reek o'th'rotten fens, whose loves I prize
As the dead carcasses of unburied men
That do corrupt my air – I banish you.
(III.3.120–3)
This is Coriolanus' vehement response to the plebeians' approval of their Tribunes' demands that he be banished from Rome as an enemy to his city and people. In the preceding scene, Coriolanus had accepted the admonition of Menenius and Volumnia and agreed to placate the common people by employing 'policy'; but the provocation of the Tribunes unleashes his virulent distaste of the plebeians' presence and values. His proud boast that he banishes them is no more than a rhetorical gesture and, when he

leaves the stage, it is for exile. The departure is greeted by the people and their Tribunes as a victory.

27 Despising
For you the city, thus I turn my back.
There is a world elsewhere.
(III.3.133–5)
The plebeians of Rome and their Tribunes have obtained the banishment of Coriolanus from the city as an enemy of the people on account of his violent abuse of them. Coriolanus proudly and defiantly turns the tables by taking an active rather than passive role in his banishment. His final phrase, on his exit from the public life of Rome, is much quoted in analogous contexts.

28 The beast
With many heads butts me away.
(IV.1.1–2)
Coriolanus' jocular reference to his banishment from Rome by the plebeians is part of his attempt to comfort his mother, Volumnia. It was a Renaissance commonplace to conceive the masses as a hydra, the many-headed monster of classical legend.

29 Anger's my meat. I sup upon myself,
And so shall starve with feeding.
(IV.2.50–1)
The essence of Volumnia's statement is evident: that she is so consumed by anger that she exhausts her own resources of energy. The source of her anger is Coriolanus' banishment by the plebeians and the comment follows her futile railing at the Tribunes of the People. Immediately after, she refers to herself as 'Juno-like' in her anger; and, indeed, she does possess the qualities of Juno, just as Coriolanus is a Mars. In Roman mythology, Juno was the wife of Jupiter and her anger was motivated by jealousy.

30 O world, thy slippery turns!
(IV.4.12)
The first phrase of Coriolanus' soliloquy on the instability of fortune and circumstance expresses its complete argument, to which the following lines serve merely as illustrations. It is uttered before the house of Aufidius in Antium, where Coriolanus has come disguised as a poor and lowly man. The visual referents of place and appearance thus reinforce the theme, so preparing the audience for Coriolanus' defection to the Volsces.

31 Thou hast a grim appearance, and thy face
Bears a command in't. Though thy tackle's torn,
Thou show'st a noble vessel. What's thy name?
(IV.5.63–5)
Aufidius is addressing Coriolanus, whose worth he instinctively recognizes despite his disguise as a poor man. Coriolanus has come to Aufidius' house at Antium after being banished from Rome by the plebeians. The image of the proud, yet ragged, vessel may refer not only to the innate merit of Coriolanus (the body as the vessel of the spirit), but also to the ship of state (whose image Coriolanus previously was at Rome). The connotations of the voyage of life are appropriate to this crucial moment of Coriolanus' destiny.

32 Peace is a very apoplexy, lethargy; mulled, deaf, sleepy, insensible; a getter of more bastard children than war's a destroyer of men.
(IV.5.230–2)
This denigration of peace comes from the lips of the first servingman in Aufidius' household. It was an Elizabethan belief that an extended peace was unhealthy and that the purging of society through war was wholesome. 'Mulled' means stupefied.

33 I'll never
Be such a gosling to obey instinct, but stand
As if a man were author of himself
And knew no other kin.
(V.3.34–7)
Coriolanus and Aufidius at the head of a Volscian army have invaded Roman territory and have the city at their mercy. These lines are the culmination of Coriolanus' meditation to himself at the sight of his wife, mother, child, and Valeria on their embassy to beg mercy of him for Rome. In the preceding scene, he has rejected the appeal of Menenius, his 'spiritual' father, and now he faces another test of his ability to determine his destiny uninfluenced by ties of kinship and emotion. Here he speaks of himself as self-begotten and self-determining, but the decisions that follow will prove otherwise.

34 Like a dull actor now
I have forgot my part and I am out,
Even to a full disgrace . . .
. . . O, a kiss
Long as my exile, sweet as my revenge!
(V.3.40–2, 44–5)

Coriolanus at the head of a Volscian army has Rome at his mercy. The appeal of his wife, Virgilia, leaves him bereft of words and undermines the resolute stance he has adopted towards his former land. Coriolanus can only briefly solicit Virgilia not to plead for Rome, before his silence is betrayed by the kiss which, as his comment acknowledges, becomes a substitute for his revenge. This action is a prelude to the greater capitulation to his mother, Volumnia, which follows.

35 The god of soldiers,
With the consent of supreme Jove, inform
Thy thoughts with nobleness, that thou mayst prove
To shame unvulnerable, and stick i'th'wars
Like a great sea-mark, standing every flaw
And saving those that eye thee!
(V.3.70–5)

Coriolanus, with Rome at his mercy, has been met by an embassy of his mother, wife, and child. These lines constitute Coriolanus' blessing of his son. Young Martius is portrayed as the image of his father; yet the desire that he manifest constant courage and resolution in battle contrasts with Coriolanus' lack of moral resolution in this situation. The simile of the 'sea-mark' appears to be drawn from the image of the 'sea' of battle.

36 O, mother, mother!
What have you done? Behold, the heavens do ope,
The gods look down, and this unnatural scene
They laugh at. O my mother, mother! O!
You have won a happy victory to Rome.
But for your son – believe it, O believe it –
Most dangerously you have with him prevailed,
If not most mortal to him.
(V.3.183–90)

The climactic moment of the play, the collapse of Coriolanus' resolve to destroy Rome, is pregnant with the city's salvation and the hero's destruction. Coriolanus has been persuaded by Volumnia's rhetoric and the silent appeal of his family's presence. The innate theatricality of the moment which Shakespeare found in his sources is emphasized by the vision of the gods witnessing the 'unnatural scene'. It is unnatural not only because of its inversion of the familiar roles (mother, wife, and child have knelt to beg their and their city's preservation), but also because it is inadequately realized by theatrical illusion.

37 If you have writ your annals true, 'tis there
That, like an eagle in a dove-cote, I

Fluttered your Volscians in Corioles.
Alone I did it. 'Boy'!
(V.6.114–17)
Coriolanus' self-destructive reference to his military feats at Corioles, which by virtue of the name given to him are almost part of his identity, is prompted by Aufidius' reproof, 'thou boy of tears' (101). On his return to Antium, Coriolanus has attempted to present the outcome of the campaign against Rome, when he yielded to his mother's pleading for Rome's salvation, as an honourable settlement. However, when he realizes Aufidius and his conspirators are intent upon his destruction, he goes to his death defiantly. The reference to the annals reveals both the hero's self-dramatization and the author's consciousness of his art of dramatic narrative.

 Cymbeline

1 CLOTEN The villain would not stand me.
SECOND LORD (*Aside*) No, but he fled forward still, toward your face.
(I.2.13–15)
Cloten's version of his swordfight with Posthumus is contradicted by the Second Lord's ironic aside. Posthumus has just been banished for marrying Imogen, Cymbeline's daughter by his first wife. Cloten, the sinister son of Cymbeline's second wife, has been rejected by Imogen but still pursues her. 'Stand' means confront.

2 Her beauty and her brain go not together. She's a good sign, but I have seen small reflection of her wit.
(I.2.27–30)
The First Lord flatters Cloten, arguing that Imogen has rejected him because, although she appears attractive ('She's a good sign'), she is not intelligent enough to appreciate his charms.

3 All of her that is out of door most rich!
If she be furnished with a mind so rare,
She is alone th' Arabian bird, and I
Have lost the wager. Boldness be my friend!
Arm me, audacity, from head to foot,
Or like the Parthian I shall flying fight.
(I.6.15–20)
The exiled Posthumus has wagered that Iachimo, an Italian gentleman, cannot persuade Imogen to make love with him. Iachimo goes to England to try to win the wager. This is his reaction on

first meeting Imogen. 'Out of door' means visible. The Arabian bird is the legendary Phoenix, which is unique, rekindling itself from its ashes when it dies. The Parthians were renowned for their ability to fire arrows over their shoulders from horseback (hence the term Parthian shot) – Iachimo means that he will be in retreat unless audacity helps him.

4 Cytherea,
How bravely thou becom'st thy bed, fresh lily,
And whiter than the sheets! That I might touch!
But kiss, one kiss! Rubies unparagoned,
How dearly they do't! 'Tis her breathing that
Perfumes the chamber thus. The flame o' th' taper
Bows toward her, and would underpeep her lids
To see th' enclosed lights, now canopied
Under these windows, white and azure laced
With blue of heaven's own tinct.
(II.2.14–23)

Iachimo, who has managed to get into her bedroom by concealing himself in a trunk, describes the sleeping Imogen. He compares her to Venus ('Cytherea') and associates her with the lily because it is a symbol of chastity. 'Bravely' means excellently; the 'Rubies unparagoned' are Imogen's lips which kiss one another, and the 'windows' are her eyelids.

5 On her left breast
A mole cinque-spotted, like the crimson drops
I' th' bottom of a cowslip.
(II.2.37–9)

Iachimo finds a physical characteristic which should convince Posthumus that he has made love with Imogen. 'Cinque-spotted' means with five spots.

6 Swift, swift, you dragons of the night, that dawning
May bare the raven's eye.
(II.2.48–9)

Iachimo adapts and reverses a line from the Roman poet Ovid's *Amores* which Marlowe had also used in *Doctor Faustus*. Unlike Ovid's lover, who wants to delay the dawn so that he can spend more time with his lover, or Doctor Faustus, who wants to delay midnight when the devils will come to fetch him to hell, Iachimo will be happy when day arrives because he will be able to get out of the trunk he has hidden in to spy on Imogen.

7 Hark hark, the lark at heaven's gate sings,
  And Phoebus gins arise,

His steeds to water at those springs
On chaliced flowers that lies;
And winking Mary-buds begin
To ope their golden eyes.
With every thing that pretty is,
My lady sweet, arise;
Arise, arise!
(II.3.19–27)

Cloten pursues Imogen in the traditional way of an aspiring lover by arranging for musicians to sing her awake with this aubade. 'Phoebus gins arise' means the sun begins to rise; 'winking Mary-buds' are closed marigold buds.

8 The thanks I give
Is telling you that I am poor of thanks
And scarce can spare them.
(II.3.88–90)

Imogen's barely polite response to Cloten's morning visit is reminiscent of Hamlet's response to Rosencrantz and Guildenstern (see *Hamlet* 89).

9 Is there no way for men to be, but women
Must be half-workers?
(II.5.1–2)

Posthumus, convinced by the circumstantial evidence that Iachimo has made love with Imogen, expresses his horror at her supposed infidelity in a generalized attack on all women. He asks rhetorically if there is no other way for men to exist ('be') without women playing a part in their creation (being 'half-workers').

10 I thought her
As chaste as unsunned snow.
(II.5.12–13)

Posthumus continues to express his horror at Imogen's supposed infidelity, using the familiar associations of coldness and snow with chastity to express her former state.

11 Could I find out
The woman's part in me! For there's no motion
That tends to vice in man but I affirm
It is the woman's part. Be it lying, note it,
The woman's; flattering, hers; deceiving, hers;
Lust and rank thoughts, hers, hers; revenges, hers;
Ambitions, covetings, change of prides, disdain,
Nice longing, slanders, mutability,
All faults that have a name, nay, that hell knows,

Why, hers, in part or all, but rather all;
For even to vice
They are not constant, but are changing still
One vice but of a minute old for one
Not half so old as that. I'll write against them,
Detest them, curse them. Yet 'tis greater skill
In a true hate to pray they have their will;
The very devils cannot plague them better.
(II.5.19–35)

Posthumus's overreaction to Imogen's supposed infidelity takes the form of assigning all vices to womankind. His extravagant reaction seems particularly petty and foolish in view of what the audience has seen of Imogen's actual dealings with Iachimo. 'Motion' means impulse; 'rank' means lascivious; 'nice' means wanton; 'mutability' means inconstancy. In the ninth line 'have a' is a conjectural emendation of a corrupt line.

12 The natural bravery of your isle, which stands
As Neptune's park, ribbed and paled in
With rocks unscalable and roaring waters,
With sands that will not bear your enemies' boats
But suck them up to th' topmast.
(III.1.18–22)

The Queen reminds Cymbeline of Britain's natural defences as part of her attempt to make him withstand the Roman demand for tribute. 'Ribbed and paled' means closed in and fenced.

13 Good wax, thy leave. Blest be
You bees that make these locks of counsel.
(III.2.35–6)

Imogen, about to open a letter from the exiled Posthumus, addresses the wax which seals the letter with mock gravity, blessing the bees for providing the wax to seal letters.

14 O, for a horse with wings!
(III.2.49)

Posthumus's letter has told Imogen to go to Milford Haven to meet him. She wishes for a winged horse like Pegasus in Greek mythology so that she can make the journey quicker. The audience will probably find Imogen's desire for speed somewhat undercut by their knowledge that Posthumus has instructed their servant Pisanio to kill her at Milford Haven.

15 A goodly day not to keep house with such
Whose roof's as low as ours! Stoop, boys. This gate
Instructs you how t' adore the heavens and bows you

To a morning's holy office. The gates of monarchs
Are arched so high that giants may jet through
And keep their impious turbans on without
Good morrow to the sun.
(III.3.1–7)

Belarius, a former courtier who stole Cymbeline's two infant sons when he was unjustly banished, has been living in disguise in the Welsh hills for many years. On his first appearance he draws a familiar Renaissance contrast between the reality of country life and the falsehood of the court. The low entrance ('gate') to their cave makes the boys, now adult, bow ('bows you') to the sun; 'jet' means strut.

16 GUIDERIUS Out of your proof you speak. We poor unfledged
Have never winged from view o' th' nest, nor know not
What air's from home. Haply this life is best,
If quiet life be best; sweeter to you
That have a sharper known, well corresponding
With your stiff age; but unto us it is
A cell of ignorance, travelling abed,
A prison, or a debtor that not dares
To stride a limit.
ARVIRAGUS What should we speak of
When we are old as you? When we shall hear
The rain and wind beat dark December, how
In this our pinching cave shall we discourse
The freezing hours away? We have seen nothing.
(III.3.27–39)

Cymbeline's stolen sons object to Belarius's arguments against the life of the court on the not unreasonable grounds that they have had no chance to make up their own minds by experiencing it for themselves. Belarius knows about life outside the nest by experience ('proof'), but Guiderius and Arviragus have only dreamt of travel ('travelling abed') like a debtor who could keep out of prison only by staying within a very narrowly defined area and dare not move outside its boundaries ('not dares / To stride a limit').

17 What shall I need to draw my sword? The paper
Hath cut her throat already. No, 'tis slander,
Whose edge is sharper than the sword, whose tongue
Outvenoms all the worms of Nile, whose breath
Rides on the posting winds and doth belie
All corners of the world. Kings, queens, and states,
Maids, matrons, nay, the secrets of the grave

This viperous slander enters.
(III.4.30–7)
Pisanio, Posthumus's and Imogen's servant, has just shown Imogen the letter in which Posthumus instructs him to kill her for her supposed adultery. Here he comments on the effects of the letter on Imogen. 'Worms' means snakes; 'posting' means speeding like a post horse.

18 Some jay of Italy,
Whose mother was her painting, hath betrayed him.
(III.4.47–8)
Imogen now believes that Posthumus has been as unfaithful as Iachimo had claimed in his attempt to seduce her. A 'jay' is a whore, making an impression through her appearance rather than her own innate qualities ('whose mother was her painting').

19 Men's vows are women's traitors!
(III.4.52)
Imogen continues to react to Posthumus's instruction to Pisanio to kill her for her supposed adultery. She sees his betrayal of his promises to her as part of a general treachery of men to women.

20 Hath Britain all the sun that shines?
(III.4.138)
Pisanio has suggested to Imogen that she should conceal herself until the nature of the mistake which has made Posthumus believe she is unfaithful is revealed. Imogen here expresses her willingness to leave the country.

21 Come, our stomachs
Will make what's homely savoury. Weariness
Can snore upon the flint, when resty sloth
Finds the down pillow hard.
(III.6.32–5)
After a successful hunting expedition, Belarius moralizes to Guiderius and Arviragus on the virtues of their spartan life. Their appetites ('stomachs') will make their plain ('homely') fare well flavoured ('savoury'), and they will rest well on hard beds whereas someone who has been lazy and indolent ('resty sloth') would find a soft pillow too hard.

22 Thy words, I grant, are bigger; for I wear not
My dagger in my mouth.
(IV.2.79–80)
Guiderius is talking to Cloten who, having followed Imogen to Wales in the hope of raping her, has met and insulted him.

23 I have sent Cloten's clotpoll down the stream.
(IV.2.185)
Guiderius, having killed Cloten and cut off his head ('clotpoll'), informs his brother of his actions. There may be an allusion to the mythological musician Orpheus, whose disembodied head also floated down a river, though the brutish Cloten has few obvious resemblances to the musician.

24 Great griefs, I see, med'cine the less.
(IV.2.244)
Imogen, disguised as a boy under the name of Fidele, has met Belarius and Guiderius and Arviragus who are, unknown to any of them at this stage, her long-lost brothers. Tired and distressed by travelling and by Posthumus's behaviour, she has taken a drug to help her recovery. This drug, given to Pisanio by the Queen in the hope that it would poison him and Imogen, is actually harmless but makes her seem to be dead. In this speech Belarius comments on the reaction of Guiderius and Arviragus to her apparent death: their griefs for Fidele's death cure ('med'cine') their grief for Cloten's.

25 Though mean and mighty, rotting
Together, have one dust, yet reverence,
That angel of the world, doth make distinction
Of place 'tween high and low.
(IV.2.247–50)
Belarius reminds Guiderius and Arviragus to pay proper attention to Cloten's burial.

26 Thersites' body is as good as Ajax'
When neither are alive.
(IV.2.253–4)
Guiderius agrees to Belarius's request to pay due attention to Cloten's burial but compares Cloten to Thersites, the ugly and malicious Greek who took part in the Trojan War, and Fidele to Ajax, one of the heroes of that war. Thersites and Ajax are significant characters in Shakespeare's earlier play *Troilus and Cressida.*

27 GUIDERIUS
Fear no more the heat o' th' sun
Nor the furious winter's rages;
Thou thy worldly task hast done,
Home art gone and ta'en thy wages.
Golden lads and girls all must,
As chimney-sweepers, come to dust.

ARVIRAGUS
Fear no more the frown o' th' great;
  Thou are past the tyrant's stroke.
Care no more to clothe and eat;
  To thee the reed is as the oak.
The sceptre, learning, physic, must
All follow this and come to dust.
GUIDERIUS
Fear no more the lightning flash,
ARVIRAGUS
  Nor th' all-dreaded thunder-stone;
GUIDERIUS
Fear not slander, censure rash;
ARVIRAGUS
  Thou hast finished joy and moan.
BOTH
All lovers young, all lovers must
Consign to thee and come to dust.
GUIDERIUS
No exorciser harm thee,
ARVIRAGUS
Nor no witchcraft charm thee.
GUIDERIUS
Ghost unlaid forbear thee;
ARVIRAGUS
Nothing ill come near thee.
BOTH
Quiet consummation have,
And renownèd be thy grave.
(IV.2.259–82)

Guiderius and Arviragus speak, rather than sing, this song over the supposedly dead body of Fidele, the disguised Imogen. It often appears in anthologies under the title of 'Fidele's Dirge'. 'As' means like; 'physic' means medicine; 'consign to thee' means meet the same fate as you; 'forbear thee' means leave you alone; 'consummation' means ultimate end.

28 Some falls are means the happier to arise.
(IV.2.406)

Lucius, commander of the invading Roman army, has discovered Imogen (disguised as Fidele) weeping over the headless body of Cloten, which she assumes from its clothing to be Posthumus's. Impressed by the fidelity of the apparent page to his dead master, he has taken her into his service. In this final line of the scene he uses conventional wisdom to try to cheer her up.

29 Fortune brings in some boats that are not steered.
(IV.3.46)
Pisanio, servant to Imogen and Posthumus, is baffled by the course of events and, ignorant of the fates of Posthumus, Imogen, and Cloten, he decides to commit himself to fate in the hope that everything will turn out well.

30 Every good servant does not all commands;
No bond but to do just ones.
(V.1.6–7)
Posthumus, having arrived in Britain with the invading Roman army, moralizes on his rashness in ordering Imogen's death. He addresses the absent Pisanio with the argument that a servant is bound only to obey just commands. In this case, fortunately for everyone, Pisanio, as the audience knows, has acted on this premise and has not carried out the unjust order.

31 Most welcome, bondage, for thou art a way,
I think, to liberty. Yet am I better
Than one that's sick o' th' gout, since he had rather
Groan so in perpetuity than be cured
By th' sure physician, Death, who is the key
T' unbar these locks.
(V.4.3–8)
In the course of the battle between the British and Roman armies Posthumus, fighting on the Roman side, has been captured and expects to be put to death. Here he welcomes prison and death as a punishment for his mistrust of Imogen.

32 A heavy reckoning for you, sir. But the comfort is, you shall be called to no more payments, fear no more tavern bills, which are often the sadness of parting.
(V.4.156–9)
Posthumus's jailer jokingly comforts him with the thought that death (the 'heavy reckoning') at least puts an end to incurring new debts.

33 Indeed, sir, he that sleeps feels not the toothache.
(V.4.171–2)
Posthumus's jailer sees the sleep of death as relieving men of the discomforts of everyday life.

Hamlet

1 You come most carefully upon your hour.
(I.1.6)
Francisco, a guard, welcomes Barnardo and draws attention to his punctuality, though 'carefully' may also have the sense of 'full of care' since, as we soon find out, odd things have been happening during their guard duties.

2 For this relief much thanks. 'Tis bitter cold,
And I am sick at heart.
(I.1.8–9)
Francisco is only a minor character but his brief comments help to establish the mood of unease and foreboding as he follows his remark about the weather with an insight into his mental state.

3 Not a mouse stirring.
(I.1.10)
Barnardo, the new guard, has asked if everything has been quiet. In his reply, Francisco uses this everyday reference which simultaneously conveys the welcome absence of trouble and the unnatural absence of movement and sound.

4 BARNARDO
What, is Horatio there?
HORATIO A piece of him.
(I.1.19)
Barnardo has asked Hamlet's friend Horatio to join them in watching for the ghost to appear again. His question builds up the nighttime atmosphere, created on the open air Renaissance stage by words rather than lighting effects. Perhaps Horatio's reply suggests his scepticism about the whole affair – is it his mind that is elsewhere?

5 What, has this thing appeared again tonight?
(I.1.21)
Marcellus, another guard, asks the assembled group if the ghost has appeared again, using an imprecise term, 'this thing', to whet the audience's appetite for further revelations.

6 Look where it comes again.
(I.1.40)
Marcellus draws our attention to the ghost's appearance.

7 But, in the gross and scope of mine opinion,
This bodes some strange eruption to our state.
(I.1.68–9)

Having seen the ghost, Horatio decides that in general terms ('the gross and scope of mine opinion') its appearance must be a warning of some major political crisis ('some strange eruption to our state').

8 In the most high and palmy state of Rome,
A little ere the mightiest Julius fell,
The graves stood tenantless and the sheeted dead
Did squeak and gibber in the Roman streets.
(I.1.113–16)

Horatio draws a parallel between the ghost's appearing and the supernatural phenomena that heralded the assassination of Julius Caesar. 'Palmy' means flourishing, and the 'sheeted dead' are in their shrouds.

9 I'll cross it, though it blast me.
(I.1.127)

Horatio says that he will attempt to stop the ghost by standing in its way. He is probably going to spread his arms in the shape of a cross, which would anger the ghost if its origins were diabolical.

10 We do it wrong, being so majestical,
To offer it the show of violence,
For it is as the air invulnerable,
And our vain blows malicious mockery.
(I.1.144–7)

After their attempts to stop the ghost have failed, Marcellus explains why their approach is misguided. The ghost cannot be harmed and their intervention is counterproductive.

11 It started, like a guilty thing
Upon a fearful summons.
(I.1.149–50)

Horatio describes the ghost's reaction to the cock crowing. It was believed that the cock summoned spirits back to hell.

12 Some say that ever 'gainst that season comes
Wherein our Saviour's birth is celebrated,
This bird of dawning singeth all night long.
And then, they say, no spirit dare stir abroad;
The nights are wholesome; then no planets strike;
No fairy takes; nor witch hath power to charm.

So hallowed and so gracious is that time.
(I.1.159–65)

Marcellus expands on the beliefs that Horatio has just articulated. This gloss on the widespread belief that the cock summoned wandering spirits is, apparently, Shakespeare's own invention. The basic suggestion is that the period before Christmas is so hallowed that normal night horrors are defused. ''Gainst' means before.

13 But look, the morn in russet mantle clad
Walks o'er the dew of yon high eastward hill.
(I.1.167–8)

Having created the cold night atmosphere in earlier speeches, Shakespeare now dispels it with Horatio's personification of dawn as a country dweller in a red or grey (russet could apply to either colour) cloak.

14 Though yet of Hamlet our dear brother's death
The memory be green ...
Yet so far hath discretion fought with nature
That we with wisest sorrow think on him
Together with remembrance of ourselves.
Therefore our sometime sister, now our Queen,
Th'imperial jointress to this warlike state,
Have we, as 'twere with a defeated joy,
With an auspicious and a dropping eye,
With mirth in funeral and with dirge in marriage,
In equal scale weighing delight and dole,
Taken to wife.
(I.2.1–2, 5–14)

Claudius has succeeded his brother Hamlet as king of Denmark and married Gertrude, Hamlet's widow, thus displacing young Hamlet, the son of Gertrude and old Hamlet. In this speech Claudius formally reminds the court of the course of events. The speech is based on a rhetorical ploy of balancing clauses against one another. Marriages between brothers- and sisters-in-law were forbidden, so Claudius's rhetoric is unlikely to have masked this from the original audience. 'Jointress' means joint inheritor and 'dole' means unhappiness.

15 CLAUDIUS
But now, my cousin Hamlet, and my son –
HAMLET (*aside*)
A little more than kin, and less than kind!

CLAUDIUS
How is it that the clouds still hang on you?
HAMLET
Not so, my lord, I am too much in the sun.
GERTRUDE
Good Hamlet, cast thy nighted colour off,
And let thine eye look like a friend on Denmark.
(I.2.64–9)

Hamlet's antagonism to Claudius is expressed through asides and puns on family relationships and natural phenomena. Claudius's first line draws our attention to the odd state of affairs, since Hamlet is both his nephew by kinship and his son by marriage. Hamlet's aside draws our attention to the fact that he is a close relative and that Claudius's behaviour is unnatural ('less than kind'). Hamlet's mourning dress presumably gives occasion to Claudius's 'clouds' and Gertrude's 'nighted colour', but Hamlet puns on 'sun' and 'son' to suggest that he is unhappy about both Claudius's attention, which keeps him in the glare of public notice, and the fact that he is now expected to behave as Claudius's son. 'Denmark' means the king of Denmark.

16 GERTRUDE
Thou knowest 'tis common. All that lives must die,
Passing through nature to eternity.
HAMLET
Ay, madam, it is common.
(I.2.72–4)

Gertrude attempts to generalize and thereby lessen Hamlet's feelings for his father. She uses 'common' to mean universal; he uses it to mean vulgar.

17 'Seems', madam? Nay, it is. I know not 'seems'.
'Tis not alone my inky cloak, good mother,
Nor customary suits of solemn black,
Nor windy suspiration of forced breath,
No, nor the fruitful river in the eye,
Nor the dejected 'haviour of the visage,
Together with all forms, moods, shapes of grief,
That can denote me truly. These indeed 'seem';
For they are actions that a man might play.
But I have that within which passes show –
These but the trappings and the suits of woe.
(I.2.76–86)

Gertrude has asked Hamlet why he seems to be taking his father's death so particularly hard. In this speech he replies that his outward appearance is a true reflection of his inner feelings.

'Windy suspiration of forced breath' means sighing uncontrollably; 'fruitful river in the eye' means weeping plentifully; ''haviour' means appearance.

18 But to persever
In obstinate condolement is a course
Of impious stubbornness. 'Tis unmanly grief.
It shows a will most incorrect to heaven,
A heart unfortified, a mind impatient
An understanding simple and unschooled.
(I.2.92–7)

Claudius's attempt at benevolent paternalism collapses into a series of platitudes aimed at shaking Hamlet out of his state of mind. 'Condolement' means sorrow; 'will most incorrect to heaven' means impious will.

19 HAMLET
I shall in all my best obey you, madam.
CLAUDIUS
Why, 'tis a loving and a fair reply.
(I.2.120–1)

Hamlet continues his uncooperative stance towards Claudius, agreeing only to his mother's request and leaving Claudius to pick up the crumbs.

20 O that this too too sullied flesh would melt,
Thaw, and resolve itself into a dew;
Or that the Everlasting had not fixed
His canon 'gainst self-slaughter. O God, God,
How weary, stale, flat, and unprofitable
Seem to me all the uses of this world!
Fie on't, ah, fie, 'tis an unweeded garden
That grows to seed. Things rank and gross in nature
Possess it merely. That it should come to this –
But two months dead, nay, not so much, not two!
So excellent a king, that was to this
Hyperion to a satyr; so loving to my mother
That he might not beteem the winds of heaven
Visit her face too roughly. Heaven and earth,
Must I remember? Why, she would hang on him
As if increase of appetite had grown
By what it fed on. And yet within a month –
Let me not think on't. Frailty, thy name is woman.
A little month, or e'er those shoes were old
With which she followed my poor father's body
Like Niobe, all tears, why she, even she –

O God, a beast that wants discourse of reason
Would have mourned longer – married with my uncle,
My father's brother, but no more like my father
Than I to Hercules. Within a month,
Ere yet the salt of most unrighteous tears
Had left the flushing in her gallèd eyes,
She married. O, most wicked speed, to post
With such dexterity to incestuous sheets!
It is not, nor it cannot come to good.
But break, my heart, for I must hold my tongue.
(I.2.129–159)

Hamlet's first soliloquy voices his unhappy state of mind occasioned by his mother marrying Claudius so soon after his father's death. At this stage he does not know that Claudius murdered his father, so his unhappiness is unfocussed and passive. 'The Everlasting' is God, a 'canon' is a religious law, and 'merely' means totally. When Hamlet compares his father and his uncle in mythological terms he sees his father as the sun god and his uncle as a bestial creature, half man half goat, which was associated with sexual licence. 'Beteem' means allow. Niobe was a mythological Queen noted for weeping over her dead children for nine days. Hercules, another mythological character, was noted for strength and courage.

21 A truant disposition, good my lord.
(I.2.169)

Horatio replies to Hamlet's question about his reasons for being in Elsinore with this joke about his disinclination to study.

22 We'll teach you to drink deep ere you depart.
(I.2.175)

Hamlet ironically promises Horatio that he will be introduced to the Danes' notorious drunken habits.

23 Thrift, thrift, Horatio. The funeral baked meats
Did coldly furnish forth the marriage tables.
(I.2.180–1)

This is Hamlet's ironic explanation of the reasons for the close proximity of his father's funeral and his mother's remarriage.

24 'A was a man. Take him for all in all,
I shall not look upon his like again.
(I.2.187–8)

Hamlet describes his father's worth in stoic terms.

25 In the dead waste and middle of the night.
(I.2.198)

Horatio is explaining the time and circumstances when Marcellus and Barnardo encountered the ghost. Some editors have preferred the reading 'dead vast' for 'dead waste'.

26 Armèd at point exactly, cap-a-pe.
(I.2.200)
Horatio is describing the physical appearance of the ghost who was wearing armour from head to foot ('cap-a-pe').

27 Distilled
Almost to jelly with the act of fear.
(I.2.204–5)
This is Horatio's description of the reaction of Marcellus and Barnardo to the ghost.

28 These hands are not more like.
(I.2.212)
Horatio ends his description of what he saw with this assertion that his hands resemble each other as much as the ghost resembles old Hamlet.

29 But answer made it none.
(I.2.215)
Horatio reports that the ghost did not reply to his questions.

30 A countenance more in sorrow than in anger.
(I.2.232)
Hamlet has asked how his father looked. This is Horatio's reply.

31 HAMLET His beard was grizzled, no?
HORATIO
It was as I have seen it in his life,
A sable silvered.
(I.2.240–2)
Hamlet is anxious to confirm the truth of Horatio's story by detailed questioning. 'Grizzled' means grey; 'sable silvered' means black with silver-grey streaks.

32 Give it an understanding but no tongue.
(I.2.250)
Hamlet asks the group who saw the ghost to keep silent about what they have seen and may see in the future.

33 My father's spirit! In arms! All is not well.
I doubt some foul play. Would the night were come!

Till then sit still, my soul. Foul deeds will rise,
Though all the earth o'erwhelm them, to men's eyes.
(I.2.255–8)

Left alone, Hamlet muses on the strangeness of the story he has just been told. 'Doubt' means suspect. For a development of the final lines see 103.

34 The chariest maid is prodigal enough
If she unmask her beauty to the moon.
Virtue itself 'scapes not calumnious strokes.
The canker galls the infants of the spring
Too oft before their buttons be disclosed.
(I.3.36–40)

Laertes, son of the court councillor Polonius, is giving his sister Ophelia some brotherly advice before setting off for France. Like his father and Claudius he is prone to sententious platitudes. The last two lines mean that disease ('canker') often injures ('galls') the young plants ('infants') before their buds ('buttons') have opened; there is also a sexual innuendo comparing the virgin Ophelia to a plant.

35 Do not, as some ungracious pastors do,
Show me the steep and thorny way to heaven
Whiles like a puffed and reckless libertine
Himself the primrose path of dalliance treads
And recks not his own rede.
(I.3.47–51)

In her reply to her brother's homilies, Ophelia draws on the biblical distinction between the difficulty of getting into Heaven and the ease of getting into Hell (see *All's Well* 26 and *Macbeth* 53). Shakespeare uses similar phrasing elsewhere to draw this comparison. An ungracious pastor is an unholy priest; 'puffed' means blown up with pride; 'recks not his own rede' means pays no attention to his own advice.

36 And these few precepts in thy memory
Look thou character. Give thy thoughts no tongue,
Nor any unproportioned thought his act.
Be thou familiar, but by no means vulgar.
Those friends thou hast, and their adoption tried,
Grapple them unto thy soul with hoops of steel.
But do not dull thy palm with entertainment
Of each new-hatched, unfledged courage. Beware
Of entrance to a quarrel. But, being in,
Bear't that th'opposèd may beware of thee.
Give every man thine ear, but few thy voice.

Take each man's censure, but reserve thy judgement.
Costly thy habit as thy purse can buy,
But not expressed in fancy; rich, not gaudy;
For the apparel oft proclaims the man...
Neither a borrower nor a lender be,
For loan oft loses both itself and friend,
And borrowing dulleth edge of husbandry.
This above all: to thine own self be true,
And it must follow, as the night the day,
Thou canst not then be false to any man.
(I.3.58–72, 75–80)

Many of Polonius's parting nuggets of advice to Laertes were already proverbial. 'In thy memory / Look thou character' means make sure you remember; 'unproportioned' means inappropriate; 'and their adoption tried' means once you are sure of their friendship; 'do not dull thy palm ... courage' means don't be too ready to make friends with every apparently brave acquaintance; 'Take each man's censure' means listen to everybody else's views; 'not expressed in fancy' means not fancifully made; 'husbandry' means good housekeeping.

37 You speak like a green girl,
Unsifted in such perilous circumstance.
(I.3.101–2)

Ophelia has told Polonius of Hamlet's interest in her. Here he accuses her of behaving like an inexperienced ('green') person with no experience ('unsifted') in such matters.

38 Ay, springes to catch woodcocks. I do know,
When the blood burns, how prodigal the soul
Lends the tongue vows. These blazes, daughter,
Giving more light than heat, extinct in both
Even in their promise, as it is a-making,
You must not take for fire.
(I.3.115–20)

Polonius sees Hamlet's vows and gifts to Ophelia as traps ('springes') for a foolish bird ('woodcock'). 'Prodigal' means prodigally. The final lines suggest that Ophelia should not take Hamlet's offers seriously because they are like sparks which fade as soon as they appear.

39 For Lord Hamlet,
Believe so much in him that he is young,
And with a larger tether may he walk
Than may be given you.
(I.3.123–6)

Polonius expresses the double standard of sexual morality to Ophelia. Hamlet as a man and a prince has more freedom of action than Ophelia. The image is of an animal whose freedom to graze is determined by the length of the rope tethering it to one place.

40 HAMLET
The air bites shrewdly. It is very cold.
HORATIO
It is a nipping and an eager air.
(I.4.1–2)
Hamlet and Horatio are watching for the ghost; these lines re-establish a sense of the scene taking place outside through the references to the weather. 'Shrewdly' and 'eager' help to personify the air as sharp and biting. In this context 'air' probably also carries the association of breeze.

41 But to my mind, though I am native here
And to the manner born, it is a custom
More honoured in the breach than the observance.
(I.4.14–16)
Hamlet is describing the custom of celebrating the king's toast drinking with fanfares. Although he has been familiar with the practice since childhood ('to the manner born'), he finds it abhorrent and thinks that it would be more proper to disregard it than to continue to observe it. 'A custom / More honoured in the breach than the observance' has come to be used generally to mean one that is less often observed than it should be.

42 So oft it chance in particular men
That – for some vicious mole of nature in them,
As in their birth, wherein they are not guilty,
Since nature cannot choose his origin –
By the o'ergrowth of some complexion,
Oft breaking down the pales and forts of reason,
Or by some habit that too much o'er-leavens
The form of plausive manners – that these men,
Carrying, I say, the stamp of one defect,
Being nature's livery or fortune's star,
His virtues else, be they as pure as grace,
As infinite as man may undergo,
Shall in the general censure take corruption
From that particular fault.
(I.4.23–36)
Hamlet muses to Horatio on the way that public opinion ('general censure') can see one natural blemish ('some vicious

mole of nature') as outweighing all a man's virtues. 'By the o'ergrowth of some complexion' means by some character trait overdeveloping; 'pales' means fences; 'o'er-leavens' means corrupts; 'plausive' means pleasing.

43 Angels and ministers of grace defend us!
Be thou a spirit of health or goblin damned,
Bring with thee airs from heaven or blasts from hell,
Be thy intents wicked or charitable,
Thou comest in such a questionable shape
That I will speak to thee.
(I.4.39–44)

Hamlet addresses the ghost. The ghost's shape is presumably 'questionable' not only because it looks like his father but because it causes doubt.

44 I do not set my life at a pin's fee.
And for my soul, what can it do to that,
Being a thing immortal as itself?
(I.4.65–7)

Hamlet responds to Horatio's attempts to dissuade him from talking to the ghost with these comments. He values his life no more than a pin which is very inexpensive to buy.

45 What if it tempt you toward the flood, my lord,
Or to the dreadful summit of the cliff
That beetles o'er his base into the sea...
The very place puts toys of desperation,
Without more motive, into every brain
That looks so many fathoms to the sea
And hears it roar beneath.
(I.4.69–71, 75–8)

Horatio's vivid description of the high cliff that overlooks ('beetles o'er his base') the sea ('flood') is part of his attempt to dissuade Hamlet from following the ghost. 'Toys of desperation' means idle thoughts of despair.

46 By heaven, I'll make a ghost of him that lets me!
(I.4.85)

Hamlet threatens Horatio and his companions with death if they try to hinder ('let') him from following the ghost.

47 Something is rotten in the state of Denmark.
(I.4.90)

Marcellus, having seen preparations for war, the ghost, and Hamlet's behaviour, makes the obvious point.

48 I am thy father's spirit,
Doomed for a certain term to walk the night.
(I.5.9–10)

The ghost confirms his identity to Hamlet and indicates that he is in purgatory since his doom is 'for a certain term' rather than eternal.

49 But that I am forbid
To tell the secrets of my prison house,
I could a tale unfold whose lightest word
Would harrow up thy soul, freeze thy young blood,
Make thy two eyes like stars start from their spheres,
Thy knotted and combinèd locks to part,
And each particular hair to stand an end
Like quills upon the fretful porpentine.
But this eternal blazon must not be
To ears of flesh and blood.
(I.5.13–22)

The ghost conjures up his picture of the horrors of purgatory through the effect that a description of them would have on the hearer. In Ptolemaic geometry the stars were thought to be fixed in spheres. The 'fretful porpentine' is an angry porcupine; 'eternal blazon' means revelation of the nature of eternity.

50 Murder most foul, as in the best it is,
But this most foul, strange, and unnatural.
(I.5.27–8)

The ghost sees his murder as particularly foul because it broke family ties and was therefore particularly against the natural order.

51 O my prophetic soul!
(I.5.40)

Since old Hamlet was murdered by Claudius, Hamlet now sees his misgivings about his uncle as prophetic.

52 But soft, methinks I scent the morning air.
(I.5.58)

The ghost interrupts his tale to remind himself of the necessity to be brief, since he has to go back to purgatory at dawn.

53 Thus was I sleeping by a brother's hand
Of life, of crown, of queen at once dispatched,
Cut off even in the blossoms of my sin,
Unhouseled, disappointed, unaneled,
No reckoning made, but sent to my account

With all my imperfections on my head.
O, horrible! O, horrible! Most horrible!
If thou hast nature in thee, bear it not.
Let not the royal bed of Denmark be
A couch for luxury and damned incest.
But howsomever thou pursues this act,
Taint not thy mind, nor let thy soul contrive
Against thy mother aught. Leave her to heaven
And to those thorns that in her bosom lodge
To prick and sting her. Fare thee well at once.
The glow-worm shows the matin to be near
And 'gins to pale his uneffectual fire.
Adieu, adieu, adieu. Remember me.
(I.5.74–91)

The ghost concludes his story with his demands for revenge on Claudius. 'Unhouseled, disappointed, unaneled' means not having received the sacrament, not prepared for death, and without having been given extreme unction. 'Nature' means natural family feelings; 'luxury' means lechery; 'matin' means morning.

54 O all you host of heaven! O earth! What else?
And shall I couple hell? O, fie! Hold, hold, my heart
And you, my sinews, grow not instant old,
But bear me stiffly up. Remember thee?
Ay, thou poor ghost, whiles memory holds a seat
In this distracted globe. Remember thee?
Yea, from the table of my memory
I'll wipe away all trivial fond records,
All saws of books, all forms, all pressures past
That youth and observation copied there,
And thy commandment all alone shall live
Within the book and volume of my brain,
Unmixed with baser matter. Yes, by heaven!
O most pernicious woman!
O villain, villain, smiling, damnèd villain!
My tables – meet it is I set it down
That one may smile, and smile, and be a villain.
At least I am sure it may be so in Denmark.
(I.5.92–109)

Hamlet reacts violently to the ghost's speech. 'Stiffly' means strongly; 'this distracted globe' probably refers to his head in which 'memory holds a seat'. Hamlet compares his memory to a memorandum notebook ('table') on which he had previously recorded aphorisms ('saws'), concepts, and general ideas ('forms') and impressions ('pressures') but which he will now wipe clean like a slate.

55 HAMLET

There's never a villain dwelling in all Denmark –
But he's an arrant knave.

HORATIO

There needs no ghost, my lord, come from the grave
To tell us this.

(I.5.123–6)

Hamlet, speaking in a distracted way after his conversation with the ghost, has promised to reveal wonderful news to Horatio and Marcellus. This is his news and Horatio's understandable response.

56 These are but wild and whirling words, my lord.

(I.5.133)

As Hamlet continues to talk distractedly, Horatio attempts to calm him.

57 It is an honest ghost, that let me tell you.

(I.5.138)

At this point Hamlet has apparently decided that the ghost is telling the truth, though his doubts resurface later in the play.

58 *The Ghost cries under the stage*

GHOST

Swear.

HAMLET

Ha, ha, boy, sayst thou so? Art thou there, truepenny?
Come on. You hear this fellow in the cellarage.

(I.5.149–51)

Hamlet now treats the ghost familiarly, using words like 'boy', 'truepenny' (which means honest fellow), and 'fellow' which carry overtones of intimacy and even condescension. The space under the stage was called the cellarage so there is a theatrical allusion here which diminishes the ghost's awesomeness as he is reduced to the level of a servant or property man under the stage.

59 *Hic et ubique*? Then we'll shift our ground.

(I.5.156)

The ghost follows Hamlet and his companions. This is Hamlet's comment on the ghost's second demand that they swear not to reveal what they have seen. '*Hic et ubique*' is Latin for here and everywhere.

60 Well said, old mole! Canst work i'th'earth so fast?
A worthy pioneer!
(I.5.162–3)
The ghost has again followed Hamlet and the others. Hamlet compares it to a mole burrowing in the earth and to a miner ('pioneer').

61 There are more things in heaven and earth, Horatio,
Than are dreamt of in your philosophy.
(I.5.166–7)
Horatio's expression of his amazement leads to this comment of Hamlet's. The exact significance of 'your' is unclear: Hamlet may be referring to Horatio's own particular brand of philosophy or he may be showing scorn of rational explanations in general.

62 To put an antic disposition on.
(I.5.172)
Hamlet is telling Horatio and Marcellus how he may act in the future, which may include fantastic behaviour ('antic disposition').

63 Rest, rest, perturbèd spirit!
(I.5.182)
Hamlet responds to the ghost's final speech with this soothing reply.

64 The time is out of joint. O, cursèd spite,
That ever I was born to set it right!
(I.5.188–9)
Hamlet laments the fact that he is destined to have to right the wrongs that are disturbing the natural order.

65 Your bait of falsehood takes this carp of truth,
And thus do we of wisdom and of reach,
With windlasses and with assays of bias,
By indirections find directions out.
(II.1.63–6)
Polonius uses a fishing image in telling his servant Reynaldo how to spy on Laertes in France. He is to use untrue stories ('bait of falsehood') about Laertes in order to find out the truth about what he is getting up to. Polonius suggests that wise and penetrating people like him ('we of wisdom and of reach') use indirect methods and oblique approaches ('windlasses' and 'assays of bias'), taking a roundabout way to find out what is going on.

66 And let him ply his music.
(II.1.73)

Polonius's final instruction to Reynaldo is to let Laertes behave as he likes, probably with pejorative overtones.

67 My lord, as I was sewing in my closet,
Lord Hamlet, with his doublet all unbraced,
No hat upon his head, his stockings fouled,
Ungartered, and down-gyvèd to his ankle,
Pale as his shirt, his knees knocking each other,
And with a look so piteous in purport
As if he had been loosèd out of hell
To speak of horrors – he comes before me...
He took me by the wrist and held me hard.
Then goes he to the length of all his arm,
And with his other hand thus o'er his brow
He falls to such perusal of my face
As 'a would draw it. Long stayed he so.
At last, a little shaking of mine arm
And thrice his head thus waving up and down,
He raised a sigh so piteous and profound
As it did seem to shatter all his bulk
And end his being. That done, he lets me go;
And, with his head over his shoulder turned,
He seemed to find his way without his eyes;
For out o'doors he went without their helps
And to the last bended their light on me.
(II.1.77–84, 87–100)
Ophelia describes Hamlet's appearance in her private room ('closet') to her father. His general appearance and behaviour are those of a conventional lover, though they are presumably part of his adoption of an antic disposition. His jacket ('doublet') was unfastened ('unbraced') and unlike a normal Elizabethan or Jacobean, who would have worn a hat indoors, he is hatless. His stockings have fallen down like fetters (gyves) round his ankles; 'purport' means expression; 'As 'a' means as if he.

68 This is the very ecstasy of love.
(II.1.102)
Polonius reads the conventional signs in Hamlet's behaviour in the conventional way, as tokens that he is mad for love.

69 CLAUDIUS
Thanks, Rosencrantz and gentle Guildenstern.
GERTRUDE
Thanks, Guildenstern and gentle Rosencrantz.
(II.2.33–4)

Rosencrantz and Guildenstern, childhood friends of Hamlet, have been summoned to court to try to find out what is wrong with Hamlet and to cheer him up. These lines of thanks have often been interpreted in the theatre as indicating their interchangeabililty. Tom Stoppard takes their apparent lack of individual identities as the starting point for his popular play *Rosencrantz and Guildenstern Are Dead.*

70 Thou still hast been the father of good news.
(II.2.42)
Claudius pays Polonius a courtly compliment. 'Still' means always.

71 Brevity is the soul of wit.
(II.2.90)
In the middle of a lengthy and rhetorical speech, Polonius indulges in an unconscious piece of self-criticism.

72 More matter, with less art.
(II.2.95)
As Polonius continues in his rhetorical vein, Gertrude interrupts to demand straight talking with more content and fewer technical flourishes.

73 That he's mad, 'tis true. 'Tis true, 'tis pity,
And pity 'tis 'tis true – a foolish figure.
But farewell it; for I will use no art.
(II.2.97–9)
Polonius is incapable of getting on with his explanation of Hamlet's madness without providing a running commentary on his own style of story-telling, disapproving here of his 'foolish figure' of speech.

74 *To the celestial, and my soul's idol, the most beautified Ophelia –*
That's an ill phrase, a vile phrase; 'beautified' is a vile phrase.
(II.2.109–11)
Polonius is reading out a letter from Hamlet to Ophelia. He interrupts his reading to comment on the style; presumably he objects to 'beautified' because it suggests that Ophelia is not naturally beautiful but has made herself beautiful. Hamlet's comments elsewhere in the play suggest that Polonius may be right to pick out this phrase.

75 *Doubt thou the stars are fire.*
Doubt that the sun doth move.
Doubt truth to be a liar.

But never doubt I love.
(II.2.115–18)
Hamlet's love poem to Ophelia, read out by Polonius, is similar to many poems of the period in its use of astronomical imagery and paradox.

76 Lord Hamlet is a prince, out of thy star.
(II.2.141)
Polonius is explaining to Gertrude and Claudius what he said to Ophelia. He use Ptolemaic astronomy to suggest that Ophelia is fixed in a lower sphere than Hamlet.

77 And he, repellèd, a short tale to make,
Fell into a sadness, then into a fast,
Thence to a watch, thence into a weakness,
Thence to a lightness, and, by this declension,
Into the madness wherein now he raves
And all we mourn for.
(II.2.146–51)
Once again Polonius embellishes his tale with rhetorical devices. Hamlet is seen as progressing downwards ('declension') through a series of states including not sleeping ('watch') and lightheadedness ('lightness') to madness.

78 Take this from this, if this be otherwise.
(II.2.156)
Polonius is probably inviting Claudius to cut off his head if what he has been saying turns out to be untrue. The line is more effective in the theatre than on the page.

79 Let me be no assistant for a state,
But keep a farm and carters.
(II.2.166–7)
Polonius says that if he is wrong in his diagnosis of Hamlet's mental state he should be demoted from his government office.

80 POLONIUS Do you know me, my lord?
HAMLET Excellent well. You are a fishmonger.
(II.2.173–4)
Although Hamlet has adopted his antic disposition, his description of Polonius as a fishmonger is unlikely to be accidental. A fishmonger deals in smelly dead animals, so Hamlet is probably alluding to the whiff of corruption he associates with him; there may also be a play on the idea of Polonius as a dealer in flesh, or a bawd.

81 To be honest, as this world goes, is to be one man picked out of ten thousand.
(II.2.178–9)
Hamlet's comment to Polonius shows that he too can indulge in commonplace wisdom, though he presumably does mean what he says.

82 POLONIUS (*aside*) Still harping on my daughter. Yet he knew me not at first. 'A said I was a fishmonger. 'A is far gone, far gone. And truly in my youth I suffered much extremity for love, very near this. I'll speak to him again. – What do you read, my lord?
HAMLET Words, words, words.
(II.2.187–93)
Polonius continues to fit all of Hamlet's behaviour into his earlier diagnosis; Hamlet continues to be enigmatic.

83 Though this be madness, yet there is method in't.
(II.2.205–6)
Polonius decides that there is still some logic ('method') in Hamlet's speech. Method here does not mean plan, for Polonius has not seen through Hamlet's antic disposition.

84 POLONIUS My honourable lord, I will most humbly take my leave of you.
HAMLET You cannot, sir, take from me anything that I will not more willingly part withal – except my life, except my life, except my life.
(II.2.213–17)
Polonius and Hamlet terminate their conversation with an exchange of civilities in which Hamlet's politeness scarcely hides his dislike of the old man. Hamlet's melancholy preoccupation with mortality is expressed in the twice-repeated final phrase.

85 GUILDENSTERN
On Fortune's cap we are not the very button.
HAMLET
Nor the soles of her shoe?
ROSENCRANTZ Neither, my lord.
HAMLET Then you live about her waist, or in the middle of her favours?
GUILDENSTERN Faith, her privates we.
HAMLET In the secret parts of Fortune? O, most true!
She is a strumpet. What news?
ROSENCRANTZ None, my lord, but that the world's grown honest.

HAMLET Then is Doomsday near.
(II.2.229–38)
Rosencrantz and Guildenstern have just met Hamlet, who has asked them how they are. Their reply leads to this bawdy personification of Fortune, who is seen as sexually promiscuous because she favours different men at different times. 'Privates' suggest both close friends and sexual organs.

86 HAMLET Denmark's a prison.
ROSENCRANTZ Then is the world one.
HAMLET A goodly one; in which there are many confines, wards, and dungeons, Denmark being one o'th'worst.
(II.2.243–6)
Hamlet's melancholy is clearly expressed in this view of existence; 'confines, wards, and dungeons' are all places of imprisonment.

87 There is nothing either good or bad but thinking makes it so.
(II.2.248–9)
Hamlet argues that it is our mental disposition that determines the worth and value of things rather than their innate qualities.

88 O God, I could be bounded in a nutshell and count myself a king of infinite space, were it not that I have bad dreams.
(II.2.253–5)
Hamlet, still being quite open with Rosencrantz and Guildenstern, develops his point that perception is more important than physical reality.

89 HAMLET But in the beaten way of friendship, what make you at Elsinore?
ROSENCRANTZ To visit you, my lord. No other occasion.
HAMLET Beggar that I am, I am even poor in thanks. But I thank you. And sure, dear friends, my thanks are too dear a halfpenny.
(II.2.269–74)
Hamlet asks why Rosencrantz and Guildenstern have come to Elsinore, using the idea of friendship as a path which has been well trodden, in the hope of getting an honest answer. His final comments are slightly obscure but seem to mean either that his thanks are not worth much or that their visit does not deserve very much in the way of thanks. It is clear, however, that he is unconvinced by Rosencrantz's answer.

90 I have of late – but wherefore I know not – lost all my mirth,

forgone all custom of exercises. And indeed it goes so heavily with my disposition that this goodly frame the earth seems to me a sterile promontory. This most excellent canopy, the air, look you, this brave o'erhanging firmament, this majestical roof fretted with golden fire – why, it appeareth nothing to me but a foul and pestilent congregation of vapours. What a piece of work is a man, how noble in reason, how infinite in faculties, in form and moving how express and admirable, in action how like an angel, in apprehension how like a god: the beauty of the world, the paragon of animals! And yet to me what is this quintessence of dust? Man delights not me – nor woman neither, though by your smiling you seem to say so.
(II.2.295–310)
Hamlet dwells on his melancholy without explaining its cause to Rosencrantz and Guildenstern. When he refers to the 'canopy' and the 'roof' he is probably referring not only to the actual heavens but also to the roof over the playhouse stage which was painted with celestial bodies. The roof 'fretted with golden fires' is, therefore, not only the sky with its heavenly bodies but also a roof with decorated bosses. Most of this passage was memorably set to music in the American musical *Hair*.

91 He that plays the king shall be welcome – his majesty shall have tribute of me.
(II.2.319–20)
Hamlet has been told that a troupe of players are on their way to Elsinore. His comments on the king can be applied to Claudius, whom he sees as a fake player king, not a real one.

92 HAMLET Do the boys carry it away?
ROSENCRANTZ Ay, that they do, my lord – Hercules and his load too.
(II.2.359–61)
Hamlet and Rosencrantz are discussing contemporary theatre politics. The popularity of child actors ('boys') led to difficulties for the adult companies like Shakespeare's. There is a direct reference to the Globe theatre where Shakespeare's company played – its sign was 'Hercules and his load', that is the mythological hero Hercules carrying the world (Globe) on his shoulders.

93 There is something in this more than natural, if philosophy could find it out.
(II.2.365–7)

Hamlet moves on from considering the strangeness of the popularity of the boys' companies to the new-found popularity of his uncle which he finds equally perplexing.

94 I am but mad north-north-west. When the wind is southerly, I know a hawk from a handsaw.
(II.2.377–8)
Hamlet tells Rosencrantz and Guildenstern that he is still fairly sane in a way that is likely to convince them that he isn't. He is saying that he is sane in 15 out of the 16 points of the compass. 'Handsaw' is usually taken as a version of 'hernshaw', a heron, though a hawk is also a tool used by plasterers. If Hamlet is using 'hawk' in the sense of a tool he is anticipating the first known printed reference by nearly seventy years.

95 That great baby you see there is not yet out of his swaddling clouts.
(II.2.381–2)
Hamlet is describing Polonius insultingly to Rosencrantz and Guildenstern. Babies were wrapped up in swaddling clothes ('clouts') to restrict their movements.

96 The best actors in the world, either for tragedy, comedy, history, pastoral, pastoral-comical, historical-pastoral, tragical-historical, tragical-comical-historical-pastoral, scene individable, or poem unlimited. Seneca cannot be too heavy, nor Plautus too light. For the law of writ and the liberty, these are the only men.
(II.2.395–401)
Polonius describes the actors' abilities in his usual style. The exhaustive inclusiveness of his list parodies prescriptive Renaissance theories of the special kinds of drama. 'Scene individable' means a play where there is no change of scene and the 'unity of place' is observed, in contrast to a 'poem unlimited' in which the classical unities of time, place, and action are not observed. The Roman dramatists Seneca (tragedies) and Plautus (comedies) had a considerable influence on Renaissance drama. The 'law of writ' again refers to plays which observe the unities, and 'liberty' to those which do not.

97 The play, I remember, pleased not the million. 'Twas caviary to the general.
(II.2.434–6)
Hamlet is remembering a play which ordinary people ('the million', 'the general') didn't like. Like caviare it was an acquired taste.

98 FIRST PLAYER
'But who, ah woe!, had seen the mobled Queen –'
HAMLET 'The mobled Queen'?
POLONIUS That's good. 'Mobled Queen' is good.
(II.2.500–2)

The player is performing a speech from a play about the fall of Troy. The queen is Hecuba, whose husband Priam has been murdered; Hamlet presumably sees parallels with his mother. Both Hamlet and Polonius pick up the unusual word 'mobled' which means muffled.

99 Good my lord, will you see the players well bestowed? Do you hear? Let them be well used, for they are the abstract and brief chronicles of the time. After your death you were better have a bad epitaph than their ill report while you live.
(II.2.520–4)

Hamlet asks Polonius to look after the actors. One imagines that Shakespeare's own sentiments may not be entirely absent from this speech.

100 Use every man after his desert, and who shall 'scape whipping?
(II.2.527–8)

This rhetorical question is part of Hamlet's response to Polonius's statement that he will look after the players 'according to their desert'. Hamlet argues that he should treat them better than they deserve since everyone is a sinner who deserves punishment.

101 O, what a rogue and peasant slave am I!
Is it not monstrous that this player here,
But in a fiction, in a dream of passion,
Could force his soul so to his own conceit
That from her working all his visage wanned,
Tears in his eyes, distraction in his aspect,
A broken voice, and his whole function suiting
With forms to his conceit? And all for nothing.
For Hecuba!
What's Hecuba to him, or he to her,
That he should weep for her? What would he do
Had he the motive and the cue for passion
That I have? He would drown the stage with tears
And cleave the general ear with horrid speech,
Make mad the guilty and appal the free,
Confound the ignorant, and amaze indeed

The very faculties of eyes and ears.
(II.2.547–563)
After the departure of Polonius and the players, Hamlet soliloquizes on the discrepancy between the player's capacity to feign violent passion and his own state. Here he puts forward a picture of the player as being able to work himself up into a high passion over the fictional sorrows of Hecuba. The player is able to use his imagination to control his faculties ('Could force his soul so to his own conceit') so that his face paled ('visage wanned') and his whole body expressed appropriately what he was imagining ('his whole function suiting / With forms to his conceit'). 'The general ear' means everybody who heard; 'amaze' means confuse. See also 102.

102 Yet I,
A dull and muddy-mettled rascal, peak
Like John-a-dreams, unpregnant of my cause,
And can say nothing, no, not for a king
Upon whose property and most dear life
A damned defeat was made. Am I a coward?
Who calls me villain? Breaks my pate across?
Plucks off my beard and blows it in my face?
Tweaks me by the nose? Gives me the lie i'th'throat
As deep as to the lungs? Who does me this?
Ha, 'swounds, I should take it. For it cannot be
But I am pigeon-livered and lack gall
To make oppression bitter, or ere this
I should ha' fatted all the region kites
With this slave's offal. Bloody, bawdy villain!
Remorseless, treacherous, lecherous, kindless villain!
O, vengeance!
Why, what an ass am I! This is most brave,
That I, the son of a dear father murdered,
Prompted to my revenge by heaven and hell,
Must like a whore unpack my heart with words
And fall a-cursing like a very drab,
A stallion!
(II.2.563–85)
Continuing his soliloquy, Hamlet moves on to consider himself rather than the player (see 101). He sees himself as passive ('muddy-mettled') and moping about ('peak') despite his genuine problems, before moving on to behave in a more 'heroic' way with his shouts of villainy and vengeance and then immediately returning to critical commentary on his own outburst. 'John-a-dreams' is a proverbial term for a dreamer; 'unpregnant of my cause' means not galvanized by my case; 'pate' means skull. 'Gives

me the lie i'th'throat / As deep as to the lungs' means makes me swallow the insult that I am a liar; ''swounds' is an oath contracted from by god's wounds. When Hamlet calls himself 'pigeon-livered' and lacking in gall he is using the idea that pigeons did not secrete gall, the supposed cause of anger, to suggest that he is lacking some vital ingredient in his make-up that would let him feel angry about his situation ('make oppression bitter'). He then moves on to a more rhetorical stance typical of the revenger in Renaissance drama with his reference to giving Claudius's ('this slave's') internal organs ('offal') to the local birds of prey ('region kites'). 'Kindless' means unnatural. Hamlet may extend the short line 'O, vengeance!' into a long cry in performance, or he may cut it short; either approach motivates his subsequent comments on his performance and continues to refer implicitly to the player's feigned violent passion. At the end Hamlet sees himself as a prostitute ('drab', 'stallion'), though some editors prefer the reading 'scullion', a kitchen boy.

103 I have heard
That guilty creatures sitting at a play
Have by the very cunning of the scene
Been struck so to the soul that presently
They have proclaimed their malefactions.
For murder, though it have no tongue, will speak
With most miraculous organ.
(II.2.586–92)

Hamlet hits on the idea of using the performance of a play to test Claudius's guilt, since criminals ('guilty creatures') have been so affected by the skill of the performance ('cunning of the scene') that they confessed. The last two lines reflect the thought that Hamlet voices in I.2; see 33.

104 The play's the thing
Wherein I'll catch the conscience of the King.
(II.2.602–3)

Hamlet ends the scene with a couplet encapsulating his hopes for the projected performance.

105 POLONIUS
'Tis too much proved, that with devotion's visage
And pious action we do sugar o'er
The devil himself.
CLAUDIUS O, 'tis too true.
(*Aside*) How smart a lash that speech doth give my conscience!
The harlot's cheek, beautied with plastering art,

Is not more ugly to the thing that helps it
Than is my deed to my most painted word.

(III.1.47–53)

Polonius and Claudius are planting Ophelia where Hamlet will come across her. Polonius has given Ophelia a prayerbook to justify her apparently solitary presence and his remarks are a gloss on his strategy. He suggests that it is only too common for the outward appearance ('visage') of religious devotion and the performance ('action') of pious acts to conceal ('sugar o'er') evil. Claudius applies this to his own state, since he too appears to be one thing when he is actually another. He modifies Polonius's idea of a sugar coating into the idea of cosmetics concealing the ugly cheek of the harlot. His word is 'painted' because it is disguised deceitfully, like the harlot's cheek.

106 To be, or not to be – that is the question;
Whether 'tis nobler in the mind to suffer
The slings and arrows of outrageous fortune
Or to take arms against a sea of troubles
And by opposing end them. To die, to sleep –
No more – and by a sleep to say we end
The heartache and the thousand natural shocks
That flesh is heir to. 'Tis a consummation
Devoutly to be wished. To die, to sleep –
To sleep – perchance to dream. Ay, there's the rub.
For in that sleep of death what dreams may come
When we have shuffled off this mortal coil
Must give us pause. There's the respect
That makes calamity of so long life.
For who would bear the whips and scorns of time,
Th'oppressor's wrong, the proud man's contumely,
The pangs of despised love, the law's delay,
The insolence of office, and the spurns
That patient merit of th'unworthy takes,
When he himself might his quietus make
With a bare bodkin? Who would fardels bear,
To grunt and sweat under a weary life,
But that the dread of something after death,
The undiscovered country, from whose bourn
No traveller returns, puzzles the will,
And makes us rather bear those ills we have
Than fly to others that we know not of?
Thus conscience does make cowards of us all;
And thus the native hue of resolution
Is sicklied o'er with the pale cast of thought,
And enterprises of great pitch and moment

With this regard their currents turn awry
And lose the name of action. Soft you now,
The fair Ophelia! – Nymph, in thy orisons
Be all my sins remembered.
(III.1.56–90)

Hamlet's meditative soliloquy is actually spoken with Ophelia onstage – he notices her in the last three lines – and with Polonius and Claudius hidden listening. Although it seems probable that Hamlet becomes aware of the presence of the concealed listeners later in the scene, it is generally assumed that this speech is not directed at them. 'Consummation' means final conclusion; 'rub' is used to mean obstruction, from its sense of an uneven surface on a bowling green. 'When we have shuffled off this mortal coil' means when we have shed our daily cares; 'respect' means consideration; 'contumely' means contempt; 'office' means officials; 'spurns / That patient merit of th'unworthy takes' means the contemptuous treatment ('spurns') that the worthy ('merit') have to suffer patiently at the hands of the unworthy. 'Quietus' comes from the Latin *quietus est*, meaning he is discharged from an obligation or debt, and is used here in the sense of final settlement. 'With a bare bodkin' means just with a dagger or large pin; 'fardels' are burdens; 'bourn' means region. The 'native hue of resolution' is the healthy natural complexion associated with resolution which becomes pallid with anxiety ('pale cast of thought'). 'Great pitch and moment' means great ambition and importance; 'with this regard' means when this is considered. 'Soft you now' is an expression of surprise; 'orisons' are prayers – Ophelia is reading a prayerbook.

107 To the noble mind
Rich gifts wax poor when givers prove unkind.
(III.1.100–1)

Ophelia, returning Hamlet's gifts to him, accuses him of being unkind, although she has been avoiding him. 'Wax' means become.

108 Get thee to a nunnery. Why wouldst thou be a breeder of sinners? I am myself indifferent honest, but yet I could accuse me of such things that it were better my mother had not borne me. I am very proud, revengeful, ambitious, with more offences at my beck than I have thoughts to put them in, imagination to give them shape, or time to act them in. What should such fellows as I do crawling between earth and heaven? We are arrant knaves all. Believe none of us. Go thy ways to a nunnery. Where's your father?
(III.1.121–30)

Hamlet is berating Ophelia, presumably as part of his 'antic disposition', though the scene is usually played as if he becomes aware of the hidden watchers only when he asks where Ophelia's father is. 'Indifferent honest' means reasonably honourable; 'beck' means bidding. It has been suggested that the slang of 'nunnery' as brothel may be present here.

109 Be thou as chaste as ice, as pure as snow, thou shalt not escape calumny.
(III.1.136–7)
Hamlet continues to berate Ophelia, offering her 'this plague for thy dowry'. Ice and snow were traditionally associated with the coldness of chastity and the purity of white.

110 I have heard of your paintings too, well enough. God hath given you one face, and you make yourselves another.
(III.1.143–5)
Hamlet's verbal assault on Ophelia now generalizes itself into an attack on women in general. He attacks the use of cosmetics ('painting') because of its element of deceit. The sense of a veneer of respectability covering an ugly truth appears throughout the play's imagery.

111 I say we will have no more marriage. Those that are married already – all but one – shall live.
(III.1.148–9)
Hamlet is obstensibly talking to Ophelia but 'all but one' appears to be directed at the concealed Claudius who is, of course, the exception Hamlet has in mind.

112 O, what a noble mind is here o'erthrown!
The courtier's, soldier's, scholar's, eye, tongue, sword,
Th'expectancy and rose of the fair state,
The glass of fashion and the mould of form,
Th'observed of all observers, quite, quite down!
And I, of ladies most deject and wretched,
That sucked the honey of his music vows,
Now see that noble and most sovereign reason
Like sweet bells jangled, out of time and harsh,
That unmatched form and feature of blown youth
Blasted with ecstasy. O, woe is me
T'have seen what I have seen, see what I see!
(III.1.151–62)
At the end of her disturbing interview with Hamlet, Ophelia paints this picture of Hamlet's qualities and her own distress. 'Expectancy and rose' means hope and flower; 'glass' means mir-

ror; 'mould of form' means model of behaviour; 'blown youth' is blooming youth and 'blasted' means withered, picking up the horticultural image from 'rose' and 'blown'.

113 Speak the speech, I pray you, as I pronounced it to you, trippingly on the tongue. But if you mouth it as many of our players do, I had as lief the town crier spoke my lines. Nor do not saw the air too much with your hand, thus. But use all gently. For in the very torrent, tempest, and, as I may say, whirlwind of your passion, you must acquire and beget a temperance that may give it smoothness. O, it offends me to the soul to hear a robustious periwig-pated fellow tear a passion to tatters, to very rags, to split the ears of the groundlings, who for the most part are capable of nothing but inexplicable dumb shows and noise. I would have such a fellow whipped for o'erdoing Termagant. It out-Herods Herod. Pray you avoid it.
(III.2.1–14)
Hamlet is instructing the player how to speak the speech he has written to be inserted in the play to be performed before Claudius. His comments also include a more general consideration of acting styles in which he expresses a preference for a more natural style rather than a crowd-pleasing rant. He feels that those who pay the lowest admission prices ('groundlings') are only capable of appreciating ('capable of nothing but') mime ('dumb shows') and noise, and objects to the coarse ('robustious') actor in a wig ('periwig-pated') who destroys an emotional passage ('passion') by overemphasis. In medieval religious drama Termagant, supposedly a Mohammedan god, and Herod were parts characterized by their wild and violent behaviour, so Hamlet is suggesting that a bad actor is excessively crude.

114 Be not too tame neither. But let your own discretion be your tutor. Suit the action to the word, the word to the action, with this special observance, that you o'erstep not the modesty of nature. For anything so o'erdone is from the purpose of playing, whose end, both at the first and now, was and is to hold, as 'twere, the mirror up to nature, to show virtue her own feature, scorn her own image, and the very age and body of the time his form and pressure. Now this overdone, or come tardy off, though it make the unskilful laugh, cannot but make the judicious grieve; the censure of the which one must in your allowance o'erweigh a whole theatre of others. O, there be players that I have seen play, and heard others

praise, and that highly, not to speak it profanely, that, neither having th'accent of Christians nor the gait of Christian, pagan, nor man, have so strutted and bellowed that I have thought some of Nature's journeymen had made men, and not made them well, they imitated humanity so abominably.
(III.2.16–34)
Hamlet continues with his advice to the player. The idea of art holding a mirror up to nature is an old one, but the length of Hamlet's comments suggests to many people that Shakespeare's own views may not be too distant from Hamlet's. Of course we do not know how the scene was originally staged and it may be that his comments were undercut by the actors. 'Come tardy off' means done badly; 'journeymen' are less accomplished workmen.

115 Let those that play your clowns speak no more than is set down for them. For there be of them that will themselves laugh to set on some quantity of barren spectators to laugh too, though in the meantime some necessary question of the play be then to be considered.
(III.2.37–42)
According to Hamlet comic actors need to be kept in check if their antics are not to distract the audience, some of whom are not too intelligent ('barren').

116 Since my dear soul was mistress of her choice
And could of men distinguish her election,
Sh'hath sealed thee for herself. For thou hast been
As one, in suffering all, that suffers nothing,
A man that Fortune's buffets and rewards
Hast ta'en with equal thanks.
(III.2.73–8)
Hamlet praises Horatio for his stoic qualities. 'Of men distinguish her election' means make a considered choice of men as friends; 'sealed' means marked.

117 Give me that man
That is not passion's slave, and I will wear him
In my heart's core, ay, in my heart of heart,
As I do thee.
(III.2.81–4)
Hamlet continues to praise Horatio for his rationality.

118 If his occulted guilt
Do not itself unkennel in one speech,
It is a damnèd ghost that we have seen,
And my imaginations are as foul

As Vulcan's stithy.
(III.2.90–4)
Hamlet expects that Claudius will reveal his hidden ('occulted') guilt, which will come out like a dog from a kennel ('unkennel') when he hears the speech Hamlet has inserted in the play to be performed before the court. As he explains to Horatio, if this does not happen the ghost is unreliable and his thoughts are as foul as the forge ('stithy') of Vulcan, the blacksmith god.

119 The chameleon's dish. I eat the air, promise-crammed. You cannot feed capons so.
(III.2.103–4)
Claudius has asked how Hamlet 'fares'. Hamlet takes this up as though Claudius were asking about his food and claims to be eating air – the chameleon's traditional food – which is crammed with Claudius's promises of the succession. Capons, castrated male chickens, were fattened for eating.

120 POLONIUS I did enact Julius Caesar. I was killed i'th'Capitol. Brutus killed me.
HAMLET It was a brute part of him to kill so capital a calf there.
(III.2.112–15)
Polonius recalls his acting triumphs and anticipates unconsciously his own death at the hands of Hamlet. Caesar's death has already been referred to by Horatio (see 8). The assassination of a tyrant is clearly relevant to Hamlet's situation at this moment.

121 Here's metal more attractive.
(III.2.119)
Gertrude has asked Hamlet to sit with her but he says that Ophelia draws him to her like a magnet.

122 HAMLET Do you think I meant country matters?
OPHELIA I think nothing, my lord.
HAMLET That's a fair thought – to lie between maids' legs.
(III.2.125–8)
Ophelia has refused Hamlet's request to lie in her lap. Here he asks if she thought he was referring to sex, making an indecent pun on cunt. Her possibly innocent reply is confounded by the common use of 'thing' to mean penis and 'nothing' to mean vagina which Hamlet picks up in his reply.

123 Die two months ago, and not forgotten yet? Then there's hope a great man's memory may outlive his life half a year. But, by'r Lady, 'a must build churches then, or else shall 'a

suffer not thinking on, with the hobby-horse, whose epitaph is 'For O, for O, the hobby-horse is forgot!'
(III.2.139–44)
Hamlet is talking to Ophelia about his father. Since prayers were said for the benefactors of churches, Hamlet ironically suggests that the sure way to be remembered after death is to 'build churches'. The hobby-horse in morris dancing was a mock horse worn by a performer who danced energetically; it thus acquired a secondary meaning of 'loose' woman which may be present here. The epitaph is presumably part of a contemporary ballad which has not survived.

124 Marry, this is miching mallecho. It means mischief.
(III.2.147–7)
This is Hamlet's comment to Ophelia on the dumb show before the play is performed to the court. The exact meaning of 'miching mallecho' is obscure, although it appears to mean something like sneaking mischief.

125 The players cannot keep counsel. They'll tell all.
(III.2.150–1)
The prologue has just entered. Hamlet remarks to Ophelia that the players cannot keep a secret ('counsel') because their job is to 'tell all'.

126 HAMLET Is this a prologue, or the posy of a ring?
OPHELIA 'Tis brief, my lord.
HAMLET As woman's love.
(III.2.161–3)
The prologue was only three lines long, so Hamlet compares it to a motto ('posy') on a ring which would inevitably be short. Hamlet's opinion of women is not high.

127 The lady doth protest too much, methinks.
(III.2.240)
Gertrude has been asked by Hamlet how she is enjoying the play, in which the player queen has just been protesting that she would never marry again if her first husband died. This is her answer.

128 CLAUDIUS Have you heard the argument? Is there no offence in't?
HAMLET No, no, they do but jest, poison in jest. No offence i'th'world.
CLAUDIUS What do you call the play?

HAMLET *The Mousetrap.*
(III.2.242–7)
Claudius has become suspicious because the play is so similar to his plot against old Hamlet. The 'argument' is the plot of the play. Agatha Christie's thriller *The Mousetrap*, which takes its title from these lines, has now run in London for over thirty years.

129 We that have free souls, it touches us not. Let the galled jade wince. Our withers are unwrung.
(III.2.251–2)
Hamlet, addressing Claudius ironically, claims that innocent people like themselves are unaffected by the play. A horse ('jade') which is chafed ('galled') should wince, but those who are untouched are like horses whose shoulder blades ('withers') are not rubbed ('unwrung') by harness.

130 Begin, murderer. Pox, leave thy damnable faces and begin. Come; the croaking raven doth bellow for revenge.
(III.2.261–3)
Hamlet curses ('Pox') the player murderer for behaving in the style he detests (see 113) by indulging in mime ('faces') before he gets to the words. 'The croaking raven …' looks like a cue for the player but his subsequent speech does not follow on directly. 'Bellow' seems inappropriate for a raven but it may be meant as part of the over-rhetorical style of the play within the play.

131 The story is extant, and written in very choice Italian.
(III.2.271–2)
As the player murderer kills the player king, Hamlet provides programme notes. Many Renaissance tragedies were, in fact, based on Italian sources.

132 What, frighted with false fire?
(III.2.275)
Claudius rises from his seat when the player king is poisoned. Hamlet believes that he has been upset by the resemblance between the fictional ('false') action and his own deeds. 'False fire' means blank cartridges.

133 Why, let the strucken deer go weep,
  The hart ungallèd play.
For some must watch, while some must sleep.
  Thus runs the world away.
(III.2.280–3)
Hamlet again contrasts the wounded ('the strucken deer') with those who are not ('hart ungallèd'), comparing the king, whose

guilt has been touched by the play, with himself. 'Watch' means stay awake. These lines may be a quotation from an old ballad.

134 O wonderful son, that can so 'stonish a mother!
(III.2.335)
Rosencrantz has told Hamlet that his mother is amazed by his behaviour. This is Hamlet's reply.

135 By these pickers and stealers.
(III.2.343)
In reply to Rosencrantz's reminder that he once loved him, Hamlet swears that he still does. Normally the oath would be 'by this hand', but Hamlet refers to the Catechism injunction to 'keep my hands from picking and stealing'.

136 'While the grass grows' – the proverb is something musty.
(III.2.351–2)
Rosencrantz has reminded Hamlet that Claudius has named him heir apparent. Hamlet's reply refers to the proverb 'While the grass grows, the horse starves'.

137 It will discourse most eloquent music.
(III.2.367)
Hamlet is referring to the recorder which he is asking Guildenstern to play.

138 You would play upon me. You would seem to know my stops. You would pluck out the heart of my mystery. You would sound me from my lowest note to the top of my compass. And there is much music, excellent voice, in this little organ. Yet cannot you make it speak. 'Sblood, do you think I am easier to be played on than a pipe? Call me what instrument you will, though you can fret me, you cannot play upon me.
(III.2.372–9)
Hamlet compares Rosencrantz and Guildenstern's willingness to try to sound him out with Guildenstern's unwillingness to try to play the recorder. 'Stops' are the finger holes in the recorder; 'sound' means fathom as well as produce sound; 'top of my compass' means top of my vocal range; 'organ' is the recorder; ''Sblood' is an oath by God's blood; 'fret' is a pun on irritate and the ridges on the fingerboard of a stringed instrument.

139 HAMLET Do you see yonder cloud that's almost in shape of a camel?
POLONIUS By th'mass, and 'tis like a camel indeed.

HAMLET Methinks it is like a weasel.
POLONIUS It is backed like a weasel.
HAMLET Or like a whale.
POLONIUS Very like a whale.
(III.2.383–9)

Hamlet continues his ironic treatment of Polonius, inviting him to share his changing perceptions of the cloud.

140 HAMLET
(*Aside*) They fool me to the top of my bent. – I will come by and by.
POLONIUS I will say so.
HAMLET
'By and by' is easily said.
(III.2.391–4)

Hamlet comments on his preceding discussions of the recorder and the cloud that the courtiers are making him play the fool to the limit of his capacity ('They fool me to the top of my bent').

141 'Tis now the very witching time of night,
When churchyards yawn, and hell itself breathes out
Contagion to this world. Now could I drink hot blood
And do such bitter business as the day
Would quake to look on.
(III.2.395–9)

Once again Hamlet adopts the language of the revenger with this invocation of the horrors of the night. The 'very witching time of night' is midnight; 'churchyards yawn' means graves gape open.

142 Let me be cruel, not unnatural.
I will speak daggers to her, but use none.
(III.2.402–3)

Hamlet reminds himself not to forget his filial obligation to his mother (to be 'not unnatural'). His remarks will be cutting but he will not be physically violent.

143 O, my offence is rank. It smells to heaven.
It hath the primal eldest curse upon't,
A brother's murder.
(III.3.36–8)

Claudius is attempting to pray for forgiveness. His offence is foul ('rank') and attracts the oldest human curse because the first murder was Cain's murder of his brother Abel.

144 What if this cursèd hand
Were thicker than itself with brother's blood,

Is there not rain enough in the sweet heavens
To wash it white as snow?
(III.3.43–6)

As Claudius continues to pray, he consoles himself with thoughts of the abundance of mercy, using imagery drawn from the Bible.

145 May one be pardoned and retain th'offence?
In the corrupted currents of this world
Offence's gilded hand may shove by justice;
And oft 'tis seen the wicked prize itself
Buys out the law. But 'tis not so above.
There is no shuffling.
(III.3.56–61)

The crucial problem for Claudius is whether he can be pardoned and still enjoy the fruits of his crime ('retain th'offence'). 'Offence's gilded hand' means the hand of the criminal bearing bribes; 'shuffling' means trickery.

146 Now might I do it pat, now 'a is a-praying.
(III.3.73)

Hamlet comes across Claudius praying and thinks it may be a good opportunity ('pat') to take his revenge ('do it'). ''A' means he.

147 Why, this is hire and salary, not revenge.
'A took my father grossly, full of bread,
With all his crimes broad blown, as flush as May;
And how his audit stands, who knows save heaven?
(III.3.79–82)

Hamlet starts to consider whether the opportunity to kill Claudius is as good as it seems. He believes that Claudius will be in a state of grace because of his prayers and would therefore go to heaven if he is killed, in which case killing him would be more like payment for services than vengeance ('hire and salary, not revenge'). He contrasts Claudius's supposed state of grace with that of his father, who was killed still full of worldly concerns (represented by 'bread') with his sins in full bloom ('broad blown, as flush as May') and with no opportunity for repentance. 'Audit' means account.

148 When he is drunk asleep, or in his rage,
Or in th'incestuous pleasure of his bed,
At game, a-swearing, or about some act
That has no relish of salvation in't –
Then trip him, that his heels may kick at heaven,
And that his soul may be as damned and black

As hell, whereto it goes. My mother stays.
This physic but prolongs thy sickly days.
(III.3.89–96)
Deciding that he should not send Claudius to heaven, Hamlet decides to catch him at a time when he is more likely to go to hell. 'This physic' is Claudius's praying, which only puts off the time of Hamlet's revenge.

149 My words fly up, my thoughts remain below.
Words without thoughts never to heaven go.
(III.3.97–8)
Ironically, in view of Hamlet's decision not to kill him because he is praying, Claudius ends his prayers by declaring that his mind ('thoughts') has not been engaged with his prayers ('words') but has remained fixed on this world ('below'). He is not in a state of grace and would presumably not have gone to heaven had Hamlet killed him.

150 Tell him his pranks have been too broad to bear with.
(III.4.2)
Polonius is instructing Gertrude how to go about her interview with Hamlet. 'Broad' means unrestrained.

151 You go not till I set you up a glass
Where you may see the inmost part of you.
(III.4.20–1)
Hamlet tells Gertrude that she is going to see her deepest thoughts ('inmost part of you') in the metaphorical mirror ('glass') that he will hold up to her.

152 How now? A rat? Dead for a ducat, dead!
(III.4.25)
Gertrude has called for help; Polonius, concealed behind a hanging (arras) has shouted out and Hamlet stabs him fatally. Hamlet has 'smelt a rat' and would wager a gold coin (ducat) that he has killed it.

153 A bloody deed – almost as bad, good mother,
As kill a king and marry with his brother.
(III.4.29–30)
Gertrude's lament over Hamlet's 'rash and bloody deed' in killing Polonius gives rise to this rejoinder from Hamlet. Gertrude is apparently unaware that Claudius killed old Hamlet.

154 Thou wretched, rash, intruding fool, farewell!
I took thee for thy better.
(III.4.32–3)

Hamlet addresses the dead Polonius. 'Better' means that Hamlet thought he had killed Claudius, Polonius's social rather than moral better.

155 Such an act
That blurs the grace and blush of modesty;
Calls virtue hypocrite; takes off the rose
From the fair forehead of an innocent love
And sets a blister there; makes marriage vows
As false as dicers' oaths; O, such a deed
As from the body of contraction plucks
The very soul, and sweet religion makes
A rhapsody of words!
(III.4.41–9)

Hamlet tells Gertrude what she has done to deserve his scolding. The 'act' is presumably her incest, which makes virtue appear deceitful ('calls virtue hypocrite'). It takes off the bloom ('rose') of an innocent love – presumably Hamlet and Ophelia's – substituting for it the mark of a branding iron which was inflicted on prostitutes. 'Contraction' means marriage contract; 'rhapsody' means meaningless jumble.

156 Ay me, what act,
That roars so loud and thunders in the index?
(III.4.52–3)

Hamlet's outburst about Gertrude's incest leaves her still baffled about the exact nature of her fault, so she asked what act he has been referring to. Here 'index' means a table of contents. Gertrude is complaining that Hamlet is going on about the awfulness of the act without getting round to saying what it is.

157 Look here upon this picture, and on this,
The counterfeit presentment of two brothers...
Could you on this fair mountain leave to feed,
And batten on this moor? Ha! Have you eyes?
You cannot call it love. For at your age
The heyday in the blood is tame; it's humble,
And waits upon the judgement.
(III.4.54–5, 67–71)

Hamlet makes Gertrude look at pictures of Claudius and old Hamlet. The pictures may be portraits hanging on the wall or they may be miniatures. It would seem more appropriate for Hamlet to have a miniature of his father while Gertrude has one of Claudius than for Gertrude to have portraits of both husbands on the wall. A 'counterfeit presentment' is an artistic representation; the idea of deceptive appearances is pervasive in the play. Hamlet sees his father as a mountain which Gertrude grazed on and his uncle as a moor on which she now gluts herself. He also puns on the sense of 'moor' as a black man in contrast with 'fair'. The image is not exact since neither mountains nor moors are ideal pasture. The 'heyday in the blood' means the excitement of sexual passion; 'waits upon' means obeys.

158 GERTRUDE
Thou turnest mine eyes into my very soul,
And there I see such black and grainèd spots
As will not leave their tinct.
HAMLET Nay, but to live
In the rank sweat of an enseamèd bed,
Stewed in corruption, honeying and making love
Over the nasty sty –
(III.4.90–5)

After Hamlet's comparison of Claudius and old Hamlet, Gertrude begins to understand. She sees herself as so deeply stained by sin that the marks will not wash out ('I see such black grainèd spots / As will not leave their tinct'). Hamlet then paints a picture of her wallowing ('enseamèd') and sweat-soaked ('stewed', probably with brothel overtones since stews were brothels) from love-making so that the bed is like a pigsty.

159 A vice of kings,
A cutpurse of the empire and the rule,
That from a shelf the precious diadem stole
And put it in his pocket.
(III.4.99–102)

Hamlet paints an unflattering picture of Claudius as like the fool in the morality plays ('vice'), and as a thief ('cutpurse') who stole the kingdom and purloined the crown ('diadem').

160 A king of shreds and patches.
(III.4.103)

Hamlet sees Claudius as a clown king wearing the fool's motley ('shreds and patches').

161 But look, amazement on thy mother sits.
O, step between her and her fighting soul!
Conceit in weakest bodies strongest works.
(III.4.113–15)

The ghost has reappeared but Gertrude, who cannot see it, is distracted by Hamlet's wild behaviour. Here the ghost draws Hamlet's attention to her distraction ('amazement'). 'Conceit' means imagination; the ghost does not appear to have a high opinion of women ('weakest bodies').

162 My pulse as yours doth temperately keep time
And makes as healthful music.
(III.4.141–2)
Gertrude, not having seen the ghost, has accused Hamlet of madness. He replies that he is as sane as she is and his pulse beats as steadily ('doth temperately keep time').

163 Mother, for love of grace,
Lay not that flattering unction to your soul,
That not your trespass but my madness speaks.
It will but skin and film the ulcerous place
Whiles rank corruption, mining all within,
Infects unseen. Confess yourself to heaven.
Repent what's past. Avoid what is to come.
(III.4.145–51)
Hamlet warns Gertrude of the danger of deluding herself with the balm ('flattering unction') that the nature of their interview has been determined by his madness rather than her crimes. In this speech the familiar idea of deceptive appearances takes the form of references to a disease working beneath the surface of the skin.

164 For in the fatness of these pursy times
Virtue itself of vice must pardon beg.
(III.4.154–5)
Hamlet tells Gertrude that the times are so gross (fat) and in such bad condition ('pursy' means short-winded) that the normal order is reversed.

165 GERTRUDE
O Hamlet, thou has cleft my heart in twain.
HAMLET
O, throw away the worser part of it,
And live the purer with the other half.
(III.4.157–9)
Gertrude claims that she has been so deeply affected by Hamlet that her heart is broken.

166 Assume a virtue, if you have it not.
(III.4.161)

Hamlet's advice to Gertrude reflects the play's concern with the relationship between appearance and truth.

167 And when you are desirous to be blest,
I'll blessing beg of you.
(III.4.172–3)
Hamlet tells Gertrude that he will not ask for a maternal blessing until she has repented and sought God's blessing.

168 I must be cruel only to be kind.
(III.4.179)
Hamlet claims that his cruel treatment of Gertrude stems from his filial duty ('kind') to his father and from his well-meaning ('kind') desire to reform her.

169 For 'tis the sport to have the enginer
Hoist with his own petar; and't shall go hard
But I will delve one yard below their mines
And blow them at the moon.
(III.4.207–10)
Hamlet is talking about Rosencrantz and Guildenstern's untrustworthiness. He uses the military analogy of a sapper ('enginer') being blown up by his own mine ('Hoist with his own petar'). It will be difficult ('shall go hard') but Hamlet will dig a countermine ('delve one yard below their mines') and blow them up.

170 I'll lug the guts into the neighbour room.
Mother, good night. Indeed, this counsellor
Is now most still, most secret, and most grave,
Who was in life a foolish prating knave.
(III.4.213–16)
Hamlet leaves his mother, taking the corpse of Polonius ('the guts') with him.

171 He keeps them, like an ape an apple, in the corner of his jaw, first mouthed, to be last swallowed.
(IV.2.17–19)
Hamlet describes to Rosencrantz and Guildenstern how the king uses such officers as them.

172 A knavish speech sleeps in a foolish ear.
(IV.2.23–4)
Hamlet remarks to Rosencrantz and Guildenstern that sarcasm ('knavish speech') is wasted ('sleeps') on the stupid listener ('foolish ear').

173 Diseases desperate grown
By desperate appliance are relieved,
Or not at all.
(IV.3.9–11)
Claudius sees Hamlet's actions in proverbial terms as a disease which needs radical treatment.

174 CLAUDIUS Now Hamlet, where's Polonius?
HAMLET At supper.
CLAUDIUS At supper? Where?
HAMLET Not where he eats, but where 'a is eaten. A certain convocation of politic worms are e'en at him. Your worm is your only emperor for diet. We fat all creatures else to fat us, and we fat ourselves for maggots.
(IV.3.16–22)
Hamlet has been brought to Claudius under guard following the murder of Polonius. The 'convocation of politic worms' is a parliament of crafty worms who are at that moment ('e'en') eating Polonius ('at him'). There appear to be allusions to the Diet (parliament) convened at the German town of Worms by the Emperor Charles V in 1521.

175 HAMLET A man may fish with the worm that hath eat of a king, and eat of the fish that hath fed of that worm.
CLAUDIUS What dost thou mean by this?
HAMLET Nothing but to show you how a king may go a progress through the guts of a beggar.
CLAUDIUS Where is Polonius?
HAMLET In heaven. Send thither to see. If your messenger find him not there, seek him i'th'other place yourself. But if indeed you find him not within this month, you shall nose him as you go up the stairs into the lobby.
CLAUDIUS (*to attendants*) Go seek him there.
HAMLET 'A will stay till you come.
(IV.3.26–38)
Hamlet extends the idea that worms do not respect human class distinctions. A 'progress' was an official royal journey conducted with pomp and ceremony. Hamlet insults Claudius with the suggestion that he could look for Polonius in hell in person ('i'th'other place yourself'). 'Nose' means smell. ''A' means he.

176 HAMLET Farewell, dear mother.
CLAUDIUS Thy loving father, Hamlet.
HAMLET My mother. Father and mother is man and wife; man and wife is one flesh; and so, my mother.
(IV.3.51–4)

Hamlet continues to insult Claudius, using the language of the marriage service.

177 Do it, England.
For like the hectic in my blood he rages,
And thou must cure me.
(IV.3.67–9)
Claudius, soliloquizing, personifies England, asking her to kill Hamlet ('Do it'), who is like a fever ('hectic') in his blood.

178 We go to gain a little patch of ground
That hath in it no profit but the name.
(IV.4.18–19)
Hamlet on his way to England has met a captain in the army of Fortinbras, the Norwegian prince, who tells him the purpose of the expedition. 'The name' means the reputation they will get for having conquered it.

179 How all occasions do inform against me
And spur my dull revenge! What is a man,
If his chief good and market of his time
Be but to sleep and feed? A beast, no more.
Sure He that made us with such large discourse,
Looking before and after, gave us not
That capability and godlike reason
To fust in us unused.
(IV.4.32–9)
Hamlet sees the Norwegian expedition as one more example to spur him on. He develops similar ideas earlier; see 20. 'Market' means profit; 'discourse' means understanding; 'fust' means go mouldy.

180 Some craven scruple
Of thinking too precisely on th'event.
(IV.4.40–1)
Hamlet is beginning to investigate the reasons for his delay. Here he wonders if cowardly ('craven') scruples about the outcome ('event') of his actions could be a factor.

181 Rightly to be great
Is not to stir without great argument,
But greatly to find quarrel in a straw
When honour's at the stake.
(IV.4.53–6)
After his conversation with the captain, Hamlet decides that true greatness does not mean rushing into action without great cause

('Rightly to be great / Is not to stir without great argument') but does involve fighting over something trivial ('a straw') if honour is involved.

182 To my shame I see
The imminent death of twenty thousand men
That for a fantasy and trick of fame
Go to their graves like beds, fight for a plot
Whereon the numbers cannot try the cause,
Which is not tomb enough and continent
To hide the slain? O, from this time forth,
My thoughts be bloody, or be nothing worth!
(IV.4.60–7)

Hamlet sees the death of the Norwegian army, going to fight for an illusion and a trifle of reputation ('a fantasy and trick of fame'), as a reproach to him for his inaction. 'Continent' means receptacle – Hamlet means that the area of ground ('plot') they are fighting over will not even be big enough to bury the dead in.

183 How should I your true-love know
From another one?
By his cockle hat and staff
And his sandal shoon.
(IV.5.23–6)

Ophelia has gone mad after the death of her father. In this scene with Gertrude she sings several songs in which grief for her dead father and lost lover appear to be mixed. The 'cockle hat and staff' are signs of a pilgrim; 'shoon' is an old plural of shoe.

184 He is dead and gone, lady.
He is dead and gone.
At his head a grass-green turf,
At his heels a stone.
(IV.5.29–32)

This is another of Ophelia's songs with sentiments appropriate to her dead father.

185 White his shroud as the mountain snow...
Larded all with sweet flowers,
Which bewept to the ground did not go
With true-love showers.
(IV.5.36, 38–40)

In the third line of Ophelia's song the rather forced rhythm suggests that she is adapting a song to the circumstances of her father's death. He was *not* wept for because he was buried without ceremony. True love tears ('showers') are more appropriate to a lover than a father.

186 Lord, we know what we are, but know not what we may be.
(IV.5.43–4)
Ophelia's comment can be applied most obviously to herself and to Hamlet, both of them transformed from normality to abnormality.

187 Tomorrow is Saint Valentine's day,
All in the morning betime,
And I a maid at your window
To be your Valentine.
Then up he rose and donned his clothes,
And dupped the chamber door;
Let in the maid, that out a maid
Never departed more.
By Gis and by Saint Charity,
Alack, and fie for shame!
Young men will do't if they come to't.
By Cock, they are to blame.
Quoth she, 'Before you tumbled me,
You promised me to wed.'
He answers:
'So would I ha' done, by yonder sun,
An thou hadst not come to my bed.'
(IV.5.48–55, 59–67)
Ophelia's song is concerned with deceit between lovers. St Valentine's day is traditionally associated with the choosing of sexual partners. 'Betime' means early; 'dupped' means opened; 'Gis' is Jesus; 'Saint Charity' is a personification rather than a real saint; 'Cock' is god, with a pun on the word for penis; 'tumbled' means made love to; 'An' means if.

188 I cannot choose but weep to think they would lay him i'th'cold ground.
(IV.5.69–70)
Ophelia laments her father's death.

189 Good night, ladies, good night. Sweet ladies, good night, good night.
(IV.5.72–3)
Ophelia leaves with a gracious farewell to a largely imaginary group of ladies. T. S. Eliot used the lines memorably in *The Waste Land.*

190 When sorrows come, they come not single spies,
But in battalions.
(IV.5.79–80)
Claudius comments on the disasters afflicting the court. Sorrows make a frontal assault like an army rather than infiltrating individually like spies.

191 We have done but greenly
In hugger-mugger to inter him.
(IV.5.84–5)
Claudius now feels that Polonius's funeral arrangements were handled naively ('greenly') since they were performed hastily and in secret ('In hugger-mugger').

192 That drop of blood that's calm proclaims me bastard,
Cries cuckold to my father, brands the harlot
Even here between the chaste unsmirchèd brows
Of my true mother.
(IV.5.119–22)
Laertes has burst in on Claudius, seeking revenge. This is his response to Gertrude's attempt to soothe him. He uses the idea that, since he inherited his blood from his parents, each calm drop is proof of his illegitimacy and that his father was a man whose wife was unfaithful ('cuckold'). His unsullied ('unsmirchèd') mother is compared to a prostitute branded on the forehead.

193 There's such divinity doth hedge a king
That treason can but peep to what it would.
(IV.5.125–6)
Claudius puts an orthodox Renaissance case that there is divine protection ('hedge') for the ruler, who is the representative of God on earth. He suggests that treason can only look from a distance at its object. An audience might find his insistence on this protection ironic in view of his own murder of the previous king.

194 To hell allegiance! Vows to the blackest devil!
Conscience and grace to the profoundest pit!
(IV.5.133–4)
Laertes swears like a good revenger.

195 Is't writ in your revenge
That, swoopstake, you will draw both friend and foe,
Winner and loser?
(IV.5.143–5)

As Claudius attempts to calm Laertes he asks whether his desire to revenge Polonius's death will include everyone in a clean sweep ('swoopstake').

196 O heavens, is't possible a young maid's wits
Should be as mortal as an old man's life?
Nature is fine in love, and where 'tis fine,
It sends some precious instance of itself
After the thing it loves.
(IV.5.161–5)
Laertes is reacting to Ophelia, who has gone mad. 'Fine' means delicate; 'instance' means token.

197 They bore him barefaced on the bier,
Hey non nony, nony, hey nony,
And in his grave rained many a tear.
(IV.5.166–8)
Ophelia sings a song with obvious applications to her father's death. 'Hey nony' is a typical Renaissance refrain.

198 There's rosemary, that's for remembrance. Pray you, love, remember. And there is pansies, that's for thoughts.
(IV.5.176–8)
Ophelia is handing out flowers to the bystanders. The flowers may be real or imaginary. 'Pansies' are for thoughts from the French *pensée*; a thought.

199 There's fennel for you, and columbines. There's rue for you, and here's some for me. We may call it herb of grace o'Sundays. O, you must wear your rue with a difference. There's a daisy. I would give you some violets, but they withered all when my father died. They say 'a made a good end.
(*sings*) For bonny sweet Robin is all my joy.
(IV.5.181–7)
Ophelia continues her flower distribution. Fennel is often associated with flattery, columbines with infidelity, rue with sorrow, daisies with deceit, and violets with faithful love. It is not clear whom these flowers are given to. 'Herb of grace' is another name for rue; ''a' means he. 'Robin' in the song is perhaps Robin Hood, but the words have not survived.

200 Thought and afflictions, passion, hell itself,
She turns to favour and to prettiness.
(IV.5.188–9)
Laertes comments on Ophelia's madness. 'Favour' means beauty.

201 And will 'a not come again?
And will 'a not come again?
No, no, he is dead.
Go to thy deathbed.
He never will come again.
His beard was as white as snow,
All flaxen was his poll.
He is gone, he is gone,
And we cast away moan.
God 'a' mercy on his soul!
(IV.5.190–9)

Ophelia's song is applicable to her father. 'All flaxen was his poll' means the hair on his head was as white as flax; ''a' means he, but in the final line means have.

202 His means of death, his obscure funeral –
No trophy, sword, nor hatchment o'er his bones,
No noble rite nor formal ostentation.
(IV.5.213–15)

Laertes complains to Claudius about the lack of ceremony in Polonius's funeral. 'Hatchment' means coat of arms.

203 Where th'offence is, let the great axe fall.
(IV.5.218)

Claudius is telling Laertes that punishment will be forthcoming for the cause of the trouble. The 'great axe' suggests some well-known part of the judicial process.

204 It warms the very sickness in my heart
That I shall live and tell him to his teeth
'Thus didest thou'.
(IV.7.54–6)

Laertes is pleased that Hamlet has returned because it gives him an opportunity to confront him face to face ('to his teeth').

205 A very riband in the cap of youth,
Yet needful too, for youth no less becomes
The light and careless livery that it wears
Than settled age his sables and his weeds,
Importing health and graveness.
(IV.7.76–80)

Claudius is describing skill in fencing to Laertes. He sees it as a necessary ('needful') skill, as appropriate to a young man as a ribbon ('riband') in his cap. Young men properly wear frivolous clothes ('light and careless livery') which would be inappropriate to old men, who wear sober fur-lined clothes ('his sables and his weeds') indicating their concern for their health and their gravity.

206 Are you like the painting of a sorrow,
A face without a heart?
(IV.7.107–8)
Claudius challenges Laertes about his father, asking if his grief is genuine, once more using the idea of an outward appearance masking an inner reality.

207 No place, indeed, should murder sanctuarize.
(IV.7.126)
Claudius's challenges to Laertes's filial loyalty have resulted in him offering to cut Hamlet's throat in a church. Claudius agrees that there should be no sanctuary for murderers, which is not an orthodox Christian position.

208 There is a willow grows askant the brook,
That shows his hoar leaves in the glassy stream.
Therewith fantastic garlands did she make
Of crowflowers, nettles, daisies, and long purples,
at dox Christian position.
That liberal shepherds give a grosser name,
But our cold maids do dead-men's-fingers call them.
There on the pendent boughs her crownet weeds
Clambering to hang, an envious sliver broke,
When down her weedy trophies and herself
Fell in the weeping brook. Her clothes spread wide,
And mermaid-like awhile they bore her up;
Which time she chanted snatches of old tunes,
As one incapable of her own distress,
Or like a creature native and indued
Unto that element. But long it could not be
Till that her garments, heavy with their drink,
Pulled the poor wretch from her melodious lay
To muddy death.
(IV.7.166–83)
Gertrude describes Ophelia's death by drowning. The willow, appropriately representing forsaken love, overhangs ('grows askant') the stream which reflects the grey ('hoar') undersides of its leaves. 'Crowflowers' are buttercups; 'long purples' are purple orchids to which the coarsely spoken ('liberal') shepherds give an obscene ('grosser') name, while the chaste ('cold') maids call them 'dead-men's-fingers' from the pale roots of some orchids. 'Crownet' means coronet; 'envious sliver' means malicious branch; 'incapable' means unaware; 'indued' means with the appropriate qualities; 'lay' means song.

209 Too much of water hast thou, poor Ophelia,
And therefore I forbid my tears. But yet
It is our trick. Nature her custom holds,
Let shame say what it will.
(IV.7.185–8)
Laertes attempts not to cry for Ophelia but finds human nature ('our trick') too much for him.

210 Is she to be buried in Christian burial when she wilfully seeks her own salvation?
(V.1.1–2)
The First Clown, digging Ophelia's grave, assumes that she has committed suicide ('wilfully seeks her own salvation') and should not therefore be buried with church services in consecrated ground. The character who speaks these lines is often referred to as the First Gravedigger; he is not a clown in the modern sense but a rustic character.

211 SECOND CLOWN Will you ha' the truth on't? If this had not been a gentlewoman, she should have been buried out o'Christian burial.
FIRST CLOWN Why, there thou sayst. And the more pity that great folk should have countenance in this world to drown or hang themselves more than their even-Christian. Come, my spade. There is no ancient gentlemen but gardeners, ditchers, and grave-makers. They hold up Adam's profession.
(V.1.23–31)
The rustics digging Ophelia's grave are quite right in their assumption that class considerations have outweighed religious scruples in the question of Ophelia's burial (see 221). 'Countenance' is privilege; 'even-Christian' means fellow Christian. The First Clown (gravedigger) believes that gardeners, ditch makers, and grave makers follow Adam's profession ('hold up') because they all dig as he did.

212 FIRST CLOWN What is he that builds stronger than either the mason, the shipwright, or the carpenter?
SECOND CLOWN The gallows-maker, for that frame outlives a thousand tenants.
FIRST CLOWN Cudgel thy brains no more about it, for your dull ass will not mend his pace with beating. And when you are asked this question next, say 'a grave-maker'. The houses he makes lasts till Doomsday.
(V.1.41–4, 56–9)
The rustics continue to pass time while digging Ophelia's grave with this riddle.

213 Has this fellow no feeling of his business? 'A sings in grave-making.
(V.1.65–6)
Hamlet has entered with Horatio and comments on the First Clown, who is singing as he digs Ophelia's grave. He wonders why he does not respond to the sombreness of his task.

214 That skull had a tongue in it, and could sing once. How the knave jowls it to the ground, as if 'twere Cain's jawbone, that did the first murder! This might be the pate of a politician, which this ass now o'erreaches; one that would circumvent God, might it not?
(V.1.75–9)
The First Clown has begun to turn up skulls from the grave. Hamlet comments on the difference between the fortunes of the living and the fortunes of their dead bodies. The reference to Cain once more takes up the theme of fratricide which is central to the play. The 'knave' and the 'ass' are both the First Clown; 'jowls' means hurls; 'pate' means skull; 'politician' normally has a derogatory sense in Shakespeare; 'o'erreaches' means has the advantage over; 'circumvent' means outwit.

215 How absolute the knave is! We must speak by the card, or equivocation will undo us.
(V.1.135–6)
Hamlet is engaging the First Clown in conversation, but as Hamlet remarks to Horatio, the Clown is insisting on exact precision in the use of language. 'By the card' means precisely; 'equivocation' means deliberate ambiguity.

216 The age is grown so picked that the toe of the peasant comes so near the heel of the courtier he galls his kibe.
(V.1.137–9)
Hamlet tells Horatio that the manners of the time ('age') have become so over-refined ('picked') that the social classes are almost indistinguishable because the usual distances between classes are not being observed; thus the peasant is walking so close to the courtier that he irritates his chilblain ('galls his kibe').

217 FIRST CLOWN He that is mad, and sent into England.
HAMLET Ay, marry, why was he sent into England?
FIRST CLOWN Why, because 'a was mad. 'A shall recover his wits there. Or, if'a do not, 'tis no great matter there.
HAMLET Why?

FIRST CLOWN 'Twill not be seen in him there. There the men are as mad as he.
(V.1.146–53)
The First Clown, who has not recognized Hamlet, is explaining that Hamlet has been sent to England. Shakespeare often uses such ironic references to England in plays set elsewhere. ''A' means he.

218 Alas, poor Yorick! I knew him, Horatio. A fellow of infinite jest, of most excellent fancy. He hath bore me on his back a thousand times. And now how abhorred in my imagination it is! My gorge rises at it. Here hung those lips that I have kissed I know not how oft. Where be your gibes now? Your gambols, your songs, your flashes of merriment that were wont to set the table on a roar? Not one now to mock your own grinning? Quite chop-fallen? Now get you to my lady's table and tell her, let her paint an inch thick, to this favour she must come. Make her laugh at that.
(V.1.181–92)
The First Clown has turned up the skull of Yorick, old Hamlet's jester. Hamlet takes the opportunity to moralize on the skull beneath the skin, the difference between appearance and the underlying truth, moving on from his inspection of Yorick's skull to an image of a woman at her dressing table who puts on a large amount of make-up ('paint an inch thick') but still ends up as unattractive as Yorick's skull ('to this favour'). 'The table on a roar' refers to the people at the dining table laughing at Yorick's antics. 'Chop-fallen' means both down in the mouth and jawless. An alternative reading to 'my lady's table' which is equally possible is 'my lady's chamber'.

219 To what base uses we may return, Horatio! Why may not imagination trace the noble dust of Alexander till 'a find it stopping a bunghole?
(V.1.199–201)
Hamlet continues to muse on the contrast between the fortunes of the living and the dead. Once dead even someone who conquered half the world like Alexander the Great becomes simply earth that can be used to close up a beer barrel.

220 Imperious Caesar, dead and turned to clay,
Might stop a hole to keep the wind away.
(V.1.209–10)
Hamlet improvises an epigram on the theme of death as a great leveller. Like Alexander (see 219), Caesar in death becomes a piece of natural material that can be used to fill up a hole.

221 PRIEST

We should profane the service of the dead
To sing a requiem and such rest to her
As to peace-parted souls.

LAERTES Lay her i'th'earth,
And from her fair and unpolluted flesh
May violets spring! I tell thee, churlish priest,
A ministering angel shall my sister be
When thou liest howling.

(V.1.232–8)

The funeral procession for Ophelia has come onto the stage. The Priest has been forced by 'great command' to ignore the doubtful circumstances of her death but will not go as far as giving her the full burial ceremonial. 'Peace-parted souls' are those who died in normal circumstances. Laertes believes that the Priest will go to hell or purgatory where he will be 'howling' in torment whereas the innocent ('unpolluted') Ophelia will go to heaven.

222 Sweets to the sweet! Farewell.
I hoped thou shouldst have been my Hamlet's wife.
I thought thy bride-bed to have decked, sweet maid,
And not have strewed thy grave.

(V.1.239–42)

Gertrude throws flowers ('Sweets') on the coffin of Ophelia ('the sweet'). Both graves and bridal beds were strewn with flowers, as Gertrude points out. Gertrude's comments are in marked contrast to Polonius's belief that a marriage between Ophelia and Hamlet was out of the question.

223 I prithee take thy fingers from my throat.
For, though I am not splenitive and rash,
Yet have I in me something dangerous,
Which let thy wisdom fear.

(V.1.256–9)

Hamlet has interrupted Ophelia's funeral and is fighting with Laertes. Hamlet's lines start with a vivid evocation of the physical situation.

224 I loved Ophelia. Forty thousand brothers
Could not with all their quantity of love
Make up my sum.

(V.1.265–7)

After an apparently genuine simple statement of his love for Ophelia, Hamlet moves rapidly back to his counter-claims against Laertes's extravagant display of emotional grief.

225 Woo't drink up eisel? Eat a crocodile?
I'll do't. Dost thou come here to whine?
To outface me with leaping in her grave?
Be buried quick with her, and so will I.
(V.1.272–5)

Hamlet continues to berate Laertes, suggesting various unpleasant or ridiculous tasks he might undertake to show his grief. 'Woo't' means would you; 'eisel' means vinegar – it has been suggested that 'Nilus', the river Nile, woud be more appropriate since drinking a river dry is more difficult than drinking vinegar; the crocodile (which would follow naturally from Nilus) was supposed to shed hypocritical tears which would be appropriate to Hamlet's accusation that Laertes is being over-emotional; 'quick' means alive.

226 This is mere madness.
And thus a while the fit will work on him.
Anon, as patient as the female dove
When that her golden couplets are disclosed,
His silence will sit drooping.
(V.1.280–4)

Gertrude attempts to excuse Hamlet's behaviour to Laertes. 'Mere' means pure; 'Anon' means soon. In the fourth line, the 'couplets' are the dove's two fledglings which are covered in golden down when they are newly hatched ('disclosed').

227 Let Hercules himself do what he may,
The cat will mew, and dog will have his day.
(V.1.287–8)

Hamlet, calming down, exits with a couplet in which he compares himself to Hercules, the classical mythological hero, and Laertes to the whining cat and dog.

228 This grave shall have a living monument.
(V.1.293)

Claudius makes a public statement that Ophelia's grave will have a lasting ('living') memorial. Laertes will presumably read it in terms of the plot against Hamlet.

229 There's a divinity that shapes our ends,
Rough-hew them how we will.
(V.2.10–11)

Hamlet has begun to learn Christian acceptance as these lines to Horatio indicate.

230 I once did hold it, as our statists do,
A baseness to write fair, and laboured much
How to forget that learning. But, sir, now
It did me yeoman's service.
(V.2.33–6)

Hamlet is explaining to Horatio how on the ship taking them to England he substituted a letter demanding Rosencrantz and Guildenstern's death for Claudius's letter demanding his. Such letters were normally written by professional scribes with good handwriting, so Hamlet congratulates himself on having abandoned the belief he shared with statesmen ('statists') that it was vulgar to write clearly ('A baseness to write fair'). His ability to write clearly was very useful, giving the kind of reliable loyal service a yeoman gave to his feudal superior.

231 But I am very sorry, good Horatio,
That to Laertes I forgot myself.
For by the image of my cause I see
The portraiture of his. I'll court his favours.
But sure the bravery of his grief did put me
Into a towering passion.
(V.2.75–80)

Hamlet realizes that Laertes is in a very similar situation to his, in that they have both lost fathers by violent means. He uses the familiar idea of mirrors and painting to associate this realization with the themes of the play. 'Favours' means friendship; 'bravery' means bravado.

232 But thou wouldst not think how ill all's here about my heart.
(V.2.206–7)

Hamlet, about to fight a supposedly friendly duel with Laertes, has a premonition that all is not well.

233 Not a whit. We defy augury. There is special providence in the fall of a sparrow. If it be now, 'tis not to come. If it be not to come, it will be now. If it be not now, yet it will come. The readiness is all.
(V.2.213–16)

Horatio, responding to Hamlet's premonition, has suggested postponing the duel with Laertes. Hamlet uses the biblical idea that God looks after even the least significant birds to suggest that everything is ordained and being prepared ('The readiness') is what matters. A similar idea is expressed in *King Lear* 89.

234 I have shot my arrow o'er the house
And hurt my brother.
(V.2.237–8)
Hamlet apologizes to Laertes for the death of Polonius in terms that suggest a childhood accident. However, 'brother' may stir up associations of fratricide such as Claudius's or of the potential brotherhood-in-law between Hamlet and Laertes which Ophelia's death has prevented.

235 A hit, a very palpable hit.
(V.2.275)
Osric, the courtier in charge of the duel between Laertes and Hamlet, judges that Hamlet has struck Laertes an easily perceptible ('very palpable') hit.

236 He's fat and scant of breath.
(V.2.281)
Gertrude comments on Hamlet's exertions in the duel. 'Fat' might mean sweaty but its normal meaning was overweight. Hamlet has earlier told us that he has been in training for some time, so this apparent contradiction may be a sign that the text here is not totally reliable.

237 Why, as a woodcock to mine own springe, Osrick.
I am justly killed with mine own treachery.
(V.2.300–1)
In the course of the duel Hamlet and Laertes have exchanged rapiers and Laertes has been wounded with the rapier he had previously poisoned. Here he compares himself to the traditionally foolish woodcock because he has walked into his own trap ('springe').

238 The point envenomed too?
Then, venom, to thy work.
(V.2.315–16)
Hamlet, told by Laertes that the rapier point is poisoned, stabs Claudius.

239 This fell sergeant, Death,
Is strict in his arrest.
(V.2.330–1)
Hamlet, fatally wounded by the poisoned rapier, compares death to a cruel sheriff's officer ('fell sergeant') who will not be put off from carrying out his task.

240 Report me and my cause aright
To the unsatisfied.
(V.2.333–4)
Hamlet asks Horatio to explain his actions to those who are perplexed by what has happened ('the unsatisfied').

241 I am more an antique Roman than a Dane.
(V.2.335)
Horatio would prefer to commit suicide like 'an antique Roman' rather than survive Hamlet. There is an implicit comparison between the stoic Romans and the hedonistic Danes.

242 O God, Horatio, what a wounded name,
Things standing thus unknown, shall I leave behind me!
If thou didst ever hold me in thy heart,
Absent thee from felicity awhile,
And in this harsh world draw thy breath in pain,
To tell my story.
(V.2.338–43)
Hamlet begs Horatio to stay alive to explain what has happened. Otherwise his reputation ('name') will be damaged ('wounded') since the cause of the events is still unknown to most people. He therefore asks Horatio to defer the joy ('felicity') of being released from the pains of 'this harsh world'.

243 The potent poison quite o'er-crows my spirit.
I cannot live to hear the news from England.
But I do prophesy th'election lights
On Fortinbras. He has my dying voice.
(V.2.347–50)
The poison is overpowering ('o'er-crows') Hamlet who gives his dying vote ('voice') for Fortinbras in the election for a new king. The news from England is of the death of Rosencrantz and Guildenstern. 'Lights / On' means falls on.

244 The rest is silence.
(V.2.352)
These are Hamlet's dying words.

245 Now cracks a noble heart. Good night, sweet Prince,
And flights of angels sing thee to thy rest!
(V.2.353–4)
Horatio speaks a brief eulogy for the dead Hamlet. In the theatre, particularly in the nineteenth century, these were often the last words of the play since Fortinbras was often omitted. The

practice is less common than it was but is by no means unknown today.

246 The ears are senseless that should give us hearing,
To tell him his commandment is fulfilled,
That Rosencrantz and Guildenstern are dead.
(V.2.363–5)

The Ambassador from England brings news of the fulfilment of Hamlet's counterplot against Rosencrantz and Guildenstern. Since he believes that they have carried out Claudius's intentions, 'The ears', 'him' and 'his' refer to Claudius.

247 Give order that these bodies
High on a stage be placèd to the view.
And let me speak to th'yet unknowing world
How these things came about. So shall you hear
Of carnal, bloody, and unnatural acts,
Of accidental judgements, casual slaughters,
Of deaths put on by cunning and forced cause,
And, in this upshot, purposes mistook
Fallen on th'inventors' heads. All this can I
Truly deliver.
(V.2.371–9)

Horatio addresses the newly arrived Fortinbras and other survivors and begins to carry out his promise to Hamlet to explain what has been happening in this brief summary of the play's action. 'Stage' means platform; 'casual' means accidental; 'put on' means provoked; 'in the upshot' means finally, as a result of this.

248 For me, with sorrow I embrace my fortune.
I have some rights of memory in this kingdom,
Which now to claim my vantage doth invite me.
(V.2.382–4)

Fortinbras becomes king, asserting that he has old claims ('rights of memory') to the throne which his good fortune ('my vantage') encourages him to claim.

249 Let four captains
Bear Hamlet like a soldier to the stage.
For he was likely, had he been put on,
To have proved most royal.
(V.2.389–92)

Fortinbras, the senior surviving character, gives the conventional eulogy in praise of the dead hero. The 'stage' is the platform Horatio asked for earlier (see 247); 'put on' means tested.

250 Go, bid the soldiers shoot.
(V.2.397)
Fortinbras speaks the play's last line. His soldiers will salute Hamlet in traditional fashion.

Henry IV Part 1

1 So shaken as we are, so wan with care,
Find we a time for frighted peace to pant,
And breathe short-winded accents of new broils
To be commenced in strands afar remote.
(I.1.1–4)
The narrative and chronology of *Henry IV Part 1* follow and develop from the events of *Richard II*. The opening lines, spoken by King Henry IV to his advisers, pick up the references to civil disturbance found in the concluding scene of that play. Henry's decision to undertake an English crusade against the infidel in the Holy Land derives from his remorse at Richard's murder and his desire to expiate the guilt. His intention is interrupted by the news from Wales and Scotland and eventually, in *Henry IV Part 2*, he dies in the Jerusalem Chamber of the Palace of Westminster, but not in Jerusalem.

2 O that it could be proved
That some night-tripping fairy had exchanged
In cradle-clothes our children where they lay,
And called mine Percy, his Plantagenet!
(I.1.85–8)
Henry IV has been informed by Sir Walter Blunt that Harry Percy (Hotspur), the son of the Earl of Northumberland, has won a victory over the Scots, under the Earl of Douglas, at Holmedon. The news prompts the King to contrast the martial prowess and honourable conduct of Hotspur with the 'riot and dishonour' of Prince Hal and enviously wish for their exchange. Shakespeare presents the characters of Hotspur and Prince Hal in dramatic contrast by making them contemporaries in age, which in reality they were not.

3 What a devil hast thou to do with the time of the day? Unless hours were cups of sack, and minutes capons, and clocks the tongues of bawds, and dials the signs of leaping-houses, and the blessed sun himself a fair hot wench in flame-coloured

taffeta, I see no reason why thou shouldst be so superfluous to demand the time of the day.
(I.2.6–12)
Prince Hal is first encountered in the company of Sir John Falstaff, a physical embodiment of appetite and disorder. Hal is berating Falstaff for the insolence of demanding to know the time of day when the conduct of his life is a disregard of the passage of time and a failure to prepare himself for death. The way Hal accuses Falstaff of spending his time is an indication of his physical and sexual appetite. 'Sack' is often identified with sherry, although it seems to have indicated an entire category of white wines imported from Spain and the Canaries. 'Leaping-houses' were brothels and red taffeta a sign of a prostitute.

4 Let us be Diana's foresters, gentlemen of the shade, minions of the moon. And let men say we be men of good government, being governed as the sea is, by our noble and chaste mistress the moon, under whose countenance we steal.
(I.2.25–9)
Falstaff is attempting to justify through elevated language his profession of highway robbery by night. Diana is the goddess of hunting and of the moon, associated with chastity, inconstancy, and control of the tides. There is a pun on 'men of good government', which can mean both well-behaved men and men who !

What, in thy quips and thy quiddities? 5
(I.2.44–5)
Falstaff's question is rhetorical. He is commenting sarcastically on Hal's wit, since he is being worsted in the arguments. A 'quiddity' is a quibble or an example of hair-splitting in argument.

6 I prithee sweet wag, shall there be gallows standing in England when thou art King? And resolution thus fubbed as it is with the rusty curb of old Father Antic the law?
(I.2.57–60)
Falstaff anticipates Hal's ascending the throne as heralding the reign of liberty and the abolition of law and punishment. Falstaff talks of crime as 'resolution' or courage and considers it is cheated ('fubbed') by the constraints of the law. The law is personified in the form of an old doctor of law, conventionally a buffoon figure in Renaissance comedy.

7 Thou hast the most unsavoury similes, and art indeed the most comparative rascalliest sweet young prince.
(I.2.79–81)

Falstaff is commenting upon Hal's facility for producing apt and unsavoury comparisons, especially regarding Falstaff himself.

8 I would to God thou and I knew where a commodity of good names were to be bought.
(I.2.82–3)
Typically, Falstaff is more concerned with reputation than morality. 'Commodity' here means supply.

9 O, thou hast damnable iteration, and art indeed able to corrupt a saint. Thou hast done much harm upon me, Hal, God forgive thee for it. Before I knew thee Hal, I knew nothing, and now am I, if a man should speak truly, little better than one of the wicked.
(I.2.90–4)
Falstaff's accusation of corruption against Hal is comically ironic. Falstaff's mimicry of the puritan idiom indicates that this is a mock repentance. Hal has just alluded to a text from Proverbs; hence 'iteration', meaning the repetition and application of texts. Hal deflates Falstaff's 'repentance' by immediately engaging him in planning a robbery.

10 Why Hal, 'tis my vocation, Hal. 'Tis no sin for a man to labour in his vocation.
(I.2.104–5)
Hal has tricked Falstaff into moving rapidly from questions of repentance to those of crime and sin. Falstaff's witty justification is that stealing in his 'vocation', both in the sense of trade and in the sense of calling. His argument is an echo of I Corinthians 7:20, a favourite text of puritan preachers.

11 How agrees the devil and thee about thy soul, that thou soldest him on Good Friday last, for a cup of Madeira and a cold capon's leg?
(I.2.113–15)
Poins' question to Falstaff depicts him as one in league with the devil. Falstaff is described as having committed the most blasphemous of acts, a compact with the devil, in the most blasphemous manner, breaking the strictest fast of the church calendar. In fact, Falstaff's characterization does derive from the Vice figure of the medieval popular drama, which was both wicked and comic.

12 There's neither honesty, manhood, nor good fellowship in

thee, nor thou camest not of the blood royal, if thou darest not stand for ten shillings.
(I.2.137–9)
Falstaff is berating Hal for being unwilling to participate in the Gad's Hill robbery. Poins has brought information concerning the planned robbery of rich pilgrims on the road to Canterbury at Gad's Hill, a place near Rochester renowned for robberies. Hal agrees to be a 'madcap' for once, but subsequently enters into another intrigue with Poins to humiliate Falstaff. 'Stand for' here means both be worth and be prepared to fight for.

13 If he fight longer than he sees reason, I'll forswear arms.
(I.2.182–3)
Poins is speaking to Hal of Falstaff, whom he has set up a trick to humiliate. With Hal, he plans to attack Falstaff and his two companions (Bardolph and Peto) in disguise, immediately after their robbery of the pilgrims at Gad's Hill. Although Poins and Hal will be outnumbered, Poins argues that they will be able to rely on the cowardice of Falstaff. The joke will be to hear Falstaff's account of the incident.

14 I know you all, and will awhile uphold
The unyoked humour of your idleness,
Yet herein will I imitate the sun,
Who doth permit the base contagious clouds
To smother up his beauty from the world,
That when he please again to be himself,
Being wanted, he may be more wondered at
By breaking through the foul and ugly mists
Of vapours that did seem to strangle him.
(I.2.193–201)
Prince Hal's soliloquy reveals his essential detachment from his low-life companions. The image of the sun breaking through clouds conveys majesty and kingship. Bolingbroke, Hal's father, used a similar image in *Richard II* (see 33) to describe the appearance of Richard on the walls of Flint Castle, but to different effect. Here Hal's sense of timing and his evaluation of his reformation's impact reveal his political acumen.

15 If all the year were playing holidays,
To sport would be as tedious as to work;
But when they seldom come, they wished-for come,
And nothing pleaseth but rare accidents.
So when this loose behaviour I throw off,
And pay the debt I never promisèd,
By how much better than my word I am,

By so much shall I falsify men's hopes.
And like bright metal on a sullen ground.
My reformation, glittering o'er my fault,
Shall show more goodly, and attract more eyes
Than that which hath no foil to set it off.
I'll so offend, to make offence a skill,
Redeeming time when men think least I will.
(I.2.202–15)

In the continuation of his first soliloquy, Hal likens the unexpected and eye-catching quality of his planned reformation amidst his dissolute life to the appearance of holidays in the working year or jewels in their settings. The relationship between the passage of time and redemption, prominent in the final couplet, links the plot of the low-life scenes with Falstaff to those concerning the affairs of state.

16 And still he smiled and talked.
And as the soldiers bore dead bodies by,
He called them untaught knaves, unmannerly,
To bring a slovenly unhandsome corpse
Betwixt the wind and his nobility.
(I.3.40–4)

Hotspur is offering Henry IV an explanation of how it could possibly have been misconstrued that he had denied the King his Scots prisoners after his victory at Holmedon. He gives a spirited account of how a dandified courtier made the demand to him immediately after the battle, when he found the messenger's manners and fashions offensive.

17 But for these vile guns
He would himself have been a soldier.
(I.3.62–3)

Hotspur is giving an account, through indirect speech, of the attitude to war of the King's messenger, who came to him after his victory over the Scots at Holmedon. Hotspur's bluntness shows that he is made for the battlefield, but not for court politics.

18 To put down Richard, that sweet lovely rose,
And plant this thorn, this canker Bolingbroke?
(I.3.173–4)

Hotspur is enraged at Henry IV's refusal to ransom his brother-in-law, Edmund Mortimer, Earl of March, who has been taken captive by Owen Glendower, the Welsh leader. Hotspur's father and uncle, Northumberland and Worcester, have explained the motivation by revealing that Mortimer had been proclaimed heir to the throne by Richard II, whom Henry IV had deposed.

(Shakespeare in fact confused two members of the Mortimer family. The Mortimer proclaimed heir was the nephew of Hotspur's wife, not the brother.) Hotspur is therefore castigating father and uncle for the part they played in Richard's deposition. 'Canker' follows the imagery of 'rose' in being a form of dog-rose, but with strong connotations for a spreading ulcer and of the canker-worm which destroys plants.

19 By heaven, methinks it were an easy leap
To pluck bright honour from the pale-faced moon,
Or dive into the bottom of the deep,
Where fathom-line could never touch the ground,
And pluck up drownèd honour by the locks.
(I.3.199–203)
Worcester, the politician, taking advantage of Hotspur's rage against Henry IV, is about to broach the topic of rebellion. He has intimated a dangerous exploit and Hotspur, without regard to its precise nature, has impulsively committed himself to any form of action. The seizure of honour serves as a symbol of a dangerous and difficult task; but Hotspur is true to a simple code of military honour. The rhetoric of the speech offers a gentle parody of the Senecan rhetoric of earlier Elizabethan drama.

20 I know a trick worth two of that.
(II.1.37–8)
The First Carrier's reply to Gadshill, the highway robber, is an idiomatic phrase meaning he is not so foolish as to comply with the request. Gadshill has asked to borrow the carrier's lantern.

21 I am bewitched with the rogue's company. If the rascal have not given me medicines to make me love him, I'll be hanged.
(II.2.16–18)
At Gad's Hill, immediately prior to the robbery, Poins and Hal have stolen away from Falstaff in accordance with their plan to double-cross and humiliate him for their amusement. Despite Falstaff's frustration at Hal's behaviour, he is besotted with his companionship.

22 Hang thyself in thine own heir-apparent garters!
(II.2.42–3)
Falstaff produces an original curse for Hal by conflating the idiomatic phrase, 'Hang thyself in thine own garters', with the concept of the Order of the Garter, held by the heir-apparent. Hal has invoked the curse by refusing to help Falstaff to his horse.

23 It would be argument for a week, laughter for a month, and a

good jest for ever.
(II.2.93–4)
Hal is predicting for Poins the response to their trick of robbing Falstaff in disguise immediately after he has robbed the pilgrims. 'Argument' means a topic of conversation. The final phrase has had its proof in the theatre whenever the play has been performed.

24 Falstaff sweats to death,
And lards the lean earth as he walks along.
Were it not for laughing I should pity him.
(II.2.106–8)
Hal is describing to Poins Falstaff's laboured and cowardly escape from their assault. Hal's reponse to it illustrates the mixture of humour and pathos in the characterization of Falstaff.

25 'Tis dangerous to take a cold, to sleep, to drink. But I tell you, my lord fool, out of this nettle, danger, we pluck this flower, safety.
(II.3.9–11)
At the opening of this scene, Hotspur is reading aloud a letter from an unnamed correspondent. It is made clear to the audience that Hotspur has sought the assistance of the writer in the Percy rebellion against Henry IV, but that the writer is diplomatically evading the commitment on account of its danger. Hotspur's rash and courageous temperament is intolerant of such cautious equivocations.

26 Why dost thou bend thine eyes upon the earth,
And start so often when thou sittest alone?
(II.3.44–5)
Hotspur's wife, named Kate in the play but not in history, has intuitively realized that her husband is embarked on a dangerous military enterprise on account of the behaviour which she describes here. The scene has some affinity of theme with that between Brutus and Portia in Julius Caesar II.1, though the boisterous love of Hotspur and Kate is presented quite differently.

27 Away, you trifler! Love! I love thee not,
I care not for thee, Kate? This is no world
To play with mammets, and to tilt with lips.
We must have bloody noses, and cracked crowns.
(II.3.93–6)
Hotspur's playful rejection of his wife and his refusal to tell her the reason for his departure are intended to protect her from knowledge of the rebellion that could be dangerous to her. It

remains true, though, that he is rejecting the private world of love and emotion for the public one of enmity and strife. 'Mammets' are dolls.

28 I have sounded the very bass string of humility.
(II.4.5–6)
Hal is recounting to Poins his experiences amongst the low-life characters of the Boar's Head Tavern in Eastcheap. Although Hal is ultimately to distance himself from these companions when he takes on his royal responsibilities, Shakespeare is insistent in this play and throughout the Histories that knowledge and understanding of the people is an essential prerequisite for successful monarchy.

29 I am not yet of Percy's mind, the Hotspur of the north, he that kills me some six or seven dozen of Scots at a breakfast, washes his hands, and says to his wife, 'Fie upon this quiet life, I want work.'
(II.4.100–3)
Hal's sarcastic account of Hotspur's industrious aggression parodies not only Hotspur's militarism but also the relationship with his wife which the audience has observed in the preceding scene.

30 If manhood, good manhood, but not forgot upon the face of the earth, then am I a shotten herring. There lives not three good men unhanged in England, and one of them is fat, and grows old.
(II.4.124–7)
Falstaff is introducing the theme of true manhood to Hal and Poins as a prologue to castigating them for not participating, as he thinks, in the robbery at Gad's Hill and not being there to defend him. This attack will rebound upon him. The allusion to the old fat man is, of course, to himself. A 'shotten herring' is a thin one, after it has shot its roe.

31 You care not who sees your back. Call you that backing of your friends? A plague upon such backing, give me them that will face me!
(II.4.144–6)
Following the Gad's Hill robbery, Falstaff has accused Prince Hal of cowardice for running away from the thieves who attacked him. Unbeknown to Falstaff, those 'thieves' were Hal and Poins. Falstaff will exaggerate their number and his brave resistance in the account that follows this accusation.

32 I am a Jew else: an Ebrew Jew.
(II.4.174)

Falstaff is attesting the veracity of a statement regarding his conduct at the Gad's Hill robbery. It is, in fact, a lie. In Elizabethan England, 'Jew' was a byword for mendacity and all forms of villainy. There were in reality no Jews in England from the time of their proscription by Edward I in 1290 until they were re-admitted by Cromwell in 1656.

33 FALSTAFF These four came all afront, and mainly thrust at me. I made me no more ado, but took all their seven points in my target, thus!
PRINCE HAL Seven? Why, there were but four even now.
(II.4.195–9)
Falstaff's spirited but mendacious account of the Gad's Hill robbery multiplies the number of his assailants from two to eleven very rapidly as he warms to his tale. Hal takes delight in exposing Falstaff's mendacity. A 'target' is a form of shield.

34 These lies are like their father that begets them, gross as a mountain, open, palpable.
(II.4.221–2)
Prince Hal is exposing to Falstaff's face his lies about the Gad's Hill robbery. The abuse extends from Falstaff's mendacity to his person.

35 Give you a reason on compulsion? If reasons were as plentiful as blackberries, I would give no man a reason upon compulsion, I.
(II.4.234–6)
Prince Hal and Poins are pressing Falstaff for explanations regarding his account of the Gad's Hill robbery. More precisely, they wish to know how he could tell that three of his assailants wore green if, as he has said, it was 'so dark'. The humour of the scene derives not only from Falstaff's exaggerated account but also from his evasiveness under this kind of pressure. A possible pun on reasons/raisins leads to 'blackberries'.

36 Mark now how a plain tale shall put you down.
(II.4.249–50)
Hal is about to expose Falstaff's vanity and mendacity to his face by giving an objective account of the Gad's Hill incident. His 'plain tale' will contrast with Falstaff's elaborate narrative.

37 Why, thou knowest I am as valiant as Hercules. But beware

instinct. The lion will not touch the true prince. Instinct is a great matter. I was now a coward on instinct.
(II.4.264–7)
The culmination of Falstaff's evasion concerning his conduct at Gad's Hill is this speech to Hal in which he claims knowledge of Hal's identity from the start and pretends that respect for the heir apparent prevented him from offering resistance. Nonetheless, the final phrase quoted above contains an ambiguity and irony that is directed back at Falstaff himself.

38 What doth gravity out of his bed at midnight?
(II.4.287)
The line is Falstaff's, in response to the Hostess's message that an elderly messenger from the King has come to the Boar's Head Tavern in search of Prince Hal. Falstaff's use of the abstraction 'gravity' creates of the messenger a morality figure to which Falstaff plays the Vice. It would, of course, be equally appropriate to direct the question at Falstaff.

39 When I was about thy years, Hal, I was not an eagle's talon in the waist – I could have crept into any alderman's thumb-ring. A plague of sighing and grief, it blows a man up like a bladder.
(II.4.322–5)
Falstaff's boast is made in reply to Hal's mocking demand to know when Falstaff last saw his own knee. His attributing his girth to worry is typical of Falstaff's comic pretence of morality. Contrary to modern practice, in the Elizabethan period rings were frequently worn on the thumb as portraits show, often by aldermen and other office-bearers as signs of their office.

40 You may buy land now as cheap as stinking mackerel.
(II.4.352–3)
Falstaff has relayed to Hal the information borne by the King's messenger that there is a threefold rebellion against his father's authority led by Douglas, Glendower, and Hotspur. His comment refers to the collapse of land and property values which always accompanies an outbreak of war.

41 I must speak in passion, and I will do it in King Cambyses' vein.
(II.4.379–80)
Falstaff and Hal have decided to act out the interview between Hal and his father, Henry IV, that must take place the following day. Falstaff is to impersonate the King's grief and anger at his son's conduct. He has called, typically, for a cup of sack to make

his eyes red, as if from weeping. The manner of passionate speech promised is to be taken from Thomas Preston's *Lamentable Tragedie, mixed full of plesant mirth, containing the Life of Cambises, King of Percia* of 1569. Shakespeare does not actually imitate in the scene that Falstaff and Hal act out the rhymed fourteener metre of Preston's play, but it had become a byword for theatrical bombast.

42 That thou art my son I have partly thy mother's word, partly my own opinion, but chiefly a villainous trick of thine eye. *(II.4.395–7)*

These words are uttered by Falstaff when he is impersonating Henry IV and rebuking Hal for his misconduct. Their irony deflates royalty as well as the moral standards of society generally.

43 There is a devil haunts thee in the likeness of an old fat man, a tun of man is thy companion. Why dost thou converse with that trunk of humours, that bolting-hutch of beastliness, that swollen parcel of dropsies, that huge bombard of sack, that stuffed cloak-bag of guts, that roasted Manningtree ox with the pudding in his belly, that reverend Vice, that grey Iniquity, that Father Ruffian, that Vanity in years? Wherein is he good, but to taste sack and drink it? Wherein neat and cleanly, but to carve a capon and eat it? Wherein cunning, but in craft? Wherein crafty, but in villainy? Wherein villainous, but in all things? Wherein worthy, but in nothing? *(II.4.435–46)*

Falstaff and Hal have decided to enact the explanation of his conduct that Hal must give the following morning to his father, Henry IV. In playing first the King, Falstaff has attempted to give a defence of himself as a grave and virtuous companion of the Prince. Outraged, Hal has reversed their roles and here, in the role of Henry IV, denounces Falstaff's character and behaviour. A 'bolting-hutch' is a sifting-bin. Manningtree is a small town in Essex but its precise association with roast ox has not been demonstrated. It could be that ox-roasting accompanied the fairs and performances of morality plays for which the town was known. The terms 'vice', 'iniquity', 'ruffian', and 'vanity' are references to the morality play.

44 If sack and sugar be a fault, God help the wicked! If to be old and merry be a sin, then many an old host that I know is damned. If to be fat be to be hated, then Pharaoh's lean kine are to be loved. No, my good lord! Banish Peto, banish Bardolph, banish Poins – but for sweet Jack Falstaff, kind Jack Falstaff, true Jack Falstaff, valiant Jack Falstaff – and there-

fore more valiant, being as he is old Jack Falstaff – banish not him thy Harry's company, banish not him thy Harry's company. Banish plump Jack, and banish all the world.
(II.4.456–65)
Falstaff, in the role of Hal, is offering a defence of himself to Hal, who is impersonating his father, Henry IV. They are enacting the interview that Hal must undergo with his father the following day. Falstaff appears to sense Hal's recall to affairs of state, since it is he who has first introduced the idea of banishment when playing the role of the King. Although Falstaff's identification of himself with abundance, liberality, and *joie de vivre* makes the idea of his rejection more difficult, his anticipation of it remains tinged with pathos. Hal's chilling reply is: 'I do, I will'; and this he actually does in *Henry IV Part 2* (see 59).

45 Play out the play!
(II.4.469)
Falstaff is referring to the dramatic interlude in which he and Hal play the roles of Hal and Henry IV in a mock examination of the Prince's conduct. The performance is interrupted by Bardolph's news of the arrival of the Sheriff and the watch pursuing the Gad's Hill robbers. Falstaff wishes to continue in order to give a further defence of himself.

46 O monstrous! But one halfpennyworth of bread to this intolerable deal of sack?
(II.4.525–6)
When the Sheriff enters the Boar's Head Tavern in pursuit of Falstaff and the Gad's Hill robbers, Falstaff is concealed behind an arras, while Hal faces the Sheriff. Afterwards, Falstaff is found asleep and Peto, on the instructions of the Prince, searches his pockets and finds a tavern bill. It indicates that Falstaff has consumed a vast quantity of wine, but very little bread.

47 GLENDOWER
At my nativity
The front of heaven was full of fiery shapes,
Of burning cressets, and at my birth
The frame and huge foundation of the earth
Shaked like a coward.
HOTSPUR Why, so it would have done
At the same season if your mother's cat
Had but kittened, though yourself had never been born.
(III.1.11–17)
The meeting of the leaders of the rebellion against Henry IV proves to be a clash of personalities which anticipates the later

divisions among the rebels. Hotspur's Northern bluntness is aroused by the prophetic and self-congratulatory rhetoric of the Welsh leader, Glendower. Hotspur repeatedly ridicules Glendower's belief of having been specially marked out by destiny.

48 These signs have marked me extraordinary,
And all the courses of my life do show
I am not in the roll of common men.
(III.1.38–40)

The signs to which Owen Glendower, the Welsh leader, is referring are extraordinary occurrences in nature which he claims accompanied his birth. The passage is illustrative of Glendower's grandiloquent boasting.

49 GLENDOWER
I can call spirits from the vasty deep.
HOTSPUR
Why, so can I, or so can any man:
But will they come when you do call for them?
GLENDOWER
Why, I can teach you, cousin, to command the devil.
HOTSPUR
And I can teach thee, coz, to shame the devil
By telling truth. Tell truth, and shame the devil.
(III.1.50–5)

Hotspur's sarcasm deflates Glendower's claims to supernatural powers. Shakespeare shares the English observation that the Celtic peoples of Britain are more given to belief in the supernatural. Hotspur makes plain that he considers such belief mere superstition. 'Tell truth, and shame the devil' was and has remained proverbial.

50 I had rather be a kitten and cry 'mew'
Than one of these same metre ballad-mongers,
I had rather hear a brazen canstick turned,
Or a dry wheel grate on the axle-tree,
And that would set my teeth nothing on edge,
Nothing so much as mincing poetry.
'Tis like the forced gait of a shuffling nag.
(III.1.123–9)

Hotspur's outburst against the artificial and effete nature of poetry is in keeping with his blunt military temperament. It is provoked by Glendower's claim to have mastered English and to have composed English poetry and set it to music while at the English court in his youth. The irony of Hotspur's statement is, of course, that it is uttered in the most natural and forceful dramatic verse, full of vivid and striking images. 'Canstick' means candlestick.

51 And such a deal of skimble-skamble stuff
As puts me from my faith.
(III.1.148–9)

Hotspur is replying to Mortimer's reproach that he argues with Glendower unnecessarily. Hotspur replies that he cannot tolerate the nonsense and superstition that Glendower utters. The phrase quoted above sums up the reply, that Glendower's superstition is so great that it makes Hotspur sceptical about his own faith (Christianity). 'Skimble-skamble' appears to be an expressive neologism of Shakespeare for nonsensical.

52 O, he is as tedious
As a tired horse, a railing wife,
Worse than a smoky house. I had rather live
With cheese and garlic in a windmill, far,
Than feed on cates and have him talk to me
In any summer house in Christendom.
(III.1.153–8)

Hotspur is expressing his view of Glendower's company to the latter's son-in-law, Mortimer. Despite his opposition to rhetorical flourish and his down-to-earth manner, Hotspur's own language is full of vivid imagery. 'Cates' means delicacies. Hotspur subsequently bears the reproof of Mortimer and Worcester for his too forthright expression.

53 I understand thy kisses, and thou mine,
And that's a feeling disputation.
(III.1.198–9)

According to the narrative of the play, Mortimer, after being taken captive by Glendower, has married his daughter. In reality, Shakespeare confused the nephew, Edmund Mortimer, who was proclaimed heir to Richard II, with the eponymous uncle who married Glendower's daughter. In this scene, the lady speaks only in Welsh with Glendower interpreting, while Mortimer can only express himself in English. Their sentimental love is contrasted with the robust relationship of Hotspur and his wife, Kate.

54 Now I perceive the devil understands Welsh.
(III.1.224)

Hotspur's comment is made to Lady Percy when Mortimer's wife, Glendower's daughter, is about to sing in Welsh. Two contrasted views of the Welsh tongue are given in this scene:

Mortimer's view of its lyrical beauty and Hotspur's view of its cacophony.

55 You swear like a comfit-maker's wife – 'Not you, in good sooth!', and 'As true as I live!', and 'As God shall mend me!', and 'As sure as day!' –
And givest such sarcenet surety for thy oaths
As if thou never walkest further than Finsbury.
Swear me, Kate, like a lady as thou art,
A good mouth-filling oath.
(III.1.241–8)

Hotspur is mocking his wife's mild oath, 'in good sooth (truth)'. He associates such mealy-mouthed expressions with petit-bourgeois, and perhaps puritan, culture. He demands the kind of full-blooded oath that befits a member of the ruling, military caste. A 'comfit-maker' was a confectioner. 'Sarcenet' was a soft, silk material and therefore Kate's 'surety' is lightweight. Finsbury, a suburb just to the north of the city, was a place of recreation for London's citizens.

56 I know not whether God will have it so
For some displeasing service I have done,
That in his secret doom out of my blood
He'll breed revengement and a scourge for me.
(III.2.4–7)

These are the first words of Henry IV in the interview with Hal that Hal and Falstaff have enacted in II.4. Henry IV's sense of guilt for the deposition of Richard II is evident in his surmise that his heir is destined by God to be his curse. The idea is pursued in the speeches that follow, when Henry IV likens Hal's disregard of public opinion to Richard's.

57 The skipping King, he ambled up and down,
With shallow jesters, and rash bavin wits,
Soon kindled and soon burnt, carded his state,
Mingled his royalty with capering fools.
(III.2.60–3)

Henry IV is giving a political lesson to Prince Hal, by explaining to him how he won the respect of the people through reserve and humility while Richard lost it through ostentatious folly and vulgarity. The picture of Richard that Henry IV evokes is almost of a stage king. 'Rash bavin' means soon ablaze ('bavin' is literally kindling). 'Carded his state' conveys that Richard degraded his regal position by mixing indiscriminately with the populace.

58 Why, Harry, do I tell thee of my foes,
Which art my nearest and dearest enemy?
(III.2.122–3)
Henry IV has just indicated to Prince Hal the gravity of the political and military situation. A mighty rebellion against his authority is led by Hotspur, with whom Henry IV has just compared Hal unfavourably. There is a pun on 'dearest', which means both most loved and most dire or most acute.

59 A hundred thousand rebels die in this.
(III.2.160)
This line is Henry IV's confident response to Prince Hal's assertion of his reformation and his determination to defeat Hotspur in battle, so reclaiming the honour and renown due to himself.

60 Well, I'll repent, and that suddenly, while I am in some liking. I shall be out of heart shortly, and then I shall have no strength to repent.
(III.3.4–7)
This scene begins with Falstaff observing to Bardolph that, since the Gad's Hill exploit, he has been in a physical and mental decline. The primary sense of the passage is clear, that Falstaff must repent while he is in the mood and before disinclination sets in. Throughout, there is an equivocation, as in 'strength', which indicates both health of the body and of the resolve, or moral will. The passage is an intimation of mortality for Falstaff, but one that he quickly throws off.

61 Company, villainous company, hath been the spoil of me.
(III.3.9–10)
Falstaff's brief contemplation of repentance immediately prior to this passage quickly turns to moral excuse and self-justification.

62 Do thou amend thy face, and I'll amend my life.
(III.3.24–5)
Bardolph has been taxing Falstaff for his disorderly life. Falstaff's counter-attack is that he will repair his life when Bardolph repairs his ruddy and imperfect complexion.

63 Shall I not take mine ease in mine inn but I shall have my pocket picked?
(III.3.79–80)
Falstaff is in dispute with the Hostess over financial affairs. In order to evade the Hostess' quite reasonable demands for payment for providing Falstaff with shirts in addition to board and lodging, Falstaff has concocted a story of theft in order to intimi-

date the Hostess with accusations of keeping a disorderly house. It was in fact Hal who had Falstaff's pocket picked.

64 Thou knowest in the state of innocency Adam fell, and what should poor Jack Falstaff do in the days of villainy? Thou seest I have more flesh than another man, and therefore more frailty.
(III.3.162–3)
Falstaff wittily subverts scriptural allusions in order to justify his villainy. The proverbial notion that 'flesh is frail' derives from Matthew 26:41 and Mark 14:38.

65 Were it good
To set the exact wealth of all our states
All at one cast? To set so rich a main
On the nice hazard of one doubtful hour?
(IV.1.45–8)
Hotspur, Worcester, and Douglas are in the rebel camp at Shrewsbury. News has just been brought to Hotspur that his father, Northumberland, is sick and is not sending forces to the rebels. Initially dismayed and angered by the news, Hotspur is here making a virtue of necessity in arguing that it may not have been wise to hazard all their forces and hopes in one battle. His imagery is drawn from the game of dice: 'main' means both strength (or here, army) and the stake in the dice-game called hazard.

66 Where is his son,
The nimble-footed madcap Prince of Wales,
And his comrades that daffed the world aside
And bid it pass?
(IV.1.94–7)
Hotspur, in the rebel camp at Shrewsbury, is questioning his cousin, Sir Richard Vernon, who has brought news of the preparations made by King Henry IV to put down the rebellion. Hotspur's sarcastic question receives in reply a description of Hal as the flower of chivalry (see 67 below). The final phrase of the quotation means to let the world go by.

67 I saw young Harry with his beaver on,
His cuishes on his thighs, gallantly armed,
Rise from the ground like feathered Mercury,
And vaulted with such ease into his seat
As if an angel dropped down from the clouds
To turn and wind a fiery Pegasus,

And witch the world with noble horsemanship.
(IV.1.104–10)
Sir Richard Vernon describes Prince Hal to Hotspur as the epitome of the chivalric ideal, both in the splendour of his armour and in his horsemanship. The description prepares the audience for the changed role of Hal. Vaulting into the saddle in armour required exceptional strength and skill and hence the reference to winged Mercury, the messenger of the gods. Pegasus, the winged horse of classical legend, would be an appropriate mount for such a figure. 'Beaver' and 'cuishes' are pieces of armour: the 'beaver' is the face-guard of a helmet; 'cuishes' offer protection for the thighs.

68 Doomsday is near. Die all, die merrily.
(IV.1.134)
Hotspur's martial spirit has been roused by Vernon's description of Hal in arms; but his confidence has been further undermined by the news that, in addition to Northumberland's evasion, Glendower's troops will not arrive in time for the battle. He embraces, nonetheless, a heroic and fatalistic philosophy.

69 I have misused the King's press damnably.
(IV.2.12–13)
In III.3. Hal had informed Falstaff that he had procured him a charge of infantry. Here Falstaff confesses that he has abused his commission for financial gain. Abuses of the royal commission for impressment were widespread in the Elizabethan period: the main abuse was that practised by Falstaff, to accept money to release the able and to replace them with the poorest and most unfit for military service.

70 I am as vigilant as a cat to steal cream.
(IV.2.56–7)
Falstaff's protestation of military vigilance to the Earl of Westmoreland ironically smacks of self-interest.

71 Tut, tut, good enough to toss, food for powder, food for powder, they'll fill a pit as well as better. Tush, man, mortal men, mortal men.
(IV.2.63–5)
Falstaff is responding cynically to Hal's observation that he has never seen such pitiful soldiers as Falstaff has pressed into service. Falstaff's acceptance that the lot of common soldiers is merely to be cannon-fodder indicates not just his venality, but exposes the inhumanity of a ruling military caste. Falstaff has earlier referred to his troops as 'the cankers of a calm world and a long peace', a

notion which derives from the Elizabethan view that an extended peace was unhealthy and that the purging of society through war was wholesome.

72 KING HENRY Will you again unknit
The churlish knot of all-abhorrèd war,
And move in that obedient orb again
Where you did give a fair and natural light,
And be no more an exhaled meteor,
A prodigy of fear, and a portent
Of broachèd mischief to the unborn times?
WORCESTER
Hear me, my liege.
For mine own part I could be well content
To entertain the lag end of my life
With quiet hours.
(V.1.15–25)

Henry IV's question is put to the Earl of Worcester, the spokesman of the rebels, at their formal exchange before the battle of Shrewsbury. Henry's imagery is based on the Elizabethan analogy between the order of the cosmos and the political and social order of the realm. In the Ptolemaic conception of the universe, the spheres rotated in fixed orbits; Worcester is given the opportunity to return to his appointed social orbit in place of being, as the rebels' messenger, like an aberrant astrological body, a portent of disaster.

73 Rebellion lay in his way, and he found it.
(V.1.28)

Henry IV has asked Worcester how he has come to be a rebel, if as he claims he has not sought conflict. Before Worcester can reply, Falstaff provides this sardonic intervention.

74 I do not think a braver gentleman,
More active-valiant or more valiant-young,
More daring or more bold, is now alive
To grace this latter age with noble deeds.
For my part, I may speak it to my shame,
I have a truant been to chivalry.
(V.1.89–94)

The first part of Prince Hal's speech to Worcester is generous praise of Hotspur's reputation, the second part an acknowledgement of his own neglect of chivalric honour. Yet the purpose of the eulogy and confession is to offer to settle the dispute in single combat with Hotspur in order to prevent the loss of other lives. Henry IV will not permit the challenge, though he does make an offer of honourable peace to the rebels.

75 FALSTAFF I would 'twere bed-time, Hal, and all well.
PRINCE HAL Why, thou owest God a death. *Exit*
FALSTAFF 'Tis not due yet – I would be loath to pay him before his day. What need I be so forward with him that calls not on me? Well, 'tis no matter, honour pricks me on. Yea, but how if honour prick me off when I come on, how then? Can honour set to a leg? No. Or an arm? No. Or take away the grief of a wound? No. Honour hath no skill in surgery then? No. What is honour? A word. What is in that word honour? What is that honour? Air. A trim reckoning! Who hath it? He that died a' Wednesday. Doth he feel it? No. Doth he hear it? No. 'Tis insensible, then? Yea, to the dead. But will it not live with the living? No. Why? Detraction will not suffer it. Therefore I'll none of it. Honour is a mere scutcheon – and so ends my catechism. *Exit*
(V.1.125–40)
Falstaff's disquisition, or mock catechism, on honour is based on the oppositon of the tangible to the intangible, love of life to love of honour. The dichotomy is picked up in the idea of honour 'pricking' or spurring on, but also 'pricking off' or marking down for death. 'Scutcheons' were ephemeral forms of heraldic devices hung in churches for funerals. Falstaff's evaluation of honour forms an ironic counterpoint to the contest for honour between Hotspur and Hal.

76 For treason is but trusted like the fox.
(V.2.7)
Worcester is arguing with Sir Richard Vernon that Hotspur should not be informed of King Henry's offer of an honourable peace; for he believes they will never be freed from the taint of rebellion but simply punished at a later date. The fox was a byword for wiliness in beast fables and was never to be trusted.

77 O gentlemen, the time of life is short!
To spend that shortness basely were too long
If life did ride upon a dial's point,
Still ending at the arrival of an hour.
(V.2.81–4)
Hotspur is addressing Worcester, Douglas, and Vernon before the battle of Shrewsbury. The prospect of death brings awareness of life's transience; but Hotspur's sense of honour proclaims

that, if it were lived basely, life would be too long even if it lasted only an hour.

78 Now, Esperance! Percy! and set on!
(V.2.96)
Hotspur's commitment to both the 'adventure of this perilous day' and to the pursuit of family and personal honour is combined in the Percy motto of *Esperance* (Hope) or *Esperance ma comforte* (Hope is my comfort).

79 Two stars keep not their motion in one sphere.
(V.4.64)
This analogy between the cosmic order and the hierarchy of the realm is employed by Prince Hal in his confrontation with Hotspur on the field of battle. The dramatic contrast of Harry Monmouth (Prince Hal) with Harry Percy (Hotspur) culminates in combat for the kingdom.

80 I better brook the loss of brittle life
Than those proud titles thou has won of me.
They wound my thoughts worse than thy sword my flesh.
But thoughts, the slaves of life, and life, time's fool,
And time, that takes survey of all the world,
Must have a stop.
(V.4.77–82)
Hotspur has been mortally wounded in battle by Prince Hal, whom he is addressing here. Even in death, Hotspur elevates the loss of honour above the loss of life, although he perceives that in death thought, life, and time all cease.

81 Fare thee well, great heart!
Ill-weaved ambition, how much art thou shrunk.
When that this body did contain a spirit,
A kingdom for it was too small a bound.
But now two paces of the vilest earth
Is room enough. This earth that bears thee dead
Bears not alive so stout a gentleman.
(V.4.86–92)
Prince Hal is generous in praise of Hotspur, whom he has killed in battle at Shrewsbury. The speech is based on the paradox of man's limitless aspiration and finite achievement. 'Stout' means valiant or resolute. In the battle scenes, Hotspur is contrasted not only with Hal but also with Falstaff, the denigrator of honour. Shortly after Hotspur's death, Falstaff arises from the 'death' he feigned to escape Douglas immediately prior to Hotspur's

receipt of the fatal wound. The audience is thus given a dual perspective of honour and death both visually and verbally.

82 What, old acquaintance, could not all this flesh
Keep in a little life? Poor Jack, farewell!
I could have better spared a better man.
(V.4.101–3)
Prince Hal speaks these words over what he takes to be the corpse of Falstaff. The frailty of the flesh is a recurrent theme of the play, explored on many levels. This panegyric is undercut by Falstaff's jumping back into life at the mention of disembowelling, since he had only feigned death to escape Douglas.

83 Lord, Lord, how this world is given to lying! I grant you I was down, and out of breath, and so was he, but we rose both at an instant, and fought a long hour by Shrewsbury clock.
(V.4.144–7)
Falstaff, having discovered the body of Hotspur, has decided to take the credit of his conquest to himself. Unfortunately, he has made the mistake of presenting his claim to the true conqueror, Prince Hal. Unabashed by Hal's revelation of the truth, Falstaff – the epitome of mendacity – laments the lack of truth in the world and invents an account of his victory.

84 If I do grow great, I'll grow less, for I'll purge, and leave sack, and live cleanly as a nobleman should do.
(V.4.162–4)
Falstaff's last lines in the play anticipate a social and pecuniary reward for his claim to have killed Hotspur. He puns on the physical and social senses of 'great', promising somewhat improbably that if he is elevated socially he will reform morally. To 'purge' in this context means to repent. 'Sack' is a category of Spanish white wines to which Falstaff has been inordinately given throughout the play.

Henry IV Part 2

1 Upon my tongues continual slanders ride,
The which in every language I pronounce,
Stuffing the ears of men with false reports.
I speak of peace while covert enmity,
Under the smile of safety, wounds the world.
(Induction 6–10)

The Induction to *Henry IV Part 2* is spoken by Rumour who, according to the Folio stage direction, is 'painted full of tongues'. Hence the reference to tongues in line 6. The personification derives from Medieval Morality and Tudor pageant traditions and perhaps has its origin in Virgil's Fama in *Aeneid* IV, 181–90. The figure was traditionally an equivocal one spreading both truth and falsehood, as again this passage makes explicit. The activity that Rumour recounts in the Induction will be enacted in the first scene of the play.

2 Rumour is a pipe
Blown by surmises, jealousies, conjectures,
And of so easy and so plain a stop
That the blunt monster with uncounted heads,
The still-discordant wavering multitude,
Can play upon it.
(Induction 15–20)

The personification of Rumour, in an emblematic coat of tongues, acts as the presenter of the drama. Rumour is speaking of its own operation under the image of a simple wind instrument whose stops (or vent-holes) are played upon by the many-headed monster, the populace. The last image is a commonplace of Elizabethan thought. The Induction serves an expository function in indicating both the true outcome of the battle of Shrewsbury, with which *Henry IV Part I* ended, and the false rumour with which this play will commence.

3 Yea, this man's brow, like to a title-leaf,
Foretells the nature of a tragic volume.
(I.1.60–1)

Northumberland recognizes in Morton's expression the tragic news he bears from Shrewsbury. The first scene of the play puts into action the function of Rumour, who presented the Induction. Northumberland has received two messengers from the battlefield: Lord Bardolph, bearing news of the rebellion's success; and Travers, bearing news of its failure. Morton brings confirmation of failure and of the death of Hotspur, Northumberland's son.

4 Thou tremblest, and the whiteness in thy cheek
Is apter than thy tongue to tell thy errand.
Even such a man, so faint, so spiritless,
So dull, so dead in look, so woe-begone,
Drew Priam's curtain in the dead of night
And would have told him half his Troy was burnt.
(I.1.68–73)

Northumberland is both addressing and describing Morton, who bears the fatal tidings of Hotspur's death and the rebellion's failure from the battlefield of Shrewsbury. King Priam's reaction to the destruction of Troy by fire at the climax of the Trojan war was a popular theme with Elizabethan poets, but the classical sources provide no precise parallel to this detail.

5 See what a ready tongue suspicion hath!
He that but fears the thing he would not know
Hath by instinct knowledge from others' eyes
That what he feared is chanced.
(I.1.85–8)

Northumberland has just anticipated the news of the death of his son, Hotspur, carried from Shrewsbury by Morton. Here he comments on his own perception.

6 Yet the first bringer of unwelcome news
Hath but a losing office, and his tongue
Sounds ever after as a sullen bell
Remembered tolling a departing friend.
(I.1.100–3)

Northumberland is articulating how he perceives the news of the death of his son, Hotspur, brought from Shrewsbury by Morton. Through Northumberland's utterances, the audience is made to receive the news as he feels it. Here Morton's voice is likened to the tolling of the funeral bell.

7 Let heaven kiss earth! Now let not Nature's hand
Keep the wild flood confined! Let order die!
And let this world no longer be a stage
To feed contention in a lingering act;
But let one spirit of the first-born Cain
Reign in all bosoms, that, each heart being set
On bloody courses, the rude scene may end,
And darkness be the burier of the dead!
(I.1.153–60)

Northumberland, according to Rumour in the Induction, had lain 'crafty-sick' at the time of the battle of Shrewsbury. However, on learning of his son's death there, Northumberland casts off the signs of his sickness, his crutch and his coif, and commits himself to arms. Here his rebellious rage involves a fratricidal curse and a vision of total anarchy in the natural and moral order.

8 But now the Bishop
Turns insurrection to religion;
Supposed sincere and holy in his thoughts,

He's followed both with body and with mind
And doth enlarge his rising with the blood
Of fair King Richard, scraped from Pomfret stones;
Derives from heaven his quarrel and his cause.
(I.1.200–6)

Morton is putting courage into Northumberland to take up arms against Henry IV. He has argued that Hotspur failed because the notion of rebellion undermined the confidence of his troops. Now that the Archbishop of York supports their cause, rebellion is transformed into a crusade drawing its power against Henry IV from the martyrdom of Richard II. Elizabeth and her governments greatly feared religious insurrection and the Tudor state used the Anglican Church as a spiritual and moral extension of its authority to condemn rebellion.

9 The brain of this foolish-compounded clay, man, is not able to invent anything that intends to laughter more than I invent, or is invented on me; I am not only witty in myself, but the cause that wit is in other men. I do here walk before thee like a sow that hath overwhelmed all her litter but one.
(I.2.6–12)

Falstaff is speaking to his page. The contrast of Falstaff's bulk with the page's small dimensions creates a comic visual effect in itself, as Falstaff observes in the last line quoted. Falstaff sees himself as the embodiment of wit and mirth, not only generating it himself but begetting and provoking it in others. This is true, for example, of his relationship with Prince Hal, who has provided him with the page. Falstaff is contemptuous of the wit of others, describing men as made of clay but compounded of folly.

10 A rascally yea-forsooth knave, to bear a gentleman in hand, and then stand upon security!
(I.2.34–6)

Falstaff is railing against his tailor. His page has just informed him that the tailor wisely will not undertake the commission for a cloak and breeches without financial securities. Falstaff's term of opprobrium satirizes the obsequious and mealy-mouthed behaviour of the puritan tradesmen of the city. He complains indignantly of having been led on in hopes only to have securities demanded of him.

11 I bought him in Paul's, and he'll buy me a horse in Smithfield. An I could get me but a wife in the stews, I were manned, horsed, and wived.
(I.2.50–2)

Falstaff is talking to the page about Bardolph who, according to the page, has gone to Smithfield to buy Falstaff a horse. Falstaff is alluding to the contemporary notion that Smithfield was the worst place to purchase a horse; St Paul's the worst place to hire a servant; and the stews (or brothels) obviously the worst place to acquire a wife. The nave of St Paul's Cathedral in the Elizabethan period was a thoroughfare of commerce, including the hiring of servants.

12 It is the disease of not listening, the malady of not marking, that I am troubled withal.

(I.2.122–3)

Falstaff is speaking to the Lord Chief Justice. Since the start of the conversation, Falstaff has been seeking to direct the Justice's attention away from his failure to respond to the Justice's summons by talking of Henry IV's 'apoplexy' or paralysis. Falstaff has observed that according to Galen, the Greek physician who was an authority to the medieval and Renaissance world, symptoms included deafness, which permits the Justice to suggest that Falstaff, too, has fallen prey to it. Falstaff then makes the above retort.

13 I am as poor as Job, my lord, but not so patient.

(I.2.127–8)

The Lord Chief Justice has just threatened Falstaff with imprisonment as a means of curing his 'deafness' (see 12 above). Falstaff seeks to extricate himself by pursuing the imagery of disease and punning on 'patient'. He likens himself to Job, the protagonist of the eponymous book of the Old Testament, in respect of poverty but not patience, for both of which Job was a byword.

14 LORD CHIEF JUSTICE Your means are very slender, and your waste is great.

FALSTAFF I would it were otherwise; I would my means were greater and my waist slenderer.

(I.2.141–4)

The Lord Chief Justice has accused Falstaff of living in 'great infamy'. Falstaff is seeking to evade the accusation by joking about the size of his girth. On stage, the Chief Justice and Falstaff present two contrasted images of old age: one the embodiment of gravity and sobriety, the other the epitome of vice.

15 Well, I am loath to gall a new-healed wound.

(I.2.149–50)

The Lord Chief Justice decides not to pursue Falstaff's involvement in the Gad's Hill exploit, unfolded in Act II of *Henry IV Part*

I, in view of Falstaff's service at the battle of Shrewsbury. His phrase has passed into the language as a metaphor for not wishing to re-open a contentious argument.

16 Do you set down your name in the scroll of youth, that are written down old with all the characters of age? Have you not a moist eye, a dry hand, a yellow cheek, a white beard, a decreasing leg, an increasing belly? Is not your voice broken, your wind short, your chin double, your wit single, and every part about you blasted with antiquity? And will you yet call yourself young?
(I.2.180–7)
Falstaff has had the effrontery to suggest that he is young, whilst the Lord Chief Justice is old. In reply, the Justice points out mercilessly the marks of age in Falstaff's person.

17 My lord, I was born about three of the clock in the afternoon, with a white head, and something a round belly. For my voice, I have lost it with hallooing, and singing of anthems. To approve my youth further, I will not. The truth is, I am only old in judgement and understanding.
(I.2.188–93)
Falstaff's response to the Lord Chief Justice's denunciation of his age is to assert the similarity of age to infancy. The truth, of course, lies in an inversion of Falstaff's claims: he is old in body, childish in judgement. Nor has any decline of his vigour, as he claims for his loss of voice, resulted from a godly life. The notion of age as a second childhood was a commonplace of the Elizabethan era as much as of our own.

18 LORD CHIEF JUSTICE Well, God send the Prince a better companion!
FALSTAFF God send the companion a better prince!
(I.2.200–3)
Falstaff's inversion of the Lord Chief Justice's wish is typical of his inversion of all moral norms. On the physical, emotional, and moral planes, he is as much a figure of rebellion as the rebels are on the social and political.

19 All you that kiss my lady Peace at home.
(I.2.209)
This contemptuous phrase of Falstaff for the civilian population in time of war is addressed to the Lord Chief Justice. The Chief Justice, in a largely expository statement, has just informed the audience that Henry IV has separated Falstaff from Prince Hal's

company by sending him north with Prince John of Lancaster against the Earl of Northumberland and the Archbishop of York.

20 It was alway yet the trick of our English nation, if they have a good thing, to make it too common.
(I.2.216–17)
Falstaff's generalization appears possibly acceptable until it is realized that it is applied to his own life. He is lamenting the potential loss of his life in the service of his country.

21 I can get no remedy against this consumption of the purse; borrowing only lingers and lingers it out, but the disease is incurable.
(I.2.238–40)
Falstaff is lamenting his poverty to his page. The imagery of disease pervades the entire scene (and play) and here is applied not only to the body but to the entire life-style of Falstaff.

22 A pox of this gout! Or a gout of this pox!
(I.2.246)
Falstaff is so consumed with diseases that he does not know to which one he should attribute the origins of his suffering.

23 When we mean to build,
We first survey the plot, then draw the model,
And when we see the figure of the house,
Then must we rate the cost of the erection,
Which if we find outweighs ability,
What do we then but draw anew the model
In fewer offices, or at least desist
To build at all?
(I.3.41–8)
Lord Bardolph is addressing his fellow rebels: the Archbishop of York, Mowbray, and Lord Hastings. His argument is based on the parable of the builder found in Luke 14:28–30. The rebels are discussing whether they can face the forces of Henry IV under Prince John of Lancaster without the support of Northumberland's troops. The essence of Bardolph's argument is that a careful evaluation of their project and its chances of success must be made.

24 An habitation giddy and unsure
Hath he that buildeth on the vulgar heart.
(I.3.89–90)
The Archbishop of York pursues the architectural metaphor of this scene in speaking to his fellow rebels, the Lords Mowbray,

Hastings, and Bardolph. The 'vulgar' heart is that of the common people and the Archbishop's speech continues by expanding his argument of the fickleness of the people's political commitment.

25 A hundred mark is a long one for a poor lone woman to bear, and I have borne, and borne, and borne, and have been fubbed off, and fubbed off, and fubbed off, from this day to that day, that it is a shame to be thought on.
(II.1.30–4)
Mistress Quickly, the Hostess of the Boar's Head Tavern, has taken out an action against Sir John Falstaff for debt, having finally grown impatient with his excuses for non-payment. She is addressing the officers, Fang and Snare, who must arrest Falstaff. 'Fubbed off' is a variant of fobbed off.

26 Away, you scullion! You rampallian! You fustilarian! I'll tickle your catastrophe!
(II.1.57–8)
The page is defending Falstaff against the attacks of the Hostess, Mistress Quickly. A 'scullion' was a kitchen servant of the lowest rank; a 'rampallian', a scoundrel; a 'fustilarian', possibly a fat frowzy woman. The final phrase means: I'll sting your backside!

27 Doth it not show vilely in me to desire small beer?
(II.2.5–6)
Prince Hal addresses the question to his companion, Poins. 'Small beer' was weak or thin beer; but the phrase, by extension, signifies the low-life and its companions.

28 Let the end try the man.
(II.2.44)
This phrase of Prince Hal to Poins was proverbial. The sense is clear: that a man should be judged by his final outcome. Prince Hal is arguing that Poins is mistaken if he considers that the Prince is as inextricably committed to vice as he and Falstaff are. He is also indicating that, contrary to popular belief, he is deeply saddened by his father's illness.

29 Well, thus we play the fools with the time, and the spirits of the wise sit in the clouds and mock us.
(II.2.135–7)
Henry IV Part 2 is marked by an oppressive sense of the passage of time and, especially, of the decay that accompanies it. Prince Hal is set apart from the idleness of his companions by his laconic detachment and is, indeed, the only character who stands to profit from the passage of time.

30 Even such kin as the parish heifers are to the town bull.
(II.2.150–1)
This is Prince Hal's riposte to the page's comment that Falstaff is to be found in the company of Doll Tearsheet, a respectable 'kinswoman' of his master. Doll, as her name implies, is a common prostitute. The Prince and Poins concoct a scheme to disguise themselves as tapsters in order to spy on Falstaff with Doll Tearsheet.

31 By his light
Did all the chivalry of England move
To do brave acts. He was indeed the glass
Wherein the noble youth did dress themselves.
(II.3.19–22)
Lady Percy, the widow of Hotspur, is remembering the glory of her husband's honour. She is addressing her father-in-law, Northumberland, whom she is urging not to join the rebels, since he failed to do so in support of Hotspur at Shrewsbury. Northumberland actually chooses flight to Scotland. In this play, the chivalric ideal that Hotspur (and Hal) stood for in *Part I* exists only as a memory.

32 Shall pack-horses,
And hollow pampered jades of Asia,
Which cannot go but thirty mile a day,
Compare with Caesars and with Cannibals,
And Troyant Greeks? Nay, rather damn them with
King Cerberus, and let the welkin roar!
(II.4.158–63)
Falstaff's ensign, Pistol, is characterized as a roaring boy and 'swaggerer'. On entering the company of Mistress Quickly and Doll Tearsheet, he immediately becomes embroiled in quarrels with them arising from the sexual equivocations in the language he uses towards them. Here, in high anger, he is out-doing the rhetoric made famous on the Elizabethan stage by Marlowe's Tamburlaine. In fact, the passage parodies *Tamburlaine Part 2*, IV.3.1–2. An even more specific source of Pistol's language has been identified by Prof. J. W. Lever in John Eliot's *Ortho-epia Gallica* of 1593.

33 Thou whoreson little tidy Bartholomew boar-pig, when wilt thou leave fighting a-days, and foining a-nights, and begin to patch up thine old body for heaven?
(II.4.226–8)
Doll Tearsheet is affectionately complimenting Falstaff on the prowess he has demonstrated in thrusting Pistol, the swaggering

soldier, out of their company. Her terms of endearment are questionable: 'tidy' means plump, a 'boar-pig' is a young boar, and 'foining' means thrusting. She is alluding especially to the tradition of roasting pig-meat at Bartholomew Fair held at Smithfield on St Bartholomew's day (24 August) and celebrated by Ben Jonson in the play of that name. Her question reinforces the theme of mortality and the passage of time. Falstaff requests her not to speak like a 'death's-head'.

34 Is it not strange that desire should so many years outlive performance?
(II.4.255–6)
Poins' observation is made to Prince Hal while these two, disguised as tapsters or barmen, are spying on Falstaff and Doll Tearsheet. Doll is sitting on Falstaff's knee and ruffling his hair.

35 You see, my good wenches, how men of merit are sought after; the undeserver may sleep, when the man of action is called on.
Falstaff is speaking to Mistress Quickly and Doll Tearsheet after he and Prince Hal have been called away from the tavern by affairs of state. While his general observation may be true, his application of it to himself is extremely dubious.

36 How many thousand of my poorest subjects
Are at this hour asleep! O sleep, O gentle sleep,
Nature's soft nurse, how have I frighted thee,
That thou no more wilt weigh my eyelids down
And steep my senses in forgetfulness?
Why rather, sleep, liest thou in smoky cribs,
Upon uneasy pallets stretching thee,
And hushed with buzzing night-flies to thy slumber
Than in the perfumed chambers of the great,
Under the canopies of costly state,
And lulled with sound of sweetest melody?
(III.1.4–14)
Henry IV's soliloquy emphasizes the burden and responsibility of kingship. While the speech may owe a debt to Sir Philip Sidney's sonnet 'Come sleepe' (*Astrophel and Stella*, 39), the contrast between the untroubled sleep of the humble and the tortured insomnia of the powerful is a literary commonplace of the period. However, sleeplessness is associated throughout Shakespeare's work with guilt, and Henry IV, in addition to his immediate problems, is also troubled by the memory of Richard's deposition.

37 Uneasy lies the head that wears a crown.
(III.1.31)

Although Henry IV's line may have its origin in Erasmus' *Institutio Principis* (1516) and although its basic idea had become proverbial by Shakespeare's day, it is in Shakespeare's phrasing that the concept has been passed down to posterity.

38 O God, that one might read the book of fate,
And see the revolution of the times
Make mountains level, and the continent,
Weary of solid firmness, melt itself
Into the sea.
(III.1.45–9)

Henry IV implicitly likens rebellion in the state to cosmic disorder. The changes described as being effected in the phenomenal world by the passage of time may owe a debt to Ovid's *Metamorphoses* XV.262 ff., available to Shakespeare in Golding's translation of 1567.

39 When Richard, with his eye brimful of tears,
Then checked and rated by Northumberland,
Did speak these words, now proved a prophecy?
'Northumberland, thou ladder by the which
My cousin Bolingbroke ascends my throne' –
Though then, God knows, I had no such intent
But that necessity so bowed the state
That I and greatness were compelled to kiss –
'The time shall come' – thus did he follow it –
'The time will come that foul sin, gathering head,
Shall break into corruption' – so went on,
Foretelling this same time's condition,
And the division of our amity.
(III.1.63–75)

Henry IV is addressing the Earl of Warwick as a witness to the events recorded in the passage. Henry IV's lines allude to Northumberland's defiance of Richard in the deposition scene (IV.1) of *Richard II* and to Richard's speech at V.1.55–68. The speech reveals Henry's sense of guilt and his continued attempts at self-justification. Henry's argument that necessity brought him to the throne is only partially sustainable.

40 There is a history in all men's lives,
Figuring the natures of the times deceased,
The which observed, a man may prophesy,
With a near aim, of the main chance of things
As yet not come to life, who in their seeds

And weak beginning lie intreasurèd.
Such things become the hatch and brood of time.
(III.1.76–82)
Warwick's response to Henry IV's recollection of Richard II's prophecy (39 above) presents a cyclic view of history, since the second line quoted means: reproducing the pattern of what has taken place. It was the humanist belief in such a cyclic view that promoted historiography and the study of history in the Renaissance, since it was believed that lessons of direct applicability could be learned. This interest also underlies Shakespeare's history plays and those of his contemporaries.

41 A soldier is better accommodated than with a wife.
(III.2.65–6)
Bardolph is replying to Justice Shallow's polite enquiry after Falstaff's wife. Shallow was a companion of Falstaff in his youth and assumes Falstaff to be married. In 'accommodated', Bardolph is bringing a London vogue word into the provinces of Gloucestershire and Shallow subsequently comments upon it with approval.

42 We have heard the chimes at midnight.
(III.2.209)
Falstaff has been reminiscing with Justice Shallow, a companion of his youth, about their misspent days at the Inns of Court. the phrase, 'the chimes at midnight', was used by Orson Welles as the title of a 1965 film based on the Falstaff episodes of the *Henry IV* plays, in which Welles played Falstaff as well as directing. This scene, like much of the play, is characterized by a sense of life-weariness and of the relentless passage of time.

43 A man can die but once; we owe God a death. I'll ne'er bear a base mind. An't be my destiny, so; an't be not, so. No man's too good to serve's prince; and, let it go which way it will, he that dies this year is quit for the next.
(III.2.228–32)
Throughout this scene Falstaff is pressing local men, provided by Shallow, to military service in Henry IV's forces. The system of impressment was subject to much corruption in the period and Falstaff's practice is no exception. Only Feeble, the least fit for military duty, expresses – albeit with some dubious logic – the correct religious and secular platitudes regarding death in military service.

44 Lord, Lord, how subject we old men are to this vice of lying!

This same starved justice hath done nothing but prate to me of the wildness of his youth, and the feats he hath done about Turnbull Street, and every third word a lie, duer paid to the hearer than the Turk's tribute. I do remember him at Clement's Inn, like a man made after supper of a cheese-paring. When 'a was naked, he was for all the world like a forked radish, with a head fantastically carved upon it with a knife.
(III.2.292–301)
After Shallow's departure, Falstaff is commenting laconically upon the way that in old age Shallow has transformed his dowdy youth into one of adventurous escapade. The generalization which introduces this disquisition on the discrepancy between Shallow's claims and reality applies ironically to Falstaff himself. Turnbull Street was notorious for vice. The 'Turk's tribute' was money exacted by the Ottoman Turks on their dependent territories in Eastern Europe (the Turkish menace to Western Europe was a constant threat in the late sixteenth century). The comic image created verbally of Shallow in old age should tally with his visual presentation on the stage.

45 Against ill chances men are ever merry,
But heaviness foreruns the good event.
(IV.2.81–2)
At Gaultree Forest, Prince John of Lancaster has encountered the leaders of the rebellion: the Archbishop of York, Lord Mowbray, and Lord Hastings. Prince John has promised that the rebels' grievances will be redressed and, on the strength of this pledge, the rebels have dismissed their forces. In this almost proverbial statement, the Archbishop of York is reassuring Mowbray, but in fact the dialogue between the Prince's faction and the rebels is shot through with an irony that anticipates the rebels' subsequent betrayal. The notion that men's inner states do not correspond with forthcoming events was commonplace. 'Against' means in the face of.

46 MOWBRAY
Is this proceeding just and honourable?
WESTMORLAND
Is your assembly so?
(IV.2.110–11)
This exchange follows immediately upon Prince John's arresting Mowbray, Hastings, and the Archbishop of York for treason. Prince John has just learned from Hastings that the rebel army has dispersed in disorder. The exchange presents succinctly the conflict depicted in the play between the anathema of rebellion and the need and right to question official policy.

47 This same, young sober-blooded boy doth not love me, nor a man cannot make him laugh – but that's no marvel, he drinks no wine.

(IV.3.86–8)

Falstaff is speaking of Prince John of Lancaster, whose cynical betrayal of the rebels is so unlike Prince Hal's honourable victory over Hotspur at the climax of *Henry IV Part I*. Although Falstaff has just taken Colevile of the Dale prisoner and has handed him over to Prince John, he knows that the Prince has no illusions about his valour and conduct.

48 A good sherris-sack hath a twofold operation in it. It ascends me into the brain, dries me there all the foolish and dull and crudy vapours which environ it, makes it apprehensive, quick, forgetive, full of nimble, fiery, and delectable shapes, which delivered o'er to the voice, the tongue, which is the birth, becomes excellent wit. The second property of your excellent sherris is the warming of the blood, which before, cold and settled, left the liver white and pale, which is the badge of pusillanimity and cowardice; but the sherris warms it, and makes it course from the inwards to the parts' extremes. It illumineth the face, which, as a beacon, gives warning to all the rest of this little kingdom, man, to arm; and then the vital commoners, and inland petty spirits, muster me all to their captain, the heart, who, great and puffed up with this retinue, doth any deed of courage; and this valour comes of sherris. So that skill in the weapon is nothing without sack, for that sets it a-work, and learning a mere hoard of gold kept by a devil, till sack commences it and sets it in act and use.

(IV.3.95–114)

Falstaff's famous panegyric on 'sherris-sack', a white wine from Xeres in Spain, attributes to the wine two major properties: stimulation of the brain and of martial vigour, or the production of wit and valour. The 'foolish and dull and crudy vapours' are perhaps melancholic, or merely dull, thoughts which are purged and replaced by 'forgetive' or inventive ones. Falstaff's account of how alcohol takes effect in the body follows Elizabethan physiology.

49 If I had a thousand sons, the first human principle I would teach them should be to forswear thin potations, and to addict themselves to sack.

(IV.3.120–2)

The conclusion to Falstaff's eulogy of 'sherris-sack' is made with particular reference to Prince Hal, whom Falstaff has just compared favourably with his 'sober-blooded' brother, Prince John. Throughout the *Henry IV* plays, Falstaff is depicted as one kind of father-figure in relation to Prince Hal.

50 For he is gracious, if he be observed;
He hath a tear for pity, and a hand
Open as day for melting charity;
Yet notwithstanding, being incensed, he is flint,
As humorous as winter, and as sudden
As flaws congealèd in the spring of day.
(IV.4.30–5)

Henry IV is dissecting Prince Hal's character for the benefit of Hal's favourite brother, Thomas, Duke of Clarence. Although his character is depicted as 'humorous' or capricious, it blends mercy with wrath in an almost godlike manner. King Henry is seeking to ensure amity amongst his sons and order in the kingdom after his death.

51 Most subject is the fattest soil to weeds.
(IV.4.54)

Henry IV is responding to the information gained from his son Thomas, Duke of Clarence, that Prince Hal is in the company of his low-life companions instead of being present at court to attend to affairs of state. 'Fattest' means richest, and the idea was proverbial.

52 O polished perturbation! Golden care!
That keepest the ports of slumber open wide
To many a watchful night! Sleep with it now!
Yet not so sound, and half so deeply sweet,
As he whose brow with homely biggen bound
Snores out the watch of night.
(IV.5.24–9)

Henry IV has been taken seriously ill in the Jerusalem Chamber at Westminster and is, in fact, dying. Ironically, this is as close as he will get to the Holy Land where he wished to conduct a crusade to expiate his guilt for Richard II's murder. Prince Hal, who is alone with his father, is addressing the crown which lies on the pillow beside the King. The Prince's words echo those of his father in III.1. (see 36 and 37 above). A 'biggen' is a night-cap.

53 This sleep is sound indeed; this is a sleep
That from this golden rigol hath divorced
So many English kings.
(IV.5.36–8)

Henry IV has been taken seriously ill in the Jerusalem Chamber at Westminster. Prince Hal, who is alone with him, believes at this moment that his father is dead. He subsequently takes the royal crown ('golden rigol'; 'rigol' is a ring or circle) that he has been contemplating and places it upon his own head, only to be reproved by the King who rouses himself from his state of unconsciousness.

54 Thy wish was father, Harry, to that thought.
(IV.5.93)

Henry IV is replying to Prince Hal's penitent statement that he feared he would never hear his father speak again. Henry IV is reproving Hal because he has precipitately removed the crown before he is entitled to wear it. The idea that Henry IV expresses here was proverbial; but it is Shakespeare's formulation of it that has come down to posterity.

55 Harry the Fifth is crowned! Up, vanity!
Down, royal state! All you sage counsellors, hence!
And to the English court assemble now,
From every region, apes of idleness!
Now, neighbour confines, purge you of your scum!
Have you a ruffian that will swear, drink, dance,
Revel the night, rob, murder, and commit
The oldest sins the newest kind of ways?
(IV.5.120–7)

Henry IV's reproof of Hal takes the form of a deathbed vision of the anarchy in the state that will follow Hal's succession. Henry IV is envisaging that the English court will become the centre of riot and disorder attracting villains from far and wide. The vision of future anarchy corresponds to the anarchy of the Falstaff-world incorporated in the play.

56 This new and gorgeous garment, majesty,
Sits not so easy on me as you think.
(V.2.43–4)

These are the first words of Henry V after his succession. They are addressed to his brothers and to the Lord Chief Justice, who fear what his exercise of power may bring. Majesty is conveyed through the image of a 'gorgeous garment', the royal robe he wears.

57 A foutre for the world and worldlings base!
I speak of Africa and golden joys.
(V.3.99–100)

Pistol has interrupted the Gloucestershire idyll of Shallow and Silence, where Falstaff and his cronies are living off the fat of the land, in order to bring from London the news of Hal's accession. His mode of expression is histrionic and hyperbolic: 'a foutre for' is a vulgar phrase expressing contempt, while Africa signified a land of legendary wealth.

58 Let us take any man's horses – the laws of England are at my commandment.
(V.3.133–5)
Falstaff is addressing Justice Shallow with reference to Pistol's news of Henry V's accession. Falstaff is determined to return to London at all speed in order, as he thinks, to share in the good fortune that has befallen Hal. He is asking Shallow to requisition horses for royal use, and his general attitude to the law promises to fulfil the picture of anarchy envisaged by Henry IV on his death-bed.

59 I know thee not, old man. Fall to thy prayers.
How ill white hairs becomes a fool and jester.
I have long dreamt of such a kind of man,
So surfeit-swelled, so old, and so profane,
But being awaked I do despise my dream.
Make less thy body hence, and more thy grace;
Leave gormandizing; know the grave doth gape
For thee thrice wider than for other men.
(V.5.50–7)
Falstaff has returned to London with Shallow, Pistol, Bardolph, and the page in the expectation of being received into the new king's favour and being showered with honours and material benefits. Unaware of Hal's transformation, Falstaff presents himself before the King only to suffer this total rejection. In Henry V's words, Falstaff is metamorphosed from a festive figure into a pathetic, even obscene, one. Some critics and audiences, whilst they recognize the moral rectitude of the King's decision, find the rejection emotionally unacceptable and repugnant.

60 Presume not that I am the thing I was.
(V.5.59)
This is the explicit statement of Hal's transformation on becoming Henry V. His speech is marked by stiff formality, though it has been speculated that the function of the remark is to forestall any jest of Falstaff which might weaken the new king's resolve.

61 Our humble author will continue the story, with Sir John in it, and make you merry with fair Katherine of France – where, for anything I know, Falstaff shall die of a sweat,

unless already 'a be killed with your hard opinions; for
Oldcastle died martyr, and this is not the man.
(Epilogue 26–31)

This passage from the Epilogue raises two issues. Firstly, *Henry V* does not continue the fortunes of Falstaff, but merely recounts his death. Therefore either the author's intention as stated here was not carried out, or *Henry V* underwent revision. Secondly, Shakespeare draws a distinction between Falstaff, the dramatic character, and Sir John Oldcastle, the historical original, who died a Wycliffite martyr.

Henry V

1 O for a Muse of fire, that would ascend
The brightest heaven of invention,
A kingdom for a stage, princes to act,
And monarchs to behold the swelling scene!
(Chorus I, 1–4)

The initial chorus is spoken by the figure of Chorus (or Prologue), most probably an actor dressed in a long black velvet coat. *Henry V* is peculiar amongst the plays of Shakespeare in having each act prefaced by a formal chorus. This convention betrays the epic nature of the dramatic narrative. The Chorus's first speech blends the play's warlike theme and its epic proportions with the divine inspiration of poetry and the author's aims at sublime expression. At the same time it exploits the discrepancy between the loftiness of theme and the limitations of Shakespeare's theatre.

2 But pardon, gentles all
The flat unraisèd spirits that hath dared
On this unworthy scaffold to bring forth
So great an object. Can this cockpit hold
The vasty fields of France? Or may we cram
Within this wooden O the very casques
That did affright the air at Agincourt?
(Chorus I, 8–14)

In his direct appeal to the audience, Chorus invites the spectators to fulfil the theatrical contract by complementing the limitations of the enactment with the exercise of their imagination. Only thus can the significance of the great victory at Agincourt be experienced. The phrase 'this wooden O' has become virtually synonymous with the circular Elizabethan public amphitheatre.

Here it is probably a reference to the *Curtain* theatre, not to the more famous *Globe* which was only under construction while Shakespeare was writing this play. 'Cockpit' also signifies a circular theatre. The form of the Elizabethan public theatres evolved, not altogether inappropriately, from the venues of blood-sports.

3 Piece out our imperfections with your thoughts.
(Chorus I, 23)
This line is the culmination of Chorus's appeal to the audience to respond imaginatively to the play.

4 Consideration like an angel came
And whipped th'offending Adam out of him.
(I.1.28–9)
The Archbishop of Canterbury is speaking to the Bishop of Ely about the reformation that overtook Henry V at the time of his accession to the throne. In *Henry IV Parts 1 and 2*, Prince Hal had been the 'madcap prince'; but, on inheriting the responsibilities of the kingdom, he has become the model king. 'Consideration' means spiritual self-examination, and 'th'offending Adam' is a reference to the unregenerate 'old man' of the Pauline epistles for which Adam's original sin was an archetype.

5 When he speaks,
The air, a chartered libertine, is still,
And the mute wonder lurketh in men's ears
To steal his sweet and honeyed sentences.
(I.1.47–50)
These lines are taken from the Archbishop of Canterbury's panegyric of the young Henry V as the model of kingship. The Archbishop has just expounded the King's mastery of all the regal arts: divinity, politics, and warfare. Henry's mastery of rhetoric adds persuasion to wisdom and will be exemplified in the play. The first scene establishes Henry as an ideal sovereign and presents the churchmen's plans to direct Henry's attention to his claims to the French throne.

6 O noble English, that could entertain
With half their forces the full pride of France,
and let another half stand laughing by,
All out of work and cold for action!
(I.2.111–14)
The Archbishop of Canterbury is persuading Henry V of the justness and feasibility of claiming the French throne. He has just alluded to the exploits of the Black Prince at Crécy.

7 For so work the honey-bees,
Creatures that by a rule in nature teach
The act of order to a peopled kingdom.
They have a king, and officers of sorts,
Where some, like magistrates, correct at home;
Others, like merchants, venture trade abroad;
Others, like soldiers, armèd in their stings,
Make boot upon the summer's velvet buds;
Which pillage they with merry march bring home
To the tent-royal of their emperor;
Who, busied in his majesty, surveys
The singing masons building roofs of gold,
The civil citizens kneading up the honey,
The poor mechanic porters crowding in
Their heavy burdens at his narrow gate,
The sad-eyed justice, with his surly hum,
Delivering o'er to executors pale
The lazy yawning drone.

(I.2.187–204)

The Archbishop of Canterbury's analogy between the society of bees and of men has a long ancestry. The two most famous sources are to be found in Virgil's *Georgics*, IV.152 ff. and in Pliny's *Natural History*, Book XI. Shakespeare could have borrowed from either or from the innumerable writers who cited one or both, including Sir Thomas Elyot and John Lyly. The model offered by the bees, as described here, is a hierarchically ordered society and this explains its attractions to Renaissance thinkers imbued with the same social concept.

8 KING HENRY
What treasure, uncle?
EXETER Tennis-balls, my liege.
KING HENRY
We are glad the Dauphin is so pleasant with us.
His present, and your pains, we thank you for.
When we have matched our rackets to these balls,
We will in France, by God's grace, play a set
Shall strike his father's crown into the hazard.

(I.2.259–64)

Henry V has just received the ambassador and the present from the Dauphin of France. The Dauphin's embassy is in response to Henry's claim to certain dukedoms of France, descending from Edward III. His present is an insult by way of allusion to Henry's riotous and sportive youth, since the manner of his reformation and his kingship is not known in France. Henry's sustained metaphor, by way of reply, offers a sporting analogy for warfare.

9 Now all the youth of England are on fire,
And silken dalliance in the wardrobe lies.
Now thrive the armourers, and honour's thought
Reigns solely in the breast of every man.
They sell the pasture now to buy the horse,
Following the mirror of all Christian kings
With wingèd heels, as English Mercuries.
For now sits expectation in the air,
And hides a sword from hilts unto the point
With crowns imperial, crowns and coronets,
Promised to Harry and his followers.
(Chorus II, 1–11)

The second chorus spoken by the Prologue describes the English preparation for the French expedition and the air of expectation surrounding it. The initial contrast is between the honour and activity of warfare and the idle luxury of peacetime. English youths become Mercuries (Mercury was the messenger of the gods, with winged heels) on account of their zeal. The vision that leads them on, the crowns to be won by conquest of the sword, may derive from a device of Edward III.

10 O England! model to thy inward greatness,
Like little body with a mighty heart,
What mightst thou do, that honour would thee do,
Were all thy children kind and natural!
(Chorus II, 16–19)

Chorus's exhortation to loyalty reflects, naturally, official Elizabethan policy which had frequently to present a case against rebellion. 'England', following Elizabethan usage, stands for both the monarch and the nation. The 'model' here is a small image or replica. The last line alludes specifically to the treachery of the Earl of Cambridge, Lord Scroop, and Sir Thomas Grey, though it has a wider reverberation.

11 The scene
Is now transported, gentles, to Southampton.
There is the playhouse now, there must you sit,
And thence to France shall we convey you safe
And bring you back, charming the narrow seas
To give you gentle pass; for, if we may,
We'll not offend one stomach with our play.
(Chorus II, 34–40)

Chorus offers a witty and gracious explanation of the Elizabethan stage's flexibility of location. Whilst fulfilling the purpose of narrative and exposition, the chorus sustains its demand on the audience's imaginative collaboration in the creation of the play.

12 O hound of Crete, think'st thou my spouse to get?
No, to the spital go,
And from the powdering tub of infamy
Fetch forth the lazar kite of Cressid's kind,
Doll Tearsheet she by name, and her espouse.
I have, and I will hold, the quondam Quickly
For the only she; and – *pauca*, there's enough.
(II.1.70–6)

The passage is a good example of Pistol's invective, which derives from and parodies the popular drama of Shakespeare's day. Pistol is jealously defying Nym, a former suitor to Mistress Quickly, Pistol's wife. He urges Nym, whose shagginess he likens to a dog, to marry the leprous whore, Doll Tearsheet. In Henryson's *Testament of Cresseid*, a late fifteenth-century work published in 1532, Cressida's infidelity had been punished by leprosy. *Pauca* is a piece of stage Latin meaning in brief.

13 BARDOLPH Would I were with him, wheresome'er he is, either in heaven or in hell!
HOSTESS Nay, sure, he's not in hell: he's in Arthur's bosom, if ever man went to Arthur's bosom. 'A made a finer end, and went away an it had been any christom child; 'a parted e'en just between twelve and one, e'en at the turning o'th'tide; for after I saw him fumble with the sheets, and play with flowers, and smile upon his fingers' ends, I knew there was but one way; for his nose was as sharp as a pen, and 'a babbled of green fields.
(II.3.7–17)

Bardolph's and the Hostess's responses are made to Pistol's news that Falstaff is dead. One of the marked changes of tone and emphasis between this play and the *Henry IV* plays results from the absence of the ebullient figure of Falstaff. The Hostess's account of Falstaff's death blends comedy and pathos. She has unwittingly secularized Abraham's bosom to Arthur's on account of Falstaff's dubious chivalry, and she offers a comic description of the traditional signs of the approach of death. The alteration by Theobald, in his 1733 edition of the *Works*, of the Folio's 'a Table of greene fields' to ''a babbled of green fields' is one of the most famous Shakespearian emendations.

14 So 'a bade me lay more clothes on his feet; I put my hand

into the bed, and felt them, and they were as cold as any stone; then I felt to his knees, and so up'ard and up'ard, and all was as cold as any stone.
(II.3.21–5)
This is the final account of Falstaff in the History plays, even though Shakespeare had promised more comic adventures in the Epilogue to *Henry IV Part 2*. Typically, Mistress Quickly's account of Falstaff's demise mixes the comic, the pathetic, and the bawdy.

15 Come, let's away. My love, give me thy lips.
Look to my chattels and my movables.
Let senses rule. The word is 'Pitch and pay!'
Trust none;
For oaths are straws, men's faiths are wafer-cakes,
And Holdfast is the only dog, my duck.
Therefore, *Caveto* be thy counsellor.
Go, clear thy crystals.
(II.3.44–50)
Pistol's version of the soldier's farewell to his wife is a mixture of affection and avarice. He and his companions are about to depart for France as part of Henry V's expedition. His main concern seems to be that Mistress Quickly should take a care to his financial interests. 'Pitch and pay' means cash only, no credit; and all the injunctions are to be wary and to trust no one, perhaps a reflection of Pistol's own dishonest nature.

16 Thus with imagined wing our swift scene flies
In motion of no less celerity
Than that of thought.
(Chorus III, 1–3)
The chorus to Act Three, which involves the transposition of the play's action to France, pursues the notion that the spectator must perceive the play through the exercise of thought and imagination.

17 Once more unto the breach, dear friends, once more,
Or close the wall up with our English dead!
In peace there's nothing so becomes a man
As modest stillness and humility:
But when the blast of war blows in our ears,
Then imitate the action of the tiger;
Stiffen the sinews, conjure up the blood,
Disguise fair nature with hard-favoured rage.
(III.1.1–8)
Henry's address to his followers at the siege of Harfleur is a patriotic appeal to adopt a martial aspect and demeanour in time

of war. The chauvinistic aspect of the play, perhaps a late manifestation of post-Armada national self-confidence, was highlighted in the famous 1944 film, in which Laurence Olivier directed himself in the title role. Until recently, many editors followed the eighteenth-century editor Rowe's emendation of 'summon' for the Folio's 'commune', in place of the now-favoured 'conjure'. 'Conjure' fits perfectly with Renaissance physiology's sense of vital spirits contained in the blood.

18 On, on, you noblest English,
Whose blood is fet from fathers of war-proof! –
Fathers that, like so many Alexanders,
Have in these parts from morn till even fought,
And sheathed their swords for lack of argument.
Dishonour not your mothers; now attest
That those whom you call fathers did beget you!
Be copy now to men of grosser blood,
And teach them how to war. And you, good yeomen,
Whose limbs were made in England, show us here
The mettle of your pasture.
(III.1.17–27)

Henry is urging on his officers and soldiers to the assault of Harfleur. His argument is that the English are derived ('fet') from fathers who have won such victories in French territory as to merit comparison with Alexander the Great. As well as expressing an English patriotism against the French, the quotation also depicts the English nation as a unity embracing the different social classes, at least from 'noblest' to 'yeomen'.

19 I see you stand like greyhounds in the slips,
Straining upon the start. The game's afoot!
Follow your spirit, and upon this charge
Cry, 'God for Harry, England, and Saint George!'
(III.1.31–4)

Following his rousing address to his troops before Harfleur, Henry sees them as greyhounds straining at their leashes ('slips') to be let loose at the game. Hunting with greyhounds was a favourite aristocratic pastime in the Middle Ages and Renaissance.

20 Would I were in an alehouse in London! I would give all my fame for a pot of ale, and safety.
(III.2.11–12)

After Henry V's rousing address to the troops before Harfleur in the previous scene, we see the reactions of the ordinary soldiers. Bardolph is urging Nym, Pistol, and the Boy to return to the assault of Harfleur, but they are reluctant. The Boy's wish quoted here shows that the spur of fame is not a sufficient stimulant to valour to overcome other attractions in all men.

21 As young as I am, I have observed these three swashers. I am boy to them all three, but all they three, though they would serve me, could not be man to me; for indeed three such antics do not amount to a man. For Bardolph, he is white-livered and red-faced; by the means whereof 'a faces it out, but fights not. For Pistol, he hath a killing tongue, and a quiet sword; by the means whereof 'a breaks words and keeps whole weapons. For Nym, he hath heard that men of few words are the best men; and therefore he scorns to say his prayers, lest 'a should be thought a coward; but his few bad words are matched with as few good deeds, for 'a never broke any man's head but his own, and that was against a post, when he was drunk.
(III.2.28–41)
The Boy is commenting upon the conduct in war of his three masters, Bardolph, Pistol, and Nym. He terms them 'swashers' or swaggerers, which indicates that they all owe a debt to the *miles gloriosus*, or swaggering soldier, of Plautine comedy, which became a Renaissance comic stereotype. Despite their pretensions, all three are cowardly: Bardolph is 'white-livered'; Pistol has a 'quiet sword'; and Nym, while he studiously avoids prayers for his own deliverance, has 'few good deeds'. The speech has all the marks of a set comic speech, deriving in particular from the Theophrastian tradition of character drawing.

22 Where have they this mettle?
Is not their climate foggy, raw, and dull,
On whom, as in despite, the sun looks pale,
Killing their fruit with frowns? Can sodden water,
A drench for sur-reined jades, their barley broth,
Decoct their cold blood to such valiant heat?
And shall our quick blood, spirited with wine,
Seem frosty?
(III.5.15–22)
The Constable of France is in conference with the King of France, the Dauphin, and the Duke of Brittany, concerning the passage of the English army through northern France. The insults ascribed to the English in this scene contrast with the terms of approval applied by Henry V in III.1. Here the Duke of Brittany has just referred to the English as 'bastard Normans, Norman bastards' and the Constable is expressing Gallic incomprehension at the mettle of the English troops, which he finds it difficult to relate to the English climate and English cuisine. 'Sodden' means

boiled; 'a drench for sur-reined jades' is a medicinal draught for over-ridden horses; and 'barley broth' is a pejorative term for beer.

23 We are in God's hand, brother, not in theirs.
(III.6.167)
Henry, with his small army, is en route for the safety of Calais to winter his troops there, when he is confronted by the French Herald, Mountjoy, who in effect demands surrender in the name of his king, which Henry rejects. The Duke of Gloucester, Henry's brother, hopes that the French army will not attack when their forces are so exhausted and depleted, so prompting Henry's statement of faith given above. Henry also rejects the possibility of his own ransom.

24 Give them great meals of beef, and iron and steel; they will eat like wolves, and fight like devils.
(III.7.145–7)
The Constable of France is speaking of the English to the Dauphin and the nobility of France on the eve of the battle of Agincourt. The association of the English with beef is of long standing.

25 Now entertain conjecture of a time
When creeping murmur and the poring dark
Fills the wide vessel of the universe.
From camp to camp, through the foul womb of night,
The hum of either army stilly sounds,
That the fixed sentinels almost receive
The secret whispers of each other's watch.
Fire answers fire, and through their paly flames
Each battle sees the other's umbered face.
Steed threatens steed, in high and boastful neighs,
Piercing the night's dull ear; and from the tents
The armourers, accomplishing the knights,
With busy hammers closing rivets up,
Give dreadful note of preparation.
(Chorus IV, 1–4)
The chorus to Act IV evokes the tense mood of expectation and the intense activity of preparation during the night before the battle of Agincourt. Shakespeare's evocative description appeals to the auditor's senses and imagination in just the way that Chorus has repeatedly appealed for the spectator's imaginative involvement in the play.

26 For forth he goes and visits all his host,
Bids them good morrow with a modest smile,
And calls them brothers, friends, and countrymen.
Upon his royal face there is no note
How dread an army hath enrounded him,
Nor doth he dedicate one jot of colour
Unto the weary and all-watchèd night,
But freshly looks, and overbears attaint
With cheerful semblance and sweet majesty;
That every wretch, pining and pale before,
Beholding him, plucks comfort from his looks.
A largess universal, like the sun,
His liberal eye doth give to every one,
Thawing cold fear, that mean and gentle all
Behold, as may unworthiness define,
A little touch of Harry in the night.
(Chorus IV, 32–47)

This well-known description of Henry visiting his small host on the eve of the battle of Agincourt has no precedent in either of Shakespeare's major historical sources, Hall's *The Union of the Two Noble Families of Lancaster and York* (1548) or Holinshed's *Chronicles* (1587). It presents a picture of ideal kingship which unites humility and courage. The description is enacted in the scene that follows.

27 Yet sit and see,
Minding true things by what their mockeries be.
(Chorus IV, 52–3)

The concluding lines of the fourth chorus confess the discrepancy between the grandeur of Shakespeare's theme, the victory of Agincourt, and the limitations of his theatrical resources, 'four or five most vile and ragged foils' (line 50). Unlike the film version, the play itself does not actually depict the battle of Agincourt, except for an ironic scene between Pistol and a French soldier.

28 Discuss unto me, art thou officer,
Or art thou base, common, and popular?
(IV.1.37–8)

Pistol is unwittingly challenging his king and commander-in-chief. 'Popular' means literally of the people. King Henry, having acknowledged the great danger of their situation to his brother, the Duke of Gloucester, and to Sir Thomas Erpingham, spends the eve of the battle in disguise, encountering his common soldiers and explaining to them the role of the king. He brings to them that 'little touch of Harry in the night' referred to in the fourth chorus.

29 The King's a bawcock, and a heart of gold,
A lad of life, an imp of fame;
Of parents good, of fist most valiant.
I kiss his dirty shoe, and from heartstring
I love the lovely bully.
(IV.1.44–8)
Pistol's enthusiastic eulogy of the King is comic not only because it is addressed unwittingly to that person, but because of its unmajestic diction. 'Bawcock' and 'bully' indicate a good lad. It is the combined expression of Henry's ideal kingship and Pistol's fervent loyalty in down-to-earth terms which produces the distinctive quality of the speech.

30 I think the King is but a man, as I am: the violet smells to him as it doth to me; the element shows to him as it doth to me; all his senses have but human conditions. His ceremonies laid by, in his nakedness he appears but a man; and though his affections are higher mounted than ours, yet when they stoop, they stoop with the like wing. Therefore, when he sees reason of fears, as we do, his fears, out of doubt, be of the same relish as ours are.
(IV.1.99–107)
Henry V, in disguise, is speaking to three English soldiers serving Sir Thomas Erpingham, in particular to John Bates, just before the dawn of Agincourt. The human attributes of kingship are a recurrent theme in Shakespeare's history plays. In his disguise, Henry is projecting himself as the ordinary man that he claims the King basically to be, despite the King having greater responsibilities and dealing with weightier matters and more powerful emotions. The imagery of 'affections' (emotions) mounting and stooping is taken from falconry.

31 Methinks I could not die anywhere so contented as in the King's company, his cause being just and his quarrel honourable.
(IV.1.122–4)
The patriotic sentiment is somewhat undercut by the speaker being the King himself, albeit in disguise. The three addressees are the English soldiers: Bates, Court, and Williams. Williams' response is quoted below (32), and the opposed views constitute a debate on the responsibilities of kingship, especially in time of war. The conversation takes place just before the dawn of Agincourt.

32 I am afeard there are few die well that die in a battle, for how

can they charitably dispose of anything when blood is their argument?
(IV.1.137–9)
Williams, an English soldier of Sir Thomas Erpingham's company, is countering the notion that death in battle in a just cause is a virtuous one. He questions how one could die in a state of Christian charity when bloodshed is the cause. His argument is prefaced by an infernal vision of the butchery and social deprivation caused by warfare. Williams is addressing the disguised king on the eve of Agincourt.

33 Every subject's duty is the King's, but every subject's soul is his own.
(IV.1.171–2)
King Henry V, in disguise, is contesting with three English soldiers, Williams in particular, the responsibilities of kingship in time of war. He is arguing that the 'King is not bound to answer the particular endings of his soldiers' (lines 151–2) and that therefore the king cannot take upon himself the spiritual responsibility of his subjects. While that may be true, the statement quoted above can also be interpreted to suggest that the subject has a higher authority than the king.

34 Upon the King! Let us our lives, our souls,
Our debts, our careful wives,
Our children, and our sins, lay on the King!
We must bear all. O hard condition.
(IV.1.223–6)
After his discussion with the common soldiers on the eve of the battle of Agincourt, Henry V is left alone to soliloquize on the responsibilities of kingship. The burdens of kingship constitute a recurrent theme of the second tetralogy of history plays from *Richard II* to *Henry V*.

35 What infinite heart's ease
Must kings neglect that private men enjoy!
And what have kings that privates have not too,
Save ceremony, save general ceremony?
And what art thou, thou idol ceremony?
(IV.1.229–32)
The passage is a continuation of Henry's soliloquy on the cares of kingship delivered before the battle of Agincourt. This particular variation on the theme places the emphasis on 'ceremony', the external trappings of state, as very inadequate compensation for the moral responsibility.

36 'Tis not the balm, the sceptre, and the ball,
The sword, the mace, the crown imperial,
The intertissued robe of gold and pearl,
The farcèd title running fore the king.
The throne he sits on, nor the tide of pomp
That beats upon the high shore of this world –
No, not all these, thrice-gorgeous ceremony,
Not all these, laid in bed majestical,
Can sleep so soundly as the wretched slave,
Who, with a body filled, and vacant mind,
Gets him to rest, crammed with distressful bread;
Never sees horrid night, the child of hell,
But, like a lackey, from the rise to set,
Sweats in the eye of Phoebus, and all night
Sleeps in Elysium.
(IV.1.253–67)
This further development of Henry's soliloquy on the responsibilities of kingship before the battle of Agincourt expands the theme of 'ceremony' (see 35 above) into a contrast between the troubled condition of the king and the blissful repose of his humble subjects. The passage parallels the musings of Henry V's father on the same theme in *Henry IV Part 2*, III.1.4–14. the 'farcèd title running fore the king' means inflated titles by which the king is addressed. 'Distressful bread' is that earned by toil. In classical mythology, Phoebus is the sun-god and Elysium the blissful resting place of the virtuous after death.

37 O God of battles, steel my soldiers' hearts;
Possess them not with fear; take from them now
The sense of reckoning, if th'opposèd numbers
Pluck their hearts from them. Not today, O Lord,
O not today, think not upon the fault
My father made in compassing the crown!
(IV.1.282–7)
This is Henry's prayer before Agincourt. He has just been recalled to conference with his nobles by Sir Thomas Erpingham, after his disguised encounter with the common soldiers and his soliloquy on the cares of kingship. The prayer first poses the physical threat, that the French forces greatly outnumber the English. It then raises a moral and spiritual threat, and a tension underlying the play, that the sins of the father (Henry IV's deposition of Richard II) may be visited upon the son.

38 O that we now had here
But one ten thousand of those men in England

That do no work today!
(IV.3.16–18)

This wish made by the Earl of Westmorland to the King before the battle of Agincourt, on the basis of the French force's numerical superiority, is denied by Henry V.

39 If we are marked to die, we are enow
To do our country loss: and if to live,
The fewer men, the greater share of honour.
(IV.3.20–2)

This is Henry V's denial of the Earl of Westmorland's wish for more troops to fight the battle of Agincourt. The great victory of Agincourt against all the odds is the culmination of Henry V's pursuit of honour which begins in the *Henry IV* plays.

40 But if it be a sin to covet honour,
I am the most offending soul alive.
(IV.3.28–9)

Henry V is confessing his pursuit of honour to the point of sin to Westmorland immediately before the battle of Agincourt, where he is to win a great victory. He is depicted as the flower of chivalry.

41 O, do not wish one more!
Rather proclaim it, Westmorland, through my host,
That he which hath no stomach to this fight,
Let him depart: his passport shall be made,
And crowns for convoy put into his purse.
We would not die in that man's company
That fears his fellowship to die with us.
(IV.3.33–9)

Henry V offers a second and more emphatic denial of Westmorland's wish for more troops to fight the battle of Agincourt. The denial illustrates Henry V's courage, magnanimity, and his demand for loyalty and commitment from his troops.

42 This day is called the Feast of Crispian:
He that outlives this day, and comes safe home,
Will stand a-tiptoe when this day is named,
And rouse him at the name of Crispian.
He that shall see this day, and live old age,
Will yearly on the vigil feast his neighbours,
And say, 'Tomorrow is Saint Crispian.'
Then will he strip his sleeve, and show his scars,
And say, 'These wounds I had on Crispin's day.'
Old men forget; yet all shall be forgot,

But he'll remember, with advantages,
What feats he did that day.
(IV.3.40–51)

Henry V's rousing speech before the battle of Agincourt rightly (and for sound psychological reasons) anticipates a great victory that will be recalled by posterity. With hindsight, Shakespeare was able to depict Agincourt as one of the great English victories against overwhelming odds and his treatment of it reflects the national pride and confidence of the post-Armada period. The variation of Crispin and Crispian arises not from confusion but from October 25 being the feast-day of two brothers, Crispinus and Crispianus, the patron saints of shoe-makers. They were martyred in 287, victims of Diocletian's oppression. 'With advantages' means with understandable exaggeration.

43 Then shall our names,...
Be in their flowing cups freshly remembered.
This story shall the good man teach his son;
And Crispin Crispian shall ne'er go by,
From this day to the ending of the world,
But we in it shall be rememberèd –
We few, we happy few, we band of brothers:
For he today that sheds his blood with me
Shall be my brother; be he ne'er so vile,
This day shall gentle his condition;
And gentlemen in England now abed
Shall think themselves accursed they were not here,
And hold their manhoods cheap, whiles any speaks
That fought with us upon Saint Crispin's day.
(IV.3.51, 55–67)

The rousing speech of Henry V before the battle of Agincourt, which anticipates a great victory, culminates in a vision of future celebrations of that triumph, taking the form of a secular act of communion in which national unity is commemorated. For an explanation of the forms 'Crispin' and 'Crispian', see 42 above.

44 There is a river in Macedon, and there is also moreover a river at Monmouth – it is called Wye at Monmouth, but it is out of my prains what is the name of the other river; but 'tis all one, 'tis alike as my fingers is to my fingers, and there is salmons in both.
(IV.7.25–9)

Fluellen, a Welsh captain and very much the stage Welshman, is comparing Henry V's (or Harry Monmouth's) victory at Agincourt to those of Alexander the Great (or 'Alexander the Pig' as his pronunciation terms him). The comparison is being pursued, somewhat improbably, through the similarities between their native lands, Monmouth and Macedon.

45 O God, Thy arm was here!
And not to us, but to Thy arm alone,
Ascribe we all!
(IV.8.105–7)
Henry V has just been informed of the losses on both sides at Agincourt. Whereas the French are said to have lost ten thousand men, including many of the leading nobility of France, the English are said to have lost only four gentlemen and a further twenty-five common soldiers. In these figures, Shakespeare is following Holinshed's *Chronicles* very closely. Modern estimates differ, though the scale of the victory is not disputed.

46 But now behold,
In the quick forge and working-house of thought,
How London doth pour out her citizens.
(Chorus V, 22–4)
The chorus to Act V narrates the return of Henry V to Calais, thence to London, and back again to France. It continues to locate the mind of the auditor as the place where the drama is realized. Since thought was associated with the elements of air and fire, 'forge' is an apt metaphor.

47 There is occasions and causes why and wherefore in all things.
(V.1.3–4)
The Welsh Captain, Fluellen, is about to explain to Gower why he is wearing a leek, even though St David's day has passed. He is planning a revenge on Pistol for mocking the leek by forcing him to eat it.

48 By this leek, I will most horribly revenge – I eat and eat, I swear –
(V.1.44)
Pistol is being forced to eat Fluellen's leek as punishment for the contempt he has shown for all things Welsh. Pistol, true to his histrionic nature, expresses his fury in a parody of the cries for revenge found in the popular revenge drama of the period.

49 Let it not disgrace me
If I demand, before this royal view,
What rub or what impediment there is
Why that the naked, poor, and mangled peace,

Dear nurse of arts, plenties, and joyful births,
Should not in this best garden of the world,
Our fertile France, put up her lovely visage?
(V.2.31–7)

The Duke of Burgundy is acting as the peacemaker between Henry V and the King of France. The peace is to be cemented in an alliance of the two royal houses through the marriage of Henry to the French King's daughter, Katherine. The actual events of the scene took place in 1420, not immediately after the battle of Agincourt in 1415. Shakespeare has telescoped time for dramatic effect.

50 But, before God, Kate, I cannot look greenly, nor gasp out my eloquence, nor I have no cunning in protestation; only downright oaths, which I never use till urged, nor never break for urging. If thou canst love a fellow of this temper, Kate, whose face is not worth sunburning, that never looks in his glass for love of anything he sees there, let thine eye be thy cook. I speak to thee plain soldier. If thou canst love me for this, take me; if not, to say to thee that I shall die is true – but for thy love, by the Lord, no – yet I love thee too. And while thou liv'st, dear Kate, take a fellow of plain and uncoined constancy; for he perforce must do thee right, because he hath not the gift to woo in other places. For these fellows of infinite tongue, that can rhyme themselves into ladies' favours, they do always reason themselves out again.
(V.2.142–57)

Henry V's courtship of Princess Katherine of France is a soldier's wooing. He makes his appeal in terms of plainness, sincerity, and constancy, claiming that he is no practitioner of either bashfulness or courtly rhetoric. The pre-Shakespearian Henry V play, the *Famous Victories of Henry V*, entered on the Stationers' Register in 1594 and surviving in a corrupt text of 1598, also contains a wooing scene between Henry and Katherine in similar, though not as skilful, terms.

51 A good leg will fall; a straight back will stoop; a black beard will turn white; a curled pate will grow bald; a fair face will wither; a full eye will wax hollow: but a good heart, Kate, is the sun and the moon – or rather, the sun, and not the moon; for it shines bright and never changes, but keeps his course truly.
(V.2.158–63)

Henry V is courting in his plain, soldierly manner Katherine, Princess of France. His appeal is made in terms of inner virtue not external attractions. Their marriage is to seal the peace between England and France.

52 Shall not thou and I, between Saint Denis and Saint George, compound a boy, half French, half English, that shall go to Constantinople and take the Turk by the beard?
(V.2.204–7)
Henry V's desire to unite the crowns of England and France is expressed in terms somewhat boisterous for the conventions of courtly love. Their offspring, assumed to be male, is envisaged as a leader of Christendom, who will relieve Europe of the Turkish menace. The idea is an anachronism on Shakespeare's part, since the Turkish threat to western Europe was a sixteenth-century phenomenon, Constantinople not falling to the Turks until 1453, while these events date from 1420.

53 O Kate, nice customs curtsy to great kings. Dear Kate, you and I cannot be confined within the weak list of a country's fashion. We are the makers of manners, Kate, and the liberty that follows our places stops the mouth of all find-faults.
(V.2.265–9)
Katherine, Princess of France, has refused Henry V a kiss on the grounds that French maids do not kiss before marriage, although she has agreed to marry him, should her father consent. Henry makes her his queen and an Englishwoman by kissing her in contempt of over-fastidious etiquette. He argues that kings are the makers not the followers of fashion.

54 God, the best maker of all marriages,
Combine your heart in one, your realms in one!
(V.2.351–2)
The prayer is that of Queen Isabel of France regarding the marriage of her daughter, Katherine, to Henry V of England. Katherine is viewed somewhat ambivalently by Henry V and, through him, by the audience, as both prospective wife and an embodiment of the realm of France, the twin objects of his desire. While he is a charmingly blunt wooer, he remains a hard negotiator. The alliance with Katherine was, in fact, the first clause of the historical treaty of Troyes. As the final chorus indicates, the joyous prospect was short-lived, for Henry V's early death led to the troubled minority and reign of Henry VI, which Shakespeare had already treated dramatically in his first tetralogy of history plays.

Henry VI Part 1

1 Hung be the heavens with black, yield day to night!
Comets, importing change of times and states,
Brandish your crystal tresses in the sky,
And with them scourge the bad revolting stars
That have consented unto Henry's death.
(I.1.1–5)

The play's opening lines, spoken by the Duke of Bedford at the funeral of King Henry V, establish a sense of gloomy foreboding about the future of the country. Since the stage was hung with black drapes for tragedy, the heavens hung with black are probably not only the skies but also the ceiling of the roof, painted with stars, that projected over the stage from the tiring house. Comets were traditionally associated with the death of rulers, disruption, and disorder in the state. Here the comets' tails ('crystal tresses') become whips to punish malign fate ('the bad revolting stars') for allowing Henry's death.

2 At pleasure here we lie, near Orleans;
Otherwhiles the famished English, like pale ghosts,
Faintly besiege us one hour in a month.
(I.2.6–8)

English forces are besieging the French at Orleans but, as Charles the Dauphin's account suggests, the siege was as difficult for the besiegers as it was for the besieged.

3 Expect Saint Martin's summer, halcyon days.
(I.2.131)

Joan la Pucelle (Joan of Arc) is convincing the French of her prowess by prophesying that she will raise the siege of Orleans. Here she promises an Indian Summer, since St Martin's feast day is 11 November and halcyon days were supposed to occur in December. St Martin, a former Roman soldier, became Bishop of Tours, which makes him doubly appropriate for Joan to mention. Halcyon days are a time of calm around the winter solstice, so called because the kingfisher ('halcyon') was believed to nest at sea then and smooth the waves during the incubation period.

4 See the coast cleared, and then we will depart.
Good God, these nobles should such stomachs bear!
I myself fight not once in forty year.
(I.3.89–91)

The Mayor of London has just broken up a street riot between the Duke of Gloucester and the Bishop of Winchester and their supporters. Although he is only a minor character, his few utterances, fleshing out Shakespeare's picture of the effects of civil strife on the whole of society, are part of a pattern of antagonistic chorus comments on the nobles' factions. 'See the coast cleared' is proverbial. The stomach was supposed to be where anger originated.

5 Yet livest thou, Salisbury? Though thy speech doth fail,
One eye thou hast to look to heaven for grace;
The sun with one eye vieweth all the world.
(I.4.82–4)
The Earl of Salisbury has been hit by French artillery fire which blew off one side of his face. Talbot, the English general, attempts to rally him with this grimly ironic encouragement to look on the bright side.

6 My thoughts are whirlèd like a potter's wheel;
I know not where I am nor what I do.
(I.5.19–20)
In battle outside Orleans, Talbot has been worsted by Joan. These lines express his bafflement that an experienced soldier like himself can be defeated by a woman.

7 A maid? and be so martial?
(II.1.21)
The English generals are discussing the reason for their difficulties with the French. Bedford's comment expresses the English belief that there is something indecent and unsporting about Joan's intervention in the wars.

8 And I have heard it said unbidden guests
Are often welcomest when they are gone.
(II.2.55–6)
Talbot, invited to visit the Countess of Auvergne, has asked his companions to join him but Bedford, anticipating the possibility of an amorous encounter between Talbot and the Countess, declines the invitation with these proverbial sentiments.

9 Between two hawks, which flies the higher pitch;
Between two dogs, which hath the deeper mouth;
Between two blades, which bears the better temper;
Between two horses, which doth bear him best;
Between two girls, which hath the merriest eye,
I have perhaps some shallow spirit of judgement;
But in these nice sharp quillets of the law,

Good faith, I am no wiser than a daw.
(II.4.11–18)
The Earl of Warwick's highly rhetorical refusal to judge between Richard Plantagenet (later Duke of York) and the Duke of Somerset is part of Shakespeare's dramatization of the origins of the Wars of the Roses which constitute the greater part of the Henry VI plays. In falconry a pitch is the highest point of the bird's flight; mouth is used here to mean voice, so that 'deeper mouth' means louder bark; 'quillets' are subtleties or quibbles; the jackdaw (daw) is proverbially stupid.

10 RICHARD
Since you are tongue-tied and so loath to speak,
In dumb significants proclaim your thoughts.
Let him that is a true-born gentleman
And stands upon the honour of his birth,
If he suppose that I have pleaded truth,
From off this briar pluck a white rose with me.
SOMERSET
Let him that is no coward nor no flatterer,
But dare maintain the party of the truth,
Pluck a red rose from off this thorn with me.
(II.4.25–33)
Although there appears to be no historical basis for this scene, Shakespeare's presentation of the choosing of the roses as emblems ('dumb significants') for the two warring factions has captured the popular imagination.

11 Defer no time; delays have dangerous ends.
(III.2.33)
Reignier, Duke of Anjou, nominal King of Naples and father of Margaret of Anjou who later marries Henry VI, speaks this proverbial line to encourage his French allies as they begin their (unhistorical) attack on Rouen.

12 I owe him little duty, and less love.
(IV.4.34)
Somerset's animosity to York appears in this line which is part of his justification for not sending him reinforcements which might have helped to save Talbot.

13 'Had Death been French, then Death had died today.'
(IV.7.28)
Talbot, eulogizing his son who has been killed in battle with the French, imagines him speaking this line.

14 Here's a silly stately style indeed!
The Turk, that two and fifty kingdoms hath,
Writes not so tedious a style as this.
Him that thou magnifiest with all these titles
Stinking and flyblown lies here at our feet.
(IV.7.72–6)
After a battle, Sir William Lucy has arrived at the French camp to discover who has been killed or taken prisoner. Joan's response is dictated by Lucy's question as to Talbot's whereabouts which takes the form of a a twelve-line rehearsal of his many titles. The Turk is the Emperor of Turkey.

15 So doth the swan her downy cygnets save,
Keeping them prisoner underneath her wings.
(V.3.56–7)
The Earl of Suffolk has captured Margaret of Anjou during a battle and been captivated by her, as these lines suggest. She becomes his mistress, marries Henry VI, and figures large in the other Henry VI plays and in *Richard III.*

16 She's beautiful, and therefore to be wooed;
She is a woman, therefore to be won.
(V.3.78–9)
Suffolk's opinion of the nature of women is not subtle. 'She' is Margaret of Anjou.

17 I am a soldier and unapt to weep
Or to exclaim on fortune's fickleness.
(V.3.133–4)
Reignier responds stoically to the news of Suffolk's capture of his daughter.

Henry VI Part 2

1 Pride went before; Ambition follows him.
While these do labour for their own preferment,
Behoves it us to labour for the realm.
(I.1.178–80)
The Earl of Salisbury applies the proverb 'Pride goes before and ambition comes after' to Cardinal Beaufort (Pride) and the Dukes of Somerset and Buckingham (Ambition), who are arguing about who should be regent for Henry VI.

2 And force perforce I'll make him yield the crown,
Whose bookish rule hath pulled fair England down.
(I.1.256–7)
The Duke of York ends his soliloquy on his plans to raise a rebellion with this soldier's criticism of Henry's scholarly ('bookish') ineffectuality as king.

3 Put forth thy hand, reach at the glorious gold.
(I.2.11)
The ambitious Duchess of Gloucester is encouraging her husband to aim at the crown ('the glorious gold') and usurp Henry, to whom he is Protector.

4 Is this the fashions in the court of England?
Is this the government of Britain's isle,
And this the royalty of Albion's king?
(I.3.41–3)
Queen Margaret complains to her lover the Duke of Suffolk, who arranged her marriage to the King, about the King's lack of status within the government.

5 She bears a duke's revenues on her back,
And in her heart she scorns our poverty.
(I.3.78–9)
Queen Margaret's main complaint is against the ambitious Duchess of Gloucester, whose dress and wealth outshine the King and Queen's.

6 Could I come near your beauty with my nails,
I could set my ten commandments on your face.
(I.3.139–40)
Queen Margaret has just provoked the Duchess of Gloucester by dropping her fan and hitting her for not picking it up, claiming that she mistook her for a lady-in-waiting. The Duchess's response is to want to scratch her face. The idea of the fingernails as the ten commandments is proverbial and apparently derives from the belief that God used his nails to scratch them on the tablets.

7 What stronger breastplate than a heart untainted!
Thrice is he armed that hath his quarrel just;
And he but naked, though locked up in steel,
Whose conscience with injustice is corrupted.
(III.2.232–5)
Henry's pious comments come immediately after the Duke of Suffolk and the Earl of Warwick have gone off to fight, and

immediately before they return with drawn swords. The context, thus, severely undercuts the content of the speech.

8 A wilderness is populous enough,
So Suffolk had thy heavenly company;
For where thou art, there is the world, itself,
With every several pleasure in the world;
And where thou art not, desolation.
I can no more. Live thou to joy thy life;
Myself no joy in naught but that thou livest.
(III.2.360–6)

The Duke of Suffolk has been banished and here he laments his state to his mistress, Queen Margaret.

9 Forbear to judge, for we are sinners all.
Close up his eyes, and draw the curtain close;
And let us all to meditation.
(III.3.31–3)

Cardinal Beaufort has just died, heavily implicated in the death of the Duke of Gloucester and apparently unrepentant. Henry typically refuses to judge, taking his cue from biblical injunctions. He is talking about drawing the curtains of a bed, as is clear from the opening stage direction for this scene in the 1594 Quarto: 'the Cardinal is discovered in his bed, raving and staring as if he were mad'.

10 The gaudy, blabbing, and remorseful day
Is crept into the bosom of the sea.
(IV.1.1–2)

The Lieutenant from the ship which has captured the banished Duke of Suffolk begins the scene in which Suffolk is murdered with a highly rhetorical piece of descriptive verse. The reasons for him describing the day as 'blabbing' and 'remorseful' are obscure.

11 True nobility is exempt from fear;
More can I bear than you dare execute.
(IV.1.131–2)

The Duke of Suffolk stakes his claim to true nobility in the face of the sailors' threats to kill him, but they do kill him.

12 Well, I say it was never merry world in England since gentlemen came up.
(IV.2.7–9)

John Holland, one of the supporters of the rebel Jack Cade, puts a traditional case against class divisions. The name may be that of the original player of the part.

13 There shall be in England seven halfpenny loaves sold for a penny; the three-hooped pot shall have ten hoops; and I will make it felony to drink small beer. All the realm shall be in common, and in Cheapside shall my palfrey go to grass ... There shall be no money; all shall eat and drink on my score; and I will apparel them all in one livery, that they may agree like brothers, and worship me their lord.
(IV.2.61–5, 68–71)
Jack Cade's reforms touch on many of the popular complaints against the inequitable nature of the economic system, such as the high cost of staple foods and the enclosure of common land. The 'three-hooped pot' held two pints, so Cade is proposing a massive increase. With no money and no trade Cheapside would revert to grazing land. 'On my score' means at my expense. 'Livery' was the uniform worn by members of a household; Cade is suggesting that everyone will be one big household with him as its head.

14 DICK The first thing we do, let's kill all the lawyers.
CADE Nay, that I mean to do. Is not this a lamentable thing, that the skin of an innocent lamb should be made parchment? That parchment, being scribbled o'er, should undo a man? Some say the bee stings, but I say 'tis the bee's wax, for I did but seal once to a thing, and I was never mine own man since.
(IV.2.72–8)
Dick the butcher, another of Cade's supporters, adds his proposal for reform which Cade takes up with a rhetorical flourish. Beeswax was used for sealing legal documents.

15 And Adam was a gardener.
(IV.2.126)
Cade is in the process of attempting to explain his claims to the crown to Sir Humphrey Stafford, who has come to put down the rebellion. The claim that since all humanity was descended from Adam and Eve all class distinctions are false was of considerable importance in various rebellions, as reflected in John Ball's famous couplet from the Peasants' Revolt of 1381: 'When Adam delved and Eve span, / Who was then the gentleman?'

16 He can speak French; and therefore he is a traitor.
(IV.2.157–8)

Cade's reason for killing Lord Say is based on the familiar anti-French prejudice as well as the claim that he sold English territory in France to the French.

17 Thou hast most traitorously corrupted the youth of the realm in erecting a grammar school; and whereas, before, our forefathers had no other books but the score and the tally, thou hast caused printing to be used; and, contrary to the King his crown and dignity, thou hast built a paper-mill. It will be proved to thy face that thou hast men about thee that usually talk of a noun and a verb, and such abominable words as no Christian ear can endure to hear. Thou hast appointed justices of the peace, to call poor men before them about matters they were not able to answer. Moreover, thou hast put them in prison; and because they could not read, thou hast hanged them; when, indeed, only for that cause they have been most worthy to live.
(IV.7.29–42)
Cade's accusations against Lord Say are populist and radically reactionary. The references to printing and to a paper-mill are anachronistic, since Caxton did not begin operating until over twenty years after Cade's death and the first known English paper-mill operated in the 1490s. Criminals who could read could escape hanging by claiming 'benefit of clergy', whereas the uneducated could not.

18 Away with him! Away with him! He speaks Latin.
(IV.7.53)
Cade's response to Lord Say's remark that Kent is '*bona terra, mala gens*' is a fair indication of the atmosphere of his kangaroo court.

19 Was ever feather so lightly blown to and fro as this multitude? The name of Henry the Fifth hales them to an hundred mischiefs and makes them leave me desolate.
(IV.8.54–7)
Lord Clifford has rallied the rebels to the King's side by stressing his descent from Henry V. In this aside Cade realizes that the rebellion is effectively over.

Henry VI Part 3

1 And, father, do but think
How sweet a thing it is to wear a crown;

Within whose circuit is Elysium.
(I.2.28–30)

Richard, later Duke of Gloucester and ultimately Richard III, is attempting to persuade his father the Duke of York to seize the crown from Henry VI. These lines are an echo of Marlowe's Tamburlaine. 'Circuit' means circumference; in Greek and Roman mythology Elysium is where the souls of the virtuous dead live, so it is often used to mean heaven.

2 O tiger's heart wrapped in a woman's hide!
(I.4.137)

Queen Margaret, leading the King's forces, has been goading the captured Duke of York. This line, part of his response to her attacks, was parodied by the writer Robert Greene (?1560–1592) in an attack on Shakespeare as 'an upstart crow, beautified with our feathers, that with his *Tiger's heart wrapped in a player's hide* supposes he is as well able to bombast out a blank verse as the best of you; and, being an absolute *Johannes fac totum* [Jack of all trades], is in his own conceit the only Shake-scene in a country'. Greene's comment, published in 1592, is the earliest known reference to Shakespeare as a dramatist.

3 This battle fares like to the morning's war,
When dying clouds contend with growing light,
What time the shepherd, blowing of his nails,
Can neither call it perfect day nor night.
(II.5.1–4)

Henry, not allowed by Margaret to join in the battle, watches the contending armies as their fortunes ebb and flow as they do throughout the play.

4 O God! Methinks it were a happy life
To be no better than a homely swain;
To sit upon a hill, as I do now;
To carve out dials quaintly, point by point,
Thereby to see the minutes how they run:
How many makes the hour full complete,
How many hours brings about the day,
How many days will finish up the year,
How many years a mortal man may live.
When this is known, then to divide the times:
So many hours must I tend my flock,
So many hours must I take my rest,
So many hours must I contemplate,
So many hours must I sport myself,...

Ah, what a life were this! How sweet! How lovely!
Gives not the hawthorn bush a sweeter shade
To shepherds looking on their silly sheep
Than doth a rich embroidered canopy
To kings that fear their subjects' treachery?
O yes, it doth; a thousand-fold it doth.
(II.5.21–34, 41–6)

Henry muses on his position, imagining how much better it would be to be an ordinary shepherd ('homely swain'), making sundials skilfully ('quaintly') and working out how to divide his time, rather than being a king.

5 I'll make my heaven to dream upon the crown,
And, whiles I live, t'account this world but hell,
Until my misshaped trunk that bears this head
Be round impalèd with a glorious crown.
(III.2.168–71)

Richard, now Duke of Gloucester, is confiding his hopes to the audience. Shakespeare's Richard is, notoriously, a hunchback ('misshapen trunk'), although his physical deformity owes more to Tudor propaganda, which postulated that the monstrosity of civil war would produce its own monster to be killed by the Duke of Richmond, founder of the Tudor dynasty as Henry VII, than it does to historical fact. 'Impalèd' means encircled.

6 Why, I can smile, and murder whiles I smile,
And cry 'Content!' to that which grieves my heart,
And wet my cheeks with artificial tears,
And frame my face to all occasions.
I'll drown more sailors than the mermaid shall;
I'll slay more gazers than the basilisk;
I'll play the orator as well as Nestor,
Deceive more slily than Ulysses could,
And, like a Sinon, take another Troy.
I can add colours to the chameleon,
Change shapes with Proteus for advantages,
And set the murderous Machiavel to school.
Can I do this, and cannot get a crown?
Tut, were it farther off, I'll pluck it down.
(III.2.182–95)

Richard explains how well fitted he is to fulfil his self-imposed task of seizing the crown. He will always wear an appropriate expression ('frame my face to all occasions'); be a siren ('mermaid') luring sailors on to the rocks; kill with a glance like the mythical basilisk; talk as well as Nestor and be as cunning as Ulysses, two of the Greek leaders in the Trojan War; deceive in order to betray like Sinon who persuaded the Trojans to take the wooden horse inside the walls of Troy; be like the sea god Proteus who could change his shape at will; and, finally, be more murderous than Machiavelli, the Florentine political thinker, who was seen in the Elizabethan theatre as a stereotyped ruthless and unprincipled schemer and power-seeker.

7 Proud setter-up and puller-down of kings!
(III.3.157)
Margaret attacks the Earl of Warwick (Warwick the Kingmaker) for disrupting the natural order and usurping the function of God, echoing the words Edward IV addressed to God in II.3. which derive ultimately from the Bible, Daniel 2:21.

8 What fates impose, that men must needs abide;
It boots not to resist both wind and tide.
(IV.3.59–60)
With these stoical words Edward IV accepts his defeat by the forces led by the Earl of Warwick. 'It boots not' means it is no use.

9 If secret powers
Suggest but truth to my divining thoughts,
This pretty lad will prove our country's bliss.
His looks are full of peaceful majesty,
His head by nature framed to wear a crown,
His hand to wield a sceptre, and himself
Likely in time to bless a regal throne.
Make much of him, my lords, for this is he
Must help you more than you are hurt by me.
(IV.6.68–76)
Henry VI has just met the future Henry VII and in this speech his prophetic ('divining') thoughts anticipate the peace which Richmond will establish when he ends the Wars of the Roses and ascends the throne.

10 A little fire is quickly trodden out;
Which, being suffered, rivers cannot quench.
(IV.8.7–8)
The Duke of Clarence, brother of Edward IV and Richard Duke of Gloucester, has defected to Henry's side and is proposing swift action to put an end to Edward's latest campaign in its early stages.

11 Thus yields the cedar to the axe's edge,
Whose arms gave shelter to the princely eagle,

Under whose shade the ramping lion slept,
Whose top branch over-peered Jove's spreading tree
And kept low shrubs from winter's powerful wind.
(V.2.11–15)

The Earl of Warwick, mortally wounded, sees his fall in symbolic terms. In Elizabethan thought the cedar, eagle, lion, and oak were all at the top of the various categories to which they belonged. Warwick sees himself as having protected the Duke of York ('princely eagle') and Henry VI (there were ramping – rampant – lions on the royal coat of arms). 'Jove's spreading tree' is the oak.

12 Lo, now my glory smeared in dust and blood!
My parks, my walks, my manors that I had,
Even now forsake me, and of all my lands
Is nothing left me but my body's length.
Why, what is pomp, rule, reign, but earth and dust?
And, live we how we can, yet die we must.
(V.2.23–8)

The Earl of Warwick contemplates the vanity of human wishes in the face of his impending death from wounds. The thought is a literary commonplace which Shakespeare also develops in *Richard II* and *Henry IV Part 1*.

Henry VIII

1 I come no more to make you laugh. Things now
That bear a weighty and a serious brow,
Sad, high, and working, full of state and woe,
Such noble scenes as draw the eye to flow,
We now present.
(Prologue, 1–5)

The Prologue indicates the nature of what is to follow, stressing its seriousness and its ability to make the audience weep ('draw the eye to flow'). The first line probably means that the play in the repertory immediately before the production of *Henry VIII* was a comedy. 'Sad, high, and working, full of state and woe' means serious, elevated, and moving, full of dignity and woe.

There has been a debate about the play's authorship since the 1850s: many scholars believe that it is a collaboration between Shakespeare and his younger contemporary John Fletcher; others believe it is entirely Shakespeare's own work. Dual authorship does not, of course, mean intellectual incoherence but if the dual authorship hypothesis is accepted all the quotations given here for *Henry VIII*, except 2, 11, 15, 16, 34 and 35, are most probably by Fletcher.

2 Heat not a furnace for your foe so hot
That it do singe yourself.
(I.2.140–1)
The Duke of Norfolk advises the Duke of Buckingham not to pursue his antagonism against Cardinal Wolsey ('your foe') to the point of endangering himself. The reference is ultimately derived from the biblical fiery furnace in the Book of Daniel.

3 If I chance to talk a little wild, forgive me;
I had it from my father.
(I.4.26–7)
At an entertainment given by Cardinal Wolsey, Lord Sands, a nobleman, joins a group of ladies, including Anne Bullen (Boleyn), with this request.

4 Drum and trumpet. Chambers discharged.
(stage direction, I.4.49)
At this point in an early production of the play (29 June 1613) a fire was accidentally started which destroyed the Globe theatre. According to contemporary reports the wadding from one of the stage cannon ('chambers') lodged in the threatre's thatched roof and started a fire which destroyed the whole building. The only human casualty, according to Sir Henry Wotton's letter describing events, was 'one man [who] had his breeches set on fire, that would perhaps have broiled him, if he had not by the benefit of a provident wit put it out with bottle ale'.

5 Go with me like good angels to my end,
And as the long divorce of steel falls on me
Make of your prayers one sweet sacrifice,
And lift my soul to heaven.
(II.1.75–8)
At the instigation of Cardinal Wolsey, the Duke of Buckingham has been condemned to death for treason. In this speech he asks his friends to accompany him to his execution where his body and soul will be separated by the executioner's axe ('the long divorce of steel falls on me').

6 Where you are liberal of your loves and counsels
Be sure you be not loose; for those you make friends
And give your hearts to, when they once perceive
The least rub in your fortunes, fall away
Like water from ye, never found again

But where they mean to sink ye.
(II.1.126–31)
The Duke of Buckingham, who has been denounced by some of his household, advises his friends to be more careful than he was. 'Loose' means careless; 'rub', a term drawn from bowls, means obstruction.

7 LORD CHAMBERLAIN
It seems the marriage with his brother's wife
Has crept too near his conscience.
SUFFOLK (*aside*) No, his conscience
Has crept too near another lady.
(II.2.15–17)
The Lord Chamberlain and the Duke of Suffolk are discussing the King's unhappiness. He had married his deceased brother's wife, Katherine of Aragon, and now, many years later, is apparently worried by theological scruples about the legitimacy of such a marriage. Suffolk, more cynical than the Chamberlain, believes that the King's attraction to Anne Bullen (Boleyn) is the true cause of this sudden attack of conscience.

8 To restore the King,
He counsels a divorce, a loss of her
That like a jewel has hung twenty years
About his neck, yet never lost her lustre;
Of her that loves him with that excellence
That angels love good men with; even of her
That, when the greatest stroke of fortune falls,
Will bless the King.
(II.2.28–35)
The Duke of Norfolk expresses his objections to Cardinal Wolsey's plan to restore the King's happiness by divorcing Katherine, whom he describes in glowing terms.

9 Heaven will one day open
The King's eyes, that so long have slept upon
This bold bad man.
(II.2.40–2)
The Lord Chamberlain hopes that eventually the King will wake up to the evil deeds of Cardinal Wolsey.

10 I would not be a queen
For all the world.
(II.3.45–6)
Anne Bullen (Boleyn), in conversation with an Old Lady, protests her disinclination to be a queen. This speech will probably be

taken ironically by the majority of audiences, who will be aware of her subsequent fate.

11 Go thy ways, Kate.
That man i'th'world who shall report he has
A better wife, let him in naught be trusted
For speaking false in that.
(II.4.133–6)

King Henry has instituted judicial proceedings to pronounce on the validity of his marriage to Katherine (Kate). She has just made a dignified protest against the process and left the court. Henry comments on her virtue.

12 Orpheus with his lute made trees,
And the mountain tops that freeze,
Bow themselves when he did sing.
To his music plants and flowers
Ever sprung, as sun and showers
There had made a lasting spring.
Everything that heard him play,
Even the billows of the sea,
Hung their heads, and then lay by.
In sweet music is such art,
Killing care and grief of heart
Fall asleep, or hearing die.
(III.1.3–14)

One of Katherine's women sings this song to her in the scene following her departure from the trial. In classical mythology the musician Orpheus tamed wild beasts and made rocks and streams obey him through the quality of his music. 'Lay by' means subdued.

13 Heaven is above all yet; there sits a judge
That no king can corrupt.
(III.1.100–1)

Katherine protests to Cardinals Wolsey and Campeius, who are trying to argue her into agreeing to a divorce from Henry, that their motives are not pure.

14 Ye have angels' faces, but heaven knows your hearts.
(III.1.145)

Katherine contends that the outward appearance of the Cardinals hides an evil interior, alluding to the proverb 'Fair face, foul heart'.

15 I know her for
A spleeny Lutheran, and not wholesome to
Our cause, that she should lie i'th'bosom of
Our hard-ruled King.
(III.2.98–101)

Cardinal Wolsey has learnt that Henry is in love with Anne Bullen (Boleyn). She is dangerous to his plans because she is a staunch Protestant ('spleeny Lutheran') who will influence the King, who is already difficult to handle ('hard-ruled').

16 And then to breakfast with
What appetite you have.
(III.2.202–3)

Henry has learnt of Cardinal Wolsey's plots through some misdirected letters which he has just returned to Wolsey, expecting that they will make him lose his appetite.

17 I have touched the highest point of all my greatness,
And from that full meridian of my glory
I haste now to my setting. I shall fall
Like a bright exhalation in the evening,
And no man see me more.
(III.2.223–7)

Cardinal Wolsey realizes that Henry's discovery of his plots means the end of his career. He compares himself to the sun or a star which has reached its highest point ('full meridian') before setting and to a meteor ('exhalation').

18 In all you writ to Rome, or else
To foreign princes, '*Ego et Rex meus*'
Was still inscribed; in which you brought the King
To be your servant.
(III.2.313–16)

The Duke of Norfolk complains to Cardinal Wolsey that in his diplomatic correspondence, conducted in Latin, he put the word *ego*, meaning I, before the word *rex*, meaning king. Although this is a normal Latin word order, Shakespeare follows his chronicle sources in assuming that Wolsey was guilty of, literally, putting himself before the king.

19 Farewell, a long farewell, to all my greatness!
This is the state of man: today he puts forth
The tender leaves of hopes, tomorrow blossoms,
And bears his blushing honours thick upon him.
The third day comes a frost, a killing frost,
And when he thinks, good easy man, full surely

His greatness is a-ripening, nips his root,
And then he falls, as I do. I have ventured,
Like little wanton boys that swim on bladders,
This many summers in a sea of glory,
But far beyond my depth. My high-blown pride
At length broke under me, and now has left me
Weary, and old with service, to the mercy
Of a rude stream that must for ever hide me.
Vain pomp and glory of this world, I hate ye.
I feel my heart new opened. O, how wretched
Is that poor man that hangs on princes' favours!
There is betwixt that smile we would aspire to,
That sweet aspect of princes, and their ruin,
More pangs and fears than wars of women have;
And when he falls, he falls like Lucifer,
Never to hope again.
(III.2.351–72)

The disgraced Cardinal Wolsey soliloquizes on his downfall. 'Wanton' means playful; 'rude' means rough; Lucifer is the devil, an angel who fell from heaven.

20 I know myself now, and I feel within me
A peace above all earthly dignities,
A still and quiet conscience.
(III.2.378–80)

Cardinal Wolsey finds his true nature in contemplation of his fortunes.

21 A load would sink a navy.
(III.2.383)

Cardinal Wolsey continues his contemplative response to his downfall, thanking the King for removing from his shoulders a burden heavy enough to sink a navy.

22 Cromwell, I charge thee, fling away ambition:
By that sin fell the angels. How can man then,
The image of his Maker, hope to win by it?
Love thyself last, cherish those hearts that hate thee;
Corruption wins not more than honesty.
Still in thy right hand carry gentle peace
To silence envious tongues. Be just, and fear not.
Let all the ends thou aim'st at be thy country's,
Thy God's, and truth's. Then if thou fall'st, O Cromwell,
Thou fall'st a blessèd martyr.
(III.2.440–9)

Cardinal Wolsey counsels his servant Thomas Cromwell, who was to follow him into high office, to avoid his mistakes. Cromwell did in fact die a 'martyr': having been Chancellor of the Exchequer, Lord Privy Seal, Lord Chamberlain, and ultimately created Earl of Essex, he was executed for high treason in 1540. 'Still' means always.

23 Had I but served my God with half the zeal
I served my King, He would not in mine age
Have left me naked to mine enemies.
(III.2.455–7)
In Holinshed's *Chronicles*, one of Shakespeare's sources, Cardinal Wolsey's words appear in the form 'If I had served God as diligently as I have done the King, He would not have given me over in my grey hairs'. In the play he speaks these lines to Thomas Cromwell, his servant, but historically they were his dying words, spoken to Sir William Kingston who is not a character in the play. Shakespeare often combines events and characters from history for dramatic effect.

24 Farewell,
The hopes of court! My hopes in heaven do dwell.
(III.2.458–9)
Cardinal Wolsey continues to take his leave of mortal affairs.

25 FIRST GENTLEMAN
God save you, sir! Where have you been broiling?
THIRD GENTLEMAN
Among the crowd i'th'Abbey, where a finger
Could not be wedged in more; I am stifled
With the mere rankness of their joy.
(IV.1.56–9)
The First Gentleman appears from time to time throughout the play in a choric role, usually discussing affairs of state from the viewpoint of the general public. The Third Gentleman has been at Westminster Abbey to see the coronation of Anne Bullen (Boleyn) which has just taken place; presumably he looks hot and sweaty, since 'broiling' means cooking. His speech confirms that he has been in an exuberant and smelly (both indicated by 'rankness') crowd packed very tight together.

26 She had all the royal makings of a queen.
(IV.1.87)
The Third Gentleman's comment about Anne Bullen (Boleyn) is actually about the ritual and ceremonial trappings of the corona-

tion ('royal makings'), but in isolation it appears to refer to her suitability to be a queen.

27 An old man, broken with the storms of state,
Is come to lay his weary bones among ye;
Give him a little earth for charity.
(IV.2.21–3)

Griffith, Katherine's servant, is telling her about Cardinal Wolsey's death. Here he quotes Wolsey's address to the abbot of the abbey where he went to die. The 'little earth' is for his grave.

28 GRIFFITH
He gave his honours to the world again,
His blessèd part to heaven, and slept in peace.
KATHERINE
So may he rest; his faults lie gently on him!
(IV.2.29–31)

Katherine comments on her servant Griffith's account of Cardinal Wolsey's death.

29 He was a man
Of an unbounded stomach, . . .

His promises were as he then was, mighty,
But his performance as he is now, nothing.
(IV.2.33–4, 41–2)

Katherine, who has little reason to like Cardinal Wolsey, sums up his character. 'Unbounded stomach' means unchecked arrogance.

30 Men's evil manners live in brass; their virtues
We write in water.
(IV.2.45–6)

Griffith, Katherine's servant, reminds her in proverbial terms that men's evil deeds tend to be remembered ('live in brass') whereas their good deeds are forgotten (written in water).

31 From his cradle
He was a scholar, and a ripe and good one,
Exceeding wise, fair-spoken, and persuading;
Lofty and sour to them that loved him not,

But, to those men that sought him, sweet as summer.
(IV.2.50–4)
Griffith, Katherine's servant, continues with his eulogy of Cardinal Wolsey.

32 After my death I wish no other herald,
No other speaker of my living actions,
To keep mine honour from corruption
But such an honest chronicler as Griffith.
(IV.2.69–72)
Katherine, impressed by her servant Griffith's fair account of Cardinal Wolsey, praises him for his honesty.

33 That comfort comes too late,
'Tis like a pardon after execution.
That gentle physic, given in time, had cured me,
But now I am past all comforts here but prayers.
(IV.2.120–4)
Lord Capuchius has brought Katherine greetings and wishes for her 'good comfort' from Henry. This is her reply. 'Here' means in this world.

34 Not ever
The justice and the truth o'th'question carries
The due o'th'verdict with it.
(V.1.129–31)
Henry, convinced of the probity of Archbishop Cranmer who has been the object of many complaints, reminds him that the righteousness of a cause ('question') does not always ('not ever') ensure the correct result ('The due o'th'verdict').

35 He has strangled
His language in his tears.
(V.1.156–7)
Henry comments on Archbishop Cranmer's response to his expression of trust in him – he has burst into tears and cannot speak.

36 Is this the honour they do one another?
'Tis well there's one above 'em yet. I had thought
They had parted so much honesty among 'em –
At least good manners – as not thus to suffer
A man of his place, and so near our favour,
To dance attendance on their lordships' pleasures,
And at the door too, like a post with packets.
(V.2.25–31)

The plotting against Archbishop Cranmer has reached the point where Cranmer is being kept waiting outside a meeting of the council. Henry is watching and commenting on events from a vantage point above the stage. The 'one above' is God, and also Henry because of his position above the conspirators. 'Parted so much honesty among 'em' means had enough decency between them; 'post with packets' means messenger with letters.

37 'Tis a cruelty
To load a falling man.
(V.3.76–7)
In the council meeting Thomas Cromwell objects to the council's treatment of Archbishop Cranmer. Neither the council nor Cromwell are aware that the King has already offered Cranmer his protection. 'Load' means oppress.

38 Is this Moorfields to muster in? Or have we some strange Indian with the great tool come to court, the women so besiege us? Bless me, what a fry of fornication is at door! On my Christian conscience, this one christening will beget a thousand: here will be father, godfather, and all together.
(V.4.33–8)
The Porter at the palace is trying to keep out a huge crowd which has gathered to try to see the christening of the future Queen Elizabeth, Anne Bullen's (Boleyn's) daughter by Henry. When the play was written, Moorfields, then on the outskirts of London, was a popular place with holiday crowds and American Indians were sometimes exhibited as curiosities. 'Tool' means penis; 'fry of fornication' means crowd of fornicators or swarming children of fornicators.

39 In her days every man shall eat in safety
Under his own vine what he plants, and sing
The merry songs of peace to all his neighbours.
God shall be truly known, and those about her
From her shall read the perfect ways of honour,
And by those claim their greatness, not by blood.
Nor shall this peace sleep with her; but as when
The bird of wonder dies, the maiden phoenix,
Her ashes new-create another heir
As great in admiration as herself.
(V.5.33–42)
Archbishop Cranmer prophesies that the future Queen Elizabeth's reign will be a time of peace and prosperity. The phoenix, a unique legendary bird rising from its own ashes, was often used as a symbol of the nature of monarchy: monarchs

were individually unique but linked to those who came before and after them. Her 'heir' was James I, who was king when the play was written. 'Read' means learn.

40 'Tis ten to one this play can never please
All that are here. Some come to take their ease,
And sleep an act or two; but those, we fear,
We've frighted with our trumpets; so, 'tis clear,
They'll say 'tis naught.
(Epilogue, 1–5)
The Epilogue begins the conventional appeal for applause by denigrating the quality of the play and almost apologizing for distressing the sleepers in the audience with the noise of the spectacular production.

Julius Caesar

1 And do you now put on your best attire?
And do you now cull out a holiday?
And do you now strew flowers in his way,
That comes in triumph over Pompey's blood?
(I.1.48–51)
Marullus, one of the Tribunes of the People, is berating the artisans of Rome for neglecting their trades in order to celebrate Caesar's triumph. 'Pompey's blood' refers to the elimination of Pompey's sons following the battle of Munda, as recounted by Plutarch in his *Life of Caesar* and available to Shakespeare in Sir Thomas North's translation, *the Lives of the Noble Grecians and Romanes*, of 1579. Gnaeus, the elder of Pompey's sons, was captured and executed in 45 BC; Sextus, the younger, was in reality put to death by Antony in 36 BC.

2 SOOTHSAYER Beware the ides of March.
CAESAR
He is a dreamer. Let us leave him.
(I.2.23–4)
The Soothsayer's warning to Caesar of the danger of the Ides of March (15th) is rejected. If we include the indirect report of the Soothsayer's words by Brutus, this is the third utterance of the warning within the space of six lines, which gives the phrase an ominous resonance and a ritualistic power within the drama. Caesar's attitude to superstition changes in the play with the approach of the Ides of March.

3 Brutus, I do observe you now of late:
I have not from your eyes that gentleness
And show of love as I was wont to have.
(I.2.32–4)

Cassius' rebuke is caused by Brutus' seeking to avoid his company. Brutus, in the lines that follow, attributes this to his introspection and inner vexations. Cassius thereby senses and seeks out Brutus' dissatisfaction with Caesar's rule.

4 What is it that you would impart to me?
If it be aught toward the general good,
Set honour in one eye, and death i'th'other,
And I will look on both indifferently;
For let the gods so speed me as I love
The name of honour more than I fear death.
(I.2.84–9)

Brutus is asking Cassius to declare his intentions openly. For his part, Brutus makes explicit that in the cause of public welfare he rates his honour as highly as his life. The topic that Cassius is about to broach is the conspiracy to assassinate Caesar.

5 I, as Aeneas, our great ancestor,
Did from the flames of Troy upon his shoulder
The old Anchises bear, so from the waves of Tiber
Did I the tired Caesar. And this man
Is now become a god, and Cassius is
A wretched creature, and must bend his body
If Caesar carelessly but nod on him.
(I.2.112–18)

Cassius is debunking the myth of Caesar's godlike nature to Brutus by narrating a series of incidents which illustrate Caesar's human frailty. He has just recounted an incident in which Caesar challenged Cassius to swim the Tiber's winter floood, only to prove incapable of the task himself. Cassius uses an epic simile to liken his feat in saving Caesar to Aeneas' carrying the aged Anchises on his back from the burning Troy. Virgil had told this story in Book II of his epic poem, *The Aeneid*, which celebrates Aeneas as the founder of Rome and Roman virtues.

6

Why, man, he doth bestride the narrow world
Like a Colossus, and we petty men
Walk under his huge legs, and peep about
To find ourselves dishonourable graves.
Men at some time are masters of their fates;

The fault, dear Brutus, is not in our stars,
But in ourselves, that we are underlings.
(I.2.134–40)

Cassius employs, as an image of Caesar's domination of the Roman world, the simile of colossal statues and their scale compared to the measure of mortal men. That Cassius conceives it merely as an image and not reality is evident in his belief that men, and not the influences of the stars, are the determiners of their own destinies. J. M. Barrie used the phrase 'dear Brutus' as the title of one of his plays (1917).

7 Why should that name be sounded more than yours?
Write them together, yours is as fair a name;
Sound them, it doth become the mouth as well;
Weigh them, it is as heavy; conjure with 'em,
'Brutus' will start a spirit as soon as 'Caesar'.
(I.2.142–6)

Cassius is maintaining to Brutus that there is nothing intrinsic to the name of Caesar, and by extension to his merit, to justify the position he holds. The idea of conjuring, or calling up, spirits is invoked to demonstrate that there is nothing magical or divine about the name of Caesar and that the name of Brutus may inspire just as much.

8 Let me have men about me that are fat,
Sleek-headed men, and such as sleep a-nights.
Yond Cassius has a lean and hungry look;
He thinks too much: such men are dangerous.
(I.2.191–4)

Caesar has returned from the games being held to celebrate the festival of the Lupercalia in angry mood, since he has reluctantly been forced, by political expediency, to reject the crown offered him. Shakespeare derived the views expressed here from those attributed to Caesar by Plutarch.

9 He reads much,
He is a great observer, and he looks
Quite through the deeds of men.
(I.2.200–2)

Caesar is contrasting Cassius' introversion with Antony's extrovert and gregarious nature. Cassius' ability to penetrate the motivation of his fellow-men has been demonstrated earlier in the scene in his understanding of Brutus' concealed fears regarding Caesar's power.

10 He put it by once; but for all that, to my thinking, he would

fain have had it. Then he offered it to him again; then he put it by again; but to my thinking, he was very loath to lay his fingers off it. And then he offered it the third time; he put it the third time by; and still as he refused it, the rabblement hooted, and clapped their chopped hands, and threw up their sweaty night-caps, and uttered such a deal of stinking breath because Caesar refused the crown, that it had, almost, choked Caesar; for he swooned, and fell down at it.
(I.2.236–46)
Casca offers a sarcastic account of Antony's thrice-repeated offer of the crown to Caesar and the latter's reluctant refusals. The narrator has witnessed the event at the games to celebrate the Lupercalia and is recounting it for the benefit of Cassius and Brutus. In fact, the off-stage sounds of the 'rabble's' response to the event will have been heard during the preceding conversation of Brutus and Cassius. Casca gives not only a vivid description of the actions but also of the crowd's noise and odour. The reference to Caesar's epilepsy, what Brutus terms the 'falling-sickness' (line 252), is another indication of his human frailty. Shakespeare's source for this detail is Plutarch.

11 CASSIUS Did Cicero say anything?
CASCA Ay, he spoke Greek.
(I.2.275–6)
Cicero was famed, in Renaissance England as in ancient Rome, as a rhetorician. Command of Greek in ancient Rome was a cultural and intellectual accomplishment which Casca ridicules. In fact, he suggests that what Cicero said made no sense by saying, 'it was Greek to me' (lines 280–1). The occasion referred to is when Caesar was offered the crown at the games of Lupercalia.

12 Well, Brutus, thou art noble; yet I see
Thy honourable mettle may be wrought
From that it is disposed: therefore it is meet
That noble minds keep ever with their likes;
For who so firm that cannot be seduced?
(I.2.305–9)
Cassius' soliloquy reveals his instinct for manipulation in contrast to the principled yet malleable nature of Brutus. Through a pun on mettle/metal, Brutus' disposition becomes the material being fashioned ('wrought') by Cassius' scheming. In fact, Cassius' speech becomes a plotting soliloquy when he plans the ruse of having 'writings', purportedly of citizens praising Brutus and hinting at Caesar's ambition, thrown through Brutus' window. To pursue the metaphor of the quotation, Brutus' tragedy is caused

by the pure metal of his principles being alloyed by the political manipulation of others.

13 Nor stony tower, nor walls of beaten brass,
Nor airless dungeon, nor strong links of iron,
Can be retentive to the strength of spirit;
But life, being weary of these worldly bars,
Never lacks power to dismiss itself.
(I.3.93–7)

Cassius has just been told by Casca a rumour that Caesar is to be made king, so sealing his commitment to assassination: 'Cassius from bondage will deliver Cassius' (line 90). This statement is an amplification of his belief that the only real imprisonment is that of the spirit.

14 It must be by his death; and for my part,
I know no personal cause to spurn at him,
But for the general. – He would be crowned.
How that might change his nature, there's the question.
It is the bright day that brings forth the adder,
And that craves wary walking. Crown him! – that!
And then, I grant, we put a sting in him
That at his will he may do danger with.
Th'abuse of greatness is when it disjoins
Remorse from power.
(II.1.10–19)

Brutus is in his 'orchard' in the early hours of the morning, sleeplessly cogitating upon the question of assassinating Caesar. The theme of the soliloquy is the effect of absolute power upon character, and the pattern of Brutus' thoughts reveals his commitment to principle and his lack of malice towards Caesar. The 'bright day' (power) brings out the 'adder' (tyranny).

15 But 'tis a common proof,
That lowliness is young ambition's ladder,
Whereto the climber-upward turns his face;
But when he once attains the upmost round,
He then unto the ladder turns his back,
Looks in the clouds, scorning the base degrees
By which he did ascend.
(II.1.21–7)

Brutus' argument is that in their ascent great men make a pretence of humility in order to gain popularity and power. Having achieved power, they reject those by whose support they have risen. The image of the ladder is also used by Shakespeare in

Richard II, V.1.55, to describe Bolingbroke's ascent of the throne through the good offices of Northumberland.

16 Between the acting of a dreadful thing
And the first motion, all the interim is
Like a phantasma or a hideous dream:
The genius and the mortal instruments
Are then in council; and the state of man,
Like to a little kingdom, suffers then
The nature of an insurrection.
(II.1.63–9)

Brutus has just confessed to himself that, since Cassius first raised the issue of assassination, he has not slept. There is a sense of suspension in time, in which the act contemplated is more present and real than the surrounding reality. Brutus depicts himself as the microcosm of a state engaged in civil war. The conflict within him is contested by 'genius' and 'mortal instruments', terms which have been subject to much interpretation. 'Genius' is usually a guardian or attendant spirit and here seems associated with psychic health and integrity. 'Mortal instruments' seems to indicate fatal, destructive, and self-destructive forces.

17 O conspiracy,
Sham'st thou to show thy dangerous brow by night,
When evils are most free? O then, by day
Where wilt thou find a cavern dark enough
To mask thy monstrous visage?
(II.1.77–81)

The conspirators have called upon Brutus at night. Lucius, Brutus' servant-boy, has just informed his master that he cannot recognize the callers because 'their hats are pluck'd about their ears / And half their faces buried in their cloaks'. Brutus is shocked by conspiracy's concealed appearance, which contrasts with his open nature. He questions rhetorically where conspiracy will be able to hide by day, like a monster in a cave, if by night, which was for Elizabethans the time associated with evil spirits, it dares not show its face.

18 What need we any spur but our own cause
To prick us to redress?
(II.1.123–4)

Brutus has committed himself to joining the conspiracy to assassinate Julius Caesar. His motivation is opposition on principle to tyranny or absolute political power. He is arguing to the other conspirators that the justness of their cause is a sufficient bond against Cassius' suggestion that they bind their commitment with an oath.

19 Let us be sacrificers, but not butchers, Caius...
Let's kill him boldly, but not wrathfully;
Let's carve him as a dish fit for the gods,
Not hew him as a carcass fit for hounds.
(II.1.166, 172–4)
Brutus is debating with (Caius) Cassius the manner of Caesar's assassination. Brutus' sense of high moral principle is evident in his imagery of sacrifice, which elevates the deed to a ritualistic and religious level. How this description will compare with the act performed in III.1 will depend upon the direction, but some degree of discrepancy will be evident.

20 Enjoy the honey-heavy dew of slumber.
(II.1.230)
Lucius, Brutus' servant-boy, has fallen asleep in the course of the conspirators' night meeting. His peaceful sleep and freedom from care contrast with his master's sleeplessness and mental turbulence. Brutus' remark is therefore illustrative of his compassionate and unenvious nature.

21 I charm you, by my once commended beauty,
By all your vows of love, and that great vow
Which did incorporate and make us one,
That you unfold to me, your self, your half,
Why you are heavy.
(II.1.271–5)
Portia has sought out Brutus in the 'orchard', following the night visit of the conspirators. Brutus wishes to keep from his wife the knowledge of the conspiracy and his fears, but she has an instinctive awareness of his mental anguish. Her appeal to be made a partner to his secrets is presented in terms of their love and the marriage bond. Brutus subsequently promises to inform her.

22 Think you I am no stronger than my sex,
Being so fathered, and so husbanded?
(II.1.296–7)
Portia's lines express a sentiment not likely to find favour with women today. It is the expression of a Roman patrician matron (and is likely to have been shared by noblewomen of Shakespeare's day). Portia's father was Cato, the politician and orator.

23 CALPHURNIA

When beggars die, there are no comets seen;
The heavens themselves blaze forth the death of princes.

CAESAR

Cowards die many times before their deaths;
The valiant never taste of death but once.
Of all the wonders that I yet have heard,
It seems to me most strange that men should fear,
Seeing that death, a necessary end,
Will come when it will come.

(II.2.30–7)

Caesar is about to depart for the Capitol on the Ides of March. Calphurnia, his wife, is seized with ominous foreboding and seeks to prevent his leaving home. Her fears are augmented by the many strange occurrences which were thought, by ancient Romans and Elizabethans alike, to presage a calamitous event. Caesar's attitude is fatalistic yet resolute, but his words prove pregnant with dramatic irony.

24 Caesar should be a beast without a heart
If he should stay at home today for fear.
No, Caesar shall not. Danger knows full well
That Caesar is more dangerous than he.
We are two lions littered in one day,
And I the elder and more terrible;
And Caesar shall go forth.

(II.2.42–8)

Caesar's tendency to speak of himself in the third person is not only an indication of his arrogance, but conveys the sense of an institution rather than a human being. Indeed, here he is having to live up to the role of fearless leader. The concept of Caesar as the twin of danger is equivocal: his role is a threat to society, but also to himself as a man.

25 She dreamt tonight she saw my statue,
Which, like a fountain with an hundred spouts,
Did run pure blood; and many lusty Romans
Came smiling, and did bathe their hands in it.

(II.2.76–9)

Caesar is recounting Calphurnia's dream (which proves an ominous prophecy) as an explanation to Decius, one of the conspirators, why he will not attend the senate. It was Decius in II.1.207–8 who had promised to bring Caesar to the Capitol through exploitation of flattery. It was Decius' interpretation of the dream as 'a vision fair and fortunate', in which Caesar is projected as the saviour and life-blood of his people, that persuades Caesar to proceed to the Capitol.

26 My heart laments that virtue cannot live
Out of the teeth of emulation.
(II.3.12–13)
This is the observation of Artemidorus, a rhetorician and sophist of Gnidos, who has prepared a paper warning Caesar of conspiracy. The source of the incident, though not the message, lies in Plutarch.

27 O constancy, be strong upon my side;
Set a huge mountain 'tween my heart and tongue!
I have a man's mind, but a woman's might.
How hard it is for women to keep counsel!
(II.4.6–9)
Portia has been made aware of Brutus' secret involvement in the conspiracy against Caesar and she is desperate that the servant-boy, Lucius, should bring news from the Capitol. Her intense anxiety is conveyed by the contradictory instructions she gives the boy, while at the same time she berates herself with Elizabethan misogynistic commonplaces. She accuses herself of inconstancy, weakness – moral and physical, indiscretion, and garrulity. See also 'Ay me, how weak a thing / The heart of woman is!' (lines 39–40).

28 CAESAR (*to the Soothsayer*) The ides of March are come.
SOOTHSAYER Ay, Caesar, but not gone.
(III.1.1–2)
The scene of assassination begins with Caesar implying the vanity of the Soothsayer's prophecy and the Soothsayer advising caution. The source of the incident is Plutarch.

29 But I am constant as the northern star,
Of whose true-fixed and resting quality
There is no fellow in the firmament.
The skies are painted with unnumbered sparks,
They are all fire, and every one doth shine;
But there's but one in all doth hold his place.
So in the world; 'tis furnished well with men,
And men are flesh and blood, and apprehensive;
Yet in the number I do know but one
That unassailable holds on his rank,
Unshaked of motion.
(III.1.60–70)

Metellus Cimber, Cassius, and Brutus are pleading with Caesar for the repeal of the decree of banishment on Metellus' brother, named as Publius by Shakespeare. The pressing of this claim gives the conspirators the opportunity to crowd around Caesar in order to effect the assassination. The form and content of Caesar's response, from which the lines above come, convince the conspirators of his tyrannical nature and alienate the audience's sympathies. The continuation of the speech unflinchingly confirms Publius Cimber's banishment. In the references to the 'firmament' and to the painted skies, Shakespeare was exploiting the resources of the Elizabethan theatre, since the canopy over the open stage was termed the firmament and bore painted symbols of the celestial bodies.

30 *Et tu, Brute?* – Then fall Caesar!
(III.1.77)
Caesar's dying line arises from his recognition of Brutus amongst the conspirators who have stabbed him. The Latin phrase (You, too, Brutus?) has no direct source in any of the classical accounts of Caesar's death, though it could derive from the Greek words ascribed to Caesar by Suetonius in his biography *Julius Caesar*. These words, however, certainly had a stage history pre-dating Shakespeare's play and possibly deriving, as Malone (the late eighteenth-century editor of Shakespeare) suggested, from *Epilogus Caesaris Interfecti*, a lost play of Richard Edes performed at Oxford in 1582. They appear in *The True Tragedy of Richard Duke of York*, published in 1595 and generally thought to be a bad quarto of *Henry VI Part 3*.

31 Ambition's debt is paid.
(III.1.83)
Brutus' words on the death of Caesar are used to quieten the people and prevent panic. Brutus' reason for joining the conspiracy to assassinate Caesar was the potential tyranny threatened by Caesar's ambition.

32 BRUTUS Fates, we will know your pleasures.
That we shall die, we know; 'tis but the time
And drawing days out, that men stand upon.
CASCA
Why, he that cuts off twenty years of life
Cuts off so many years of fearing death.
(III.1.98–102)
These statements follow shortly on the assassination of Caesar, when the conspirators are anxiously awaiting the response of the people to the deed. The contrast of the certainty of death with

the uncertainty of its moment was proverbial. Casca's stoic utterance is his last in the play, for he then disappears from the action.

33 How many ages hence
Shall this our lofty scene be acted over,
In states unborn, and accents yet unknown!
(III.1.111–13)

Shakespeare frequently draws attention to the theatrical and illusionistic aspects of his drama. Cassius' words parallel the historical event of assassination with its theatrical enactment. The life and death of Julius Caesar was a popular subject with Renaissance dramatists, both academic and commercial. In the case of Shakespeare's play, the words have proved prophetic.

34 O mighty Caesar! Dost thou lie so low?
Are all thy conquests, glories, triumphs, spoils
Shrunk to this little measure?
(III.1.148–50)

Mark Antony's first sight of the corpse of Caesar prompts a public rhetorical outburst based on the tragic theme of the fall of great men (*de casibus virum illustrorum*). The 'little measure' is, of course, Caesar's body, the little world of man, as opposed to the larger world he ruled by conquest. The play is, in fact, structured on two *de casibus* patterns: the literal and physical one of Caesar, and the mental and spiritual one of Brutus.

35 Had I as many eyes as thou hast wounds,
Weeping as fast as they stream forth thy blood,
It would become me better than to close
In terms of friendship with thine enemies.
(III.1.200–3)

Mark Antony is ostensibly making friends with the conspirators. However, his contemplation of Caesar's corpse and the parallel he establishes between its flowing wounds and his tears takes the argument in another direction, leading to a reproof from Cassius.

36 Thou art the ruins of the noblest man
That ever livèd in the tide of times.
(III.1.256–7)

Antony's private lament over the corpse of Caesar employs more natural speech rhythms than his earlier public rhetorical outburst. The 'tide of times' means literally the passage of time, but the image of the tide is closely linked in the play with the ebbing and flowing of men's destinies.

37 And Caesar's spirit, ranging for revenge,
With Ate by his side, come hot from hell,
Shall in these confines with a monarch's voice
Cry havoc and let slip the dogs of war,
That this foul deed shall smell above the earth
With carrion men, groaning for burial.
(III.1.270–5)

Antony's vision of the retribution exacted by Caesar's ghost releases his anger against the conspirators, before whom he has been compelled to express himself diplomatically. Ate, according to Hesiod the daughter of Strife, was to Shakespeare a figure of discord and vengeance. The phrase, 'the dogs of war', has passed into the language as a term for mercenaries and undisciplined troops.

38 Passion, I see, is catching.
(III.1.283)

Mark Antony's sorrow at the death of Caesar is revived by the instinctive tears of the servant of Octavius on seeing the corpse. 'Passion' means emotion, and more specifically here, grief. The alliance of Octavius Caesar with Mark Antony provides a political counterbalance to the fortunes of the conspirators.

39 If then that friend demand why Brutus rose against Caesar, this is my answer: not that I loved Caesar less, but that I loved Rome more ... As Caesar loved me, I weep for him; as he was fortunate, I rejoice at it; as he was valiant, I honour him; but, as he was ambitious, I slew him.
(III.2.19–26)

This is the kernel of Brutus' succinct and straightforward address to the people of Rome in the Forum explaining the motivation of the assassination of Caesar. Typically of Brutus, his address elevates principle above personal feeling. It had been agreed with Mark Antony that Brutus should address the Roman people first to explain the assassination and that afterwards Antony should deliver a funeral oration over Caesar's body. While Brutus speaks plainly and directly in prose, Antony is given the more emotive medium of verse.

40 Who is here so base that would be a bondman? If any, speak; for him have I offended. Who is here so rude that would not be a Roman? If any, speak; for him have I offended. Who is here so vile that will not love his country? If any, speak; for him have I offended.
(III.2.28–33)

In his address to the Roman people explaining the motivation of Caesar's assassination, Brutus appeals to the principles of liberty and patriotism. His use of these concepts and the rhetorical patterns in which they are couched are a way of manipulating the crowd's response. 'Rude' means savage or ignorant.

41 As I slew my best lover for the good of Rome, I have the same dagger for myself, when it shall please my country to need my death.
(III.2.44–7)
Brutus, in his explanation of the motivation behind Caesar's assassination, has proclaimed to the people that he measures himself by the same principles he applied to Caesar. Immediately prior to these lines, Mark Antony has entered the Forum with the body of Caesar to begin the funeral oration allowed him by the conspirators, largely at Brutus' behest. Brutus' words prove prophetic, since he does in fact die by his own hand in V.5.

42 Friends, Romans, countrymen, lend me your ears;
I come to bury Caesar, not to praise him.
The evil that men do lives after them,
The good is oft interrèd with their bones;
So let it be with Caesar. The noble Brutus
Hath told you Caesar was ambitious.
If it were so, it was a grievous fault,
And grievously hath Caesar answered it.
Here, under leave of Brutus and the rest –
For Brutus is an honourable man;
So are they all, all honourable men –
Come I to speak in Caesar's funeral.
He was my friend, faithful and just to me;
But Brutus says he was ambitious,
And Brutus is an honourable man.
(III.2.74–88)
Mark Antony's funeral oration over the body of Caesar is to turn the fickle crowd's sympathy against Brutus who, after addressing the people on the motivation of the assassination, has unwisely left the Forum. Antony plays cleverly upon Brutus' accusation of Caesar's ambition and ironically upon the notion of the conspirators being 'honourable' and having acted from principle. The last two lines quoted are repeated (with the substitution of 'yet' for 'but') at 95–6 and 100–1, while the term 'honourable men' is further employed at lines 125 and 128.

43 O judgement! thou art fled to brutish beasts,
And men have lost their reason.
(III.2.105–6)
Shakespeare makes Antony exploit the tenet of Renaissance humanism which distinguished man from the beasts by virtue of his powers of reason. The opposition of the human to the bestial was a Renaissance commonplace (compare *Hamlet* 20, 179).

44 ALL
The will, the will! We will hear Caesar's will!
ANTONY
Have patience, gentle friends; I must not read it.
It is not meet you know how Caesar loved you.
You are not wood, you are not stones, but men;
And being men, hearing the will of Caesar,
It will inflame you, it will make you mad.
(III.2.140–5)
The presentation of Caesar's will, which Antony claims to have found in Caesar's closet, is the masterstroke of Antony's oration. Antony's suggestion that the people are Caesar's 'heirs' (line 146) outweighs Brutus' offer of a 'place in the commonwealth' (line 43), which was won by the assassination. There is a pun on 'wood' at line 143, since it also means mad.

45 If you have tears, prepare to shed them now.
You all do know this mantle. I remember
The first time ever Caesar put it on;
'Twas on a summer's evening in his tent,
That day he overcame the Nervii.
Look, in this place ran Cassius' dagger through;
See what a rent the envious Casca made:
Through this, the well-belovèd Brutus stabbed.
(III.2.170–7)
Having engaged the plebeians' attention with the promise of Caesar's will, Antony descends from the 'pulpit' and makes the crowd form a circle around Caesar's body. Before proceeding to the tangible benefits of the will, he unleashes the most emotional part of the oration, dwelling on Caesar's military service for the state and on the envy and ingratitude of the conspirators. The victory over the Nervii was one of Caesar's most decisive and acclaimed battles in the Gallic War of 57 BC.

46 This was the most unkindest cut of all;
For when the noble Caesar saw him stab,
Ingratitude, more strong than traitors' arms,
Quite vanquished him: then burst his mighty heart;

And in his mantle muffling up his face,
Even at the base of Pompey's statue,
Which all the while ran blood, great Caesar fell.
O, what a fall was there, my countrymen!
Then I, and you, and all of us fell down,
Whilst bloody treason flourished over us.
O, now you weep, and I perceive you feel
The dint of pity. These are gracious drops.
(III.2.184–95)

This passage from Antony's funeral oration refers to Brutus' blow and the ingratitude it represented. It recreates in narrative form the climax of the assassination as it was enacted in III.1. 'Unkindest' combines the sense of most cruel and most unnatural (contrary to the instinct of mankind). The double superlative, 'most unkindest', was a standard feature of Elizabethan English. 'Dint' means force. In the course of the speech, Antony has transformed the conspirators' blow for liberty into an act of treason within the minds of the people, so rousing their pity and tears.

47 I come not, friends, to steal away your hearts;
I am no orator, as Brutus is,
But, as you know me all, a plain blunt man,
That love my friend; and that they know full well
That gave me public leave to speak of him.
For I have neither wit, nor words, nor worth,
Action, nor utterance, nor the power of speech
To stir men's blood.
(III.2.217–24)

Antony's statement is richly ironic. Brutus' speech to the people was very direct and unadorned in comparison with Antony's rhetoric, which has roused the plebeians to a frenzy of anger against the conspirators. The 'friend' is Caesar, over whose body Antony has delivered the funeral oration to the people. The qualities that Antony claims not to possess are the traditional attributes of the classical orator.

48 Here was a Caesar! When comes such another?
(III.2.253)

Antony's exclamation and rhetorical question follow his reading of Caesar's will. The plebeians in their anger and indignation at the conspirators had forgotten the will, but Antony artfully employs its bequests of money and public parks as the final straws to incite the people into violent rebellion. At the beginning of Act IV, the Triumvirs (Antony, Octavius, and Lepidus) decide to use some of the will's bequests for their own purposes.

49 Mischief, thou art afoot,
Take thou what course thou wilt.
(III.2.262–3)

The fury of the mutinous plebeians is personified in Antony's remark. The nature of the remark suggests that Antony is driven more by the desire to avenge Ceasar's death than by any clear political design. The uncontrollable force of mischief that Antony has incited in the people through his oratory is witnessed in the following scene, III.4, when Cinna the poet is murdered by the mob in mistake for Cinna the conspirator.

50 Fortune is merry,
And in this mood will give us anything.
(III.2.268–9)

Antony has just learned that Octavius has arrived in Rome and has decided to meet him at the house of Lepidus. In the aftermath of Caesar's assassination and the mutiny of the plebs against the conspirators, these three are to become the Triumvirs of the Roman world. Antony's ecstatic remark suggests he is an opportunist rather than a scheming politician.

51 Tear him for his bad verses, tear him for his bad verses!
(III.3.30)

The Fourth Plebeian's attitude epitomizes the uncontrollable fury of the mob. In seeking vengeance upon the conspirators for the murder of Caesar, the mob has mistaken Cinna the poet for Cinna the conspirator. His protestations to this effect carry no weight and he is killed, since the mob is bent upon having blood.

52 This is a slight unmeritable man,
Meet to be sent on errands.
(IV.1.12–13)

Antony's slighting reference to Lepidus, made to Octavius, reveals tensions within the triumvirate of the three men, established to rule the Roman world after the murder of Caesar. Historically, the three decided to make a threefold division of the government of state in 43 BC.

53 When love begins to sicken and decay,
It useth an enforcèd ceremony.
There are no tricks in plain and simple faith.
(IV.2.20–2)

After the assassination of Caesar, relationships between the main conspirators become subject to strain, especially under the pressure of the war against the triumvirate of Antony, Octavius, and Lepidus for control of the Roman world. Brutus, encamped with his troops near Sardis, is questioning his officer, Lucilius, on his reception by Cassius. This remark is made when Brutus learns that Lucilius was received with 'courtesy and respect enough' but not with 'free and friendly conference'.

54 You yourself
Are much condemned to have an itching palm.
(IV.3.9–10)
Brutus and Cassius have withdrawn to Brutus' tent before Sardis, out of view of their officers and troops, in order to settle the differences that have arisen between them. Brutus' accusation that Cassius has a mercenary and avaricious streak gets the discussion off on the wrong foot.

55 Shall we now
Contaminate our fingers with base bribes,
And sell the mighty space of our large honours
For so much trash as may be graspèd thus?
I had rather be a dog, and bay the moon,
Than such a Roman.
(IV.3.23–8)
Brutus and Cassius have withdrawn to Brutus' tent near Sardis to settle the differences between them. Brutus is appealing to the high principles of Roman virtue. He is castigating Cassius and his officers for involvement in bribery, which he sees not only as corrupt in itself but contrary to the principles of justice for which the murder of Caesar was performed. The image of a dog (or wolf) baying at the moon was proverbial.

56 I'll use you for my mirth, yea, for my laughter,
When you are waspish.
(IV.3.49–50)
In the course of the argument between Brutus and Cassius in Brutus' tent near Sardis, Cassius asserts that he is the more experienced soldier. Brutus at first reacts angrily to Cassius' own anger but then, in these lines, turns to ridicule. He repeatedly accuses Cassius of 'rash choler' (line 39), of being 'choleric' (43) and of 'testy humour' (46).

57 CASSIUS
Do not presume too much upon my love;
I may do that I shall be sorry for.
BRUTUS
You have done that you should be sorry for.
There is no terror, Cassius, in your threats;
For I am armed so strong in honesty

That they pass by me as the idle wind,
Which I respect not.

(IV.3.63–9)

This exchange is representative of the argument between the two leaders of the conspirators which takes place in Brutus' tent before Sardis. Cassius' anger and indignation are as evident as Brutus' sense of moral principle and self-righteousness. 'Honesty' has the more general signification of moral integrity.

58 A friend should bear his friend's infirmities.

(IV.3.85)

Cassius is arguing that Brutus is magnifying his faults when it is the function of a friend to be patient of shortcomings. Brutus has accused Cassius of refusing him the money to pay his legions, a charge denied by Cassius. The dispute takes place in Brutus' tent near Sardis.

59 Cassius is aweary of the world;
Hated by one he loves; braved by his brother.

(IV.3.94–5)

The argument between Cassius and Brutus in Brutus' tent near Sardis grieves them both. A sense of world-weariness has entered their spirits, because the assassination of Caesar has not created the dawn of liberty and fraternity they anticipated, but merely division, dissension, and conflict. Cassius is speaking of himself and referring to Brutus.

60 BRUTUS
O Cassius, I am sick of many griefs.
CASSIUS
Of your philosophy you make no use,
If you give place to accidental evils.

(IV.3.143–5)

Brutus' line explains the unaccustomed anger he has shown towards Cassius in their quarrel at Sardis. The sources of the griefs follow: the death of Portia, Brutus' wife, by her own hand and the ominous military situation. Cassius offers consolation by arguing that Brutus' stoicism should not leave him prey to chance evils.

61 BRUTUS
Why, farewell, Portia. We must die, Messala.
With meditating that she must die once,
I have the patience to endure it now.
MESSALA
Even so great men great losses should endure.

CASSIUS
I have as much of this in art as you,
But yet my nature could not bear it so.
(IV.3.188–93)

The Folio text of *Julius Caesar* contains in this scene two contradictory accounts of Portia's death: one at lines 146–56 and this second account some 40 lines later. The consensus of editorial opinion is that the second account was probably a first version which was not cancelled with sufficient clarity in the copy from which the Folio was printed. The Folio is the only authentic text of *Julius Caesar*. The account given above stresses Brutus' stoicism but diminishes his humanity: in fact, this point is made in Cassius' lines where he states that his own knowledge of philosophy is inadequate to cope with the human response.

62 Good reasons must of force give place to better.
(IV.3.201)

Cassius and Brutus are discussing military tactics in Brutus' tent near Sardis. Cassius has argued that they should await the attack of Antony and Octavius at Sardis, while Brutus is to argue for meeting their forces at Philippi. Hence, in his view, he is about to counter Cassius' 'good reasons' with 'better'. His advice proves disastrous to their cause.

63 The enemy increaseth every day;
We, at the height, are ready to decline.
There is a tide in the affairs of men,
Which, taken at the flood, leads on to fortune;
Omitted, all the voyage of their life
Is bound in shallows and in miseries.
On such a full sea are we now afloat,
And we must take the current when it serves,
Or lose our ventures.
(IV.3.214–22)

Brutus' argument encapsulates the ebb and flow of political, military, and personal fortunes in the play. The tide imagery matches the *de casibus virum illustrorum* concept of the tragedy, which traces the rise and fall of great men. In fact, the passage is a mixture of metaphor and what that represents: 'tide' leads to 'fortune' and 'shallows' is explained by the following 'miseries'. 'Omitted' in this context means missed (of a tide), while 'ventures' brings the sea/tide imagery back to issues of gain or loss by signifying commercial cargoes committed to the seas for profit. The military situation in question concerns the relative strengths of the armies of Antony and Octavius on the one hand, and Brutus and Cassius on the other. The third line is alluded to in

Byron's *Don Juan*, canto VI stanza I, and parodied, with reference to women, in the following stanza.

64 The deep of night is crept upon our talk,
And nature must obey necessity,
Which we will niggard with a little rest.
(IV.3.224–6)
Brutus suddenly realizes that the discussions with Cassius, held in Brutus' tent near Sardis, have lasted into the night and that rest is necessary for the military exertions ahead of them. In fact, Brutus does not sleep but asks for music and then intends to read. Throughout the play, Brutus is characterized by sleeplessness caused by the weight of conscience.

65 This was an ill beginning of the night;
Never come such division 'tween our souls!
(IV.3.232–3)
Cassius is referring to the argument with Brutus and the lengthy discussions that followed from it which took place in Brutus' tent near Sardis. The divisions in their friendship are healed before the battle at Philippi.

66 I should not urge thy duty past thy might.
(IV.3.259)
Although it is extremely late by the time Brutus and Cassius have finished their discussions, Brutus has asked his servant-boy, Lucius, to provide music for him. Lucius has stated that it is his duty to play despite his tiredness, so prompting Brutus' remark. The Renaissance, following Platonic traditions, believed music to be restorative of the soul's harmony. Shakespeare has telescoped dramatic time to give the impression that the meeting between Brutus and Cassius at Sardis took place on the eve of the battle at Philippi. In reality the Sardis meeting took place early in 42 BC and the battle of Philippi in the following autumn.

67 How ill this taper burns! Ha! Who comes here?
I think it is the weakness of mine eyes
That shapes this monstrous apparition.
It comes upon me. Art thou any thing?
Art thou some god, some angel, or some devil,
That mak'st my blood cold, and my hair to stare?
(IV.3.273–9)
Brutus is in his tent at Sardis, awake amongst his sleeping men, when the ghost of Caesar appears. The fright to Brutus' soul contrasts with the restorative harmony of the music that his boy, Lucius, has just played. Caesar's ghost has come to warn Brutus

that he shall see him again at Philippi. It was an Elizabethan superstitious belief that devils could assume the form of ghosts and lure men to destruction.

68 But for your words, they rob the Hybla bees,
And leave them honeyless.
(V.1.34–5)
Cassius makes this retort to Antony before the battle at Philippi. The two armies are drawn up for battle, but the generals wish to exchange words first. Antony has just accused Brutus of hypocrisy, of using fair words when performing violent acts – as in the assassination of Caesar. Cassius, defending Brutus, replies that, while Antony's 'blows' are an unknown quantity, the power of his rhetoric is known – an allusion to his incitement of the people with his funeral oration over Caesar's body. Hybla was a mountain (and town) in Sicily famed for its honey.

69 If we do meet again, why, we shall smile;
If not, when then this parting was well made.
(V.1.117–18)
These are Brutus' words at his leave-taking with Cassius before the battle of Philippi. Cassius, contrary to his sceptical nature, has been smitten with a sense of ill omen and has obliged Brutus to contemplate the prospect of defeat in battle. Neither man is willing to lose liberty, nor to grace Antony's and Octavius' triumph. Implicitly, therefore, they are committed in defeat to death in battle or suicide, and hence the finality of their farewell, should fate not offer them another victorious meeting.

70 O, that a man might know
The end of this day's business ere it come!
But it sufficeth that the day will end,
And then the end is known.
(V.1.122–5)
Brutus' last wish before the battle at Philippi is a natural but impossible one. The conclusion of his thought illustrates his patient, stoical attitude to human destiny.

71 This day I breathèd first. Time is come round,
And where I did begin, there shall I end.
My life is run his compass.
(V.3.23–5)
Cassius had indicated at V.1.71 that the day of the battle of Philippi was his birthday. Having learned that Antony's troops have overrun his own and are sacking his camp, he foresees that the day will also be his last. The cyclical pattern of existence he

posits derives from the Elizabethan concept of the wheel of Fortune.

72 Mistrust of good success hath done this deed.
O hateful Error, Melancholy's child,
Why dost thou show to the apt thoughts of men
The things that are not?
(V.3.66–9)

Messala's response to finding Cassius dead reveals that Cassius was over-hasty in his despair. Brutus' success against Octavius' troops counterbalances Cassius' losses against Antony. Error is personified as the offspring of Melancholy, whose actions kill the mother (Melancholy) and the melancholic (Cassius). 'Apt' means quick to learn.

73 O Julius Caesar, thou art mighty yet!
Thy spirit walks abroad, and turns our swords
In our own proper entrails.
(V.3.94–6)

When Brutus discovers that not only is Cassius dead, but that Titinius, Cassius' officer and friend, has also committed suicide, he attributes the destructive power abroad to the ghost of Caesar. Following his apprehension of Caesar's ghost at Sardis in IV.3, Brutus interprets these acts as vengeance, not despair.

74 My heart doth joy that yet in all my life
I found no man but he was true to me.
(V.5.34–5)

Brutus is aware that he has lost the second (or rather renewed) battle of Philippi. He has stated at line 20: 'I know my hour is come'. His companions (Clitus, Dardanius, and Volumnius) are extremely reluctant to aid him in the act of suicide, though Strato eventually does so. As the statement indicates, Brutus dies, despite his defeat, with his ideals and his noble concept of humanity intact.

75 This was the noblest Roman of them all.
All the conspirators save only he
Did that they did in envy of great Caesar;
He only, in a general honest thought
And common good to all, made one of them.
His life was gentle, and the elements
So mixed in him, that Nature might stand up
And say to all the world, 'This was a man!'
(V.5.68–75)

Antony's panegyric on the dead Brutus constitutes one of the most famous and most anthologized passages of Shakespeare. While Antony's fluency of rhetoric remains evident, the features of Brutus' character and motivation to which he refers are generally confirmed by the play. The last two lines are based on the notion, Platonic in origin, that the four elements which constituted the world also composed the nature of man. Hence Nature (the macrocosm) could in Brutus (the microcosm) recognize a true image of itself. The essence of Antony's oration is to be found in Plutarch.

King John

1 Madam, an if my brother had my shape
And I had his . . .
And, to his shape, were heir to all this land –
Would I might never stir from off this place,
I would give it every foot to have this face;
I would not be Sir Nob in any case!
(I.1.138–9, 144–7)

These lines constitute the sardonic reply of the Bastard to Queen Eleanor's question whether he would rather be deemed Sir Robert Faulconbridge's legitimate heir or the bastard of her son, the former king, Richard Coeur-de-Lion. They earn him a knighthood, recognition as a Plantagenet, and a chance to win fame and fortune in Eleanor's service in the French wars. However, the manner in which King John and Eleanor decide the dispute between the Bastard and the legitimate Robert Faulconbridge raises questions concerning freedom and property in the realm.

2 Well, now can I make any Joan a lady.
'Good den, Sir Richard' – 'God 'a' mercy, fellow' –
And if his name be George, I'll call him Peter;
For new-made honour doth forget men's names.
(I.1.184–7)

In his soliloquy, the Bastard is musing cynically upon the power and pride of the aristocracy. In speaking to his half-brother earlier he had maintained the distinction between aristocratic and materialistic values in retorting: 'My father gave me honour, yours gave land' (line 165). 'Joan' was a generic name for a country girl.

3 Sweet, sweet, sweet poison for the age's tooth.
(I.1.213)

The Bastard is cynical in his acute observation of the age's obsequiousness and his determination to rise socially through exploitation of it.

4 That white-faced shore,
Whose foot spurns back the ocean's roaring tides
And coops from other lands her islanders,
... that England, hedged in with the main,
That water-wallèd bulwark, still secure
And confident from foreign purposes.
(II.1.23–8)

The forces that support the claim of Arthur, Duke of Brittany, King John's nephew, to the throne of England are met before the town of Angers. These words form part of the pledge of the Archduke of Austria to support young Arthur's rights. Passages extolling the invincibility of the English as an island race were popular on the Elizabethan stage after the defeat of the Armada in 1588. This passage anticipates the well-known speech of Gaunt in *Richard II*, II.1.40–60.

5 For courage mounteth with occasion.
(II.1.82)

The Archduke of Austria's response to news that King John's forces have arrived at Angers means that emergencies promote courage. The notion was proverbial.

6 Fortune shall cull forth
Out of one side her happy minion,
To whom in favour she shall give the day,
And kiss him with a glorious victory.
(II.1.391–4)

The citizens of Angers are refusing to open their gates until the rightful sovereign of England is established. The Bastard spurs the rival monarchs to unite in destroying the town before settling their own differences. His commitment to the powers of Fortune reveals his dynamism and amorality.

7 That smooth-faced gentleman, tickling commodity;
Commodity, the bias of the world.
(II.1.573–4)

'Commodity', here personified as a flattering and deceitful gentleman, means self-interest. The Bastard's observation on the way of the world has been prompted by the bargain struck between King John of England and King Philip of France to marry the former's niece to the latter's son, so settling their differences to the detriment of the claims of Arthur.

8 Well, whiles I am a beggar, I will rail
And say there is no sin but to be rich;
And being rich, my virtue then shall be
To say there is no vice but beggary.
(II.1.593–6)
In the preceding section of the soliloquy the Bastard has shown how the power of 'commodity' or self-interest destabilizes the world by its power to draw all men its way. He acknowledges that he is only railing at 'commodity' because he has not been courted by it, but recognizes in the lines above how it would change his attitudes.

9 A woman, naturally born to fears.
(III.1.14)
Constance is describing her vulnerability as a woman and a widow in the world of power-politics. She has just learned from Salisbury that the King of France has reneged on his promises to support the claims of her son, Arthur, to the English throne. Arthur is the object of her fears.

10 No Italian priest,
Shall tithe or toll in our dominions;
But as we, under God, are supreme head,
So, under Him, that great supremacy
Where we do reign we will alone uphold.
(III.1.153–7)
King John's reply to the demands of the papal legate, Pandulph, is designed to appeal to the Protestantism and patriotism of the Elizabethan audience. Its concepts and phrasing owe more to the history of the Reformation than of the Middle Ages.

11 Old Time the clock-setter, that bald sexton Time.
(III.1.324)
In the Bastard's line, the emblematic figure of Father Time and a homely image of the sexton, the church officer responsible for the clock, are conflated. Philip of France has decided to take up arms against England in accordance with the papal legate's injunction, while King John has just warned him that he will repent the decision within the hour.

12 Bell, book, and candle shall not drive me back
When gold and silver becks me to come on.
(III.3.13–14)

The Bastard has been ordered back to England by King John with the instruction to obtain money from the English church. His statement indicates that not even the threat of excommunication, or religious authority more generally, will overcome his desire for financial gain.

13 Grief fills the room up of my absent child,
Lies in his bed, walks up and down with me,
Puts on his pretty looks, repeats his words,
Remembers me of all his gracious parts,
Stuffs out his vacant garments with his form;
Then have I reason to be fond of grief?
(III.4.93–8)

This is the most powerful image of Constance's lament to the French party following separation from her son Arthur, taken prisoner to England by King John. Grief is personified and occupies the place vacated by her son.

14 Life is as tedious as a twice-told tale,
Vexing the dull ear of a drowsy man,
And bitter shame hath spoiled the sweet world's taste,
That it yields naught but shame and bitterness.
(III.4.108–11)

This reflection of Lewis, the Dauphin, on the bitterness of life is prompted by the defeat of the French party and by Constance's despair.

15 Methinks nobody should be sad but I.
Yet I remember, when I was in France,
Young gentlemen would be as sad as night
Only for wantonness.
(IV.1.13–16)

In his imprisonment in England, Arthur is thinking nostalgically of France and contrasting his real cause for sadness with the courtier-gallant's affectation of melancholy. 'Wantonness' here means affectation. Unbeknown to Arthur, Hubert (the former citizen of Angers, now his jailer) is preparing on King John's instructions to have him blinded with hot irons. In the course of the scene, Arthur's goodness and pathos will persuade Hubert to disobey his master and let the boy live.

16 Ah, none but in this iron age would do it!
(IV.1.60)

Arthur has read King John's instructions to Hubert to put out his eyes with hot irons and has ascertained Hubert's intentions to fulfil them. The phrase 'iron age', meaning cruel and wicked time, alludes to the myth found in Hesiod of the golden age and its subsequent degeneration into the silver age, brass age, and so on. 'Iron age' thus represents an advanced stage of degeneration.

17 Why do you bend such solemn brows on me?
Think you I bear the shears of destiny?
Have I commandment on the pulse of life?
(IV.2.90–2)
King John has just announced to the English nobles the news of Arthur's death, supposedly of a sickness. Salisbury and Pembroke are suspicious of the King's motives and decide to take up Arthur's cause. In reality, Arthur is not dead. John's second line above refers to the Fates who cut the threads of life.

18 It is the curse of kings to be attended
By slaves that take their humours for a warrant
To break within the bloody house of life.
(IV.2.208–10)
King John is seeking to shift the moral responsibility for Arthur's supposed murder from himself to the jailer, Hubert. 'Humours' here are whims. The idea is pursued when John argues that Hubert's willingness to follow villainous instructions begot in him evil designs.

19 Heaven take my soul, and England keep my bones!
(IV.3.10)
Arthur's dying line appeals to both piety and patriotism. He has leapt from the walls of the castle of his imprisonment in an attempt to escape.

20 Whate'er you think, good words, I think, were best.
(IV.3.28)
The Bastard is giving his usual brand of cynical advice to the English nobles, Pembroke, Salisbury, and Bigot, who are indignant at King John's conduct of the realm. The nobles have established contact with an embassy of the Dauphin of France.

21 What, shall they seek the lion in his den,
And fright him there?
(V.1.57–8)
The Bastard is urging King John to take action in defence of his realm against the alliance of the invading French forces and the rebel lords. John, as King of England, would bear the lion on his coat of arms.

22 I do not ask you much –
I beg cold comfort; and you are so strait
And so ingrateful you deny me that.
(V.7.41–3)

These are the words of the dying John to his son, Prince Henry, and the English nobles. The demand for 'cold comfort' is literal, since John is possessed by fever caused by the poison administered at Swinstead Abbey (Shakespeare's error for Swineshead) where the King rested from the battle. 'Strait' signifies mean or niggardly.

23 This England never did, nor never shall,
Lie at the proud foot of a conqueror...
Naught shall make us rue
If England to itself do rest but true!
(V.7.112–13, 117–18)

The concluding lines of the play permit the Bastard to express a patriotic sentiment, despite the deficiencies of the reign of King John. The confidence in England's future, if only she remain true to her traditions, is representative of the patriotism of the post-Armada period.

King Lear

1 Nothing will come of nothing. Speak again.
(I.1.90)

King Lear has divided his kingdom between his three daughters: Gonerill, Regan, and Cordelia. The division is made according to their protestations of love for him. Gonerill and Regan offer fulsome and hypocritical testimonies of their devotion; but Cordelia, Lear's youngest and favourite child, feels unable to enter this public contest of flattery. Consequently, in reply to Lear's demand for her statement, she merely answers 'Nothing', so provoking this response of Lear. He is referring to the Latin tag *ex nihilo nihil fit* and the notion of man's reduction to nothingness will be prominent in the play.

2 LEAR So young, and so untender?
CORDELIA So young, my lord, and true.
LEAR
Let it be so! Thy truth then be thy dower!
(I.1.106–8)

Despite Lear's predilection for Cordelia, her refusal to comply with the terms of the love-test enrages him. Despite her imminent betrothal, he disinherits her and deprives her of the dowry normally essential for marriage. Materially, she is reduced to the 'nothing' she has uttered; but, in reality, Lear has deprived himself of the more valuable asset by banishing truth and good sense from his kingdom. 'Untender' has the sense of inflexible and insensitive.

3 Here I disclaim all my paternal care,
Propinquity and property of blood,
And as a stranger to my heart and me
Hold thee from this for ever. The barbarous Scythian,
Or he that makes his generation messes
To gorge his appetite, shall to my bosom
Be as well neighboured, pitied, and relieved
As thou my sometime daughter.
(I.1.113–20)

The terms of Lear's formal oath, ritually disinheriting Cordelia for her refusal to acknowledge publicly her love for Lear in order to gain a third of the kingdom, prove ironic in that it is Lear who becomes the victim of such conduct at the hands of his other daughters, Gonerill and Regan. The Scythians, a people of central Asia, were a byword for barbarity with the Roman poets, who transmitted this notion to the Renaissance. Here the Scythian is seen devouring his children in an act of gluttony.

4 See better, Lear, and let me still remain
The true blank of thine eye.
(I.1.158–9)

Of the British court, the Earl of Kent is the only member (apart from Cordelia) to offer good and disinterested counsel. Nonetheless, his protest at the insane treatment of Cordelia, who has been disinherited for her failure to participate in Lear's public trial of his daughters' love, results in the banishment of his loyalty, though he later returns to serve Lear in disguise. Here he is replying to Lear's first utterance of banishment from his sight with the request to be allowed to continue to guide Lear's perception. The 'true-blank' is the direct line of sight, for Kent is pursuing a metaphor from archery. True perception, by exercise of the senses, is a major theme of the play.

5 If I want that glib and oily art
To speak and purpose not.
(I.1.224–5)

The King of France and Duke of Burgundy have been at Lear's court as suitors for Cordelia's hand. After disinheriting her, Lear asks Burgundy whether he will accept her without a dowry and receives a negative reply. At this point, Cordelia intervenes to demand that it be made known that her rejection results from her lack of unctuous sycophancy, not from any vicious or unchaste action. The construction 'If for I want' means: if it is because I lack.

6 It is no vicious blot, murder or foulness,
No unchaste action or dishonoured step
That hath deprived me of your grace and favour,
But even for want of that for which I am richer:
A still-soliciting eye and such a tongue
That I am glad I have not, though not to have it
Hath lost me in your liking.
(I.1.227–33)

Cordelia is demanding that Lear make publicly known to her suitors, the Duke of Burgundy and King of France, the reason for his angry disinheritance of her, since he is asking the suitors to accept her without a dowry. Lear has depicted her 'crime' as so unnatural that she is listing what might be of such gravity to merit a parent's total rejection. 'A still-soliciting eye' is one always alert to the main chance.

7 Love's not love
When it is mingled with regards that stands
Aloof from th'entire point.
(I.1.238–40)

The King of France, before he accepts Cordelia for her merit alone, repeats Lear's offer of a dowerless Cordelia to Burgundy, arguing that love which has a regard to material considerations cannot truly be considered love. His action is a contrast to the calculated protestations made by Gonerill and Regan.

8 Fairest Cordelia, that art most rich, being poor,
Most choice, forsaken, and most loved, despised
Thee and thy virtues here I seize upon...
Gods, gods! 'Tis strange that from their cold'st neglect
My love should kindle to inflamed respect.
(I.1.250–5)

These are the words with which the King of France makes the dowerless Cordelia his wife and queen. His act of love and charity contrasts with the sycophancy and calculating greed of Gonerill and Regan.

9 Time shall unfold what plighted cunning hides;
Who covers faults, at last with shame derides.
(I.1.281–2)

Despite disinheritance by Lear, Cordelia has been taken as queen and wife by the King of France, who urges her to take leave of her sisters. In doing so, Cordelia draws attention to the function of time as the revealer of deceit. Her statement proves prophetic of her sisters' evil.

10 'Tis the infirmity of his age. Yet he hath ever but slenderly known himself.
(I.1.292–3)

After the formal court ritual of Lear's division of the kingdom, Gonerill and Regan are left alone. Regan observes how Lear's limited self-awareness results in grosser misjudgements in old age. With her sister, she decides to take advantage of this weakness in her own interest. The analysis of Lear's lack of self-knowledge and his painful struggle to awareness constitutes the central experience of the play.

11 Thou, Nature, art my goddess; to thy law
My services are bound. Wherefore should I
Stand in the plague of custom and permit
The curiosity of nations to deprive me,
For that I am some twelve or fourteen moonshines
Lag of a brother? Why bastard? Wherefore base?
When my dimensions are as well-compact,
My mind as generous, and my shape as true
As honest madam's issue?
(I.2.1–9)

Edmund, the bastard son of the Duke of Gloucester, has a ruthless determination to rise in the world and here he dedicates himself to the power which, he believes, will enable him to do it. 'Nature' is a key word in the play and is conceived in more than one way. Edmund's notion anticipates the Hobbesian view of nature as a condition of pre-civilized man and is akin to Tennyson's nature 'red in tooth and claw'. His viewpoint poses an anarchic threat to the Jacobean concept of a divinely ordained hierarchy in the universe and in human society.

12 Now gods stand up for bastards!
(I.2.22)

This is the concluding line of Edmund's soliloquy of self-consecration to the force of nature. His appeal to the gods to support his programme of ruthless self-assertion is a threat to the Jacobean social and moral order, but Shakespeare's having set the play in pre-Christian Britain renders the standpoint ambiguous.

13 These late eclipses in the sun and moon portend no good to us. Though the wisdom of nature, can reason it thus and thus, yet nature finds itself scourged by the sequent effects: love cools, friendship falls off, brothers divide. In cities, mutinies; in countries, discord; in palaces, treason; and the bond cracked 'twixt son and father. This villain of mine comes under the prediction: there's son against father; the King falls from bias of nature: there's father against child. We have seen the best of our time.
(I.2.103–12)
The superstitious and credulous Duke of Gloucester is reacting to the wickedly false information provided by his bastard son, Edmund, that his legitimate son, Edgar, is plotting against his life. The suggestion fits in with the disorder that Gloucester has observed in the court and so he falls prey to it. Gloucester's fatalistic belief in the power of the stars to determine human destiny reveals an unwillingness to take moral responsibility. 'The wisdom of nature' is science.

14 This is the excellent foppery of the world, that when we are sick in fortune – often the surfeits of our own behaviour – we make guilty of our disasters the sun, the moon, and stars, as if we were villains on necessity, fools by heavenly compulsion, knaves, thieves, and treachers by spherical predominance, drunkards, liars, and adulterers by an enforced obedience of planetary influence; and all that we are evil in by a divine thrusting-on. An admirable evasion of whoremaster man, to lay his goatish disposition to the charge of a star. My father compounded with my mother under the Dragon's tail, and my nativity was under Ursa Major, so that it follows I am rough and lecherous. Fut! I should have been that I am had the maidenliest star in the firmament twinkled on my bastardizing.
(I.2.118–32)
This is the sceptical response of Edmund, the bastard son, to Gloucester's belief in astrology. Although his argument is superficially attractive to the modern mind, ultimately it only swaps one form of determinism for another, since Edmund, too, refuses to exercise moral control and merely gives free rein to the natural man. 'Spherical predominance' is the influence of a planet in the ascendant. A 'goatish disposition' was a lecherous one, as the phrase 'whoremaster man' suggests. The 'Dragon's tail' was an astrological term for an intersection of the moon's orbit with the

line of the sun. 'Ursa Major' is, of course, the Great Bear. Edmund's horoscope is dominated by Mars and Venus and characterizes him as violent and lecherous, as the action of the play confirms.

15 Pat he comes, like the catastrophe of the old comedy. My cue is villainous melancholy.
(I.2.133–4)
Edmund is speaking first of his brother Edgar and then of himself in terms of conventional theatrical roles. In fact, both their roles in the play blend elements of comedy and tragedy, though in different ways.

16 KENT You have that in your countenance which I would fain call master.
LEAR What's that?
KENT Authority.
(I.4.27–30)
Kent, having been banished by Lear, is now in disguise seeking to ingratiate himself into Lear's service in order to protect his master from the troubles he foresees ahead. Kent's term 'authority' is a reminder of Lear's place and responsibility in the kingdom, which Gonerill and Regan are to contest.

17 LEAR Dost thou call me fool, boy?
FOOL All thy other titles thou hast given away; that thou wast born with.
(I.4.146–8)
The Fool's curious language, made up of maxims, proverbial sayings, rhymes, and songs, serves the purpose of pointing Lear to the truth and to a realization of the error he has committed in banishing Cordelia and placing himself at the mercy of his other daughters. Through a rhyme, he has just promised to teach Lear the difference between a sweet and bitter fool, which he concludes by pointing at Lear. The suggestion is that not only is Lear a born fool, but that folly is part of the human condition.

18 Thou hadst little wit in thy bald crown when thou gavest thy golden one away.
(I.4.160–1)
The Fool makes this blunt statement of the truth to Lear in developing a riddle about the exchange of two crowns for an egg. The Fool's strategy of mercilessly confronting Lear with his error and folly helps promote Lear's conflict with Gonerill later in this scene.

19 I marvel what kin thou and thy daughters are. They'll have me whipped for speaking true; thou'lt have me whipped for lying; and sometimes I am whipped for holding my peace.
(I.4.178–81)
The Fool (or Jester) was a licensed figure, permitted to make observations and to defy authority in a manner forbidden to other members of the court. Shakespeare has used this social convention to great theatrical effect in *King Lear.* Nonetheless, the Fool points out the limitations imposed in an autocratic society upon even this traditional outlet of criticism.

20 Ingratitude, thou marble-hearted fiend,
More hideous when thou showest thee in a child
Than the sea-monster!
(I.4.256–8)
Lear is berating Gonerill for filial ingratitude. Gonerill has provoked a quarrel concerning the conduct of Lear's retinue (although it is only fair to observe that the terms of kingship Lear had sought to reserve to himself were authority without responsibility). Lear cannot, in effect, tolerate any check to his egotism. The sea-monster referred to could merely be generic; or, it might be a reference to the sea-monster of Seneca's *Phaedra* (available in a 1581 translation), since it destroyed Hippolytus on the power of a curse of filial ingratitude.

21 Hear, Nature, hear! Dear goddess, hear!
Suspend thy purpose, if thou didst intend
To make this creature fruitful.
Into her womb convey sterility,
Dry up in her the organs of increase,
And from her derogate body never spring
A babe to honour her.
(I.4.272–8)
Like Edmund, Lear also invokes nature as a destructive power. His terrible curse is uttered against Gonerill for her criticism of the conduct of Lear's retinue of knights. Lear's curse is essentially a repudiation of the positive forces of nature operative in human society through the procreative function of woman. 'Derogate' means dishonoured or degraded, and is used of Gonerill in contrast to the function of children to honour parents according to the Fourth Commandment.

22 If she must teem,
Create her child of spleen, that it may live
And be a thwart disnatured torment to her.
Let it stamp wrinkles in her brow of youth,

With cadent tears fret channels in her cheeks,
Turn all her mother's pains and benefits
To laughter and contempt, that she may feel
How sharper than a serpent's tooth it is
To have a thankless child!
(I.4.278–86)

Lear is cursing Gonerill for her filial ingratitude. He has uttered a chilling invocation to nature to render Gonerill sterile. This continuation of the curse argues that, if she must breed, her child should prove to be a torment to her. 'Teem' means breed or 'thwart disnatured' signifies unnatural and perverse. 'Cadent' tears are falling tears which cut ('fret') channels in the cheeks.

23 O let me not be mad, not mad, sweet heaven!
Keep me in temper; I would not be mad!
(I.5.43–4)

Lear has left Gonerill's palace in high rage – with the intention of seeking refuge with Regan. In this short scene, the Fool makes Lear face the unpalatable truth that he has committed a gross wrong to Cordelia and a gross error in giving power to the ungrateful Gonerill and Regan. The Fool has just told Lear bluntly that he should not have grown old before he had been wise. The insoluble conflict of emotions in Lear's consciousness prompts his first anticipation of madness.

24 Such smiling rogues as these,
Like rats, oft bite the holy cords atwain,
Which are t'intrinse t'unloose.
(II.2.71–3)

Kent, in disguise as Lear's servant, is speaking to the Earl of Cornwall (Regan's husband) of Oswald, Gonerill's messenger. Kent and Oswald have arrived at the same time at Gloucester's palace and have fallen into dispute. Cornwall has asked Kent for an explanation of his anger and Kent is indicating that it lies within the nature and function of sycophants such as Oswald. The 'holy cords' are the bonds of amity which bind together a Christian society.

25 Goose, if I had you upon Sarum Plain,
I'd drive ye cackling home to Camelot.
(II.2.81–2)

This contemptuous expression of Kent is directed at Oswald, the sycophantic messenger of Gonerill. It is difficult to explicate; but it originates in the idea that Oswald's giddy loquaciousness is comparable to the behaviour and sound of a goose, which he wishes to put to noisy flight. 'Sarum Plain' is Salisbury Plain, and it is true that in the Elizabethan period Arthur's Camelot was identified by some with nearby Winchester; but, why these places should occur to Kent at this moment is not clear.

26 Nothing almost sees miracles
But misery.
(II.2.163–4)
For insolence to Gonerill's messenger, Oswald, Kent (disguised as a serving man of Lear) is enduring the punishment of the stocks inflicted on him by Cornwall and Regan. Left alone, Kent decides to read a letter he has received from Cordelia, which promises redress of the wrongs perpetrated in Britain. Kent's proverbial saying suggests that those in the most miserable situations are best placed to apprehend miracles.

27 Fortune, good night; smile once more; turn thy wheel.
(II.2.171)
Kent has been placed in the stocks before Gloucester's palace at the instructions of the Earl of Cornwall and Regan for his insolence towards them and towards Oswald, Gonerill's messenger. He has just read the letter from Cordelia promising redress of the situation in Britain. He decides to sleep, cheered by this prospect of a change for the better. Fortune's wheel was an emblematic representation of the force of circumstance: after reaching its lowest point, the wheel was bound to rise. Tragedy conventionally dealt with the fall of fortune's wheel.

28 Edgar I nothing am.
(II.3.21)
Edgar has been proclaimed an outlaw by his father, Gloucester, who has been tricked by his bastard son, Edmund, into believing that Edgar was plotting to murder him and seize his inheritance. In a desperate attempt to escape detection and survive, Edgar resolves to adopt the naked and filthy disguise of a lunatic beggar. In being declared an outlaw of society, he has in effect been stripped of his identity and so adopts the most basic form of human existence. His role becomes a symbol of reduction to basic human needs, an image of nothingness.

29 Nature in you stands on the very verge
Of his confine.
(II.4.142–3)
Regan is addressing Lear, her father, before Gloucester's palace. Lear is seeking from her redress and consolation for the wrongs inflicted on him by Gonerill, but Regan is replying in much the

same terms as her sister. She is drawing attention to Lear's age (he confesses later in the play to being over eighty) and by implication to his lack of judgement.

30 All's not offence that indiscretion finds
And dotage terms so.
(II.4.191–2)
The lines are Gonerill's response to Lear's implicit accusation of an offence when he is shocked that Regan should welcome her so warmly. The family is assembled at Gloucester's palace, where Lear is affronted to find his servant (the disguised Kent) in the stocks. The two sisters repeatedly attack Lear's age and lack of judgement: 'indiscretion' means want of judgement.

31 But yet thou art my flesh, my blood, my daughter –
Or rather a disease that's in my flesh,
Which I must needs call mine. Thou art a boil,
A plague-sore, or embossed carbuncle,
In my corrupted blood.
(II.4.216–20)
Lear has just stated that he never wishes to see Gonerill again, because she refuses to accommodate him on his terms. He finds himself torn beteen paternal responsibility and a hatred intensified by the paternal bond. Lear's recognition that Gonerill is part of himself is telling in many ways. The inner battle within Lear's consciousness that results in madness embraces conflicts of character externalized in the narrative of the daughters. The image applied to Gonerill forms part of a pattern of disease imagery in the play: 'embossed' means swollen.

32 O, reason not the need! Our basest beggars
Are in the poorest thing superfluous.
Allow not nature more than nature needs –
Man's life is cheap as beast's.
(II.4.259–62)
Gonerill and Regan have been badgering Lear into reducing his retinue of knights, until Regan finally demands to know what need he has of a single retainer. Lear's response is that comfort and civilized society are constituted of more than basic human needs. His inability to resolve this conflict of wills results in his madness and in his being driven onto the heath in the storm to suffer a life as 'cheap as beast's'.

33 But for true need –
You heavens, give me that patience, patience I need!
You see me here, you gods, a poor old man,

As full of grief as age, wretched in both.
(II.4.265–8)

Gonerill and Regan have been brow-beating Lear into the reduction, even abolition, of his retinue. Their frustration of Lear's will and their curtailment of the trappings of royalty, to which he has been accustomed, provoke in Lear not only anger, but also a questioning of his true needs. At this moment, patience is the foremost of his needs.

34 Touch me with noble anger,
And let not women's weapons, water drops,
Stain my man's cheeks. No, you unnatural hags,
I will have such revenges on you both
That all the world shall – I will do such things –
What they are yet I know not; but they shall be
The terrors of the earth.
(II.4.271–7)

Gonerill and Regan have been insisting that Lear has no need of a retinue. The frustration of Lear's will by his daughters provokes an insoluble crisis in Lear's identity. Stripped of the authority which would permit him to vent his rage, the only releases for his anger are tears or madness. Immediately after this speech and as the storm approaches, Lear leaves Gloucester's palace for the heath with his faithful followers, the Fool and the disguised Kent.

35 Contending with the fretful elements:
Bids the wind blow the earth into the sea,
Or swell the curlèd waters 'bove the main,
That things might change or cease; tears his white hair,
Which the impetuous blasts with eyeless rage
Catch in their fury and make nothing of;
Strives in his little world of man to out-storm
The to-and-fro conflicting wind and rain.
(III.1.4–11)

This is the description of Lear in the storm on the heath given by the gentleman to Kent. Given the resources of the Jacobean theatre, Shakespeare had to create the impact of the storm largely through the poetry. His use of pathetic fallacy, by which the physical storm parallels that in Lear's mind, means that the description serves a double function. In fact, the 'little world of man' refers to the classically-derived Renaissance concept of the microcosm and its analogy to the macrocosm, the phenomenal world. Lear is seen as both victim and agent of the storm, since in his fury he wills the angry weather ('fretful elements') to create the state of chaos which existed at the Creation, before the separation of the land from the waters.

36 Blow, winds and crack your cheeks! Rage! Blow!
You cataracts and hurricanoes, spout
Till you have drenched our steeples, drowned the cocks!
You sulphurous and thought-executing fires,
Vaunt-curriers of oak-cleaving thunderbolts,
Singe my white head! And thou all-shaking thunder,
Strike flat the thick rotundity o'the world,
Crack Nature's moulds, all germens spill at once
That makes ingrateful man!
(III.2.1–9)

Lear and the Fool are now exposed to the full violence of the storm in the hostile environment of the heath, the doors of Gloucester's palace having been barred against them at the instructions of Lear's daughters. The language in which Lear urges on the storm to still greater violence not only creates the storm, in the Jacobean theatre's absence of many other theatrical resources, but displays the conflict of passions within Lear's mind. Lear is willing a second flood or a return to the primeval state of chaos which existed at Creation before the separation of land and water. Significantly, this was before the creation of man, since Lear's misanthropy desires the destruction of mankind. 'Hurricanoes' are water-spouts; 'cocks' refer to weathercocks on the tops of steeples; 'germens' are the seeds by which species are propagated. Lines 5–6 refer to the lightning which presages thunder.

37 Rumble thy bellyful! Spit, fire! Spout, rain!
Nor rain, wind, thunder, fire are my daughters.
I tax not you, you elements, with unkindness;
I never gave you kingdom, called you children.
You owe me no subscription; then let fall
Your horrible pleasure. Here I stand, your slave,
A poor, infirm, weak, and despised old man.
(III.2.15–20)

Lear, with the Fool, is exposed to the violence of the storm on the heath, having had the doors of Gloucester's palace barred against him by Gonerill and Regan. Despite the violence of the storm and his bodily suffering, Lear feels this less keenly than the torment of his mind at his daughters' filial ingratitude. He begins to see himself simply as a man, rather than a king.

38 Let the great gods
That keep this dreadful pudder o'er our heads
Find out their enemies now.
(III.2.49–51)

Lear is speaking to Kent, who is disguised as a serving-man. They are caught in the storm on the heath near Gloucester's palace, which Lear left in fury at Gonerill and Regan's demands that he dismiss his retinue and live on their terms. Lear sees the storm as a form of divine retribution and, since he suffered its violence, implicitly acknowledges guilt here. 'Pudder' is a variant of pother, meaning noise or hubbub.

39 Close pent-up guilts,
Rive your concealing continents, and cry
These dreadful summoners grace. I am a man
More sinned against than sinning.
(III.2.57–60)

Lear, on the heath, sees the storm as an act of divine retribution punishing secret offenders. Here he urges hidden guilts to break out from their hiding places in order to beg mercy of the elements which represent divine justice. Although Kent (in disguise) and the Fool are present, Lear's utterances are not so much means of communication as the release of inner promptings. Despite the concluding lines of self-justification, the statement applies as much to Lear as to others.

40 The art of our necessities is strange
And can make vile things precious.
(III.2.70–1)

Lear's physical and psychological suffering in the storm on the heath promotes a re-evaluation of himself and of human needs. He is being directed by Kent (in disguise) to a hovel for shelter. Aware of his physical suffering and his incipient madness, Lear gratefully accepts shelter which as a king he would have despised. In showing consideration for the sufferings of the Fool, Lear shows compassion for another for the first time.

41 When the mind's free
The body's delicate; this tempest in my mind
Doth from my senses take all feeling else
Save what beats there. – Filial ingratitude!
(III.4.11–14)

Lear is speaking to Kent (in disguise) before the hovel on the heath, having left and subsequently been barred from Gloucester's palace. The physical storm, to which Lear has been exposed, parallels that in his mind; and here Lear acknowledges that, when the mind is so tormented, the body is no longer conscious of pain. The source of his emotional suffering is the ingratitude shown by Gonerill and Regan, between whom he has divided the kingdom.

42 Poor naked wretches, wheresoe'er you are,
That bide the pelting of this pitiless storm,
How shall your houseless heads and unfed sides,
Your looped and windowed raggedness, defend you
From seasons such as these?
(III.4.28–32)

Lear's physical and mental suffering on the heath has prompted within him compassion for the poor and homeless, whose lives are subject to deprivation. His egotism is checked and his first act of compassion is to allow the Fool to enter the hovel before him, while he prays for the poor. 'Looped and windowed raggedness' is a vivid image of the tattered rags of the poor, perhaps prompted by 'houseless'.

43 O, I have ta'en
Too little care of this! Take physic, pomp;
Expose thyself to feel what wretches feel,
That thou mayst shake the superflux to them
And show the heavens more just.
(III.4.32–6)

After praying for the poor and homeless before the hovel on the heath, Lear acknowledges the application of his new perception of suffering to his former attitudes and administration. 'Pomp' is a personification of the pompous man in authority, which Lear himself was. Authority's attitude is conceived of as a social disease which can only be cured if the surfeit of the rich is removed in order to provide a more just and equitable distribution.

44 LEAR
Judicious punishment! 'Twas this flesh begot
Those pelican daughters.
EDGAR
Pillicock sat on Pillicock Hill.
Alow, alow, loo, loo!
FOOL This cold night will turn us all to fools and madmen.
(III.4.71–6)

When the Fool enters the hovel on the heath, he encounters Edgar in the guise of a mad beggar and is terrified by the apparition. In his madness, Lear identifies with this vision of man reduced to his naked and most basic form. He believes the man must have been so reduced by giving away his goods to his daughters. According to medieval bestiaries, pelicans killed their fathers. Edgar, feigning madness, puns on pelican to produce 'pillicock', a term for the penis, and in an obscene quibble pursues the notion of sexuality and procreation as a source of evil. The

Fool draws attention to the strange conclave they constitute: a professional fool, one feigning insane beggary, and a mad king.

45 A servingman, proud in heart and mind, that curled my hair, wore gloves in my cap, served the lust of my mistress' heart and did the act of darkness with her, swore as many oaths as I spake words and broke them in the sweet face of heaven; one that slept in the contriving of lust and waked to do it.
(III.4.82–7)
In his insanity, Lear is fascinated by the figure of Poor Tom, the mad beggar (Edgar's disguise to evade arrest as an outlaw). Lear sees Poor Tom, because of his madness and destitution, as an *alter ego* and enquires of him his identity. Edgar creates in response an image of a fashionable servant and lover whose whole life is dominated by lust. Curled hair for men was fashionable in the Jacobean period, while lovers wore the gloves of their beloved in their caps as love-tokens. The 'act of darkness' is the sexual act.

46 Keep thy foot out of brothels, thy hand out of plackets, thy pen from lenders' books, and defy the foul fiend.
(III.4.92–4)
Edgar, in the role of the possessed beggar, Poor Tom, is addressing Lear and the Fool on the heath. They have discovered him sheltering in the hovel and he has just given a fictitious account of his former self as a lust-crazed servant. The moral advice given here is determined by the role he is playing. 'Plackets' were openings in petticoats and the sins castigated here were, presumably, common weaknesses of young servingmen of the period.

47 Is man no more than this? Consider him well. Thou owest the worm no silk, the beast no hide, the sheep no wool, the cat no perfume. Ha! Here's three on's are sophisticated. Thou art the thing itself! Unaccommodated man is no more but such a poor, bare, forked animal as thou art. Off, off, you lendings!
(III.4.99–105)
Lear meets the mad beggar, Poor Tom (the disguise of Edgar in order to escape detection as a fugitive from justice). Their encounter takes place at the hovel on the heath, for both have fled Gloucester's palace. In his madness, Lear perceives in this adopted figure of Edgar basic humanity and true human need. 'Unaccommodated' covers both homeless and unclothed, while 'forked' is suggested by the naked human form. Clothes are referred to as 'lendings', things borrowed and not part of essential humanity, when Lear wishes to identify with Poor Tom by stripping himself naked.

48 The prince of darkness is a gentleman; Modo he's called and Mahu.
(III.4.136–7)
Gloucester has sought out the King on the heath in order to offer some assistance, contrary to Gonerill and Regan's wishes. Poor Tom's statement is prompted by Gloucester's adverse comment upon the company in which he finds Lear, the Fool and a mad beggar. Poor Tom is the disguise of Edgar, Gloucester's wrongly outlawed son. According to contemporary demonology, Modo and Mahu were leaders of devils, but the reference to 'gentleman' may also contain a social criticism.

49 Poor Tom's a-cold.
(III.4.140)
Poor Tom, the mad beggar, is the identity that Edgar has adopted to evade arrest as an outlaw. His pathetic cry is a reminder of the physical sufferings of those on the heath and of the poor in general.

50 I will keep still with my philosopher.
(III.4.170)
In his madness, Lear perceives a wisdom in Poor Tom's basic humanity and dubs him a 'philosopher'. Poor Tom, the naked, mad beggar, is in fact Edgar, Gloucester's legitimate son, disguised to evade arrest as an outlaw. When Gloucester and Kent offer assistance to Lear on the heath, he refuses to be separated from Tom.

51 Child Roland to the dark tower came;
His word was still 'Fie, foh, and fum,
I smell the blood of a British man.'
(III.4.176–8)
Edgar, as the mad beggar Poor Tom, utters a nonsense rhyme. It conflates a reference to a romance involving Roland, one of the knights of Charlemagne, with an allusion to the fairy-tale giant of Jack and the Beanstalk. It suggests irrational violence and fear. The first line provided the inspiration for the famous poem of Robert Browning, 'Childe Roland to the Dark Tower Came' (1855).

52 He's mad that trusts in the tameness of a wolf, a horse's health, a boy's love, or a whore's oath.
(III.6.18–19)
Lear is on the heath in the company of the Fool and Poor Tom (the assumed role of Edgar). In his madness, he is obsessed with ideas of justice and revenge, and he is about to institute a 'trial'

of Gonerill and Regan over which the three 'madmen' will preside. The Fool, as these lines indicate, continues to point out the irreversible laws of nature and the gross error of judgement that Lear has committed. Horses were obviously considered particularly subject to disease.

53 The little dogs and all –
Trey, Blanch and Sweetheart – see, they bark at me.
(III.6.61–2)
Lear, in his madness on the heath, has instituted an insane trial of Gonerill with himself, the Fool, and Poor Tom as judges. In this pathetic line, which does so much to convey Lear's total insanity by this stage, he envisages the lap-dogs, presumably of Gonerill, who defend their mistress against his attack. Despite the setting in primitive pre-Christian Britain, there are many touches which suggest a lavish Jacobean court.

54 Then let them anatomize Regan, see what breeds about her heart. Is there any cause in nature that makes these hard hearts?
(III.6.75–7)
Lear, now totally insane, moves from the idea of trying Gonerill for crimes against her father to dissecting Regan in order to discover the cause of such filial ingratitude. The phrase 'hard hearts' is taken from a theological context, where absence of grace is the cause, but here a physiological explanation is sought.

55 LEAR We'll go to supper i'the morning.
FOOL And I'll go to bed at noon.
(III.6.82–3)
Exhausted by his mad visions, Lear is persuaded by Kent (still disguised as the serving-man) to rest. The King, presumably remembering that he has not eaten, appears to be saying no more than supper can be postponed until the morning. The Fool, however, plays upon the phrase to suggest the insanity of the world they inhabit. These are the last words in the play of the Fool, who appears physically destroyed by his sufferings on the heath. Some critics have found in the line a suggestion of premature death. Others, insisting on the doubling of the Fool's role with Cordelia's, have argued that his disappearance is necessary for practical reasons.

56 When we our betters see bearing out woes,
We scarcely think our miseries our foes...
How light and portable my pain seems now,

When that which makes me bend makes the King bow.
(III.6.100–7)
Edgar, in his disguise as Poor Tom, has become witness to Lear's sufferings, which are akin to his own. In the second part of the play, he provides a stoic commentary upon his own, his father's, and the King's miseries. Here he is suggesting that the observation of prominent people suffering similar tribulations to our own relieves our sense of pain and grief.

57 I am tied to the stake, and I must stand the course.
(III.7.53)
On the information of Edmund, Gloucester has been arrested by Regan and her husband, the Duke of Cornwall, and is being interrogated about the King's whereabouts and the landing of French troops. Gloucester, previously so fatalistically convinced that the stars control human destiny, here makes a moral stand. The image he uses is taken from the popular blood-sport of bear-baiting, where a bear tied to a stake was attacked and tormented by dogs.

58 Because I would not see thy cruel nails
Pluck out his poor old eyes; nor thy fierce sister
In his anointed flesh rash boarish fangs.
(III.7.55–7)
This is Gloucester's defiant response to Regan's demand to know why he has sent the King to Dover, where Cordelia's army has landed. Regrettably, Gloucester's hypothetical image of cruelty, the plucking out of eyes, comes to be practised upon Gloucester himself. The sisters, Gonerill and Regan, are increasingly described in brutal, animal images.

59 CORNWALL
Out, vile jelly!
Where is thy lustre now?
GLOUCESTER
All dark and comfortless.
(III.7.82–4)
The putting-out of Gloucester's eyes is one of the most violent and barbaric acts in Jacobean tragedy. The sadism of Cornwall's repeated act is reinforced by the contemptuous terms in which he refers to the precious gift of sight. Gloucester, in his search for comfort, asks for his son Edmund, only to discover that he has been responsible for his arrest, and therefore indirectly for his mutilation.

60 Yet better thus, and known to be contemned,
Than still contemned and flattered. To be worst,
The lowest and most dejected thing of fortune,
Stands still in esperance, lives not in fear.
The lamentable change is from the best;
The worst returns to laughter.
(IV.1.1–6)

Edgar is using his reduction to the naked poverty of Poor Tom to re-evaluate human experience. His argument relates to the fall and rise of Fortune's wheel; for he is suggesting that to be in an abject condition has the consolation that any change must be for the better. Immediately after this soliloquy, he encounters his blinded father. This meeting undermines his philosophy, by reducing him to a deeper level of misery, but strengthens his resolve to endure and survive.

61 I have no way and therefore want no eyes;
I stumbled when I saw.
(IV.1.18–19)

These are the blinded Gloucester's words to his guide. They demonstrate clearly the way that the imagery of sight and blindness functions in the play to convey more general notions of perception. When Gloucester had his sight, he misjudged between Edgar and Edmund. Now, without his sight and believing he has lost Edgar irrevocably, he has no direction in life. Unbeknown to him, Edgar is in his presence and is to take on the role of his guide and mentor.

62 Might I but live to see thee in my touch
I'd say I had eyes again.
(IV.1.23–4)

The blinded Gloucester is speaking of the son he has wronged, Edgar. 'To see thee in my touch' exploits synaesthesia, the blending of sense experience, to convey the intensity of Gloucester's desire to be re-united with his legitimate son. Unbeknown to Gloucester, Edgar – in his disguise of Poor Tom – is a witness to this pitiful spectacle of his father.

63 Who is't can say 'I am at the worst'?
I am worse than e'er I was.
(IV.1.25–6)

Edgar's statement is a refutation of the position that he adopted at the beginning of the scene (see 60 above). The narrative of *King Lear* repeatedly takes characters (and spectators) to greater pitches of suffering than they imagined possible. Edgar's comment results from his observation – in the guise of Poor Tom – of his father's blindness and suffering.

64 As flies to wanton boys are we to the gods;
They kill us for their sport.
(IV.1.36–7)
Gloucester, from having held a deterministic view of man's destiny, has come to a belief that the gods' attitude to human suffering is negligent and arbitrary. The treatment meted out by the gods to mankind is likened to the sadistic pleasure boys take in toying with and killing flies. The blinded Gloucester is being observed by his son Edgar in his disguise as the bedlam beggar, a figure who, Gloucester has just remarked to his guide, brought his son into his mind.

65 'Tis the time's plague when madmen lead the blind.
(IV.1.46)
The blinded Gloucester has decided to take as his guide the mad beggar, Poor Tom, without knowing that it is his son Edgar in disguise. The notion of the blind led by the mad seems to him an appropriate image of the inverted values of the age. *King Lear* is full of visual and verbal images of a world turned upside-down.

66 That nature which contemns its origin
Cannot be bordered certain in itself.
She that herself will sliver and disbranch
From her material sap perforce must wither
And come to deadly use.
(IV.2.32–6)
The Duke of Albany unexpectedly takes a moral stand against the actions of his wife, Gonerill, who is planning to add adultery with Edmund to the violence shown to her father. Albany's image is drawn from botany: 'sliver and disbranch' means cut herself off or tear herself away from and the 'material sap' is that which gives physical (and moral) life. 'Cannot be bordered certain in itself' means that such a nature cannot be trusted of lack of restraint.

67 Wisdom and goodness to the vile seem vile;
Filths savour but themselves.
(IV.2.38–9)
The Duke of Albany is repudiating the totally perverted values of his wife, Gonerill. He is arguing that to the vile filth is attractive, while virtue appears repugnant.

68 If that the heavens do not their visible spirits
Send quickly down to tame these vile offences,

It will come –
Humanity must perforce prey on itself
Like monsters of the deep.
(IV.2.46–50)
The Duke of Albany is denouncing the immorality of his wife, Gonerill. The two elements of his argument are: first, that the wickedness of Gonerill and her accomplices should provoke divine retribution; and second, that even without such intervention the logic of evil is self-destructive. The evil will destroy one another, as sea-monsters devour one another. This argument is fulfilled in the play when Gonerill, Regan, and Edmund are destroyed by their own lust and violence.

69 This shows you are above,
You justicers, that these our nether crimes
So speedily can venge!
(IV.2.78–80)
The Duke of Albany has just been informed by a messenger that the Duke of Cornwall has been killed by a servant as he was about to gouge out the second eye of Gloucester. To Albany, the news of Cornwall's death while engaged on such a sadistic act appears confirmation that the gods will intervene to assert divine justice. Whether the play as a whole sustains or negates this contention is a much-debated critical issue. The gods are conceived as divine judges looking down upon the crimes of the 'nether' (lower) world.

70 Patience and sorrow strove
Who should express her goodliest.
(IV.3.16–17)
The Gentleman's description to Kent of Cordelia's reactions to the news of her father's sufferings depicts her as an ideal balance of feeling and self-control. Her grief and her control contend for possession of her expression, each one outdoing the other in beauty. Cordelia has landed with a French army at Dover in an attempt to restore her father's fortunes.

71 It is the stars,
The stars above us govern our conditions.
(IV.3.32–3)
The reasoning behind Kent's statement to the Gentleman lies in the difference of character between Cordelia and her sisters, which appears to deny any sense of heredity. It must therefore be the moment of birth that determines temperament. Astrology was a Renaissance preoccupation, though Shakespeare may also

be exploiting the belief to give the play a pre-Christian atmosphere.

72 Alack, 'tis he! Why, he was met even now
As mad as the vexed sea, singing aloud,
Crowned with rank fumiter and furrow-weeds,
With hardokes, hemlock, nettles, cuckoo-flowers,
Darnel, and all the idle weeds that grow
In our sustaining corn.
(IV.4.1–6)

In Cordelia's description of her father, King Lear, two concepts of nature are evident: a benign and fertile aspect which produces the 'sustaining corn', and a wild, uncontrollable element which produces the weeds and the violence of the sea that serves as an image of Lear's madness. The herbs referred to are bitter ones, symbolizing remorse and mortification.

73 All blest secrets,
All you unpublished virtues of the earth,
Spring with my tears! Be aidant and remediate
In the good man's distress.
(IV.4.15–18)

Cordelia is discussing with the Doctor the means of restoring Lear to his senses. Her prayer conceives nature as a secret storehouse of materials designed for man's sustenance. 'Virtues' has the sense of powers. Cordelia's tears have connotations of fruitfulness and grace. 'Aidant and remediate' are unusual forms, meaning helpful and remedying.

74 How fearful
And dizzy 'tis to cast one's eyes so low!
The crows and choughs that wind the midway air
Show scarce so gross as beetles. Halfway down
Hangs one that gathers sampire – dreadful trade!
Methinks he seems no bigger than his head.
The fishermen that walk upon the beach
Appear like mice, and yon tall anchoring bark
Diminished to her cock; her cock, a buoy
Almost too small for sight. The murmuring surge
That on th'unnumbered idle pebble chafes
Cannot be heard so high.
(IV.6.11–22)

Edgar, now in the disguise of a peasant, is describing to his father, the blinded Gloucester, an imaginary Dover cliff. Gloucester wishes to be brought to the cliff edge in order to commit suicide; but his loving son is ensuring his preservation, physical and spiritual. The passage is a masterpiece of verbal perspective, capturing the vertiginous sense of peering over a cliff. 'Choughs' are a species of crow; 'sampire' or samphire is a rock herb used for pickling; and the bark's 'cock' is its cock-boat or dinghy.

75 Is wretchedness deprived that benefit
To end itself by death? 'Twas yet some comfort
When misery could beguile the tyrant's rage
And frustrate his proud will.
(IV.6.61–4)

Gloucester, in his blindness, believes that he has hurled himself from the top of Dover cliff in a suicide attempt. In fact, his son Edgar (disguised as a peasant) has deceived him into thinking flat ground the cliff, and has so preserved him. Adopting the role of another peasant, Edgar pretends to have seen Gloucester fall and to have found him at the foot of the cliff. Initially, Gloucester resents the incapacity to determine his end by suicide, the traditional escape from oppression – especially for the Roman stoics.

76 EDGAR
Therefore, thou happy father,
Think that the clearest gods, who make them honours
Of men's impossibilities, have preserved thee.
GLOUCESTER
I do remember now. Henceforth I'll bear
Affliction till it do cry out itself
'Enough, enough', and die.
(IV.6.72–7)

Gloucester, following his blinding by Cornwall, believes that he has thrown himself from the top of Dover cliff in a suicide attempt. In reality, he has been deceived by his son Edgar, who is disguised as a peasant, into merely casting himself headlong on the ground. Edgar, assuming the persona of another peasant, pretends to have discovered him at the foot of the cliff and inculcates in his father a sense of miraculous preservation. Edgar's presentation of the gods as pure and honoured by men for performing impossible tasks removes Gloucester's desperate urge to self-destruction. 'Father' simply means old man.

77 LEAR
They told me I was everything. 'Tis a lie: I am not ague-proof.
GLOUCESTER
The trick of that voice I do well remember.
Is't not the King?

LEAR Ay, every inch a king.
(IV.6.104–7)

Gloucester, though blind, recognizes King Lear by his voice, despite the madness of his utterances. The reason within Lear's madness lies in the distinction he is making between the sycophantic image of kingship and the reality of his humanity. The 'trick' of the voice is a quality of voice or a speech mannerism.

78 Die for adultery? No.
The wren goes to't, and the small gilded fly
Does lecher in my sight.
Let copulation thrive.
(IV.6.111–14)

When Gloucester recognizes the King by his voice, he instinctively kneels to him. In his insanity, Lear takes this as an acknowledgement of guilt and assumes the cause to be an illicit sexual relationship. In his mind, two ideas are confused: a vision of the world dominated by rampant sexuality and a false conviction that bastards prove kinder than legitimate children. The latter belief is based on the false conviction that Edmund has been loyal to Gloucester.

79 The fitchew nor the soilèd horse goes to't
With a more riotous appetite.
Down from the waist they are centaurs,
Though women all above;
But to the girdle do the gods inherit,
Beneath is all the fiends –
There's hell, there's darkness, there is the sulphurous pit – burning, scalding, stench, consumption! Fie, fie, fie! Pah, pah! Give me an ounce of civet; good apothecary, sweeten my imagination.
(IV.6.122–31)

Lear's mad outpouring has been prompted by his taking Gloucester for an adulterer. Lear's sufferings at the hands of his daughters, Gonerill and Regan have created in Lear's diseased imagination a loathing of female sexuality. A 'fitchew' is a weasel and a term for a prostitute, while a 'soilèd horse' is one fed on fresh grass and therefore full of (sexual) vigour. Centaurs were creatures of Greek mythology, men above the waist and horses below. They traditionally symbolized man's animal instincts. When Lear's disgust at female sexuality moves from animal to diabolic imagery, his expression breaks down into prose. 'Civet' was used as a perfume.

80 GLOUCESTER O, let me kiss that hand!
LEAR Let me wipe it first; it smells of mortality.
GLOUCESTER
O ruined piece of nature! This great world
Shall so wear out to naught.
(IV.6.133–6)
Gloucester, blinded by Cornwall, wishes to perform an act of obeisance to his sovereign, Lear. The King, on the other hand, is obsessed in his madness with his fallen humanity. Gloucester perceives in the mad King, who as man represents the perfection of Creation, and as king the apex of the social pyramid, the ruinous collapse of the microcosm (or little world of man) which presages the destruction of the macrocosm (the universe).

81 A man may see how this world goes with no eyes. Look with thine ears. See how yon justice rails upon yon simple thief. Hark in thine ear – change places and, handy-dandy, which is the justice, which is the thief?
(IV.6.151–5)
This passage is often taken to epitomize the total inversion of values found in the world of this play. The blinded Gloucester has told the mad Lear that he sees how the world goes 'feelingly', which means both keenly and imperfectly (because by touch alone). Responding to the second interpretation, the reason in Lear's madness retorts that all (sense) experience of this world points to the same conclusion: that the social and moral distinctions made by the world are hypocritical and invalid.

82 Thou rascal beadle, hold thy bloody hand.
Why dost thou lash that whore? Strip thy own back.
Thou hotly lusts to use her in that kind
For which thou whipp'st her.
(IV.6.161–4)
In his madness, Lear perceives the justice of the everyday world to be a perversion of true justice. He breaks down the barriers of justicer and wrong-doer in an image of violent sexuality. Public whipping was the normal punishment for prostitution in Jacobean times.

83 Thorough tattered clothes great vices do appear;
Robes and furred gowns hide all.
(IV.6.165–6)
The reason of Lear's madness draws attention to the social injustice in the application of the law. The rich in high positions are able to conceal their crimes, while small offences in the poor are represented as great because more evident.

84 O matter and impertinency mixed,
Reason in madness!
(IV.6.175–6)
Edgar, disguised as a peasant guide to his blind father, Gloucester, is an observer of the latter's meeting with the mad Lear. His statement is an overt comment upon the social and moral perception contained within Lear's insane outpourings.

85 When we are born we cry that we are come
To this great stage of fools.
(IV.6.183–4)
In his torment, Lear perceives the whole of human existence as a tragedy symbolized by a new-born child's first cry. The ability to see the stage as the world and the world as a stage was a commonplace of Renaissance thought.

86 A most poor man made tame to fortune's blows,
Who, by the art of known and feeling sorrows,
Am pregnant to good pity.
(IV.6.221–3)
Edgar describes himself in this manner to Gloucester, following the latter's encounter with Lear. He is presenting himself to his blind father as a peasant guide. He suggests that he is disposed to feel pity on account of experiencing his and others' sufferings, to which he has become resigned. Immediately after Gloucester's acceptance of his aid, Edgar defends his father against Oswald and, on killing him, discovers the letter to Edmund revealing Gonerill's plot to make Edmund her husband in Albany's place.

87 You do me wrong to take me out o'the grave.
Thou art a soul in bliss; but I am bound
Upon a wheel of fire, that mine own tears
Do scald like molten lead.
(IV.7.45–8)
Lear is in the care of Cordelia, Kent, and the Doctor in the French camp. The Doctor is applying all means of restoration to his patient: he has been dressed in clean clothes, allowed to sleep, and music – associated by the Renaissance Platonic tradition with the restoration of psychic harmony – has been played. Lear's words are addressed to Cordelia upon his waking. To Lear's mind, Cordelia appears an angel in paradise, while he remains a tormented soul in hell, scalded by his tears of guilt. The wheel of fire had become a conventional Christian mode of conceiving the torments of hell.

88 Pray do not mock me.
I am a very foolish fond old man,
Four score and upward, not an hour more nor less,
And, to deal plainly,
I fear I am not in my perfect mind...
Do not laugh at me,
For, as I am a man, I think this lady
To be my child Cordelia.
(IV.7.59–63, 68–70)

Lear is in the French camp at Dover in the care of Cordelia, Kent, and the Doctor. He has awoken from his restorative sleep and the rage of his madness is past. When Cordelia begs his blessing, he kneels to her and makes confession of his infirmity. His act of recognition has the full power of Aristotelian anagnorisis, for it constitutes perception of himself as well as identification of another.

89 Men must endure
Their going hence even as their coming hither;
Ripeness is all.
(V.2.9–11)

The final phrase of the quotation is one of the most gnomic utterances in the Shakespearian canon. The context is the aftermath of the battle in which Cordelia's army loses to the forces of her sisters. After the restoration of Lear to Cordelia in IV.7., their defeat sabotages the audience's expectations of a felicitous resolution of their sufferings. After the defeat, Gloucester merely wishes for annihilation, but Edgar's experience as Poor Tom has taught him the art of survival and stoical endurance, which he seeks to impart to his father in these words.

90 No, no, no, no! Come let's away to prison.
We two alone will sing birds i'the cage;
When thou dost ask me blessing I'll kneel down
And ask of thee forgiveness; so we'll live,
And pray, and sing, and tell old tales, and laugh
At gilded butterflies, and hear poor rogues
Talk of court news; and we'll talk with them too –
Who loses and who wins, who's in, who's out –
And take upon's the mystery of things
As if we were God's spies; and we'll wear out,
In a walled prison, packs and sects of great ones
That ebb and flow by the moon.
(V.3.8–19)

Cordelia and Lear are the captives of Edmund, following their defeat in battle. Lear refuses, in these lines, to see Gonerill and Regan and proposes to Cordelia a prospect of captivity which is a still refuge from the mutability of political life. The reference to a single 'God' is curious, given the setting of pre-Christian Britain and the references elsewhere to the pagan gods.

91 Upon such sacrifices, my Cordelia,
The gods themselves throw incense.
(V.3.20–1)
Edmund has ordered Lear and Cordelia to captivity in prison. Lear, convinced of the justness of his and Cordelia's cause against Gonerill and Regan, sees himself and Cordelia as a sacrifice fit for the gods.

92 EDGAR
The gods are just, and of our pleasant vices
Make instruments to plague us:
The dark and vicious place where thee he got
Cost him his eyes.
EDMUND Th'hast spoken right. 'Tis true.
The wheel is come full circle.
(V.3.168–72)
Edgar has just revealed his identity to Edmund after defeating him in single combat. The information gained of Gonerill's plot against Albany, her husband, from the letter he took from Oswald, had permitted Edgar to approach Albany with the request to challenge Edmund as a traitor. Edgar's words assert the justice of man's destiny, and Edmund's responding reference to the wheel of Fortune concurs. 'Pleasant vices' are those which give pleasure.

93 I asked his blessing, and from first to last
Told him my pilgrimage; but his flawed heart – ...
'Twixt two extremes of passion, joy and grief,
Burst smilingly.
(V.3.193–4, 196–7)
Edgar is recounting to Albany the manner of his father, Gloucester's death. He informs Albany that only shortly before Gloucester's death, when he was armed to face Edmund in combat and prove him a traitor, did he reveal his identity to his blind father and give an account of his experiences. Gloucester dies because his heart is subjected to extremes of contrary emotions, joy and grief. It is not a death of despair, which he has more than

once desired in the play, but a death in the full knowledge of life's good and evil.

94 Howl, howl, howl! O, you are men of stones!
Had I your tongues and eyes I'd use them so
That heaven's vault should crack.
(V.3.255–7)

Lear is bearing the dead Cordelia in his arms. Edmund had given instruction for their execution in prison and, although after defeat by Edgar in combat he repents and revokes the order, the reprieve arrives too late to save Cordelia from being hanged. Lear's reference to 'men of stones', addressed to Albany, Edgar, and Kent, conflates their lack of feeling (in Lear's view) with their petrified state when confronted with this tableau of suffering and of fate's most bitter irony.

95 If it be so,
It is a chance which does redeem all sorrows
That ever I have felt.
(V.3.263–5)

Lear is referring to the possibility that there remain life and breath in Cordelia. She has been hanged in prison on Edmund's orders, his reprieve having arrived too late. While Lear really knows that she is dead, he cannot help hoping otherwise and searches for a sign of breath with a looking-glass and a feather. Cordelia's death proves the final sorrow that destroys Lear.

96 Her voice was ever soft,
Gentle and low – an excellent thing in woman.
(V.3.271–2)

Lear is speaking of Cordelia as he cradles her dead form in his arms. He is speaking before Albany, Edgar, Kent, and their officers. Cordelia has been hanged on the orders of Edmund.

97 And my poor fool is hanged! No, no, no life!
Why should a dog, a horse, a rat have life,
And thou no breath at all? Thou'lt come no more;
Never, never, never, never, never.
Pray you undo this button. Thank you, sir.
Do you see this? Look on her! Look, her lips!
Look there! Look there!
(V.3.303–9)

Lear's last lines in the play have been the subject of much discussion. He has borne in his arms the dead Cordelia, who has been hanged in prison on Edmund's instructions. 'Poor fool', which was a term of endearment, undoubtedly refers to Cordelia; but there are suggestions that the word 'fool' may have been prompted by the doubling of the roles of the Fool and Cordelia. This remains speculation. The attention that Lear draws to Cordelia's lips tends to indicate that he is deluded into seeing a sign of life. Even if this is so, it is no proof of the state of mind or spirit in which Lear dies.

98 Vex not his ghost. O, let him pass. He hates him
That would upon the rack of this tough world
Stretch him out longer.
(V.3.311–13)
Kent is urging Edgar to allow Lear to die peacefully and not to seek to rouse his consciousness. Lear's passing has been caused by the bitter irony and ultimate sorrow of Cordelia's death. Kent conceives existence in this world as a rack, an instrument of torture, which stretches both body and soul beyond the limits of endurance.

99 The weight of this sad time we must obey;
Speak what we feel, not what we ought to say.
The oldest hath borne most; we that are young
Shall never see so much nor live so long.
(V.3.321–4)
The Folio gives these formal lines of conclusion to the tragedy to Edgar, though the Quarto had attributed them to Albany, perhaps according to the convention that the senior survivor proffers the final moral. Edgar's references to speaking in accord with feeling and to the extent of Lear's suffering are in keeping with the audiences's experience of the play.

Love's Labour's Lost

1 Let fame, that all hunt after in their lives,
Live registered upon our brazen tombs,
And then grace us in the disgrace of death;
When, spite of cormorant devouring Time,
Th'endeavour of this present breath may buy
That honour which shall bate his scythe's keen edge,
And make us heirs of all eternity.
(I.1.1–7)
The King of Navarre addresses Berowne, Longaville and Dumaine, the three noblemen who are going to join him in a proposed three-year period of study and abstinence from food, sleep, and contact with women. He sees this project, which is detailed later

in the scene, as one way in which they can achieve everlasting fame and defeat death. 'Brazen tombs' means brass funeral monuments and probably derives ultimately from the Latin poet Horace's influential claim in his *Odes* to have written poetry more durable than brass (see also Sonnet 55). The cormorant was symbolic of ravenous appetite; 'bate' means blunt.

2 O, these are barren tasks, too hard to keep,
Not to see ladies, study, fast, not sleep.
(I.1.47–8)
Berowne voices his objections to the King's proposals, stressing their unnaturalness.

3 Study is like the heaven's glorious sun,
   That will not be deep-searched with saucy looks.
Small have continual plodders ever won,
   Save base authority from others' books.
These earthly godfathers of heaven's lights,
   That give a name to every fixèd star,
Have no more profit of their shining nights
   Than those that walk and wot not what they are.
(I.1.84–91)
Berowne develops his arguments against the uselessness of book-learning. The play's concern with the relationship between words and acts is reflected in the reference to astronomy where the astronomers who give names to stars are seen as being like god-fathers who give names to children but achieve nothing by doing so. 'Wot' means know.

4 At Christmas I no more desire a rose
Than wish a snow in May's new-fangled shows,
But like of each thing that in season grows.
(I.1.105–7)
Berowne uses the traditional idea that there is a fit time for everything to argue against the unnaturalness of the King's plans.

5 If I break faith, this word shall speak for me:
I am forsworn on mere 'necessity'.
(I.1.151–2)
Although the courtiers have sworn an oath not to see women, the Princess of France's arrival means that they will have to break the oath almost before they have started their three years of abstention. The King has remarked that the Princess will have to stay at the court out of 'mere necessity'. This is part of Berowne's mocking response.

6 One who the music of his own vain tongue
Doth ravish like enchanting harmony.
(I.1.164–5)
The King describes Don Armado, the Spanish traveller. Many audiences and critics, to say nothing of the ladies of France in the play, would apply these terms to the majority of the male characters of the play, whose besetting sin is one form of word-mangling or another.

7 KING Did you hear the proclamation?
COSTARD I do confess much of the hearing it, but little of the marking of it.
(I.1.272–4)
Costard, a countryman who plays something of the clown role in the play, has been accused of consorting with the country-woman Jaquenetta, contrary to the King's proclamation. He claims to have heard the words of the proclamation but paid no attention to their meaning. Again there are links between his attitude to words and those of the other male characters.

8 Welcome the sour cup of prosperity! Affliction may one day smile again, and till then sit thee down, sorrow!
(I.1.300–2)
As this speech shows, Costard is as given to misusing words as the other male characters, albeit his misusages are errors rather than equivocations or affectations. The occasion of these remarks is his sentence to a week's diet of bran and water for consorting with Jaquenetta.

9 I am ill at reckoning. It fitteth the spirit of a tapster.
(I.2.40–1)
Don Armado, the Spanish traveller, tells his page Moth that he is too refined to add up properly like a barman ('tapster').

10 The world was very guilty of such a ballad some three ages since, but I think now 'tis not to be found.
(I.2.106–7)
Don Armado has asked his page Moth about the ballad of the king and the beggar which presumably has some bearing on his attraction to the lowly Jaquenetta. Moth replies that the ballad is out of date.

11 Assist me, some extemporal god of rhyme, for I am sure I shall turn sonnet. Devise, wit; write, pen; for I am for whole volumes in folio.
(I.2.176–8)

Don Armado proposes to act as a conventional lover should, by writing love poetry. Here he invokes some god of impromptu verse ('extemporal god of rhyme') to inspire him. 'Turn sonnet' means compose sonnets. As his language is characterized by rhetorical tricks and verbosity, it is not surprising that his poetic effusions will fill whole volumes in the largest format ('folio').

12 Beauty is bought by judgement of the eye,
Not uttered by base sale of chapmen's tongues.
(II.1.15–16)
The Princess of France, arriving in Navarre on a diplomatic mission on behalf of her ailing father, rebukes her courtier Boyet for his conventional praise of her beauty. Throughout the play the Princess and her ladies insist on the importance of words reflecting real qualities – as in this instance where she argues that beauty is in the eye of the beholder, not put up for sale by tradesmen ('Not uttered … tongues').

13 Berowne they call him – but a merrier man,
Within the limit of becoming mirth,
I never spent an hour's talk withal.
(II.1.66–8)
Rosaline, one of the Princess of France's ladies, describes Berowne to the others. There may be a pun on brown and Berowne which would give point to the 'but' by suggesting a contrast between the melancholy traditionally associated with the colour brown and Berowne's actual temperament. 'Withal' means with.

14 Did not I dance with you in Brabant once?
(II.1)
This line, spoken by Berowne and repeated by Rosaline, is part of an initial exchange between them which is widely regarded as one of a number of accidental survivals from an earlier draft of the play. In the edition used as copy text for this book it is not printed in the main text and has no line number; it would appear after line 113.

15 BEROWNE Your wit's too hot, it speeds too fast, 'twill tire.
ROSALINE Not till it leave the rider in the mire.
(II.1)
This is part of the initial exchange between Berowne and Rosaline which appears to be a survival of an earlier draft (see 14 above). Rosaline's wit is compared to a horse.

16 Thy own wish wish I thee in every place.
(II.1.179)

The King responds to the Princess's wish to sweet health and fair desires.

17 Warble, child; make passionate my sense of hearing.
(III.1.1–2)
As befits a besotted lover, Armado seeks opportunities to indulge in a conventional lover's melancholy behaviour. Here he uses his normal overblown style to ask Moth to sing.

18 Now will I look to his remuneration. 'Remuneration'! O, that's the Latin word for three farthings. Three farthings – remuneration. 'What's the price of this inkle?' 'One penny.' 'No, I'll give you a remuneration.' Why, it carries it! 'Remuneration'! Why, it is a fairer name than French crown. I will never buy and sell out of this word.
(III.1.133–40)
Costard examines the money Armado has given him to carry a letter to Jaquenetta. Armado naturally used the pretentious word 'remuneration' for the tiny sum he gave Costard. A farthing was a quarter of an old penny; 'inkle' is linen tape; Costard imagines that a shopkeeper could be impressed by the big word into selling cheap. A French crown is not only a coin but also the bald head associated with syphilis; 'out of this word' means using any other word. See also 19.

19 Guerdon, O sweet guerdon! Better than remuneration – elevenpence farthing better. Most sweet guerdon! I will do it, sir, in print. Guerdon! Remuneration!
(III.1.166–9)
Berowne has given Costard money to carry a letter to Rosaline. Like Armado (see 18) he has used a fancy word – 'guerdon', meaning reward – to describe his gift. Here Costard compares the shilling Berowne gave him as 'guerdon' with Armado's three farthings 'remuneration'. 'In print' means carefully. Presumably the final two words are addressed in appropriate tones of voice to the coins held in each of Costard's hands.

20 And I, forsooth, in love!
I, that have been love's whip,
A very beadle to a humorous sigh,
A critic, nay, a night-watch constable,
A domineering pedant o'er the boy,
Than whom no mortal so magnificent!
This wimpled, whining, purblind, wayward boy,
This Signor Junior, giant-dwarf, Dan Cupid,
Regent of love-rhymes, lord of folded arms,

Th'anointed sovereign of sighs and groans,
Liege of all loiterers and malcontents,
Dread prince of plackets, king of codpieces.
(III.1.170–81)

Berowne soliloquizes on having fallen in love with Rosaline, contrasting his previous scorn for lovers with his current state. The beadle was a parish official charged with whipping (sexual) offenders; 'humorous' means moody; 'pedant' means schoolmaster; 'wimpled' means blindfolded and 'purblind' means totally blind – both refer to the usual depiction of Cupid, the god of love, as a blindfolded boy. 'Signor' puns on senior, drawing attention to the paradox of the giant power of the apparently powerless small child. 'Dan', a variant of the contraction for the Latin *dominus*, means lord or master. Folded arms, loitering, and being unhappy ('malcontent') were all attributes of the melancholy lover. As distinctive parts of female and male clothes, 'plackets' (openings in petticoats) and 'codpieces' (pouches on breeches, covering the genitals) came to be used in a bawdy sense for women and men.

21 A whitely wanton with a velvet brow,
With two pitch-balls stuck in her face for eyes;
Ay, and, by heaven, one that will do the deed
Though Argus were her eunuch and her guard!
And I to sigh for her, to watch for her,
To pray for her! Go to, it is a plague
That Cupid will impose for my neglect
Of his almighty dreadful little might.
Well, I will love, write, sigh, pray, sue, and groan;
Some men must love my lady, and some Joan.
(III.1.193–202)

Berowne continues to berate himself for having fallen in love with a woman who does not match the conventional picture of the ideal beloved. She has a sallow complexion ('whitely') with a soft ('velvet') forehead and has dark eyes ('pitch-balls'). According to him, she is so promiscuous ('one that will do the deed') that even the many-eyed Argus who, in classical mythology, was set to guard Io from the amorous attentions of Jupiter would be unable to stop her. 'Watch' means be sleepless. Since Joan was often used as a generic name for a woman of low social status, Berowne is again degrading Rosaline by using it for her.

22 Sir, he hath never fed of the dainties that are bred in a book.
He hath not eat paper, as it were; he hath not drunk ink.
(IV.2.24–6)

Nathaniel the curate describes Dull the constable to Holofernes the schoolmaster. Dull does not share the general obsession with words.

23 Old Mantuan, old Mantuan! Who understandeth thee not, loves thee not.
(IV.2.98–9)
Holofernes, displaying his erudition to Nathaniel, Costard, Dull, and Jaquenetta, makes an obvious point. The Latin *Eclogues* of the Italian poet Mantuan (1447–1516) were a standard part of the Elizabethan grammar school curriculum, so it is not unreasonable for Holofernes to have some knowledge of them.

24 Here are only numbers ratified; but, for the elegancy, facility, and golden cadence of poesy, *caret*. Ovidius Naso was the man; and why indeed 'Naso' but for smelling out the odoriferous flowers of fancy, the jerks of invention?
(IV.2.121–5)
Holofernes is commenting on Berowne's love poem to Rosaline which Costard has mistakenly delivered to Jaquenetta. 'Numbers ratified' are metrically correct verses; '*caret*' is Latin for it is lacking. 'Ovidius Naso' is the Latin form of the name of the highly influential Roman poet Ovid, whose family name – Naso – means nose. 'Jerks of invention' means strokes of wit.

25 All hid, all hid – an old infant play.
Like a demi-god here sit I in the sky,
And wretched fools' secrets heedfully o'er-eye.
More sacks to the mill! O heavens, I have my wish!
Dumaine transformed! Four woodcocks in a dish!
(IV.3.76–80)
Berowne has concealed himself and heard the King and Longaville confess that they are in love, each believing himself to be alone. Thus Berowne has overheard the King who has overheard Longaville. In the fourth line the proverbial expression 'More sacks to the mill', which means lots more to come, marks the arrival of Dumaine, who is also in love. 'All hid' was a cry in the children's game of Hoodman Blind – Berowne is referring to himself, probably concealed in the gallery above the stage, and the King and Longaville, probably hiding behind the downstage pillars which supported the canopy over the acting area in Elizabethan theatres. The woodcock was a proverbially silly bird, so Berowne is saying they are all in the same boat.

26 Walk aside the true folk, and let the traitors stay.
(IV.3.211)

After Berowne has berated his companions for falling in love, Costard and Jaquenetta have brought Berowne's misdirected love letter to them, thus forcing Berowne to own up to his fall from grace. When the King dismisses Costard and Jaquenetta, Costard replies with this accurate judgement of the situation.

27 O paradox! Black is the badge of hell,
The hue of dungeons, and the school of night.
(IV.3.252–3)

The King objects to Berowne's praise of Rosaline's dark complexion. Although there seems to be no real difficulty about reading the 'school of night' to mean black is the school which teaches the night to be black, there has been a great deal of speculation, much of it now discredited, that the phrase is an allusion to an atheistic coterie associated with Sir Walter Raleigh. This view was particularly fashionable at a time when the play's theatrical strengths were undervalued; but recent productions, and the growing interest in and understanding of the play's preoccupation with the nature of language, have largely removed the need for special pleading to justify what were once deemed to be the play's failings.

28 But love, first learnèd in a lady's eyes,
Lives not alone immurèd in the brain,
But with the motion of all elements
Courses as swift as thought in every power,
And gives to every power a double power,
Above their functions and their offices.
It adds a precious seeing to the eye:
A lover's eyes will gaze an eagle blind.
A lover's ear will hear the lowest sound
When the suspicious head of theft is stopped.
Love's feeling is more soft and sensible
Than are the tender horns of cockled snails.
Love's tongue proves dainty Bacchus gross in taste.
For valour, is not Love a Hercules,
Still climbing trees in the Hesperides?
Subtle as Sphinx; as sweet and musical
As bright Apollo's lute, strung with his hair.
And when Love speaks, the voice of all the gods
Make heaven drowsy with the harmony.
Never durst poet touch a pen to write
Until his ink were tempered with Love's sighs.
(IV.3.303–23)

The King, Longaville, and Dumaine have called on Berowne to justify them breaking their oath, which he does in a lengthy speech full of specious justifications. According to Berowne, love, unlike other forms of study, enriches the body as well as the brain. 'Immured' means walled up; 'power' means faculty. 'When the suspicious head of theft is stopped' means when the thief who is listening intently for a sound cannot hear anything. 'Cockled' means with shells. The Hesperides were actually the daughters of Hesperus, in whose garden grew the golden apples which Hercules had to gather as the last of his labours, but here, as often, the term is applied to the garden. The Theban Sphinx was 'subtle' because it posed the riddle which Oedipus eventually answered.

29 From women's eyes this doctrine I derive:
They sparkle still the right Promethean fire;
They are the books, the arts, the academes,
That show, contain, and nourish all the world.
(IV.3.326–9)

Berowne continues to justify the nobles' abandonment of the academy by arguing that they have found the true source of knowledge in their love. Prometheus stole fire from heaven for the benefit of the human race. The original texts of *Love's Labour's Lost* preserve a first version of Berowne's speech of justification. In that version, the second and third lines of this quotation run thus: 'They are the ground, the books, the academes, / From whence doth spring the true Promethean fire'.

30 For where is any author in the world
Teaches such beauty as a woman's eye?
(IV.3)

These lines from the first version of Berowne's long speech of justification do not appear in the main text of the edition used for this book, but as they have often been quoted they are presented here.

31 Let us once lose our oaths to find ourselves,
Or else we lose ourselves to keep our oaths.
It is religion to be thus forsworn,
For charity itself fulfils the law,
And who can sever love from charity?
(IV.3.337–41)

Berowne concludes his long attempt to justify the nobles' breaking their oath with a desperate juggling of terms.

32 He draweth out the thread of his verbosity finer than the staple of his argument. I abhor such fanatical phantasimes, such insociable and point-device companions, such rackers of

orthography, as to speak 'dout' *sine* 'b', when he should say 'doubt', 'det' when he should pronounce 'debt' – d, e, b, t, not d, e, t. He clepeth a calf 'cauf', half 'hauf'; neighbour *vocatur* 'nebour', neigh abbreviated 'ne'. This is abhominable, which he would call 'abominable'.
(V.1.16–24)
Holofernes, in conversation with Nathaniel and Dull, is objecting to Armado's verbal mannerisms. 'Staple' means fibre. As a pedantic schoolmaster Holofernes dislikes extravagant fantastic people ('fantastical phantasimes') who are impossible to associate with ('insociable'), affectedly precise ('point-device'), and who are torturers of spelling ('rackers of orthography') because of their pronunciation. Holofernes believes that pronunciation should follow spelling, hence his objections to the various pronunciations which to us, and to many Elizabethans, would be preferable to the ones he adopts. 'Clepeth' means calls; '*vocatur*' is Latin for is called; 'abhominable' was the usual Elizabethan spelling, arising from a mistaken etymology, of abominable.

33 *Bone*? '*Bone*' for '*bene*'! Priscian a little scratched; 'twill serve.
(V.1.28–9)
Holofernes comments on Nathaniel's use of '*bone*' instead of the Latin *bene*, meaning well. Nathaniel seems to be confusing and conflating the French *bon* and the Latin *bene*. Priscian was a Latin grammarian, so Holofernes means the Latin is not perfect.

34 MOTH They have been at a great feast of languages and stolen the scraps.
COSTARD O, they have lived long on the alms-basket of words! I marvel thy master hath not eaten thee for a word, for thou are not so long by the head as *honorificabilitudinitatibus*. Thou art easier swallowed than a flap-dragon.
(V.1.36–42)
Moth and Costard comment on the linguistic posturing of Armado, Holofernes, and Nathaniel. The alms-basket was used to collect leftovers to give to the poor. Costard is probably punning on the French *mot* – a word – and Moth's name (probably pronounced mote) when he refers to Armado eating him for a word. '*Honorificabilitudinitatibus*', which is the ablative or dative plural of a medieval Latin word, was believed to be the longest word in existence. Its meaning, irrelevant in this context, is the state of being honoured. A 'flap-dragon' was a burning raisin floating in alcohol.

35 It is the King's most sweet pleasure and affection to congrat-

ulate the Princess at her pavilion in the posteriors of this day, which the rude multitude call the afternoon.
(V.1.82–5)
Armado informs Holofernes and Nathaniel of the King's plans in his usual style.

36 HOLOFERNES *Via*, goodman Dull! Thou hast spoken no word all this while.
DULL Nor understood none neither, sir.
(V.1.142–4)
At the end of a scene of characteristic linguistic extravagance, Dull offers an apt comment. '*Via*' means come on, probably with the sense of cheer up.

37 Had she been light, like you,
Of such a merry, nimble, stirring spirit,
She might ha' been a grandam ere she died.
And so may you, for a light heart lives long.
(V.2.15–18)
Katharine, one of the Princess of France's ladies, is comparing her sister who died of love-melancholy with Rosaline, punning on various meanings of 'light' such as merry, casual, promiscuous, and lightweight. 'Grandam' means grandmother; 'a light heart lives long' is proverbial.

38 Some thousand verses of a faithful lover;
A huge translation of hypocrisy,
Vilely compiled, profound simplicity.
(V.2.50–2)
Katharine describes to the Princess her love poem from Dumaine. 'Translation' means communication.

39 KING
All hail, sweet madam, and fair time of day.
PRINCESS
'Fair' in 'all hail' is foul, as I conceive.
KING
Construe my speeches better, if you may.
(V.2.339–41)
Even the King's attempt at a greeting provides opportunities for (deliberate) misunderstanding as the Princess chooses to interpret 'hail' as hailstorm rather than welcome. This reflects the play's concern with the whole question of how people can interpret ('construe') each other's words and how words can be accurately related to deeds.

40 Taffeta phrases, silken terms precise,
Three-piled hyperboles, spruce affection,
Figures pedantical – these summer flies
Have blown me full of maggot ostentation.
I do forswear them; and I here protest
By this white glove – how white the hand, God knows! –
Henceforth my wooing mind shall be expressed
In russet yeas and honest kersey noes.
And, to begin: wench – so God help me, law! –
My love to thee is sound, *sans* crack or flaw.
(V.2.406–15)

After several fumbling attempts to woo the ladies, the men have been thoroughly discomforted. Here Berowne addresses Rosaline, attempting to abandon his previous methods of wooing because of their insincerity. Unfortunately, as this speech indicates, with its convoluted clothing imagery, the habits are ingrained. 'Taffeta phrases' means fine phrases; 'three-piled' was the richest form of velvet and it is used here to mean best quality; 'spruce affection' means elegant affectation; 'figures' are rhetorical tricks. Russet is the red-brown colour associated with peasants' clothing and kersey is a coarse woollen cloth. 'Wench', inappropriate for a court lady, marks the beginning of Berowne's attempts at plain country wooing but '*sans*' (French for without) is an affected word. 'Law' is an exclamation more often associated with rustic than with noble characters.

41 A foolish mild man; an honest man, look you, and soon dashed. He is a marvellous good neighbour, faith, and a very good bowler; but for Alisander, alas, you see how 'tis – a little o'erparted.
(V.2.577–81)

In the Pageant of the Nine Worthies arranged to entertain the Princess and her ladies, Nathaniel, playing Alexander the Great ('Alisander'), has been put off by the nobles' heckling. Here Costard eulogizes his everyday qualities. 'A little o'erparted' means that he is not quite up to playing the part. Presumably Nathaniel plays bowls, though the phrase 'a very good bowler' may mean a very good sport.

42 The sweet war-man is dead and rotten. Sweet chucks, beat not the bones of the buried. When he breathed, he was a man.
(V.2.658–60)

Armado, playing the Trojan hero Hector in the Pageant of the Nine Worthies, answers the nobles' continued heckling with this dignified response. 'Chucks' is a term of endearment.

43 Worthies, away! The scene begins to cloud.
(V.2.717)
Berowne terminates the Pageant of the Nine Worthies in response to the news of the death of the King of France, the Princess's father.

44 Honest plain words best pierce the ear of grief.
(V.2.748)
After the princess has failed to understand the King's convoluted declaration of love, Berowne begins his explanation of the nobles' situation with this line. Once again he rejects the rhetorical devices which he then goes on to use.

45 KING
Now, at the latest minute of the hour,
Grant us your loves.
PRINCESS A time, methinks too short
To make a world-without-end bargain in.
(V.2.782–4)
The King makes a last attempt to save something from the thwarted wooing.

46 To move wild laughter in the throat of death?
It cannot be; it is impossible;
Mirth cannot move a soul in agony.
(V.2.844–6)
Rosaline has told Berowne that she will not marry him unless he first spends a year visiting the desperately ill and trying to make them laugh. This is his response.

47 A jest's prosperity lies in the ear
Of him that hears it, never in the tongue
Of him that makes it.
(V.2.850–2)
Rosaline explains why Berowne needs to spend his year trying to make the sick laugh; he has the wrong attitude to humour.

48 BEROWNE
Our wooing doth not end like an old play;
Jack hath not Jill. These ladies' courtesy
Might well have made our sport a comedy.
KING
Come, sir, it wants a twelvemonth and a day,
And then 'twill end.
BEROWNE That's too long for a play.
(V.2.863–7)

Berowne draws our attention to the play's unusual ending, in which the couples are not going to be married in the course of the play. 'Courtesy' means kind agreement.

49 When daisies pied and violets blue
And lady-smocks all silver-white
And cuckoo-buds of yellow hue
Do paint the meadows with delight,
The cuckoo then, on every tree,
Mocks married men; for thus sings he:
'Cuckoo!
Cuckoo, cuckoo!' O, word of fear,
Unpleasing to a married ear!
When shepherds pipe on oaten straws,
And merry larks are ploughmen's clocks,
When turtles tread, and rooks, and daws,
And maidens bleach their summer smocks,
The cuckoo then, on every tree, etc.
(V.2.883–900)

The play concludes with the contrasting songs of the cuckoo and the owl. Presumably the songs, which are assigned to Ver, the spring, and Hiems, the winter, were sung by the best available singers. 'Lady-smocks' are cuckoo-flowers; 'cuckoo-buds' may be buttercups. The cuckoo's song mocks married men because of its resemblance to cuckold; 'turtles' are turtle doves; 'daws' are jackdaws.

50 When icicles hang by the wall,
And Dick the shepherd blows his nail.
And Tom bears logs into the hall,
And milk comes frozen home in pail,
When blood is nipped, and ways be foul,
Then nightly sings the staring owl:
'Tu-whit
Tu-who!' – a merry note,
While greasy Joan doth keel the pot.
When all aloud the wind doth blow,
And coughing drowns the parson's saw,
And birds sit brooding in the snow,
And Marian's nose looks red and raw,
When roasted crabs hiss in the bowl,
Then nightly sings the staring owl: etc.
(V.2.901–18)

This song is sung by Hiems, winter, at the end of the play (see 49). 'Blows his nail' means blows on his fingers to keep warm and stands idle; 'ways be foul' means roads are muddy. Joan is a generic name for a woman of low social status; it is used earlier in the play when Berowne is denigrating Rosaline (see 21). 'Keel' means cool; 'saw' means moral maxim; 'crabs' are crab apples.

51 The words of Mercury are harsh after the songs of Apollo. You that way; we this way.
(V.2.919–20)
The first sentence appears in the 1598 quarto edition of the play without any speech prefix, but in the First Folio the speech is assigned to Armado and the final phrases appear. Although some editors have discarded these final phrases, they have proved very effective in the theatre, giving a double-edged sense of the parting of the French ladies from the court of Navarre and of the audience from the actors. The contrast between Apollo and Mercury is also particularly resonant: Apollo can be associated not only with the songs of the immediate context but also with the love poetry of the whole play, whereas Mercury, the messenger of the gods, can be associated with Marcade, the messenger who brought the 'harsh' words that finally disrupted the courtly wooing, as well as with the truly difficult tasks the men will have to undertake in the world beyond the play.

Macbeth

I FIRST WITCH
When shall we three meet again?
In thunder, lightning, or in rain?
SECOND WITCH
When the hurly-burly's done,
When the battle's lost and won.
THIRD WITCH
That will be ere the set of sun.
FIRST WITCH
Where the place?
SECOND WITCH Upon the heath.
THIRD WITCH
There to meet with Macbeth.
FIRST WITCH
I come, Grey-Malkin.
SECOND WITCH Padock calls!
THIRD WITCH Anon!
ALL
Fair is foul, and foul is fair.

Hover through the fog and filthy air.
(I.1.1–10)

The play's opening lines, with their emphasis on the disruption of natural order and on equivocation, quickly establish its mood and its preoccupations. Shakespeare often uses couplets for magic charms and in scenes involving the supernatural. 'Hurly-burly' is confusion; Grey-Malkin and Padock are the names of the Witches' familiars, probably a cat and a toad.

2 What bloody man is that?
(I.2.1)

Duncan, King of Scotland, asks his nobles the identity of the 'bleeding Captain' who brings news of Macbeth's triumph in battle. In a famous production by Barry Jackson at the Birmingham Repertory Theatre in the late 1920s, set in the period of the First World War, Duncan – dressed as a Field Marshal – turned the word 'bloody' into an expletive.

3 For brave Macbeth – well he deserves that name –
Disdaining fortune, with his brandished steel,
Which smoked with bloody execution,
Like valour's minion carvèd out his passage
Till he faced the slave –
Which ne'er shook hands nor bade farewell to him
Till he unseamed him from the nave to the chops,
And fixed his head upon our battlements.
(I.2.16–23)

The Captain recounts the story of Macbeth's victory over the rebellious Macdonald ('the slave') to the King and his nobles. 'From the nave to the chops', which means from the navel to the jaws, is the first indication that Macbeth can be seen as a butcher.

4 So they
Doubly redoubled strokes upon the foe.
Except they meant to bathe in reeking wounds
Or memorize another Golgotha
I cannot tell.
(I.2.38–42)

The Captain describes the reactions of the army commanders Macbeth and Banquo to a renewed Norwegian assault. 'Memorize another Golgotha' means make the battlefield as memorable for its deaths as Calvary was for the death of Christ.

5 Bellona's bridegroom, lapped in proof,
Confronted him with self-comparisons,
Point against point-rebellious, arm 'gainst arm,

Curbing his lavish spirit; and to conclude,
The victory fell on us.
(I.2.56–60)

Ross, a lord, has brought more news of Macbeth's triumphs to the King. 'Bellona's bridegroom' is Macbeth, married to the goddess of war, who triumphs over the rebellious Thane of Cawdor ('him'). 'Lapped in proof' means well armoured. There is anticipatory irony in 'Confronted him with self-comparisons', which overtly means matched with equal courage, but can also be applied to Macbeth's future treachery when he is Thane of Cawdor. 'Point' is swordpoint; 'lavish' means pushy.

6 A sailor's wife had chestnuts in her lap,
And munched and munched and munched. 'Give me,' quoth I.
'Aroint thee, witch!' the rump-fed ronyon cries.
Her husband's to Aleppo gone, master o'the *Tiger*.
But in a sieve I'll thither sail
And like a rat without a tail
I'll do, I'll do, and I'll do.
(I.3.4–10)

The First Witch tells the others what she has been doing since they last met. 'Aroint thee' obviously means something like get lost, but 'aroint' is unknown except here and in *King Lear*. The most obvious interpretation of 'rump-fed' is fed on best-quality meat; 'ronyon' is a term of abuse. A ship called the *Tiger* sailed to Aleppo in 1583 and had an adventurous voyage in 1604–6 which was common knowledge when the play was written. It was popularly believed that the animals witches turned themselves into lacked tails. 'I'll do' means I will do him some (unspecified) harm.

7 Sleep shall neither night nor day
Hang upon his penthouse lid.
He shall live a man forbid.
Weary sev'n-nights nine times nine
Shall he dwindle, peak, and pine.
Though his bark cannot be lost,
Yet it shall be tempest-tossed.
(I.3.19–25)

The First Witch's description to the other Witches of the things she will do to the master of the *Tiger* anticipates what they will do to Macbeth. The historical *Tiger*, which was in the news in 1606, was actually away for 568 days, one more than the Witch calculates; seven and nine are magic numbers. 'Penthouse lid' means drooping eyelid; 'forbid' means cursed; 'peak' means grow thin. If we apply the final couplet to Macbeth, it suggests that the

Witches themselves cannot destroy Macbeth without his own connivance.

8 Here I have a pilot's thumb,
Wracked as homeward he did come.
(I.3.27–8)
The First Witch mentions an ingredient of a magic potion to the others. Macbeth himself is also a pilot wrecked ('wracked') on his way home.

9 THIRD WITCH
A drum! a drum!
Macbeth doth come.
ALL
The Weird Sisters, hand in hand,
Posters of the sea and land,
Thus do go, about, about;
Thrice to thine, and thrice to mine,
And thrice again, to make up nine.
Peace! The charm's wound up.
(I.3.29–36)
The Witches prepare for Macbeth's arrival. 'Weird' was a name given to one of the Three Fates, who were sometimes called 'The Weird Sisters', hence the use of weird to mean supernatural, and then simply strange or odd. 'Posters' means travellers. Presumably the Witches move in a circle, first clockwise and then anti-clockwise (or vice-versa) to wind the charm up.

10 So foul and fair a day I have not seen.
(I.3.37)
Macbeth's opening remark to Banquo picks up the Witches' 'Fair is foul' (see 1), thus immediately linking him with their world before they have even met. Presumably Macbeth means the weather is bad but their victory is good.

11 What are these,
So withered and so wild in their attire,
That look not like the inhabitants o'the earth,
And yet are on't? Live you? Or are you aught
That man may question? You seem to understand me
By each at once her choppy finger laying
Upon her skinny lips. You should be women;
And yet your beards forbid me to interpret
That you are so.
(I.3.38–46)

Banquo draws Macbeth's attention to the Witches and then addresses them. Perhaps they put their chapped, rough ('choppy') fingers to their lips to indicate they have secrets to tell, or perhaps it is to discourage Banquo from speaking since they say nothing until Macbeth speaks to them.

12 Good sir, why do you start, and seem to fear
Things that do sound so fair?
(I.3.50–1)
Banquo asks Macbeth why he has reacted so strongly to the Witches' greeting him as Thane of Glamis (which he is already) and of Cawdor and 'king hereafter'. 'Fair' again picks up 'Foul is fair' and the whole question of the relationship between outward appearance and inner truth. The strength of Macbeth's reaction has been taken as evidence that he already had ambitions of becoming king.

13 If you can look into the seeds of time
And say which grain will grow and which will not,
Speak then to me who neither beg nor fear
Your favours nor your hate.
(I.3.57–60)
Banquo, taking a rather different attitude to the Witches from Macbeth's, asks them if they can tell him anything about his future.

14 Stay, you imperfect speakers! Tell me more!
(I.3.69)
Macbeth addresses the Witches as they begin to leave. As he will find out to his cost, they are indeed imperfect speakers.

15 Say from whence
You owe this strange intelligence; or why
Upon this blasted heath you stop our way
With such prophetic greeting?
(I.3.74–7)
Macbeth tries to get the Witches to give him more information. 'Owe this strange intelligence' means get this strange news.

16 The earth hath bubbles as the water has,
And these are of them.
(I.3.78–9)
Banquo comments to Macbeth on the Witches' disappearance.

17 Were such things here as we do speak about?
Or have we eaten on the insane root

That takes the reason prisoner?
(I.3.82–4)
Macbeth asks Banquo if the Witches were really there. An 'insane root' is one that makes people mad if they eat it.

18 The Thane of Cawdor lives. Why do you dress me
In borrowed robes?
(I.3.107–8)
Macbeth responds with surprise to Ross greeting him as Thane of Cawdor. Later in the play Macbeth is seen as someone who has 'borrowed' the crown (see 120).

19 And oftentimes, to win us to our harm,
The instruments of darkness tell us truths;
Win us with honest trifles, to betray's
In deepest consequence.
(I.3.122–6)
Banquo warns Macbeth against trusting the Witches. 'Darkness' means evil; 'betray's' is betray us.

20 Two truths are told
As happy prologues to the swelling Act
Of the imperial theme.
(I.3.126–8)
Macbeth muses aside on the Witches' greeting. The 'Two truths' are that he is now Thane of Glamis and Cawdor. He sees becoming king ('the imperial theme') as part of the magnificent play proper (suggested by 'the swelling Act') which follows the prologues. The theatrical references are also significant later in the play (see 128 in particular).

21 This supernatural soliciting
Cannot be ill, cannot be good. If ill,
Why hath it given me earnest of success
Commencing in a truth? I am Thane of Cawdor.
If good, why do I yield to that suggestion
Whose horrid image doth unfix my hair,
And make my seated heart knock at my ribs
Against the use of nature? Present fears
Are less than horrible imaginings.
My thought, whose murder yet is but fantastical,
Shakes so my single state of man
That function is smothered in surmise,
And nothing is but what is not.
(I.3.129–141)

Macbeth debates the meaning of the Witches' news in a lengthy aside which begins with a balancing of good and ill reminiscent of 'Fair is foul'. He sees the Witches as tempting ('soliciting') him even though they do not suggest he should do anything to fulfil their prophesies. The 'horrid image' is of murdering the King – since 'horrid' literally means bristling, it links neatly with his hair standing on end (unfixed). 'Present fears / Are less than horrible imaginings' means that the potential horrors of the future are more scaring than the immediate things that frighten us (presumably because we know the scale of our present problems). 'Whose murder yet is but fantastical' means whose murder is still in the imagination; 'single' means individual. 'That function is smothered in surmise' means so that my power to act is smothered by speculation so that the only thing that exists for me in the present is thoughts of the future ('nothing is but what is not').

22 If chance will have me king, why chance may crown me
Without my stir.
(I.3.143–4)
Macbeth continues to muse aside on the Witches' prophesies. 'Without my stir' means without my doing anything about it.

23 Come what come may,
Time and the hour runs through the roughest day.
(I.3.146–7)
Macbeth, still turning over the possibilities of becoming king, decides that come what may, whatever is going to happen will happen.

24 MALCOLM Nothing in his life
Became him like the leaving it. He died
As one that had been studied in his death
To throw away the dearest thing he owed
As 'twere a careless trifle.
DUNCAN There's no art
To find the mind's construction in the face.
He was a gentleman on whom I built
An absolute trust.
(I.4.8–15)
Malcolm, Duncan's son, describes the death of the original treacherous Thane of Cawdor to Duncan. 'As one that had been studied' means like someone who had learned his part; 'owed' means owned. Duncan now proceeds to put as much misplaced trust in Macbeth, who enters on the word 'trust', as he did in the original Thane of Cawdor.

25 Stars, hide your fires,
Let not light see my black and deep desires.
The eye wink at the hand; yet let that be
Which the eye fears, when it is done, to see.
(I.4.51–4)
In an aside Macbeth reacts to Duncan's nomination of Malcolm as his successor before the nobles. 'The eye wink at the hand; yet let that be / Which the eye fears, when it is done, to see' means let the eye stay shut while the hand is doing an act (murdering Duncan) the consequences of which the eye will be afraid to look on when it is done.

26 Glamis thou art, and Cawdor, and shalt be
What thou art promised. Yet do I fear thy nature:
It is too full o'the milk of human-kindness
To catch the nearest way. Thou wouldst be great,
Art not without ambition, but without
The illness should attend it. What thou wouldst highly
That wouldst thou holily, wouldst not play false,
And yet wouldst wrongly win. Thou'dst have, great Glamis,
That which cries, 'Thus thou must do' if thou have it,
And that which rather thou dost fear to do
Than wishest should be undone. Hie thee hither
That I may pour my spirits in thine ear,
And chastise with the valour of my tongue
All that impedes thee from the golden round
Which fate and metaphysical aid doth seem
To have thee crowned withal.
(I.5.13–28)
Lady Macbeth, alone, reacts to Macbeth's letter informing her what the Witches have told him. 'The milk of human-kindness' refers to natural fellow-feelings of common humanity – the modern sense of 'kindness' is scarcely present. The 'nearest way' is the shortest route to the crown; 'illness' means evil; 'highly' means greatly. Lines 20–3 mean: if you want the crown you will have to perform evil acts which you are scared to do, even though you would not wish them undone if they were already done. 'Round' means crown; 'metaphysical' means supernatural.

27 The raven himself is hoarse
That croaks the fatal entrance of Duncan
Under my battlements. Come, you spirits
That tend on mortal thoughts, unsex me here
And fill me from the crown to the toe top-full
Of direst cruelty. Make thick my blood;
Stop up the access and passage to remorse,

That no compunctious visitings of nature
Shake my fell purpose, nor keep peace between
The effect and it. Come to my woman's breasts
And take my milk for gall, you murdering ministers,
Wherever, in your sightless substances,
You wait on nature's mischief. Come, thick night,
And pall thee in the dunnest smoke of hell,
That my keen knife see not the wound it makes,
Nor heaven peep through the blanket of the dark
To cry, 'Hold, hold!'
(I.5.36–52)

A messenger has brought news that Duncan plans to spend the night at Macbeth's castle. Left alone, Lady Macbeth anticipates the future and invokes spirits to remove her humanity. 'Mortal thoughts' are deadly designs; 'unsex' means make me unnatural; the crown refers to the crown of the head. 'Make thick my blood; / Stop up the access and passage to remorse' means make my blood thick so that it cannot take pity ('remorse') along my veins to my heart. 'Fell' means evil; 'keep peace between / The effect and it' means come between my purpose and putting it into effect. 'Take my milk for gall' means substitute gall for my milk, make me unnatural, echoing her complaint that Macbeth was 'too full of the milk of human-kindness'; 'sightless' means invisible; 'pall' means wrap; 'dunnest' means darkest; 'Hold' means stop.

28 Your face, my thane, is as a book where men
May read strange matters. To beguile the time
Look like the time, bear welcome in your eye,
Your hand, your tongue; look like the innocent flower,
But be the serpent under't. He that's coming
Must be provided for.
(I.5.60–5)

Lady Macbeth sets to work on the newly arrived Macbeth. 'To beguile the time / Look like the time' means in order to deceive people you must appear as they expect you to appear.

29 DUNCAN
This castle hath a pleasant seat; the air
Nimbly and sweetly recommends itself
Unto our gentle senses.
BANQUO This guest of summer,
The temple-haunting martlet, does approve
By his loved mansionry that the heaven's breath
Smells wooingly here; no jutty, frieze,
Buttress, nor coign of vantage, but this bird

Hath made his pendent bed and procreant cradle;
Where they most breed and haunt I have observed
The air is delicate.

(I.6.1–10)

Duncan and Banquo arrive at Macbeth's castle. Just as Duncan found it impossible to see into the previous Thane of Cawdor's mind, so he and Banquo mistake the castle's air of tranquillity for a mark of its inhabitants' attitudes. The audience, of course, already knows better. 'Seat' means location; 'nimbly' means promptly; 'approve' means show, prove; 'By his loved mansionry' means by liking to build here; 'jutty' means projection; 'coign of vantage' means convenient corner; 'pendent bed' means hanging nest.

30 If it were done when 'tis done, then 'twere well
It were done quickly. If the assassination
Could trammel up the consequence, and catch
With his surcease success – that but this blow
Might be the be-all and the end-all! – here,
But here, upon this bank and shoal of time,
We'd jump the life to come. But in these cases
We still have judgement here – that we but teach
Bloody instructions, which, being taught, return
To plague the inventor. This even-handed justice
Commends the ingredience of our poisoned chalice
To our own lips. He's here in double trust:
First, as I am his kinsman and his subject,
Strong both against the deed; then, as his host,
Who should against his murderer shut the door,
Not bear the knife myself. Besides, this Duncan
Hath borne his faculties so meek, hath been
So clear in his great office, that his virtues
Will plead like angels, trumpet-tongued against
The deep damnation of his taking-off;
And Pity, like a naked new-born babe
Striding the blast, or heaven's cherubin, horsed
Upon the sightless curriers of the air,
Shall blow the horrid deed in every eye,
That tears shall drown the wind. I have no spur
To prick the sides of my intent but only
Vaulting ambition which o'erleaps itself
And falls on the other.

(I.7.1–28)

Macbeth soliloquizes about the forthcoming murder of Duncan and its consequences. 'If it were done when 'tis done, then 'twere well / It were done quickly' means if committing the murder was all there was to it, it would be best to get it over with. 'Trammel up the consequence' means prevent any consequences; 'catch / With his surcease success' means obtain success through his death or, if 'his' is taken to mean its, by putting an end to the consequences. In 'bank and shoal of time', time is seen as a sea surrounding a sandbank which is life; 'shoal' is an emendation of the Folio reading 'Schoole' which has been defended as fitting in with 'bank' meaning bench, so that the phrase would mean school for eternity. 'Jump' means skip, not worry about; 'that we but teach' means so we simply offer; 'ingredience' means ingredients; 'faculties' are powers; 'clear' means guiltless; 'taking-off' means murder; 'Striding the blast' means astride the storm of indignation (and of the trumpet); 'sightless curriers' are the invisible winds. In the final sentence, Macbeth sees his plan ('intent') as a horse spurred on by ambition which is then seen as a rider who attempts to jump ('vault') into the saddle but falls on the other side.

31 MACBETH

We will proceed no further in this business.
He hath honoured me of late, and I have bought
Golden opinions from all sorts of people
Which would be worn now in their newest gloss,
Not cast aside so soon.
LADY Was the hope drunk
Wherein you dressed yourself? Hath it slept since?
And wakes it now to look so green and pale
At what it did so freely? From this time
Such I account thy love. Art thou afeard
To be the same in thine own act and valour
As thou art in desire? Wouldst thou have that
Which thou esteem'st the ornament of life,
And live a coward in thine own esteem,
Letting 'I dare not' wait upon 'I would',
Like the poor cat i'the adage?

(I.7.31–45)

Both Lady Macbeth and Macbeth use clothing imagery as Macbeth attempts to call off the murder of Duncan ('this business'). 'Green and pale' means hung over; 'that / Which thou esteem'st the ornament of life' is the crown. The cat in the proverb ('i'the adage') wanted to eat fish but didn't want to get her feet wet.

32 MACBETH

I dare do all that may become a man;
Who dares do more is none.
LADY What beast was't then

That made you break this enterprise to me?
When you durst do it, then you were a man;
And to be more than what you were, you would
Be so much more the man. Nor time nor place
Did then adhere, and yet you would make both.
They have made themselves, and that their fitness now
Does unmake you. I have given suck, and know
How tender 'tis to love the babe that milks me;
I would while it was smiling in my face
Have plucked my nipple from his boneless gums
And dashed the brains out, had I so sworn as you
Have done to this.

MACBETH If we should fail?

LADY We fail!
But screw your courage to the sticking place,
And we'll not fail.

(I.7.46–61)

Lady Macbeth continues her attempt to stiffen Macbeth's resolution. In his opening lines, Macbeth argues that he is willing to do anything that it is proper for a man to do, but that to be too daring is to be inhuman. 'Durst' means dared; 'adhere' means come together. The fact that we never see the child Lady Macbeth mentions here and that Macduff later appears to say that Macbeth has no children (see 111) may appear inconsistent in a reading, though few members of an audience are likely to be troubled by it; the tendency to treat characters in drama as real people with lives outside their fictional context persists despite useful correctives such as L. C. Knights's essay 'How many children had Lady Macbeth?'.

33 Bring forth men-children only!
For thy undaunted mettle should compose
Nothing but males.

(I.7.72–4)

Macbeth accepts Lady Macbeth's version of what constitutes manliness (that is, killing Duncan in order to get the crown) and praises her accordingly.

34 False face must hide what the false heart doth know.

(I.7.82)

Macbeth's final words in the scene, addressed to Lady Macbeth, referring to the need to conceal their planned treachery by appearing unconcerned, again take up the idea that outward appearance is no index to inner nature.

35 There's husbandry in heaven:
Their candles are all out.
(II.1.4–5)

Banquo, walking late with his son Fleance, comments that the night is starless. 'Husbandry' means thrift.

36 A heavy summons lies like lead upon me
And yet I would not sleep. Merciful powers,
Restrain in me the cursèd thoughts that nature
Gives way to in repose.
(II.1.6–9)

In his late night walk with his son Fleance, Banquo is reflecting on his meeting with the Witches and resisting 'the cursèd thoughts' that Macbeth is proving to be incapable of withstanding.

37 Is this a dagger which I see before me,
The handle toward my hand? Come, let me clutch thee –
I have thee not and yet I see thee still!
Art thou not, fatal vision, sensible
To feeling as to sight? Or art thou but
A dagger of the mind, a false creation,
Proceeding from the heat-oppressèd brain?
I see thee yet, in form as palpable
As this which now I draw.
Thou marshall'st me the way that I was going,
And such an instrument I was to use. –
Mine eyes are made the fools o'the other senses,
Or else worth all the rest. – I see thee still;
And, on thy blade and dudgeon, gouts of blood,
Which was not so before. There's no such thing.
It is the bloody business which informs
Thus to mine eyes.
(II.1.33–49)

Macbeth soliloquizes just before the murder of Duncan. It is as though he sleepwalks into the murder, conscious of the enormity of what he is doing but unable to stop himself. 'Sensible' means perceptible; 'heat-oppressed' means fevered. 'Mine eyes are made the fools o'the other senses, / Or else worth all the rest' means either my eyes are deceiving me or I am having a vision that transcends what I could learn from my other senses. 'Dudgeon' means wooden handle: 'informs' means presents this picture.

38 Now o'er the one half-world
Nature seems dead, and wicked dreams abuse
The curtained sleep. Witchcraft celebrates

Pale Hecat's offerings; and withered Murder,
Alarumed by his sentinel the wolf,
Whose howl's his watch, thus with his stealthy pace,
With Tarquin's ravishing strides, towards his design
Moves like a ghost. Thou sure and firm-set earth,
Hear not my steps, which way they walk, for fear
Thy very stones prate of my whereabout
And take the present horror from the time
Which now suits with it. – Whiles I threat, he lives:
Words to the heat of deeds too cold breath gives.
A bell rings
I go, and it is done; the bell invites me.
Hear it not, Duncan, for it is a knell
That summons thee to heaven or to hell.
(II.1.49–64)

Macbeth continues to soliloquize as he draws closer to the murder of Duncan. There is a continued sense of detachment from the act he is about to commit which is reflected in the generalized atmospheric invocation of night, in the description of Murder personified, and in the specific invocation to the earth not to hear his steps. 'Half-world' means hemisphere; 'curtained' means both behind bed curtains and hidden from control by the consciousness. Hecate, the goddess of witchcraft, was associated with the moon (hence 'Pale'); 'offerings' means ritual sacrifices; 'Alarumed' means alarmed, woken up. In Roman legend Tarquin raped Lucrece, hence his stride is 'ravishing'. 'Prate' means tell; 'whereabout' means whereabouts; 'take the present horror from the time' means break this horrible silence; 'suits with' means is appropriate to; 'Whiles' means while; 'gives' means give.

39 That which hath made them drunk hath made me bold;
What hath quenched them hath given me fire.
(II.2.1–2)

Lady Macbeth enters while Macbeth is murdering Duncan, confiding to the audience that the drink which has made the grooms guarding Duncan's room sleepy ('quenched them') has made her bold.

40 It was the owl that shrieked, the fatal bellman
Which gives the stern'st good-night.
(II.2.3–4)

Lady Macbeth, who is very jittery, is startled by an owl's hooting which she instantly assumes to be a human scream. A 'bellman' was sent to condemned prisoners on the night before their execution, so the 'stern'st good-night' is the last goodnight.

41 The attempt and not the deed
Confounds us.
(II.2.10–11)
Lady Macbeth, hearing noises from Duncan's bedchamber, thinks that Macbeth has been discovered before he can commit the murder.

42 Had he not resembled
My father as he slept, I had done't.
(II.2.12–13)
Lady Macbeth, still alone and waiting for Macbeth to come back from committing the murder, reveals the first chink in her apparently resolute facade.

43 MACBETH
I have done the deed. Didst thou not hear a noise?
LADY
I heard the owl-scream and the cricket's cry.
(II.2.14–15)
Macbeth greets Lady Macbeth after the murder of Duncan. Although her reply suggests that the natural order is undisturbed, both owls and crickets were associated with death.

44 MACBETH
But wherefore could not I pronounce 'Amen'?
I had most need of blessing, and 'Amen'
Stuck in my throat.
LADY These deeds must not be thought
After these ways; so, it will make us mad.
(II.2.31–4)
Macbeth and Lady Macbeth are in a panicky and hysterical state after the murder. Macbeth overheard Malcolm and Donalbain, the King's sons, saying their prayers but could not join in their 'Amen'. Lady Macbeth foresees all too accurately the result of giving the imagination too much free play.

45 Methought I heard a voice cry, 'Sleep no more!
Macbeth does murder sleep – the innocent sleep,
Sleep that knits up the ravelled sleave of care,
The death of each day's life, sore labour's bath,
Balm of hurt minds, great nature's second course,
Chief nourisher in life's feast'.
(II.2.35–40)
As Lady Macbeth and Macbeth continue in a hysterical state after the murder of Duncan, he tells her of an imagined cry he heard after he had done the murder. The cry, which is presumably his

conscience, reflects the way that the murder of Duncan initiates an overthrow of natural order at every level, from lack of sleep (which affects both Macbeth and Lady Macbeth) and broken banquets to more murders. The 'ravelled sleave' is a tangled skein; in feasts the 'second course' was the meat course, hence 'Chief nourisher'.

46 'Glamis hath murdered sleep, and therefore Cawdor
Shall sleep no more, Macbeth shall sleep no more.'
(II.2.42–3)
Macbeth continues to tell Lady Macbeth what he thought the voice said. He appears to be damned to sleeplessness in all aspects of his existence.

47 You do unbend your noble strength, to think
So brain-sickly of things.
(II.2.45–6)
Lady Macbeth tries to calm Macbeth's hysteria.

48 MACBETH I'll go no more.
I am afraid to think what I have done;
Look on't again I dare not.
LADY Infirm of purpose!
Give me the daggers. The sleeping and the dead
Are but as pictures. 'Tis the eye of childhood
That fears a painted devil. If he do bleed,
I'll gild the faces of the grooms withal,
For it must seem their guilt.
(II.2.50–7)
Lady Macbeth wants Macbeth to take the daggers he brought with him from the murder back into Duncan's room but he refuses. Lady Macbeth's pun on 'gild' and 'guilt' is grimly appropriate and again draws on the idea that the face may not be an accurate indicator of the inner person.

49 Whence is that knocking?
How is't with me when every noise appals me?
What hands are here! Ha – they pluck out mine eyes!
Will all great Neptune's ocean wash this blood
Clean from my hand? No, this my hand will rather
The multitudinous seas incarnadine,
Making the green one red.
(II.2.57–63)
Macbeth, left alone, reacts badly to the sound of knocking and then, apparently for the first time, notices that his hands are bloodstained. 'Incarnadine' means make red. Although the punc-

tuation of the last line has been disputed, it clearly means making the green sea a uniform red colour.

50 A little water clears us of this deed.
(II.2.67)
Lady Macbeth scolds Macbeth, arguing that they can wash the blood off their hands with a little water. There is obviously a contrast between her little water and his ocean (see 49) and there are also overtones of Pontius Pilate and, ironically, of baptism where a little water makes a child into a Christian. Lady Macbeth's sleepwalking scene shows how wrong her assessment is (see 113).

51 Here's a knocking indeed! If a man were porter of hell-gate he should have old turning the key.
Knock
Knock, knock, knock! Who's there i'the name of Belzebub? Here's a farmer that hanged himself on the expectation of plenty.
(II.3.1–5)
The Porter of Macbeth's castle has been awoken by the same knocking that disturbed Macbeth and Lady Macbeth. His prose grumbling to himself and the audience changes the atmosphere drastically after the feverish intensity of the previous scene, but there is a grim irony in his pretending to be the porter of Hell (a familiar character from the medieval drama) when his master and mistress have just turned the castle into a hell. Although the Porter's initial speech and exchanges with Macduff and Lennox were condemned by both Pope and Coleridge as unShakespearian interpolations, Thomas De Quincey's powerful defence 'On the Knocking at the Gate in *Macbeth*' (1823) established the importance and integrity of the scene. 'He should have old turning the key' means he would be kept busy turning the key to let people in.

52 Knock, Knock! Who's there in the other devil's name? Faith, here's an equivocator that could swear in both the scales against either scale, who committed treason enough for God's sake, yet could not equivocate to heaven. O, come in, equivocator.
(II.3.7–11)
Macbeth's Porter continues to play the porter of Hell. Although he cannot remember another devil's name, he still welcomes the equivocator. The play is much concerned with equivocation of all kinds, particularly by Macbeth who is already beginning to discover that he cannot 'equivocate to heaven', but there appears

to be a specific reference here to the 1605 Gunpowder Plot to blow up King James. There was great moral outrage when it turned out in the trials which followed the plot's discovery that the Provincial of the Jesuit Order, Father Henry Garnet, had equivocated, that is, given sworn evidence while making a mental reservation that the evidence was untrue. The 'scales' are the scales of justice.

53 Knock, knock! Never at quiet! What are you? – But this place is too cold for hell. I'll devil-porter it no further. I had thought to have let in some of all professions that go the primrose way to the everlasting bonfire.

Knock

Anon, anon! I pray you remember the porter.

(II.3.15–19)

The Porter finally decides to abandon his comic routine as the porter of Hell and answer the door. Shakespeare uses the idea that the easy path to damnation is strewn with flowers in *All's Well* (see 26) and *Hamlet* (see 35) as well as here. The final sentence, a request for a tip, is presumably addressed directly to the audience.

54 PORTER Faith, sir, we were carousing till the second cock; and drink, sir, is a great provoker of three things.

MACDUFF What three things does drink especially provoke?

PORTER Marry, sir, nose-painting, sleep, and urine. Lechery, sir, it provokes and unprovokes: it provokes the desire but it takes away the performance.

(II.3.22–8)

The Porter, having let Macduff and Lennox in, goes into another comic routine, using Macduff as his straight man. Even in the Porter's casual reference to the time there is an allusion to Christ's betrayal by Peter before the cock crowed thrice. 'Nose-painting' refers to the red nose of the drunkard.

55 The labour we delight in physics pain.

(II.3.47)

Macduff responds to Macbeth's greeting small talk with some of his own. There may be a degree of irony if the remark is applied to Macbeth, whose labour (killing Duncan) does not result in joy. 'Physics' means cures.

56 LENNOX

The night has been unruly. Where we lay,
Our chimneys were blown down, and, as they say,
Lamentings heard i'the air, strange screams of death

And prophesying, with accents terrible,
Of dire combustion and confused events
New-hatched to the woeful time. The obscure bird
Clamoured the live-long night. Some say the earth
Was feverous and did shake.

MACBETH 'Twas a rough night.

(II.3.51–8)

While they wait for Macduff to come back from waking Duncan, Lennox fills the time with an account of unnatural disorders in the night. Macbeth, distracted by his knowledge that Macduff will find Duncan murdered, can manage only a flat prosaic response to Lennox's list of the kind of events in nature which were held to accompany major disturbances in the human world. 'New-hatched' means newly born; the 'obscure bird' is the owl, a herald of death.

57 O horror, horror, horror!
Tongue nor heart cannot conceive nor name thee!

(II.3.60–1)

Macduff enters to Macbeth and Lennox from having discovered Duncan dead.

58 Confusion now hath made his masterpiece;
Most sacrilegious murder hath broke ope
The Lord's anointed temple and stole thence
The life o'the building.

(II.3.63–6)

Macduff begins to tell Macbeth and Lennox what has happened. Shakespeare's choice of words directs our attention to the full horror of the murder by stressing the sacrilege of killing a king. 'Ope' means open; 'The Lord's anointed temple', combining two biblical references (2 Corinthians 6:16 and 1 Samuel 24:10), is the body of the king.

59 Shake off this downy sleep, death's counterfeit,
And look on death itself! Up, up, and see
The Great Doom's image!

(II.3.73–5)

Macduff rouses the inhabitants of the castle to see Duncan's body. The 'Great Doom' is Judgement Day.

60 MACDUFF
Our royal master's murdered.

LADY Woe, alas!
What, in our house!

BANQUO Too cruel, anywhere.
(II.3.84–5)
Although Lady Macbeth's reaction to Macduff's statement that Duncan has been murdered has been defended as an innocent hostess's natural response, it has also been seen as an ill-judged gambit striking a false note. Presumably the tone in which Banquo's line is delivered will determine audience response.

61 Had I but died an hour before this chance
I had lived a blessèd time; for from this instant
There's nothing serious in mortality.
All is but toys, renown and grace is dead,
The wine of life is drawn, and the mere lees
Is left this vault to brag of.
(II.3.88–93)
Macbeth, who had gone off with Lennox into Duncan's chamber, re-enters to the assembled nobles. His lines, meant to convince them of his innocence and integrity, are presumably hypocritical yet they come to seem only too accurate in their assessment as the play proceeds. 'Mortality' is human life; 'lees' are dregs; 'vault', taking up the wine imagery, is a wine vault – it is also the sky and a tomb, as well as picking up the idea of a room left empty from earlier in the scene (see 58).

62 MACBETH
Who can be wise, amazed, temperate and furious,
Loyal and neutral, in a moment? No man.
The expedition of my violent love
Outrun the pauser reason. Here lay Duncan,
His silver skin laced with his golden blood,
And his gashed stabs looked like a breach in nature
For ruin's wasteful entrance; there the murderers,
Steeped in the colours of their trade, their daggers
Unmannerly breeched with gore. Who could refrain,
That had a heart to love, and in that heart
Courage to make's love known?
LADY (*swooning*) Help me hence, ho!
MACDUFF
Look to the lady!
(II.3.105–16)
Macbeth attempts to justify his killing of Duncan's grooms to the assembled nobles in response to a suspicious question from Macduff. Lady Macbeth's reaction has been interpreted as a genuine response to the power of Macbeth's speech and as a ploy to distract attention from his discomfort which some critics see as being reflected in a forced quality in his speech. 'Expedition'

means hastiness; 'the pauser reason' is reason which should delay such hastiness. Duncan's skin is presumably grey and his blood is 'golden' because it is precious. The grooms' 'Unmannerly breeched' daggers are unsheathed but covered instead with the blood of the king they should have protected – 'breeched' takes up 'breach' from earlier in the speech and continues the play's clothing imagery. 'Make's' means make his.

63 Where we are
There's daggers in men's smiles. The nea'er in blood
The nearer bloody.
(II.3.136–8)
Malcolm and Donalbain, Duncan's sons, left alone after the murder, decide to flee abroad to different destinations. Donalbain voices their belief that people closely related to them are more likely to kill them.

64 'Tis unnatural,
Even like the deed that's done. On Tuesday last,
A falcon towering in her pride of place
Was by a mousing owl hawked at and killed.
(II.4.10–13)
An Old Man, introduced as a chorus figure, adds another portent to Ross's account of unnatural events. The 'deed' is Duncan's murder. The falcon is circling to the highest point of its flight ('towering in her pride of place') when it is attacked ('hawked at'), in a reversal of the natural order, by an owl which would normally fly low in its hunt for mice ('mousing').

65 Thou hast it now: King, Cawdor, Glamis, all
As the weird women promised; and I fear
Thou playedst most foully for't.
(III.1.1–3)
Banquo soliloquizes about Macbeth's sudden rise to power and his methods of obtaining that power.

66 BANQUO
Go not my horse the better,
I must become a borrower of the night
For a dark hour or twain.
MACBETH Fail not our feast.
(III.1.25–7)
Macbeth, plotting Banquo's death, has asked how long he is planning to ride. 'Go not my horse the better' means if my horse does not go well enough. Macbeth's command that Banquo

should be at the banquet that evening is fulfilled by the appearance of his ghost (see 81).

67 To be thus is nothing;
But to be safely thus!
(III.1.47–8)

Macbeth soliloquizes about the kingship: there is no point in being king unless your rule is unchallenged.

68 FIRST MURDERER We are men, my liege.
MACBETH
Ay, in the catalogue ye go for men,
As hounds and greyhounds, mongrels, spaniels, curs,
Shoughs, water-rugs, and demi-wolves are clept
All by the name of dogs.
(III.1.90–3)

Macbeth is talking to the Murderers he is hiring to kill Banquo. He taunts them in terms which recall Lady Macbeth taunting him about his masculinity. 'Shoughs' are shaggy-haired dogs; 'water-rugs' are probably rough-haired water dogs and 'demi-wolves' are cross-breeds, dogs crossed with wolves; 'clept' means called.

69 SECOND MURDERER I am one, my liege,
Whom the vile blows and buffets of the world
Hath so incensed that I am reckless what I do
To spite the world.
FIRST MURDERER And I another,
So weary with disasters, tugged with fortune,
That I would set my life on any chance
To mend it or be rid on't.
(III.1.107–113)

The Murderers are trying to convince Macbeth of their readiness to murder Banquo. 'Tugged with' means battered by; 'set' means stake.

70 Leave no rubs nor botches in the work.
(III.1.133)

Macbeth instructs the Murderers to kill Banquo's son Fleance in order to make the job perfect. 'Rubs' and 'botches' are rough spots and mistakes.

71 Naught's had, all's spent,
Where our desire is got without content.
(III.2.4–5)

Macbeth briefly soliloquizes: he has done everything but achieved nothing ('Naught's had, all's spent') because he cannot enjoy the crown unchallenged.

72 LADY Things without all remedy
Should be without regard; what's done is done.
MACBETH
We have scorched the snake, not killed it;
She'll close and be herself, whilst our poor malice
Remains in danger of her former tooth.
But let the frame of things disjoint, both the worlds suffer
Ere we will eat our meal in fear, and sleep
In the affliction of these terrible dreams
That shake us nightly; better be with the dead
Whom we, to gain our peace, have sent to peace,
Than on the torture of the mind to lie
In restless ecstasy. Duncan is in his grave;
After life's fitful fever he sleeps well;
Treason has done his worst. Nor steel, nor poison,
Malice domestic, foreign levy, nothing
Can touch him further.
(III.2.11–26)

Lady Macbeth's attempts to rally her husband, disturbed by his lack of sleep, fail. 'Scorched' means slashed, wounded – the eighteenth-century editor Lewis Theobald's famous emendation 'scotch'd' has been rejected by more recent editors. 'Former tooth' means the snake's fangs, as dangerous as they were before it was wounded. 'Let the frame of things disjoint, both the worlds suffer' means let everything fall apart and the earthly and heavenly worlds suffer. 'Whom we, to gain our peace, have sent to peace' means whom we, to satisfy our ambition and attain peace of mind, have sent to the peace of the grave. 'On the torture of the mind to lie / In restless ecstasy' suggests that now his sleep is full of bad dreams, Macbeth's bed has become like a rack on which he is tormented by his nightmares and fantasies. A 'foreign levy' is a foreign army.

73 Ere the bat hath flown
His cloistered flight, ere to black Hecat's summons
The shard-borne beetle, with his drowsy hums,
Hath rung night's yawning peal, there shall be done
A deed of dreadful note.
(III.2.40–4)

Macbeth tells Lady Macbeth that something will happen before night to make them happier. Bats fly indoors and are associated with churches, hence 'cloistered'. Hecate is the goddess of witchcraft and the moon. The beetle may be dung-bred or it may be carried on scaly wings, depending on how 'shard-borne' is interpreted.

74 Be innocent of the knowledge, dearest chuck,
Till thou applaud the deed. Come, seeling night,
Scarf up the tender eye of pitiful day,
And with thy bloody and invisible hand
Cancel and tear to pieces that great bond
Which keeps me pale. Light thickens
And the crow makes wing to the rooky wood;
Good things of day begin to droop and drowse,
Whiles night's black agents to their preys do rouse.
Thou marvell'st at my words; but hold thee still.
Things bad begun make strong themselves by ill.
(III.2.45–55)
Macbeth replies to Lady Macbeth's question about what he is planning. The contrast between the endearment 'dearest chuck' and the murder of Banquo is striking. 'Come, seeling night, / Scarf up the tender eye of pitiful day' draws on the language of falconry in which the falconer sews up ('seels') the eyes of a hawk as part of its training; 'scarf up' means blindfold. The 'great bond' may refer to legal prohibitions of murder or to Nature's agreement by which Banquo and Fleance live. 'To their preys do rouse' means get ready to go hunting.

75 The west yet glimmers with some streaks of day.
Now spurs the lated traveller apace
To gain the timely inn.
(III.3.5–7)
The First Murderer's beautiful description of sunset, grimly apposite to Banquo, the belated traveller who will never reach safety, is spoken to the other two Murderers as they wait for Banquo and Fleance. 'Timely' means convenient.

76 Ourself will mingle with society
And play the humble host.
(III.4.3–4)
Macbeth tells his guests at the banquet that he will mingle with them. As Lady Macbeth stays sitting, he is forced to face Banquo's ghost without her support when it first appears.

77 There's blood upon thy face!
(III.4.13)

Macbeth talks to the First Murderer on the fringes of the banquet. In this case the outward appearance is a true indication of what has been happening.

78 Then comes my fit again. I had else been perfect,
Whole as the marble, founded as the rock,
As broad and general as the casing air;
But now I am cabined, cribbed, confined, bound in
To saucy doubts and fears.
(III.4.20–4)
This is Macbeth's reaction to the First Murderer's news that Fleance escaped from the ambush. 'Founded' means solid; 'broad and general' means unrestrained; 'casing' means encasing, surrounded. 'Cabined, cribbed, confined, bound in' all mean shut in – the repetition suggests Macbeth's obsessive intensity. 'Saucy' means impudent.

79 There the grown serpent lies. The worm that's fled
Hath nature that in time will venom breed,
No teeth for the present.
(III.4.28–30)
Macbeth comforts himself with the thought that Banquo ('the grown serpent') is dead and Fleance ('The worm') is currently powerless to harm him.

80 Now good digestion wait on appetite,
And health on both!
(III.4.37–8)
This general address to the guests is Macbeth's response to Lady Macbeth reminding him of his duties as a host which he has been neglecting while talking to the Murderer and then soliloquizing.

81 Which of you have done this?
(III.4.48)
Macbeth responds to the appearance of Banquo's ghost by asking who killed him, thus baffling the guests, who are unable to see the ghost and remain puzzled throughout Macbeth's encounter with it.

82 Thou canst not say I did it; never shake
Thy gory locks at me.
(III.4.49–50)
Macbeth addresses the ghost, apparently thinking that since he did not physically kill Banquo himself he is, in some peculiar way, innocent of the murder. The guests witness Macbeth's behaviour but do not see the ghost.

83 If charnel-houses and our graves must send
Those that we bury, back, our monuments
Shall be the maws of kites.
(III.4.70–2)

Macbeth, unnerved by the ghost's appearance, suggests that if the normal burial places are sending their occupants back, it will be necessary for bodies to be disposed of to birds of prey. 'Charnel-houses' are places where bones are kept; 'maws' are stomachs. The guests are present throughout this outburst.

84 The times has been
That, when the brains were out, the man would die,
And there an end.
(III.4.77–9)

Still in the presence of the guests, Macbeth continues to object that Banquo's murder ought to have been the end of him.

85 What man dare, I dare.
Approach thou like the rugged Russian bear,
The armed rhinoceros, or the Hyrcan tiger,
Take any shape but that, and my firm nerves
Shall never tremble. Or be alive again,
And dare me to the desert with thy sword:
If trembling I inhabit then, protest me
The baby of a girl. Hence, horrible shadow!
Unreal mockery, hence!
(III.4.98–106)

Macbeth continues to react to the ghost despite Lady Macbeth's attempts to gloss over the situation to the guests. In Roman literature tigers were often associated with Hyrcania in Persia. 'If trembling I inhabit then' means if I tremble then; 'baby' probably means doll, although it could be intended to give a double image of helplessness in company with 'girl'.

86 You have displaced the mirth, broke the good meeting
With most admired disorder.
(III.4.108–9)

Lady Macbeth's rebuke can be applied not only to her husband's specific behaviour at the banquet but also to his general destruction of the civilized virtues throughout the kingdom.

87 Stand not upon the order of your going;
But go at once.
(III.4.118–19)

Lady Macbeth tries to get the guests away before Macbeth's behaviour can do any more damage to their reputation. The abruptness of the guests' departure contrasts with the ceremonial opening of the banquet.

88 MACBETH
It will have blood, they say; blood will have blood.
Stones have been known to move and trees to speak;
Augurs and understood relations have
By maggot-pies, and choughs, and rooks brought forth
The secret'st man of blood. What is the night?
LADY
Almost at odds with morning, which is which.
(III.4.121–6)
After the guests' departure, Macbeth continues to muse distractedly on the theme of 'murder will out' until he asks Lady Macbeth the time. Various inanimate and animate parts of nature will reveal the crime despite the murderer's best efforts to conceal it. 'Augurs' are predictions; 'understood relations' is somewhat obscure but may mean understood reports or connections established; 'maggot-pies' are magpies; 'choughs' are birds of the crow family. Lady Macbeth's reply, with its reference to a struggle between night and day, has wider applications.

89 I am in blood
Stepped in so far, that, should I wade no more,
Returning were as tedious as go o'er.
(III.4.135–7)
Macbeth, telling Lady Macbeth his plans, comments accurately on his predicament, trapped by his own actions, insecure in his position and beginning to discover the banality of evil.

90 You lack the season of all natures, sleep.
(III.4.140)
Lady Macbeth's line to Macbeth is presumably motivated by the immediate context of their sleepless night following the banquet, but it also applies to the wider context in which Macbeth has murdered Sleep. 'Season' means preservative, spice.

91 And you all know security
Is mortals' chiefest enemy.
(III.5.32–3)
In a scene often regarded as an interpolation, Hecate, after complaining to the Witches that they have not been involving her in their plots, makes the point that overconfidence ('security') is the greatest enemy of human beings. Even if the lines are not Shakespeare's, they are clearly apposite to the way in which Mac-

beth is lulled into a false sense of 'security' by the Witches' equivocation.

92 Thrice the brinded cat hath mewed.
(IV.1.1)
A new scene with the Witches opens with the First Witch's statement. Presumably the streaked ('brinded') cat is the Witch's familiar.

93 FIRST WITCH
Round about the cauldron go;
In the poisoned entrails throw:
Toad that under cold stone
Days and nights has thirty-one
Sweltered venom, sleeping got,
Boil thou first i'the charmèd pot.
ALL
Double, double, toil and trouble;
Fire burn, and cauldron bubble.
(IV.1.4–11)
The Witches are concocting a charm. 'Sweltered venom, sleeping got' means venom exuded while the toad was asleep.

94 Eye of newt, and toe of frog,
Wool of bat, and tongue of dog,
Adder's fork, and blind-worm's sting,
Lizard's leg and howlet's wing,
For a charm of powerful trouble,
Like a hell-broth, boil and bubble.
(IV.1.14–19)
The Second Witch adds her ingredients to the cauldron. 'Fork' means forked tongue; the slow worm ('blind-worm') is, in fact, harmless; a 'howlet' is a young owl.

95 Liver of blaspheming Jew,
Gall of goat, and slips of yew
Slivered in the moon's eclipse,
Nose of Turk, and Tartar's lips,
Finger of birth-strangled babe,
Ditch-delivered by a drab,
Make the gruel thick and slab.
(IV.1.26–32)
These are some of the Third Witch's ingredients. The Jew, Turk, Tartar, and 'birth-strangled babe' are particularly valuable sources of ingredients for the Witches because they are all unchristened. The liver was believed to be the seat of the passions; 'blasphem-

ing' is applied to the Jew because he does not accept the divinity of Christ. 'Slips of yew' are seedlings of the yew, which often grows in graveyards and is poisonous. 'Slab' means thick, viscous.

96 SECOND WITCH

By the pricking of my thumbs,
Something wicked this way comes.
Open, locks, whoever knocks!

Enter Macbeth

MACBETH

How now, you secret, black, and midnight hags!
What is't you do?

ALL A deed without a name.

(IV.1.44–8)

Macbeth arrives to seek help from the Witches. The Witches' deed is so horrible it does not have a name.

97 Be bloody, bold and resolute; laugh to scorn
The power of man; for none of woman born
Shall harm Macbeth.

(IV.1.78–80)

In response to Macbeth's desire to know what will happen in the future, the Witches produce a series of Apparitions. The Second Apparition who speaks these lines is 'a bloody child', presumably representing Macduff. As Macbeth later discovers, the Apparition is equivocating (see 133).

98 But yet I'll make assurance double sure,
And take a bond of fate.

(IV.1.82–3)

Convinced by the Second Apparition, Macbeth at first decides to let Macduff (whom he assumes to be naturally born) live, but then decides to make a bond to make everything doubly sure by killing him anyway.

99 Macbeth shall never vanquished be, until
Great Birnan Wood to high Dunsinane Hill
Shall come against him.

(IV.1.91–3)

The Third Apparition, a crowned child with a tree in its hand who is presumably Malcolm carrying a branch of Birnan Wood, equivocates with Macbeth in the same way as the Second Apparition (see 98).

100 Show his eyes and grieve his heart;
Come like shadows, so depart.
(IV.1.109–10)

Despite their warnings, Macbeth has asked the Witches to tell him if Banquo's family will ever rule Scotland. Here they summon up a display of future kings descended from Banquo.

101 What, will the line stretch out to the crack of doom?
(IV.1.116)

Macbeth reacts in horror to the apparently endless succession of kings descended from Banquo that the Witches have conjured up. 'Line' means both queue and line of succession.

102 The very firstlings of my heart shall be
The firstlings of my hand.
(IV.1.146–7)

Macbeth, informed by Lennox of Macduff's flight to England, decides that in future he will act as soon as he decides to do something.

103 When our actions do not,
Our fears do make us traitors.
(IV.2.3–4)

Lady Macduff, left behind when her husband fled to England, complains to Ross that Macduff's flight will be interpreted by Macbeth as treachery.

104 He loves us not.
He wants the natural touch; for the poor wren,
The most diminutive of birds, will fight,
Her young ones in her nest, against the owl.
(IV.2.8–11)

Lady Macduff complains to Ross that Macduff's leaving her and their family behind shows his lack of natural family feelings. In terms of the broader movement of the play we can see how Macbeth's unnaturalness is beginning to influence everyone's behaviour.

105 SON
And must they all be hanged that swear and lie?
LADY MACDUFF Every one.
SON Who must hang them?
LADY MACDUFF Why, the honest men.
SON Then the liars and swearers are fools; for there are liars and swearers enow to beat the honest men and hang up them.
(IV.2.52–8)

After Ross's departure, Lady Macduff has told her son that Macduff was a traitor, which she defines for him as 'one that swears and lies'. This scene of domestic pathos, which ends with the murder of Lady Macduff and her son, shows how limitless Macbeth's capacity for trying to find peace of mind by exterminating sources of potential opposition has become.

106 Angels are bright still though the brightest fell.
(IV.3.22)
Malcolm is suspicious of Macduff, who has joined him in England. Here he suggests that Macduff should excuse his doubts, which cannot alter Macduff's true worth, just as Lucifer's fall from heaven has not altered the worth of the angels. At this stage they do not know that Lady Macduff has been murdered.

107 Such welcome and unwelcome things at once
'Tis hard to reconcile.
(IV.3.138–9)
Macduff's violent and despairing reaction to Malcolm's pretence to be more evil than Macbeth has convinced Malcolm that he is not one of Macbeth's agents and he has told him that an English army is already on the point of setting out for Scotland. Macduff's reaction continues the play's concern with the problem of how to tell good from evil, fair from foul, inner truth from outward appearance, all of which have been considered in the testing of Macduff. They are still unaware of Lady Macduff's death.

108 MACDUFF
Stands Scotland where it did?
ROSS Alas, poor country,
Almost afraid to know itself! It cannot
Be called our mother, but our grave.
(IV.3.164–6)
Ross, newly arrived in England, has met Macduff and Malcolm but not yet told them of Lady Macduff's murder. An audience, expecting this revelation, will probably see the specific event behind his generalized comments.

109 The dead man's knell
Is there scarce asked for who, and good men's lives
Expire before the flowers in their caps,
Dying or ere they sicken.
(IV.3.170–3)
Ross paints a picture of the general state of affairs in Scotland for Malcolm and Macduff, still not mentioning the murder of Lady

Macduff. Death is so commonplace that no one takes any notice of the bells that mark funerals. 'Or ere' means before.

110 What, man! Ne'er pull your hat upon your brows.
Give sorrow words: the grief that does not speak
Whispers the o'erfraught heart and bids it break.
(IV.3.208–10)

Ross has finally managed to tell Macduff of his family's murder. Malcolm's lines comment on Macduff's initial silent reaction. In the Renaissance period hats were worn indoors as well as outside and exact locations were seldom specified, but in modern productions this scene is often set outside so that Macduff can plausibly be wearing a hat. 'O'erfraught' means overloaded.

111 MALCOLM Be comforted.
Let's make us medicines of our great revenge
To cure this deadly grief.
MACDUFF He has no children.
All my pretty ones? Did you say all?
O hell-kite! All? What, all my pretty chickens
And their dam, at one fell swoop?
MALCOLM
Dispute it like a man.
MACDUFF I shall do so;
But I must also feel it as a man.
I cannot but remember such things were
That were most precious to me.
(IV.3.213–22)

Malcolm attempts to comfort Macduff after Ross has told him about the deaths of his whole household. 'He has no children' has been variously interpreted as meaning that Malcolm cannot understand Macduff's grief because he has no children, that Macbeth has no children whom Macduff can kill in revenge, and that if Macbeth had had any children he would have been incapable of killing Macduff's. Macduff sees Macbeth as a hellish bird of prey swooping on his nest (unconsciously echoing Lady Macduff's bird images, see 104). 'Chicken' is still used as a term of endearment, although it is suggested here by the use of 'kite'; 'dam' means mother. 'At one fell swoop' means in one evil attack – birds of prey swoop on their victims – but it has come to be misapplied in popular usage to mean simply all at once.

112 DOCTOR You see her eyes are open.
GENTLEWOMAN Ay, but their sense are shut.
(V.1.24–5)

Lady Macbeth's Gentlewoman has asked the Doctor to watch her as she walks in her sleep. Here they comment on her.

113 Out, damned spot! Out, I say! – One: two: why then, 'tis time to do't. – Hell is murky! – Fie, my lord, fie! A soldier and afeard? – What need we fear who knows it, when none can call our power to accompt? – Yet who would have thought the old man to have had so much blood in him?
(V.1.34–9)
Lady Macbeth, watched by the Doctor and her Gentlewoman as she walks in her sleep, goes through the motions of trying to get Duncan's blood off her hands and relives part of the murder. Her disjointed speech marks the degree of her mental disturbance, while her inability to clean her hands and, symbolically, remove her guilt is in sharp contrast to her earlier beliefs (see 50). 'One: two' refers to the time of Duncan's murder; 'accompt' means account.

114 The Thane of Fife had a wife; where is she now? – What, will these hands ne'er be clean? – No more o'that, my lord, no more o'that. You mar all with this starting.
(V.1.41–3)
Lady Macbeth, still watched by the Doctor and her Gentlewoman as she walks in her sleep, moves on to talk of Lady Macduff's murder and Macbeth's jumpiness, while still attempting to wash Duncan's blood off her hand. The jingle of 'Fife' and 'wife' can be used effectively in the theatre to suggest the disintegration of her mind.

115 Here's the smell of the blood still. All the perfumes of Arabia will not sweeten this little hand. Oh! Oh! Oh!
(V.1.48–9)
Still watched by the Doctor and the Gentlewoman as she sleepwalks, Lady Macbeth begins to despair of cleaning her hands and thus, figuratively, of purging her guilt for the murder of Duncan.

116 I would not have such a heart in my bosom for the dignity of the whole body.
(V.1.51–2)
After hearing Lady Macbeth's sleepwalking secrets, the horrified Gentlewoman comments to the Doctor. 'Dignity' means worth.

117 Wash your hands; put on your nightgown; look not so pale. I tell you yet again, Banquo's buried; he cannot come out on's grave.
(V.1.58–60)

Lady Macbeth's sleepwalking résumé of crimes, overheard by the Doctor and the Gentlewoman, now reaches Banquo's murder. 'Out on's' means out of his.

118 To bed, to bed! There's knocking at the gate. Come, come, come, come, give me your hand. What's done cannot be undone. To bed, to bed, to bed.
(V.1.62–4)
Lady Macbeth's sleepwalking, overheard by the Gentlewoman and the Doctor, ends with the knocking at the gate after Duncan's murder. 'What's done cannot be undone' ironically recalls her earlier 'What's done is done' (see 72).

119 Foul whisperings are abroad, unnatural deeds
Do breed unnatural troubles; infected minds
To their deaf pillows will discharge their secrets.
More needs she the divine than the physician.
(V.1.67–70)
The Doctor's choric comment to the Gentlewomen after the exit of the sleepwalking Lady Macbeth can be applied to the wider situation as well as to Lady Macbeth's specific condition.

120 Those he commands move only in command,
Nothing in love. Now does he feel his title
Hang loose about him like a giant's robe
Upon a dwarfish thief.
(V.2.19–22)
Angus, a lord in Malcolm and Macduff's army, describes Macbeth and his followers to his fellow officers. The clothing imagery here takes up other references earlier in the play (see 18 for an example). 'Only in command / Nothing in love' means because they have to, not because they want to.

121 Bring me no more reports; let them fly all.
Till Birnan Wood remove to Dunsinane
I cannot taint with fear.
(V.3.1–3)
Macbeth, who has entered with the Doctor and attendants, appears to have been told that his supporters ('them') are leaving him and reacts by reaffirming his faith in the Witches' prophesies.

122 The devil damn thee black, thou cream-faced loon!
Where got'st thou that goose look?
(V.3.11–12)
Macbeth reacts explosively to the arrival of a messenger with news. The messenger is presumably pale-faced with fear, hence

'cream-faced' and 'goose look' (which means cowardly appearance); 'loon' means rascal. In Sir William Davenant's Restoration adaptation of the play, first staged in 1672, the first line became 'Now Friend what means thy change of countenance', in which decorum triumphs effortlessly over vigour.

123 I have lived long enough: my way of life
Is fallen into the sere, the yellow leaf;
And that which should accompany old age,
As honour, love, obedience, troops of friends,
I must not look to have; but, in their stead,
Curses, not loud, but deep, mouth-honour, breath
Which the poor heart would fain deny and dare not.
(V.3.22–8)

Macbeth soliloquizes about the decline in his moral fortunes which has followed his attaining power. 'Sere' means (the state of being) withered. In the last two lines Macbeth describes how his subjects curse him under their breath ('not loud, but deep'), pay him lip-service ('mouth-honour'), and speak polite words ('breath') only because they are too faint-hearted to speak the truth ('Which the poor heart would fain deny and dare not'); in other words, he is surrounded by equivocators.

124 MACBETH
Canst thou not minister to a mind diseased,
Pluck from the memory a rooted sorrow,
Raze out the written troubles of the brain,
And with some sweet oblivious antidote
Cleanse the stuffed bosom of that perilous stuff
Which weighs upon the heart?
DOCTOR Therein the patient
Must minister to himself.
MACBETH
Throw physic to the dogs! I'll none of it.
(V.3.40–7)

Macbeth questions the Doctor about Lady Macbeth. 'Raze out' means erase; 'written' means recorded permanently, fixed; 'stuffed' means clogged.

125 Were I from Dunsinane away and clear,
Profit again should hardly draw me here.
(V.3.61–2)

The Doctor who has observed Lady Macbeth sleepwalking as well as Macbeth's behaviour comments aside to end the scene.

126 Hang out our banners on the outward walls.
The cry is still, 'They come.' Our castle's strength
Will laugh a siege to scorn.
(V.5.1–3)
Macbeth is preparing for the arrival of Malcolm and Macduff's army.

127 I have almost forgot the taste of fears.
The time has been my senses would have cooled
To hear a night-shriek, and my fell of hair
Would at a dismal treatise rouse and stir
As life were in't. I have supped full with horrors:
Direness, familiar to my slaughterous thoughts,
Cannot once start me.
(V.5.9–15)
Macbeth comments on his unsurprised reaction to the sudden wailing of women which, unknown to him, marks Lady Macbeth's death. 'Fell' means skin, hence scalp; 'dismal treatise' means woeful story; 'supped full with' means had my fill of; 'start' means startle.

128 She should have died hereafter.
There would have been a time for such a word –
Tomorrow, and tomorrow, and tomorrow,
Creeps in this petty pace from day to day
To the last syllable of recorded time;
And all our yesterdays have lighted fools
The way to dusty death. Out, out, brief candle!
Life's but a walking shadow, a poor player
That struts and frets his hour upon the stage
And then is heard no more. It is a tale
Told by an idiot, full of sound and fury,
Signifying nothing.
(V.5.17–28)
Told by Seyton that Lady Macbeth is dead, Macbeth reacts numbly with his vision of the futility of their lives. This is one of those speeches which are sometimes regarded as representing Shakespeare's own 'philosophy of life', but we should always remember its context and not be fooled by the quality of the writing into assuming that it must, therefore, represent Shakespeare's own views. There has been some controversy over the meaning of the first line, which has been taken to mean she would have died at some time anyway or she should have died at a time when it would have been possible to pay her proper attention – perhaps both interpretations are possible. 'Word' means news; 'in this petty pace' probably refers to Macbeth pacing around but it

could also refer to the rhythm of 'Tomorrow, and tomorrow, and tomorrow', thus meaning in a minor key. 'To the last syllable of recorded time' perhaps means to the end of the last recorded word, but has also been explained as referring to the Last Judgement or to the end of an individual's words. The comparison of life to a candle leads to the shadow which in turn suggests the actor who is both to be pitied because his part is short and a poor actor.

129 If this which he avouches does appear,
There is nor flying hence nor tarrying here.
I 'gin to be aweary of the sun,
And wish the estate o'the world were now undone. –
Ring the alarum bell! – Blow wind, come wrack,
At least we'll die with harness on our back.
(V.5.47–52)

Macbeth, told by a Messenger that Birnan wood appears to be moving towards Dunsinane, realizes that if what the messenger says ('he avouches') is true ('doth appear') he has run out of options, but at least he will go down fighting. The 'estate o'the world' is the universe; 'wrack' means wreck; 'harness' is armour.

130 They have tied me to a stake, I cannot fly,
But bear-like I must fight the course.
(V.6.11–12)

In battle, Macbeth reflects that he is trapped like a bear in the so-called sport of bear-baiting. 'Course' is a technical term for one round of the fight between the bear and the dogs.

131 We have met with foes
That strike beside us.
(V.6.38–9)

As the battle to defeat Macbeth continues, Malcolm comments to Old Seyward, the commander of the English troops who are fighting on his side, that Macbeth's army is not fighting them. The lines have been interpreted as meaning both join in alongside and miss us deliberately with their weapons.

132 Why should I play the Roman fool and die
On mine own sword?
(V.6.40–1)

As the battle continues, Macbeth re-enters and decides against adopting the traditional response of defeated Roman leaders such as Brutus or Antony.

133 MACBETH

I bear a charmèd life which must not yield
To one of woman born.

MACDUFF Despair thy charm,
And let the angel whom thou still hast served
Tell thee Macduff was from his mother's womb
Untimely ripped.

MACBETH

Accursèd be that tongue that tells me so;
For it hath cowed my better part of man;
And be these juggling fiends no more believed
That palter with us in a double sense,
That keep the word of promise to our ear
And break it to our hope. I'll not fight with thee.

(V.6.51–61)

In the long-awaited confrontation between Macbeth and Macduff, Macbeth discovers that his sense of 'security' has been misplaced because the Witches have equivocated with him. 'Despair' means have no faith in; 'angel' means bad angel; 'juggling' means cheating; 'palter with us in a double sense' means equivocate with us, speak with double meanings.

134 Lay on, Macduff;
And damned be him that first cries, 'Hold, enough!'

(V.6.72–3)

Macbeth summons up his last reserves for a final combat with Macduff. The first line is often misquoted as 'Lead on, Macduff'.

135 The time is free.

(V.6.94)

Macduff re-enters with Macbeth's severed head to confirm Malcolm's victory. His words suggest that a burden has been lifted from the natural processes themselves and that the natural order is restored.

136 This dead butcher and his fiend-like queen.

(V.6.108)

Malcolm gives his final judgement on Macbeth and Lady Macbeth.

Measure for Measure

1 I'll privily away: I love the people,
But do not like to stage me to their eyes;
Though it do well, I do not relish well

Their loud applause and aves vehement,
Nor do I think the man of safe discretion
That does affect it.
(I.1.67–72)
The Duke of Vienna, having decided to leave the government in the hands of a deputy, Angelo, explains why he is departing without ceremony to Angelo and his fellow deputy Escalus. 'Aves' are cries of acclamation, from the Latin *ave*.

2 LUCIO Thou conclud'st like the sanctimonious pirate, that went to sea with the Ten Commandments, but scraped one out of the table.
SECOND GENTLEMAN 'Thou shalt not steal'?
LUCIO Ay, that he razed.
(I.2.7–11)
Lucio, a man about town, is in conversation with two gentlemen who, anticipating a possible military campaign against Hungary, have prayed for peace, 'but not the King of Hungary's!' 'Table' means list, with a reference to the tablets of stone on which the Ten Commandments were originally written. 'Razed' means erased.

3 Groping for trouts in a peculiar river.
(I.2.89)
Pompey, servant to the bawd Mistress Overdone, tells her that a man, presumably Claudio, has been sent to prison for illicit sexual activity – the analogy is with poaching. 'Peculiar' means private.

4 Our natures do pursue,
Like rats that ravin down their proper bane,
A thirsty evil, and when we drink we die.
(I.2.127–9)
Claudio, who believes that his secret marriage to the pregnant Juliet is legally binding, has been arrested for fornication on the orders of the Duke's deputy Angelo. Here he describes to Lucio how people pursue liberty to excess, like rats that greedily devour their special poison ('ravin down their proper bane').

5 Whether it be the fault and glimpse of newness,
Or whether that the body public be
A horse whereon the governor doth ride,
Who, newly in the seat, that it may know
He can command, lets it straight feel the spur;
Whether the tyranny be in his place,
Or in his eminence that fills it up,
I stagger in – but this new governor

Awakes me all the enrollèd penalties
Which have, like unscoured armour, hung by th'wall
So long that nineteen zodiacs have gone round
And none of them been worn, and for a name
Now puts the drowsy and neglected act
Freshly on me. 'Tis surely for a name.
(I.2.157–70)

Claudio explains to Lucio his understanding of Angelo's reasons for reviving the unused sanctions against fornication. 'Fault and glimpse of newness' probably means a rash faulty judgement due to inexperience; 'be in his place, / Or in his eminence that fills it up' means stems from the nature of the office itself or from the self-importance of the office-bearer; 'I stagger in' means I don't know. 'Awakes me all the enrollèd penalties' means reapplies the prescribed penalties; 'unscour'd' means unpolished; 'for a name' may refer both to Angelo's desire to make his reputation and to Claudio and Juliet not having openly declared their marriage: Claudio believes that he is being punished for a minor procedural fault. Later in the play, the Duke says that it has been fourteen years since the laws were used – the discrepancy between his figure and Claudio's may be an authorial error or it may be that each character has his own reason for exaggerating or minimizing the period of laxity (see 8).

6 In her youth
There is a prone and speechless dialect,
Such as move men.
(I.2.181–3)

Claudio wants his sister Isabella (who is just about to become a nun) to plead his case to Angelo, and describes her qualifications for the task to Lucio. Although his words are overtly to do with her powers of persuasion, the possible sexual overtones of 'prone' and 'move' begin to create the ambiguous atmosphere of sexuality that surrounds Isabella. 'Prone' may mean apt or refer to the prone position associated with supplication; 'dialect' means language.

7 Believe not that the dribbling dart of love,
Can pierce a complete bosom.
(I.3.2–3)

The Duke is explaining to the Friar, whom he is asking to help him disguise himself as a friar, that he is not wanting to do so because he is in love. The Duke's confidence in his own invulnerability is misplaced, since he later proposes marriage to Isabella. The 'dribbling dart of love' is Cupid's feeble arrow which cannot pierce the Duke's impenetrable ('complete') bosom.

8 We have strict statutes and most biting laws,
The needful bits and curbs to headstrong weeds,
Which for this fourteen years we have let slip;
Even like an o'ergrown lion in a cave,
That goes not out to prey. Now, as fond fathers,
Having bound up the threatening twigs of birch,
Only to stick it in their children's sight
For terror, not to use, in time the rod
Becomes more mocked than feared, so our decrees,
Dead to infliction, to themselves are dead,
And liberty plucks justice by the nose;
The baby beats the nurse, and quite athwart
Goes all decorum.
(I.3.19–31)

The Duke gives the Friar one of his explanations for handing over the government of Vienna to Angelo (see also 10). Since 'bits and curbs' are used to control horses, some editors have amended 'weeds' to 'steeds' or 'jades'. The Duke says his laxity has lasted for fourteen years, Claudio says nineteen (see 5). 'Fond' means foolish. 'Dead to infliction, to themselves are dead' means are as good as dead if they cannot be made effective.

9 Sith 'twas my fault to give the people scope,
'Twould be my tyranny to strike and gall them
For what I bid them do: for we bid this be done
When evil deeds have their permissive pass
And not the punishment.
(I.3.35–9)

The Duke continues to explain to the Friar why he could not reasonably reinstate the legal penalties himself. 'Sith' means since; 'have their permissive pass' means are allowed to go unchecked.

10 Lord Angelo is precise,
Stands at a guard with envy, scarce confesses
That his blood flows, or that his appetite
Is more to bread than stone. Hence shall we see,
If power change purpose, what our seemers be.
(I.3.50–4)

The Duke now gives the Friar a different reason for his temporary abdication. As 'seemers' suggests that the Duke is already suspicious of Angelo, his motives appear rather confused (see 8). 'Precise' means (over) rigid, puritanical; 'Stands at a guard with envy' means is on his guard against being malicious; 'his appetite / Is more to bread than stone' means he needs natural sustenance.

11 I hold you as a thing enskied and sainted,
By your renouncement an immortal spirit
And to be talked with in sincerity,
As with a saint.
(I.4.34–7)

Lucio's attempt to enlist Isabella (who is about to become a nun) in Claudio's defence is foundering on her displeasure at his racy language; here he tries to make amends. 'Renouncement' refers to the nun's renunciation of the world.

12 Your brother and his lover have embraced.
As those that feed grow full, as blossoming time
That from the seedness the bare fallow brings
To teeming foison, even so her plenteous womb
Expresseth his full tilth and husbandry.
(I.4.40–4)

Lucio tells Isabella what Claudio and Juliet have done. 'That from the seedness the bare fallow brings / To teeming foison' means that brings the bare field sown with seed to teeming harvest; 'plenteous' means full, bursting; 'tilth' means tillage; 'husbandry' puns on the state of being a husband and cultivation.

13 A man whose blood
Is very snow-broth, one who never feels
The wanton stings and motions of the sense,
But doth rebate and blunt his natural edge
With profits of the mind, study, and fast.
(I.4.57–61)

Lucio describes Angelo to Isabella. 'Snow-broth' is melted snow, suggesting his unnatural coldness; 'stings and motions of the sense' are physical urges and desires; 'rebate' means make dull.

14 Our doubts are traitors
And make us lose the good we oft might win,
By fearing to attempt.
(I.4.77–9)

Lucio encourages Isabella to put aside her doubts about persuading Angelo to be merciful to Claudio.

15 When maidens sue,
Men give like gods; but when they weep and kneel,
All their petitions are as freely theirs
As they themselves would owe them.
(I.4.80–3)

Lucio is telling Isabella that she must convince Angelo to grant her petition for Claudio's life. The last two lines mean: they are granted all their requests as readily as if they themselves were responsible for granting them.

16 We must not make a scarecrow of the law,
Setting it up to fear the birds of prey,
And let it keep one shape, till custom make it
Their perch and not their terror.
(II.1.1–4)

Angelo explains to Escalus his reasons for reapplying the unused laws. 'Fear' means scare.

17 'Tis one thing to be tempted, Escalus,
Another thing to fall. I not deny,
The jury, passing on the prisoner's life,
May in the sworn twelve have a thief or two
Guiltier than him they try; what's open made to justice,
That justice seizes; what knows the laws
That thieves do pass on thieves? 'Tis very pregnant,
The jewel that we find, we stoop and take't
Because we see it; but what we do not see
We tread upon, and never think of it.
You may not so extenuate his offence
For I have had such faults; but rather tell me,
When I, that censure him, do so offend,
Let mine own judgement pattern out my death
And nothing come in partial. Sir, he must die.
(II.1.17–31)

Escalus has suggested that if an opportunity had arisen even Angelo might have been tempted to commit a similar crime to Claudio's. Angelo's reply is ironic in view of his subsequent designs on Isabella which make him liable to the same punishment as Claudio for the same crime. 'Passing' means reaching a verdict. 'What knows the laws / That thieves do pass on thieves?' means who knows what sentences, or what does the law know of the sentences, that thieves pass on thieves? 'Pregnant' means obvious; 'nothing come in partial' means let there be no attempt at mitigation.

18 This will last out a night in Russia
When nights are longest there.
(II.1.128–9)

Angelo's reaction to a muddled case involving the Constable Elbow, Pompey, and Froth, a gentleman, is to leave it to Escalus.

19 There is a vice that most I do abhor,
And most desire should meet the blow of justice,

For which I would not plead, but that I must,
For which I must not plead, but that I am
At war 'twixt will and will not.
(II.2.29–33)

Isabella, pleading with Angelo for Claudio's life, makes the point that her sisterly feelings for Claudio force her to minimize her moral scruples. Her reaction to his vice is extreme and, some would argue, unchristian.

20 Condemn the fault, and not the actor of it?
(II.2.37)

Angelo responds sceptically to Isabella's suggestion that he should condemn the crime and not the criminal.

21 No ceremony that to great ones longs,
Not the king's crown, nor the deputed sword,
The marshal's truncheon, nor the judge's robe,
Become them with one half so good a grace
As mercy does.
(II.2.59–63)

Isabella tries to persuade Angelo to show mercy to Claudio. 'Longs' means belongs; 'deputed sword', 'marshal's truncheon', and 'judge's robe' are all symbols of office.

22 O, 'tis excellent
To have a giant's strength, but it is tyrannous
To use it like a giant.
(II.2.107–9)

Isabella tries another argument in her attempt to persuade Angelo to be merciful to Claudio.

23 Could great men thunder
As Jove himself does, Jove would ne'er be quiet,
For every pelting, petty officer
Would use his heaven for thunder,
Nothing but thunder. Merciful heaven,
Thou rather with thy sharp and sulphurous bolt
Splits the unwedgeable and gnarlèd oak
Than the soft myrtle; but man, proud man,
Dressed in a little brief authority,
Most ignorant of what he's most assured,
His glassy essence, like an angry ape
Plays such fantastic tricks before high heaven
As makes the angels weep.
(II.2.110–22)

Isabella develops her case against Angelo's use of his authority to condemn Claudio. 'Pelting' means insignificant; 'unwedgeable' means unsplittable by human means. 'Gnarlèd', meaning knotted, appears to be a Shakespearian coinage, if it is not just an error for 'knarled'; 'glassy essence' means man's essence as it appears in the mirror.

24 Great men may jest with saints: 'tis wit in them,
But in the less, foul profanation.
(II.2.127–8)
Isabella is saying to Angelo that we should not judge people by our own standards. The 'less' are ordinary people.

25 That in the captain's but a choleric word
Which in the soldier is flat blasphemy.
(II.2.130–1)
Isabella continues to offer examples of not judging people by our own standards. 'Choleric' means angry.

26 What's this? What's this? Is this her fault or mine?
The tempter, or the tempted, who sins most?
(II.2.162–3)
Left alone, Angelo begins to voice his dismay at finding himself sexually attracted to Isabella.

27 O cunning enemy that, to catch a saint,
With saints dost bait thy hook. Most dangerous
Is that temptation that doth goad us on
To sin in loving virtue. Never could the strumpet
With all her double vigour, art and nature,
Once stir my temper; but this virtuous maid
Subdues me quite. Ever till now,
When men were fond, I smiled and wondered how.
(II.2.180–7)
Angelo muses to himself about the irony that Isabella's sanctity has sparked off his lust. The 'cunning enemy' is Satan; 'fond' means infatuated.

28 Might there not be a charity in sin
To save this brother's life?
(II.4.63–4)
Angelo initiates the process of tempting Isabella. She assumes that the sin would be in him not applying the law, but he means her sinning by committing an act of fornication with him.

29 Th'impression of keen whips I'd wear as rubies,
And strip myself to death as to a bed
That long I have been sick for, ere I'd yield
My body up to shame.
(II.4.101–4)
Isabella replies in vivid terms to Angelo's offer to trade her virginity for her brother's life. Although Isabella is overtly talking of baring herself for punishment, many readers and audiences have seen the sado-masochistic connotations of the association of sex, death, and punishment as psychologically revealing.

30 I something do excuse the thing I hate
For his advantage that I dearly love.
(II.4.119–20)
Isabella tells Angelo that her attempt to help Claudio means that she has to condone to some extent ('something do excuse') behaviour that she deplores.

31 More than our brother is our chastity.
(II.4.185)
Isabella, left alone after Angelo's verbal assaults on her virginity, voices her own conviction. The use of 'our', usually associated with kings, may be a pointer to her character.

32 CLAUDIO
The miserable have no other medicine
But only hope:
I have hope to live, and am prepared to die.
DUKE
Be absolute for death: either death or life
Shall thereby be the sweeter. Reason thus with life:
If I do lose thee, I do lose a thing
That none but fools would keep; a breath thou art,
Servile to all the skyey influences
That dost this habitation where thou keep'st
Hourly afflict. Merely, thou art death's fool,
For him thou labour'st by thy flight to shun,
And yet runn'st toward him still.
(III.1.2–13)
The Duke, who has disguised himself as a friar, offers the condemned Claudio a mélange of advice on how to face death. 'Servile' means subject; 'skyey' means of the planets, astrological; 'habitation' means body; 'keep'st' means live.

33 Thou'rt by no means valiant,
For thou dost fear the soft and tender fork

Of a poor worm. Thy best of rest is sleep.
And that thou oft provok'st, yet grossly fear'st
Thy death, which is no more. Thou art not thyself,
For thou exists on many a thousand grains
That issue out of dust.
(III.1.15–21)

The Duke, disguised as a friar, continues to console Claudio by telling him how to reason against death. 'Fork' means forked tongue; 'worm' means snake; 'exists' means exist.

34 If thou art rich, thou'rt poor,
For, like an ass, whose back with ingots bows,
Thou bear'st thy heavy riches but a journey,
And death unloads thee. Friend hast thou none,
For thine own bowels, which do call thee sire,
The mere effusion of thy proper loins,
Do curse the gout, serpigo, and the rheum
For ending thee no sooner. Thou hast nor youth nor age,
But as it were an after-dinner's sleep,
Dreaming on both, for all thy blessed youth
Becomes as agèd, and doth beg the alms
Of palsied eld: and when thou art old and rich,
Thou hast neither heat, affection, limb, nor beauty
To make thy riches pleasant. What's yet in this
That bears the name of life? Yet in this life
Lie hid more thousand deaths; yet death we fear,
That makes these odds all even.
(III.1.25–41)

The disguised Duke concludes his attempt to reconcile the condemned Claudio to death with a picture of the discomforts of old age. 'Bowels' means offspring (who curse the elderly for not dying earlier so that they can inherit). 'Gout, serpigo, and the rheum' are diseases; 'eld' is old age which begs arms for support, punning on alms (money) which the young beg of the old; 'heat, affection, limb' are desire, passion, strength.

35 Dar'st thou die?
The sense of death is most in apprehension,
And the poor beetle that we tread upon
In corporal sufferance finds a pang as great
As when a giant dies.
(III.1.80–4)

Isabella, who has not yet told him that Angelo is willing to trade her virginity for his life, asks Claudio if he is willing to die. 'Corporal sufferance' means bodily suffering.

36 If I must die,
I will encounter darkness as a bride,
And hung it in mine arms.
(III.1.86–8)

Claudio reassures Isabella of his readiness to die in terms which recall her blending of references to sexuality and death in 29.

37 O, were it but my life,
I'd throw it down for your deliverance
As frankly as a pin.
(III.1.107–9)

Isabella has told Claudio of Angelo's offer and reassures him that she would be willing to suffer death, but not the loss of her virginity, to secure his release. 'Frankly' means readily.

38 CLAUDIO Death is a fearful thing.
ISABELLA
And shamèd life a hateful.
CLAUDIO
Ay, but to die, and go we know not where,
To lie in cold obstruction and to rot;
This sensible warm motion to become
A kneaded clod; and the delighted spirit
To bathe in fiery floods, or to reside
In thrilling region of thick-ribbèd ice,
To be imprisoned in the viewless winds
And blown with restless violence round about
The pendent world; or to be worse than worst
Of those that lawless and incertain thought
Imagine howling, 'tis too horrible.
The weariest and most loathèd worldly life
That age, ache, penury, and imprisonment
Can lay on nature is a paradise
To what we fear of death.
(III.1.119–35)

Claudio gives memorable expression to his fear of death which outweighs his regard for Isabella's religious scruples about her virginity. This picture of torments after death derives ultimately from the Italian poet Dante and the Roman poet Virgil. 'Cold obstruction' means rigor mortis; 'sensible warm motion' means warm body capable of feeling (in opposition to 'cold obstruction'); 'delighted' means capable of delight; 'viewless' means invisible; 'pendent' means hanging. 'Lawless and incertain thought' appears to refer to beliefs which had no Christian authority ('lawless') or were dubious ('incertain'); 'imagine' means imagines.

39 O, fie, fie, fie!
Thy sin's not accidental, but a trade.
Mercy to thee would prove itself a bawd,
'Tis best that thou diest quickly.
(III.1.151–4)
Isabella explodes at Claudio's willingness for her to prostitute herself to Angelo. She sees his sexual activity with Juliet ('sin') as not an isolated mistake ('accidental') but a sign of his normal behaviour ('trade'), so that being merciful to him would make Mercy a bawd.

40 The hand that hath made you fair hath made you good.
(III.1.182–3)
The Duke, disguised as a friar, compliments Isabella.

41 Virtue is bold, and goodness never fearful.
(III.1.210)
The disguised Duke offers Isabella another moral commonplace.

42 There, at the moated grange, resides this dejected Mariana.
(III.1.265–6)
The disguised Duke is proposing that Mariana, Angelo's rejected fiancée, should be substituted for Isabella so that Angelo will make love to her in the belief that she is Isabella. Tennyson's *Mariana* is a meditation on Mariana's feelings in the time after Angelo deserted her.

43 Some report a sea-maid spawned him. Some that he was begot between two stock-fishes. But it is certain that when he makes water his urine is congealed ice.
(III.2.102–4)
Lucio showers a stream of gossip about Angelo on the disguised Duke. A 'sea-maid' is a mermaid; 'stock-fishes', dried cod, was use metaphorically of people without sexual appeal.

44 Why, what a ruthless thing is this in him, for the rebellion of a cod-piece to take away the life of a man!
(III.2.108–9)
Lucio, addressing the disguised Duke, denounces Angelo's severity. 'Cod-piece', the ornamental covering for the male genitals, is used here with sexual connotations.

45 A very superficial, ignorant, unweighing fellow.
(III.2.132)

Lucio's description of the Duke to the friar who is actually the disguised Duke does not endear him to the Duke in the play's dénouement – see 61. 'Unweighing' means undiscriminating.

46 Take, O take those lips away
  That so sweetly were forsworn;
And those eyes, the break of day,
  Lights that do mislead the morn:
But my kisses bring again, bring again;
Seals of love, but sealed in vain, sealed in vain.
(IV.1.1–6)
A boy sings this appropriately melancholy song of forsworn love to Mariana on her first appearance.

47 ABHORSON A bawd, sir? Fie upon him, he will discredit our mystery.
PROVOST Go to, sir, you weigh equally. A feather will turn the scale.
(IV.2.25–8)
The Provost in charge of the gaol has offered Pompey the bawd as assistant to Abhorson the executioner. The Provost's remarks continue the play's theme of measure for measure. A 'mystery' is a skilled trade or profession.

48 Every true man's apparel fits your thief.
(IV.2.40)
In the course of a complex attempt to prove to Pompey that being a hangman is a profession, Abhorson makes the point that a thief will steal anything.

49 A man that apprehends death no more dreadfully but as a drunken sleep; careless, reckless, and fearless of what's past, present, or to come; insensible of mortality, and desperately mortal.
(IV.2.139–42)
The Provost describes the prisoner Barnardine to the disguised Duke. Shakespeare appears to be deliberately drawing our attention to the Duke's (and the dramatist's?) inability to order life as tidily as he wants to: Barnardine at first appears to be a plot device intended to provide a head that can be substituted for Claudio's, but his refusal to be executed means that another prisoner, who has already conveniently died of natural causes, has to be introduced (see 52). 'Apprehends' means understands; 'insensible of mortality' means with no feelings about death; 'desperately mortal' means a hopeless case.

50 Drunk many times a day, if not many days entirely drunk.
(IV.2.146–7)
The Provost describes Barnardine to the disguised Duke.

51 O, death's a great disguiser.
(IV.2.170)
The disguised Duke, who has suggested that Barnardine's head should be substituted for Claudio's, answers the Provost's objection that the two men do not look alike.

52 BARNARDINE I swear I will not die today for any man's persuasion.
DUKE But hear you.
BARNARDINE Not a word. If you have anything to say to me, come to my ward, for thence will not I today.
(IV.3.57–61)
The disguised Duke's plan founders on the rock of Barnardine's intractability (see 49).

53 The old fantastical Duke of dark corners.
(IV.3.155–6)
Lucio continues to store up trouble for himself with this comment to Isabella which is made in front of the disguised Duke.

54 I am a kind of burr, I shall stick.
(IV.3.175)
Lucio adopts a proverbial phrase to justify his accompanying the disguised Duke.

55 O, your desert speaks loud, and I should wrong it
To lock it in the wards of covert bosom,
When it deserves with characters of brass
A forted residence 'gainst the tooth of time
And razure of oblivion.
(V.1.9–13)
The Duke, who has reappeared as himself, praises Angelo to his face. His use of a prison metaphor in 'wards of covert bosom', meaning cells of undisclosed affection, is ironic. The references to brass are ultimately to the *Odes* of the Roman poet Horace; Shakespeare also uses the idea in *Love's Labour's Lost* (see 1) and the *Sonnets* (see 22). 'Razure' means erasure.

56 Respect to your great place, and let the devil
Be sometime honoured for his burning throne.
(V.1.290–1)

The Duke, who has left Angelo and Escalus to try Mariana and Isabella's case against Angelo, has reappeared in his friar's disguise. This speech, a response to Escalus's 'know you where you are?', may be divided into two parts, the first aimed at Escalus, the second – with its references to the devil – at Angelo. 'Let the devil / Be sometime honoured for his burning throne' means let us honour even the devil because he has authority in hell.

57 My business in this state
Made me a looker-on here in Vienna,
Where I have seen corruption boil and bubble
Till it o'errun the stew. Laws for all faults,
But faults so countenanced that the strong statutes
Stand like the forfeits in a barber's shop,
As much in mock as mark.
(V.1.314–20)

The disguised Duke, describes the moral degradation of Vienna to the court without conscious irony, despite the fact that he is ultimately responsible for the state of affairs he describes. 'Stew' also means brothel. The 'forfeits in a barber's shop' which become objects of merriment ('mock') rather than a warning ('mark') have been variously explained as lists of penalties for bad behaviour, extracted teeth (since the barbers were also dentists), or even, since the barbers were also surgeons, parts of the dissected bodies of criminals!

58 Haste still pays haste, and leisure answers leisure,
Like doth quit like, and Measure still for Measure.
(V.1.407–8)

The Duke, who has had his disguise pulled off by Lucio, proceeds to judgement on Angelo, whom he has forced to marry Mariana. The Duke wishes to apply the strict Old Testament law in applying the same penalty to Angelo that Claudio has supposedly suffered.

59 They say best men are moulded out of faults,
And, for the most, become much more the better
For being a little bad. So may my husband.
(V.1.436–8)

Mariana pleads with the Duke not to execute her newly acquired husband Angelo.

60 If he be like your brother, for his sake
Is he pardoned, and for your lovely sake,
Give me your hand and say you will be mine.

He is my brother too. But fitter time for that.
(V.1.487–90)

The Duke produces Claudio alive and proposes to Isabella. Many interpretations of the play depend on the value assigned to Isabella's remaining silent from Claudio's unveiling to the end of the play and to the Duke's second proposal (see 62). Since the Duke does propose again, it appears that here at least she does not agree to marry the Duke.

61 Marrying a punk, my lord, is pressing to death, whipping, and hanging.
(V.1.519–20)

When the Duke was in disguise, Lucio told him how he had escaped marrying a woman who was pregnant by him. The Duke has punished Lucio for slandering him by decreeing that he should marry her. Here Lucio protests that marrying a whore ('punk') is a combination of cruel punishments. 'Pressing to death' was a punishment using weights to crush someone to death; here it also has sexual overtones. Many modern readers and audiences find the Duke's unforgiving attitude to Lucio difficult to reconcile with his willingness to condone other apparently more serious crimes.

62 Dear Isabel,
I have a motion much imports your good,
Whereto if you'll a willing ear incline,
What's mine is yours, and what is yours is mine.
(V.1.531–4)

The Duke appears to renew his proposal to Isabella, who still does not reply. Silence may indicate consent but powerful arguments have been advanced, both by literary critics and in the theatre, against assuming too readily that the ending is a happy one since at least two of the four potential couples – Lucio and his punk, Angelo and Mariana – have one less than willing partner. Do Claudio and Juliet and the Duke and Isabella provide a balancing foursome? In John Barton's memorable 1970 production Isabella was left alone onstage at the end – other productions offer different solutions and interpretation of the ending will depend on the way in which other parts of the play have been treated.

The Merchant of Venice

1 ANTONIO
In sooth I know not why I am so sad.

It wearies me, you say it wearies you;
But how I caught it, found it, or came by it,
What stuff 'tis made of, whereof it is born,
I am to learn;
And such a want-wit sadness makes of me
That I have much ado to know myself.

SALERIO

Your mind is tossing on the ocean,
There where your argosies with portly sail,
Like signors and rich burghers on the flood,
Or as it were the pageants of the sea,
Do overpeer the petty traffickers
That curtsy to them, do them reverence,
As they fly by them with their woven wings.

(I.1.1–14)

The play opens with the merchant Antonio telling his companions Salerio and Solanio that he does not know the cause of his melancholy. Critics have variously explained it as arising from Bassanio's imminent departure, from a premonition of his difficulties, from the ennui of the rich and, inevitably, as a survival from an earlier version. Whatever its cause, at this stage in the play it must remain unexplained because we have no other information on which to base a judgement. 'In sooth' means truly; 'I am to learn' means I don't know; 'argosies' are large merchant ships; 'portly' means majestic. 'Pageants' were large mobile scenic units in the form of ships etc. that were used in medieval theatre and in civic displays; 'overpeer the petty traffickers' means look down on the small boats, which bob up and down in their wake ('curtsy to them'); 'woven wings' are sails.

2 My ventures are not in one bottom trusted,
Nor to one place; nor is my whole estate
Upon the fortune of this present year.

(I.1.42–4)

Antonio tells Salerio and Solanio that they are wrong to think that his melancholy stems from concern for his trading ventures. It is the confidence he voices here that makes him willing to agree to Shylock's 'merry bond'. 'Bottom' means ship; 'Upon' means staked upon.

3 Now by two-headed Janus,
Nature hath framed strange fellows in her time.

(I.1.50–1)

Solanio has decided that Antonio is sad because he is not merry, and compares him to Janus, the two-headed Roman god of entrances and beginnings, whose name is preserved in January, the month that looks back to the old year and forward to the new. It has been claimed that one of Janus's faces was happy and one sad.

4 You have too much respect upon the world;
They lose it that do buy it with much care.
(I.1.74–5)
Gratiano, another of Antonio's friends who has entered with Bassanio and Lorenzo, carries on where Solanio and Salerio left off, trying to shake Antonio out of his melancholy. 'Respect upon' means regard for.

5 I hold the world but as the world, Gratiano,
A stage where every man must play a part,
And mine a sad one.
(I.1.77–9)
Antonio replies to Gratiano's attempt to cheer him up with a commonplace.

6 There are a sort of men whose visages
Do cream and mantle like a standing pond,
And do a wilful stillness entertain
With purpose to be dressed in an opinion
Of wisdom, gravity, profound conceit,
As who should say, 'I am Sir Oracle,
And when I ope my lips, let no dog bark.'
O my Antonio, I do know of these
That therefore only are reputed wise
For saying nothing.
(I.1.88–97)
Gratiano develops an argument, aimed at Antonio, against men who adopt serious appearances in order to make an impression on the world. 'Do cream and mantle' means are covered with a pale sour mask; 'a wilful stillness entertain' means maintain a deliberate silence. 'With purpose to be dressed in an opinion' means so that they get a reputation; 'conceit' means understanding; 'ope' means open.

7 But fish not with this melancholy bait
For this fool gudgeon, this opinion.
(I.1.101–2)
Gratiano concludes his attempt to snap Antonio out of what he takes to be a false melancholy. A 'gudgeon' is a small fish used as bait, here it means a gullible fool – Gratiano is saying that Antonio should not use melancholy as a means to get a reputation ('opinion') which depends on the gullibility of fools.

8 Silence is only commendable
In a neat's tongue dried and a maid not vendible.
(I.1.111–12)

Gratiano leaves, after his attempts to make Antonio happier and more talkative, with another warning against silence. A 'neat's tongue' is an ox tongue; 'vendible' means marriageable.

9 Gratiano speaks an infinite deal of nothing, more than any man in all Venice. His reasons are as two grains of wheat hid in two bushels of chaff: you shall seek all day ere you find them, and when you have them they are not worth the search.
(I.1.114–18)

Bassanio encourages Antonio not to take Gratiano too seriously.

10 My purse, my person, my extremest means
Lie all unlocked to your occasions.
(I.1.138–9)

Antonio expresses his willingness to help Bassanio in his attempt to recoup his fortunes by any means at his disposal. 'Occasions' are needs.

11 In Belmont is a lady richly left,
And she is fair, and, fairer than that word,
Of wondrous virtues. Sometimes from her eyes
I did receive fair speechless messages.
(I.1.161–4)

Economic and amatory considerations coexist in Bassanio's explanation to Antonio of his reasons for wanting to marry Portia. 'Fairer than that word' means better than that.

12 PORTIA By my troth, Nerissa, my little body is aweary of this great world.
NERISSA You would be, sweet madam, if your miseries were in the same abundance as your good fortunes are; and yet for aught I see, they are as sick that surfeit with too much as they that starve with nothing. It is no mean happiness, therefore, to be seated in the mean; superfluity comes sooner by white hairs, but competency lives longer.
(I.2.1–9)

Nerissa, Portia's Gentlewoman, offers moral platitudes to rally Portia from the melancholy which links her with Antonio in Venice. The first 'mean' means little and the second refers to the Golden Mean – having neither too much nor too little. 'Superfluity' means excess; 'competency' means moderation.

13 If to do were as easy as to know what were good to do, chapels had been churches, and poor men's cottages princes' palaces. It is a good divine that follows his own instructions. I can easier teach twenty what were good to be done than to be one of the twenty to follow mine own teaching. The brain may devise laws for the blood, but a hot temper leaps o'er a cold decree, such a hare is madness the youth to skip o'er the meshes of good counsel the cripple.
(I.2.12–20)
Portia answers Nerissa's moral platitudes with a string of her own. 'Chapels' refers to the small separately dedicated areas within large churches. 'Blood' and 'hot temper' are contrasted with 'brain' and 'cold decree': the cold rational brain makes laws which hot-blooded passion ignores.

14 I had rather be married to a death's-head with a bone in his mouth.
(I.2.48–9)
Portia comments to Nerissa on one of her suitors, the Count Palatine. A 'death's-head' is a skull.

15 God made him and therefore let him pass for a man. ... If I should marry him, I should marry twenty husbands.
(I.2.53–4, 58–9)
Portia gives Nerissa her verdict on her French suitor Monsieur Le Bon, who has so many attributes that marrying him would be like marrying twenty husbands.

16 I say nothing to him, for he understands not me, nor I him. He hath neither Latin, French, nor Italian, and you will come into the court and swear that I have a poor pennyworth in the English. He is a proper man's picture, but alas, who can converse with a dumb-show? How oddly he is suited! I think he bought his doublet in Italy, his round hose in France, his bonnet in Germany, and his behaviour everywhere.
(I.2.64–71)
Portia's cataloguing of her suitors for Nerissa now arrives at the English Lord Falconbridge. Complaints about English travellers abroad were a common feature of Renaissance literature and drama. Portia's claim to speak little ('a poor pennyworth') English is a typical Shakespearian reminder to the audience of the play's fictional status.

17 I will do anything, Nerissa, ere I will be married to a sponge.
(I.2.92–3)

Portia's German suitor, the Duke of Saxony's nephew, is unacceptable to her because of his excessive drinking – he soaks up alcohol like a sponge.

18 I am glad this parcel of wooers are so reasonable, for there is not one among them but I dote on his very absence, and I pray God grant them a fair departure.
(I.2.102–5)
All of the suitors Portia has catalogued to Nerissa have decided to leave because they are unwilling to try to win her in accordance with her dead father's conditions which involve choosing between three caskets. This is Portia's reaction to the news. 'Parcel' means group.

19 But ships are but boards, sailors but men; there be land rats and water rats, water thieves and land thieves, I mean pirates; and then there is the peril of waters, winds, and rocks.
(I.3.21–4)
Shylock, a Jewish financier, who has been approached by Bassanio seeking financial support for his proposed trip to woo Portia in Belmont on Antonio's security, enumerates to Bassanio some of the hazards which threaten Antonio's ventures and which may reduce his credit-worthiness. There is probably a pun (pi-rats) on pirates.

20 How like a fawning publican he looks.
I hate him for he is a Christian;
But more, for that in low simplicity
He lends out money gratis and brings down
The rate of usance here with us in Venice.
If I can catch him once upon the hip,
I will feed fat the ancient grudge I bear him.
He hates our sacred nation and he rails
Even there where merchants most do congregate
On me, my bargains, and my well-won thrift,
Which he calls interest. Cursèd be my tribe
If I forgive him.
(I.3.38–49)
In a long aside Shylock voices his dislike of Antonio, who has just joined Bassanio. The mixture of pathos, comedy, and melodrama which contributes to Shylock's character makes him a difficult character for modern audiences, who will find the anti-Semitic elements particularly distasteful. Yet as an old father suspicious of his daughter, a miser, and a usurer he is a traditional comic figure, and as a pantomime ogre figure implacably seeking Antonio's death he is understandable and unsympathetic. If he were simply

an ebullient Machiavellian figure like the Jew Barabas in Marlowe's *Jew of Malta* there would be fewer difficulties in coming to terms with the blend of contradictory influences and impulses which go into Shylock's character. He is a villain, but his defences of his humanity give him a complexity which is more lifelike than the majority of fictional characters. Moreover, his villainy is carefully presented as a response to the general persecution of the Jews, to Antonio's treatment of him, and to Jessica's running away from him.

Historically, Jews had tended to become money-lenders because Christians were forbidden to lend money at interest. Anti-Jewish hostility thus often arose because of the natural tendency of debtors not to like the people they owe money to, as well as xenophobia which identified the Jews as a group with their own habits and customs and a crude hostility which identified the Jews as the killers of Christ. Although Edward I officially expelled the Jews from England, there was a Jewish community in London in Shakespeare's time, conforming outwardly to Christianity. One of them, a Portuguese called Roderigo Lopez, became doctor to the Queen but became involved in political plots which led to his denunciation and execution for high treason in 1594.

The publicans were Jewish tax-gatherers in Roman times: Shylock may be referring to the one mentioned in Luke 18 who 'fawned' on God and may also dislike them because they gathered taxes from the Jews on behalf of foreign masters. 'Gratis' means for nothing; 'usance' means interest; 'upon the hip', a wrestling term, means at a disadvantage, with a probable reference to the story of Jacob wrestling with the angel in Genesis 32.

21 The devil can cite Scripture for his purpose.
An evil soul producing holy witness
Is like a villain with a smiling cheek,
A goodly apple rotten at the heart.
O what a goodly outside falsehood hath!
(I.3.95–9)

Antonio expresses his hatred of Shylock to Bassanio in very strong terms. Shakespeare often contrasts inner reality with outward appearance, a theme which is developed throughout the play in the caskets story, Portia's disguise, and Jessica's escape among other elements.

22 Signor Antonio, many a time and oft
In the Rialto you have rated me
About my moneys and my usances.
Still have I borne it with a patient shrug,

For sufferance is the badge of all our tribe.
You call me misbeliever, cut-throat dog,
And spit upon my Jewish gaberdine,
And all for use of that which is mine own.
(I.3.102–10)

Shylock responds to Antonio's question as to whether he will provide the finance for Bassanio's expedition by stating his grievances against him, thus softening the picture formed by his earlier aside (see 20). The Rialto is the Venetian stock exchange; 'rated' means berated; the 'Jewish gaberdine' is a distinctive coat worn by Jews.

23 You, that did void your rheum upon my beard
And foot me as you spurn a stranger cur
Over your threshold, moneys is your suit
What should I say to you? Should I not say,
'Hath a dog money? Is it possible
A cur can lend three thousand ducats?' Or
Shall I bend low, and in a bondman's key,
With bated breath and whispering humbleness,
Say this:
'Fair sir, you spat on me on Wednesday last,
You spurned me such a day, another time
You called me dog, and for these courtesies
I'll lend you thus much moneys'?
(I.3.114–26)

Shylock develops his list of complaints against Antonio, thus eliciting more sympathy from the audience by demonstrating what he has to suffer as a daily routine. 'Void your rheum' means spit; 'foot me' means kick me.

24 If you repay me not on such a day,
In such a place, such sum or sums as are
Expressed in the conditon, let the forfeit
Be nominated for an equal pound
Of your fair flesh, to be cut off and taken
In what part of your body pleaseth me.
(I.3.143–8)

Shylock agrees to lend Antonio the money to finance Bassanio's expedition to Belmont in return for this guarantee. The story of the pound of flesh is originally a folk tale from the east which figures in several medieval literary works. As so often in folk tales and myths, it is crucial to get the wording of the agreement exactly right, as Shylock discovers when he is allowed only 'an equal pound of flesh', no more and no less, in Portia's judgement in the trial scene.

25 O father Abram, what these Christians are,
Whose own hard dealings teaches them suspect
The thoughts of others! Pray you tell me this:
If he should break his day, what should I gain
By the exaction of the forfeiture?
(I.3.157–61)
Shylock counters Bassanio's objections to Antonio's entering into the agreement by pointing out that there would be no commercial advantage to him in enforcing the claim to a pound of Antonio's flesh. 'Break his day' means be unable to pay when the money is due.

26 This merry bond.
(I.3.170)
Shylock presents his agreement to lend money to finance Bassanio's trip in return for a pound of Antonio's flesh if he cannot repay on time as a joke.

27 ANTONIO
The Hebrew will turn Christian; he grows kind.
BASSANIO
I like not fair terms and a villain's mind.
ANTONIO
Come on. In this there can be no dismay;
My ships come home a month before the day.
(I.3.175–8)
Antonio dismisses Bassanio's doubts about the agreement with Shylock. The terms are 'fair' because Shylock has asked for no interest, only the pound of flesh which he has presented as a joke, but Bassanio mistrusts him.

28 Mislike me not for my complexion,
The shadowed livery of the burnished sun,
To whom I am a neighbour and near bred.
(II.1.1–3)
Morocco, another of Portia's suitors, opens his wooing by asking her not to despise his colour. He sees himself as heavily tanned, wearing the dark ('shadowed') uniform ('livery') appropriate to a member of the sun's household.

29 Well, my conscience hanging about the neck of my heart says very wisely to me, 'My honest friend Launcelot', being an honest man's son or rather an honest woman's son, for indeed my father did something smack, something grow to, he had a kind of taste – well, my conscience says, 'Launcelot, budge not.' 'Budge,' says the fiend. 'Budge not,' says my con-

science. 'Conscience,' say I, 'you counsel well.' 'Fiend,' say I, 'you counsel well.' To be ruled by my conscience, I should stay with the Jew my master who, God bless the mark, is a kind of devil; and to run away from the Jew, I should be ruled by the fiend, who, saving your reverence, is the devil himself. Certainly the Jew is the very devil incarnation; and in my conscience, my conscience is but a kind of hard conscience to offer to counsel me to stay with the Jew. The fiend gives the more friendly counsel. I will run, fiend; my heels are at your commandment; I will run.
(II.2.11–28)
Launcelot Gobbo, Shylock's Christian servant, is debating with himself and the audience whether he should stay with Shylock or leave him. He dramatizes his indecision in the form of a debate between his conscience and the devil. Presumably it is filial piety which makes him stop short of directly accusing his father of fornication in 'my father did something smack, something grow to, he had a kind of taste', where all the expressions indicate his predilections. 'God bless the mark' and 'saving your reverence' are both phrases used to apologize for profane or indecent remarks; 'incarnation' is Launcelot's mistake for incarnate.

30 The boy was the very staff of my age, my very prop.
(II.2.60–1)
Old Gobbo, Launcelot's father, has such poor eyesight that he is not aware that the person who has just told him Launcelot is dead is, in fact, Launcelot himself. This is his reaction to the news.

31 It is a wise father that knows his own child.
(II.2.70–1)
Launcelot, who has begun to try to make himself known to his father, appropriates this proverbial saying. As so often in Shakespeare, the comic plot reinforces or comments on the themes of the main plot: Old Gobbo has been deceived by an outward appearance.

32 Truth will come to light; murder cannot be hid long.
(II.2.72–3)
As he continues his attempts to convince his father that he is Launcelot, Launcelot deploys two more familiar proverbs.

33 There is some ill a-brewing towards my rest,
For I did dream of money bags tonight.
(II.5.17–18)
Shylock, who has been asked to dine with Bassanio, is rightly suspicious that something is being plotted against him as his

daughter Jessica, who is present with Launcelot as he says these lines, is planning to elope with Lorenzo in his absence.

34 I will not say you shall see a masque, but if you do, then it was not for nothing that my nose fell a-bleeding on Black Monday last at six o'clock i'th'morning, falling out that year on Ash Wednesday was four year in th'afternoon.
(II.5.22–6)
Launcelot, attempting to persuade Shylock that he should go to Bassanio's for dinner, adopts a nonsensical and portentous style of prophecy and prognostication in an attempt to entice him with promises of entertainment. 'Black Monday' is Easter Monday.

35 What, are there masques? Hear you me, Jessica:
Lock up my doors; and when you hear the drum
And the vile squealing of the wry-necked fife,
Clamber not you up to the casements then,
Nor thrust your head into the public street
To gaze on Christian fools with varnished faces;
But stop my house's ears, I mean my casements;
Let not the sound of shallow foppery enter
My sober house. By Jacob's staff I swear
I have no mind of feasting forth tonight.
(II.5.27–36)
Launcelot's attempts to persuade him to go out almost have the opposite effect on Shylock, who reacts with this speech. The 'wry-necked fife' probably refers to the fife player who looks away from his instrument; 'varnished' may refer to cosmetics or to masks, both of which cover the face underneath and are associated with deceit. 'Foppery' means foolishness; 'forth' means out.

36 But love is blind, and lovers cannot see
The pretty follies that themselves commit.
(II.6.36–7)
Jessica, wearing male clothing, is eloping with Lorenzo. This gives extra point to these lines which she speaks to Lorenzo, who is waiting for her with his companions. In the Renaissance theatre the part of Jessica would, of course, have been played by a male actor.

37 What, must I hold a candle to my shames?
(II.6.41)

As part of the elopement, Jessica, in her male clothing, is to be Lorenzo's torch-bearer. In this line she says that carrying a light will make her unusual appearance even more obvious.

38 *Who chooseth me must give and hazard all he hath.*
Must give, for what? For lead! Hazard for lead?
This casket threatens; men that hazard all
Do it in hope of fair advantages.
A golden mind stoops not to shows of dross;
I'll then nor give nor hazard aught for lead.
(II.7.16–21)

Morocco is now trying to win Portia by opening the casket which contains her picture. He has a choice of three – gold, silver, and lead. As with the pound of flesh story, the story of the caskets has folk tale origins. In these lines Morocco reads and comments on the lead casket's inscription. See 39 and 40 for the inscriptions of the other caskets.

39 What says the silver with her virgin hue?
Who chooseth me shall get as much as he deserves.
(II.7.22–3)

Morocco now considers the silver casket. See 38 and 40 for the other caskets' inscriptions. 'Virgin hue' refers to silver's associations with the moon and with chastity.

40 *Who chooseth me shall gain what many men desire.*
Why that's the lady! All the world desires her;
From the four corners of the earth they come
To kiss this shrine, this mortal breathing saint.
(II.7.37–40)

Morocco now views and comments on the golden casket. See 38 and 39 for the other caskets' inscriptions.

41 *All that glisters is not gold;*
Often have you heard that told.
Many a man his life hath sold
But my outside to behold.
Gilded tombs do worms infold.
Had you been as wise as bold,
Young in limbs, in judgement old,
Your answer had not been inscrolled.
Fare you well, your suit is cold.
(II.7.65–73)

Morocco has chosen the golden casket, inside which he finds this message. The first line is proverbial.

42 'My daughter! O my ducats! O my daughter!
Fled with a Christian! O my Christian ducats!
Justice! The law! My ducats and my daughter!'
(II.8.15–17)

Solanio quotes to Salerio Shylock's reaction to finding that Jessica has eloped, taking with her some of his wealth. The linking of ducats and daughter suggests that Shylock's miserliness is as important as his paternal feelings, but the fact that the speech is only reported lessens its impact on the audience.

43 What many men desire; that 'many' may be meant
By the fool multitude that choose by show,
Not learning more than the fond eye doth teach,
Which pries not to th'interior, but like the martlet
Builds in the weather on the outward wall,
Even in the force and road of casualty.
I will not choose what many men desire,
Because I will not jump with common spirits
And rank me with the barbarous multitudes.
(II.9.25–33)

Arragon, another of Portia's suitors trying to pick the right casket in order to win her as his bride, comments on the inscription of the golden one (see 40). 'Fond' means foolish; 'Even in the force and road of casualty' is somewhat obscure, but the general meaning is even in the power and way of mischance; 'jump' means agree, go along.

44 Let none presume
To wear an undeservèd dignity.
O that estates, degrees, and offices
Were not derived corruptly, and that clear honour
Were purchased by the merit of the wearer!
How many then should cover that stand bare,
How many be commanded that command;
How much low peasantry would then be gleaned
From the true seed of honour, and how much honour
Picked from the chaff and ruin of the times
To be new varnished.
(II.9.39–49)

Arragon, having rejected the golden casket, moves on to the silver one (see 39). 'Degrees and offices' are ranks and positions; 'cover' means wear hats – since hats were taken off in the presence of those of superior status, Arragon is saying that honest men would achieve the status their honesty deserved. He than says that if merit received its due rewards some of the current nobility would be thrown out and some who had fallen on hard times would be restored to their former glories; 'gleaned' means picked out and discarded; 'seed' means offspring as well as seed; 'new varnished' means restored to their former outward appearance of nobility.

45 What's here? The portrait of a blinking idiot
Presenting me a schedule!
(II.9.54–5)
Arragon chose the silver casket, whose contents he describes in these lines. A 'schedule' is a document.

46 *Some there be that shadows kiss;*
Such have but a shadow's bliss.
(II.9.66–7)
Arragon reads these lines, which are part of the verses written on the 'schedule' in the silver casket. 'Shadows' may mean portraits as well as shadows.

47 Thus hath the candle singed the moth.
O these deliberate fools! When they do choose,
They have the wisdom by their wit to lose.
(II.9.79–81)
Portia comments to Nerissa on Arragon's failure. The first line is proverbial.

48 Yet it lives there unchecked that Antonio hath a ship of rich lading wracked on the narrow seas, the Goodwins I think they call the place, a very dangerous flat, and fatal, where the carcasses of many a tall ship lie buried as they say, if my gossip Report be an honest woman of her word.
(III.1.2–7)
Solanio tells Salerio of an uncontradicted ('unchecked') rumour on the Rialto ('there'). Shakespeare again uses an incidental reference to remind the audience of the fictional status of the theatrical event by making Solanio describe the Goodwin Sands, a familiar hazard to shipping in the English Channel ('the narrow seas'), as being far away. 'Wracked' means wrecked; 'gossip' means godmother, but is used here as a title of 'Report', thus meaning Dame Rumour.

49 Let him look to his bond. He was wont to call me usurer. Let him look to his bond. He was wont to lend money for a Christian courtesy. Let him look to his bond.
(III.1.43–5)
Shylock rages about Antonio to Salerio and Solanio. 'For a Christian courtesy' may mean as an act of benevolence or in return for

no more than an expression of thanks – 'curtsey' and 'courtesy' were not fully differentiated in Shakespeare's time.

50 SALERIO Why, I am sure if he forfeit thou wilt not take his flesh. What's that good for?
SHYLOCK To bait fish withal. If it will feed nothing else, it will feed my revenge. He hath disgraced me and hindered me half a million, laughed at my losses, mocked at my gains, scorned my nation, thwarted my bargains, cooled my friends, heated mine enemies, and what's his reason? I am a Jew. Hath not a Jew eyes? Hath not a Jew hands, organs, dimensions, senses, affections, passions? Fed with the same food, hurt with the same weapons, subject to the same diseases, healed by the same means, warmed and cooled by the same winter and summer as a Christian is? If you prick us, do we not bleed? If you tickle us, do we not laugh? If you poison us, do we not die? And if you wrong us, shall we not revenge? If we are like you in the rest, we will resemble you in that. If a Jew wrong a Christian, what is his humility? Revenge. If a Christian wrong a Jew, what should his sufferance be by Christian example? Why, revenge! The villainy you teach me I will execute, and it shall go hard but I will better the instruction.
(III.1.46–66)
Salerio cannot believe that Shylock would enforce his bond if Antonio cannot repay by the due date. Although part of Shylock's speech can be read as an impassioned defence of the Jews' humanity, the context locates the shared humanity between Christian and Jew in their shared desire for revenge.

51 Thou stick'st a dagger in me. I shall never see my gold again. Fourscore ducats at a sitting, fourscore ducats!
(III.1.100–2)
Tubal, another Jew, has just told Shylock that Jessica has spent eighty ducats in one night in Genoa. This is Shylock's response.

52 TUBAL One of them showed me a ring that he had of your daughter for a monkey.
SHYLOCK Out upon her! Thou torturest me, Tubal. It was my turquoise; I had it of Leah when I was a bachelor. I would not have given it for a wilderness of monkeys.
(III.1.108–13)
Tubal refers to 'One' of Antonio's creditors with whom he came back to Venice. Jessica is clearly enjoying herself, but Shylock's reaction shows the range of Shakespeare's characterization of

him: the old man's sentimental regard for his wife's youthful present to him cuts across his miser role. 'Out on her' means damn her.

53 Let music sound while he doth make his choice,
Then if he lose he makes a swanlike end,
Fading in music.
(III.2.43–5)
Portia, who loves him, orders music to be played while Bassanio is making up his mind which casket to choose. The swan was believed to sing beautifully just before its death, hence 'swanlike end'.

54 Tell me where is fancy bred,
Or in the heart, or in the head?
How begot, how nourishèd?
  Reply, reply.
It is engendered in the eyes,
With gazing fed, and fancy dies
In the cradle where it lies.
  Let us all ring fancy's knell.
  I'll begin it – Ding, dong, bell.
(III.2.63–71)
This song is sung (by whom is not stated) while Bassanio is deciding which casket to choose. Although it has been suggested that the song (in which 'bred', 'head', and 'nourishèd' all rhyme with lead) is intended to tell Bassanio which casket to choose, it seems more likely that any connection between the song and Bassanio's choice lies in the resemblance between its stress on the superficiality of 'fancy', love based only on the senses, which dies in its eyes, and Bassanio's view that appearances are misleading.

55 So may the outward shows be least themselves.
The world is still deceived with ornament.
In law, what plea so tainted and corrupt,
But being seasoned with a gracious voice,
Obscures the show of evil? In religion,
What damnèd error but some sober brow
Will bless it and approve it with a text,
Hiding the grossness with fair ornament?
There is no vice so simple but assumes
Some mark of virtue on his outward parts.
(III.2.73–82)

As he decides which casket to choose, Bassanio muses on the familiar Shakespearian theme of the relationship between appearance and reality. A 'text' is a biblical reference.

56 Thus ornament is but the guilèd shore
To a most dangerous sea, the beauteous scarf
Veiling an Indian beauty; in a word,
The seeming truth which cunning times put on
To entrap the wisest. Therefore thou gaudy gold,
Hard food for Midas, I will none of thee;
Nor none of thee, thou pale and common drudge
'Tween man and man. But thou, thou meagre lead
Which rather threaten'st than dost promise aught,
Thy paleness moves me more than eloquence,
And here choose I. Joy be the consequence!
(III.2.97–107)

Bassanio works his way towards choosing the correct casket. 'Guilèd' means treacherous. In classical mythology Midas was granted the wish that everything he touched should turn to gold – unfortunately this turned out to include his food; there are parallels between this story and the pound of flesh story in the need to make the bargain in unambiguous words. 'Pale and common drudge' refers to the use of silver in coins; 'meagre' means unprepossessing.

57 How all the other passions fleet to air:
As doubtful thoughts, and rash-embraced despair,
And shudd'ring fear, and green-eyed jealousy.
(III.2.108–10)

Portia reacts joyfully to Bassanio's choosing the correct casket. 'Fleet to' means fly off into; 'As' means such as.

58 You see me, Lord Bassanio, where I stand,
Such as I am. Though for myself alone
I would not be ambitious in my wish
To wish myself much better, yet for you
I would be trebled twenty times myself,
A thousand times more fair, ten thousand times
More rich, that only to stand high in your account,
I might in virtues, beauties, livings, friends,
Exceed account; but the full sum of me
Is sum of something, which to term in gross,
Is an unlessoned girl, unschooled, unpractisèd,
Happy in this, she is not yet so old
But she may learn; happier than this,

She is not bred so dull but she can learn.
(III.2.149–62)
Portia responds to Bassanio's request that she should confirm that he has chosen correctly with a long speech which includes these lines. The language of trade and economics figures prominently in the speech, linking Portia with the commercial ethos of Venice. 'Livings' means possessions.

59 I wish you all the joy that you can wish.
(III.2.190)
Gratiano congratulates Portia and Bassanio on their betrothal.

60 Here are a few of the unpleasant'st words
That ever blotted paper!
(III.2.251–2)
No sooner have Bassanio and Portia learnt that Gratiano and Nerissa also intend to marry, than Lorenzo, Jessica, and Salerio arrive from Venice. Salerio gives Bassanio a letter from Antonio telling of his misfortunes. In these lines, Bassanio describes the contents of the letter to Portia. The words blot the paper in the sense of marring it by their contents as well as being written in ink dried with a blotting agent.

61 I will have my bond.
(III.3.17)
Shylock repeats this phrase several times as Antonio attempts to talk to him. In insisting on the letter of the law, Shylock makes himself vulnerable to Portia's equally legalistic counterattack.

62 This comes too near the praising of myself,
Therefore no more of it.
(III.4.22–3)
Portia is telling Nerissa, Lorenzo, and Jessica that she is happy to have provided money with which she hopes Antonio can be saved by Bassanio, who has already left for Venice. She breaks off with this piece of modesty.

63 We were Christians enow before, e'en as many as could well live one by another. This making of Christians will raise the price of hogs; if we grow all to be pork-eaters, we shall not shortly have a rasher on the coals for money.
(III.5.19–23)
Launcelot, who did leave Shylock's service, jokingly complains to Jessica that her conversion to Christianity will lead to a shortage of pork since she will no longer be prohibited from eating pigs by

her religion. 'Enow' means enough; 'one by another' means together; 'a rasher' is a rasher of bacon.

64 How every fool can play upon the word! I think the best grace of wit will shortly turn into silence, and discourse grow commendable in none only but parrots.
(III.5.40–2)
Lorenzo, who has joined Launcelot and Jessica, objects to Launcelot's punning. 'Grace' means virtue; 'discourse' means the ability to talk.

65 Wilt thou show the whole wealth of thy wit in an instant? I pray thee understand a plain man in his plain meaning.
(III.5.51–3)
Lorenzo loses his temper with Launcelot's verbal games.

66 We all expect a gentle answer, Jew.
(IV.1.34)
The Duke of Venice, presiding over the judicial process, concludes with this line a lengthy speech suggesting that Shylock will give up his plan to take a pound of Antonio's flesh. There is a pun on 'gentle' and 'Gentile' which suggests the improbability of Shylock giving a gentle answer.

67 You'll ask me why I rather choose to have
A weight of carrion flesh than to receive
Three thousand ducats. I'll not answer that,
But say it is my humour. Is it answered?
(IV.1.40–3)
Shylock addresses the Duke and the assembled Venetian notables who include Antonio, Bassanio, and Gratiano. 'Humour' means whim.

68 Some men there are love not a gaping pig,
Some that are mad if they behold a cat,
And others, when the bagpipe sings i'th'nose,
Cannot contain their urine; for affection,
Master of passion, sways it to the mood
Of what it likes or loathes. Now for your answer:
As there is no firm reason to be rendered
Why he cannot abide a gaping pig,
Why he a harmless necessary cat,
Why he a woollen bagpipe, but of force
Must yield to such inevitable shame
As to offend, himself being offended;
So can I give no reason, nor I will not,

More than a lodged hate and a certain loathing
I bear Antonio, that I follow thus
A losing suit against him. Are you answered?
(IV.1.47–62)

Shylock continues to give reasons for his behaviour towards Antonio, which he ascribes to natural antipathy. A 'gaping pig' is one prepared for eating, with a fruit in its jaws; a 'harmless necessary cat' is one which is not a witch's familiar and is needed to catch mice; 'woollen' means covered in woollen cloth; 'of force' means of necessity. The 'shame' is the result of urinating uncontrollably; 'lodged' means fixed; 'certain' means determined. Shylock sees his case ('suit') as a losing one because he will get only a pound of flesh for his 3000 ducats – there is anticipatory irony, however, since his case turns out to involve much greater loss.

69 I am not bound to please thee with my answers.
(IV.1.65)

Shylock responds to an intervention from Bassanio. 'Bound' picks up the various ideas associated with 'bond'.

70 BASSANIO
Do all men kill the things they do not love?
SHYLOCK
Hates any man the thing he would not kill?
(IV.1.66–7)

Bassanio and Shylock trade matched rhetorical questions. The balancing of the sentences suggests the impasse between Shylock and the Christians.

71 DUKE
How shalt thou hope for mercy, rendering none?
SHYLOCK
What judgement shall I dread, doing no wrong?
(IV.1.88–9)

The Duke intervenes with a reference to the Lord's Prayer (Forgive us our trespasses as we forgive them that trespass against us) which is answered by Shylock's insistence on the law. Again the rhetorical balancing of the sentences suggests the stalemate between Shylock and the Christians. These lines support the contention that the play is in part a contest between an Old Testament morality characterized by a stress on the letter of the law and a New Testament morality characterized by a stress on charity.

72 I am a tainted wether of the flock,
Meetest for death. The weakest kind of fruit
Drops earliest to the ground, and so let me.
(IV.1.114–16)
Antonio tells Bassanio that he sees himself as an appropriate sacrificial victim. Why he should see himself as a diseased ram ('tainted wether') is not entirely clear, though he is something of a melancholy misfit whose fortunes do parallel Shylock's in some ways.

73 *I never knew so young a body with so old a head.*
(IV.1.161–2)
The Duke reads a letter from Bellario, a learned Doctor of Laws, commending a young lawyer called Balthazar who is actually Portia in male disguise.

74 PORTIA Then must the Jew be merciful.
SHYLOCK
On what compulsion must I? Tell me that.
PORTIA
The quality of mercy is not strained,
It droppeth as the gentle rain from heaven
Upon the place beneath. It is twice blest,
It blesseth him that gives and him that takes.
'Tis mightiest in the mightiest, it becomes
The thronèd monarch better than his crown.
His sceptre shows the force of temporal power,
The attribute to awe and majesty,
Wherein doth sit the dread and fear of kings;
But mercy is above this sceptred sway,
It is enthronèd in the hearts of kings,
It is an attribute to God himself,
And earthly power doth then show likest God's
When mercy seasons justice. Therefore, Jew,
Though justice be thy plea, consider this:
That in the course of justice none of us
Should see salvation. We do pray for mercy,
And that same prayer doth teach us all to render
The deeds of mercy.
(IV.1.179–99)
Portia, disguised as a lawyer, has ascertained that the facts of the case are not in dispute and suggests that Shylock ought to be ('must be') merciful. Shylock takes 'must' in its normal sense, and this leads to Portia's well-known speech on mercy. The ideas in the speech are not unusual, though Shakespeare gives them memorable expression, and it is significant in the context of the

play that soon after this speech Portia proceeds to exact a merciless judgement on Shylock. This may be justified, since he has rejected mercy in the first place, but it does show the importance of not taking a speech out of context and inflating it into the author's own views. 'Strained' means compelled; the prayer reference is to the end of the Lord's Prayer (see 71).

75 My deeds upon my head! I crave the law.
(IV.1.203)
Shylock responds to Portia's eloquent plea in favour of mercy by demanding justice; ultimately he receives a verdict marked only by justice, which is alleviated somewhat by Antonio's charity.

76 Wrest once the law to your authority,
To do a great right, do a little wrong.
(IV.1.212–13)
Bassanio urges the Duke (or, possibly, Portia?) to bend the law in order to save Antonio's life.

77 PORTIA
It must not be. There is no power in Venice
Can alter a decree establishèd.
'Twill be recorded for a precedent,
And many an error by the same example
Will rush into the state. It cannot be.
SHYLOCK
A Daniel come to judgement! Yea, a Daniel!
O wise young judge, how I do honour thee!
(IV.1.215–21)
Portia, in her lawyer's disguise, rejects Bassanio's request to bend the law. Venice was, in fact, renowned for the strict enforcement of its laws. 'Error' means miscarriage of justice; Daniel is a wise young judge in the Bible.

78 An oath, an oath! I have an oath in heaven;
Shall I lay perjury upon my soul?
No, not for Venice!
(IV.1.225–7)
Shylock continues to demand his rights, thus making it inevitable that when the situation is reversed he has a smaller claim to our sympathies.

79 I charge you by the law,
Whereof you are a well-deserving pillar,
Proceed to judgement.
(IV.1.235–7)

Shylock demands that the disguised Portia should give her judgement.

80 The court awards it, and the law doth give it.
(IV.1.297)
Portia, in her role as the lawyer, agrees in formal legal terms that Shylock is entitled to his pound of flesh.

81 Thyself shalt see the act,
For, as thou urgest justice, be assured
Thou shalt have justice more than thou desir'st.
(IV.1.311–13)
Portia, having pointed out that Shylock is not entitled under the terms of the bond to take any of Antonio's blood, then proceeds to turn the tables on him by promising him justice without mercy such as he demanded (urged) for Antonio.

82 A second Daniel! A Daniel, Jew!
Now, infidel, I have you on the hip!
(IV.1.330–1)
Gratiano reacts joyfully to Portia's claim that Shylock will be liable to death and confiscation of all his goods if he takes any blood or more or less than a pound of Antonio's flesh, turning Shylock's own sentiments (see 77) against him. Although Gratiano was not present when Shylock used the term 'catch him once upon the hip' (see 20), there is dramatic logic in his adopting a phrase Shylock used to describe his desire to get Antonio at a disadvantage.

83 A Daniel still say I, a second Daniel!
I thank thee, Jew, for teaching me that word.
(IV.1.337–8)
Gratiano continues to gloat at Shylock's discomforting at Portia's hands.

84 Nay, take my life and all! Pardon not that!
You take my house when you do take the prop
That doth sustain my house. You take my life
When you do take the means whereby I live.
(IV.1.371–4)
The court, at Portia's prompting, has confiscated Shylock's goods but the Duke has pardoned his life. Shylock responds with these lines.

85 PORTIA
Art thou contented, Jew? What dost thou say?

SHYLOCK
I am content.
(IV.1.390–1)
At the end of the judgement Shylock has also been told to become a Christian and promise to leave his estate to Lorenzo and Jessica when he dies. Obviously Shylock is not 'contented' in the everyday sense but he does agree, because he has no option.

86 I pray you give me leave to go from hence,
I am not well; send the deed after me,
And I will sign it.
(IV.1.392–4)
With these lines Shylock leaves the court and the play. Although he has forfeited sympathy by his vengeful pursuit of Antonio, the piling on of punishments in this scene tends to problematize the Christians' victory and it is hard to see his defeat as simply the appropriate punishment for an ogre figure. The deed is the deed of gift to Lorenzo and Jessica.

87 He is well paid that is well satisfied,
And I delivering you am satisfied.
(IV.1.412–13)
The disguised Portia tells Antonio that she is happy to have saved him and does not want the fee he and Bassanio have offered.

88 I pray you know me when we meet again.
(IV.1.416)
The disguised Portia is apparently asking Bassanio and Antonio to regard their meeting as a formal introduction, but for herself, and for the audience, there is also the knowledge that Bassanio has been unable to penetrate her male disguise and therefore will not know the lawyer when he meets him/her as Portia.

89 I see, sir, you are liberal in offers.
You taught me first to beg, and now methinks
You teach me how a beggar should be answered.
(IV.1.435–7)
The disguised Portia complains that Bassanio will not give her the ring she has asked for in response to his request that she should take something as a souvenir. It is, of course, the ring she gave him before he left Belmont and he is naturally reluctant to part with it. Ultimately he does so at Antonio's request, thus storing up trouble for himself in the final act.

90 The moon shines bright. In such a night as this,
When the sweet wind did gently kiss the trees

And they did make no noise, in such a night
Troilus methinks mounted the Troyan walls,
And sighed his soul toward the Grecian tents
Where Cressid lay that night.
(V.1.1–6)
Lorenzo opens the last act with these lines to Jessica. They exchange famous examples of love before locating themselves within that tradition (see 91). The examples they offer are, like Troilus, double-edged: Troilus remained faithful to Cressida when she was forced to leave Troy and join her father in the camp of the besieging Greeks, but she did not. Thus, although the mood certainly changes from that of the trial scene, the change is not to an unchallenged happiness.

91 LORENZO In such a night
Did Jessica steal from the wealthy Jew,
And with an unthrift love did run from Venice
As far as Belmont.
JESSICA In such a night
Did young Lorenzo swear he loved her well,
Stealing her soul with many vows of faith,
And ne'er a true one.
LORENZO In such a night
Did pretty Jessica, like a little shrew,
Slander her love, and he forgave it her.
(V.1.14–22)
Lorenzo and Jessica conclude their debate about love by placing themselves within the great tradition created by the examples they have quoted (see 90). 'Steal' may be both rob and steal away.

92 Who comes so fast in silence of the night?
(V.1.25)
Lorenzo and Jessica have heard footsteps. Lorenzo challenges the new arrival, who is a messenger bringing news of Portia's imminent arrival.

93 How sweet the moonlight sleeps upon this bank!
Here will we sit and let the sounds of music
Creep in our ears; soft stillness and the night
Become the touches of sweet harmony.
Sit, Jessica. Look how the floor of heaven
Is thick inlaid with patens of bright gold.
There's not the smallest orb which thou beholdest
But in his motion like an angel sings,
Still quiring to the young-eyed cherubins;

Such harmony is in immortal souls,
But whilst this muddy vesture of decay
Doth grossly close it in, we cannot hear it.
(V.1.54–65)

Lorenzo suggests that he and Jessica should await Portia's arrival outside. He is planning to listen to Portia's household musicians, whom he has asked to play to welcome her arrival, and he also refers to the music of the spheres which were held to support the stars in Ptolemaic astronomy. The 'floor of heaven' is the sky inlaid with stars which shine like communion dishes ('patens') and also the roof covering part of the stage area in a theatre like the Globe which, painted with stars and moons, was called the 'heavens'. 'Quiring' means making music; 'muddy vesture of decay' means the body – earthly clothing subject to decay.

94 I am never merry when I hear sweet music.
(V.1.69)

Jessica reacts to the music of Portia's musicians by telling Lorenzo that she responds to music with melancholy.

95 The man that hath no music in himself,
Nor is not moved with concord of sweet sounds,
Is fit for treasons, stratagems, and spoils,
The motions of his spirit are dull as night,
And his affections dark as Erebus.
Let no such man be trusted.
(V.1.83–8)

Lorenzo replies to Jessica's response to music (see 94) by stressing its virtues. 'Spoils' means plunder; 'motions' means impulses; 'Erebus' is, effectively, the underworld.

96 PORTIA
That light we see is burning in my hall;
How far that little candle throws his beams!
So shines a good deed in a naughty world.
NERISSA
When the moon shone we did not see the candle.
PORTIA
So doth the greater glory dim the less.
A substitute shines brightly as a king
Until a king be by, and then his state
Empties itself, as doth an inland brook
Into the main of waters.
(V.1.89–97)

Portia and Nerissa arrive home, undisguised. 'Naughty' was a much stronger word in Shakespeare's day, meaning evil; 'main' means main body – a lake or the sea.

97 The crow doth sing as sweetly as the lark
When neither is attended, and I think
The nightingale, if she should sing by day
When every goose is cackling, would be thought
No better a musician than the wren.
How many things by season seasoned are
To their right praise and true perfection!
(V.1.102–8)
Portia's comments to Nerissa follow on from her feeling that her musicians' music sounds sweeter than it does by day. 'Attended' probably means in company but it may mean listened to; 'by season seasoned are' means are valued by the right occasion.

98 How the moon sleeps with Endymion,
And would not be awaked.
(V.1.109–10)
Portia comments to Nerissa on the sleeping Lorenzo and Jessica. In classical mythology Diana the moon goddess loved Endymion, whom she made sleep for ever so that she could look at his beauty for ever.

99 This night methinks is but the daylight sick.
(V.1.124)
Portia says to Lorenzo, Jessica, and Nerissa that dawn is approaching, perhaps deliberately changing the subject since Bassanio and Gratiano are arriving and she has just been warning Lorenzo and Jessica not to say that she and Nerissa have been away.

100 Let me give light, but let me not be light,
For a light wife doth make a heavy husband.
(V.1.129–130)
Portia, welcoming Bassanio, puns on the sense of 'light' as sexually promiscuous and lightweight as she lights him onto the stage. 'Heavy' means sad as well as heavy.

101 Now by this hand, I gave it to a youth,
A kind of boy, a little scrubbèd boy
No higher than thyself, the judge's clerk,
A prating boy that begged it as a fee.
(V.1.161–4)

Gratiano is in trouble with Nerissa because he gave her ring to the lawyer's clerk who was actually, unknown to him, Nerissa herself. His description of the clerk adds insult to injury and allows the audience opportunities for knowing laughter at his expense. 'Scrubbèd' means stunted; 'prating' means talkative.

102 For by these blessèd candles of the night,
Had you been there I think you would have begged
The ring of me to give the worthy doctor.
(V.1.220–2)

Bassanio is trying to defend his action in giving Portia's ring to the lawyer who was, unknown to him, Portia herself in disguise. The 'candles of the night' are stars.

103 You shall not know by what strange accident
I chancèd on this letter.
(V.1.278–9)

Portia, having revealed that she and Nerissa were the lawyer and clerk who saved Antonio, now produces a letter which says that three of Antonio's ships have made successful voyages. Shakespeare presumably wanted to give Antonio's ventures a happy ending but did not choose to develop any further plot complications. Portia's remark conveys the necessary information and apparently closes off the possibility of further questioning without asking the audience to take it too seriously as anything other than a plot device.

The Merry Wives of Windsor

1 I will make a Star-Chamber matter of it.
(I.1.1–2)

The threat of Robert Shallow, a country justice of the peace, to bring his dispute with Sir John Falstaff before the Star Chamber is comic because he attributes great importance to a relatively petty matter, although at this point only the manner of delivery can convey this to the audience. The Star Chamber took its name from a room in the royal palace of Westminster whose ceiling was painted with stars and where the Queen's Council sat as a judicial body. It did exercise jurisdiction in disputes between the gentry and nobility and later, in the Jacobean period, came to abuse its authority to do so. The dispute with Falstaff arises from 'riot' or unrestrained lawlessness: Falstaff has forcibly entered Shallow's hunting lodge, beaten his men, and killed his deer.

2 I'll ne'er be drunk whilst I live again, but in honest, civil, godly company, for this trick. If I be drunk, I'll be drunk with those that have the fear of God, and not with drunken knaves.

(I.1.167–70)

The statement is a fine illustration of Slender's stupidity. It arises from his inability to prove that Pistol and Nym, Falstaff's low-life companions, have picked his pocket. His charge founders as a result of their counter-accusation of his drunkenness.

3 I had rather than forty shillings I had my Book of Songs and Sonnets here.

(I.1.183–4)

Slender, one of the suitors to Mistress Anne Page, is depicted as a country booby. When left alone, as here, he is incapable of entertaining himself for a single moment. The line is probably a reference to the immensely popular Tottel's *Miscellany* (the *Songs and Sonnets* of Henry Howard, Earl of Surrey, and others), which was published in 1557 and went through eight or more editions before the turn of the century.

4 'Convey', the wise it call. 'Steal'? Foh,
A fico for the phrase!

(I.3.26–7)

Pistol is discussing the art of theft with Nym and the two are castigating the lack of dexterity of Bardolph, whom Falstaff has just demoted to the tapster's trade to serve the host of the Garter Inn at Windsor. Throughout the play, Pistol casts himself in the role of a player and employs an elevated, histrionic turn of phrase, often borrowed and parodied from popular plays of the period. 'A fico [Spanish, 'fig'] for' was a contemptuous expression of the age, frequently accompanied by an obscene gesture.

5 She is a region in Guiana, all gold and bounty. I will be cheaters to them both, and they shall be exchequers to me. They shall be my East and West Indies, and I will trade to them both.

(I.3.63–7)

Falstaff's plot to seduce and cheat both Mistress Ford and Mistress Page is the initial intrigue upon which *The Merry Wives of Windsor* is structured. The description of his design not only projects Falstaff as a Saturnalian figure, vigorous and unscrupulous in sexual and monetary scheming, but employs the commercial and geographical imagery popular in the love poetry of the period to present the two women as objects of desire. The specific reference to Guiana may have been prompted by Ralegh's voyage of 1595 to discover the fabled wealth of Eldorado and other such enterprises. Later in the scene, Pistol and Nym, Falstaff's accomplices, decide to subvert the plan.

6 Here will be an old abusing of God's patience and the King's English.
(I.4.4–5)
This observation of Mistress Quickly, the housekeeper of the French physician Doctor Caius, is made to John Rugby, another household servant. 'Old' means 'great' and reference to the 'King's English' seems to have already been proverbial by the age of Elizabeth I. It is not therefore an indication that the play was revised in the reign of James I, nor really evidence that Shakespeare conceived the action as taking place in the reigns of Henry IV or Henry V, the context of the other Falstaff plays. The abuse of language and godliness referred to would take place if Doctor Caius should find a stranger in his house. Mistress Quickly is receiving Peter Simple, who is pleading Abraham Slender's case with Anne Page. Later in the scene, Simple has to hide in a closet in a vain attempt to escape Caius's detection.

7 O, wicked, wicked world! One that is well-nigh worn to pieces with age to show himself a young gallant!
(II.1.19–21)
This is Mistress Page's reaction to Falstaff's declaration of love by letter. Her reference to him in the preceding line as a 'Herod of Jewry', an allusion to the vice figure of the late medieval miracle plays, indicates that she views him as absurd and comic as well as wicked.

8 I shall think the worse of fat men as long as I have an eye to make difference of men's liking. And yet he would not swear; praised women's modesty; and gave such orderly and well-behaved reproof to all uncomeliness that I would have sworn his disposition would have gone to the truth of his words. But they do no more adhere and keep place together than the Hundredth Psalm to the tune of 'Greensleeves'. What tempest, I trow, threw this whale, with so many tuns of oil in his belly, ashore at Windsor? How shall I be revenged on him? I think the best way were to entertain him with hope till the wicked fire of lust have melted him in his own grease.
(II.1.51–63)

The speech expresses Mistress Ford's indignation at Falstaff's importuning her. The discrepancy between Falstaff's pretence of virtue and his practice of vice is conveyed by a contrast between the divine and solemn music of the psalms and a popular love song, still well-known to-day. The emendation of Rowe, an eighteenth-century editor of Shakespeare, of 'Hundredth Psalm' for 'hundred Psalms' has now generally won approval. The imagery of Mistress Ford's speech emphasizes Falstaff's obesity and bestiality, while in her last comment lies the seed of the two women's counter-plot and revenge.

9 I will find you twenty lascivious turtles ere one chaste man.
(II.1.75–6)
Mistress Page's comment is a female view of male infidelity. The 'turtles' are not the sea-creatures but 'turtledoves', a by-word for faithfulness.

10 Faith, thou hast some crotchets in thy head now.
(II.1.144–5)
Mistress Ford's observation on her husband's behaviour is taken from a contemporary proverb meaning to entertain absurd notions. It is a response to Ford's choleric instruction to his wife to go home.

11 If he should intend this voyage toward my wife, I would turn her loose to him; and what he gets more of her than sharp words, let it lie on my head.
(II.1.169–72)
Page's words to Ford, in their discussion of the trustworthiness of Pistol and Nym's information on Falstaff's attempts to seduce their wives, reveal his faith in his wife in contrast to Ford's obsessive jealousy. Ford's response twists the last phrase into an allusion to the cuckold's horns. The use of the term 'voyage' for the attempt at seduction picks up Falstaff's own language of sexual and commercial adventure (see 5 above).

12 There is either liquor in his pate or money in his purse when he looks so merrily.
(II.1.178–9)
Page's reference to the Host of the Garter Inn at Windsor, which actually existed in Shakespeare's time, draws on the conventional attributes of the publican as bibulous and avaricious.

13 Why then, the world's mine oyster,
Which I with sword will open.
(II.2.2–3)

Pistol's response to Falstaff's refusal to lend him money makes use of a contemporary proverb based on the idea of opening an oyster at the distance of a dagger for fear of finding it rotten. In the face of poverty, Pistol is suggesting that he will resort to extorting money by violence from a corrupt society.

14 FALSTAFF Of what quality was your love, then?
FORD Like a fair house built on another man's ground, so that I have lost my edifice by mistaking the place where I erected it.
(II.2.208–11)
Ford is disguised as Brook, a supposed suitor to Mistress Ford, and is recounting his imagined love for another man's wife in order to test Falstaff's integrity. His image possibly alludes both to the contemporary law by which property belonged to the owner of the land upon which it was erected. Burbage, the theatrical entrepreneur for whom Shakespeare wrote, encountered such problems before the construction of The Globe.

15 I will rather trust a Fleming with my butter, Parson Hugh the Welshman with my cheese, an Irishman with my aqua-vitae bottle, or a thief to walk my ambling gelding, than my wife with herself.
(II.2.286–90)
Ford's characteristic outburst of jealousy results from his plan to penetrate Falstaff's intentions (by means of his disguise as Brook) having backfired. 'Brook' has asked Falstaff to seduce Mistress Ford on the grounds that, once her virtue has been overcome by Falstaff's irresistible charms, she will be more pliant towards 'Brook' himself. Falstaff, in his desire to obtain 'Brook's' gold, has just revealed that Mistress Ford has already established an assignation with him for that evening, so prompting, on Falstaff's exit, Ford's soliloquy of jealousy. The comparisons are based on the irresistible attraction of each nationality or character-type to the object indicated.

16 He capers, he dances, he has eyes of youth, he writes verses, he speaks holiday, he smells April and May.
(III.2.60–2)
The description is the Host's view of Fenton, the true suitor of Anne Page. It expresses the vigour traditionally associated with the young lover. Love is linked not only to Spring but to festivity and the licence of holiday.

17 O, what a world of vile ill-favoured faults
Looks handsome in three hundred pounds a year!
(III.4.32–3)
Anne Page is contrasting the 'glitter' of Slender, the suitor chosen by her father on account of mercenary considerations, with the true 'gold' of Fenton, the man of her inclinations. Slender, the country booby, is rich, though his wealth sits uncomfortably on his lack of education; whereas Fenton, the gentleman, is impecunious, having wasted his estate. The social contrasts and the opposition of love and money were features of the citizen comedy genre in which Shakespeare, somewhat exceptionally, wrote this play.

18 Well, if I be served such another trick, I'll have my brains ta'en out and buttered, and give them to a dog for a new-year's gift.
(III.5.5–8)
Falstaff is castigating himself for having been duped by Mistress Ford and Mistress Page. He has just recounted how, after being carried out of Mistress Ford's house concealed in a linen basket to escape the jealous wrath of her husband (as the audience has witnessed in scene 3 of this Act), he has been tipped unceremoniously into the Thames along with the dirty washing.

19 And you may know by my size that I have a kind of alacrity in sinking. If the bottom were as deep as hell, I should down.
(III.5.10–12)
These sentences are part of Falstaff's account of his involuntary 'dip' in the Thames. While the statement is not strictly true according to the laws of physics, it contributes to the comedy of the scene that the audience is being encouraged to imagine. Falstaff's self-irony in the description is one of the redeeming features of his roguery.

20 If I find not what I seek, show no colour for my extremity. Let me for ever be your table sport. Let them say of me 'As jealous as Ford, that searched a hollow walnut for his wife's leman'.
(IV.2.150–4)
Ford's ironical statement about himself is made while he is vainly emptying his wife's linen basket in search of Falstaff, who he has learned was previously concealed there. It is made shortly before the appearance of Falstaff disguised as the fat woman of Brainford (Brentford), a person that Ford loathes as a witch and subsequently beats out of doors. The trick played by Mistress Ford therefore has the dual purpose of punishing Falstaff for his lech-

ery and Ford for his insane jealousy. Ford's phrase 'show no colour' appears to mean 'offer no excuse'. A 'hollow walnut' was proverbially tiny and therefore an implausible hiding place, while a 'leman' was an unlawful lover or paramour.

21 I rather will suspect the sun with cold
Than thee with wantonness. Now doth thy honour stand,
In him that was of late an heretic,
As firm as faith.
(IV.4.5–9)
Ford's repentant statement to his wife, after learning how Mistress Ford and Mistress Page have tricked Falstaff, is appropriately based on an illogical and impossible suspicion. The religious terms of 'faith' and 'heretic' appear to be drawn from the language of courtly love with its associations of ennobled feeling, though they may also reinforce the notion of the sacrament of marriage. The elevated feeling is deflated by Page's comment: 'Be not as extreme in submission / As in offence'.

22 This is the third time; I hope good luck lies in odd numbers ... They say there is divinity in odd numbers, either in nativity, chance, or death.
(V.1.1–4)
Falstaff is playing upon the idea of 'third time lucky' in his hope to seduce Mistress Ford at the third attempt. The audience, however, is cognizant of the third trick of the women to be practised upon him at Herne's Oak, where he is to appear wearing a buck's head, the horns of which will mark him out for social mockery just like the cuckolds he would make other men.

23 When gods have hot backs, what shall poor men do?
(V.5.11)
Falstaff is justifying his lechery by comparing his assignation with the women to the amorous escapades of Jupiter. This train of thought has been prompted by the comparison of the horns he is wearing to those of Jupiter when, assuming the form of a bull, he effected the rape of Europa.

24 EVANS I smell a man of middle earth.
FALSTAFF Heavens defend me from that Welsh fairy, lest he transform me to a piece of cheese.
(V.5.80–2)
This exchange serves as the cue for the comic climax of the play. Evans, in the guise of a satyr, is directing the 'fairies' in their

mock ritual. At this point they are supposed to become aware of the presence of Falstaff, a mortal, who is lying prostrate on the ground. At the instructions of the 'Fairy Queen' (Mistress Quickly), they put Falstaff to a trial by fire, suggesting that if he be chaste he will not feel pain. Of course, Falstaff is tortured by their lighted tapers and so, according to the ritual, proves his desires corrupted. The elaborate dramatic trick enacted upon Falstaff by the Windsor community is masque-like in proving virtue and castigating vice, while its broad humour is reminiscent of the anti-masque within the court masque. The comic ritual is also the climax of the plot relating to Anne Page, since Slender and Doctor Caius are duped into eloping with substitutes, while Fenton claims Anne. Falstaff's derogatory reference to Evans is based on the notion that the Welsh are great eaters of cheese.

A Midsummer Night's Dream

1 THESEUS
Now, fair Hippolyta, our nuptial hour
Draws on apace. Four happy days bring in
Another moon – but O, methinks how slow
This old moon wanes! She lingers my desires,
Like to a stepdame or a dowager
Long withering out a young man's revenue.
HIPPOLYTA
Four days will quickly steep themselves in night;
Four nights will quickly dream away the time:
And then the moon – like to a silver bow
New-bent in heaven – shall behold the night
Of our solemnities.
(I.1.1–11)

In the play's opening speech Theseus, the duke of Athens, who is to marry Hippolyta, queen of the Amazons, introduces the idea of marriage which frames the play. The moon presides over the imagery and the action. The idea of aged relatives thwarting youthful aspirations anticipates Egeus's attempts to order the amatory relationships of his daughter Hermia with her suitors Lysander and Demetrius. Hippolyta's speech counters Theseus's views with an immediate contradiction and amplification in a way typical of the play and introduces the idea of 'dream' which is so significant in the play.

2 Fair Hermia, question your desires,
Know of your youth, examine well your blood,
Whether, if you yield not to your father's choice,
You can endure the livery of a nun,
For aye to be in shady cloister mewed,
To live a barren sister all your life,
Chanting faint hymns to the cold fruitless moon.
Thrice blessèd they that master so their blood
To undergo such maiden pilgrimage;
But earthlier happy is the rose distilled
Than that which, withering on the virgin thorn,
Grows, lives, and dies in single blessedness.
(I.1.67–78)

Theseus explains the options open to Hermia if she refuses to marry Demetrius, her father's choice. Although the reference to nuns is strictly anachronistic, the Renaissance theatre did not operate on the so-called realistic conventions of some later theatres. The choice of vocabulary directs our sympathies against the 'maiden pilgrimage', and the moon makes one of its frequent appearances.

3 Ay me! For aught that I could ever read,
Could ever hear by tale or history,
The course of true love never did run smooth.
(I.1.132–4)

Lysander, left alone with Hermia, generalizes their predicament by reference to the great tradition of star-crossed lovers in fiction ('tale') and fact ('history'). The third line has become proverbial.

4 Or if there were a sympathy in choice,
War, death, or sickness did lay siege to it,
Making it momentany as a sound,
Swift as a shadow, short as any dream,
Brief as the lightning in the collied night,
That in a spleen unfolds both heaven and earth,
And – ere a man hath power to say 'Behold!' –
The jaws of darkness do devour it up.
So quick bright things come to confusion.
(I.1.141–9)

Lysander again offers comfort in the fact that he and Hermia are only suffering what every lover suffers. The references to dream and night anticipate the events in the wood and help to establish atmosphere. 'Momentany' means momentary and 'collied' means blackened.

5 I swear to thee by Cupid's strongest bow,
By his best arrow with the golden head,
By the simplicity of Venus' doves,
By that which knitteth souls and prospers loves,
And by that fire which burned the Carthage queen
When the false Trojan under sail was seen,
By all the vows that ever men have broke –
In number more than ever women spoke, –
In that same place thou hast appointed me
Tomorrow truly will I meet with thee.
(I.1.169–78)

Hermia's vow to meet Lysander in the wood so that they can escape the law identifies her with the great tradition of love represented by Cupid and Venus, but her references to Aeneas, the false Trojan, deserting Dido, and to men's broken vows are ironically prophetic of her fate in the wood.

6 Your eyes are lodestars, and your tongue's sweet air
More tuneable than lark to shepherd's ear
When wheat is green, when hawthorn buds appear.
(I.1.183–5)

Helena, Hermia's friend, is in love with Demetrius, who is in love with Hermia. Here she complains that Hermia's beauty has drawn Demetrius to her. A lodestar is a guiding star, probably with overtones of Hermia exerting a magnetic attraction on her suitors.

7 Things base and vile, holding no quantity,
Love can transpose to form and dignity.
Love looks not with the eyes, but with the mind,
And therefore is winged Cupid painted blind.
(I.1.232–5)

Helena's soliloquy, in which she laments Demetrius's spurning of her, develops into a more general discussion of the way that true love stems from the mind rather than from external appearances and empirical evidence. This stress on the imagination's ability to shape events is fundamental to the play.

8 Our play is *The most lamentable comedy and most cruel death of Pyramus and Thisbe.*
(I.2.11–12)

Quince the carpenter, head of a group of amateur actors who are hoping to perform as part of Theseus's wedding celebrations, reads the title of their play. Before Shakespeare burlesqued Pyramus and Thisbe they were tragic figures whose story, told in Ovid's *Metamorphoses*, was available to Shakespeare in an English version of dubious quality by Arthur Golding published in 1567. See also 58.

9 That will ask some tears in the true performing of it. If I do it, let the audience look to their eyes! I will move storms. I will condole, in some measure. To the rest. – Yet my chief humour is for a tyrant. I could play Ercles rarely, or a part to tear a cat in, to make all split:

The raging rocks
And shivering shocks
Shall break the locks
Of prison gates,
And Phibbus' car
Shall shine from far
And make and mar
The foolish Fates.

This was lofty! – Now name the rest of the players. – This is Ercles' vein, a tyrant's vein. A lover is more condoling.
(I.2.22–37)
Bottom the weaver is the star of Quince's group. His account of the effect of his proposed performance as Pyramus reflects his own estimate of his talents. 'Ercles' is Hercules, a tyrant rather than a lover and therefore given to the rant and swagger associated with the idea of tearing a cat. 'Phibbus' car' is the chariot of the sun god Phoebus.

10 Nay, faith, let not me play a woman – I have a beard coming.
(I.2.43–4)
Francis Flute the bellows-mender has just been told by Quince that he is to play the part of Thisbe. In the English theatre of Shakespeare's time female roles were played by male actors. Flute's protest is an attempt to suggest he is too mature for a female part, although it does appear that the 'boys' who played these parts could be as old as 24.

11 SNUG Have you the lion's part written? Pray you, if it be, give it me; for I am slow of study.
QUINCE You may do it extempore; for it is nothing but roaring.
BOTTOM Let me play the lion too. I will roar that I will do any man's heart good to hear me. I will roar that I will make the Duke say 'Let him roar again; let him roar again!'
(I.2.62–9)
Snug the joiner is to play the lion that frightens Thisbe, but his modest doubts provide an opportunity for Bottom's mega-

lomaniac tendency to want to play anything, particularly if it involves roaring.

12 I will aggravate my voice so that I will roar you as gently as any sucking dove. I will roar you an 'twere any nightingale.
(I.2.76–8)
After objections from the other members of Quince's group that too much realism in the lion's roaring would frighten the audience, Bottom proposes to roar quietly but his malapropism 'aggravate' for 'mitigate' ruins the effect. He also appears to conflate the sitting dove and the sucking lamb into the 'sucking dove'. These confusions, typical of Bottom, also serve to help create the sense of a natural landscape which is so important in the following scenes and which would not have been presented naturalistically on the Elizabethan stage.

13 You can play no part but Pyramus; for Pyramus is a sweet-faced man; a proper man as one shall see in a summer's day; a most lovely, gentlemanlike man. Therefore you must needs play Pyramus.
(I.2.79–82)
Quince, the diplomatic director, soothes his star Bottom into aquiescence in only playing one part by the usual methods of flattering his ego and implicitly denigrating the abilities of the other actors.

14 Enough; hold, or cut bowstrings.
(I.2.103)
Bottom closes the scene with a line whose exact meaning is much disputed, although the general sense appears to be 'keep your agreement [to meet in the wood for a rehearsal] or be disgraced if you don't'.

15 PUCK
How now, spirit; whither wander you?
FAIRY
Over hill, over dale,
Thorough bush, thorough briar,
Over park, over pale,
Thorough flood, thorough fire –
I do wander everywhere
Swifter than the moon's sphere,
And I serve the Fairy Queen,
To dew her orbs upon the green.
The cowslips tall her pensioners be;
In their gold coats spots you see –

Those be rubies, fairy favours;
In those freckles live their savours.
I must go seek some dewdrops here,
And hang a pearl in every cowslip's ear.
(II.1.1–15)

This is the first appearance of the fairies. At this stage we learn little about Puck but the Fairy establishes the nature of the fairies through the verse, which contrasts with the verse and prose used for the mortals, the wealth of nature imagery, and the reference to 'tall' cowslips which marks the beginning of the stress on the fairies' diminutive size. Queen Elizabeth I's 'pensioners' were the gentlemen of the royal bodyguard. Fashionable Elizabethans of both sexes often wore jewels as ear decorations.

16 That all their elves for fear
Creep into acorn cups and hide them there.
(II.1.30–1)

The Fairy's description of the elves' reaction to the arguments between Oberon and Titania, king and queen of the fairies, about who is to have the Indian boy, economically suggests the size of the fairies, the nature of their environment, and the depth of the dispute.

17 FAIRY
Either I mistake your shape and making quite,
Or else you are that shrewd and knavish sprite
Called Robin Goodfellow. Are not you he
That frights the maidens of the villagery,
Skim milk, and sometimes labour in the quern,
And bootless make the breathless housewife churn,
And sometime make the drink to bear no barm,
Mislead night-wanderers, laughing at their harm?
Those that 'Hobgoblin' call you, and 'Sweet Puck',
You do their work, and they shall have good luck.
Are not you he?
PUCK Thou speakest aright:
I am that merry wanderer of the night.
I jest to Oberon, and make him smile
When I a fat and bean-fed horse beguile,
Neighing in likeness of a filly foal;
And sometime lurk I in a gossip's bowl
In very likeness of a roasted crab;
And when she drinks, against her lips I bob,
And on her withered dewlap pour the ale.
(II.1.32–50)

The Fairy's speech and Puck's reply list many of the characteristics associated with this representative hobgoblin. Puck was once a generic name, as is Robin Goodfellow. On the evidence of these speeches, Puck appears to be a more domestic creature than Oberon and Titania, responsible for minor irritations and given to practical jokes. 'Quern' means churn; 'bootless' means in vain; a 'crab' is a crab apple.

18 PUCK
But room, Fairy: here comes Oberon.
FAIRY
And here my mistress. Would that he were gone!
(II.1.58–9)

The antagonism between Oberon and Titania over the Indian boy is neatly conveyed by splitting the couplet between their followers and pointing up the quarrel by rhyming Oberon with 'gone'.

19 Ill met by moonlight, proud Titania!
(II.1.60)

Oberon's greeting to Titania not only anticipates the general action of the following scenes, in which all meetings by moonlight tend to be ill, but emphasizes the night setting. In the Elizabethan theatre performances usually took place in the open air by daylight, so the impression of night had to be created verbally.

20 These are the forgeries of jealousy;
And never since the middle summer's spring
Met we on hill, in dale, forest, or mead,
By pavèd fountain or by rushy brook,
Or in the beachèd margent of the sea
To dance our ringlets to the whistling wind,
But with thy brawls thou hast disturbed our sport.
Therefore the winds, piping to us in vain,
As in revenge have sucked up from the sea
Contagious fogs which, falling in the land,
Hath every pelting river made so proud
That they have overborne their continents.
The ox hath therefore stretched his yoke in vain,
The ploughman lost his sweat, and the green corn
Hath rotted ere his youth attained a beard.
The fold stands empty in the drownèd field,
And crows are fatted with the murrion flock.
The nine men's morris is filled up with mud,
And the quaint mazes in the wanton green

For lack of tread are indistinguishable.
(II.1.81–100)

Titania's description of the adverse effects of the argument between herself and Oberon identifies them as being responsible for the good order of nature, which is threatened by their discord. In fact this version of what has been happening to the weather is not confirmed by anyone else in the play, so it can be seen as an example of the limited subjective perception which is typical of so many characters in the play, as well as an explicit evocation of the relationship between the personal and the pastoral. The speech is sometimes thought to be topical, but there is often bad weather in British summers. A 'pelting' river is an insignificant one and its 'continents' are its banks. The 'murrion flock' have been stricken with a sheep plague. The 'nine men's morris' is an outdoor playing area for the game of the same name.

21 The human mortals want their winter cheer.
No night is now with hymn or carol blessed.
Therefore the moon, the governess of floods,
Pale in her anger, washes all the air,
That rheumatic diseases do abound;
And thorough this distemperature we see
The seasons alter; hoary-headed frosts
Fall in the fresh lap of the crimson rose,
And on old Hiems' thin and icy crown
An odorous chaplet of sweet summer buds
Is as in mockery set. The spring, the summer,
The childing autumn, angry winter change
Their wonted liveries, and the mazèd world
By their increase now knows not which is which.
And this same progeny of evils
Comes from our debate, from our dissension.
We are their parents and original.
(II.1.101–17)

Titania continues her account of the effects of her disagreement with Oberon. 'Hiems' is winter personified.

22 His mother was a votaress of my order,
And in the spicèd Indian air by night
Full often hath she gossiped by my side,
And sat with me on Neptune's yellow sands
Marking th'embarkèd traders on the flood,
When we have laughed to see the sails conceive
And grow big-bellied with the wanton wind;
Which she with pretty and with swimming gait
Following – her womb then rich with my young squire –

Would imitate, and sail upon the land
To fetch me trifles, and return again
As from a voyage, rich with merchandise.
But she, being mortal, of that boy did die,
And for her sake do I rear up her boy;
And for her sake I will not part with him.
(II.1.123–37)

Titania's description of her friendship with the Indian boy's mother remains an outstanding evocation of the joys and pains of pregnancy and childbirth.

23 OBERON
My gentle Puck, come hither. Thou rememberest
Since once I sat upon a promontory
And heard a mermaid on a dolphin's back
Uttering such dulcet and harmonious breath
That the rude sea grew civil at her song,
And certain stars shot madly from their spheres
To hear the sea-maid's music?
PUCK I remember.
OBERON
That very time I saw – but thou couldst not –
Flying between the cold moon and the earth
Cupid all armed. A certain aim he took
At a fair vestal thronèd by the west,
And loosed his loveshaft smartly from his bow
As it should pierce a hundred thousand hearts;
But I might see young Cupid's fiery shaft
Quenched in the chaste beams of the watery moon,
And the imperial votaress passed on
In maiden meditation, fancy-free.
Yet marked I where the bolt of Cupid fell:
It fell upon a little western flower,
Before, milk-white; now purple with love's wound:
And maidens call it 'love in idleness'.
(II.1.148–68)

Oberon's account of the origins of the flower 'love-in-idleness' which is to serve as a love charm contains some kind of topical allusion to Queen Elizabeth. Although the exact nature of the compliment is disputed, it is clear that the 'fair vestal' is the queen who was chaste, as were the Vestal Virgins of ancient Rome.

24 I'll put a girdle round about the earth
In forty minutes!
(II.1.175–6)

Puck's boast of how long it will take him to get the flower was, as Jan Kott remarked, an accurate anticipation of the time the first sputnik took to do the same journey. A girdle is associated with Drake's circumnavigation in an Emblem book of 1586.

25 But who comes here? I am invisible,
And I will overhear their conference.
(II.1.186–7)

Oberon's remark as he sees Demetrius and Helena entering reminds us of the sophistication of Elizabethan audiences and dramaturgy. He may have used a cloak like the 'robe for to goo invisibell' which appears in the property and costume list of the contemporary theatre manager Phillip Henslowe, or the audience may simply have been expected to accept his statement.

26 I know a bank where the wild thyme blows,
Where oxlips and the nodding violet grows,
Quite overcanopied with luscious woodbine,
With sweet muskroses and with eglantine.
There sleeps Titania some time of the night,
Lulled in these flowers with dances and delight.
And there the snake throws her enamelled skin,
Weed wide enough to wrap a fairy in.
And with the juice of this I'll streak her eyes
And make her full of hateful fantasies.
(II.1.249–58)

Oberon is going to enchant Titania so that when she wakes she will fall in love with the next living thing she meets. This atmospheric invocation of the night-time wood is often quoted, and has been set to music, without the last two lines in which the beauty of the landscape, already qualified by the presence of the snake, is modified by the nature of the deed to be performed within it. 'Weed' means piece of clothing.

27 FIRST FAIRY
You spotted snakes with double tongue,
Thorny hedgehogs, be not seen.
Newts and blindworms, do no wrong,
Come not near our Fairy Queen.
CHORUS
Philomel with melody
Sing in our sweet lullaby,
Lulla, lulla, lullaby; lulla, lulla, lullaby.
Never harm
Nor spell nor charm
Come our lovely lady nigh.

So good night, with lullaby.
FIRST FAIRY
Weaving spiders, come not here;
Hence, you longlegged spinners, hence!
Beetles black, approach not near,
Worm nor snail, do no offence.
CHORUS
Philomel with melody *etc.*
Titania sleeps
SECOND FAIRY
Hence, away! Now all is well.
One aloof stand sentinel!
(II.2.9–33)

The fairies sing Titania to sleep with what proves to be a deeply ironic lullaby, since Oberon is about to appear and enchant her. It is typical of the play's methods that the less attractive side of nature should be summoned up but contained within the harmony of a song. 'Blindworms' are slow-worms.

28 Night and silence. – Who is here?
Weeds of Athens he doth wear.
(II.2.76–7)

Puck, having failed to find Demetrius (whom he is supposed to enchant so that he will love Helena), comes across the sleeping Lysander and, not knowing that there are two male Athenians in the wood, makes the mistake which begins the lovers' real troubles. 'Weeds' means clothes.

29 HELENA
Lysander, if you live, good sir, awake!
LYSANDER (*wakes*)
And run through fire I will for thy sweet sake!
(II.2.108–9)

Helena's concern for Lysander leads to the inevitable conclusion of Puck's mistake since Lysander, like Titania, loves the first thing he sees when he wakes. The couplet rhyme gives added force to the moment.

30 Here's a marvellous convenient place for our rehearsal. This green plot shall be our stage, this hawthorn brake our tiring-house, and we will do it in action as we will do it before the Duke.
(III.1.2–5)

The mechanicals, Quince's group of actors, arrive for their rehearsal in the wood. Quince's lines remind us of the theatricality of the play, since the hawthorn brake and green plot he refers to would have actually been the tiring-house (the dressing room whose wall provides the stage facade) and stage in the Elizabethan theatre.

31 Masters, you ought to consider with yourself, to bring in – God shield us – a lion among ladies is a most dreadful thing; for there is not a more fearful wildfowl than your lion living; and we ought to look to't.
(III.1.27–30)
The mechanicals' production is fraught with difficulties, including the problem of how to present a lion in performance safely. Bottom's eloquent statement of the problem is marred only by his malapropism 'wild-fowl'. The problem is ultimately solved by giving Snug, who plays the lion, a speech of explanation.

32 What hempen homespuns have we swaggering here
So near the cradle of the Fairy Queen?
What, a play toward? I'll be an auditor –
An actor too, perhaps, if I see cause.
(III.1.70–3)
Puck's entrance speech draws attention back to Titania, who has been asleep onstage throughout the mechanicals' rehearsal, and prepares us for his intervention.

33 A stranger Pyramus than e'er played here.
(III.1.83)
Puck anticipates his transformation of Bottom and draws the audience's attention to the changes Shakespeare is making to the Pyramus and Thisbe story.

34 I'll follow you, I'll lead you about a round,
Thorough bog, thorough bush, thorough brake, thorough briar,
Sometime a horse I'll be, sometime a hound,
A hog, a headless bear, sometime a fire,
And neigh, and bark, and grunt and roar and burn
Like horse, hound, hog, bear, fire at every turn.
(III.1.100–5)
Puck's catalogue of projected torments for the mechanicals includes many of the tricks traditionally associated with hobgoblins and will o'the wisps ('fires').

35 Bless thee, Bottom! Bless thee! Thou art translated!
(III.1.112–3)

Quince's response to Bottom's monstrous reappearance with an ass's head has become more comic with the modern tendency to regard 'translated' as a malapropism.

36 I see their knavery! This is to make an ass of me, to fright me, if they could.
(III.1.114–15)
Bottom's comments on his friends' behaviour draw our attention to the gap between their perception and his – he is an ass already.

37 BOTTOM (*sings*)
The ousel cock so black of hue,
With orange-tawny bill,
The throstle with his note so true,
The wren with little quill.
TITANIA (*wakes*)
What angel wakes me from my flowery bed?
BOTTOM (*sings*)
The finch, the sparrow, and the lark,
The plainsong cuckoo grey,
Whose note full many a man doth mark
And dares not answer 'Nay'.
(III.1.118–26)
Bottom's song is presumably rather different in quality from the one that sent Titania to sleep, thus enhancing the comic effect. Perhaps the references to the natural world here relate to those in the fairies' earlier song, since the birds would eat insects. The irony in Titania's waking speech is very clear.

38 The moon methinks looks with a watery eye;
And when she weeps, weeps every little flower,
Lamenting some enforcèd chastity.
(III.1.193–5)
Titania probably sees the moon as Diana, the chaste goddess who weeps (creates dew in the context of flowers) over violated chastity, but 'enforcèd' could also carry the sense of maintained against the will, which would tie in with Hermia's possible fates.

39 How now, mad spirit?
What night-rule now about this haunted grove?
(III.2.4–5)
Oberon's greeting to Puck is a reminder of the differences between the rational daylight world of Athens and the ways in which the wood and night operate.

40 Shall we their fond pageant see?
Lord, what fools these mortals be!
(III.2.114–15)

Puck encourages us to see the forthcoming arguments at cross purposes between the Athenian lovers in theatrically distanced terms with his reference to 'pageant'. The second line has become almost proverbial, but in its original context these particular mortals' foolishness is abetted by fairy magic.

41 We grew together
Like to a double cherry, seeming parted
But yet an union in partition,
Two lovely berries moulded on one stem,
So with two seeming bodies but one heart.
(III.2.208–12)

Helena's rebuke to Hermia for joining with Lysander and Demetrius in mocking her offers various images of their longstanding friendship, including this picture of a 'union in partition'. Helena is quite mistaken about the true nature of events since Lysander and Demetrius, both under the magic spell, do actually love her at this moment.

42 O, when she is angry she is keen and shrewd.
She was a vixen when she went to school,
And though she be but little, she is fierce.
(III.2.323–5)

Helena's predicament – apparently being wooed in jest by Lysander and Demetrius – leads her to abandon her previous protestations of longstanding friendship for Hermia in favour of recollections of her longstanding vices. 'Vixen' is appropriate to the general atmosphere of woodland flora and fauna as well as to the slanging match. The reference to Hermia's physique presumably reflects the relative stature of the original players of Helena and Hermia.

43 PUCK
My fairy lord, this must be done with haste,
For night's swift dragons cut the clouds full fast,
And yonder shines Aurora's harbinger,
At whose approach ghosts wandering here and there
Troop home to churchyards. Damnèd spirits all
That in crossways and floods have burial
Already to their wormy beds are gone.
For fear lest day should look their shames upon
They wilfully themselves exile from light,
And must for aye consort with black-browed night.

OBERON
But we are spirits of another sort.
I with the morning's love have oft made sport,
And like a forester the groves may tread
Even till the eastern gate all fiery red
Opening on Neptune with fair blessèd beams
Turns into yellow gold his salt green streams.
But notwithstanding, haste, make no delay;
We may effect this business, yet ere day.
(III.2.378–395)

Puck's account of the arrival of dawn and Oberon's contrasting version show Shakespeare's interest in presenting a full picture of the associations of a particular moment. The actual description of dawn is superfluous in plot terms, since what matters is the disenchanting of Lysander and Titania, but important thematically. Night's 'swift dragons' draw her chariot; Aurora is a personification of dawn, so her harbinger is the morning star; Neptune, the god of the sea, here stands for the sea itself.

44 Yet but three? Come one more,
Two of both kinds makes up four.
Here she comes, curst and sad.
Cupid is a knavish lad
Thus to make poor females mad.
(III.2.437–41)

Puck's comment, occasioned by the late arrival of the distressed and cross ('curst') Hermia to join the other three sleeping lovers, draws attention to the fact that the women have not been cushioned by magic and have therefore experienced the effects of the cross-purposes of the night directly – unlike Lysander and Demetrius, who were cushioned by the effects of magic.

45 Jack shall have Jill;
Naught shall go ill.
The man shall have his mare again, and all shall be well.
(III.2.461–3)

These lines, the end of Puck's speech disenchanting Lysander so that the two pairs of lovers can be properly reestablished, deflates their previous pretensions to be like the great lovers of antiquity. Jack and Jill and the man and his mare were both proverbial before Shakespeare. The monosyllabic words create an appropriate atmosphere of simplicity and authority.

46 Come, sit thee down upon this flowery bed
While I thy amiable cheeks do coy,
And stick muskroses in thy sleek, smooth head,

And kiss thy fair large ears, my gentle joy.
(IV.1.1–4)
Titania's endearments to Bottom draw attention to his unsuitability to be her lover by referring to his asshead. 'Coy' means caress.

47 I must to the barber's, Monsieur, for methinks I am marvellous hairy about the face. And I am such a tender ass, if my hair do but tickle me, I must scratch.
(IV.1.23–6)
Bottom is asking 'Monsieur' Mustardseed, one of Titania's fairies, to join in scratching his head. He assumes he is itchy because he has not shaved – the ass reference again ironically underlines Bottom's unawareness of his true position. Presumably he addresses the fairies as 'Monsieur' because of some notion of proper gentlemanly behaviour.

48 I have a reasonable good ear in music. Let's have the tongs and the bones.
(IV.1.28–9)
Bottom's reply to Titania's question whether he would like to hear some music reveals the gap between his own belief in his connoisseurship and his actual taste, since the tongs and bones were primitive instruments.

49 Methinks I have a great desire to a bottle of hay. Good hay, sweet hay hath no fellow.
(IV.1.32–3)
Titania has asked Bottom what he would like to eat. Naturally, being an ass, he wants hay. 'Bottle of hay' simply means a measure of hay; it was not a malapropism in Shakespeare's time even though it is usually treated as one in the modern theatre.

50 I pray you, let none of your people stir me. I have an exposition of sleep come upon me.
(IV.1.37–8)
This is Bottom's final request to Titania before they are released from their spells. 'Your people' are Titania's fairies; 'exposition' is a malapropism for disposition.

51 PUCK
Fairy king, attend, and mark:
I do hear the morning lark.
OBERON
Then, my queen, in silence sad,
Trip we after night's shade.

We the globe can compass soon,
Swifter than the wandering moon.

TITANIA

Come, my lord, and in our flight
Tell me how it came this night
That I sleeping here was found
With these mortals on the ground.

(IV.1.92–101)

Puck again reminds Oberon of the approach of dawn and the fairies depart, reminding us once more of their nature with references to the moon and to flying. Shakespeare is able to cut short the explanations of the night's events which the audience already knows by having the story told offstage.

52 I never heard
So musical a discord, such sweet thunder.

(IV.1.116–17)

Theseus and Hippolyta have arrived in the wood on a hunting trip. Hippolyta's description of the baying hounds she heard on another hunt is a striking example of the play's characteristic use of reconciled paradox.

53 Good morrow, friends – Saint Valentine is past!
Begin these woodbirds but to couple now?

(IV.1.138–9)

Theseus's irony permeates his first speech to the newly awakened lovers who have just been disturbed by the hunting party. His use of 'friends' points up the fact that when he last heard of them they were at loggerheads. 'St Valentine' and 'woodbirds' relate to the belief that birds chose their mates on St Valentine's day. The lines also appear to contain an implicit stage direction that the lovers should have been lying as two couples.

54 I have had a most rare vision. I have had a dream past the wit of man to say what dream it was. Man is but an ass if he go about to expound this dream.

(IV.1.203–5)

Bottom, having just woken up, remembers his adventures as a dream. Comedy arises from the discrepancy between his understanding of events and ours, reinforced by another unconscious mention of the ass. The last sentence remains a salutary reminder to commentators of the dangers of commenting ...

55 The eye of man hath not heard, the ear of man hath not seen,

man's hand is not able to taste, his tongue to conceive, nor his heart to report what my dream was!
(IV.1.208–11)
Bottom continues his waking speech, confusing the functions of the various organs of perception in a way which recalls the other perceptual confusions in the play. The lines parody a passage in the Bible, I Corinthians 2:9.

56 HIPPOLYTA
'Tis strange, my Theseus, that these lovers speak of.
THESEUS
More strange than true. I never may believe
These antique fables, nor these fairy toys.
Lovers and madmen have such seething brains,
Such shaping fantasies, that apprehend
More than cool reason ever comprehends.
The lunatic, the lover, and the poet
Are of imagination all compact.
One sees more devils than vast hell can hold.
That is the madman. The lover, all as frantic,
Sees Helen's beauty in a brow of Egypt.
The poet's eye, in a fine frenzy rolling,
Doth glance from heaven to earth, from earth to heaven.
And as imagination bodies forth
The forms of things unknown, the poet's pen
Turns them to shapes, and gives to airy nothing
A local habitation and a name.
Such tricks hath strong imagination
That if it would but apprehend some joy,
It comprehends some bringer of that joy.
Or in the night, imagining some fear,
How easy is a bush supposed a bear?
(V.1.1–22)
Theseus's response to Hippolyta's puzzlement over the lovers' story leads him into an explicit discussion of the nature and function of the imagination in constructing our view of the world. Because this speech is often anthologized, it is often forgotten that it is only one speech by a character who has an imperfect idea of the true nature of the events in the wood and whose view is corrected in Hippolyta's next speech. 'Helen' is Helen of Troy, presumably fair in comparison to the dark complexion of a gipsy ('brow of Egypt'), although there may be an unconscious reminiscence of the complexions of Hermia and Helena. Are we meant to remember that Theseus himself is an antique fable? See also 63.

57 But all the story of the night told over,
And all their minds transfigured so together,
More witnesseth than fancy's images,
And grows to something of great constancy;
But howsoever, strange and admirable.
(V.1.23–7)
Hippolyta's judgement of the lovers' story is a fitting epigraph for a play that blends so many apparently disparate elements into a coherent whole.

58 *A tedious brief scene of young Pyramus*
And his love Thisbe; 'very tragical mirth'.
Merry and tragical? Tedious and brief?
That is, hot ice and wondrous strange snow.
How shall we find the concord of this discord?
(V.1.56–60)
Theseus is reading the list of productions available for him to see as part of the wedding celebrations. The full title of 'Pyramus and Thisbe' appears to be a burlesque of such play titles as Thomas Preston's *Cambyses* (published circa 1570) which is described as 'a lamentable tragedy mixed full of pleasant mirth'. But it also shows Shakespeare's concern to reconcile the apparently paradoxical which is further reflected in Theseus's comments. See also 8.

59 Where I have come, great clerks have purposèd
To greet me with premeditated welcomes,
Where I have seen them shiver and look pale,
Make periods in the midst of sentences,
Throttle their practised accent in their fears,
And in conclusion dumbly have broke off,
Not paying me a welcome. Trust me, sweet,
Out of this silence yet I picked a welcome,
And in the modesty of fearful duty
I read as much as from the rattling tongue
Of saucy and audacious eloquence.
Love, therefore, and tongue-tied simplicity
In least speak most, to my capacity.
(V.1.93–105)
Theseus's speech to Hippolyta expands his reasons for hearing 'Pyramus and Thisbe', accepting the will for the deed. It is also, however, an accurate prophecy of Quince's prologue. There appears to be a tribute in these lines to Queen Elizabeth's behaviour on such occasions in real life.

60 If we offend it is with our good will.
That you should think we come not to offend
But with good will. To show our simple skill,
That is the true beginning of our end.
Consider then we come but in despite.
We do not come as minding to content you,
Our true intent is. All for your delight
We are not here. That you should here repent you
The actors are at hand, and by their show
You shall know all that you are like to know.
(V.1.108–18)

Quince's prologue to 'Pyramus and Thisbe' is ruined by his phrasing, which destroys the intended sense.

61 Whereat with blade – with bloody, blameful blade –
He bravely broached his boiling bloody breast.
(V.1.145–6)

This part of the second prologue to 'Pyramus and Thisbe', again spoken by Quince, describes Pyramus's death. Alliteration on this scale was regarded as extremely old-fashioned in English verse by this date and the effect is deliberately comic.

62 With the help of a surgeon he might yet recover, and prove an ass.
(V.1.298–9)

Theseus's comment on Pyramus's death recalls Bottom's previous incarnation as an ass and often provokes a response from Bottom on stage, wondering how much Theseus knows. Extra point is given to the remark if, as happened most memorably in Peter Brook's 1970 production, Oberon and Theseus are doubled. The speech also recalls the St George mumming plays in which the Turkish knight is resurrected by a doctor.

63 The iron tongue of midnight hath told twelve.
Lovers, to bed; 'tis almost fairy time.
(V.1.353–4)

Theseus's last speech takes the mortals off to bed. The reference to fairy time somewhat undercuts Theseus's earlier dismissal of 'fairy toys' (see 56), as well as anticipating the arrival of the fairies in an 'innocent' remark about the lateness of the hour.

64 Now the hungry lion roars
And the wolf behowls the moon,
Whilst the heavy ploughman snores
All with weary task foredone.
(V.1.361–4)

As the mortals depart, Puck arrives as herald of the fairies who are to bless the palace. Perhaps the mention of a lion picks up the mechanicals' lion as well as referring to the wild beast.

65 Not a mouse
Shall disturb this hallowed house.
I am sent with broom before
To sweep the dust behind the door.
(V.1.377–80)

Puck is traditionally associated with midnight house-cleaning, so his last two lines before Oberon and Titania appear are doubly appropriate: he is clearing the way for their royal progress and performing one of his traditional tasks.

66 Now until the break of day
Through this house each fairy stray.
To the best bride bed will we,
Which by us shall blessèd be;
And the issue there create
Ever shall be fortunate.
So shall all the couples three
Ever true in loving be,
And the blots of nature's hand
Shall not in their issue stand.
Never mole, harelip, nor scar,
Nor mark prodigious, such as are
Despisèd in nativity,
Shall upon their children be.
With this field dew consecrate
Every fairy take his gait,
And each several chamber bless
Through this palace with sweet peace;
And the owner of it blessed
Ever shall in safety rest.
Trip away; make no stay.
Meet me all by break of day.
(V.1.391–412)

Oberon's blessing rounds off the play's themes by making the future safe for the characters whose love tangles we have followed through the play. There is some argument as to whether this is the song referred to a few lines earlier. See also *The Two Noble Kinsmen* 1.

67 If we shadows have offended,
Think but this, and all is mended:
That you have but slumbered here

While these visions did appear.
And this weak and idle theme,
No more yielding but a dream.
(V.1.413–18)

Puck's epilogue plays on the idea of fairies as shadows and players as shadows, proposing to escape bad opinions by relegating the play to the insubstantial status of a dream.

68 Give me your hands if we be friends,
And Robin shall restore amends.
(V.1.427–8)

The play ends with Puck's plea for applause, which has been taken literally in recent productions, such as Peter Brook's 1970 revival in which the cast shook hands with the audience as well as asking them to clap. Joining hands is a powerful element in magic and clapping is a way of warding off evil spirits, so both activities demand the audience's active involvement in making the play work.

Much Ado About Nothing

1 A victory is twice itself when the achiever brings home full numbers.
(I.1.8–9)

The comedy opens with the messenger's account to Leonato, Governor of Messina, of the victory without loss of life attained by Don Pedro of Aragon over Don John, his bastard brother. The triumphal return of Don Pedro's retinue to Messina is the dramatic pretext for bringing Claudio (a Florentine) and Benedick (a Paduan) into the household of Leonato. Notions of conflict and betrayal are thus present in the comedy from the first scene.

2 He hath borne himself beyond the promise of his age, doing, in the figure of a lamb, and feats of a lion.
(I.1.13–15)

The messenger's description of Claudio, who has been much honoured by Don Pedro, combines attributes of youth and gentleness with those of courage and ferocity. Claudio is to become the suitor to Leonato's daughter, Hero.

3 He set up his bills here in Messina, and challenged Cupid at

the flight; and my uncle's fool, reading the challenge, subscribed for Cupid, and challenged him at the bird-bolt.
(I.1.36–9)
The tone and content of Beatrice's portrait of Benedick not only establishes the contest of wits between them, but deflates Benedick both as a warrior and as a ladies' man. The gist of Beatrice's caricature is that Benedick has proclaimed himself a great lover by challenging Cupid to a shooting match using flight arrows, but that her uncle's jester has mockingly adopted the role of Cupid and accepted a contest using bird-bolts, blunt arrows used for shooting birds which were also associated with Cupid.

4 BEATRICE I wonder that you will still be talking, Signor Benedick; nobody marks you.
BENEDICK What, my dear Lady Disdain! Are you yet living?
(I.1.108–11)
The first exchange of Beatrice and Benedick is indeed an example of the 'skirmish of wit' promised by Leonato. The sexual antagonism of the war of words becomes the first motif of the comedy. Benedick's riposte to Beatrice as 'Lady Disdain' alludes to the characteristic stance of the Petrarchan mistress.

5 Why i'faith, methinks she's too low for a high praise, too brown for a fair praise, and too little for a great praise; only this commendation I can afford her, that were she other than she is, she were unhandsome; and being no other but as she is, I do not like her.
(I.1.161–5)
Benedick is speaking to Claudio of Hero as a 'professed tyrant to their [women's] sex'. His aim is to amuse and to demonstrate his wit rather than to give a true opinion. The witty expression is not to Claudio's amusement, since the young warrior has fallen in love with Hero on sight; and the comedy arises from the contrasted attitudes to love of the two men.

6 Shall I never see a bachelor of threescore again? Go to, i'faith; an thou wilt needs thrust thy neck into a yoke, wear the print of it, and sigh away Sundays.
(I.1.185–9)
Benedick is uttering the bachelor's lament at hearing his friend Claudio's intention to marry Hero. Marriage is characterized as a state of thraldom for men, symbolized by the yoke borne by oxen or bulls, and promises only a prospect of tedious Sundays, the Elizabethans' day of entertainment. The proverbial image of

the bull bearing the yoke is used later in the scene: 'In time the savage bull doth bear the yoke' (line 241).

7 Because I will not do them the wrong to mistrust any, I will do myself the right to trust none; and the fine is, for the which I may go the finer, I will live a bachelor.
(I.1.224–7)
Benedick's witty justification of the stance he has adopted towards women amounts to a declaration. These are, of course, the words he will be forced to eat in the course of the play's action. The second part of his sentence is based on the pun of 'fine', meaning end or conclusion, being transformed into 'finer', which means richer.

8 I had rather be a canker in a hedge than a rose in his grace, and it better fits my blood to be disdained of all than to fashion a carriage to rob love from any. In this, though I cannot be said to be a flattering honest man, it must not be denied but I am a plain-dealing villain.
(I.3.25–30)
Don John is expressing his inability to conceal his envy and malice in reply to Conrade's advice to bide his time. Don John is depicted as a melancholic and a malcontent, and his reproof of Conrade, that he is not conforming to his birth-star of Saturn, suggests that he himself is saturnine in temperament. Don John's bastardy is not mentioned in the play until IV.1.186, after his last appearance, but it is a feature of his characterization throughout. Here we see the connotations of bastardy in the vigour of nature, the dog-rose ('canker') in the hedge, as opposed to the grace and cultivation of the civilized world.

9 Will it serve for any model to build mischief on?
(I.3.42–3)
Borachio, the drunkard, is bringing Don John the news of Claudio's intended match with Hero and of how Don Pedro plans to forward it by wooing her on Claudio's behalf. Don John's reaction reveals his instinct for malice and his plot provides the spring of the potential tragedy in the Claudio-Hero narrative. The line constitutes a consistent architectural analogy, 'model' indicating a design.

10 LEONATO Well, niece, I hope to see you one day fitted with a husband.
BEATRICE Not till God make men of some other metal than earth. Would it not grieve a woman to be overmastered with a

piece of valiant dust? To make an account of her life to a clod of wayward marl?
(II.1.50–5)
Beatrice's witty response to Leonato is constructed by linking the social reality of woman's subservience to man with the origin of man as recounted in Genesis. She thus demonstrates the illogicality of woman's subordination to 'dust'. In the lines that follow, she also demonstrates that, since all men are sons of Adam and all women daughters of Eve, marriage is a form of incest and therefore unnatural.

11 Speak low, if you speak love.
(II.1.88)
These are Don Pedro's words to Hero. Under the disguise of a masked reveller, Don Pedro is initiating the courtship of Hero on behalf of Claudio.

12 Friendship is constant in all other things
Save in the office and affairs of love.
(II.1.160–1)
Claudio has just been informed by Don John and Borachio that Don Pedro woos Hero for himself. Taking advantage of the masks the men are wearing, they have deliberately mistaken Claudio for Benedick in order to impart their information. Even though the whole play is structured on misapprehensions of the feelings and intentions of oneself and of others, Claudio demonstrates the superficiality of his love for Hero.

13 I would not marry her, though she were endowed with all that Adam had left him before he transgressed.
(II.1.229–31)
Benedick's vow to Don Pedro is characteristically hyperbolic and derogatory to Beatrice. He is claiming that he would reject her, even if her dowry were the whole of Creation over which Adam had dominion before the Fall. The vow invites retribution, and this will be achieved through Don Pedro's conspiracy to match Beatrice and Benedick.

14 I will go on the slightest errand now to the Antipodes that you can devise to send me on. I will fetch you a tooth-picker now from the furthest inch of Asia; bring you the length of Prester John's foot; fetch you a hair off the great Cham's beard; do you any embassage to the Pigmies, rather than hold three words' conference with this harpy.
(II.1.242–8)

In an extreme example of hyperbole, Benedick is indicating impossible tasks that he would sooner perform than speak with Beatrice. The exotic places and peoples referred to are drawn from writers of the fantastic travel literature of the Middle Ages, probably from Marco Polo and Sir John Mandeville. Prester John was believed to be the priest-emperor of a realm of untold wealth in the East. The 'great Cham' refers to the Great Khan or Mongol emperor, also reputed to be fabulously rich.

15 Silence is the perfectest herald of joy; I were but little happy, if I could say how much.
(II.1.282–3)
These words are Claudio's, on hearing that Don Pedro has won Hero's consent to marriage on his behalf. Their cold formality is typical of Claudio's utterance and it conceals the suspicion about Don Pedro's motivation, implanted in him by Don John.

16 I was born to speak all mirth and no matter.
(II.1.304–5)
Beatrice's deprecation of her own wit is uttered as an apology to Don Pedro, whom she has light-heartedly rejected as a suitor because he would be 'too costly to wear every day'.

17 I do much wonder that one man, seeing how much another man is a fool when he dedicates his behaviours to love, will, after he hath laughed at such shallow follies in others, become the argument of his own scorn by falling in love; and such a man is Claudio. I have known when there was no music with him but the drum and the fife, and now had he rather hear the tabor and the pipe.
(II.3.8–15)
Benedick is musing about the transformation of Claudio from a soldier to a lover and from a sceptic of love to an enthusiast. The drum and the fife represent martial music, the tabor and the pipe amatory strains. The pattern he describes will, ironically, also match his own progress in the play.

18 One woman is fair, yet I am well; another is wise; yet I am well; another virtuous, yet I am well; but till all graces be in one woman, one woman shall not come in my grace. Rich she shall be, that's certain; wise, or I'll none; virtuous, or I'll never cheapen her; fair, or I'll never look on her; mild, or come not near me; noble, or not I for an angel; of good discourse, an excellent musician, and her hair shall be of what colour it please God.
(II.3.25–31)

The passage is a notable example of Benedick's assumed misogyny. His terse and pithy inventory of woman's graces and his response to them is interrupted by the approach of Don Pedro, Leonato, Claudio, and musicians, who will put into practice their plan of allowing Benedick to overhear their account of Beatrice's desperate love for him. Their account is a fiction aimed to induce love of Beatrice in Benedick.

19 Sigh no more, ladies, sigh no more,
  Men were deceivers ever,
One foot in sea and one on shore,
  To one thing constant never:
Then sigh not so, but let them go,
  And by you blithe and bonny,
Converting all your sounds of woe
  Into Hey nonny, nonny.
(II.3.60–7)
The first verse of Balthasar's song expresses the theme of deception in love which lies at the heart of the narrative and thematic structure of *Much Ado About Nothing*. In context, it is doubly ironic. The hidden Benedick sees it as part of Claudio's indulgence of romantic love, while the conspirators are employing the emotional appeal of its theme and music as a preface to their tale of Beatrice's unrequited love for him.

20 Sits the wind in that corner?
(II.3.99–100)
Benedick employs this proverbial saying when he is incredulous at hearing of Beatrice's supposed love for him. Her 'love' is a fiction of Don Pedro, Claudio, and Leonato, who have conspired that Benedick should overhear their conversation in order to induce love of Beatrice in him.

21 I will be horribly in love with her. I may chance have some odd quirks and remnants of wit broken on me, because I have railed so long against marriage; but doth not the appetite alter? A man loves the meat in his youth that he cannot endure in his age. Shall quips and sentences and these paper bullets of the brain awe a man from the career of his humour? No, the world must be peopled. When I said I would die a bachelor, I did not think I should live till I were married.
(II.3.228–36)
Benedick, following his deception, shows himself as enthusiastic in courtship as before he had been in railing at women. The comedy of the passage lies in its combination of enthusiasm with rationalization, culminating in Benedick's embrace of the divine injunction

to procreate. The speech is a cue for the entry of Beatrice, whom Benedick now sees and treats in a reverential manner, so creating another source of comedy.

22 The pleasant'st angling is to see the fish
Cut with her golden oars the silver stream,
And greedily devour the treacherous bait.
(III.1.26–8)
This image is employed by Ursula, an attendant of Hero, to describe the gulling of Beatrice which they are about to perpetrate, and which will parallel that of Benedick in the preceding scene. They are to persuade Beatrice that Benedick is in love with her.

23 Some Cupid kills with arrows, some with traps.
(III.1.106)
The two ways of falling in love that Hero suggests here form the plot of *Much Ado About Nothing*: direct physical attraction, as in the case of Claudio and Hero, and being brought together through intrigues, as with Benedick and Beatrice.

24 What fire is in mine ears? Can this be true?
  Stand I condemned for pride and scorn so much?
Contempt, farewell! and maiden pride, adieu!
  No glory lives behind the back of such.
(III.1.107–10)
Beatrice's response to her gulling has an emotional intensity that contrasts with Benedick's comic enthusiasm. She speaks verse for the first time in the play. Indeed, her entire gulling scene has been conducted in verse while Benedick's was in prose. Her first utterance condenses the fire of love in her heart with her acute perception of the news of Benedick's attraction. The pride and scorn she abandons are the qualities for which Hero and Ursula have criticized her in the act of gulling.

25 Well, everyone can master a grief but he that has it.
(III.2.26–7)
Benedick is responding to the mockery of his companions. At this point, he has not told them that he is in love, but that he has toothache. Toothache and love were curiously associated in Elizabethan literature, presumably as both being sources of pain and torment.

26 If he be not in love with some woman, there is no believing

old signs. 'A brushes his hat o'mornings; what should that bode?
(III.2.37–9)
Claudio is here mocking Benedick, a noted opponent of love, by drawing attention to the 'old signs' of the male lover: attention to dress, recourse to the barber, the use of perfumes.

27 To be a well-favoured man is the gift of fortune; but to write and read comes by nature.
(III.3.14–16)
The opposition of the gifts of Fortune to those of Nature was a commonplace of Elizabethan debate. See, for example, the discussion of Rosalind and Celia in *As You Like It* I.3., where Rosalind states that 'Fortune reigns in the gifts of the world, not in the lineaments of Nature'. Dogberry, the dim-witted Constable of the Watch, typically confuses the gifts of Fortune and Nature in speaking to the watchman.

28 You are thought here to be the most senseless and fit man for the constable of the watch; therefore bear you the lantern. This is your charge: you shall comprehend all vagrom men.
(III.3.21–5)
Dogberry's instructions to the watchmen contain two of his many malapropisms: 'senseless' for sensible and 'comprehend' for apprehend. 'Vagrom' means vagrant. The Elizabethan authorities were much concerned with the problems of vagrancy. The passage also clearly illustrates that satire of the forces of law and order, and of the slow-witted country 'bobby' in particular, has a long stage history.

29 The most peaceable way for you, if you do take a thief, is to let him show himself what he is and steal out of your company.
(III.3.56–8)
The logic of Dogberry's advice to the Watch not only reveals his idiocy, but also contains an unwitting satiric observation on the efficiency and practice of the law.

30 VERGES Yes, I thank God I am as honest as any man living that is an old man and no honester than I.
DOGBERRY Comparisons are odorous; *palabras*, neighbour Verges.
(III.5.13–16)
This passage is a good example of the comic dialogue of Dogberry, the Constable of the Watch, and his second-in-command, Verges. Shakespeare uses the stock comic techniques of misunderstandings, lack of logic in speech, and malapropisms to expose

their bumbling incompetence. The Spanish tag *palabras* (*pocas palabras* = few words), taken from the vogue for such tags on the contemporary stage, is particularly appropriate to the situation. Despite the men's garrulity, the scene has an underlying tension, because the Watch has unwittingly apprehended the perpetrators of the plot against Hero and Claudio.

31 A good old man, sir, he will be talking; as they say, 'When the age is in, the wit is out.'
(III.5.32–3)
The observation of Dogberry, the Constable, on Verges is ironical for two reasons: he himself is the more garrulous, and Verges is actually close to conveying relevant information to Leonato concerning the arrest of Borachio and Conrade, who have been involved in Don John's plot against Claudio and Leonato's daughter, Hero. The statement is based on the traditional association of senility and garrulity.

32 God's a good man.
(III.5.35)
This is the clearest example of Dogberry's speech being full of truisms, proverbs, and commonplaces.

33 O, what men dare do! What men may do!
What men daily do, not knowing what they do!
(IV.1.17–18)
Claudio's sarcastic response is made to Leonato, who has 'dared' state that there is no impediment on Claudio's part to marriage with Hero. In the section of the scene that follows, Claudio renounces Hero at the altar, believing – through the machinations of Don John – that she is Borachio's lover. Claudio's language is marked by rhetoric and lack of direct speech.

34 But fare thee well, most foul, most fair! Farewell,
Thou pure impiety and impious purity!
For thee I'll lock up all the gates of love,
And on my eyelids shall conjecture hang,
To turn all beauty into thoughts of harm,
And never shall it more be gracious.
(IV.1.101–6)
Claudio's denunciation and renunciation of Hero at the altar is both bitter and mannered. Wordplay is not necessarily inimical to the presentation of deep feeling, but there remains a suggestion of self-indulgent expression. 'Conjecture' is suspicion, which will henceforth transform all his apprehension of women's beauty

into a warning of their infidelity. Claudio has been tricked into believing Hero false by the plot of Don John.

35 O that I were a man for his sake, or that I had any friend would be a man for my sake! But manhood is melted into curtsies, valour into compliment, and men are only turned into tongue, and trim ones too. He is now as valiant as Hercules that only tells a lie and swears it. I cannot be a man with wishing, therefore I will die a woman with grieving.
(IV.1.312–18)
Beatrice's desire to avenge the honour of her cousin, Hero, following the latter's denunciation for unchastity by Claudio, makes her realize acutely the limitations imposed upon her sex by the conventions of her society. Her willingness to depend upon Benedick at this point and his decision to challenge Claudio cements their love, for the first time openly acknowledged earlier in this scene.

36 Flat burglary as ever was committed.
(IV.2.48)
This comment is the indignant response of Dogberry, the Constable, to learning that Borachio had been bribed by Don John to defame Hero. Needless to say, Dogberry applies a mistaken term for the crime.

37 O villain! Thou wilt be condemned into everlasting redemption for this.
(IV.2.54–5)
This illustration of Dogberry's moral indignation at Borachio's villainy is one of his most delightful malapropisms.

38 I am a wise fellow, and, which is more, an officer; and, which is more, a householder; and, which is more, as pretty a piece of flesh as any is in Messina.
(IV.2.77–80)
Dogberry's assertion of his merit and self-esteem is made in response to Conrade's calling him an ass. The pride in his humble achievements and attainments has an element of pathos; but it remains true that it was the common-sense Sexton who pursued the investigation successfully. Dogberry and Verges merely cause comic confusion.

39 Patch grief with proverbs.
(V.1.17)
The phrase is taken from Leonato's rejection of the consolation offered by his brother, Antonio, following the dishonour and sup-

posed death of Hero. Leonato is arguing that, only if a father with similar griefs were to offer consoling moral tags and proverbial sayings, would he not find them mere platitudes. His view is elaborated in the lines that shortly follow: 'there was never yet philosopher / That could endure the toothache patiently'.

40 In a false quarrel there is no true valour.
(V.1.119)
The line is Benedick's, in response to Claudio and Don Pedro, who have just given a flippant account of how the elderly Leonato and Antonio had nearly engaged them in fight as a result of Hero's dishonour and supposed death. Benedick has himself come to challenge Claudio at Beatrice's behest and is therefore sensitive to the cause of true valour.

41 No, I was not born under a rhyming planet, nor I cannot woo in festival terms.
(V.2.39–40)
Benedick is one of several blunt but honest lovers in Shakespeare's plays. Although awaiting the arrival of Beatrice, he decides to dismiss the poeticizing of the Elizabethan courtly lover.

Othello

1 A fellow almost damned in a fair wife –
That never set a squadron in the field,
Nor the division of a battle knows
More than a spinster.
(I.1.21–4)
Iago is complaining to Roderigo that he has been passed over as Othello's lieutenant in favour of Michael Cassio, whom he is describing in pejorative terms. His complaint is that Cassio's knowledge of war is only theoretical, while he himself has proved his worth to Othello in the field. The first line quoted poses a problem, since Cassio is not married in Shakespeare's play, though he was in the source, Cinthio's novella, which Shakespeare may have intended to follow more closely. It may just be a sneer at Cassio's sexual prowess.

2 'Tis the curse of service:
Preferment goes by letter and affection,
And not by old gradation, where each second

Stood heir to th'first.
(I.1.35–8)

Iago is expounding to Roderigo his cynical observation of the world that promotion is achieved through letters of recommendation and by the inclinations of those in authority and not through seniority. He bears a grudge for being passed over for the position of Othello's lieutenant, which has gone to Michael Cassio.

3 You shall mark
Many a duteous and knee-crooking knave
That, doting on his own obsequious bondage,
Wears out his time, much like his master's ass,
For naught but provender, and when he's old – cashiered!
(I.1.44–8)

Iago has just observed that, despite his resentment at not having been promoted to Othello's lieutenant, he will continue to serve him in order to get even with him. The irony of the passage indicates clearly that Iago has no intention of offering a lifetime of loyalty to be rewarded with bare sustenance and ultimate dismissal.

4 In following him, I follow but myself.
(I.1.59)

This line is the culmination of Iago's exposition to Roderigo of how he will use his service of Othello as a tool for his revenge at having been passed over for the lieutenancy. It offers verbal evidence for those critics who see Iago as an *alter ego* of Othello.

5 For when my outward action doth demonstrate
The native act and figure of my heart
In compliment extern, 'tis not long after,
But I will wear my heart upon my sleeve
For daws to peck at – I am not what I am.
(I.1.62–6)

Iago is explaining to Roderigo how he will conceal his intentions from the world, for to expose them would be as good as to wear his heart on his sleeve for birds to peck at. 'Figure' means intention or purpose, while 'compliment extern' is outward show. This attitude and the overt statement in the last phrase are typical of the stage Machiavel. If the final phrase is also an inversion of *Exodus* 3:14, God's statement 'I am that I am', Iago's diabolic nature is even more evident.

6 You'll have your daughter covered with a Barbary horse;

you'll have your nephews neigh to you, you'll have coursers for cousins, and jennets for germans.
(I.1.111–14)
Iago and Roderigo have woken Brabantio at night with the news that his daughter, Desdemona, has eloped with Othello. Iago goads Brabantio to rage by speaking of Othello's marriage to Desdemona as robbery and by dwelling on the sexual act in terms of animal imagery. The Barbary coast was a term for North Africa, then famous for horse breeding, and so a 'Barbary horse' stands for Othello, the Moor. 'Nephews' means grandchildren, because in Latin *nepotes* covers both relationships. 'Coursers' and 'jennets' are types of horse, while 'germans' are blood-relations.

7 Your daughter and the Moor are now making the beast with two backs.
(I.1.116–18)
Iago uses animal imagery to debase the sexual relationship of Othello and Desdemona. It is specifically designed to enrage Brabantio, Desdemona's father, who has just been informed of the elopement. Iago's images also suggest his and his society's racial prejudice, especially in the sphere of sexual relationships.

8 Though I do hate him as I do hell pains,
Yet for necessity of present life
I must show out a flag and sign of love,
Which is indeed but sign.
(I.1.155–8)
This is an explicit statement of Iago's plan to mask his hatred of Othello and desire for revenge with a show of love. The simile of the first line quoted is equivocal in its effect: it appears to equate Othello with diabolic imagery, but actually Othello constitutes Iago's hell, suggesting Iago is the damned one.

9 Though in the trade of war I have slain men,
Yet do I hold it very stuff o'th'conscience
To do no contrived murder: I lack iniquity
Sometimes to do me service.
(I.2.1–4)
Although the distinction between killing in war and premeditated murder is a valid one, the moral stance that Iago is adopting, as Othello's loyal and scrupulous follower, is a pose. It becomes apparent, for example, that he has attributed his own abuse of Othello, which the audience has heard in the previous scene, to Roderigo. The mask of villainy, including the explicit denial of his

own vicious nature, is in keeping with the conduct promised in the first scene and with the conventions of the stage Machiavel.

10 My parts, my title, and my perfect soul
Shall manifest me rightly.
(I.2.31–2)
Othello's sense of his own righteousness hovers on the borderline between nobility and vainglory. Iago has just suggested that Othello avoids meeting Brabantio (presumably, in order to create possibilities of further enmity between them and to cast on Othello the appearance of guilt). 'Parts' are natural abilities, and 'perfect soul' suggests a conscience ever ready to render its final account.

11 Keep up your bright swords, for the dew will rust them.
(I.2.59)
Critics have offered differing interpretations of this much-quoted line: some have suggested that it illustrates Othello's tendency to self-dramatization, others that it reflects his dignity and authority. Othello is intervening between Iago and Roderigo after the latter has arrived with Brabantio to accuse Othello of the 'theft' of Desdemona.

12 Damned as thou art, thou hast enchanted her:
For I'll refer me to all things of sense,
If she in chains of magic were not bound,
Whether a maid, so tender, fair, and happy,
So opposite to marriage that she shunned
The wealthy curlèd darlings of our nation,
Would ever have – t'incur a general mock –
Run from her guardage to the sooty bosom
Of such a thing as thou: to fear, not to delight.
(I.2.63–71)
Brabantio, in accusing Othello of having seduced Desdemona away from him and all natural feeling, associates Othello's power over her with witchcraft and damnation. He projects the irrational prejudice of his society towards the Moor, which Desdemona's love has rejected. 'Guardage' is guardianship.

13 For my particular grief
Is of so flood-gate and o'erbearing nature
That it engluts and swallows other sorrows
And yet is still itself.
(I.3.55–8)
Brabantio is excusing himself to the Duke of Venice for having neglected the business of state. Brabantio is overwhelmed by the

news of Desdemona's marriage to Othello and, together with the Moor, has come before the Senate to plead his case. The Duke and Senate, however, are preoccupied with the news of a Turkish expedition against the Venetian territory of Cyprus. Brabantio's image of a 'flood-gate' suggests the uncontrollable force of emotion and its expression in tears.

14 Rude am I in my speech
And little blessed with the soft phrase of peace;
For since these arms of mine had seven years' pith
Till now some nine moons wasted, they have used
Their dearest action in the tented field;...
I will a round unvarnished tale deliver
Of my whole course of love: what drugs, what charms,
What conjuration and what mighty magic –
For such proceedings I am charged withal –
I won his daughter.
(I.3.81–5, 90–4)

Despite Othello's protestations to the contrary, he is endowed with powerful rhetoric and his account of his courtship of Desdemona conveys the fascination his tales could have held for her. At the same time, his speech identifies Othello with the violence of warfare, its uncomplicated values, and the company of men.

15 A maiden never bold;
ushed at herself.
of Brabantio pose problems of lineation and punctuaBlushed at herself.
(I.3.94–6)

These lines of Brabantio pose problems of lineation and punctuation, as well as meaning, though the arrangement given above is now generally accepted. 'Motion' is normally taken to mean natural impulse and 'herself' to refer back to this, since the word can also signify 'itself'. Nonetheless, the sense of the passage, especially in a dramatic context, would appear to derive from its general drift rather than analysis of its component parts.

16 Her father loved me, oft invited me,
Still questioned me the story of my life
From year to year – in battles, sieges, fortunes
That I have passed.
I ran it through, even from my boyish days
To th'very moment that he bade me tell it:
Wherein I spake of most disastrous chances,
Of moving accidents by flood and field,

Of hair-breadth scapes i'th'imminent deadly breach,
Of being taken by the insolent foe,
And sold to slavery; of my redemption thence,
And portance in my travels' history:
Wherein of antres vast and deserts idle,
Rough quarries, rocks, and hills whose heads touch heaven,
It was my hint to speak – such was the process:
And of the Cannibals that each other eat,
The Anthropophagi, and men whose heads
Do grow beneath their shoulders.
(I.3.127–44)

Othello offers the Duke of Venice an account of how he won Desdemona's love, while Iago has been dispatched to bring Desdemona before the Senate. Othello gives an account, first, of his life of battle and adventure and, second, of the strange places and people he has encountered. The details of the latter probably derive ultimately from Pliny's *Natural History*, as transmitted through medieval and Elizabethan travel narratives. 'Portance' means behaviour, 'antres' caves, and 'idle' infertile and uninhabited.

17 My story being done,
She gave me for my pains a world of sighs:
She swore, in faith 'twas strange, 'twas passing strange,
'Twas pitiful, 'twas wondrous pitiful;
She wished she had not heard it, yet she wished
That heaven had made her such a man. She thanked me,
And bade me, if I had a friend that loved her,
I should but teach him how to tell my story,
And that would woo her. Upon this hint I spake:
She loved me for the dangers I had passed,
And I loved her, that she did pity them.
This only is the witchcraft I have used.
(I.3.157–68)

The final section of Othello's account to the Senate of Venice of his courtship describes Desdemona's response to his tales and refutes the accusation of witchcraft made by Brabantio, Desdemona's father. Desdemona enters immediately after this speech.

18 I do perceive here a divided duty.
(I.3.179)

Desdemona, before the Senate of Venice, acknowledges her conflicting loyalties, to father and to husband. In following the pattern of her mother in preferring husband to father, she earns

Brabantio's rejection and provides him with an opportunity to warn Othello of her propensity for deception.

19 The robbed that smiles steals something from the thief;
He robs himself that spends a bootless grief.
(I.3.206–7)
The Duke of Venice unavailingly seeks to reconcile Brabantio to Desdemona's marriage by counselling him, somewhat sententiously, to make the best of a bad job. 'Bootless' here means pointless. Brabantio replies somewhat tartly that, if the Duke's counsel is valid, the loss of Cyprus to the Turks could be accepted with a smile.

20 The tyrant, custom, most grave Senators,
Hath made the flinty and steel couch of war
My thrice-driven bed of down.
(I.3.227–9)
Othello, in accepting the Senate's commission against the Turks' Cyprus expedition, acknowledges that 'custom' (force of circumstance) has transformed the soft bed of marriage into the 'couch of war'. The notion of 'custom' as a tyrant was proverbial.

21 That I did love the Moor to live with him,
My downright violence and storm of fortunes
May trumpet to the world. My heart's subdued
Even to the very quality of my lord.
I saw Othello's visage in his mind
And to his honours and his valiant parts
Did I my soul and fortunes consecrate.
(I.3.245–51)
Desdemona is pleading with the Duke of Venice the right to accompany her husband on the Cyprus expedition. The passage is significant in showing Desdemona's appreciation of Othello's inner virtues and her embrace of his destiny.

22 Look to her, Moor, if thou hast eyes to see.
She has deceived her father, and may thee.
(I.3.289–90)
Brabantio's parting-shot to Othello perhaps sows the first seed of doubt of Desdemona's fidelity in Othello's mind. It would appear to be provoked merely by fatherly jealousy and bitterness, since he is distraught at Desdemona's precipitate marriage and the prospect of her loss.

23 Virtue? A fig! 'Tis in ourselves that we are thus, or thus. Our

bodies are our gardens, to the which our wills are gardeners.
(I.3.316–18)
Iago is counselling the foolish Roderigo against despair and suicide in the cause of love. Iago has previously accepted money from Roderigo to forward a marriage with Desdemona and, now that is no longer possible, holds open the possibility of her seduction in order to continue fleecing him. Like other Shakespearian Machiavels, Iago is convinced that each man is the determiner of his own destiny. The concept of the body as a garden appears to derive from that nexus of classical and biblical sources which the Middle Ages and Renaissance elaborated as an analogy for order/disorder in the individual (and the state). 'Will' condenses in one term the three notions of volition, theological free-will, and sexual desire.

24 These Moors are changeable in their wills – fill thy purse with money. The food that to him now is as luscious as locusts shall be to him shortly as acerbe as the coloquintida. She must change for youth: when she is sated with his body she will find the error of her choice. Therefore put money in thy purse. If thou wilt needs damn thyself, do it a more delicate way than drowning. Make all the money thou canst. If sanctimony and a frail vow betwixt an erring barbarian and a super-subtle Venetian be not too hard for my wits and all the tribe of hell, thou shalt enjoy her – therefore make money. A pox of drowning thyself!
(I.3.342–53)
Iago's deception of Roderigo into following the wars in the vain hope of seducing Desdemona permits him to express his hatred of Othello and his contempt of human sexuality. The passage is skilfully wrought on the opposition of attraction and repulsion, and it interweaves the ideas of money, sex, and destruction (by drowning and as a consequence of the plan Iago is concocting). The perplexing 'locusts' are now normally taken to refer to the cobs of the carob tree, while 'coloquintida' or colocynth is a type of bitter apple used for purgative drugs. 'Acerbe' means bitter. 'Super-subtle' suggests excessively sophisticated, in opposition to 'barbarian'.

25 There are many events in the womb of time, which will be delivered.
(I.3.364–5)
Iago is confiding to Roderigo the hatching of his plot against Othello; but the notion of Time the Revealer was a Renaissance commonplace.

26 Cassio's a proper man: let me see now;
To get his place and to plume up my will
In double knavery. How? How? Let's see.
After some time, to abuse Othello's ear
That he is too familiar with his wife;
He hath a person and a smooth dispose
To be suspected, framed to make women false.
The Moor is of a free and open nature,
That thinks men honest that but seem to be so,
And will as tenderly be led by th'nose
As asses are.
I have't. It is engendered. Hell and night
Must bring this monstrous birth to the world's light.
(I.3.386–98)
Iago is engaged in a plotting soliloquy, a convention of the Elizabethan stage associated with the Machiavel. This section of the soliloquy hints to the audience the bald outline of the plot; it contrasts the appearance and temperament of Cassio and Othello; it illustrates Iago's cynical manipulation of men; and, finally, it advances the play's thematic contrast of light and dark, with all their connotations of virtue and diabolism. 'Proper' means good-looking.

27 Tempests themselves, high seas, and howling winds,
The guttered rocks and congregated sands,
Traitors enscarped to clog the guiltless keel,
As having sense of beauty, do omit
Their mortal natures, letting go safely by
The divine Desdemona.
(II.1.68–73)
Cassio is describing Desdemona's safe passage to Cyprus through the storm which has scattered the Turkish fleet. While Desdemona's beauty appears to protect her from this mortal danger and accord her a divine status, it will not prove potent against Iago's malevolence. Cassio's courtliness, here evident in his diction, will provide a basis of suspicion for Iago to exploit. The Folio reads 'ensteeped' for 'enscarped' and 'common' for 'mortal', which means deadly.

28 You are pictures out of doors, bells in your parlours, wild-cats in your kitchens, saints in your injuries, devils being offended, players in your housewifery, and housewives in your beds.
(II.1.108–11)
Iago's misogynistic description of women is prompted by Cassio's greeting his wife, Emilia, with a kiss. The picture is essentially one

of feminine hypocrisy and mock-modesty. Silence out of doors ('pictures') is contrasted with turmoil within ('bells'). Women are idlers ('players') at work and hussies ('housewives') in bed.

29 I am nothing if not critical.
(II.1.118)
Iago's assessment of himself is made to distract Desdemona for insisting that he give his opinion of her. Iago has been defaming women.

30 With as little a web as this will I ensnare as great a fly as Cassio.
(II.1.165–6)
Iago is observing the courtliness of Cassio towards Desdemona, whom Cassio has just taken by the hand. His poisoned imagination perceives the potential for deadly mischief. His manipulative plotting will constitute the web in which his victims will become helplessly ensnared. The image of the web is repeated in the play.

31 OTHELLO If it were now to die,
'Twere now to be most happy; for I fear
My soul hath her content so absolute
That not another comfort like to this
Succeeds in unknown fate.
DESDEMONA The heavens forbid
But that our loves and comforts should increase,
Even as our days do grow.
(II.1.183–9)
This exchange takes place between Othello and Desdemona on their being reunited in Cyprus after their separation at sea and the dangers of the sea-storm. In view of their subsequent fates, the passage is pregnant with dramatic irony.

32 IAGO
A slipper and subtle knave, a finder out of occasions; that has an eye can stamp and counterfeit advantages, though true advantage never present itself; a devilish knave! Besides, the knave is handsome, young, and hath all those requisites in him that folly and green minds look after. A pestilent complete knave; and the woman hath found him already.
RODERIGO I cannot believe that in her: she's full of most blessed condition.
IAGO Blessed fig's end! The wine she drinks is made of grapes.
(II.1.235–45)

Iago's plot is to persuade Roderigo that Desdemona is on the verge of an affair with Cassio. After abusing Desdemona for excessive sexual appetite, Iago denounces to Roderigo the supposed cunning of Cassio. Roderigo's response projects the respect generally held for Desdemona's virtue, but again Iago contemptuously dismisses the notion, returning to an image of appetite.

33 Make the Moor thank me, love me, and reward me
For making him egregiously an ass,
And practising upon his peace and quiet,
Even to madness. 'Tis here, but yet confused:
Knavery's plain face is never seen till used.
(II.1.299–303)

Iago is an arch-opportunist in adapting his plan for revenge to the occasions presented him. His account of his motivation is also changeable. In this second plotting soliloquy, Iago advances the motivation of sexual jealousy (his suspicions that Othello and Cassio have 'leaped' into his 'seat'), rather than missed promotion. Editors and critics have not always given much credence to the motivation Iago attributes to himself, Coleridge speaking of his 'motiveless malignity'. Certainly, Iago betrays the conventional attitudes of the Machiavellian malcontent, including the instinct for concealment revealed in the last line.

34 I have very poor and unhappy brains for drinking. I could well wish courtesy would invent some other custom of entertainment.
(II.3.30–2)

Cassio's reply to Iago's invitation to drink is confirmed by his later drunkenness. Iago is exploiting Othello's injunction to celebrate his marriage and the destruction of the Turkish fleet with a view to advancing his plot against Cassio and Othello.

35 CASSIO Is your Englishman so expert in his drinking?
IAGO Why, he drinks you with facility your Dane dead drunk; he sweats not to overthrow your Almaine; he gives your Hollander a vomit, ere the next pottle can be filled.
(II.3.75–9)

This exchange between Cassio and Iago takes place at the revel held in Cyprus to celebrate Othello's marriage and the destruction of the Turkish fleet. It would seem to appeal to a curious kind of chauvinism on the part of Shakespeare's audience. An 'Almaine' is a German.

36 Thy honesty and love doth mince this matter.
(II.3.241)

Othello's line to Iago is rich in irony, since he believes Iago is protecting Cassio from blame for Montano's wound. Iago has, in fact, stage-managed a brawl between Cassio and Roderigo, of which Montano has become the innocent victim. Cassio is drunk as a result of Iago's insistence that he drink against his own inclination and better judgement. 'Honesty' is a term repeatedly (and ironically) applied to Iago throughout the play. 'Honest' in Elizabethan English had a wider range of reference than the modern word, being closer to honourable.

37 Reputation, reputation, reputation! O, I have lost my reputation! I have lost the immortal part of myself, and what remains is bestial. My reputation, Iago, my reputation!
(II.3.255–8)
Even in his remorse for his drunken action of wounding Montano, Cassio does not suspect the machinations of Iago, to whom this speech is addressed. In identifying reputation as immortal, Cassio is relating it to fame, which lives after men.

38 Drunk! And speak parrot! And squabble! Swagger! Swear! And discourse fustian with one's own shadow! O, thou invisible spirit of wine, if thou hast no name to be known by, let us call thee devil.
(II.3.272–5)
Cassio is remorseful that his drunken action of wounding Montano has lost him the good opinion of Othello, and is denouncing alcohol. Iago, the person addressed, is seeking to persuade him that Othello's respect can be re-won, since the next part of his plot is to get Cassio to obtain Desdemona's services in this suit. To 'speak parrot' is to speak nonsense.

39 O God, that men should put an enemy in their mouths to steal away their brains! That we should with joy, pleasance, revel and applause transform ourselves into beasts!
(II.3.281–4)
Cassio's remorseful diatribe against alcohol follows his having wounded Montano in a drunken brawl that Iago has engineered. Loss of human reason was associated with bestiality in Renaissance thought.

40 Come, come; good wine is a good familiar creature if it be well used: exclaim no more against it.
(II.3.300–1)
Iago, having allowed Cassio's remorse to run its course, is about to further his plot by advising Cassio to enlist Desdemona's sup-

port in re-winning Othello's confidence. 'Familiar' may have the sense of attendant spirit, in addition to friendly. The line is ironic in that Iago may be alluding to the good service wine has done him in furthering his plot. Iago persuaded Cassio to drink heavily against his better judgement.

41 So will I turn her virtue into pitch,
And out of her own goodness make the net
That shall enmesh them all.
(II.3.350–2)

The tragic plot of *Othello* turns upon the ability of Iago's malice to transform good into apparent evil. In this third plotting soliloquy, he has just unfolded to the audience that he will get Desdemona to plead for Cassio, at the same time as poisoning Othello's mind with the notion that Cassio is Desdemona's lover. Once again the image of a 'net' or web is used to describe the plot.

42 How poor are they that have not patience!
What wound did ever heal but by degrees?
(II.3.359–60)

These sententious lines are ironical on the lips of Iago, since he is manipulating Roderigo, who has become exasperated at having spent his money, having been beaten by Cassio, and having made none of the promised progress with Desdemona. Roderigo is easily satisfied by excuses and Iago continues to exercise his own patience in plotting.

43 O thereby hangs a tail.
(III.1.8)

The Clown is mocking musicians of wind instruments. Apart from the pun on tail/tale, the Clown is indulging in a bawdy quibble on 'tail'. It was an Elizabethan custom for a newly married couple to be awoken with music, and this is being prepared for Othello and Desdemona.

44 I never knew a Florentine more kind and honest.
(III.1.39)

Cassio's observation on Iago is full of dramatic irony. Iago is ostensibly helping Cassio to enlist Desdemona's aid for his re-instatement through the services of his wife, Emilia. His real plan is to incite Othello with murderous jealousy of Cassio.

45 My lord shall never rest.
I'll watch him tame and talk him out of patience;
His bed shall seem a school, his board a shrift;

I'll intermingle everything he does
With Cassio's suit.
(III.3.22–6)

Desdemona's frank promise to Cassio that she will urge his re-instatement with Othello is shot through with the irony that this conduct is bound to enrage her husband as a consequence of Iago's incitement to jealousy. 'Watch him tame' is a term from the training of hawks, which were tamed by being denied sleep. 'His board a shrift' means that Othello's table will become a confessional.

46 Why, this is not a boon:
'Tis as I should entreat you wear your gloves
Or feed on nourishing dishes, or keep you warm,
Or sue to you to do a peculiar profit
To your own person. Nay, when I have a suit
Wherein I mean to touch your love indeed
It shall be full of poise and difficult weight,
And fearful to be granted.
(III.3.76–83)

Desdemona is arguing with Othello that the re-instatement of Cassio is not a favour to her so much as an act for Othello's own good. To strengthen her case, she questions rhetorically what the response would be if she had a request of some importance to her.

47 Excellent wretch! Perdition catch my soul
But I do love thee! And when I love thee not,
Chaos is come again.
(III.3.90–2)

Othello is speaking of his love for Desdemona. 'Wretch' was a common term of affection. The passage opposes the bliss of Othello's love for Desdemona with the state of damnation and anarchy that its negation portends. The lines prove prophetic as Othello is transformed by Iago's malice from Christian nobility to a diabolic fiend. In the course of this scene, Othello moves from tender love to murderous intent.

48 By heaven, he echoes me,
As if there were some monster in his thought
Too hideous to be shown.
(III.3.105–7)

Othello's rhetorical utterance refers to Iago, who has deliberately repeated Othello's words about Cassio – especially the term 'honest' meaning chaste/virtuous – as a means of arousing suspicion in Othello's mind. In fact, the 'monster' – later identified with jealousy – comes to be created in Othello's mind, though its original genesis could be said to take place within Iago.

49 Who has a breast so pure,
But some uncleanly apprehensions
Keep leets and law-days, and in session sit
With meditations lawful?
(III.3.137–40)

Iago is responding to Othello's request that he reveal his inner thoughts about Cassio in such a way that he places doubts in Othello's mind without making any specific accusation. 'Apprehensions' are acts of mental perception, while 'leets' were local courts of justice.

50 Good name in man and woman, dear my lord,
Is the immediate jewel of their souls.
Who steals my purse, steals trash; 'tis something, nothing;
'Twas mine, 'tis his, and has been slave to thousands:
But he that filches from me my good name
Robs me of that which not enriches him
And makes me poor indeed.
(III.3.154–60)

Iago is uttering the proverbial notions of reputation and good name. His prevarication increases Othello's desire to be told plainly Iago's opinion of Cassio, while ironically it heightens the audience's awareness of the damnable act Iago is about to commit. Iago is to defame both Cassio and Desdemona as lovers.

51 O, beware, my lord, of jealousy!
It is the green-eyed monster, which doth mock
The meat it feeds on.
(III.3.163–5)

Ironically, Iago warns Othello of the state of mind into which he is leading him. The colour green is associated with jealousy, while the monster is seen as consuming (perhaps from within) the victim it taunts.

52 I would not have your free and noble nature,
Out of self-bounty, be abused. Look to't.
I know our country disposition well:
In Venice they do let God see the pranks
They dare not show their husbands; their best conscience
Is not to leave't undone, but keep't unknown.
(III.3.197–202)

Iago, in preparation for convincing Othello of Desdemona's adultery, plays upon his comparative unfamiliarity with Venetian society and his social insecurity as a Moor (negro). He encourages Othello to see himself as the innocent victim of Desdemona's vice as a consequence of his 'noble nature'. 'Self-bounty' is natural generosity.

53 I humbly do beseech you of your pardon
For too much loving you.
(III.3.210–11)
Iago is ironically excusing himself for speaking too frankly of Desdemona to Othello. He has been arousing Othello's suspicions that Desdemona is an adulteress and Cassio her lover.

54 If I do prove her haggard,
Though that her jesses were my dear heart-strings,
I'd whistle her off, and let her down the wind
To prey at fortune. Haply, for I am black
And have not those soft parts of conversation
That chamberers have; or for I am declined
Into the vale of years – yet that's not much –
She's gone: I am abused, and my relief
Must be to loathe her. O, curse of marriage!
That we can call these delicate creatures ours
And not their appetites! I had rather be a toad
And live upon the vapour of a dungeon
Than keep a corner in the thing I love
For others' uses.
(III.3.257–70)
Othello's soliloquy, after Iago has implanted the suspicions of Desdemona's adultery, reveals the possessive nature of his love as well as the confusion of his mind. The first image is taken from hawking: 'haggard' means untrained, and 'jesses' were the short straps by which the hawk was fastened to the leash. The second sentence portrays Othello's social and racial insecurity, his envy of 'chamberers' or smooth gallants. Toads were considered loathsome and contemptible objects.

55 If she be false, O, then heaven mocks itself!
I'll not believe't.
(III.3.275–6)
Othello's declaration is made upon seeing Desdemona when she enters immediately after his soliloquy of jealousy and suspicion (see 54 above). Her radiant virtue is self-evident.

56 Trifles light as air
Are to the jealous confirmations strong

As proofs of holy writ.
(III.3.319–21)

Iago is referring to the handkerchief of Desdemona, the first gift of Othello to her, which Emilia has obtained for her husband through Desdemona's negligence. His plan is to pass it into the possession of Cassio as proof of Desdemona's infidelity. The observation further displays Iago's mastery of human psychology.

57 Not poppy, nor mandragora,
Nor all the drowsy syrups of the world,
Shall ever medicine thee to that sweet sleep
Which thou owed'st yesterday.
(III.3.326–9)

Iago has just observed that Othello has already begun to change as a result of the suspicions sown. This is proven to be true on Othello's entry, which is accompanied by Iago's remark that he will never again know the sleep of peace and contentment.

58 I had been happy if the general camp,
Pioners and all, had tasted her sweet body,
So I had nothing known. O, now, for ever
Farewell the tranquil mind! Farewell content!
Farewell the plumèd troops and the big wars
That make ambition virtue – O, farewell!
Farewell the neighing steed, and the shrill trump,
The spirit-stirring drum, th'ear-piercing fife,
The royal banner and all quality,
Pride, pomp and circumstance of glorious war!
And , O you mortal engines, whose rude throats
Th'immortal Jove's dread clamours counterfeit,
Farewell! Othello's occupation's gone.
(III.3.342–54)

Othello's speech confirms the observation of Iago that his peace of mind has been destroyed (see 57 above). His suspicions of Desdemona's infidelity have destroyed not only his married bliss but also his image of himself as a noble and valiant leader of men. His identity, inner and outer, is totally undermined, perhaps because he is already intent upon Desdemona's murder, which must also result in his own destruction.

59 Villain, be sure thou prove my love a whore;
Be sure of it: give me the ocular proof,
Or by the worth of mine eternal soul,
Thou hadst been better have been born a dog
Than answer my waked wrath!
(III.3.356–60)

Othello demands of Iago the proof of Desdemona's adultery that will justify the actions he is planning to take. If proof cannot be provided, Iago himself will become the object of Othello's rage.

60 O monstrous world! Take note, take note, O world!
To be direct and honest is not safe.
(III.3.374–5)

This is one of the many examples of Iago's flagrant hypocrisy. After tainting Othello's mind with suspicion of Desdemona's infidelity, Iago is seeking to direct his master's fury away from himself as the discovererd of Desdemona's 'adultery'.

61 But this denoted a foregone conclusion.
(III.3.425)

Iago, as proof of Desdemona's adultery, has fabricated the implausible situation that Cassio, when sleeping with Iago, dreamed of Desdemona, spoke of her in his dreams, and kissed Iago as Desdemona. Having enraged Othello, he protests that it was no more than a dream on Cassio's part, to which Othello makes the reply given above. Iago then adds the 'proof' of Desdemona's handkerchief, which he has obtained from his wife, Emilia, who waits upon Desdemona.

62 Like to the Pontic sea,
Whose icy current and compulsive course
Ne'er feels retiring ebb, but keeps due on
To the Propontic and the Hellespont,
Even so my bloody thoughts with violent pace
Shall ne'er look back, ne'er ebb to humble love,
Till that a capable and wide revenge
Swallow them up.
(III.3.450–7)

Opinions have differed upon Othello's expression of his desire for revenge upon Desdemona's 'adultery'. Swinburne thought it 'one of the most precious jewels that ever the prodigal after-thought of a great poet bestowed upon the rapture of his readers'. The simile is not found in the First Quarto and Pope agreed that it should be omitted. It derives from Pliny's *Natural History* but is adapted as a cry for revenge.

63 'Tis true: there's magic in the web of it.
A sibyl, that had numbered in the world
The sun to course two hundred compasses,
In her prophetic fury sewed the work:
The worms were hallowed that did breed the silk,
And it was dyed in mummy, which the skilful

Conserved of maidens' hearts.
(III.4.69–75)

Othello is describing to Desdemona the handkerchief which he gave her as his first remembrance and which Iago has obtained from Emilia in order to further his machinations. Othello has asked Desdemona to produce the handkerchief. In his previous speech, he has told how his mother had the handkerchief from an Egyptian enchantress and how it has the power to subdue the owner's lover, but how loss of it loses the lover's good favour. 'Mummy' was a liquor believed to originate from mummified bodies and to have medicinal or magical properties. The lines here derive from Ariosto's *Orlando Furioso* xlvi.80ff.

64 But jealous souls will not be answered so;
They are not ever jealous for the cause,
But jealous for they're jealous. It is a monster
Begot upon itself, born on itself.
(III.4.155–8)

Emilia's lines are in response to Desdemona's protestation that she never gave Othello cause for jealousy. The irrationality of jealousy is a prominent element in the tragedy of *Othello*, which here Emilia articulates explicitly. If we accept Iago's references to his own jealous suspicions, this could explain Emilia's apprehension of the emotion.

65 What! Keep a week away? Seven days and nights?
Eight score eight hours? And lovers' absent hours
More tedious than the dial eight score times!
O weary reckoning!
(III.4.169–72)

Bianca, Cassio's courtesan, is chiding him for his absence with the rigour of a lover's reckoning. Cassio passes to Bianca the handkerchief of Desdemona that Iago has placed in his lodgings, only to become in turn the victim of her jealous suspicions. It is a feature of Shakespearian dramaturgy that the major theme of jealousy should be explored on different levels.

66 O, it comes o'er my memory
As doth the raven o'er the infected house,
Boding to all!
(IV.1.20–2)

Othello has been prompted by Iago to recall Desdemona's loss of the handkerchief which was his first remembrance to her. The raven was believed to be not only a bird of ill-omen but a carrier of infection.

67 Work on,
My medicine, work! Thus credulous fools are caught,
And many worthy and chaste dames even thus,
All guiltless, meet reproach.
(IV.1.44–7)
Iago has tormented Othello with images of adultery until Othello has collapsed physically in an epileptic fit. Iago's first line is ironical, since his malice is poisonous and destructive, not medicinal and restorative, as the 'reproach' (shame) of innocent women illustrates.

68 Think every bearded fellow that's but yoked
May draw with you. There's millions now alive
That nightly lie in those unproper beds
Which they dare swear peculiar.
(IV.1.66–9)
Iago's diseased vision of marriage is offered as a malicious comfort to Othello. Othello despises himself as a cuckold ('A hornèd man's a monster and a beast' – line 62), but Iago urges him to see this condition as a natural consequence of marriage, linking the marriage yoke to the hornèd beast's yoke.

69 'Tis the strumpet's plague
To beguile many and be beguiled by one.
(IV.1.96–7)
Iago is generalizing from the situation of Bianca, a courtesan who dotes upon Cassio. Iago has set up the situation in which he will question Cassio about Bianca, while Othello observes Cassio's gestures and expressions, believing the topic of conversation to be Desdemona.

70 She shall not live! No, my heart is turned to stone: I strike it, and it hurts my hand. – O, the world hath not a sweeter creature! She might lie by an emperor's side and command him tasks.
(IV.1.181–4)
In his jealous passion, Othello oscillates between his furious desire for revenge and his tender adoration of Desdemona's qualities. He believes he has just seen Cassio confirm Desdemona's infidelity when Cassio gave Desdemona's handkerchief to Bianca.

71 O, she will sing the savageness out of a bear!
(IV.1.187–8)
Othello offers a regretful eulogy of Desdemona's charms. The Orphic tradition of music, which the Renaissance inherited from

classical sources, carried the notion that it had the power to tame savage beasts. The untameable beast here is Othello himself.

72 But yet the pity of it, Iago! O, Iago, the pity of it, Iago!
(IV.1.194–5)
Othello's recollection of Desdemona's qualities and charm provokes his realization of a tragic waste, an experience shared by the audience, though for different reasons. His dependence on lago at this point is sadly evident in the repetition of his name.

73 O, well-painted passion!
(IV.1.259)
Othello uses the phrase to describe Desdemona's tears after he has struck her. Othello has just received from Lodovico his order from Venice to return, leaving Cassio in his place, a decision of which Desdemona has expressed her approval. 'Painted' may refer to speech as well as to looks and gesture.

74 Goats and monkeys!
(IV.1.265)
After accepting his orders from Venice, Othello leaves the stage, enraged at Desdemona's apparent open approval of her 'lover's' promotion. His parting remark is a reference to the lascivious behaviour associated with both goats and monkeys.

75 Is this the nature
Whom passion could not shake? Whose solid virtue
The shot of accident nor dart of chance
Could neither graze nor pierce?
(IV.1.267–70)
Lodovico, the Senate's messenger from Venice, is astounded at Othello's violent treatment of Desdemona. His lines not only emphasize the transformation within Othello's conduct, but act as a reminder of the 'solid virtue' for which Othello was esteemed at Venice.

76 Your mystery, your mystery! Nay, dispatch!
(IV.2.29)
Othello is dismissing Emilia, Desdemona's waiting woman, from their company. 'Mystery' means trade, and that of Emilia is here assumed by Othello to be a procuress. Othello wishes to be alone with Desdemona in order to interrogate her about her supposed adultery.

77 Had it pleased heaven
To try me with affliction, had they rained
All kinds of sores and shames on my bare head,
Steeped me in poverty to the very lips,
Given to captivity me and my utmost hopes,
I should have found in some place of my soul
A drop of patience. But alas, to make me
A fixèd figure for the time of scorn
To point his slow unmoving finger at!
Yet could I bear that too, well, very well:
But there where I have garnered up my heart,
Where either I must live, or bear no life,
The fountain from the which my current runs,
Or else dries up – to be discarded thence
Or keep it as a cistern for foul toads
To knot and gender in! Turn thy complexion there,
Patience, thou young and rose-lipped cherubin,
Ay, there look grim as hell!
(IV.2.46–63)
Othello's expression of pain at being marked out as a figure of mockery and shame is addressed to Desdemona. The last three lines of the speech constitute one of the most insoluble cruxes in Shakespeare. It is uncertain whether a personification of Patience is being rhetorically addressed or whether Othello is seeking in Desdemona's face the transformation from patient beauty to hellish ugliness that he believes would correspond to her sin.

78 O, thou weed,
Who art so lovely fair, and smell'st so sweet
That the sense aches at thee, would thou hadst ne'er been born!
(IV.2.66–8)
Othello's attitude to Desdemona oscillates between desire for her beauty and detestation of her supposed corruption. The First Quarto has 'black weed' and in both the First Quarto and the Folio the lineation differs from the arrangement given here.

79 I cry you mercy then:
I took you for that cunning whore of Venice
That married with Othello. (*Calling*) You, mistress,
That have the office opposite to Saint Peter
And keep the gate of hell!
(IV.2.87–91)
Othello's ironical address to Desdemona is made in response to her denial of whoredom. Othello's unspecific accusation of infidelity prevents Desdemona from refuting the charge ade-

quately. The last three lines are directed at Emilia, who Othello believes to be Desdemona's bawd.

80 Those that do teach young babes
Do it with gentle means and easy tasks:
He might have chid me so, for, in good faith,
I am a child to chiding.
(IV.2.110–13)

Desdemona is explaining to Emilia and Iago how feelingly she takes Othello's reproofs, since she has not been used to reprimands. The lines emphasize Desdemona's youth and innocence.

81 EMILIA
I will be hanged if some eternal villain,
Some busy and insinuating rogue,
Some cogging, cozening slave, to get some office,
Have not devised this slander; I'll be hanged else.
IAGO
Fie, there is no such man! It is impossible.
DESDEMONA
If any such there be, heaven pardon him.
EMILIA
A halter pardon him and hell gnaw his bones!
(IV.2.129–35)

The passage illustrates the variety of responses to Othello's accusation of adultery offered by Desdemona, Emilia, and Iago. Desdemona's charity, Emilia's forthright honesty, and Iago's hypocrisy are all evident.

82 Unkindness may do much,
And his unkindness may defeat my life,
But never taint my love.
(IV.2.158–60)

Desdemona is speaking to Iago of Othello's cruelty towards her and requesting his intervention on her behalf. There is no suspicion of Iago's complicity in the plot against her honour. Her lines prove prophetic.

83 EMILIA
I would you had never seen him.
DESDEMONA
So would not I: my love doth so approve him
That even his stubbornness, his checks, his frowns
... have grace and favour in them.
(IV.3.17–20)

The quality of Desdemona's love for Othello remains constant despite his inexplicable cruelty towards her. Desdemona is preparing for bed with the assistance of Emilia. She plans to re-win Othello's love, while he has plotted her destruction. The scene is shot through with Desdemona's melancholy reminiscences and her premonition of death.

84 My mother had a maid called Barbary:
She was in love: and he she loved proved mad
And did forsake her. She had a song of willow;
An old thing 'twas; but it expressed her fortune,
And she died singing it. That song tonight
Will not go from my mind.
(IV.3.25–30)

Desdemona's recollection of the willow song of the forsaken maid casts a sombre shadow over her preparations for Othello's bed, which she has had laid with her wedding sheets. The song, and its context, is a good example of Shakespeare's atmospheric use of music. Verdi makes equally effective use of the willow song in his operatic version of *Otello* (1887).

85 The poor soul sat sighing by a sycamore tree,
  Sing all a green willow;
Her hand on her bosom, her head on her knee,
  Sing willow, willow, willow;
The fresh streams ran by her and murmured her moans;
  Sing willow, willow, willow;
Her salt tears fell from her and softened the stones –
  Sing willow, willow, willow –
Sing all a green willow must be my garland.
(IV.3.38–48)

The willow song, which Desdemona sings and attributes to a wronged maid of her mother, is in fact an adaptation of a popular song of Shakespeare's time, in which the forsaken lover was a man. The song does not occur in the First Quarto, perhaps because it had been omitted in performance. The last lines of the stanza are interspersed with Desdemona's instructions to Emilia (here omitted).

86 Mine eyes do itch:
Does that bode weeping?
(IV.3.55–6)

The itching of Desdemona's eyes, foreshadowing weeping, is another premonition of her tragic fate. Emilia's response, ''Tis neither here nor there', remains a colloquial phrase of modern

English. Desdemona is preparing for bed, with Emilia's assistance, on the night of her murder.

87 The world's a huge thing: it is a great price for a small vice.
(IV.3.67–8)
Desdemona has asked Emilia whether she believes women are capable of such a gross sin as adultery. Emilia's pragmatic responses, of which this is one, suggest that everything has its price. Emilia's frank acknowledgement of the ways of the world highlights Desdemona's total innocence.

88 Let husbands know
Their wives have sense like them: they see and smell,
And have their palates both for sweet and sour
As husbands have. What is it that they do,
When they change us for others? Is it sport?
I think it is. And doth affection breed it?
I think it doth. Is't frailty that thus errs?
It is so too. And have not we affections,
Desires for sport, and frailty, as men have?
(IV.3.92–100)
Emilia's feminist manifesto occurs in a play in which women are very much the victims of male aggression. The person addressed, Desdemona, is not protected from male domination, nor from ultimate destruction, despite her orthodox acceptance of her society's code of relationships.

89 He hath a daily beauty in his life
That makes me ugly.
(V.1.19–20)
Iago is speaking of Cassio, for whom he has just set Roderigo in ambush. The line demonstrates envy as the source of much of Iago's malice. Roderigo subsequently wounds Cassio in the leg and receives a wound in return.

90 This is the night
That either makes me, or fordoes me quite.
(V.1.128–9)
This aside of Iago is the prelude for the tragic climax of the play and, in the conventional division of the play into scenes, immediately precedes the final scene. Up to this point, Iago's plot has succeeded admirably: Cassio, his rival, has been maimed; Roderigo, who has outlived his usefulness to Iago and has become a potential threat, has been eliminated by Iago's own hand; and Iago now awaits the final success, the destruction of Desdemona and Othello.

91 It is the cause, it is the cause, my soul:
Let me not name it to you, you chaste stars!
It is the cause. Yet I'll not shed her blood,
Nor scar that whiter skin of hers than snow,
And smooth as monumental alabaster:
Yet she must die ...
... but once put out thy light,
Thou cunning'st pattern of excelling nature,
I know not where is that Promethean heat
That can thy light relume. When I have plucked thy rose,
I cannot give it vital growth again,
It needs must wither. I'll smell it on the tree.
He kisses her
O balmy breath, that dost almost persuade
Justice to break her sword! One more, one more.
Be thus when thou art dead and I will kill thee,
And love thee after. One more, and this the last.
So sweet was ne'er so fatal. I must weep.
But they are cruel tears; this sorrow's heavenly –
It strikes where it doth love.
(V.2.1–6, 10–22)

This soliloquy of Othello is delivered beside the bed of the sleeping Desdemona. It is clear that he conceives the act of murder he is about to commit as one of justice, not revenge. The 'cause' of the first line is Desdemona's 'infidelity'. Throughout the soliloquy, Desdemona is associated with light and life which, once extinguished, can never be restored. Prometheus was the legendary bringer of fire (and light) to men. The sword is an emblem of justice, of which Othello sees himself an instrument even when it demands he strike where he loves.

92 That death's unnatural that kills for loving.
(V.2.42)

Othello has declared his intention to kill Desdemona and has urged her to confess her sins. She claims that she has none other than her 'loves' to Othello, but he insists that is the cause of her death. Her response answers not only the immediate point, but in the structure of the scene as a whole counters Othello's presentation of her murder as a dutiful and loving act of justice.

93 Kill me tomorrow: let me live tonight!
(V.2.81)

Desdemona pleads for an extension of her life. Othello loses control of the sacrificial act he intends to commit when Desdemona weeps at being told that Cassio is dead. He becomes enraged, believing that her tears are confirmation of her adultery with Cassio.

94 Methinks it should be now a huge eclipse
Of sun and moon, and that th'affrighted globe
Should yawn at alteration.
(V.2.100–2)
Othello, with Emilia knocking on the chamber door for entry, realizes for the first time the enormity of the crime he has committed in murdering Desdemona. Eclipses and earthquakes were believed to accompany portentous events.

95 Then murder's out of tune,
And sweet revenge grows harsh.
(V.2.117–18)
Emilia has just informed Othello that Roderigo has been killed but not Cassio, as Othello had believed. In the new context, Othello's murder of Desdemona, as yet undiscovered by Emilia, begins to take on the colouring of revenge not justice, as he had conceived it.

96 DESDEMONA
A guiltless death I die.
EMILIA
O, who hath done this deed?
DESDEMONA
Nobody – I myself – farewell.
Commend me to my kind lord – O, farewell!
(V.2.123–6)
Emilia has discovered the body of Desdemona, who revives briefly to utter a futile exoneration of Othello, for he immediately acknowledges responsibility to Emilia. Desdemona's lines offer one of the many touches of pathos in the scene.

97 OTHELLO
She's like a liar gone to burning hell:
'Twas I that killed her.
EMILIA O, the more angel she,
And you the blacker devil!
(V.2.130–2)
Othello is still persuaded of Desdemona's guilt. This conviction is only undermined after Emilia learns of Iago's part in persuading Othello of Desdemona's adultery. At the end of the play Othello is transformed from the noble Moor into a black devil contrasted with the radiant angel of Desdemona.

98 Nay, had she been true,
If heaven would make me such another world
Of one entire and perfect chrysolite,
I'd not have sold her for it.
(V.2.142–5)

The audience's sense of loss at this point is even greater than Othello's, for the audience knows Desdemona, the object of discussion here, to have been faithful. This passage answers the earlier cynical observation of Emilia, the person addressed here, which is quoted as 87 above. A 'chrysolite' is a precious stone, green in colour.

99 Thou hast not half that power to do me harm
As I have to be hurt.
(V.2.161–2)

Emilia grows in stature in the final scene as she realizes the villainy of her husband, Iago, and the gross injustice exacted upon Desdemona. She denounces Othello's action courageously, and later confronts the threats of her husband. Her statement here means that she takes the death of her mistress more feelingly than any pain Othello can inflict.

100 You told a lie, an odious damnèd lie:
Upon my soul, a lie, a wicked lie!
(V.2.179–80)

This is the manner in which Emilia bravely denounces Iago's confirmation that he accused Desdemona of infidelity to Othello.

101 Are there no stones in heaven
But what serve for the thunder?
(V.2.232–3)

Othello is invoking divine justice upon Iago, for Emilia has just provided the proof of her husband's villainy and Desdemona's innocence. She has revealed that she gave Desdemona's handkerchief to Iago. 'Stones' are thunderbolts, which Othello wishes would strike Iago down. At this point, Othello makes a rush at Iago, but is disarmed by Montano, while Iago takes advantage of the confusion to stab Emilia.

102 But why should honour outlive honesty?
(V.2.243)

Othello has been denied the opportunity to vent his rage on Iago by Montano. He questions why concern for reputation should linger after the demise of a virtuous life.

103 I will play the swan
And die in music.
(V.2.245–6)

Emilia, fatally stabbed by Iago for revealing his villainous plot, dies singing the refrain from the willow song that Desdemona sang before her death (see 85 above). The line is an allusion to the belief that swans, otherwise unharmonious, sing immediately prior to death.

104 Who can control his fate? – 'Tis not so now.
Be not afraid, though you do see me weaponed:
Here is my journey's end, here is my butt
And very sea-mark of my utmost sail.
(V.2.263–6)

Othello is musing upon the mystery of human destiny. He has drawn a second weapon and is obviously determined to exercise such control over destiny as he can through death. 'Butt' is an aim or goal, and 'sea-mark' a beacon. The analogy between human life and a sea-voyage was a Renaissance commonplace.

105 O ill-starred wench
Pale as thy smock! When we shall meet at compt
This look of thine will hurl my soul from heaven
And fiends will snatch at it. Cold, cold, my girl,
Even like thy chastity.
O cursèd, cursèd slave! Whip me, ye devils,
From the possession of this heavenly sight!
Blow me about in winds! Roast me in sulphur!
Wash me in steep-down gulfs of liquid fire!
(V.2.270–8)

Othello's lines are addressed to the corpse of Desdemona. 'Compt' is the day of judgement, when the final reckoning will be rendered. Othello envisages an eternal separation, with Desdemona's soul attaining heaven and his being hurled into everlasting torment. The vision of hell conveys his state of damnation: he already sees himself as a black devil.

106 An honourable murderer, if you will:
For naught did I in hate, but all in honour.
(V.2.291–2)

This late appeal of Othello to Lodovico to have his actions, however erroneous, considered honourable is only partially acceptable. It is true that, unlike Iago, his actions were not committed out of malice; but his indulgence of his passion, his acting on insubstantial evidence, and his failure to recognize

Desdemona's virtue and to remain true to her, all place him beyond the pale of 'honour'.

107 I have done the state some service and they know't:
No more of that. I pray you in your letters
When you shall these unlucky deeds relate
Speak of me as I am; nothing extenuate,
Nor set down aught in malice. Then must you speak
Of one that loved not wisely, but too well;
Of one, not easily jealous but, being wrought,
Perplexed in the extreme; of one whose hand
Like the base Indian threw a pearl away
Richer than all his tribe; of one whose sùbdued eyes,
Albeit unusèd to the melting mood,
Drop tears as fast as the Arabian trees
Their med'cinable gum. Set you down this:
And say, besides, that in Aleppo once
Where a malignant and a turbaned Turk
Beat a Venetian and traduced the state,
I took by th'throat the circumcisèd dog
And smoke him thus.
(V.2.335–52)
In his last long speech, Othello re-establishes the image of himself as an honourable man, a servant of the Venetian state, and a true lover, whose good deeds have been undermined by the distraction of jealousy. The sense of tragic waste is conveyed in the allusion to the Indian throwing away the valuable pearl. It should be noted that the Folio reads 'Iudean' for Indian, which could also make sense. The references to the Orient and to exotic lands reinforce a sense of Othello's extreme actions being those of an alien in Venetian society. As he has destroyed Venice's enemies, so he now destroys himself for having traduced its code of honour.

108 GRATIANO All that's spoke is marred!
OTHELLO
I kissed thee, ere I killed thee: no way but this,
Killing myself, to die upon a kiss.
(V.2.353–5)
Gratiano's line refers to Othello's speech given above as 107. Fatally wounded by his own hand, Othello embraces the dead Desdemona and dies with a kiss, so enacting a frequent equivocation of the love-poets of the Renaissance, since 'die' can also signify to reach orgasm. More importantly, the deaths of Desdemona and Othello reiterate that association of sexual passion and death which is so deeply rooted in Western culture.

Pericles

1 See where she comes, apparelled like the spring.
(I.1.13)
In this line Pericles describes the daughter of Antiochus, king of Antioch, whom he is trying to win as his bride by answering a riddle. Although recent revivals have demonstrated the play's theatrical vitality, and despite its obvious thematic links with Shakespeare's other late plays, the text of *Pericles*, as we have it, appears to be, at best, a mangled version of the original. It is generally agreed that the text is a debased rendering of an original which may well have been a collaborative effort between Shakespeare and another writer, perhaps his younger contemporary John Fletcher with whom he wrote *Henry VIII* and *The Two Noble Kinsmen.*

2 Few love to hear the sins they love to act.
(I.1.93)
Pericles has realized that the answer to the riddle which would allow him to marry Antiochus's daughter is that Antiochus and his daughter are committing incest. Pericles, challenged to give the answer by Antiochus, begins with this line.

3 The blind mole casts
Copped hills towards heaven, to tell the earth is thronged
By man's oppression, and the poor worm doth die for't.
(I.1.101–3)
Pericles continues his answer to Antiochus by pointing out why he would be unwise to give the answer, using the image of the mole which throws up its heaped ('Copped') hills in protest against the earth being crushed ('thronged') by men but then dies because its protest gives it away. 'Worm' means creature.

4 'Tis time to fear when tyrants seems to kiss.
(I.2.79)
Pericles has returned to Tyre, fearful that Antiochus will try to murder him to prevent him revealing the secret of his incest. In this speech he is confiding his fears to Helicanus, one of his noblemen. Antiochus had appeared friendly but Pericles did not trust him.

5 Well, I perceive he was a wise fellow and had good discretion that, being bid to ask what he would of the king, desired he might know none of his secrets.
(I.3.3–6)

Thaliard, sent by Antiochus to kill Pericles, muses on the dangers of getting involved in the affairs of kings. He refers to the classical writer Plutarch's story of the poet Philippides who, offered a gift by his king, had declined to know any of his secrets because knowing them would make him vulnerable.

6 THIRD FISHERMAN
Master, I marvel how the fishes live in the sea?
FIRST FISHERMAN
Why, as men do a-land: the great ones eat up the little ones.
(II.1.26–9)
Pericles, having left Tyre to avoid provoking Antiochus, has been shipwrecked at Pentapolis where three fisherman are talking on the seashore.

7 A man whom both the waters and the wind,
In that vast tennis-court, hath made the ball
For them to play upon entreats you pity him.
(II.1.59–61)
Pericles asks the fishermen to pity him, using the common idea of man as a tennis ball to the gods.

8 Opinion's but a fool, that makes us scan
The outward habit by the inward man.
(II.2.55–6)
Simonides, king of Pentapolis, has just watched a parade of knights in which Pericles has appeared in shabby armour. His comment reverses the normal idea that outward appearances do not necessarily reflect inner characteristics; presumably this is a mistake by whoever was responsible for preserving the text as we have it, but the mistake has been preserved in the couplet rhyme.

9 O you gods!
Why do you make us love your goodly gifts
And snatch them straight away?
(III.1.22–4)
Pericles has married Thaisa, daughter of Simonides, who has apparently died in childbirth on board ship in a storm en route to Tyre. This is Pericles's reaction to her death.

10 Now, mild may be thy life!
For a more blusterous birth had never babe;
Quiet and gentle thy conditions! for
Thou are the rudeliest welcome to this world

That ever was prince's child. Happy what follows!
Thou has as chiding a nativity
As fire, air, water, earth, and heaven can make
To herald thee from the womb. [Poor inch of nature!]
Even at the first thy loss is more than can
Thy portage quit, with all thou canst find here.
Now the good gods throw their best eyes upon't.
(III.1.27–37)
Pericles prays for his infant daughter Marina, born in a storm at sea. 'Conditions' means way of life; 'Poor inch of nature!' is supplied from a prose narrative, George Wilkins's *The Painful Adventures of Pericles, Prince of Tyre*, published in 1608, which was probably an early attempt to capitalize on the success of the play. The ninth and tenth lines mean that Marina has lost more by her mother's death at the beginning of her life than she can hope to gain in the rest of her life to pay for her passage through life ('portage').

11 A terrible childbed hast thou had, my dear;
No light, no fire; th'unfriendly elements
Forgot thee utterly. Nor have I time
To give thee hallowed to thy grave, but straight
Must cast thee, scarcely coffined, in the ooze,
Where, for a monument upon thy bones,
And e'er-remaining lamps, the belching whale
And humming water must o'erwhelm thy corpse
Lying with simple shells.
(III.1.56–64)
Pericles addresses Thaisa, who is about to be buried at sea after her apparent death in childbirth. 'E'er-remaining lamps' are votive candles burning forever; 'belching' means spouting.

12 By you being pardoned, we commit no crime
To use one language in each several clime
Where our scene seems to live.
(IV.4.5–7)
John Gower, a medieval writer used by Shakespeare as the play's chorus figure, draws the audience's attention to the dramatic convention whereby the characters in a play all speak English, despite the changing locations ('several clime').

13 SECOND GENTLEMAN Come, I am for no more bawdy houses. Shall's go hear the vestals sing?
FIRST GENTLEMAN I'll do anything now that is virtuous, but I am out of the road of rutting for ever.
(IV.5.6–9)

After many adventures, Marina, Pericles's daughter, has been consigned to a brothel where her purity converts her prospective clients. These Gentlemen have just been transformed by meeting her. The 'vestals' are virgin priestesses; 'rutting' means fornication.

14 Fie, fie upon her! She's able to freeze the god Priapus and undo a whole generation.
(IV.6.3–4)
The Bawd of the brothel in which Marina has been confined is worried by her ability to convert the clients to chastity. Priapus is a fertility god.

15 Thou that beget'st him that did thee beget.
(V.1.196)
Pericles has been reunited with his daughter Marina, whose musical skill has awakened him from a trance brought on by his misfortunes. Unlike Antiochus's daughter, Marina has given a fruitful new life to her father. This line has been seen as a key to *The Winter's Tale* and *The Tempest* as well as *Pericles.*

Richard II

1 The blood is hot that must be cooled for this.
(I.1.51)
Henry Bolingbroke, Duke of Hereford and son of John of Gaunt, Duke of Lancaster, has accused Thomas Mowbray, Duke of Norfolk, of high treason before King Richard. According to the political and chivalric conventions of the age in which the play is set, the resolution of the accusation must be through armed combat. Mowbray is thus stating that the combatants' anger can only be assuaged through death. In Shakespeare's source, Holinshed's *Chronicles*, the challenge takes place at Windsor Castle.

2 KING RICHARD
Give me his gage. Lions make leopards tame.
MOWBRAY
Yea, but not change his spots. Take but my shame
And I resign my gage. My dear dear lord,
The purest treasure mortal times afford
Is spotless reputation. That away,
Men are but gilded loam, or painted clay.
(I.1.174–9)

Bolingbroke, Duke of Hereford, has challenged Mowbray, Duke of Norfolk, to armed combat in support of his accusation of treason against him. Mowbray has accepted the challenge by also throwing down his gage. King Richard has intervened in an attempt at mediation, but the two combatants are reluctant to withdraw their challenges. Mowbray's argument elevates honour and reputation above life and, by implictation, above obedience to the sovereign. Richard's reference to 'lions' and 'leopards' alludes to the heraldic devices representing himself and Mowbray. Mowbray's notion that leopards cannot change their spots derives from Jeremiah 13:23, but was probably proverbial.

3 We were not born to sue, but to command.
(I.1.196)
Richard employs the royal 'we' in making this statement of royal prerogative. In reality, his will has been frustrated by Bolingbroke and Mowbray, who have refused to withdraw their challenges at his request. Consequently, trial by combat in the lists is declared for St Lambert's day at Coventry.

4 Edward's seven sons, whereof thyself art one,
Were as seven vials of his sacred blood,
Or seven fair branches springing from one root.
Some of those seven are dried by nature's course,
Some of those branches by the destinies cut.
But Thomas, my dear lord, my life, my Gloucester,
One vial full of Edward's sacred blood,
One flourishing branch of his most royal root,
Is cracked, and all the precious liquor spilt;
Is hacked down, and his summer leaves all faded,
By envy's hand, and murder's bloody axe.
(I.2.11–21)
The Duchess of Gloucester is seeking redress from John of Gaunt, her brother-in-law, for the murder of Gloucester at, as she believes, Richard's instigation. In this highly emblematic description, she depicts an outrage upon the sanctity of the royal blood of Edward III, Richard's grandfather. Her imagery is based on the concept of a family tree, with the branches stemming from the root of the family's founder.

5 God's is the quarrel.
(I.2.37)
John of Gaunt's response to the Duchess of Gloucester's appeal that he revenge the death of Gloucester at Richard's instigation is not merely political evasion. The lines that follow raise the concept of kingship around which the play revolves. Gaunt argues

that, since the king is God's anointed deputy within his realm, only God may take action against the king, even when he is culpable.

6 The language I have learnt these forty years,
My native English, now I must forgo,
And now my tongue's use is to me no more
Than an unstringèd viol or a harp,
Or like a cunning instrument cased up –
Or being open, put into his hands
That knows no touch to tune the harmony.
Within my mouth you have engaoled my tongue,
Doubly portcullised with my teeth and lips,
And dull unfeeling barren ignorance
Is made my gaoler to attend on me.
(I.3.159–69)

At the lists in Coventry, King Richard interrupts the armed combat of Bolingbroke and Mowbray and issues decrees of banishment upon them, life banishment for Mowbray. Mowbray's poignant response to his banishment, that denial of self-expression is a form of imprisonment, implies praise of the beauty and flexibility of his mother tongue. The Renaissance saw the rapid development and appreciation of vernacular languages. Shakespeare's own art and the rhetoric of this play is just one example of it.

7 How long a time lies in one little word!
Four lagging winters and four wanton springs
End in a word – such is the breath of kings.
(I.3.213–15)

Richard has banished Bolingbroke for ten years because of his refusal to withdraw his challenge of treason against Mowbray. Seeing the effect of his decree upon the aged John of Gaunt, Bolingbroke's father, Richard reduces the sentence by four years. Gaunt points out here (and more explicitly in lines 226–32) that, while the breath of kings has the godlike power to utter sentence and take away life, it has not the godlike power to extend or give life. He knows he will not live to see his son's return.

8 Things sweet to taste prove in digestion sour.
(I.3.236)

John of Gaunt is explaining to his nephew, Richard, through a proverbial saying, why he now resents as a father the banishment of Bolingbroke, although he had given his assent as a judge together with his fellow peers. It is a minor example of the contrast found throughout the play between public role and private feeling.

9 Must I not serve a long apprenticehood
To foreign passages, and in the end,
Having my freedom, boast of nothing else
But that I was a journeyman to grief?
(I.3.271–4)

Bolingbroke is expressing to his father the futility of his banishment by Richard. His extended metaphor is based on an apprenticeship to foreign travel under a hard master, grief. Editors have found inconsistencies of terminology or tense in the image, since becoming a 'journeyman' or skilled artisan should logically be identified with freedom from the apprenticeship and not co-exist with it.

10 All places that the eye of heaven visits
Are to a wise man ports and happy havens.
Teach thy necessity to reason thus:
There is no virtue like necessity.
(I.3.275–8)

Bolingbroke has been banished from Richard's realm for six years for his refusal to withdraw his accusation of treason against Thomas Mowbray, Duke of Norfolk. His father, John of Gaunt, is offering stoical advice on making a virtue of necessity.

11 O, who can hold a fire in his hand
By thinking on the frosty Caucasus,
Or cloy the hungry edge of appetite
By bare imagination of a feast,
Or wallow naked in December snow
By thinking on fantastic summer's heat?
(I.3.294–9)

Gaunt has urged Bolingbroke to reconcile himself to banishment by transforming restraint to liberty by the exercise of the mind. Bolingbroke's response here shows his pragmatic nature, his awareness of reality, and his rejection of the power of the imagination. These themes will recur in relation to Richard's reactions to his deposition and his imprisonment.

12 Ourself and Bushy
Observed his courtship to the common people,
How he did seem to dive into their hearts
With humble and familiar courtesy;
What reverence he did throw away on slaves,
Wooing poor craftsmen with the craft of smiles

And patient underbearing of his fortune,
As 'twere to banish their affects with him.
(I.4.23–30)

Richard offers a jaundiced account of Bolingbroke's 'courtship' of the common people to his cousin Aumerle, son of the Duke of York. Initially, Richard is only shown in an aristocratic milieu and is depicted as being extremely conscious of his role as king, its divinity and powers. His penchant for rhetoric and rhetorical gesture is contrasted with Bolingbroke's more pragmatic and down-to-earth conduct and expression.

13 Pray God we may make haste and come too late!
(I.4.64)

Richard has been informed by Bushy, one of his 'flatterers', that John of Gaunt, Duke of Lancaster and Bolingbroke's father, is 'grievous sick'. Richard wishes his death in order that he may seize Lancaster's property to pay for the wars in Ireland on which he is about to embark. The flippancy of the line is an expression of Richard's thoughtless cynicism.

14 O, but they say the tongues of dying men
Enforce attention like deep harmony...
More are men's ends marked than their lives before.
The setting sun, and music at the close,
As the last taste of sweets, is sweetest last,
Writ in remembrance more than things long past.
(II.1.5–6, 11–14)

John of Gaunt, from his deathbed, has sent for his nephew, King Richard, in order to give him final counsel. It was a contemporary belief that men were possessed of greater spiritual insight at death. Ironically, this proves true of Richard himself, although he rejects the advice offered here. A 'close' was the concluding cadence of a musical phrase. This speech was anthologized in *England's Parnassus* of 1600 in the section on 'Death'.

15 Methinks I am a prophet new-inspired,
And thus, expiring, do foretell of him:
His rash fierce blaze of riot cannot last;
For violent fires soon burn out themselves.
(II.1.31–4)

John of Gaunt, on his deathbed, is inspired to foretell the fate of Richard if he should persevere in his neglect of the realm. Gaunt's images of the 'blaze of riot' and 'violent fires' suggest a negative side to the imagery of the sun-king which Richard employs about himself. Gaunt's prophecy is delivered to his brother, the Duke of York. Richard arrives too late to hear it.

16 This royal throne of kings, this sceptred isle,
This earth of majesty, this seat of Mars,
This other Eden – demi-paradise –
This fortress built by nature for herself
Against infection and the hand of war,
This happy breed of men, this little world,
This precious stone set in the silver sea,
Which serves it in the office of a wall,
Or as a moat defensive to a house
Against the envy of less happier lands;
This blessèd plot, this earth, this realm, this England,
This nurse, this teeming womb of royal kings,
Feared by their breed, and famous by their birth.
Renownèd for their deeds as far from home
For Christian service and true chivalry
As is the sepulchre in stubborn Jewry
Of the world's ransom, blessèd Mary's son;
This land of such dear souls, this dear dear land,
Dear for her reputation through the world,
Is now leased out – I die pronouncing it –
Like to a tenement or pelting farm.
(II.1.40–60)

John of Gaunt's vision of England's rich inheritance of freedom and valour and its degeneration in Richard's hands to a mere tenanted farm draws on many traditions of describing and eulogizing the nation. Essentially, England is seen as a blessed and fertile garden enclosed and protected by the sea. The passage relates notions of kingship and true chivalry to religious concepts, just as the play as a whole depicts kingship as a theologico-political issue. A 'tenement' is property held by a tenant, while 'pelting' means paltry. It was the taxation of the realm that Richard had actually 'leased out'.

17 England, bound in with the triumphant sea,
Whose rocky shore beats back the envious siege
Of watery Neptune, is now bound in with shame,
With inky blots and rotten parchment bonds.
That England that was wont to conquer others
Hath made a shameful conquest of itself.
(II.1.61–6)

The continuation of Gaunt's vision of England places increased emphasis on the role of the sea in England's destiny. After the defeat of the Armada in 1588, eulogies of England which depicted her as mistress of the seas were very popular. The central concept of this section of the speech is that England cannot be conquered except from within. There are many parallels with the Bastard's speech in *King John,* V.7. 112–18.

18 Thy deathbed is no lesser than thy land,
Wherein thou liest in reputation sick;
And thou, too careless patient as thou art,
Committest thy anointed body to the cure
Of those 'physicians' that first wounded thee.
A thousand flatterers sit within thy crown,
Whose compass is no bigger than thy head,
And yet, encagèd in so small a verge,
The waste is no whit lesser than thy land.
(II.1.95–103)

John of Gaunt is giving his dying counsel to King Richard. He has contrasted his own physical decay but intellectual and spiritual perception with Richard's physical well-being but lack of political and moral wisdom. Gaunt is able to apply his imagery through the macrocosm/microcosm analogy by which Richard stands both for his realm and for himself. In the course of the scene, the visual image of Gaunt's deathbed upon the stage is extended to encompass the whole realm as well as Richard's inner condition.

19 Take Hereford's rights away, and take from Time
His charters and his customary rights.
Let not tomorrow then ensue today.
Be not thyself; for how art thou a king
But by fair sequence and succession?
(II.1.195–9)

The Duke of York is rebuking his nephew, King Richard, for his decision to confiscate upon his death the property of his uncle, John of Gaunt, Duke of Lancaster, which is the natural inheritance of the banished Henry Bolingbroke. York's argument is that Richard is committing an act of rebellion against himself by breaking those laws of succession and inheritance by which he claims the throne. The narrative of the play, with Richard's loss of role and identity, is to endorse York's statement.

20 I will despair and be at enmity
With cozening hope.
(II.2.68–9)

Queen Isabel has just learned from Green that Bolingbroke has landed in England and that the Earl of Worcester has resigned his stewardship of the royal household and has defected to the invader. King Richard has just left England for the Irish wars.

Throughout the scene, Isabel has had a presentiment of doom, but Bushy has sought to relieve her gloom. 'Cozening' means cheating or deceitful.

21 The task he undertakes
Is numbering sands and drinking oceans dry.
(II.2.144–5)
Green uses two proverbial phrases for attempting the impossible to communicate to Bushy and Bagot the dimension of the Duke of York's task in trying to muster support for Richard against the invasion of Bolingbroke.

22 I count myself in nothing else so happy
As in a soul remembering my good friends.
(II.3.46–7)
Harry Percy (Hotspur), the son of the Duke of Northumberland, has just pledged his service to Bolingbroke, following the latter's invasion of England. In view of Bolingbroke's treatment of the Percy family after becoming Henry IV, this courtly and diplomatic reception of his valuable ally proves ironic.

23 Tut, tut, grace me no grace, nor uncle me no uncle!
(II.3.86)
The Duke of York is reproving his nephew, Bolingbroke, for addressing him, the regent of England, as 'gracious uncle' when Bolingbroke is acting as rebel by invading the realm. The word-play of the line demonstrates Shakespeare's ability, when occasion demands, to render colloquial the rhetoric of this highly stylized and ritualized play.

24 The caterpillars of the commonwealth.
(II.3.165)
This phrase of Bolingbroke refers to Bushy, Bagot, and their accomplices, who are seen as 'flatterers' or evil counsellors of King Richard. In the following line, Bolingbroke announces his intention 'to weed and pluck away' these persons, and Bushy and Green are subsequently executed by him at Bristol Castle. The imagery anticipates that of the garden scene (III.4.), with Bolingbroke demonstrating himself a proficient 'gardener' here.

25 Things past redress are now with me past care.
(II.3.170)
The Duke of York finds himself compromised as regent of the realm by Bolingbroke's invasion, whose might he is unable to resist. He declares himself neutral in the dispute, while the plot as a whole shows him subscribing to the policy that 'might is right'.

His statement is based on the proverbial notion, 'past cure, past care', but he is using it to rationalize his position.

26 Eating the bitter bread of banishment.
(III.1.21)
Bolingbroke is denouncing Bushy and Green prior to his execution of them at Bristol Castle. The section of the speech from which the line is taken refers to the injuries inflicted on himself through their malice. This very tangible manner of speaking of the bitter experience of exile derives from the Old Testament, I Kings 22:27.

27 So when this thief, this traitor Bolingbroke,
Who all this while hath revelled in the night
Whilst we were wandering with the Antipodes,
Shall see us rising in our throne, the east,
His treasons will sit blushing in his face,
Not able to endure the sight of day,
But self-affrighted, tremble at his sin.
(III.2.47–53)
Richard has returned from Ireland to confront the invasion of Bolingbroke. He believes that Bolingbroke has returned in his absence like a thief in the night. The quotation is the second part of an extended metaphor in which Richard likens his return to the rising sun. The analogy suggests not only the majesty of the sun-king, but is potentially blasphemous in its connotations of Christ triumphant. Richard's statement to his cousin, Aumerle, is overtly rhetorical and demonstrates little grasp of Bolingbroke's character and situation. The sun was Richard's personal emblem.

28 Not all the water in the rough rude sea
Can wash the balm off from an anointed king.
The breath of worldly men cannot depose
The deputy elected by the Lord.
For every man that Bolingbroke hath pressed
To lift shrewd steel against our golden crown,
God for his Richard hath in heavenly pay
A glorious angel. Then if angels fight,
Weak men must fall; for heaven still guards the right.
(III.2.54–62)
The quotation is the continuation of 27 above. In it Richard expounds the doctrine of the sanctity of monarchy as Tudor constitutional lawyers had developed it from medieval sources. Essentially, it is the doctrine that has come to be known as 'the divine right of kings'. Once again Richard mistakes rhetoric for political reality.

29 Awake, thou coward majesty; thou sleepest.
Is not the King's name twenty thousand names?
Arm, arm, my name! A puny subject strikes
At thy great glory.
(III.2.84–7)

Throughout the scene of his return from Ireland, Richard vacillates between despair and vaunting rhetoric. Richard has despaired at Salisbury's information on the defection of his Welsh troops to Bolingbroke. This revival of courage is made in response to Aumerle's encouragement that Richard remember his position.

30 Of comfort no man speak.
Let's talk of graves, of worms, and epitaphs;
Make dust our paper, and with rainy eyes
Write sorrow on the bosom of the earth.
Let's choose executors and talk of wills.
(III.2.144–8)

Richard has just been informed by Sir Stephen Scroop of Bolingbroke's execution of Bushy and Green at Bristol Castle. Only a few lines earlier Richard had denounced them as 'Judases' when Scroop, breaking the news gently, told him that they had made their peace with Bolingbroke. The speech has a *de contemptu mundi* strain, demonstrating the vanity of earthly power and pleasure.

31 For God's sake let us sit upon the ground
And tell sad stories of the death of kings –
How some have been deposed, some slain in war,
Some haunted by the ghosts they have deposed,
Some poisoned by their wives, some sleeping killed,
All murdered. For within the hollow crown
That rounds the mortal temples of a king
Keeps death his court; and there the antic sits,
Scoffing his state and grinning at his pomp,
Allowing him a breath, a little scene,
To monarchize, be feared, and kill with looks,
Infusing him with self and vain conceit,
As if this flesh which walls about our life
Were brass impregnable; and humoured thus,
Comes at the last, and with a little pin
Bores through his castle wall, and – farewell, king!
(III.2.155–70)

Richard's catalogue of the demise of kings is based on the fall of famous men tradition of tragedy (*de casibus virum illustrorum*), such as could be found in *The Mirror for Magistrates* of 1578 and of which, at one level, *Richard II* is an example. The description of the death's head appearing within the monarch's crown seems to derive from an emblematic or other iconographic tradition illustrating the vanity of terrestrial power, but no precise parallel has been identified. The phrase 'the hollow crown' provided the Royal Shakespeare Company in 1961 with the title for a very successful performance based on readings from the history plays.

32 I live with bread, like you; feel want,
Taste grief, need friends.
(III.2.175–6)
Richard is addressing his followers, Aumerle, Scroop, and the Bishop of Carlisle, following his despairing catalogue of the death of kings (31 above). The passage shows the first promptings of Richard's awareness of his shared humanity, as opposed to his regal status.

33 See, see, King Richard doth himself appear,
As doth the blushing, discontented sun
From out the fiery portal of the east
When he perceives the envious clouds are bent
To dim his glory and to stain the track
Of his bright passage to the occident.
(III.3.62–7)
Bolingbroke is describing Richard's appearance on the walls of Flint Castle. The upper stage of the Elizabethan theatre was undoubtedly used for this effect. Bolingbroke unwittingly uses one of Richard's own comparisons, that of the rising sun of majesty, only this time the redness of the morning sun signifies Richard's anger. Bolingbroke's son, Prince Hal, is later to use a similar image in *Henry IV Part I*, I.2.193–201, to describe his emergence from obscurity into majesty.

34 He is come to open
The purple testament of bleeding war.
(III.3.93–4)
Richard from the walls of Flint Castle is denouncing Bolingbroke's invasion as an act of treason and asserting, somewhat vainly, his own constitutional and divine authority. The term 'testament' carries, appropriately, both legal and religious connotations.

35 O that I were as great
As is my grief, or lesser than my name,
Or that I could forget what I have been,

Or not remember what I must be now!
(III.3.136–9)

At Flint Castle, Northumberland has demanded on Bolingbroke's behalf repeal of the latter's banishment and restoration of his 'lineal royalties' (line 113). Richard is forced to concede; but, as this statement to Aumerle indicates, the action provokes a conflict within him between emotion and public role.

36 What must the King do now? Must he submit?
The King shall do it. Must he be deposed?
The King shall be contented. Must he lose
The name of king? A God's name, let it go.
I'll give my jewels for a set of beads,
My gorgeous palace for a hermitage,
My gay apparel for an almsman's gown,
My figured goblets for a dish of wood,
My sceptre for a palmer's walking-staff,
My subjects for a pair of carvèd saints,
And my large kingdom for a little grave,
A little, little grave, an obscure grave;
Or I'll be buried in the King's highway,
Some way of common trade where subjects' feet
May hourly trample on their sovereign's head,
For on my heart they tread now whilst I live,
And buried once, why not upon my head?
(III.3.143–59)

Richard is anticipating the further demands to be made by Bolingbroke at Flint Castle. Mentally, he is already preparing himself for the transformation of identity that must take place: the crown of kingship is to be exchanged for that of martyrdom, the extent of the realm for the limits of a grave. In choosing the role of the palmer or pilgrim, Richard is now undertaking an imitation of Christ as the Man of Sorrows as opposed to Christ the King, and seeing himself as the suffering servant and victim of his people rather than as their master.

37 Down, down I come like glistering Phaethon,
Wanting the manage of unruly jades.
In the base-court – base-court, where kings grow base
To come at traitors' calls, and do them grace.
In the base-court.
(III.3.178–82)

This image of Richard is enacted physically in the staging of the play as well as serving symbolically the thematic structure. After this speech Richard leaves the upper-stage of the Elizabethan theatre and re-enters the main arena on the same level as

Bolingbroke. His image is also the culmination of the sun imagery used about himself. Phaethon, the son of Apollo, drove his father's sun-chariot so near the earth that Zeus struck him with a thunderbolt to avoid the conflagration of the world. The simile conveys a rash and precipitous fall. Richard, seeing his descent as a degradation, puns on the 'base' of base-court, meaning the lower or outer courtyard of a castle.

38 GARDENER

Go thou, and like an executioner
Cut off the heads of too fast-growing sprays
That look too lofty in our commonwealth.
All must be even in our government.
You thus employed, I will go root away
The noisome weeds which without profit suck
The soil's fertility from wholesome flowers.

FIRST MAN

Why should we, in the compass of a pale,
Keep law and form and due proportion,
Showing as in a model our firm estate,
When our sea-wallèd garden, the whole land,
Is full of weeds, her fairest flowers choked up,
Her fruit trees all unpruned, her hedges ruined,
Her knots disordered, and her wholesome herbs
Swarming with caterpillars?

(III.4.33–47)

The garden scene is a highly emblematic inset into the narrative of *Richard II* which recapitulates the imagery of England as a sea-walled garden, a demi-paradise, which unfortunately has run to seed owing to the gardener's (monarch's) lack of attention (see 16 and 24 above). The Gardener's instruction to the First Man recalls Bolingbroke's execution of Bagot, Bushy, and Green, which is later discussed by the gardeners. The extended comparison between toiling in the garden and maintaining order in society has a wealth of sources, biblical and classical.

39 Thou, old Adam's likeness, set to dress this garden.

(III.4.73)

Queen Isabel, who has overheard the gardeners discussing the probable deposition of Richard, likens the Gardener to Adam, so furthering the comparison of England to Paradise.

40 Here in this place
I'll set a bank of rue, sour herb of grace.
Rue even for ruth here shortly shall be seen

In the remembrance of a weeping Queen.
(III.4.104–7)

The emblematic garden scene concludes in the Gardener's decision to plant a bank of rue in commemoration of Queen Isabel's tears for Richard's plight. The lines are based on complex punning: 'rue' was also called 'herb of grace', but to 'rue' meant to repent and repentance was seen to stem from God's grace. The 'rue' will replace the 'ruth' (pity), symbolized by the Queen's fallen tear, but the medicinal properties of the herb will serve the cause of 'ruth'.

41 Thieves are not judged but they are by to hear
Although apparent guilt be seen in them;
And shall the figure of God's majesty,
His captain, steward, deputy elect,
Anointed, crownèd, planted many years,
Be judged by subject and inferior breath
And he himself not present?
(IV.1.123–9)

York has brought to Bolingbroke the news of Richard's willingness to abdicate in his favour and Bolingbroke has stated his intention to ascend the throne. The Bishop of Carlisle here objects to Richard's deposition taking place in his absence and offers the most explicit statement of the Tudor view of kingship. For his pains, he is arrested by Bolingbroke on a charge of treason.

42 Alack, why am I sent for to a king
Before I have shook off the regal thoughts
Wherewith I reigned? I hardly yet have learned
To insinuate, flatter, bow, and bend my knee.
Give sorrow leave awhile to tutor me
To this submission.
(IV.1.162–7)

Richard has been summoned before Bolingbroke to affect formally his own deposition. Throughout the deposition scene, he is in search of a new identity to replace the lost role of king.

43 Here, cousin – seize the crown. Here, cousin –
On this side, my hand; and on that side, thine.
Now is this golden crown like a deep well
That owes two buckets, filling one another,
The emptier ever dancing in the air,
The other down, unseen, and full of water.
That bucket down and full of tears am I,

Drinking my griefs whilst you mount up on high.
(IV.1.181–8)

Richard's speech, and the gesture determined by it, is an example of this play's use at key moments of ritualized action and symbolic properties. Richard uses the crown, symbol of kingship, to convey the pattern of his fall and Bolingbroke's rise. The movement of the buckets in the well is an inversion of that of the scales of the balance employed by the Gardener in III.4.84–9. Richard here depicts himself weighed down by grief.

44 You may my glories and my state depose,
But not my griefs. Still am I king of those.
(IV.1.191–2)

Richard is explaining to Bolingbroke that, while he may dispossess him of the status of kingship, he cannot relieve him of the griefs occasioned by his loss of the crown. The emphasis on his grief throughout the deposition scene portrays him as a man of sorrows and prepares his martyrdom.

45 Now mark me how I will undo myself.
I give this heavy weight from off my head,
And this unwieldy sceptre from my hand,
The pride of kingly sway from out my heart.
With mine own tears I wash away my balm,
With mine own hands I give away my crown,
With mine own tongue deny my sacred state,
With mine own breath release all duteous oaths.
(IV.1.202–9)

Richard effectively resolves for Bolingbroke the thorny constitutional and theological issue of the right to depose a king by 'undoing' himself. He enacts a ritual scene of deposition, acting the traitor to himself.

46 Though some of you – with Pilate – wash your hands,
Showing an outward pity, yet you Pilates
Have here delivered me to my sour cross,
And water cannot wash away your sin.
. . .
Mine eyes are full of tears. I cannot see.
And yet salt water blinds them not so much
But they can see a sort of traitors here.
Nay, if I turn mine eyes upon myself
I find myself a traitor with the rest.
(IV.1.238–41, 243–7)

Richard is responding to Northumberland's demand, made on behalf of Bolingbroke and the other peers, that Richard read out and confess his crimes against the nation. His diction again depicts him as the martyred Christ, although he ultimately acknowledges his own act of treachery and rebellion against himself.

47 A brittle glory shineth in this face.
As brittle as the glory is the face.
(IV.1.286–7)
In his search for an identity after his deposition, Richard has asked that a looking-glass be brought that he may examine his face stripped of royal authority. He has refused to read the list of his crimes against the nation, instead referring to himself as 'the very book indeed / Where all my sins are writ' (lines 273–4). The mirror is an equivocal symbol indicating both Richard's former vanity and his present search for and confrontation of the truth. Immediately after these lines, he shatters the mirror in a hundred pieces in a ritual act of self-destruction.

48 The shadow of your sorrow hath destroyed
The shadow of your face.
(IV.1.291–2)
On shattering the mirror, Richard warns Bolingbroke to note how quickly sorrow has destroyed his face. Bolingbroke's reply insinuates that Richard's action has been yet another rhetorical gesture by playing on the word 'shadow'. The suggestion is that the shadow cast by Richard's sorrow has only destroyed an unreal image of Richard's face and identity, not the true substance. The lines could be seen to rebound ironically on the speaker.

49 Learn, good soul,
To think our former state a happy dream,
From which awaked the truth of what we are
Shows us but this. I am sworn brother, sweet,
To grim Necessity, and he and I
Will keep a league till death.
(V.1.17–22)
Richard is being led under guard to the Tower of London. Queen Isabel has placed herself along the route to obtain a last meeting. Richard instructs the Queen to perceive the truth of their situation and to acknowledge the illusion under which they previously lived. 'But this' means the fact that it was just a dream. Richard uses the chivalric image of a 'sworn brother' to stress the conscious and courageous acceptance of his destiny.

50 In winter's tedious nights sit by the fire
With good old folks, and let them tell thee tales

Of woeful ages long ago betid;
And ere thou bid goodnight, to quite their griefs
Tell thou the lamentable tale of me,
And send the hearers weeping to their beds.
(V.1.40–5)

In his last meeting with his queen, Richard advises her to take refuge in France. The memory that he wishes her to retain of him shows his tendency towards self-pity and towards dramatizing his existence. The passage also illustrates Shakespeare's own consciousness of his narrative and dramatic art.

51 Northumberland, thou ladder wherewithal
The mounting Bolingbroke ascends my throne,
The time shall not be many hours of age
More than it is ere foul sin, gathering head,
Shall break into corruption.
(V.1.55–9)

Northumberland has interrupted the last meeting of Richard and Queen Isabel with the news that Richard is to be taken to Pomfret (Pontefract) and that the Queen must flee to France. Richard denounces him, prophesying the conflicts that will ensue between Northumberland and Bolingbroke and which, in fact, constitute the basis of *Henry IV Parts 1 and 2.*

52 As in a theatre the eyes of men,
After a well graced actor leaves the stage,
Are idly bent on him that enters next,
Thinking his prattle to be tedious:
Even so, or with much more contempt, men's eyes
Did scowl on gentle Richard.
(V.2.23–8)

The Duke of York is recounting to the Duchess the entry into London of the triumphant Bolingbroke and the humiliated Richard. The image draws attention to the theatrical nature of kingship and public life and, at the same time, to Shakespeare's consciousness of his dramatic art.

53 I have been studying how I may compare
This prison where I live unto the world;
And for because the world is populous,
And here is not a creature but myself,
I cannot do it. Yet I'll hammer it out.
My brain I'll prove the female to my soul,
My soul the father, and these two beget
A generation of still-breeding thoughts,

And these same thoughts people this little world.
(V.5.1–9)

Richard's long soliloquy at the opening of this scene, set in a prison at Pomfret (Pontefract) Castle, conveys a new maturity in Richard's thought and expression through its imagery, syntax, and rhythm. The direct, though no less dramatic, style here, reproducing the natural movements of human thought, is in marked contrast to Richard's formal rhetoric earlier in the play. Richard is peopling the microcosm (or little world) of the prison with thoughts so that it corresponds to the macrocosm in order that he may reason out his identity within that world.

54 Thus play I in one person many people,
And none contented. Sometimes am I king.
Then treasons make me wish myself a beggar;
And so I am. Then crushing penury
Persuades me I was better when a king.
Then am I kinged again; and by and by
Think that I am unkinged by Bolingbroke,
And straight am nothing.
(V.5.31–8)

In prison Richard's mind oscillates between being all things and being nothing. In his search for identity, his mind inhabits the 'people' (thoughts or possibilities) that his mind has generated in order to populate the prison. The formulation and order of the thoughts suggests a mind in turmoil, endlessly rotating upon itself, with the only escape annihilation.

55 How sour sweet music is
When time is broke, and no proportion kept.
So is it in the music of men's lives.
(V.5.42–4)

Richard is in prison at Pomfret (Pontefract) Castle. He can hear music being played, whose time and harmony according to Renaissance beliefs of Platonic origin were, ideally, analogous to the order and harmony of the well-tempered soul. In this case, the music is out of time, so reminding Richard of the disorder he permitted in himself and in his state.

56 I wasted time, and now doth time waste me;
For now hath time made me his numbering clock.
My thoughts are minutes, and with sighs they jar
Their watches on unto mine eyes, the outward watch
Whereto my finger, like a dial's point,
Is pointing still in cleansing them from tears.
Now, sir, the sound that tells what hour it is

Are clamorous groans which strike upon my heart,
Which is the bell. So sighs, and tears, and groans
Show minutes, times, and hours. But my time
Runs posting on in Bolingbroke's proud joy,
While I stand fooling here, his jack of the clock.
(V.5.49–60)

Richard's prison contemplation of the analogy between badly played music and the disorder of his government leads naturally (through the notion of 'time' in music) to a consideration of his neglect of the passage of time. The image transforms him into a mechanical clock, and finally its mannikin that stikes the hours, recording the passing of his meaningless existence in the context of Bolingbroke's rise to power.

57 Mount, mount, my soul. Thy seat is up on high,
Whilst my gross flesh sinks downward here to die.
(V.5.111–12)

Richard's material descent in the play has been paralleled by a spiritual ascent: as he has declined as a king, he has risen as a man. His last lines in the play, uttered at the moment of his murder in a prison of Pomfret (Pontefract) Castle by Sir Piers of Exton, mark the release of his spirit.

58 With Cain go wander thorough shades of night,
And never show thy head by day nor light.
(V.6.43–4)

Sir Piers of Exton has brought the body of King Richard, whom he has murdered in prison, before Bolingbroke, now Henry IV. Exton had committed the murder in hope of favour, on the basis of a remark of Bolingbroke wishing relief from the 'living fear' that Richard constituted. Bolingbroke's reaction to the killing is to condemn it and to exile Exton as a primal murderer. Since the final scene also contains news of a rebellion, there is no sense of the dawn of a new order.

Richard III

1 Now is the winter of our discontent
Made glorious summer by this sun of York,
And all the clouds that loured upon our house
In the deep bosom of the ocean buried.
(I.1.1–4)

The play opens with Richard's brother Edward IV apparently secure on the throne of England. In the opening speech Richard soliloquizes about his family's change of fortune, punning on 'sun', which was also a Yorkist emblem, and son – Richard, Edward, and the Duke of Clarence were the sons of the Duke of York. 'Loured' means looked threateningly; 'house' means family.

2 Grim-visaged war hath smoothed his wrinkled front,
And now, instead of mounting barbèd steeds
To fright the souls of fearful adversaries,
He capers nimbly in a lady's chamber
To the lascivious pleasing of a lute.
But I, that am not shaped for sportive tricks
Nor made to court an amorous looking-glass;
I, that am rudely stamped, and want love's majesty
To strut before a wanton ambling nymph;
I, that am curtailed of this fair proportion,
Cheated of feature by dissembling Nature,
Deformed, unfinished, sent before my time
Into this breathing world, scarce half made up,
And that so lamely and unfashionable
That dogs bark at me as I halt by them –
Why I, in this weak piping time of peace,
Have no delight to pass away the time,
Unless to spy my shadow in the sun
And descant on mine own deformity.
And therefore, since I cannot prove a lover
To entertain these fair well-spoken days,
I am determined to prove a villain
And hate the idle pleasures of these days.
(I.1.9–31)

Richard continues to soliloquize about the political situation which gives him little scope for his talents. Although Shakespeare stresses Richard's physical and spiritual deformity throughout the play, the historical Richard appears to have been an able administrator, of good moral character and scarcely physically deformed. Shakespeare was writing during the reign of the last monarch descended from the Duke of Richmond who defeated Richard and succeeded him as Henry VII, so it is not surprising that he follows his chronicle sources in emphasizing Richard's bad points, drawing also on the Vice character from the medieval Morality plays and the more recent figure of the Machiavellian villain to complete the picture. 'Wrinkled front' means frowning face; 'barbèd' means armoured; 'lascivious pleasing' means pleasingly lascivious music; 'rudely stamped' means badly moulded; 'feature' means bodily shape; 'lamely' means imperfectly, presum ably with a reference to Richard's lameness; 'halt' means limp; 'piping time of peace' means that the characteristic sounds of peace are unmartial music and women's and children's high voices; 'descant' means comment, continuing the musical references; 'am determined' means have decided; 'idle' means frivolous.

3 Simple plain Clarence, I do love thee so
That I will shortly send thy soul to heaven,
If heaven will take the present at our hands.
(I.1.118–20)
Richard, alone, addresses his brother the Duke of Clarence, who has been committed to the Tower of London as a result of Richard's machinations. Clarence is simple and plain because he has not realized that Richard is responsible for his disgrace.

4 God take King Edward to His mercy
And leave the world for me to bustle in!
(I.1.151–2)
Richard's characteristic response to the news of Edward's illness is spoken when he is alone on stage. Like so many of Richard's speeches, its effect is to privilege the audience over the other characters, who do not have similar access to his motivations, thereby almost enlisting them as his accomplices.

5 No beast so fierce but knows some touch of pity.
(I.2.71)
Lady Anne, the widow of Henry VI's son Edward, Prince of Wales, has been stopped by Richard as she takes Henry's corpse to be buried. She sees Richard as worse than a beast because of his many crimes, which include murdering her husband and father-in-law.

6 Teach not thy lip such scorn; for it was made
For kissing, lady, not for such contempt.
(I.2.171–2)
Richard is attempting to woo Lady Anne. Her scornful look presumably stems from her dislike of the man who murdered her husband and father-in-law.

7 Was ever woman in this humour wooed?
Was ever woman in this humour won?
(I.2.227–8)
Richard comments to the audience on the lack of logic in Lady Anne's acceptance of his advances despite his previous dealings

with her family, which include murdering her husband and father-in-law.

8 Cannot a plain man live and think no harm,
But thus his simple truth must be abused
With silken, sly, insinuating Jacks?
(I.3.51–3)
Richard, playing the part of a plain-speaking man, enters with his ally Lord Hastings, voicing a complaint aimed at annoying Queen Elizabeth (Edward's wife) and her family, whom he persists in regarding as low-born upstarts. Jack, which also means knave, was a generic name given to men of low social status.

9 The world is grown so bad
That wrens make prey where eagles dare not perch.
Since every Jack became a gentleman
There's many a gentle person made a Jack.
(I.3.69–72)
Richard continues with his complaint about the Queen and her family, whom he regards as being low down the pecking order – wrens and jacks rather than eagles and gentlemen. He argues that their elevation has led to the degradation of their social betters.

10 Poor painted queen, vain flourish of my fortune!
Why strew'st thou sugar on that bottled spider
Whose deadly web ensnareth thee about?
(I.3.240–2)
Queen Margaret, widow of Henry VI, has been cursing Queen Elizabeth and Richard who, despite their mutual animosity, have united against her insults. She regards herself as the true Queen and Elizabeth as a fake ('painted') and an empty show ('vain flourish'). She refers to the belief that animals can be caught by putting salt on their tails when she asks rhetorically why Elizabeth is encouraging Richard by strewing sugar on him. Richard is seen as swollen ('bottled') because of his hunchback, and as a spider because spiders were believed to be poisonous.

11 And thus I clothe my naked villainy
With odd old ends stolen forth of Holy Writ,
And seem a saint, when most I play the devil.
(I.3.335–7)
Richard again confides his working methods to the audience (compare *Merchant of Venice* 21).

12 O, I have passed a miserable night,
So full of fearful dreams, of ugly sights,

That, as I am a Christian faithful man,
I would not spend another such a night
Though 'twere to buy a world of happy days,
So full of dismal terror was the time.
(I.4.2–7)

The Duke of Clarence confides in the Keeper of the Tower of London, in which he is a prisoner.

13 O Lord! Methought what pain it was to drown!
What dreadful noise of waters in mine ears!
What sights of ugly death within mine eyes!
Methoughts I saw a thousand fearful wracks;
A thousand men that fishes gnawed upon;
Wedges of gold, great anchors, heaps of pearl,
Inestimable stones, unvalued jewels,
All scattered in the bottom of the sea.
Some lay in dead men's skulls, and in the holes
Where eyes did once inhabit, there were crept,
As 'twere in scorn of eyes, reflecting gems,
That wooed the slimy bottom of the deep
And mocked the dead bones that lay scattered by.
(I.4.21–33)

Clarence tells his dream to the Keeper of the Tower of London. It is ironically prophetic of his forthcoming fate of being drowned in a butt of Malmsey wine. 'Wracks' are wrecks; 'invalued' means priceless.

14 Clarence is come – false, fleeting, perjured Clarence.
(I.4.55)

In Clarence's dream, which he is telling to the Keeper of the Tower of London, he arrives in the underworld where he is greeted with these words by the ghost of Edward, Prince of Wales. According to Shakespeare, Clarence (who was Edward's brother-in-law and fought on both sides in the Wars of the Roses), Edward IV, and Richard murdered Edward, Prince of Wales, after the Battle of Tewkesbury.

15 Faith, some certain dregs of conscience are yet within me.... I'll not meddle with it; it makes a man a coward. A man cannot steal, but it accuseth him; a man cannot swear, but it checks him; a man cannot lie with his neighbour's wife, but it detects him. 'Tis a blushing shamefaced spirit that mutinies in a man's bosom. It fills a man full of obstacles. It made me once restore a purse of gold that by chance I found. It begd cities gars any man that keeps it. It is turned out of towns and

for a dangerous thing, and every man that means to live well endeavours to trust to himself and live without it.
(I.4.122–3, 136–46)
The Second Murderer, one of two sent by Richard to murder Clarence, has been afflicted with a sudden unexpected and unwelcome attack of conscience. In a grimly ironic discussion with the other murderer he manages to put it aside. Richard himself suffers a similar attack just before the Battle of Bosworth at the end of the play (see 41, 42, 45). To 'live well' is to enjoy life or, to the contrary, to live a properly moral life.

16 I do not know that Englishman alive
With whom my soul is any jot at odds
More than the infant that is born tonight.
I thank my God for my humility!
(II.1.71–4)
Richard enjoys himself in fake bonhomie with the assembled court, knowing that their ignorance of Clarence's death will soon give him an opportunity to destroy the putatively reconciliatory atmosphere. Presumably the irony of the last line is apparent only to the audience.

17 Some tardy cripple bare the countermand,
That came too lag to see him buried.
(II.1.91–2)
Richard offers his false explanation of how Clarence came to be killed despite the King's reprieve. Audiences, but not the assembled court, are presumably meant to apply the cripple reference ironically to Richard himself. 'Lag' means late.

18 Woe to that land that's governed by a child!
(II.3.11)
In a choric scene in which three citizens discuss Edward IV's death and the succession of the young Edward V, the Third Citizen voices the proverbial and well-founded distrust of rule by minors and their guardians.

19 You are too senseless-obstinate, my lord,
Too ceremonious and traditional.
(III.1.44–5)
Alarmed at the prospect of Richard seizing power, Queen Elizabeth (Edward V's mother) has taken sanctuary with her younger son Richard, Duke of York. Here the Duke of Buckingham, one of Richard's allies, argues with Cardinal Bourchier that he is being too old-fashioned in his attitudes to sanctuary: sanctuary was

given to criminals, therefore it cannot be extended to the innocent! 'Ceremonious' means scrupulous about legal niceties.

20 So wise so young, they say, do never live long.
(III.1.79)
Richard's sardonic aside on the childish wisdom of Edward V anticipates his subsequent murder in the Tower of London.

21 Thus, like the formal Vice, Iniquity,
I moralize two meanings in one word.
(III.1.82–3)
Richard comments on the way that he has converted his aside (see 20) into an accessible public statement. The 'formal Vice, Iniquity', is the stock Vice character of the medieval Morality plays. 'I moralize two meanings in one word' means I interpret the hidden meaning of a phrase.

22 Short summers lightly have a forward spring.
(III.1.94)
Richard again offers an ironic aside on the boy King's wisdom in anticipation of his forthcoming death. 'Forward' means early and precocious.

23 My Lord of Ely, when I was last in Holborn
I saw good strawberries in your garden there.
I do beseech you send for some of them.
(III.4.31–3)
Richard makes this request at a Council meeting. It appears to be a deliberately irrelevant comment made to avoid saying anything about his coronation. Later in the play the Bishop of Ely is a foe of Richard's.

24 I think there's never a man in Christendom
Can lesser hide his love or hate than he,
For by his face straight shall you know his heart.
(III.4.51–3)
Hastings, who is about to be denounced and executed without trial by Richard, is spectacularly wrong in his assessment of the relationship between Richard's outward appearance and his inner motives.

25 Talk'st thou to me of ifs? Thou art a traitor.
Off with his head! Now by Saint Paul I swear
I will not dine until I see the same!
(III.4.75–7)

Richard is swift to remove Hastings, who has reacted conditionally to his sweeping condemnation of Queen Elizabeth and Jane Shore for conspiring against him.

26 I can counterfeit the deep tragedian.
(III.5.5)
Richard and Buckingham are about to try to convince the Lord Mayor of London that Hastings was a traitor. Buckingham assures Richard that he can play his part well.

27 Here's a good world the while! Who is so gross
That cannot see this palpable device?
Yet who's so bold but says he sees it not?
Bad is the world, and all will come to naught
When such ill dealing must be seen in thought.
(III.6.10–14)
The Scrivener (professional scribe) who prepared the indictment of Hastings tells the audience that it was all done while Hastings was still at liberty. 'The while' means now; 'gross' means stupid.

28 LORD MAYOR
See where his grace stands, 'tween two clergymen.
BUCKINGHAM
Two props of virtue for a Christian prince,
To stay him from the fall of vanity;
And see, a book of prayer in his hand –
True ornaments to know a holy man.
(III.7.94–8)
As part of their careful stage management of a scene in which Richard is to be pressured into taking the crown by Buckingham and the Lord Mayor, Buckingham and Richard have arranged for him to appear in suitably pious guise.

29 O, do not swear, my lord of Buckingham.
(III.7.219)
As part of the game designed to impress the Lord Mayor, Richard has refused the crown and Buckingham has stormed off swearing. Richard's improbably pious sentiment is, of course, part of the act.

30 Pity, you ancient stones, those tender babes
Whom envy hath immured within your walls –
Rough cradle for such little pretty ones!
Rude ragged nurse, old sullen playfellow
For tender princes – use my babies well!

So foolish sorrow bids your stones farewell.
(IV.1.98–103)
Queen Elizabeth addresses the Tower of London, in which her children, the young Edward V and his brother the young Duke of York, have been imprisoned ('immured') by Richard.

31 Uncertain way of gain! But I am in
So far in blood that sin will pluck on sin.
Tear-falling pity dwells not in this eye.
(IV.2.62–4)
Richard tells the audience his latest plans, which are hazardous because they involve murdering his nephews (Edward V and the Duke of York) and his wife Anne and then marrying his niece.

32 I am not in the giving vein today.
(IV.2.115)
Richard, who has fallen out with Buckingham over the murder of Edward V and the Duke of York, shows his displeasure by refusing to honour him with the previously promised earldom of Hereford. 'Vein' means mood.

33 The sons of Edward sleep in Abraham's bosom.
(IV.3.38)
Richard reviews the progress of his plans with the audience. Although some modern historians have questioned whether Richard was responsible for the murder of the princes in the Tower, the general view remains that the person who had most to gain from their deaths was the person most likely to have arranged them. 'Abraham's bosom' is heaven.

34 Thou cam'st on earth to make the earth my hell.
A grievous burden was thy birth to me;
Tetchy and wayward was thy infancy;
Thy schooldays frightful, desperate, wild, and furious;
Thy prime of manhood daring, bold, and venturous;
Thy age confirmed, proud, subtle, sly, and bloody,
More mild, but yet more harmful – kind in hatred.
What comfortable hour canst thou name
That ever graced me with thy company?
(IV.4.167–75)
The Duchess of York denounces her son Richard to his face, enhancing the audience's sense of his unnaturalness since a mother would normally be expected to be biased in favour of her child. 'Prime of manhood' means early manhood; 'age' means maturity.

35 An honest tale speeds best being plainly told.
(IV.4.358)
Queen Elizabeth replies to Richard's request that she should help to woo her daughter on his behalf. Since Richard is the girl's uncle, one presumes that Elizabeth is using the term 'honest' ironically.

36 Harp not on that string, madam; that is past.
(IV.4.364)
As part of his attempt to enlist Queen Elizabeth's help in wooing her daughter (who is, of course, his niece) Richard briskly suggests that she should forget that she has already murdered her other two children, the princes in the Tower.

37 Out on you, owls! Nothing but songs of death?
(IV.4.507)
Richard is angry with the stream of messengers bringing bad news, although the one who takes the brunt of this outburst actually has good news when he is eventually allowed to speak. 'Out on you' is an expletive; the owl was traditionally associated with death.

38 CATESBY My liege, the Duke of Buckingham is taken.
[RICHARD Off with his head! So much for Buckingham.]
(IV.4.531)
The line following the news of Buckingham's capture is probably the most famous addition to Shakespeare in the many reworkings of his plays that held the stage in the eighteenth and nineteenth centuries. It first appeared in the actor-playwright Colley Cibber's adaptation, first performed at Drury Lane in 1700, and it still sometimes appears in modern productions of Shakespeare's play; perhaps the most famous example is Laurence Olivier's film version of 1955.

39 True hope is swift and flies with swallow's wings;
Kings it makes gods, and meaner creatures kings.
(V.2.23–4)
The Duke of Richmond, the future Henry VII, who has arrived in England to try to overthrow Richard, injects a note of health and hopefulness into the grim political situation.

40 Besides, the King's name is a tower of strength,
Which they upon the adverse faction want.
(V.3.12–13)
Richard bolsters himself and his forces with an assertion of the power of the name of king. Presumably Richard has conveniently

forgotten all those other kings whose title ('name') had not helped them, going back to Richard II whose weakness and deposition were the ultimate cause of the Wars of the Roses. 'Want' means both lack and desire.

41 Give me another horse! Bind up my wounds!
Have mercy, Jesu! – Soft! I did but dream.
O coward conscience, how dost thou afflict me!
(V.3.178–80)
Before the Battle of Bosworth, Richard is visited in his sleep by the ghosts of those he has killed. He anticipates his fate in the dream from which he wakes in the course of this speech.

42 My conscience hath a thousand several tongues,
And every tongue brings in a several tale,
And every tale condemns me for a villain.
(V.3.194–6)
After waking from his dream on the night before the Battle of Bosworth, Richard muses on the enormity of his crimes and his unexpected attack of conscience. 'Several' means different.

43 I shall despair. There is no creature loves me;
And if I die, no soul will pity me.
Nay, wherefore should they, since that I myself
Find in myself no pity to myself?
(V.3.201–4)
Richard continues to sound the depths of his conscience before the Battle of Bosworth.

44 By the apostle Paul, shadows tonight
Have struck more terror to the soul of Richard
Than can the substance of ten thousand soldiers
Armèd in proof and led by shallow Richmond.
(V.3.217–20)
Richard confesses to his follower Sir Richard Ratcliffe that ghosts and dreams (both suggested by 'shadows') have terrified him more than the reality ('substance') of the heavily armoured ('Armèd in proof') army of the lightweight ('shallow') Richmond.

45 Conscience is but a word that cowards use,
Devised at first to keep the strong in awe.
(V.3.310–11)
In an aside before the battle, Richard rejects the claims of conscience in terms that recall the Second Murderer (see 15).

46 If we be conquered, let men conquer us,
And not these bastard Britains, whom our fathers
Have in their own land beaten, bobbed, and thumped.
(V.3.333–5)
In his address to his army before the Battle of Bosworth, Richard denigrates Richmond's army as foreigners – 'Britains' means Bretons.

47 A horse! A horse! My kingdom for a horse!
(V.4.7)
In the course of battle Richard has been unhorsed and cries out for another one. There is probably also the sense that his kingdom will be lost for want of a horse.

48 Slave, I have set my life upon a cast,
And I will stand the hazard of the die.
(V.4.9–10)
Richard rejects an offer from his follower Sir William Catesby to help him to a horse. He has staked his life on a throw ('cast') of the dice ('die' is the correct singular form of dice) and he will await the outcome.

49 The day is ours; the bloody dog is dead.
(V.5.2)
The victorious Richmond dismisses Richard, who has been compared throughout the play to various unsavoury animals, as a mad dog.

Romeo and Juliet

1 From forth the fatal loins of these two foes
A pair of star-crossed lovers take their life.
(Prologue, 5–6)
The prologue, spoken by the figure of Chorus, constitutes a sonnet, in keeping with the courtly love traditions of the play's subject matter and the linguistic formality of their expression. The sonnet is a fourteen-line poem, believed to be of Arabic origin, which was made popular in Western Europe by the Provençal lyric poets of the Middle Ages and by the Tuscan poets of the fourteenth century, above all by Francesco Petrarca (1304–74) or Petrarch as he became known to the English. Here the sonnet presents the argument of the play and the thematic opposition of love and strife. The 'two foes' are the opposing

Verona families of Montague and Capulet, while 'star-crossed' suggests the enmity of fate.

2 The fearful passage of their death-marked love
And the continuance of their parents' rage,
Which, but their children's end, naught could remove,
Is now the two hours' traffic of our stage.
(Prologue, 9–12)
The third quatrain of Chorus's sonnet outlines the narrative of the action to follow and conveys a sense of tragic awe for the impending doom of the protagonists. The reference to the 'two hours' traffic of our stage' has given rise to much unresolved debate by theatre historians concerning the timing and conditions of performance in the Elizabethan theatre, since modern productions clearly take considerably longer.

3 I do not bite my thumb at you, sir. But I bite my thumb, sir.
(I.1.49–50)
The reply of Sampson, a retainer of the house of Capulet, to the challenge of Abram, a serving-man of the Montagues ('Do you bite your thumb at us, sir?'), is representative of the opening scene, which depicts the conflict of the two great households at the level of their servants. The gesture of inserting the thumb into the mouth, and possibly making a noise by jerking it out with the nail against the upper teeth, was one of defiance.

4 TYBALT
What, art thou drawn among these heartless hinds?
Turn thee, Benvolio, look upon thy death.
BENVOLIO
I do but keep the peace. Put up thy sword.
(I.1.65–7)
These are the first words in the play of the 'fiery' Tybalt, addressed to Benvolio, whom he has found intervening between the fighting servants of the houses of Montague and Capulet. They establish Tybalt, the nephew of Lady Capulet and cousin of Juliet, as both a violent and witty figure, since 'heartless hinds' is a pun suggesting both cowardly inferiors and female deer lacking a hart to protect them. Tybalt is contrasted here with Benvolio, nephew of Montague and cousin of Romeo, who – as his name indicates – is well-meaning.

5 Here's much to-do with hate, but more with love.
Why then, O brawling love, O loving hate,
O anything, of nothing first create!
(I.1.175–7)

Romeo's expression of his love melancholy, caused by his frustrated passion for the Capulet maiden, Rosaline, and confided to his cousin Benvolio, anticipates the greater conflict that his love for Juliet, Capulet's daughter, will provoke. Romeo is son and heir to Montague, head of the rival family. The final line is an inversion of the Latin tag *ex nihilo nihil fit* (nothing can be created of nothing).

6 She will not stay the siege of loving terms
Nor bide th'encounter of assailing eyes,
Nor ope her lap to saint-seducing gold.
(I.1.212–14)

Romeo's description of Rosaline, his beloved, to Benvolio characterizes her as the chaste and disdainful mistress of Petrarchan sonnets. The third line refers to Jupiter's sexual possession of Danaë in the form of a shower of gold, so transforming an image of incorruptibility into an erotic one. The language of *Romeo and Juliet* owes a great debt to the diction and imagery of various traditions of European love poetry which England's late Renaissance made popular in the 1580s and early 1590s.

7 'Tis not hard, I think,
For men so old as we to keep the peace.
(I.2.2–3)

Old Capulet's comment to his kinsman Paris, the suitor of Juliet, follows an injunction of Prince Escalus that the two families should keep the peace in Verona. The Prince had summoned the two heads of household to hear his sentence when he had interrupted the brawl in I.1. The saying has become a byword for older statesmen.

8 PARIS
Younger than she are happy mothers made.
CAPULET
And too soon marred are those so early made.
(I.2.12–13)

The exchange of Capulet and Paris, Juliet's suitor, concerns the readiness of Juliet for marriage. Capulet has just indicated that Juliet is not yet fourteen. In fact, Shakespeare emphasized Juliet's youth, for in the two principal sources, the Italian prose narrative by Matteo Bandello and Arthur Brooke's moralistic poem of 1562, she was eighteen and sixteen respectively. Capulet's line could be based on a proverbial saying, since Puttenham in *The Arte of English Poesie (1589)* employs a similar phrase.

9 O, then I see Queen Mab hath been with you.
She is the fairies' midwife, and she comes
In shape no bigger than an agate stone
On the forefinger of an alderman,
Drawn with a team of little atomies
Over men's noses as they lie asleep...

And in this state she gallops night by night
Through lovers' brains, and then they dream of love;
O'er courtiers' knees, that dream on curtsies straight;
O'er lawyers' fingers, who straight dream on fees;
O'er ladies' lips, who straight on kisses dream,
Which oft the angry Mab with blisters plagues,
Because their breaths with sweetmeats tainted are.
Sometime she gallops o'er the courtier's nose,
And then dreams he of smelling out a suit.
And sometime comes she with a tithe-pig's tail
Tickling a parson's nose as 'a lies asleep;
Then he dreams of another benefice.
Sometimes she driveth o'er a soldier's neck;
And then dreams he of cutting foreign throats,
Of breaches, ambuscados, Spanish blades,
Of healths five fathom deep; and then anon
Drums in his ear, at which he starts and wakes,
And being thus frighted, swears a prayer or two
And sleeps again...

This is the hag, when maids lie on their backs,
That presses them and learns them first to bear,
Making them women of good carriage.
(I.4.53–8, 70–88, 92–4)

This much-anthologized speech of Mercutio, the friend of Romeo, is a response to the latter's confession that he had dreamed the previous night. Mercutio, drawing probably on English folklore and magic, creates the figure of Queen Mab, whose task it is to deliver the dreams and fancies of minds in repose. 'Queen', as the speech reveals, may indicate a hag or low person, for the fairy world to the Elizabethans was a threatening, not a pretty, one. The tone of Mercutio's speech displays his scepticism of the significance attributed to dreams in the Renaissance, since in his vision the dreams that Queen Mab delivers are so appropriate to the dreamers that they appear subconscious desires of these dreamers which lie concealed during waking hours. The speech characterizes Mercutio as a wit and sceptic, for it is full of acute, even cynical, social observation and moves from fantastic mockery of lovers to a deflating, bawdy quibble.

Mercutio, Benvolio, and Romeo are planning to attend the Capulet feast disguised as masquers, where Romeo hopes to see Rosaline. Mercutio is mocking Romeo's love melancholy.

10 For you and I are past our dancing days.
(I.5.32)
Old Capulet makes this remark to an elderly kinsman at the feast being held in his house. Capulet has broached with Juliet the matter of Paris's marriage proposal and instructed her to observe him at the feast in order to ascertain whether she will consent. It is at the feast that Romeo and Juliet first catch sight of one another.

11 O, she doth teach the torches to burn bright!
It seems she hangs upon the cheek of night
As a rich jewel in an Ethiop's ear –
Beauty too rich for use, for earth too dear!
(I.5.44–7)
Romeo's first words on catching sight of Juliet at the Capulet feast end on a note of foreboding, despite the imagery of light with which Juliet is associated throughout the play. Elizabethans used the term 'Ethiop' for any black African. These lines are often quoted with the Second Folio misreading of 'Her beauty'. Romeo's perception is that Juliet's beauty is too exquisite for the everyday world.

12 ROMEO
If I profane with my unworthiest hand
This holy shrine, the gentle sin is this.
My lips, two blushing pilgrims, ready stand
To smooth that rough touch with a tender kiss.
JULIET
Good pilgrim, you do wrong your hand too much,
Which mannerly devotion shows in this.
For saints have hands that pilgrims' hands do touch,
And palm to palm is holy palmers' kiss.
ROMEO
Have not saints lips, and holy palmers too?
JULIET
Ay, pilgrim, lips that they must use in prayer.
ROMEO
O, then, dear saint, let lips do what hands do!
They pray: grant thou, lest faith turn to despair.
JULIET
Saints do not move, though grant for prayers' sake.

ROMEO
Then move not while my prayer's effect I take.
(I.5.93–106)
The first exchange of Romeo and Juliet, at the Capulet feast, is cast appropriately in the form of a sonnet which employs the Petrarchan diction of the religion of love. Francesco Petrarca of Petrarch (1304–74) had made the sonnet the vehicle of the expression of courtly love by the success of his *Canzoniere*, dedicated to his mistress, Laura. Elevation of the mistress to a quasi-divine object of adoration and cultivation of the religion of love were features of the Petrarchan sonnet tradition which swept Europe in the fifteenth and sixteenth centuries. Romeo and Juliet's sonnet culminates in the kiss which Juliet has parried at the end of the second quatrain with a meeting of hands.

13 My only love, sprung from my only hate!
Too early seen unknown, and known too late!
Prodigious birth of love it is to me
That I must love a loathèd enemy.
(I.5.138–41)
Juliet's exclamation is patterned upon the play's thematic opposition of love and hatred. It is made on learning from the Nurse that her masked wooer at the Capulet feast is Romeo, son of her father's enemy, Montague.

14 Now old desire doth in his deathbed lie,
And young affection gapes to be his heir.
(Prologue 2, 1–2)
The Second Prologue, spoken by Chorus, again takes the form of a sonnet. It begins, by means of the impersonal formulation given above, to recount the violent change of Romeo's affection from Rosaline to Juliet.

15 He jests at scars that never felt a wound.
Enter Juliet above
But soft! What light through yonder window breaks?
It is the East, and Juliet is the sun!
(II.2.1–3)
Romeo's first line responds to his companions' bawdy and insensitive mockery of his infatuation. The second and third constitute a comment upon the vision of Juliet who, unaware of Romeo's presence, appears at this moment on the upper stage. The narrative assumes that Romeo has entered the Capulets' orchard in order to catch a glimpse of Juliet; the flexibility of Elizabethan staging permits unbroken movement from Romeo's scene with

his companions to this one with Juliet. The scene is popularly known as the 'balcony scene', but there is no reference to such a structure in it. The First Quarto indicates that Juliet appears at a window.

16 It is my lady. O, it is my love!
O that she knew she were!
(II.2.10–11)
Romeo's words draw attention to the irony of situation in this scene, when he is observing Juliet from the Capulets' orchard. According to the dramatic conventions of the scene, neither character can initially hear the other's statements. In this way, Romeo is to overhear Juliet's declaration of her love for him.

17 See how she leans her cheek upon her hand!
O that I were a glove upon that hand,
That I might touch that cheek!
(II.2.23–5)
Romeo, unseen and unheard, is observing Juliet from the Capulets' orchard. His rather conventional expressions of unsatisfied passion also act as a commentary upon Juliet's expressions and gestures of unrequited love.

18 O Romeo, Romeo! – wherefore art thou Romeo?
Deny thy father and refuse thy name.
Or, if thou wilt not, be but sworn my love,
And I'll no longer be a Capulet.
(II.2.33–6)
Juliet's rebellious statement overthrows social convention in setting personal happiness and sexual and emotional fulfilment above obligations to kin and obedience to patriarchal authority. Identification with the young lovers was no doubt tempered in Shakespeare's day by an awareness of such responsibilities, despite the dramatist's sympathetic portrayal of their characters and situation. Arthur Brooke's poem, *The Tragical History of Romeus and Juliet* of 1562, was a moralistic condemnation of illicit love.

19 What's Montague? It is nor hand nor foot
Nor arm nor face nor any other part
Belonging to a man. O, be some other name!
What's in a name? That which we call a rose
By any other word would smell as sweet.
So Romeo would, were he not Romeo called,
Retain that dear perfection which he owes

Without that title.
(II.2.40–7)
The central lines of Juliet's speech have passed into the language, despite the passage being textually problematic. The reading now normally followed is essentially that of Malone, the eighteenth-century editor of Shakespeare, which preserves good sense and does not violate the text, at the same time as incorporating the readings of the First and Second Quartos. The proverbial saying gives the First Quarto reading of 'name' for 'word' in line 44, since this was included in many older editions of Shakespeare.

20 With love's light wings did I o'erperch these walls.
For stony limits cannot hold love out,
And what love can do, that dares love attempt.
(II.2.66–8)
Romeo's response to Juliet's pragmatic and practical questions concerning his presence in the Capulets' orchard offers only a hyperbolic statement of the all-conquering power of love. The wings of love are those of Cupid; but there is a pun on 'light', which can also mean wanton. Romeo has come to the orchard to catch a glimpse of his beloved and, on overhearing her declaration of love for him, has addressed her.

21 Fain would I dwell on form – fain, fain deny
What I have spoke. But farewell compliment!
(II.2.88–9)
Juliet confesses that it is futile and impossible not to acknowledge the passion that Romeo has overheard her express from his position of hiding in the Capulets' orchard. Juliet has just stated that, were it not for the night, he would see a maiden blush 'bepaint' her cheek. 'Compliment' in this context signifies the formal modesty of speech and behaviour demanded by social convention.

22 At lovers' perjuries,
They say, Jove laughs.
(II.2.92–3)
Juliet's mistrust of the lovers' vows, proffered by Romeo from the orchard, goes back to Ovid's *Art of Love*, I.633. Her line contributes to the sense of inevitable doom surrounding the lovers.

23 O, swear not by the moon, th'inconstant moon,
That monthly changes in her circled orb,
Lest that thy love prove likewise variable.
(II.2.109–11)
Juliet's fear of lovers' oaths is reinforced by their frequent invocation of the moon, which was associated not only with lovers

but also with fickleness and inconstancy. The two connotations of the moon are not unrelated, as Juliet feelingly perceives. The protestations of love have been made by Romeo after he has heard Juliet's secret declaration of love from his position of hiding in the Capulets' orchard.

24 I have no joy of this contract tonight.
It is too rash, too unadvised, too sudden;
Too like the lightning, which doth cease to be
Ere one can say 'It lightens'. Sweet, good night!
This bud of love, by summer's ripening breath,
May prove a beauteous flower when next we meet.
(II.2.117–22)
Romeo and Juliet have just exchanged vows of love, following Romeo's entry into the Capulets' orchard to observe his beloved. Juliet's farewell juxtaposes the promise of love with an awareness that the impetuosity and violence of its passion forbodes ill.

25 My bounty is as boundless as the sea,
My love as deep. The more I give to thee,
The more I have, for both are infinite.
(II.2.133–5)
Juliet's comparison of the extent of her love to the vastness of the ocean is a theme repeated throughout the Shakespearian canon, most notably in the thematic structure of *The Merchant of Venice* and the Romances. 'Bounty' indicates generosity. Juliet is speaking to Romeo after their exchange of lovers' vows.

26 Love goes toward love as schoolboys from their books;
But love from love, toward school with heavy looks.
(II.2.156–7)
Romeo's image, on taking his leave of Juliet after their exchange of vows, is resonant of the youth of the lovers. It is akin to the image of the schoolboy employed by Jaques in the Seven Ages of Man speech in *As You Like It* (see 40).

27 'Tis almost morning. I would have thee gone.
And yet no farther than a wanton's bird,
That lets it hop a little from his hand,
Like a poor prisoner in his twisted gyves,
And with a silken thread plucks it back again,
So loving-jealous of his liberty.
(II.2.176–8)
Juliet is urging Romeo to leave the Capulets' orchard before daybreak to ensure his safety, when she would prefer to retain

his company. Her speech reveals the contrary pulls upon the emotions of the protagonists through the image of a child's treatment of a pet bird. The oxymoron 'loving-jealous' encapsulates the twin emotions within the lover's desire to retain the beloved. 'Gyves' are bonds or fetters.

28 JULIET

Good night, good night! Parting is such sweet sorrow
That I shall say goodnight till it be morrow.
Exit Juliet

ROMEO

Sleep dwell upon thine eyes, peace in thy breast!
Would I were sleep and peace, so sweet to rest!

(II.2.184–7)

The exchange of couplets that marks Romeo and Juliet's parting at the conclusion of this scene after their reciprocal declarations of love constitutes a passage of textual confusion. The Second Quarto divides the second couplet between the two speakers, even though it is a response to the first. The Second Quarto also divides the first line quoted here between the speakers. The first phrase of the second sentence in the first couplet has passed into the language as a proverbial saying.

29 BENVOLIO Why, what is Tybalt!

MERCUTIO More than Prince of Cats, I can tell you. O, he's the courageous captain of compliments. He fights as you sing pricksong: keeps time, distance, and proportion. He rests his minim rests, one, two and the third in your bosom.

(II.4.18–23)

Warburton, an eighteenth-century editor of Shakespeare, explained Mercutio's mystifying reply to Benvolio's question by pointing out that Tybert was the name given to the prince of cats in the medieval stories of *Reynard the Fox*. Mercutio's description of the 'fiery' Tybalt offers a thumb-nail sketch by pursuing a parallel between the arts of singing and fencing. 'Pricksong' was part-harmony or descant, while 'compliments' refers to the rules and formal courtesies of fencing.

30 BENVOLIO Here comes Romeo, here comes Romeo!

MERCUTIO Without his roe, like a dried herring. O flesh, flesh, how art thou fishified!

(II.4.36–8)

Mercutio's witty response to Benvolio's statement is an example of multiple punning. There are possible puns on: (i) the first syllable of 'Romeo', leaving him half a man and possibly with only 'meo' or 'O me', the lament of the unrequited lover; (ii) 'roe' or deer/dear; (iii) the first syllable of Rosaline, whom Mercutio still takes to be Romeo's beloved; and (iv) the milt or sperm of male fish. It is the last and bawdiest meaning which is picked up in the last sentence, where Romeo is mocked for his obsession with sex and his lifeless, melancholy attitude.

31 I am the very pink of courtesy.
(II.4.56)
Mercutio's assessment of himself ironically follows his bawdy raillery of Romeo's love (which Mercutio still takes to be for Rosaline). Romeo has, in fact, come from his meeting with Juliet. 'Pink' indicates an ideal, a perfect example, and the entire phrase has passed into the language, though it is often used with the same self-irony as Mercutio employs.

32 A gentleman, Nurse, that loves to hear himself talk and will speak more in a minute than he will stand to in a month.
(II.4.144–6)
Romeo's evaluation of Mercutio for the Nurse, though it is characterized by gentle irony, possibly concludes in one of the phallic images that the Nurse has observed to be so prominent in Mercutio's speech. The term 'stand' frequently indicated tumescence. The Nurse has come with a message from Juliet for Romeo.

33 Thy head is as full of quarrels as an egg is full of meat; and yet thy head hath been beaten as addle as an egg for quarrelling.
(III.1.21–3)
The key phrase from Mercutio's accusation that Benvolio is as quarrelsome a fellow as any in Italy is an example of the many comic instances that Mercutio cites of Benvolio's temperament. This phrase, in which 'meat' signifies food generally, was proverbial.

34 Men's eyes were made to look, and let them gaze.
I will not budge for no man's pleasure, I.
(III.1.53–4)
Mercutio and Benvolio with men of the house of Montague have encountered Capulets, led by the 'fiery' Tybalt, in the streets of Verona. Mercutio's lines reject the sagacious advice of Benvolio to withdraw, and indicate his intention to brazen out the confrontation with Tybalt.

35 No, 'tis not so deep as a well, nor so wide as a church door.

But 'tis enough. 'Twill serve. Ask for me tomorrow, and you shall find me a grave man.
(III.1.96–8)
Mercutio is referring to the wound he has received when Tybalt struck him under Romeo's arm as the latter attempted to come between them and prevent their fighting. The comment is made in response to Romeo's remark of consolation that the hurt cannot be serious. The formulation of Mercutio's reply, including the pun on 'grave', is typical of Mercutio's cynical humour, which stays with him even to the point of death.

36 A plague a'both your houses!
They have made worms' meat of me.
(III.1.106–7)
This is the third utterance of Mercutio's curse upon the houses of Montague and Capulet within the space of twenty lines, the first time being when he realizes he has been fatally wounded by Tybalt. Mercutio, a friend of the house of Montague, received the fatal wound as Romeo attempted to intervene in his fight with Tybalt. The phrase has passed into the language as an expression of frustration when an individual finds himself the victim of two contending parties.

37 O, I am fortune's fool!
(III.1.136)
Romeo's realization that he is the plaything of fortune occurs after he has killed Tybalt in a swordfight, following the news of Mercutio's death at Tybalt's hands. He has thus killed the kinsman of Juliet, whom he has just married in secret, and so exacerbated the feud between the two families. In the immediate context, Benvolio has just informed Romeo that the citizens of Verona have been alerted to the strife and that, if he is taken, Prince Escalus is certain to condemn him to death. The situation leads to Romeo's exile and the consequent tragic circumstances.

38 Gallop apace, you fiery-footed steeds,
Towards Phoebus' lodging! Such a waggoner
As Phaëton would whip you to the West
And bring in cloudy night immediately.
Spread thy close curtain, love-performing night,
That runaway's eyes may wink and Romeo
Leap to these arms untalked of and unseen.
Lovers can see to do their amorous rites
By their own beauties; or, if love be blind,
It best agrees with night. Come, civil night,
Thou sober-suited matron, all in black,

And learn me how to lose a winning match,
Played for a pair of stainless maidenhoods.
(III.2.1–13)

Juliet is awaiting the arrival of Romeo by night to consummate their secret marriage. Her invocation to night is a masterpiece of erotic poetry in the tradition of the Latin poet of love, Ovid. By means of personifications drawn from classical mythology, she describes the passage of the sun to the West and the arrival of night. But Shakespeare adds to the erotic associations of night a sense of tragic foreboding presaged in the figure of Phaeton, the reckless and tragic charioteer of the sun. 'Runaway's' in the sixth line constitutes a famous Shakespearian crux which has eluded complete explanation. It would seem to refer most naturally to the sun and to Phaeton, whose chariot careered out of control. It has been taken also to refer to night, to Romeo, and even to Cupid, who was depicted as a runaway. The paradox of 'lose a winning match' conveys that Juliet will gain her love by yielding herself to him.

39 Come, night. Come, Romeo. Come, thou day in night;
For thou wilt lie upon the wings of night
Whiter than new snow upon a raven's back.
Come, gentle night. Come, loving, black-browed night.
Give me my Romeo. And when I shall die,
Take him and cut him out in little stars,
And he will make the face of heaven so fine
That all the world will be in love with night
And pay no worship to the garish sun.
O I have bought the manion of a love,
But not possessed it; and though I am sold,
Not yet enjoyed.
(III.2.17–28)

Juliet is awaiting the arrival of Romeo by night to consummate their secret marriage. Her anticipation of his possession of her exploits the term 'die' to suggest orgasm and sexual ecstasy. This usage was a commonplace of the erotic poetry of the period. She envisages Romeo's 'death' as the apotheosis of her lover, in a manner comparable to the climax of Ovid's *Metamorphoses.* The auditor/reader cannot, however, be unaware of the tragic import of the death imagery and the passage further cements the thematic bonding of love with death.

40 Affliction is enamoured of thy parts,
And thou art wedded to calamity.
(III.3.2–3)

Friar Laurence is speaking to Romeo at his cell, where Romeo has taken refuge following his murder of Tybalt. It is ironic that the Friar's statement that Romeo seems marked out for misfortune should unwittingly play on the ideas of love and matrimony, so reinforcing the inevitable linking of love and destruction in the play.

41 Thou cuttest my head off with a golden axe
And smilest upon the stroke that murders me.
(III.3.22–3)
Romeo has just learned from Friar Laurence, at whose cell he has taken refuge following the murder of Tybalt, that the Prince's sentence for his crime is exile from Verona, not death. Romeo equates exile with death, because he will be separated from Juliet – his source of life. The essence of Romeo's statement is that the judgement appears merciful to the speaker but is not so to the auditor.

42 Adversity's sweet milk, philosophy.
(III.3.56)
'Philosophy' is the consolation and counsel that Friar Laurence offers Romeo on his banishment from Verona for the murder of Tybalt. Though his actions are equivocal, the Friar's statements represent the accepted opinions of his day and his utterances are cast in a sententious form.

43 Hang up philosophy!
Unless philosophy can make a Juliet,
Displant a town, reverse a prince's doom,
It helps not, it prevails not.
(III.3.58–61)
Romeo rejects Friar Laurence's consolations of philosophy on pragmatic grounds. He has just learned from the Friar that Prince Escalus has exiled him from Verona for the murder of Tybalt and so separated him from Juliet, whom he has secretly married.

44 Night's candles are burnt out, and jocund day
Stands tiptoe on the misty mountain tops.
(III.5.9–10)
Romeo has come to Juliet in secret at night to consummate their clandestine marriage. One of Shakespeare's many evocative descriptions of early morning heralds their parting. Romeo must leave Verona under the Prince's sentence of exile for his murder of Tybalt. The lines are Romeo's response to Juliet's attempt to persuade him that the bird they have heard is the nightingale, a bird of night and love, and not the lark, the herald of the dawn.

45 I have more care to stay than will to go.
(III.5.23)
Romeo must leave Verona and Juliet, whom he is addressing, for exile. 'Care' means desire.

46 O Fortune, Fortune! All men call thee fickle.
(III.5.60)
Juliet's apostrophe to Fortune, the Renaissance descendant of the classical goddess Fortuna, ascribes the conventional attribute of fickleness to her power. In the Renaissance, Fortune was depicted emblematically as a blindfolded female figure perched precariously on a wheel or globe, so illustrating her unpredictability. Juliet's exclamation is occasioned by the departure of Romeo for exile immediately after the consummation of their love.

47 Villain and he be many miles asunder.
(III.5.81)
Lady Capulet has named Romeo a villain to Juliet for the murder of their kinsman, Tybalt. Juliet's response is deliberately equivocal, as many of her statements in this scene have to be. The phrase ostensibly means that Romeo and Tybalt are far apart, separated by distance and death, but it carries the covert meaning that Romeo is far from being a villain. In this scene, Lady Capulet conveys the information that Romeo is in exile in Mantua and reveals her intention to have him poisoned there.

48 Thank me no thankings, nor proud me no prouds.
(III.5.152)
Old Capulet has proposed to Juliet a marriage with Count Paris, a kinsman of Prince Escalus. His testy reproof of Juliet's attempts at courteous evasion of the proposal picks up the terms 'thank' and 'proud' (in the sense of honoured) that his daughter has repeatedly used.

49 Utter your gravity o'er a gossip's bowl,
For here we need it not.
(III.5.174–5)
Capulet's contemptuous dismissal of the Nurse's advice and attempt at mediation occurs when he is enraged at Juliet's refusal to marry Paris. Juliet is, of course, secretly married to Romeo. Capulet's statement conveys a vivid picture of the Nurse gossiping with her cronies.

50 Is there no pity sitting in the clouds
That sees into the bottom of my grief?
(III.5.197–8)

Juliet's lines refer to her unhappiness at the prospect of marrying Paris. They are addressed to her mother, Lady Capulet, but for the audience they have a wider significance. Juliet cannot confide to her mother her secret marriage to Romeo and her grief at his exile for the murder of her cousin, Tybalt. Lady Capulet, aware only of a reluctance to marry Paris and assumed grief at Tybalt's death, rejects her daughter's appeals.

51 Romeo's a dishclout to him.
(III.5.220)

The Nurse's counsel that Juliet should marry Paris and forget Romeo completes Juliet's misery and tragic isolation. The bawdiness and moral laxity of the Nurse suddenly takes on a sinister colouring and confirms Juliet in her resolve to die, if she cannot find a remedy in the counsel of Friar Laurence. The tragic die is cast.

52 Farewell! God knows when we shall meet again.
I have a faint cold fear thrills through my veins
That almost freezes up the heat of life.
I'll call them back again to comfort me.
Nurse! – What should she do here?
My dismal scene I needs must act alone.
(IV.3.14–19)

The opening of Juliet's soliloquy, on the eve of the marriage to Paris, portrays the total isolation of the young heroine. She is gathering courage to drink the potion that Friar Laurence has provided. The potion will simulate the effects of death and so remove Juliet from her predicament.

53 Out alas! she's cold,
Her blood is settled, and her joints are stiff.
Life and these lips have long been separated.
Death lies on her like an untimely frost
Upon the sweetest flower of all the field.
(IV.5.25–9)

Juliet has taken a potion which simulates the appearance of death in order to evade marriage with Paris. Capulet's lament for his supposedly dead child employs an image of frost destroying a flower, so conveying the youth of Juliet and the untimeliness of her death.

54 Is it e'en so? Then I defy you, stars!
(V.1.24)

Romeo, in exile in Mantua, has learned from Balthasar, his servant, the news of Juliet's supposed death as it is reported at Verona. Romeo defies his destiny. The weight of textual argument favours 'defy' and not 'deny'.

55 Being holiday, the beggar's shop is shut.
(V.1.56)
Romeo, on learning of Juliet's supposed death, has decided to procure poison from an apothecary, to return to Verona from his exile in Mantua, and to commit suicide there at the Capulets' tomb. Initially, he finds the apothecary's shop closed, but subsequently the apothecary appears. 'Beggar' means wretch or poor man.

56 ROMEO
The world is not thy friend, nor the world's law.
The world affords no law to make thee rich.
Then be not poor, but break it and take this.
APOTHECARY
My poverty but not my will consents.
ROMEO
I pay thy poverty and not thy will.
(V.1.72–6)
The exchange between Romeo and the apothecary summarizes the age-old conflict between law or moral principle and necessity or material advantage. The apothecary has indicated that the law of Mantua forbids the sale of poison, but Romeo wins him over by an appeal to his poverty. Romeo intends to commit suicide, having learned of Juliet's supposed death at Verona.

57 Tempt not a desperate man.
(V.3.59)
This injunction, which has become proverbial, is part of Romeo's admonition to Paris before the tomb of Juliet. Paris has come to perform his obsequies, while Romeo, distraught with grief, is intent upon joining Juliet in death by taking poison. Paris, on seeing Romeo back in Verona, has attempted to arrest him. Unbeknown to both men, Juliet is merely in the power of a potion administered by Friar Laurence which simulates the effects of death.

58 O, give me thy hand,
One writ with me in sour misfortune's book.
(V.3.81–2)

Romeo has encountered Paris at the tomb of Juliet and has reluctantly been forced to kill him in self-defence. His words to the dying Paris unite the two men as victims of fate and as the rival betrothed of Juliet. The idea of the book of fate in which all destinies are written is pagan in origin but was assimilated into Christian culture. This notion reinforces the sense of predestination in the play and the helplessness of the human victims.

59 Death, that hath sucked the honey of thy breath,
Hath had no power yet upon thy beauty.
Thou art not conquered. Beauty's ensign yet
Is crimson in thy lips and in thy cheeks,
And death's pale flag is not advancèd there.
(V.3.92–6)

Romeo has entered the Capulet tomb and is contemplating what he takes to be the lifeless form of Juliet. His address to her beauty exploits the interplay of physical and religious love in the Petrarchan tradition. Though Juliet is believed to be dead, she remains a source of light in the darkness of the tomb and appears to have triumphed over death in a physical as much as spiritual way. The second sentence employs military metaphor to depict the battle of life and death for Juliet.

60 Shall I believe
That unsubstantial death is amorous,
And that the lean abhorrèd monster keeps
Thee here in dark to be his paramour?
For fear of that I still will stay with thee
And never from this palace of dim night
Depart again. Here, here will I remain
With worms that are thy chambermaids. O here
Will I set up my everlasting rest
And shake the yoke of inauspicious stars
From this world-wearied flesh.
(V.3.102–12)

Romeo is contemplating the apparently lifeless form of Juliet in the Capulet tomb. His sustained personification of Death transforms the figure from an aggressor to a violator, who seeks to possess Juliet. In the thematic pattern of the scene, Juliet's marriage proves to be her death and her tomb becomes her bridal bed, the place of consummation and inseparable union with Romeo. Romeo again defies the influence of the stars which have crossed his love, but his action, in taking poison, completes their design.

61 Come, bitter conduct, come, unsavoury guide!
Thou desperate pilot, now at once run on
The dashing rocks thy seasick weary bark!
Here's to my love! (*He drinks*) O true Apothecary!
Thy drugs are quick. Thus with a kiss I die.
(V.3.116–20)

Romeo, on learning of Juliet's supposed death, has returned to Verona from exile in Mantua and he is contemplating the apparently lifeless form of Juliet in the Capulet tomb. His lines are addressed to the poison he has obtained from the Mantuan apothecary with the intention of committing suicide at the tomb. The poison is conceived as a reckless 'pilot' endangering the 'bark' (or ship) of his life. He dies embracing Juliet. When Juliet awakes from the influence of Friar Laurence's potion, which merely simulated death, she joins Romeo in an eternal union by dispatching herself with his dagger.

The Taming of the Shrew

1 Look in the Chronicles, we came in with Richard Conqueror.
(Induction 1.3–4)

Christopher Sly, a drunken tinker, is arguing with the Hostess of an inn. His claim to ancient lineage is spoiled by his confusing Richard the Lionheart with William the Conqueror.

2 And if the boy have not a woman's gift
To rain a shower of commanded tears,
An onion will do well for such a shift,
Which in a napkin being close conveyed,
Shall in despite enforce a watery eye.
(Induction 1.122–6)

A Lord is playing a practical joke on Sly by furnishing him with a wife, one of the lord's pages in disguise, and a performance by a group of travelling players. This performance constitutes the main action of the play. At this point the Lord is giving instructions as to how the page can counterfeit the tears of the distressed wife overjoyed at her husband's restoration to health. The Lord's opinion of women is as low as that of many other characters in the play.

3 No profit grows where is no pleasure ta'en.
In brief, sir, study what you most affect.
(I.1.39–40)

Tranio is advising his master Lucentio on the best way to go about his programme of self-improvement.

4 'Tis a very excellent piece of work, madam lady.
Would 'twere done!
They sit and mark
(I.1.250–1)

Sly has watched the first scene of the play proper with the page disguised as his wife. The stage direction indicates that they continue to watch, but there are no more interruptions from Sly in the text as we have it. In *The Taming of a Shrew*, published in 1594, there are further scenes with Sly, but the exact relationship between the two plays is disputed. Many productions of *The Shrew* include the Sly scenes from *A Shrew.*

5 Such wind as scatters young men through the world
To seek their fortunes farther than at home,
Where small experience grows.
(I.2.49–51)

Hortensio, a resident of Padua, has asked Petruchio, newly arrived from Verona, 'what happy gale' blows him there. Petruchio's commonplace answer is not the whole story; see the next entry.

6 I come to wive it wealthily in Padua;
If wealthily, then happily in Padua.
(I.2.74–5)

Petruchio reveals the true motive for his journey to Padua, thus offering Hortensio a possible solution to the difficulties he faces in wooing Bianca, the younger daughter of Baptista, who will not let her marry until his elder daughter, Katherine or Kate (the shrew of the title), has a husband.

7 Why, nothing comes amiss, so money comes withal.
(I.2.80–1)

Grumio, Petruchio's servant, comments on his master's motivation.

8 She is your treasure, she must have a husband,
I must dance bare-foot on her wedding-day,
And for your love to her lead apes in hell.
(II.1.32–4)

Kate is angry because her father appears to favour his younger and more conventional daughter over the independent-minded and older Kate. Her comments are based on the custom that an older unmarried sister danced barefoot at her younger sister's wedding and the belief that unmarried women, having no children to lead to heaven, led apes in hell.

9 Say that she rail, why then I'll tell her plain
She sings as sweetly as a nightingale.
Say that she frown, I'll say she looks as clear
As morning roses newly washed with dew.
Say she be mute and will not speak a word,
Then I'll commend her volubility,
And say she uttereth piercing eloquence.
If she do bid me pack, I'll give her thanks,
As though she bid me stay by her a week.
If she deny to wed, I'll crave the day
When I shall ask the banns, and when be married.
(II.1.170–80)

Petruchio is going to attempt to woo Kate, thus removing the obstacle in the way of Bianca's various suitors. In this speech he outlines his plan of action to the audience.

10 You lie, in faith, for you are called plain Kate,
And bonny Kate, and sometimes Kate the curst.
But Kate, the prettiest Kate in Christendom,
Kate of Kate Hall, my super-dainty Kate,
For dainties are all Kates, and therefore, Kate,
Take this of me, Kate of my consolation.
(II.1.185–90)

Kate has claimed that she is normally called Katherine, but Petruchio responds with this speech in which he puns on 'cates' meaning delicacies.

11 We will have rings, and things, and fine array,
And kiss me, Kate, we will be married o' Sunday.
(II.1.316–17)

Despite Kate's protestations, Petruchio continues his policy of whirlwind wooing, culminating in this declaration of intent. *Kiss me Kate* is the title of a musical by Cole Porter based on Shakespeare's play.

12 No shame but mine. I must forsooth be forced
To give my hand, opposed against my heart,
Unto a mad-brain rudesby, full of spleen,
Who wooed in haste and means to wed at leisure.
(III.2.8–11)

Petruchio is late for his wedding. Kate is understandably upset, since no one took any notice of her protests and misgivings. A 'rudesby' is a rough coarse man; the spleen was thought to be the seat of the emotions, so Kate is accusing Petruchio of being both uncouth and emotionally unstable. Her final line is an ironic variant on the proverbial 'Marry in haste; repent at leisure'.

13 To me she's married, not unto my clothes.
Could I repair what she will wear in me
As I can change these poor accoutrements,
'Twere well for Kate and better for myself.
(III.2.116–19)

Petruchio has arrived for the wedding in unsuitable clothes, but brushes aside objections in these lines in which he refutes the proverbial idea that, as Polonius puts it, 'the apparel oft proclaims the man' (see *Hamlet* 36).

14 Thus have I politicly begun my reign,
And 'tis my hope to end successfully.
My falcon now is sharp and passing empty,
And till she stoop she must not be full-gorged,
For then she never looks upon her lure.
Another way I have to man my haggard,
To make her come and know her keeper's call,
That is, to watch her, as we watch these kites
That bate and beat and will not be obedient.
She eat no meat today, nor none shall eat.
Last night she slept not, nor tonight she shall not.
As with the meat, some undeservèd fault
I'll find about the making of the bed,
And here I'll fling the pillow, there the bolster,
This way the coverlet, another way the sheets.
Ay, and amid this hurly I intend
That all is done in reverend care of her.
And, in conclusion, she shall watch all night,
And if she chance to nod I'll rail and brawl,
And with the clamour keep her still awake.
This is a way to kill a wife with kindness,
And thus I'll curb her mad and headstrong humour.
He that knows better how to tame a shrew,
Now let him speak – 'tis charity to show.
(IV.1.174–97)

Petruchio again favours the audience with an account of his taming programme. The comparison of Kate to a falcon is apt, since Petruchio uses the same methods of sensory deprivation to tame her as were used in falconry. Although attempts are sometimes made to defend Petruchio's actions in terms of the traditions of farce, on the face of it these lines manifest a brutal and degrading attitude to women. In falconry the wild bird was called a haggard; to stoop means to fly to the lure which attracts the bird back to the falconer. 'These kites / That bate and beat' are the birds which flutter and flap their wings. 'Hurly' means upset or commotion, and 'watch' means stay awake. 'To kill with kindness' proverbially meant causing harm by being too indulgent – Petruchio is being ironic. The speech ends with an invitation to the audience which shows the close contact possible between the stage and audience in Elizabethan theatrical conditions.

15 PETRUCHIO
I will not go today, and ere I do,
It shall be what o'clock I say it is.
HORTENSIO
Why, so this gallant will command the sun.
(IV.3.190–2)
Petruchio, continuing to demand unquestioning obedience from Kate, changes his mind about setting out for her father's house because Kate has contradicted him about the correct time.

16 I knew a wench married in an afternoon as she went to the garden for parsley to stuff a rabbit.
(IV.4.95–7)
Biondello's observation is occasioned by Tranio having arranged for their master Lucentio to marry Bianca in secret.

17 Then, God be blessed, it is the blessèd sun.
But sun it is not, when you say it is not,
And the moon changes even as your mind.
What you will have it named, even that it is,
And so it shall be so for Katherine.
(IV.5.18–22)
Kate finally submits to Petruchio by agreeing that the sun is the moon, although there is still some element of defiance in her remark on the changeability of Petruchio's mind.

18 My cake is dough, but I'll in among the rest,
Out of hope of all but my share of the feast.
(V.1.128–9)
Gremio, a disappointed suitor of Bianca's, uses a proverbial expression to acknowledge his failure.

19 Thy husband is thy lord, thy life, thy keeper,
Thy head, thy sovereign; one that cares for thee,
And for thy maintenance; commits his body
To painful labour both by sea and land,
To watch the night in storms, the day in cold,
Whilst thou liest warm at home, secure and safe;...
Such duty as the subject owes the prince,
Even such a woman oweth to her husband.
And when she is froward, peevish, sullen, sour,
And not obedient to his honest will,
What is she but a foul contending rebel
And graceless traitor to her loving lord?
I am ashamed that women are so simple
To offer war where they should kneel for peace,
Or seek for rule, supremacy, and sway,
When they are bound to serve, love, and obey.
(V.2.145–50, 154–63)

Kate's long speech in praise of wifely submission has been interpreted in many different ways: she has been seen as truly tamed, as being ironic at her husband's expense, and as having arrived at a mutually affectionate relationship with him. The ideas in the speech have been regarded as marking an improvement over medieval attitudes to women and as showing how unemancipated women still were in the Elizabethan period.

20 HORTENSIO
Now go thy ways, thou hast tamed a curst shrew.
LUCENTIO
'Tis a wonder, by your leave, she will be tamed so.
(V.2.187–8)

Although Hortensio appears to believe Petruchio has successfully tamed Kate, the final line of the play appears to leave room for some debate.

The Tempest

1 What cares these roarers for the name of king?
(I.1.16–17)

The play opens in a storm at sea. The Boatswain, hampered by the noble passengers, points out that the elements are unimpressed by human distinctions. The overthrow of normal order, which is of great thematic importance in the play, is also contained in the word 'roarers' which refers not only to the roaring seas but also to the contemporary term for rowdies. 'Cares' means care.

2 I have great comfort from this fellow. Methinks he hath no drowning-mark upon him: his complexion is perfect gallows. Stand fast, good Fate, to his hanging. Make the rope of his destiny our cable, for our own doth little advantage. If he be not born to be hanged, our case is miserable.
(I.1.28–33)
Gonzalo, a Neapolitan lord who is a passenger on the ship, tells the audience that the passengers' best hope of survival lies in the truth of the proverbial idea that a man who is doomed to hang need not fear drowning, which he thinks may apply to the unfriendly Boatswain. A 'drowning-mark' probably refers to the positioning of a mole which was believed to indicate the manner of a person's death. 'His complexion is perfect gallows' means that his appearance shows he is destined to be hanged.

3 Now would I give a thousand furlongs of sea for an acre of barren ground. Long heath, brown furze, anything. The wills above be done, but I would, fain die a dry death.
(I.1.61–4)
Gonzalo ends the scene confiding his thoughts to the audience. 'Furze' is gorse.

4 O, I have suffered
With those that I saw suffer! A brave vessel,
Who had, no doubt, some noble creature in her,
Dashed all to pieces. O, the cry did knock
Against my very heart! Poor souls, they perished.
(I.2.5–9)
Miranda tells her father Prospero, the exiled Duke of Milan, her reactions to the apparent destruction of the ship which, unknown to her, is carrying Prospero's usurping brother Antonio amongst other noble passengers.

5 The direful spectacle of the wrack, which touched
The very virtue of compassion in thee,
I have with such provision in mine art
So safely ordered, that there is no soul –
No, not so much perdition as an hair
Betid to any creature in the vessel
Which thou heard'st cry, which thou sawst sink.
(I.2.26–32)

Prospero tells Miranda that the wreck ('wrack') has caused no harm. Prospero is often seen throughout the play as a presenter of shows, so his choice of the word 'spectacle' is significant.

6 What seest thou else
In the dark backward and abysm of time?
(I.2.49–50)
Prospero, in tellng Miranda how they came to be exiled on the island, has discovered that she remembers a little of her life before they were banished, even though she was very young. He now asks if she remembers anything else. 'Abysm' means abyss.

7 Your tale, sir, would cure deafness.
(I.2.106)
Prospero has paused in his lengthy exposition of how he and Miranda came to be on the island to ask her if she is paying attention. Some directors and actresses have chosen to play this line as though Miranda is bored, but there is no justification for such an interpretation apart from the director's inability to pace the scene.

8 Me, poor man, my library
Was dukedom large enough.
(I.2.109–10)
Prospero tells Miranda that his interest in study has led his brother Antonio to decide that he was incapable of governing anything except his books.

9 The still-vexed Bermoothes.
(I.2.229)
Ariel, Prospero's spirit servant, refers to the Bermudas in the course of explaining that he has brought the ship safely into harbour and dispersed the passengers about the island. One of Shakespeare's sources for the play was the narratives of the wreck of the *Sea-Venture* off Bermuda in 1609. The islands were associated with continual storms (hence 'still-vexed') and magic. Ariel's sex is not clear and the part has been played by both men and women. Since the spirit is told to adopt the disguise of a sea nymph there is a case for talking of it as female, but this has tended to a romanticization of the relationship between Ariel and Prospero which is not justified by the text; in this book, therefore, Ariel is treated as male.

10 Thou dost; and think'st it much tread the ooze
Of the salt deep,
To run upon the sharp wind of the north,

To do me business in the veins o'th'earth
When it is baked with frost.
(I.2.252–6)

Prospero accuses Ariel of being unwilling to serve him properly.

11 A freckled whelp, hag-born.
(I.2.283)

Prospero describes to Ariel his other servant, Caliban. Unlike Ariel, who is a spirit of the air, Caliban (whose name is an anagram of cannibal) is distinctly earthbound. Although different characters vary in their descriptions of him he appears to be semi-human and is endowed with the capacity for speech. His mother was a witch, Sycorax, and Prospero claims that his father was the devil.

12 PROSPERO
If thou more murmur'st, I will rend an oak,
And peg thee in his knotty entrails, till
Thou hast howled away twelve winters.
ARIEL Pardon, master
I will be correspondent to command,
And do my spriting gently.
(I.2.294–8)

Prospero terminates his argument with Ariel by threatening to torment him with the same kind of tortures that Sycorax had inflicted on him. 'Correspondent' means obedient.

13 I must eat my dinner.
This island's mine, by Sycorax my mother,
Which thou tak'st from me. When thou cam'st first,
Thou strok'st me, and made much of me, wouldst give me
Water with berries in't, and teach me how
To name the bigger light, and how the less,
That burn by day and night. And then I loved thee,
And showed thee all the qualities o'th'isle,
The fresh springs, brine-pits, barren place and fertile.
Cursed be I that did so! All the charms
Of Sycorax – toads, beetles, bats light on you!
For I am all the subjects that you have,
Which first was mine own king; and here you sty me
In this hard rock, whiles you do keep from me
The rest o'th'island.
(I.2.330–44)

On his first appearance, Caliban grumbles that Prospero is interrupting his meal and voices his counter-claim that Prospero has usurped him to Prospero and Miranda. His complaint echoes

Prospero's complaints about Antonio and is part of a whole pattern of rebellions and usurpations which pervades the play. 'By' in the second line means by inheritance from; 'whiles' means whilst.

14 You taught me language, and my profit on't
Is, I know how to curse. The red plague rid you
For learning me your language!
(I.2.363–5)

Caliban continues to berate Prospero and Miranda for usurping his title to the island. The 'You' of the first line probably refers to both Miranda (who has said in her last speech that she taught him to speak) and Prospero. The 'red plague' is one that produces red sores; 'rid' means destroy.

15 Come unto these yellow sands,
And then take hands.
Curtsied when you have and kissed
The wild waves whist,
Foot it featly here and there;
And, sweet sprites, the burden bear.
Hark, hark!
(*Burden, dispersedly*) Bow-wow!
The watch-dogs bark.
(*Burden, dispersedly*) Bow-wow!
Hark, hark! I hear
The strain of strutting chanticleer
Cry cock-a-diddle-dow!
(I.2.375–87)

Ariel, who is invisible to all the characters except Prospero, enters singing this song to one of the passengers from the ship, Ferdinand, son of Alonso, the King of Naples. The refrain ('Burden') is sung by other spirits dispersed about the playing area. The exact syntax of 'Curtsied when you have and kissed / The wild waves whist' is unclear, but it appears to mean that the ceremonies associated with the beginning of dancing (taking hands and curtseying) quieten the waves. 'Featly' means neatly; 'chanticleer' is a generic name for cocks.

16 Where should this music be? I'th'air or th'earth?
It sounds no more; and sure it waits upon
Some god o'th'island. Sitting on a bank,
Weeping again the King my father's wrack,
This music crept by me upon the waters,
Allaying both their fury and my passion
With its sweet air.
(I.2.388–94)

Ferdinand, who has come ashore from the apparently sinking ship, speculates on the source of the music being played by the invisible Ariel. The haunting effect of the fourth and fifth lines derives from the suppression of the logical subject 'I' and its replacement by 'music'. 'Wrack' means wreck.

17 Full fathom five thy father lies,
Of his bones are coral made;
Those are pearls that were his eyes;
Nothing of him that doth fade,
But doth suffer a sea-change
Into something rich and strange.
Sea-nymphs hourly ring his knell:
(*Burden*) Ding-dong.
Hark! Now I hear them – Ding-dong bell.
(I.2.397–405)
The invisible Ariel and the spirits sing another song to Ferdinand.

18 The fringèd curtains of thine eye advance.
(I.2.409)
Prospero invites Miranda to look at Ferdinand, using a formal tone to establish the almost ritual quality of the lovers' first meeting. The 'fringèd curtains' are eyelids; 'advance' means raise.

19 At the first sight
They have changed eyes.
(I.2.441–2)
Prospero tells us that Ferdinand and Miranda have done the proper thing for a hero and heroine in a Romance by falling in love at first sight.

20 Why speaks my father so ungently? This
Is the third man that e'er I saw; the first
That e'er I sighed for. Pity move my father
To be inclined my way.
(I.2.445–7)
Miranda, puzzled at Prospero's harshness to Ferdinand, voices her dismay. There is a slight problem for a very close reader in Miranda's reference to Ferdinand as the third man she has ever seen: the three would appear to be Prospero, Caliban, and Ferdinand, but she later says she has seen only two, Ferdinand and Prospero.

21 What, I say,
My foot my tutor?
(I.2.469–70)

Prospero, angry at Miranda's intervention on Ferdinand's behalf, reminds her that she should be subservient to him. He is the head which exerts control over the inferior foot, and by her actions she is usurping his function.

22 He receives comfort like cold porridge.
(II.1.10–11)
All the noble passengers from the ship except Ferdinand have landed together. Alonso, King of Naples, believes that Ferdinand, his son, is dead, but Gonzalo has been trying to cheer him up. In this speech, Sebastian, Alonso's brother, comments to Antonio, Prospero's brother, on Alonso's response to Gonzalo's efforts.

23 Look, he's winding up the watch of his wit. By and by it will strike.
(II.1.14–15)
In an aside to Antonio, Sebastian again derides Gonzalo's attempts to cheer Alonso up.

24 The truth you speak doth lack some gentleness,
And time to speak it in. You rub the sore,
When you should bring the plaster.
(II.1.139–41)
Gonzalo chides Sebastian's forthright condemnation of Alonso for getting them into their current predicament.

25 We all were sea-swallowed, though some cast again,
And, by that destiny, to perform an act
Whereof what's past is prologue, what to come,
In yours and my discharge.
(II.1.255–8)
While the other shipwrecked nobles sleep, Antonio is trying to persuade Sebastian into murdering Alonso in order to become King of Naples. In this speech he is ending his account of how they came to be on the island and anticipating a possible future. 'Cast', which means thrown ashore, introduces a series of words with theatrical connotations as well as everyday meanings, including 'discharge' which means the playing of a part.

26 O, that you bore
The mind that I do! What a sleep were this
For your advancement!
(II.1.271–3)
Antonio continues to persuade Sebastian to murder Alonso in his sleep.

27 They'll take suggestion as a cat laps milk.
(II.1.293)
Antonio tells Sebastian that, after they have murdered Alonso and Gonzalo, the other nobles will fall in with their plans as readily as a cat drinks milk.

28 All the infections that the sun sucks up
From bogs, fens, flats, on Prosper fall, and make him
By inch-meal a disease!
(II.2.1–3)
Caliban enters alone, cursing Prospero. 'Inch-meal' means inch by inch.

29 A very ancient and fishlike smell ... A strange fish! Were I in England now, as once I was, and had but this fish painted, not a holiday fool there but would give a piece of silver. There would this monster make a man. Any strange beast there makes a man. When they will not give a doit to relieve a lame beggar, they will lay out ten to see a dead Indian.
(II.2.25–6, 27–32)
The jester Trinculo, a survivor of the wreck, examines Caliban, who has hidden under his cloak in the belief that Trinculo is one of Prospero's spirits sent to torment him. Although Trinculo at first believes that Caliban is a fish, he later decides that he is an islander and more like a human being. As Trinculo describes Caliban to the audience, Shakespeare adopts his familiar device of making a character who is supposedly in another country refer to England, thus creating a dual perspective on events. The painting of the fish would serve as an advertisement outside a fairground booth. 'This monster make a man' means both that this monster could be exhibited as a man and this monster would make a man's fortune. A 'doit' is a coin of low value. American Indians were frequently exhibited in England during this period, either dead or alive.

30 Misery acquaints a man with strange bed-fellows. I will here shroud till the dregs of the storm be past.
(II.2.39–40)
Trinculo, caught in a storm, decides he will have to hide under Caliban's cloak. In view of his propensity for drink, his use of 'dregs' to mean end is appropriate.

31 Well, here's my comfort.
He drinks and then sings
The master, the swabber, the boatswain, and I,
The gunner and his mate,

Loved Mall, Meg and Marian, and Margery,
But none of us cared for Kate.
For she had a tongue with a tang,
Would cry to a sailor, 'Go hang!'
She loved not the savour of tar nor of pitch,
Yet a tailor might scratch her where'er she did itch.
(II.2.44–52)

Stephano, Alonso's drunken butler, has also escaped from the supposed wreck and arrives singing drunkenly. A 'swabber' was a seaman who washed (swabbed) the decks.

32 Four legs and two voices – a most delicate monster. His forward voice now is to speak well of his friend. His backward voice is to utter foul speeches and to detract.
(II.2.88–91)

Stephano has now discovered Caliban and Trinculo, who are still under Caliban's cloak with one head at each end of it.

33 That's a brave god, and bears celestial liquor.
(II.2.115)

Caliban reacts positively to Stephano giving him a drink.

34 No more dams I'll make for fish,
Nor fetch in firing
At requiring,
Nor scrape trenchering, nor wash dish.
Ban, Ban, Cacaliban
Has a new master – get a new man!
Freedom, high-day! High-day, freedom! Freedom, high-day, freedom!
(II.2.176–83)

The drunken Caliban has rejected his old master Prospero in favour of Stephano and his drink. Here he sings his rejection of his previous menial tasks. 'Firing' is firewood; 'trenchering' is plates.

35 Full many a lady
I have eyed with best regard, and many a time
Th'harmony of their tongues hath into bondage
Brought my too diligent ear. For several virtues
Have I liked several women; never any
With so full soul but some defect in her
Did quarrel with the noblest grace she owed,
And put it to the foil. But you, O you,
So perfect and so peerless, are created

Of every creature's best.
(III.1.39–48)
Ferdinand declares his love to Miranda in extravagant terms. 'Several' means individual, different; 'put it to the foil' means cancelled it out.

36 FERDINAND Wherefore weep you?
MIRANDA
At mine unworthiness, that dare not offer
What I desire to give, and much less take
What I shall die to want. But this is trifling;
And all the more it seeks to hide itself,
The bigger bulk it shows. Hence, bashful cunning!
And prompt me, plain and holy innocence.
I am your wife, if you will marry me.
If not, I'll die your maid. To be your fellow
You may deny me, but I'll be your servant
Whether you will or no.
FERDINAND My mistress, dearest,
And I thus humble ever.
MIRANDA My husband, then?
FERDINAND
Ay, with a heart as willing
As bondage e'er of freedom. Here's my hand.
MIRANDA
And mine, with my heart in't.
(III.1.76–90)
Ferdinand and Miranda declare their loves. There are various references to secret pregnancy and sexual activity in Miranda's long speech which give some interesting overtones to the exchange.

37 Why thou deboshed fish, thou, was there ever man a coward that hath drunk so much sack as I today?
(III.2.25–7)
Trinculo objects to Caliban saying to Stephano that he is not valiant. 'Deboshed' means debauched; 'sack' is a type of wine.

38 Flout 'em and scout 'em,
And scout 'em and flout 'em!
Thought is free.
(III.2.122–4)
Stephano sings a song whose words mean: be rude to people and deride them, you can think what you like.

39 He that dies pays all debts.
(III.2.132)

Stephano, terrified by the invisible Ariel playing the tune of the song the drunkards have been singing, adopts a proverbial saying to bolster his failing courage.

40 Be not afeard; the isle is full of noises,
Sounds, and sweet airs, that give delight and hurt not.
Sometimes a thousand twangling instruments
Will hum about mine ears; and sometime voices
That, if I then had waked after long sleep,
Will make me sleep again; and then, in dreaming,
The clouds methought would open, and show riches
Ready to drop upon me, that when I waked
I cried to dream again.
(III.2.136–44)
Caliban calms Trinculo and Stephano, who have been terrified by Ariel's music.

41 My old bones aches. Here's a maze trod indeed,
Through forthrights and meanders!
(III.3.2–3)
Gonzalo tells Alonso that he is exhausted by their wanderings about the island. 'Forthrights and meanders' are straight and winding paths.

42 Methought the billows spoke, and told me of it;
The winds did sing it to me; and the thunder,
That deep and dreadful organ-pipe, pronounced
The name of Prosper: it did bass my trespass.
Therefore my son i'th'ooze is bedded, and
I'll seek him deeper than e'er plummet sounded,
And with him there lie mudded.
(III.3.98–104)
Alonso is distracted, following Ariel's appearance as a harpy to remind him of his crimes. 'Bass' means provided the bass note for the tune the elements sang to him.

43 Our revels now are ended. These our actors,
As I foretold you, were all spirits, and
Are melted into air, into thin air;
And like the baseless fabric of this vision,
The cloud-capped towers, the gorgeous palaces,
The solemn temples, the great globe itself,
Yea, all which it inherit, shall dissolve,
And, like this insubstantial pageant faded,
Leave not a rack behind. We are such stuff
As dreams are made on; and our little life

Is rounded with a sleep.
(IV.1.148–58)
Prospero, forced to terminate the betrothal masque of Ferdinand and Miranda when he remembers Caliban's conspiracy against him, reassures Ferdinand that all is well. Such terms as 'revels', 'pageant', and 'rack' have specific theatrical connotations as well as their general meanings. The Globe was one of the main theatres used by Shakespeare's company; 'rack' is both a cloud and a stage cloud.

44 A devil, a born devil, on whose nature
Nurture can never stick; on whom my pains,
Humanely taken, all, all lost, quite lost.
And as with age his body uglier grows,
So his mind cankers.
(IV.1.188–92)
Prospero soliloquizes on Caliban's intractability.

45 Monster, I do smell all horse-piss, at which my nose is in great indignation.
(IV.1.199–200)
Caliban, Trinculo, and Stephano have just escaped from a scum-covered pool. Here Trinculo complains to Caliban, whose plotting against Prospero has led them into this state of affairs.

46 I do begin to have bloody thoughts.
(IV.1.220–1)
Stephano, reminded by Caliban of the benefits of killing Prospero, turns his mind back to business.

47 We shall lose our time,
And all be turned to barnacles, or to apes
With foreheads villainous low.
(IV.1.247–9)
Caliban objects to Trinculo and Stephano that their absorption in the clothes which Prospero has deployed to delay them will result in the collapse of the conspiracy.

48 Hast thou, which art but air, a touch, a feeling
Of their afflictions, and shall not myself,
One of their kind, that relish all as sharply
Passion as they, be kindlier moved than thou art?
(V.1.21–4)
This is Prospero's response to Ariel's compassion for the shipwrecked nobles. 'Kindlier' means both more sympathetically and

more in accordance with the humanity Prospero shares with the nobles.

49 The rarer action is
In virtue than in vengeance.
(V.1.27–8)
Prospero abandons his thoughts of revenge in favour of forgiveness. 'Rarer' means both scarcer and nobler.

50 Ye elves of hills, brooks, standing lakes, and groves,
And ye that on the sands with printless foot
Do chase the ebbing Neptune, and do fly him
When he comes back; you demi-puppets that
By moonshine do the green, sour ringlets make,
Whereof the ewe not bites; and you whose pastime
Is to make midnight mushrumps, that rejoice
To hear the solemn curfew, by whose aid –
Weak masters though ye be – I have bedimmed
The noontide sun, called forth the mutinous winds,
And 'twixt the green sea and the azured vault
Set roaring war; to the dread rattling thunder
Have I given fire, and rifted Jove's stout oak
With his own bolt; the strong-based promontory
Have I made shake, and by the spurs plucked up
The pine and cedar; graves at my command
Have waked their sleepers, oped, and let 'em forth
By my so potent art. But this rough magic
I here abjure ...
I'll break my staff,
Bury it certain fathoms in the earth,
And deeper than did ever plummet sound
I'll drown my book.
(V.1.33–51, 54–7)
Prospero first invokes his spirits and then abjures his magic art. This passage derives from a speech by the witch Medea in the Roman poet Ovid's *Metamorphoses*. 'Neptune' is a personification of the sea; 'demi-puppets' are small fairies; 'green, sour ringlets' are fairy rings in the grass; 'midnight mushrumps' are mushrooms that appear overnight. The curfew bell marks the beginning of night when the spirits can operate; 'spurs' are roots. The staff and the book of spells are traditional attributes of magicians. The penultimate line echoes one of Alonso's, in which, believing that Ferdinand has been drowned he proposes to seek him 'deeper than e'er plummet sounded' (see 42).

51 Where the bee sucks, there suck I,
In a cowslip's bell I lie;
There I couch when owls do cry.
On the bat's back I do fly
After summer merrily.
Merrily, merrily shall I live now,
Under the blossom that hangs on the bough.
(V.1.88–94)
Ariel sings this final song, celebrating his forthcoming freedom, while helping Prospero to put on his ducal robes before the meeting of all the individual groups that have been on the island unknown to one another.

52 MIRANDA O, wonder!
How many goodly creatures are there here!
How beauteous mankind is! O brave new world,
That has such people in't!
PROSPERO 'Tis new to thee.
(V.1.181–4)
Miranda responds to her first sight of the party of nobles with an undifferentiated comment which includes the evil as well as the good members of the group. Prospero provides a more wordly-wise corrective. Miranda's lines are the source of the title of Aldous Huxley's novel *Brave New World.*

Timon of Athens

1 'Tis not enough to help the feeble up,
But to support him after.
(I.1.111–12)
Timon, a wealthy and powerful Athenian lord, is beset with suitors begging aid and money. Timon has just offered to pay the debts of Ventidius and so free him from prison. His offer of sustenance is an indication of his magnanimity.

2 The strain of man's bred out
Into baboon and monkey.
(I.1.254–5)
The view of Apemantus, a Cynic, is that the race of man has degenerated into apes. Apemantus' Cynical philosophy contrasts with and is opposed to Timon's magnanimity throughout the first scene.

3 I wonder men dare trust themselves with men.
Methinks they should invite them without knives:
Good for their meat, and safer for their lives.
(I.2.42–4)
Apemantus, a Cynic, conceives the communal act of eating as a vision of man devouring man.

4 Grant I may never prove so fond
To trust man on his oath or bond.
(I.2.63–4)
The couplet is taken from 'Apemantus' Grace', a misanthropic parody of graces which Apemantus delivers before joining the eating and drinking at the banquet in Timon's house. Apemantus is a Cynical philosopher, with a churlish disposition.

5 Men shut their doors against a setting sun.
(I.2.142)
Apemantus, a Cynic, has just expressed his contempt for the ladies' masque of Amazons presented at Timon's banquet. He expresses the view that those who now dance before Timon would be prepared to stamp on him, if he fell from wealth and power. In this proverbial phrase, he encapsulates the idea that men shun a declining power.

6 'Tis pity bounty had not eyes behind,
That man might ne'er be wretched for his mind.
(I.2.160–1)
Timon's steward is aware that his master is bankrupting himself through his 'bounty', or generosity of mind, which he translates directly into magnanimous action or gift. As the scene progresses, the steward's revelations of the reality of Timon's economic situation increase. The steward is here expressing regret that the quality of bounty is not more cautious or prudent: to have 'eyes behind' was a proverbial image of cautious behaviour. 'That man' refers not to Timon specifically but to any man.

7 Nothing emboldens sin so much as mercy.
(III.5.3)
Alcibiades, the military leader, has come before the senators of Athens to plead for mercy on behalf of a friend who is facing the death penalty. His grounds of appeal are that the friend has done worthy military service for the state. This comment of the first senator represents the senators' rigorous and punitive attitude. Alcibiades' outspoken denunciation of the senators' ingratitude (they made money while the friend's military service kept them

safe) earns him banishment. Thus Alcibiades' narrative acts as a counterpoint to Timon's situation in the play.

8 May you a better feast never behold,
You knot of mouth-friends! Smoke and lukewarm water
Is your perfection. This is Timon's last,
Who, stuck and spangled with your flatteries,
Washes it off, and sprinkles in your faces
Your reeking villainy.
(III.6.88–93)

Timon, pressed by his creditors and denied money by his 'friends', invites the flattering lords to one last banquet. After patiently bearing the unctuous excuses for their denials of money, he uncovers the dishes to reveal only warm water, which he flings in their faces as he denounces them.

9 Nothing I'll bear from thee
But nakedness, thou detestable town.
(IV.1.32–3)

Timon, ruined by the demands of his creditors and his rejection by his former friends, has delivered an extremely vituperative curse upon his native city of Athens. He has decided to take to the woods outside Athens as a naked outcast.

10 Let's shake our heads and say,
As 'twere a knell unto our master's fortunes,
'We have seen better days'.
(IV.2.25–7)

Unlike Timon's former friends, his steward and other household servants remain loyal to him after his fall. These are the steward's words to the servants at their separation. The final phrase has passed into the language to express former prosperity.

11 O the fierce wretchedness that glory brings us!
Who would not wish to be from wealth exempt,
Since riches point to misery and contempt?
(IV.2.30–2)

This is the steward's sententious observation upon the fall of his master, Timon, and the latter's rejection by his former friends, despite his previous generosity towards them. The language of the play is marked by such maxims, just as its structure is informed by the moral fable.

12 This yellow slave
Will knit and break religions, bless th'accursed,
Make the hoar leprosy adored, place thieves,

And give them title, knee, and approbation,
With senators on the bench.
(IV.3.34–8)
Timon, now a naked outcast in the woods, has ironically discovered gold ('this yellow slave'), while digging in the earth for roots as sustenance. His contemptuous apostrophe to gold depicts it as the source of evil in the world.

13 The middle of humanity thou never knewest, but the extremity of both ends.
(IV.3.302–3)
Apemantus, the Cynical philosopher, has sought out Timon in the woods, having learned that Timon's attitude to mankind has changed completely. Still rejected by Timon, Apemantus asserts that Timon's character has only known the extremes of magnanimity and misanthropy.

14 What is amiss, plague and infection mend!
Graves only be men's works, and death their gain!
Sun, hide thy beams. Timon hath done his reign.
(V.1.219–21)
Timon's steward and the senators of Athens have come to his cave to seek his assistance against Alcibiades' march on their city. Timon rejects their appeals and is intent upon the preparation of his own tomb and epitaph, which is discovered by a soldier in V.3. The only solution that Timon can offer the citizens of Athens is the one he has learned for himself – complete removal from the vicissitudes of fortune, ultimately in death.

Titus Andronicus

1 She is a woman, therefore may be wooed;
She is a woman, therefore may be won;
She is Lavinia, therefore must be loved.
What, man! More water glideth by the mill
Than wots the miller of, and easy it is
Of a cut loaf to steal a shive, we know.
(II.1.82–7)
Demetrius, son of the Empress Tamora, is describing his desire for Lavinia, the daughter of Titus Andronicus, who is married to Bassianus, the Emperor's brother. The 'man' he refers to may be either his brother Chiron or Aaron the Moor, Tamora's clandestine lover, since both of them are onstage. His low opinion of

women's fidelity informs the image of a married woman as a cut loaf from which it is easy to take an extra slice ('shive').

2 *Enter the Empress' sons with Lavinia, her hands cut off, and her tongue cut out, and ravished.*
(opening stage direction, II.4.)
On Aaron's advice, Chiron and Demetrius ('the Empress' sons') have raped Lavinia, cutting her hands off and her tongue out in order to prevent her telling who was responsible. The play is heavily influenced by the Roman writer Seneca whose works, probably written for recitation rather than production, contain many similar gory and horrific descriptions.

3 Why, foolish Lucius, dost thou not perceive
That Rome is but a wilderness of tigers?
Tigers must prey, and Rome affords no prey
But me and mine.
(III.1.53–6)
Lucius is the last survivor of Titus's twenty-five sons – twenty-one have been killed in battle, Titus has killed one for rebellion, and two are on the point of being executed for the murder of Bassianus. In fact Bassianus was killed by Chiron and Demetrius before they raped Lavinia. Here Titus is comforting Lucius, arguing that he is foolish to resent being banished for attempting to rescue his wrongly condemned brothers, since it will remove him from Rome's hostile environment.

4 Bear thou my hand, sweet wench, between thy teeth.
(III.1.282)
In a cruel deception, Aaron the Moor had persuaded Titus that he could save his two condemned sons by cutting off one of his hands. That hand has now been returned, together with the heads of the two executed sons. Titus now asks Lavinia ('sweet wench') to carry the hand between her teeth. Although the stage picture at this point may appear rather ludicrous if not well handled – with the handless tongueless Lavinia carrying her father's hand like a dog a bone, Titus carrying one son's head, and his brother Marcus another – recent stagings have shown that the play can be more than an early equivalent of a horror film.

5 Come and take choice of all my library,
And so beguile thy sorrow.
(IV.1.34–5)
Titus encourages Lavinia to console herself with reading until they discover who raped her. In fact Lavinia is looking for a copy of the Roman poet Ovid's *Metamorphoses*, which contains the

story of Philomel, who suffered a very similar fate to her. By pointing to the story and using her stumps to hold a stick with which she draws names in the sand, she manages to tell her family who was responsible.

6 Coal-black is better than another hue,
In that it scorns to bear another hue;
For all the water in the ocean
Can never turn the swan's black legs to white,
Although she lave them hourly in the flood.
(IV.2.99–103)
The villainous Aaron defends his colour. The immediate occasion of this speech is the birth of his inappropriately coloured son to the white Empress, who is married to a white Emperor. 'Lave' means wash; 'flood' means stream.

7 Is the sun dimmed, that gnats do fly in it?
The eagle suffers little birds to sing
And is not careful what they mean thereby,
Knowing that with the shadow of his wings
He can at pleasure stint their melody.
(IV.4.83–7)
The Empress Tamora encourages her husband Saturninus to stand firm in the face of discontent at home and the arrival of a hostile army led by Lucius, Titus's last surviving son. 'Is not careful' means does not worry about; 'stint' means stop.

8 Why, there they are both, baked in that pie.
(V.3.60)
Titus's revenge on Tamora and her sons for all the horrors they have inflicted on his family is to invite her to a meal in which the main course is a pie made of their crushed bodies. Such cannibal banquets in which parents unwittingly eat their dead children occur on several occasions in classical mythology. Shakespeare may well have been most influenced by Ovid's treatment of the story of Procne in the *Metamorphoses* and Seneca's version of the story of Thyestes. Many Renaissance tragedies of revenge end with equally bizarre revenges.

9 If one good deed in all my life I did,
I do repent it from my very soul.
(V.3.189–90)
Aaron remains true to his creed to the very end. Throughout the play he has acted as an out-and-out villain, expressing tender feelings only for his child by Tamora.

Troilus and Cressida

1 You have here a new play, never staled with the stage, never clapper-clawed with the palms of the vulgar.
(Epistle to the Reader, 1–2)
The opening sentence from the Epistle to the Reader of the 1609 Quarto of *Troilus and Cressida* strongly implies that the play had not been performed in the public theatre.

2 Now expectation, tickling skittish spirits,
On one and other side, Troyan and Greek,
Sets all on hazard.
(Prologue, 20–2)
The Prologue, who describes himself as 'suited / In like conditions as our argument', introduces the context of the drama, the Trojan War. He describes how the Greek expedition has for years been laying siege to Troy in an attempt to wrest Helen (the wife of the Greek prince, Menelaus) from Paris, a Trojan prince. These lines depict the keenness with which the contest is daily fought and the eager anticipation of the outcome shared by each side. 'Skittish' means lively.

3 O, that her hand,
In whose comparison all whites are ink,
Writing their own reproach; to whose soft seizure
The cygnet's down is harsh, and spirit of sense
Hard as the palm of ploughman.
(I.1.54–8)
The twin themes of *Troilus and Cressida* are love and war: the play's narrative and its pattern of scenes interlace the twin arguments. In the first scene, Troilus, a son of King Priam of Troy, is explaining to Pandarus, the uncle of Cressida, how his appetite for battle against the Greeks has been undermined by the war within him, his passion for Cressida. Cressida is the daughter of a Trojan priest and seer, Calchas, who has deserted to the Greek camp because he has foreseen the destruction of Troy. The construction 'that her hand' means that hand of hers. The eulogy of the whiteness of the mistress' hand is a feature of the Petrarchan, courtly love tradition.

4 Helen must needs be fair,
When with your blood you daily paint her thus.
(I.1.89–90)
Helen's seizure from her husband, Menelaus, by Paris, a prince of Troy, was the cause of the Trojan War. Helen's beauty was leg-

endary. In the Renaissance, she was traditionally viewed as the archetype of female beauty; but, in *Troilus and Cressida*, Shakespeare debunks the myth. Here Troilus implies that the sacrifice made by the Trojans in Helen's name results in their attributing such value to her.

5 Why, have you any discretion, have you any eyes, do you know what a man is? Is not birth, beauty, good shape, discourse, manhood, learning, gentleness, virtue, youth, liberality, and such like, the spice and salt that season a man?
(I.2.243–7)
Pandarus is observing, with his niece Cressida, the passing of the Trojan troops, with the princes of Troy in the van and the common soldiers following. His aim is to draw Cressida's attention to Troilus in the hope of promoting a liaison between them. Cressida, who is not blind to her uncle's intentions nor unsusceptible to Troilus' attractions, is teasing Pandarus by suggesting that the Greek warrior, Achilles, is a better man than Troilus, so prompting this contemptuous response. Pandarus' voyeuristic involvement in forwarding Troilus' sexual interests portrays him as an equivocal figure.

6 But more in Troilus thousandfold I see
Than in the glass of Pandar's praise may be.
Yet hold I off: women are angels, wooing;
Things won are done, joy's soul lies in the doing.
That she beloved knows nought that knows not this:
Men prize the thing ungained more than it is;
That she was never yet, that ever knew
Love got so sweet as when desire did sue.
Therefore this maxim out of love I teach:
Achievement is command; ungained, beseech.
(I.2.276–85)
Cressida's soliloquy, after Pandarus' approach to her on Troilus' behalf, reveals a full awareness of her situation. Cressida has been interpreted both as a *femme fatale*, a sensual creature who plays the game with Troilus and then, despite her involvement, succumbs to Diomedes' attentions, and as a victim, both of the war and of her position as a woman in this society, who must adopt such strategies in order to survive. Dual perspectives are a feature of this play and Cressida's character is not exempt from this. Cressida's acute assessment of the pattern of male sexual passion shows affinities with sonnet 129.

7 Checks and disasters
Grow in the veins of actions highest reared.
(I.3.4–5)

Agamemnon, the General of the expedition against Troy, is holding council in the Greek camp. He gives an account of the opposition of Fate to the Greek enterprise which has resulted in Troy not having fallen despite a seven years' siege. These misfortunes, he argues, are 'the protractive trials of great Jove / To find persistive constancy in men' (lines 20–1).

8 In the reproof of chance
Lies the true proof of men.
(I.3.33–4)

The aged Nestor takes up the theme of Agamemnon, the Greek General, that the true test of men lies in their facing the trials of fortune. The precise age of Nestor is not recorded, but he refers to having known the grandfathers of grown men.

9 Degree being vizarded,
Th' unworthiest shows as fairly in the mask.
The heavens themselves, the planets, and this centre
Observe degree, priority, and place,
Insisture, course, proportion, season, form,
Office, and custom, in all line of order.
(I.3.83–8)

Ulysses, Prince of Ithaca, argues in the Greek council that the reason for the expedition's failure to date lies in the factious nature of the Greeks and their failure to observe 'degree' or hierarchy. Ulysses' theme of hierarchy as the binding force of the cosmos and of society was a common sixteenth-century argument. However, in context, the speech is ironic and has little effect. Ulysses himself was a byword for guile and deceit and it is he who stirs up enmity between Ajax and Achilles. The speech has been taken to represent the 'Elizabethan World Order'; but, if such an order ever existed, it was only in the fragile constructs of official propaganda.

10 O, when degree is shaked,
Which is the ladder of all high designs,
The enterprise is sick. How could communities,
Degrees in schools, and brotherhoods in cities,
Peaceful commerce from dividable shores,
The primogenity and due of birth,
Prerogative of age, crowns, sceptres, laurels,
But by degree, stand in authentic place?
(I.3.101–8)

This section of Ulysses' speech on 'degree' (hierarchy) is applying the hierarchical order perceived in the cosmos to the social order. Analogous arguments are to be found in Book I of Richard Hooker's *Laws of Ecclesiastical Polity* (1593), which was largely an official apology of the Elizabethan settlement in church and state. Nonetheless, it would be wrong to take this speech as the central statement of the play, to which its action is merely illustrative. The entire presentation of the Trojan War is equivocal.

11 Take but degree away, untune that string,
And hark what discord follows. Each thing meets
In mere oppugnancy.
(I.3.109–11)
Before he applies his theme of 'degree' (hierarchy) to the situation of the Greek expedition, Ulysses concludes his argument with a vision of the total anarchy that must follow, if hierarchy is not observed. The same argument was used by propagandists of the Tudor dynasty as a powerful weapon against rebellion. Ulysses is speaking in the Greek camp before Agamemnon and the Greek generals.

12 But we are soldiers;
And may that soldier a mere recreant prove,
That means not, hath not, or is not in love!
(I.3.286–8)
Agamemnon is replying to the challenge made by Aeneas on behalf of Hector which has interrupted the council in the Greek camp. The challenge that Aeneas has delivered links the twin themes of love and war, since Hector has challenged the Greek warriors to combat in defence of their women's beauty. He has vaunted the beauty and honour of his wife, Andromache, above all Grecian women. Despite the setting of the Trojan War, Shakespeare conceives the conflict in chivalric terms, like medieval writers before him, and Hector is the epitome of the chivalric warrior.

13 The plague of Greece upon thee, thou mongrel beef-witted lord!
(II.1.11–12)
This is the curse of Thersites, a scurrilous Greek, upon Ajax for having struck him. Ajax is described as 'mongrel' because he was half-Trojan and half-Greek: his mother, Hesione, was the sister of King Priam of Troy. It was generally believed that a heavy diet of beef dulled the intelligence. Ajax is depicted in the play as a per-

son of brute strength and little intelligence. In fact, Ajax requires Thersites to read for him the proclamation of Hector's challenge.

14 'Tis mad idolatry
To make the service greater than the god.
(II.2.56–7)

Hector is disputing with Troilus in the Trojan council. Hector has argued that Helen does not merit the loss of life shed for her keeping; but Troilus' idealism has led him to object that it is a point of honour and that all things have only the value attributed to them. Hector's reply may owe a debt to the arguments against the Scribes and Pharisees found in Matthew 23.

15 I take to-day a wife, and my election
Is led on in the conduct of my will –
My will enkindled by mine eyes and ears,
Two traded pilots 'twixt the dangerous shores
Of will and judgement.
(II.2.61–5)

Troilus is continuing his argument with Hector about intrinsic versus attributed value by means of a hypothetical situation, the choice of a wife. Troilus is, in fact, giving too much weight to the operation of will, when it is judgement that should evaluate the sense experience gained from 'eyes and ears'. His reasoning is that of a young man in the grip of passion and, although the situation is hypothetical, Cressida may be in his thoughts.

16 He touched the ports desired,
And for an old aunt whom the Greeks held captive
He brought a Grecian queen, whose youth and freshness
Wrinkles Apollo's and makes stale the morning.
Why keep we her? The Grecians keep our aunt.
Is she worth keeping? Why, she is a pearl
Whose price hath launched above a thousand ships
And turned crowned kings to merchants.
(II.2.76–83)

This is Troilus' account to the Trojan council of Paris' rape of Helen which, he argues, had the full backing of Troy. The 'old aunt' was Hesione, sister of King Priam, who was due to be sacrificed to a sea-monster, but was rescued by Herakles and given to Telamon. Line 82 echoes Marlowe's vision of Helen in *Dr Faustus* (V.1.107): 'Was this the face that launched a thousand ships?'

17 Thus to persist
In doing wrong extenuates not wrong,

But makes it much more heavy.
(II.2.186–8)
Hector is countering the arguments of Troilus and Paris regarding the merits of keeping Helen at the cost of continued bloodshed. Troilus has argued that one is honour-bound to stick by one's decisions, while Paris has gone further in arguing that 'honourable keeping' can erase the 'soil' of her rape. Despite the logical and moral strength of his position, Hector capitulates to his younger brothers on another point of honour, that to submit to the Greeks' demands would touch upon their 'joint and several dignities'. It is a decision that leads ultimately to his destruction by Achilles.

18 All the argument is a whore and a cuckold, a good quarrel to draw emulous factions and bleed to death upon.
(II.3.68–70)
This is the succinct and cynical view of the Trojan War held by Thersites, a deformed and scurrilous follower of the Greek expedition. His satirical observations upon the issues of the war represent a debasement not only of the chivalric views found in Shakespeare's medieval sources (Chaucer, Caxton, and Lydgate) but also of the elevated respect with which the Renaissance viewed all things classical.

19 I do hate a proud man, as I do hate the engendering of toads.
(II.3.154–5)
Ajax's rather childish and wooden expression of contempt for pride is directed at Achilles. He is speaking to Agamemnon and Nestor who, together with the devious Ulysses, are manipulating Ajax in order to stir Achilles into action against Hector through rivalry with Ajax. As Nestor points out, the comment is ironical. Toads were a proverbial object of loathing in the period.

20 I stalk about her door
Like a strange soul upon the Stygian banks
Staying for waftage. O, be thou my Charon,
And give me swift transportance to those fields
Where I may wallow in the lily-beds
Proposed for the deserver.
(III.2.7–12)
Troilus is describing to Pandarus his conduct towards Cressida, which is that of the unrequited courtly lover. His imagery, however, likens the consummation of his passion to death, for he depicts himself as a departed soul requiring the assistance of the boatman, Charon, for passage across the river Styx to the Elysian fields. At least subconsciously, therefore, whilst requesting the

assistance of Pandarus as a go-between, he sees the liaison with Cressida as potentially destructive and annihilating.

21 I am giddy; expectation whirls me round.
Th'imaginary relish is so sweet
That it enchants my sense. What will it be
When that the wat'ry palates taste indeed
Love's thrice-repurèd nectar? Death, I fear me,
Sounding destruction, or some joy too fine,
Too subtle, potent, tuned too sharp in sweetness
For the capacity of my ruder powers.
(III.2.16–23)

Pandarus has just told Troilus that he will immediately bring Cressida to him. Troilus' soliloquy depicts the intensity of sexual anticipation. He imagines that, if this is the experience of anticipation, that of fulfilment must be either beyond the comprehension of his senses or destructive. 'Wat'ry' means watering. The Quarto's reading of 'repured' is now generally preferred to the Folio's 'reputed': 'thrice-repurèd' suggests a super-refined distillation.

22 My heart beats thicker than a feverous pulse,
And all my powers do their bestowing lose,
Like vassalage at unawares encount'ring
The eye of majesty.
(III.2.34–7)

Troilus is describing the physical and emotional sensation of sexual anticipation, caused by the imminent approach of Cressida to a meeting engineered by her uncle, Pandarus. 'Bestowing' means use or function, while 'vassalage' simply means vassals. Troilus compares the meeting with his beloved to that of tongue-tied inferiors unexpectedly encountering their sovereign.

23 This is the monstruosity in love, lady, that the will is infinite and the execution confined; that the desire is boundless and the act a slave to limit.
(III.2.76–9)

Troilus is acknowledging to Cressida the discrepancy between lovers' aspirations and desires and the possibility of their realization. The discussion takes place as a prelude to their first sexual encounter. The implication is that love must always remain a delusion.

24 Your silence,
Cunning in dumbness, from my weakness draws

My very soul of counsel.
(III.2.127–9)

At the meeting arranged by Pandarus, Cressida confesses to Troilus that she was easily 'won' and only 'hard to seem won'. She instinctively perceives the sexual relationship as a battle for domination and conceives her ploy as a defence mechanism. The relationship of Troilus and Cressida is conditioned by its context of a world endlessly at war.

25 For to be wise and love
Exceeds man's might.
(III.2.148–9)

Cressida cites this proverbial saying after acknowledging that her confession of love might have been a trick to tempt Troilus to a full revelation of his feelings. As he has not made such a statement, she suggests that he is either wise or not in love.

26 Let all pitiful goers-between be called to the world's end after my name; call them all Pandars; let all constant men be Troiluses, all false women Cressids, and all brokers-between Pandars!
(III.2.196–200)

Shakespeare exploits his audience's knowledge of the Troilus and Cressida tale to imbue his characters' promises of fidelity with a cruel irony. By Shakespeare's day, their names had become bywords for the constant lover and the false woman. 'Pandar' has passed into the language as a term for a pimp or go-between. In such a context, the swearing of the oath as a religious, almost sacramental, act has a chilling effect.

27 Time hath, my lord, a wallet at his back,
Wherein he puts alms for oblivion,
A great-sized monster of ingratitudes.
Those scraps are good deeds past, which are devoured
As fast as they are made, forgot as soon
As done. Perseverance, dear my lord,
Keeps honour bright; to have done, is to hang
Quite out of fashion, like a rusty mail
In monumental mock'ry.
(III.3.145–53)

Ulysses is cunningly spurring Achilles into taking up the challenge of Hector. He has spoken to Achilles of the praise that Achilles' rival, Ajax, is receiving, as if he had already defeated Hector and, with him, Troy. Achilles, whom the Greek generals are deliberately spurning, asks whether his earlier deeds have been forgotten, so prompting this cynical but accurate observation of

Ulysses. The last lines quoted refer to the practice of placing the armour of great warriors on their tombs.

28 For time is like a fashionable host,
That slightly shakes his parting guest by th' hand,
And with his arms outstretched, as he would fly,
Grasps in the comer. The welcome ever smiles,
And farewell goes out sighing.
(III.3.165–9)

Ulysses cynically views the achievements of men in relation to the passage of time in terms of winners and losers. He places emphasis on the relentless changes of fashion, with the newest achievement the most welcome and those past neglected. The emblematic winged figure of time is transformed into a fashionable host on the threshold of success and popularity. The final sentence quoted illustrates the compression of syntax which is a feature of this play: 'welcome' and 'farewell' must indicate the persons welcomed and taken leave of. The purpose of the speech is to stir Achilles into emulation of Ajax and so to prompt his answering the challenge of Hector.

29 For beauty, wit,
High birth, vigour of bone, desert in service,
Love, friendship, charity, are subjects all
To envious and calumniating time.
(III.3.170–3)

Ulysses is expounding to Achilles the devouring power of time to destroy all the achievements of men. 'Vigour of bone' stands for physical strength. Ulysses' aim is to spur Achilles into rivalry with Ajax and into renewed military achievement by answering the challenge of Hector.

30 A plague of opinion! A man may wear it on both sides like a leather jerkin.
(III.3.263–4)

Thersites is speaking to Achilles about Ajax who, having agreed to answer the challenge of Hector, is strutting about the Greek camp. 'Opinion' here has not its modern sense, but that of a favourable view of oneself, either in the sense of overweening pride or in the sense of self-confidence. Thersites is suggesting that both aspects derive from pride and that 'opinion' is therefore comparable to a reversible jerkin.

31 The bitter disposition of the time
Will have it so.
(IV.1.49–50)

Paris is commenting to Aeneas upon the news that Cressida is to be sent to her father, Calchas, in the Greek camp in exchange for Antenor, a son of King Priam, and upon the effect that this news will have on Troilus. The harshness of a time of war is seen as impinging bitterly upon the lives and emotions of those caught up in its turmoil.

32 How my achievements mock me!
(IV.2.69)
Troilus has just been informed by his brother Aeneas that the Trojan council has ratified the exchange of Cressida for their brother, Antenor. Cressida is to join her father, the seer Calchas, in the Greek camp.

33 The grief is fine, full, perfect, that I taste.
(IV.4.3)
Cressida is speaking to Pandarus of her grief at being forced to leave Troy and Troilus as a result of the Trojan council's agreement to her exchange for Antenor. Her uncle, Pandarus, is advising moderation.

34 My love admits no qualifying dross.
(IV.4.9)
Cressida, in her anger and desperation at being separated from Troilus by a decision of the Trojan council to exchange her for Antenor, asserts the absolute perfection of her love. She is responding to her uncle Pandarus' appeal for moderation.

35 What a pair of spectacles is here!
(IV.4.13)
Pandarus is making a facetious and inappropriate observation upon the woeful expressions of Troilus and Cressida, who have both learned of the decision to send Cressida to her father, Calchas, in the Greek camp in exchange for Antenor. A 'pair of spectacles' is, of course, an anachronism in the context of the Trojan War.

36 We two, that with so many thousand sighs
Did buy each other, must poorly sell ourselves
With the rude brevity and discharge of one.
Injurious time now with a robber's haste
Crams his rich thiev'ry up.
(IV.4.38–42)
Troilus, in his farewell to Cressida, places emphasis on the malign and destructive power of time. Cressida is about to be taken to her father, Calchas, in the Greek camp in exchange for Antenor.

'Discharge' means both payment (of a debt) and exhalation (of a sigh).

37 There's language in her eye, her cheek, her lip;...
O, these encounterers, so glib of tongue,...
... set them down
For sluttish spoils of opportunity
And daughters of the game.
(IV.5.55, 58, 61–3)
Ulysses is speaking of Cressida to Nestor and the other Greek commanders after her arrival in the Greek camp accompanied by Diomedes. Ulysses judges Cressida a sexual opportunist on account of her witty tongue and physical attraction. On her reception in the Greek camp, she has in fact been the victim of male opportunism, when all the Greek generals have taken the opportunity to kiss her welcome. An 'encounterer' is a person prepared to meet someone half-way.

38 The end crowns all,
And that old common arbitrator, Time,
Will one day end it.
(IV.5.224–6)
Hector, the epitome of honour, has just fought with Ajax in the lists. He has refused to continue, on the grounds that Ajax is half-Trojan and a cousin, his mother being Hesione, sister of Priam. After the combat, Hector is received honourably in the Greek camp; but Ulysses reminds him of his prophecy made on his first embassy to Troy that refusal to return Helen will result in the destruction of the city. In this detail, Shakespeare is following John Lydgate's *Troy Book*. Hector is stating through a proverbial saying that only time and the final outcome of the war will reveal the truth.

39 CRESSIDA
Ah, poor our sex! this fault in us I find,
The error of our eye directs our mind.
What error leads must err. O, then conclude
Minds swayed by eyes are full of turpitude.
THERSITES
A proof of strength she could not publish more,
Unless she say, 'My mind is now turned whore.'
(V.2.107–12)
In the Greek camp, Cressida has become the object of Diomedes' attentions. In this scene, Ulysses malevolently and

secretly brings Troilus to a place where he may observe a meeting between Cressida and Diomedes. After some vacillation, Cressida establishes an assignation with Diomedes and gives him the sleeve, Troilus' token of love, that she had brought from Troy as a pledge of fidelity. In addition to Troilus' commentary of disillusion and rage, Thersites provides a scurrilous commentary which reduces all human motivations to the most basic instincts. Here he debases Cressida's assertion that the frailty of her sex lies in its judgement being swayed by sense experience.

40 If beauty have a soul, this is not she;
If souls guide vows, if vows be sanctimonies,
If sanctimony be the gods' delight,
If there be rule in unity itself,
This was not she.
(V.2.136–40)
After witnessing Cressida establish an assignation with Diomedes and give him his own pledge of love, Troilus' disillusion and loss of faith is such that he cannot believe that the Cressida he has observed is the one he loved. Despite its logical and rhetorical formulation, the speech operates primarily at the emotional level, conveying the collapse of all that gave order to Troilus' world.

41 Lechery, lechery; still wars and lechery; nothing else holds fashion.
(V.2.193–4)
This is Thersites' vision of the age, which succinctly, though pejoratively, links the themes of love and war. Thersites has just observed, together with Ulysses and Troilus, Cressida's act of infidelity with Diomedes. He has just heard that Hector is arming himself in preparation for another day of battle against the Greeks in defence of Paris' seizure of Helen from Menelaus.

42 Words, words, mere words, no matter from the heart.
(V.3.108)
Troilus is indicating to Pandarus the contents of a letter from Cressida that Pandarus has brought him. Unbeknown to both Cressida and Pandarus, Troilus has observed Cressida's meeting with Diomedes in the Greek camp and has lost all faith in her fidelity. He is determined to join Hector in the field of battle and win from Diomedes his love-token to Cressida, or die in the attempt.

43 Hector is dead; there is no more to say.
(V.10.22)

Hector, the epitome both of chivalry and of chaste marital love in the play, has aroused the fury of Achilles by killing in battle Patroclus, Achilles' male lover. Achilles plots with his myrmidons to trap Hector and destroy him. Hector, taken unawares and unarmed, is slain. His body is then dishonoured by being dragged by horses through the field of battle. Hector's destruction symbolizes the collapse of Trojan idealism and foreshadows the total destruction of Troy. Here Troilus is giving the news of Hector's death to the other Trojan princes: Aeneas, Paris, Antenor, and Deiphobus.

44 O world, world! thus is the poor agent despised. O traitors and bawds, how earnestly are you set a-work, and how ill requited! Why should our endeavour be so loved, and the performance so loathed?

(V.10.35–9)

Pandarus is given the last speech in the play. He has just been cursed with ignominy and shame by Troilus, whose disillusion at the infidelity of Cressida has been completed by Achilles' destruction of Hector. Pandarus' lines pursue the play's exploration of the discrepancy between idealistic anticipation of love's joys and contempt for the experience of love. By leaving the stage finally to Pandarus, the play suggests the collapse of idealism and the reign of a totally fallen world.

Twelfth Night

1 If music be the food of love, play on,
Give me excess of it, that, surfeiting,
The appetite may sicken, and so die.
That strain again! It had a dying fall.
O, it came o'er my ear like the sweet sound
That breathes upon a bank of violets,
Stealing and giving odour. Enough, no more!
'Tis not so sweet now as it was before.
O spirit of love, how quick and fresh art thou,
That notwithstanding thy capacity
Receiveth as the sea, naught enters there,
Of what validity and pitch soe'er,
But falls into abatement and low price
Even in a minute. So full of shapes is fancy
That it alone is high fantastical.

(I.1.1–15)

Orsino, ruler of Illyria, opens the play in characteristic style. Although he claims to be in love with Olivia, he shows this love mainly in extravagant and often, as here, abstract language spoken when she is safely absent. The changeability of the conventional lover is well expressed in his attitude to music. This initial choice of vocabulary, with its insistence on excess, surfeit, and sickening, sets the tone of a play in which the pain of love is never far from the surface. 'Dying fall' means final cadence.

2 O, when mine eyes did see Olivia first,
Methought she purged the air of pestilence.
That instant was I turned into a hart,
And my desires, like fell and cruel hounds,
E'er since pursue me.
(I.1.20–4)

Orsino names his love, puns on 'hart' and 'heart', and compares himself to Actaeon who, in classical legend, saw the goddess Diana bathing; she turned him into a stag and his dogs tore him to pieces.

3 Away before me to sweet beds of flowers!
Love thoughts lie rich when canopied with bowers.
(I.1.41–2)

Orsino ends the scene with a couplet whose banal rhyme does little to enhance his credibility. His wooing remains essentially passive and conventional, almost part of the good courtier's education rather than something to do with love for a real woman.

4 VIOLA
What country, friends, is this?
CAPTAIN
This is Illyria, lady.
VIOLA
And what should I do in Illyria?
My brother, he is in Elysium.
(I.2.1–4)

Viola appears in sharp contrast to Orsino. Her dialogue, although she believes her brother died in the shipwreck, is much more purposeful. The country's name, Illyria, suggests the world of Romance which the play acknowledges with its tale of shipwrecked twins reunited. Elysium, the name of the place where the virtuous dead live in classical mythology, is used instead of heaven to enhance the Romance atmosphere.

5 I prithee – and I'll pay thee bounteously –
Conceal me what I am, and be my aid

For such disguise as haply shall become
The form of my intent. I'll serve this Duke.
Thou shalt present me as an eunuch to him.
It may be worth thy pains, for I can sing
And speak to him in many sorts of music
That will allow me very worth his service.
What else may hap to time I will commit.
Only shape thou thy silence to my wit.
(I.2.53–62)

Viola may be a Romance heroine, as her decision to adopt male clothes and serve Orsino indicates, but her offer to pay the captain for his help is typical of her practicality. Women in male disguise in Shakespeare's plays are often freed from the restrictive social inhibitions of the period, but Viola's disguise causes her a good deal of pain, trapping her as well as liberating her. In Shakespeare's theatre female parts were played by male actors.

6 You must confine yourself within the modest limits of order.
(I.3.7–8)

Maria, Olivia's waiting-gentlewoman, is attempting to calm the excesses of Sir Toby Belch, a relative of Olivia, whose late nights and drunkenness are a major problem to the household. This is one of many lines in the play which reflect a concern with the relationship between excess and restraint.

7 He plays o'the viol-de-gamboys, and speaks three or four languages word for word without book, and hath all the good gifts of nature.
(I.3.23–5)

Sir Toby is describing the musical accomplishments of Sir Andrew Aguecheek, a foolish knight whose pretensions to Olivia he encourages whilst fleecing him of his money. The viol-de-gamboys is the Renaissance equivalent of the violoncello. As we find later, Sir Andrew is being overpraised.

8 Methinks sometimes I have no more wit than a Christian or an ordinary man has; but I am a great eater of beef, and I believe that does harm to my wit.
(I.3.80–3)

Sir Andrew may be foolish and bewildered by Sir Toby, but he is not entirely unaware of his own nature. Since a normal man would be a Christian, it is likely that 'ordinary' here is a pun on the word for an eating house where the public could eat, thus also introducing the idea of food. Contemporary medical writers argued that too much meat eating slowed the wits.

9 I would I had bestowed that time in the tongues that I have in fencing, dancing, and bear-baiting. O, had I but followed the arts!
(I.3.88–91)
Sir Andrew gives a more accurate picture of his educational attainments than Sir Toby did earlier. 'Tongues' means languages. Bear-baiting was a popular pastime in the period.

10 Wherefore are these things hid? Wherefore have these gifts a curtain before 'em? Are they like to take dust, like Mistress Mall's picture? Why dost thou not go to church in a galliard and come home in a coranto? My very walk should be a jig. I would not so much as make water but in a sink-apace. What dost thou mean? Is it a world to hide virtues in? I did think by the excellent constitution of thy leg it was formed under the star of a galliard.
(I.3.118–26)
Sir Toby's response to Sir Andrew's list of his dancing abilities makes use of the names of contemporary dances. 'Sink-apace' is the cinquepas, a lively five-step dance similar to the galliard. 'Mistress Mall's picture' is probably a contemporary allusion. Paintings were often protected by curtains, but the reference to dust suggests that Mall is in some kind of disgrace. Critics who believe that Malvolio is a satirical portrait of Sir William Knollys, Controller of the Queen's Household, identify Mall with his ward Mary Fitton, with whom he was infatuated.

11 They shall yet belie thy happy years
That say thou art a man. Diana's lip
Is not more smooth and rubious. Thy small pipe
Is as the maiden's organ, shrill and sound,
And all is semblative a woman's part.
(I.4.30–4)
In describing the characteristics of his new servant Cesario, the disguised Viola, Orsino reminds the audience of her true identity by drawing attention to Cesario's apparently female characteristics. In the early productions, when Viola would have been played by a male actor, there would have been a further possible level of irony. 'Rubious' means ruby red; 'pipe' means voice; 'semblative' means like.

12 Many a good hanging prevents a bad marriage.
(I.5.18)
Feste, the professional fool attached to Olivia's household, is engaging in a battle of wits with Maria. Many of his comments, like this one, are semi- or mock-proverbial.

13 Well, go thy way, if Sir Toby would leave drinking, thou wert as witty a piece of Eve's flesh as any in Illyria.
(I.5.24–6)
One of the professional fool's characteristics in Shakespeare's plays is clearsightedness. Here Feste points the way to the marriage between Maria, to whom he is talking, and Sir Toby. In his mock sanctimonious style Maria is seen as a descendant of the first sinful woman, Eve.

14 For what says Quinapalus? 'Better a witty fool than a foolish wit'.
(I.5. 32–3)
Feste, a witty fool, makes his point about folly and wisdom with the help of the usual pedantic reference to an obscure authority which typified Renaissance scholarship. Quinapalus is a name coined for the occasion, suggestive of the legion of Latin commentators on classical and sacred texts.

15 Lady, *cucullus non facit monachum*; that's as much to say as I wear not motley in my brain.
(I.5.50–2)
Feste continues to demonstrate his wisdom as he begins to argue Olivia out of her sterile commitment to mourning for her dead brother. 'Cucullus non facit monachum' is a proverbial phrase meaning 'the cowl does not make the monk', i.e. an outward appearance is no guarantee of a person's character. Feste's clothing is 'motley', the professional fool's traditional garb, but that does not mean he is stupid.

16 Good my mouse of virtue, answer me.
(I.5.57–8)
Feste now takes on the role of a parson catechizing a small child in his attempt to break Olivia's mood. Later in the play he develops this part, tormenting Malvolio as Sir Topas the curate. 'Mouse' was often used as a term of endearment in the period.

17 O, you are sick of self-love, Malvolio, and taste with a distempered appetite. To be generous, guiltless, and of free disposition, is to take those things for bird-bolts that you deem cannon bullets. There is no slander in an allowed fool, though he do nothing but rail; nor no railing in a known discreet man, though he do nothing but reprove.
(I.5.85–91)
Malvolio, Olivia's steward, has just been denigrating professional fools. Olivia shows her basic good sense in her response. Malvolio is not the only character in the play who has a distempered

appetite; Olivia herself and Orsino are other obvious candidates. A bird-bolt is a blunt arrow used in hunting birds – Olivia is accusing Malvolio of making a mountain out of a molehill. An allowed fool is one like Feste who has a licence to jest.

18 A plague o'these pickle-herring!
(I.5.115)
Pickle herring was a notorious cause of indigestion, but Sir Toby is probably attempting to hide the true cause of his problems – over-indulgence in alcohol. Since references to pickle herring often occur in company with references to alcohol, Sir Toby's fiction is unlikely to have hidden the truth.

19 OLIVIA Cousin, cousin, how have you come so early by this lethargy?
SIR TOBY Lechery! I defy lechery!
(I.5.118–120)
Olivia is accusing Sir Toby of being drunk, using lethargy as a euphemism. Sir Toby's mishearing of lethargy as lechery shows that she is correct, even if he manages to get the doctrinal position correct.

20 Not yet old enough for a man, nor young enough for a boy; as a squash is before 'tis a peascod, or a codling when 'tis almost an apple. 'Tis with him in standing water between boy and man. He is very well-favoured, and he speaks very shrewishly. One would think his mother's milk were scarce out of him.
(I.5.151–6)
Malvolio describes Cesario, the disguised Viola, to Olivia with many rhetorical flourishes. A squash is an unripe peapod ('peascod'), a codling is an unripe apple, and standing water is the turn of the tide. The last sentence is proverbial.

21 I would be loath to cast away my speech; for besides that it is excellently well penned, I have taken great pains to con it.
(I.5.165–7)
Viola, disguised as Cesario, has been sent to woo Olivia on Orsino's behalf. Olivia and Maria meet her but Olivia is veiled. Viola begins her conventional praise but then breaks off with this frank admission of the artificiality of her enterprise. 'Con' means learn.

22 OLIVIA Whence came you, sir?
VIOLA I can say little more than I have studied, and that question's out of my part.
(I.5.170–2)
Viola's answer emphasizes her status as a proxy playing the lover on behalf of someone else and, since Olivia's question touches on the sensitive area of her origins, serves as a reminder that Viola is playing two roles – Cesario as well as Orsino's messenger.

23 OLIVIA Are you a comedian?
VIOLA No, my profound heart; and yet, by the very fangs of malice, I swear I am not that I play.
(I.5.175–7)
The emphasis on role-playing continues with Olivia asking directly if Cesario (Viola) is an actor ('comedian'). Viola's response plays on the audience's knowledge of her disguise. The sense of the first part of Viola's lines is that Olivia has been clever in spotting Viola's role-playing as Orsino's proxy but harsh in her question.

24 VIOLA Alas, I took great pains to study it, and 'tis poetical.
pared speech. ia is ded on it.
olivia It is the more like to be feigned.
pared speech. *(I.5.187–8)*
Olivia has asked Cesario (Viola) to skip her prepared speech. Here Viola emphasizes the hard work she has put in, but Olivia is suspicious of poetry precisely because so much effort is expended on it.

25 OLIVIA We will draw the curtain and show you the picture. Look you, sir, such a one I was this present. Is't not well done?
VIOLA Excellently done – if God did all.
OLIVIA 'Tis in grain, sir, 'twill endure wind and weather.
VIOLA
'Tis beauty truly blent, whose red and white
Nature's own sweet and cunning hand laid on.
Lady, you are the cruellest she alive,
If you will lead these graces to the grave,
And leave the world no copy.
OLIVIA O, sir, I will not be so hard-hearted. I will give out divers schedules of my beauty. It shall be inventoried, and every particle and utensil labelled to my will. As, item: two lips, indifferent red; item: two grey eyes, with lids to them; item: one neck, one chin, and so forth.
(I.5.223–37)

Olivia and Viola's negotiations have now reached the stage where Olivia, at Viola's request, removes her veil. She compares herself to her own portrait hidden behind a curtain – her veil – thus opening the way for a comparison between portrait and cosmetic painting which underlies the sparring of the subsequent lines. 'In grain' means natural; 'blent' means blended. When Viola says 'copy' she means child, but Olivia deliberately mis-takes her to mean a literal copy. The whole exchange is much concerned with the relationship between outer appearances and inner realities which characterizes so much of Shakespeare's work.

26 VIOLA

Make me a willow cabin at your gate,
And call upon my soul within the house;
Write loyal cantons of contemnèd love
And sing them loud even in the dead of night;
Hallow your name to the reverberate hills
And make the babbling gossip of the air
Cry out 'Olivia!' O, you should not rest
Between the elements of air and earth,
But you should pity me.

OLIVIA You might do much.

(I.5.257–65)

Olivia has asked what Cesario (Viola) would do if he (she) loved her as much as Orsino does and were rejected. Viola replies with this speech, which presumably reflects her unrequited love for Orsino. It also has the effect of reinforcing Olivia's growing passion for her which is reflected in the very simple statement with which she ends Viola's line. Willows are traditionally associated with rejected love; 'my soul within the house' is Olivia; 'cantons' are songs; 'contemned' means despised, rejected; 'Hallow' means both cry out and bless; 'reverberate' means reverberating; and 'babbling gossip' is a personification of echo.

27 'What is your parentage?'
'Above my fortunes, yet my state is well.
I am a gentleman.' I'll be sworn thou art.
Thy tongue, thy face, thy limbs, actions, and spirit
Do give thee fivefold blazon. Not too fast! soft, soft –
Unless the master were the man. How now?
Even so quickly may one catch the plague?

(I.5.278–84)

Olivia begins her speech immediately after Viola's exit by quoting her own earlier question and Viola's reply. A blazon is a coat of arms; Olivia is saying that Viola's appearance is as good a guarantee of her gentlemanly status as a coat of arms would be. She has fallen in love with Viola at first meeting and like Orsino she sees love in terms of disease (plague).

28 She is drowned already, sir, with salt water, though I seem to drown her remembrance again with more.
(II.1.26–8)
Sebastian, Viola's twin brother, has also been saved from the shipwreck but, like her, believes that his twin is dead. In describing her to Antonio, who saved him from the wreck, Sebastian finds himself crying; salt water suggests both tears and the sea.

29 I am bound to the Count Orsino's court.
(II.1.37–8)
Sebastian's decision to go to Orsino's court is a necessary precondition for the reunion of brother and sister and the sorting out of the confused emotional situation between Viola, Olivia, and Orsino, since his presence will offer Olivia an appropriate channel for her affections. The placing of this scene between Olivia falling in love with Viola and Viola learning of Olivia's love is very important to the comic development of the play since it suggests the eventual outcome to the audience, thus defusing the seriousness of the situation.

30 Fortune forbid my outside have not charmed her!
None of my lord's ring? Why, he sent her none.
I am the man! If it be so – as 'tis –
Poor lady, she were better love a dream.
Disguise, I see thou art a wickedness
Wherein the pregnant enemy does much.
How will this fadge? My master loves her dearly;
And I, poor monster, fond as much on him;
And she, mistaken, seems to dote on me.
What will become of this? As I am man,
My state is desperate for my master's love.
As I am woman – now, alas the day,
What thriftless sighs shall poor Olivia breathe!
O time, thou must untangle this, not I!
It is too hard a knot for me t'untie.
(II.2.18, 24–8, 33–41)
Olivia has sent Malvolio to give a ring to Cesario (Viola), pretending that she is returning one of Orsino's gifts. After Malvolio's exit Viola realizes that her male disguise has fooled Olivia as well as Orsino, with the result that the unfortunate Olivia has fallen in love with a women disguised as a man. Viola's soliloquy summarizes her current knowledge of the state of affairs and is a useful recapitulation of the events in this plot to precede a lengthy

subplot scene. A common complaint against the theatre was that it involved people being deceitful by pretending to be other people and this appears to lie behind Viola's reference to the cunning Devil (pregnant enemy). 'Fadge' means turn out. Viola is a monster because she is neither man nor woman.

31 SIR TOBY Approach, Sir Andrew. Not to be abed after midnight, is to be up betimes, and *dilucolo surgere*, thou knowest –
SIR ANDREW Nay, by my troth, I know not; but I know to be up late is to be up late.
SIR TOBY A false conclusion! I hate it as an unfilled can. To be up after midnight and to go to bed then is early; so that to go to bed after midnight is to go to bed betimes. Does not our lives consist of the four elements?
SIR ANDREW Faith, so they say; but I think it rather consists of eating and drinking.
(II.3.1–11)
Sir Toby and Sir Andrew appear after Viola's exit and continue the emphasis on time from a different perspective. Whereas Viola trusts to time, Sir Toby is trying to distort time: as we find out later in the scene, it is very late at night. Sir Andrew, despite his foolishness, has a truer understanding of what they are about. '*Diluculo surgere*' is part of a Latin sentence in Lilly's Latin Grammar, a sixteenth-century schoolbook; Sir Toby quotes 'to get up at dawn' – the rest of the sentence is 'is most healthy'. Sir Toby's reference to the four elements is to the theory that matter was made up of earth, air, fire, and water in various combinations.

32 I did impetticoat thy gratillity.
(II.3.25)
Feste's mock gravity extends to this elevated way of saying that he accepted sixpence Sir Andrew sent him in payment for some previous entertainment. Both 'impetticoat' (pocket) and 'gratillity' (a little gratuity) were coined for this occasion.

33 O mistress mine! Where are you roaming?
O, stay and hear: your true love's coming,
   That can sing both high and low.
Trip no further, pretty sweeting;
Journeys end in lovers meeting,
   Every wise man's son doth know.
What is love? 'Tis not hereafter;
Present mirth hath present laughter,
   What's to come is still unsure.

In delay there lies no plenty –
Then come kiss me, sweet and twenty,
  Youth's a stuff will not endure.
(II.3.37–42, 45–50)

Feste's song is sung to Sir Toby and Sir Andrew. A somewhat melancholy love song, it is more appropriate to the adventures of the main plot characters than to the two knights. 'Present laughter' has been used as a play title by Noël Coward, while the title of R. C. Sherriff's *Journey's End* perhaps derives from the phrase 'journeys end' here. There are two settings of a tune with this title from the period – Thomas Morley's was published in 1599, William Byrd's in 1619 – although we cannot be absolutely certain that Shakespeare meant to use this tune.

34 Am not I consanguineous? Am I not of her blood?
(II.3.76)

Sir Toby reminds us that his presence in Olivia's household is due to him being a relative. It is often assumed that, since he calls her niece, he is Olivia's uncle, but the word, like cousin, was used less precisely in Shakespeare's time than in ours.

35 He does it with a better grace, but I do it more natural.
(II.3.81–2)

Sir Andrew, in commenting on Sir Toby's ability to play the fool, manages to suggest that he, Sir Andrew, is naturally foolish.

36 Is there no respect of place, persons, nor time in you?
(II.3.90–1)

Malvolio has been called up by Olivia to stop the drunken revelry. His question is, therefore, highly proper, but he is the enemy of all holiday behaviour, standing at the opposite pole from Sir Toby, who wants to extend holiday until there is nothing else.

37 Dost thou think, because thou art virtuous, there shall be no more cakes and ale?
(II.3.110–12)

Sir Toby puts the counter-argument to Malvolio. Cakes and ale were associated with church feasts and would be particularly obnoxious to a Puritan such as Maria claims Malvolio to be.

38 Sometimes he is a kind of puritan.
(II.3.134)

Maria, who joined the company before Malvolio arrived to tell them off, accuses Malvolio of being a Puritan. He is certainly a puritan in the wider sense of being a killjoy but, although there are references to such English sects as the Brownists in the play, he is not characterized as a member of a specific sect. Puritans were often opposed to the theatre, making no distinction between deceit and fiction and disliking the disorder which sometimes accompanies public gatherings. They are, unsurprisingly, seldom presented favourably in Renaissance drama.

39 I will drop in his way some obscure epistles of love; wherein, by the colour of his beard, the shape of his leg, the manner of his gait, the expressure of his eye, forehead, and complexion, he shall find himself most feelingly personated. I can write very like my lady, your niece; on a forgotten matter we can hardly make distinction of our hands.

(II.3.148–54)

Maria explains to Sir Toby the scheme by which Malvolio's pretensions will be revealed. 'Expressure' means expression; 'feelingly personated' means described vividly, with overtones of impersonation which relate to the play's thematic concerns.

40 I was adored once, too.

(II.3.174)

Sir Toby has just remarked that Maria adores him. Sir Andrew's melancholic recollection of past glory is both characteristically self-aware and a source of amusement for the audience.

41 ORSINO If ever thou shalt love,
In the sweet pangs of it, remember me.
For such as I am, all true lovers are:
Unstaid and skittish in all motions else,
Save in the constant image of the creature
That is beloved. How dost thou like this tune?
VIOLA
It gives a very echo to the seat
Where love is throned.

(II.4.15–22)

Music is being played to Orsino and Cesario (Viola) throughout this speech, in which Orsino dilates on the nature of true love. There is an ironic contrast in the situation of the supposed lover prattling about the nature of true love to the true lover beside him, who is deeply affected by the tune of the sad song that Feste sings later. See also 42 and 43.

42 ORSINO
Let still the woman take
An elder than herself; so wears she to him;
So sways she level in her husband's heart.

For, boy, however we do praise ourselves,
Our fancies are more giddy and unfirm,
More longing, wavering, sooner lost and worn,
Than women's are.

VIOLA I think it well, my lord.

ORSINO
Then let thy love be younger than thyself,
Or thy affection cannot hold the bent.
For women are as roses whose fair flower,
Being once displayed, doth fall that very hour.

VIOLA
And so they are. Alas, that they are so,
To die, even when they to perfection grow.

(II.4.29–41)

Orsino continues to offer sententious advice to Viola. There is considerable irony in his confiding his thoughts about men to a disguised woman who is in love with him. As in the play's opening scene, Orsino rapidly contradicts himself (see 41 and 43). Orsino suggests that a younger wife will adapt ('wears') to her husband and thus remain loved as much as she was.

43 Come away, come away, death,
And in sad cypress let me be laid.
Fie away, fie away, breath!
I am slain by a fair cruel maid.
My shroud of white, stuck all with yew,
O, prepare it!
My part of death, no one so true
Did share it.

(II.4.50–7)

Feste sings this song to Orsino and Viola. The tune was being played throughout their earlier discussion in this scene (see 41 and 42), so it suggests their rather melancholic attitude to love. Cypress and yew are both trees traditionally associated with death and graveyards.

44 There is no woman's sides
Can bide the beating of so strong a passion
As love doth give my heart; no woman's heart
So big to hold so much, they lack retention.
Alas, their love may be called appetite,
No motion of the liver, but the palate,
That suffer surfeit, cloyment, and revolt.
But mine is all as hungry as the sea,
And can digest as much. Make no compare
Between that love a woman can bear me

And that I owe Olivia.
(II.4.92–102)
Viola has raised the possibility that there could be a woman who loved Orsino as much as he claims to love Olivia. In this reply, Orsino is moved to an extravagant and eloquent account of his passion which is undercut by the fact that he is himself using as his go-between a woman who loves him far more than he loves Olivia. The central strand of imagery is physiological, starting with 'sides' and running through 'retention', a medical term meaning the ability to retain. The liver was regarded as a seat of the passions.

45 VIOLA
My father had a daughter loved a man –
As it might be perhaps, were I a woman,
I should your lordship.
ORSINO And what's her history?
VIOLA
A blank, my lord. She never told her love,
But let concealment, like a worm i'the bud,
Feed on her damask cheek. She pined in thought,
And with a green and yellow melancholy,
She sat like Patience on a monument,
Smiling at grief. Was not this love indeed?
We men may say more, swear more, but indeed
Our shows are more than will; for still we prove
Much in our vows, but little in our love.
ORSINO
But died thy sister of her love, my boy?
VIOLA
I am all the daughters of my father's house,
And all the brothers too; and yet, I know not.
(II.4.106–20)
The dialogue between Cesario (Viola) and Orsino moves on to dangerous ground as Viola compares herself to the woman she actually is and voices her actual feelings for Orsino. The 'damask cheek' compares the supposed sister's complexion to the damask rose being eaten from within by the 'worm i'the bud'. Melancholy is described as green and yellow because of the pallor of the sick face. 'Patience on a monument' is presumably an allegorical figure on a tomb or in an emblem book.

46 Get ye all three into the box-tree. Malvolio's coming down this walk, he has been yonder i'the sun practising behaviour to his own shadow this half-hour.
(II.5.15–17)

The conspirators, Sir Andrew, Sir Toby, the shadowy figure of Fabian, and Maria, are ready to spring their trap on Malvolio. Maria's statement about Malvolio's behaviour is borne out when he appears, and it is an important confirmation that he deserves his punishment. Box is a kind of shrub used in borders and hedges, but what form the box-tree took in the original production is not clear.

47 The lady of the Strachy married the yeoman of the wardrobe.
(II.5.38–9)
Before he finds the letter Maria has left for him, Malvolio is already musing on examples of socially advantageous marriages. Despite many brave and some foolhardy attempts to identify the two people Malvolio mentions they remain unsatisfactorily identified.

48 Seven of my people, with an obedient start, make out for him. I frown the while, and perchance wind up my watch, or play with my *(fingering his steward's chain of office)* – some rich jewel. Toby approaches, curtsies there to me.
(II.5.57–61)
Malvolio is fantasizing about his revenge on Sir Toby when he has married Olivia. In the middle of the fantasy, which occurs before he has picked up the letter, the tangible chain of his steward's office has to be redefined as an object more appropriate to his new status; the stage direction is editorial but the action and its object are strongly implied. As befits his elevated position, 'Count' Malvolio drops the 'Sir' from Toby's name.

49 Though our silence be drawn from us with cars, yet peace!
(II.5.63–4)
The conspirators find it hard to keep quiet in the face of Malvolio's posturing but Fabian reminds them of the necessity of silence. 'Drawn from us with cars' is presumably analogous to 'wild horses couldn't drag it out of us'.

50 *I may command where I adore;*
But silence, like a Lucrece' knife,
With bloodless stroke my heart doth gore;
M.O.A.I. doth sway my life.
(II.5.103–6)
Malvolio has found the letter and is now reading Maria's riddling verse. He takes the writing to be Olivia's and therefore assumes that it is she who loves where she may command. Malvolio has just told us that the letter was sealed with Olivia's seal, a Lucretia, so the reference in the verse to Lucretia confirms his mistaken impression. The Roman Lucretia was a symbol of chas-

tity, and Shakespeare wrote a poem on her. The riddle of the last line has defied satisfactory solution, although I AM O (i.e. Olivia) is quite attractive.

51 *If this fall into thy hand, revolve. In my stars I am above thee, but be not afraid of greatness. Some are born great, some achieve greatness, and some have greatness thrust upon 'em.*
(II.5.139–42)
Malvolio gives up on the riddle and starts to read the letter. The lines about greatness have become proverbial. 'Revolve' means consider but it is often interpreted literally in the theatre, providing an opportunity for the conspirators to exploit avoiding Malvolio's gaze to comic effect.

52 *Remember who commended thy yellow stockings and wished to see thee ever cross-gartered.*
(II.5.148–9)
The letter continues. As Maria tells us later, Olivia actually hates both yellow and cross-gartering. Yellow is a holiday colour; most Malvolios wear black earlier in the play so that the reversal will seem greater. Cross-gartering was out of fashion by the time the play was written.

53 FESTE Now Jove, in his next commodity of hair, send thee a beard!
VIOLA By my troth, I'll tell thee, I am almost sick for one – (*aside*)though I would not have it grow on my chin.
(III.1.43–7)
In the course of their discussion Cesario (Viola) has given Feste a coin. His thanks typically take the form of a mock invocation to the gods, asking that Cesario should soon reach maturity. She, equally characteristically, takes the opportunity to remind the audience of her disguise and her plight.

54 This fellow is wise enough to play the fool;
And to do that well craves a kind of wit.
He must observe their mood on whom he jests,
The quality of persons, and the time,
And, like the haggard, check at every feather
That comes before his eye. This is a practice
As full of labour as a wise man's art.
For folly that he wisely shows is fit;
But wise men, folly-fallen, quite taint their wit.
(III.1.58–66)
After Feste's departure Viola muses on his artistic abilities. Such observations about the wisdom and aptitude of professional fools

are quite common in the Renaissance but Shakespeare, a professional writer and actor, often returns to the subject, which can also be related to the difference between outward appearance and the true nature, another of his major interests. The 'haggard' is the wild hawk, which changes direction to attack ('check') smaller birds ('every feather'); the point of the comparison is that Feste has to seize every opportunity to make a joke that comes his way.

55 SIR TOBY Taste your legs, sir; put them to motion.
VIOLA My legs do better under-stand me, sir, than I understand what you mean by bidding me taste my legs.
(III.1.76–8)
Cesario (Viola) and SirToby are sparring in an affected exchange of compliments which leads to Viola's pun on 'understand', meaning support as well as comprehend. 'Taste' means try.

56 VIOLA Most excellent, accomplished lady, the heavens rain odours on you!
SIR ANDREW (*aside*) That youth's a rare courtier. 'Rain odours'! Well!
(III.1.81–3)
Cesario (Viola) greets Olivia with the typically hyperbolic compliment of the conventional lover. Sir Andrew, lingering about the scene, is deeply impressed by Viola's verbal facility, which begins to convince him of the futility of his pretensions to Olivia.

57 My servant, sir? 'Twas never merry world
Since lowly feigning was called compliment.
(III.1.95–6)
Cesario (Viola) continues in her hyperbolic vein, thus earning this rebuke from Olivia. In the courtly love tradition the lover regarded himself as the servant of his mistress; this is what Olivia is referring to here in the second line. The first line means things have deteriorated or never been the same.

58 OLIVIA
There lies your way, due west.
VIOLA Then westward ho!
(III.1.131)
Olivia dismisses Cesario (Viola) at the end of their discussion. Viola's reply is the traditional cry of the watermen who ran a water-taxi service on the Thames when they were intending to go from the City to Westminster.

59 O, what a deal of scorn looks beautiful
In the contempt and anger of his lip!
(III.1.142–3)
Olivia and Cesario (Viola) have been sparring about who they are, and Viola has become angry. Olivia's aside reveals that she finds even this angry face attractive.

60 Love sought, is good; but given unsought, is better.
(III.1.153)
In declaring her love for Cesario (Viola), Olivia makes this reasonable point which is inevitably undercut by the audience's knowledge of the true situation.

61 She did show favour to the youth in your sight only to exasperate you, to awake your dormouse valour, to put fire in your heart and brimstone in your liver. You should then have accosted her, and with some excellent jests fire-new from the mint, you should have banged the youth into dumbness. This was looked for at your hand, and this was baulked.
(III.2.17–23)
Sir Andrew has decided to give up his wooing of Olivia. Fabian and Sir Toby are attempting to keep him interested by reinterpreting to Sir Andrew's advantage the favours Olivia has shown to Cesario. Here Fabian argues that Sir Andrew has missed an opportunity to see off his rival because of his 'dormouse' (sleeping and timid) valour; 'fire-new from the mint' is the equivalent of hot from the press.

62 You are now sailed into the north of my lady's opinion; where you will hang like an icicle on a Dutchman's beard, unless you do redeem it by some laudable attempt either of valour or policy.
(III.2.24–8)
Fabian continues to castigate Sir Andrew for failing to seize the opportunity to woo Olivia. Fabian claims that Olivia now regards Sir Andrew coldly – he is in 'the north of my lady's opinion'. The only way back into her favour is by doing a brave deed or finding a stratagem ('policy') to defeat Cesario (Viola). The icy Dutchman is presumably William Barentz, who sailed in the Arctic in 1596–7 and gave his name to the Barents Sea. His name appears on the 'new map' mentioned by Maria later in the scene; see 67.

63 I had as lief be a Brownist as a politician.
(III.2.30)
Sir Andrew rejects Fabian's suggestion that he should win Olivia by a trick, on the grounds that he hates trickery. 'I had as lief be'

means I would as soon be. Politician is usually derogatory in Shakespeare, as it is here, meaning a plotter or intriguer rather than a person involved in affairs of state. The Brownists were a puritan sect, ancestors of the Congregationalists, so Sir Andrew is saying that he dislikes trickery as much as he dislikes puritans.

64 Taunt him with licence of ink. If thou 'thou'-est him some thrice it shall not be amiss, and as many lies as will lie in thy sheet of paper – although the sheet were big enough for the bed of Ware in England, set 'em down, go about it.
(III.2.42–6)
Sir Toby has decided that Sir Andrew should duel with Cesario (Viola) and is suggesting the form of the challenge. 'Thou' was used to intimates, as by Sir Toby here, and to social inferiors, so Sir Toby is suggesting that Sir Andrew should use an insulting form of address in the challenge. The Great Bed of Ware, more than ten feet long and broad, was a famous Elizabethan tourist attraction which is now in the Victoria and Albert Museum in London; Ware is a town in Hertfordshire. Shakespeare often has characters remind us of the supposed foreign setting of his plays by making them refer to aspects of English life as though they were foreign.

65 For Andrew, if he were opened and you find so much blood in his liver as will clog the foot of a flea, I'll eat the rest of the anatomy.
(III.2.58–60)
As preparations for the duel continue, Sir Toby explains to Fabian that Sir Andrew is as cowardly as they suspect Cesario (Viola) to be. The liver was supposed to be the source of blood, which is associated with valour, so that Sir Toby is suggesting that an autopsy would discover that Sir Andrew was lily-livered; 'anatomy' here means corpse.

66 Look where the youngest wren of nine comes.
(III.2.63)
Sir Toby draws Fabian's attention to Maria's entrance. Wrens were supposed to lay nine eggs, of which the last to hatch produced the smallest bird. Maria is often described as being small in stature, which presumably reflects the size of the original player.

67 He does smile his face into more lines than is in the new map with the augmentation of the Indies.
(III.2.74–6)
Maria is explaining how Malvolio is behaving now that he has digested the instructions in the letter. His smiling creases his face

into a grid of lines like those on the map of the world on a new projection published by Emmeric Mollineux in 1599.

68 In the south suburbs, at the Elephant,
Is best to lodge.
(III.3.40–1)
Antonio and Sebastian have now arrived in Orsino's territory. The Elephant, Antonio's recommended lodging place, was an inn in Southwark close to the Globe theatre. Once again Shakespeare is making a reference to a familiar part of his original audience's life.

69 Your store,
I think, is not for idle markets, sir.
(III.3.46–7)
Antonio has given Sebastian his purse as part of Shakespeare's preparation for the series of mistaken identities between Viola and Sebastian which lead to the denouement. Here Antonio justifies his decision by referring delicately to Sebastian's limited supply of money ('store') which is not enough to buy luxuries.

70 Sad, lady? I could be sad; this does make some obstruction in the blood, this cross-gartering.
(III.4.19–20)
Olivia, encountering the transformed Malvolio for the first time, has remarked that she sent for him on serious ('sad') business. He, however, has his own problems since his comically inappropriate holiday wear, adopted to liberate him from his everyday limitations, is itself a source of constriction.

71 I think we do know the sweet Roman hand.
(III.4.27)
The 'sweet Roman hand' is what Malvolio believes to be Olivia's handwriting in the letter which gave him the instructions as to the behaviour which is now puzzling Olivia. 'Roman hand' is the then new Italic script.

72 Why, this is very midsummer madness.
(III.4.56)
Olivia's surprise at Malvolio's extraordinary behaviour leads her to this proverbial description of it. It was popularly supposed that the great heat of midsummer made dogs mad.

73 And when she went away now – 'let this fellow be looked to'. Fellow! Not 'Malvolio', nor after my degree, but 'fellow'! Why, everything adheres together, that no dram of a scruple,

no scruple of a scruple, no obstacle, no incredulous or unsafe circumstance – what can be said? – nothing that can be, can come between me and the full prospect of my hopes. Well, Jove, not I, is the doer of this, and he is to be thanked.
(III.4.76–83)
Because of Malvolio's strange behaviour Olivia is making arrangements to have him specially looked after. In the course of giving instructions she has described him as 'fellow', an appropriate term for a person of high rank being polite about an inferior. Malvolio, however, takes it in the sense of companion, and finds all her concerned behaviour proof of her love for him. When he talks of scruples, Malvolio is playing on the two meanings 'doubt' and 'tiny amount'.

74 Which way is he, in the name of sanctity? If all the devils of hell be drawn in little and Legion himself possessed him, yet I'll speak to him.
(III.4.84–6)
Sir Toby has been sent to look after Malvolio and therefore makes his entrance in a burst of sententious religiosity, invoking holy protection before facing the supposed madman. Legion was the name given to the host of devils who possessed the madman in the Bible, St Mark 5:9.

75 What, man, defy the devil! Consider, he's an enemy to mankind.
(III.4.97–8)
Sir Toby continues to treat Malvolio as a madman, encouraging him with commonplaces.

76 Go, hang yourselves all. You are idle, shallow things; I am not of your element.
(III.4.122–3)
Wrapped in his own good opinion of himself, Malvolio brushes off his tormentors. He sees himself as made of finer stuff than they are, existing on a different plane ('not of your element').

77 If this were played upon a stage now, I could condemn it as an improbable fiction.
(III.4.126–7)
Fabian's response to Malvolio's behaviour is typical of Shakespeare's dramaturgy. He often has characters draw our attention to the improbability of events, thus both reminding us that his plays are fictions and reinforcing their credibility, in the same way that we say 'it was incredible' to emphasize that something did actually happen.

78 More matter for a May morning!
(III.4.141)
Fabian is commenting on the arrival of Sir Andrew with his challenge just after Malvolio has left. May is associated with holiday and games, so Fabian is reminding us of the suspension of normal order associated with festivals such as Mayday or Twelfth Night itself.

79 Still you keep o' the windy side of the law.
(III.4.162)
As Sir Toby reads out Sir Andrew's challenge, Fabian comments on the phrasing. Since duelling was illegal, Sir Andrew has tried to write in a way which will clear him of any charge of starting the quarrel. Fabian suggests that he is managing thereby to keep on the safe side of the law; 'windy' meaning safe because the scent of a hunted animal would not carry against the wind.

80 *Fare thee well, and God have mercy upon one of our souls. He may have mercy upon mine, but my hope is better – and so, look to thyself. Thy friend as thou usest him, and thy sworn enemy, Andrew Aguecheek.*
(III.4.165–8)
Sir Toby continues to read the challenge but Sir Andrew's attempts at careful phrasing have come unstuck. He hopes he will survive and that therefore God will have mercy on Cesario's (Viola's) soul, but manages to suggest that he is hoping for something better than salvation.

81 Nay, let me alone for swearing.
(III.4.181)
Sir Andrew is by no means sure about his capacity to fight, but he is quite confident about the swearing that precedes the duel.

82 He is knight dubbed with unhatched rapier and on carpet consideration – but he is a devil in private brawl. Souls and bodies hath he divorced three.
(III.4.230–2)
Sir Toby is now terrifying Cesario (Viola) with tales of Sir Andrew's knightly prowess. In fact it appears that Sir Andrew's knighthood, like many at the court of James I, is a reward for financial or other unmartial services to the crown; 'on carpet consideration' suggest that he may have received it in return for a donation. This is further suggested by the 'unhatched' sword which has either never been drawn or not marked in battle.

83 I am one that had rather go with Sir Priest than Sir Knight.
(III.4.264–5)

The build-up to the duel involves Sir Toby offering to try to make Cesario's (Viola's) peace with Sir Andrew. In accepting the offer Viola stresses her peaceful nature and perhaps her preference for marriage ('go with Sir Priest') over fighting.

84 A little thing would make me tell them how much I lack of a man.

(III.4.293–4)

As the duel with Sir Andrew appears increasingly likely to happen, Viola confides her state of mind to the audience. She is playing on the sense of 'man' as manly quality or bravery as well as on the literal meaning.

85 For the fair kindness you have showed me here,
And part being prompted by your present trouble,
Out of my lean and low ability,
I'll lend you something. My having is not much.

(III.4.332–5)

The duel between Sir Andrew and Viola has been interrupted by the intercession of Antonio who assumes that Viola is Sebastian. Antonio has then been arrested because of his previous war service against Orsino and has asked his supposed friend for the money he lent him earlier. This is Viola's reply which, naturally, seems inadequate to Antonio.

86 VIOLA
I hate ingratitude more in a man
Than lying, vainness, babbling drunkenness,
Or any taint of vice whose strong corruption
Inhabits our frail blood –
ANTONIO O heavens themselves!

(III.4.345–8)

Viola continues to protest her innocence of Antonio's charges, thus increasing his anger.

87 In nature, there's no blemish but the mind;
None can be called deformed, but the unkind.

(III.4.358–9)

Antonio is stung into denouncing the supposed Sebastian's ingratitude. The lines suggest that although there may appear to be outward blemishes in nature the only true deformity is in those who behave unnaturally, as Antonio thinks Sebastian is behaving in apparently rejecting his friend.

88 What relish is in this? How runs the stream?
Or I am mad, or else this is a dream.
Let fancy still my sense in Lethe steep;
If it be thus to dream, still let me sleep!
(IV.1.59–62)

Confusion mounts as Olivia talks to Sebastian in the mistaken belief that he is Cesario (Viola). Sebastian's aside is in couplets which mark the sense of unreality that he feels. He, luckily for everybody, is happy to go along with Olivia. In trying to make sense of his bewildering experiences – he has also been attacked by Sir Toby and Sir Andrew – Sebastian asks what he is to make of it all ('What relish is in this'). 'Or ... or' is a Renaissance version of 'Either ... or'. Drinking the waters of Lethe, one of the rivers in the classical Greek underworld, made the spirits of the dead forget their lives on earth, so Sebastian is saying he is quite happy to forget his former life as this one has so much to offer.

89 Out, hyperbolical fiend, how vexest thou this man! Talkest thou nothing but of ladies?
(IV.2.25–6)

Feste, visiting Malvolio who has been confined in a dark house as treatment for his madness, is pretending to be Sir Topas the curate. Malvolio has asked him to go to Olivia, and his response is to pretend to think he is possessed by a sexually obsessed spirit. 'Hyperbolical' here means unruly or boisterous.

90 Fie, thou dishonest Satan! I call thee by the most modest terms, for I am one of those gentle ones that will use the devil himself with courtesy.
(IV.2.31–3)

Feste, as Sir Topas the curate, continues to talk to the demon supposedly possessing Malvolio.

91 Madman, thou errest. I say there is no darkness but ignorance, in which thou art more puzzled than the Egyptians in their fog.
(IV.2.42–4)

The curate would naturally talk in pious platitudes, so Feste laces his discussion with Malvolio with ringing biblical cadences and references. The Egyptian fog, three days of darkness, was one of the plagues of Egypt described in the Bible, Exodus 10.

92 FESTE What is the opinion of Pythagoras concerning wildfowl?
MALVOLIO That the soul of our grandam might haply inhabit a bird.

FESTE What thinkest thou of his opinion?
MALVOLIO I think nobly of the soul, and no way approve his opinion.
FESTE Fare thee well; remain thou still in darkness. Thou shalt hold the opinion of Pythagoras ere I will allow of thy wits, and fear to kill a woodcock lest thou dispossess the soul of thy grandam. Fare thee well.
(IV.2.49–59)
In desperation Malvolio has asked Feste, the supposed Sir Topas, to test his sanity by asking him about some everyday topic. Although he gives what would normally be regarded as the correct answer, since the ideas of the Greek philosopher Pythagoras about the transmigration of souls were regarded as heretical, Feste has decided to reverse conventional wisdom and merely being right is not enough to get Malvolio freed. 'Grandam' means grandmother.

93 Leave thy vain bibble-babble.
(IV.2.96–7)
Still pretending to be the curate, Feste uses a common phrase to denigrate Malvolio's basically sane statements.

94 [He] grew a twenty years' removèd thing
While one would wink.
(V.1.87–8)
Antonio is describing, to Orsino, Viola's behaviour when he intervened to save her from Sir Andrew. He believes that she is Sebastian and thus describes how the person he thought of as his friend rapidly distanced himself from him.

95 I'll sacrifice the lamb that I do love
To spite a raven's heart within a dove.
(V.1.128–9)
Orsino has realized that Olivia is in love with Viola and is proposing to do some mischief to Cesario (Viola), who is the lamb he refers to, in order to get back at Olivia, whom he sees as a dove with a raven's heart because she looks peaceful and loveable but is actually preying on Orsino. Once again Orsino talks extravagantly but to little purpose.

96 Since when, my watch hath told me, toward my grave
I have travelled but two hours.
(V.1.160–1)
The priest has been called by Olivia to testify that she is married to Cesario (Viola). In fact the marriage was between Olivia and Sebastian, but the priest does not know this when he testifies.

He is basically only saying that the marriage took place two hours previously, but the phrasing is both apt for a priest and voices the melancholic attitude often found in the play.

97 We took him for a coward, but he's the very devil incardinate.
(V.1.177–9)
As the denouement gathers pace, Sir Andrew enters, having been beaten by Sebastian, whom he and Sir Toby had attacked in the belief that he was Cesario (Viola). This is his description of their apparent misjudgement of Cesario. 'Incardinate' is an error for incarnate.

98 One face, one voice, one habit, and two persons!
A natural perspective, that is and is not.
(V.1.213–14)
After all the mistakes Viola and Sebastian are finally seen on stage together and Orsino voices the assembled company's surprise. A perspective was a device whereby one image appeared as two.

99 FESTE And thus the whirligig of time brings in his revenges.
MALVOLIO
I'll be revenged on the whole pack of you! *Exit*
OLIVIA
He hath been most notoriously abused.
(V.1.373–6)
The plot of Malvolio has been revealed and Feste claims his revenge for the insults Malvolio has heaped on him earlier, suggesting that time is like a spinning top. Malvolio, however, cannot be included within the comic synthesis, and his exit line and Olivia's remark contribute to the by no means entirely happy atmosphere of the play's ending.

100 Cesario, come;
For so you shall be, while you are a man.
But when in other habits you are seen –
Orsino's mistress, and his fancy's queen!
(V.1.382–5)
There is something slightly odd about the visual picture at the end of the play with two couples of lovers made up of three 'men' and a single woman. Orsino's remarks remind the audience of this, and it is perhaps disturbing that he is still talking in the same terms as he did at the beginning of the play.

101 When that I was and a little tiny boy,
With hey-ho, the wind and the rain;

A foolish thing was but a toy,
  For the rain it raineth every day.
But when I came to man's estate,
  With hey-ho, the wind and the rain;
'Gainst knaves and thieves men shut their gate,
  For the rain it raineth every day.
But when I came, alas, to wive,
  With hey-ho, the wind and the rain;
By swaggering could I never thrive,
  For the rain it raineth every day.
But when I came unto my beds,
  With hey-ho, the wind and the rain;
With tosspots still had drunken heads,
  For the rain it raineth every day.
A great while ago the world began,
  With hey-ho, the wind and the rain;
But that's all one, our play is done,
  And we'll strive to please you every day.

(V.1.386–405)

The play ends with Feste alone on stage singing this song. It may be a folk song and it also appears in a shorter and different form in *King Lear*. In the theatre it is now generally treated as melancholic, since Feste is an individual excluded from the various couples established at the end of the play. It ends with a compliment aimed at the audience, eliciting applause. 'Toy' means trifle and a 'tosspot' is a drunkard.

The Two Gentlemen of Verona

1 Home-keeping youth have ever homely wits.

(I.1.2)

Valentine is to leave Verona for Milan. Proteus, his friend, has evidently been trying to persuade him to remain. Valentine is mockingly suggesting that he understands Proteus' desire to remain at home on account of his attachment to Julia. The opposition of *amicitia* (male friendship) to *amor* (sexual love) is one of the major themes of romantic comedy, the genre in which *The Two Gentlemen of Verona* is written.

2 He after honour hunts, I after love.
He leaves his friends to dignify them more;
I leave myself, my friends, and all for love.
Thou, Julia, thou hast metamorphosed me,
Made me neglect my studies, lose my time,
War with good counsel, set the world at naught;
Made wit with musing weak, heart sick with thought.
(I.1.63–9)

Proteus is contrasting Valentine's active pursuit of fame at the court of Milan with his own dedication to the religion of love. The effect of love is likened to a metamorphosis, appropriate in view of the inconstancy and the name of Proteus, which signifies a classical sea-god capable of changing form. The protean nature of man was a preoccupation of Renaissance moral philosophy. Ovid's *Metamorphoses*, especially in Arthur Golding's translation of 1567, was also a strong influence on Elizabethan literature. The effects of love which Proteus describes in the last three lines are stereotypical.

3 Fie, fie! How wayward is this foolish love,
That, like a testy babe, will scratch the nurse,
And presently, all humbled, kiss the rod.
(I.2.57–9)

Julia has been debating with her maid, Lucetta, whether she should fall in love with any of her suitors. Lucetta has produced a letter from Proteus, but Julia has feigned anger and disdain. Left alone, Julia muses on the contradictory impulses of love which determine all her actions in this scene from aggression to submission.

4 O, hateful hands, to tear such loving words.
Injurious wasps, to feed on such sweet honey,
And kill the bees that yield it with your stings.
(I.2.105–7)

In the presence of her maid, Lucetta, Julia has torn in pieces the letter from Proteus, but left alone she gathers the pieces together and berates herself for her ingratitude to the forlorn lover. Bees (and wasps) were associated with love in the emblematic arts of the Renaissance on account of the stings of love and the sweetness of its honey.

5 O, how this spring of love resembleth
  The uncertain glory of an April day,
Which now shows all the beauty of the sun,
  And by and by a cloud takes all away.
(I.3.84–7)

Proteus has just been informed that his father desires that he join Valentine in Milan. The news has come bitterly hard upon Julia's welcoming his suit of love. In fact, his pretending the letter from Julia was news from Valentine (lest his father object to his love) has actually prompted his father's plan to send him abroad to gain experience of life. The uncertainty and unpredictability of love's course and love's experience is central to the play and is encapsulated in Proteus' image of the variability of spring weather.

6 VALENTINE Why, how know you that I am in love?
SPEED Marry, by these special marks: first, you have learned, like Sir Proteus, to wreathe your arms, like a malcontent; to relish a love-song, like a robin-redbreast; to walk alone, like one that had the pestilence; to sigh, like a schoolboy that had lost his ABC; to weep, like a young wench that had buried her grandam; to fast, like one that takes diet; to watch, like one that fears robbing; to speak puling, like a beggar at Hallowmas. You were wont, when you laughed, to crow like a cock; when you walked, to walk like one of the lions; when you fasted, it was presently after dinner; when you looked sadly, it was for want of money. And now you are metamorphosed with a mistress, that, when I look on you, I can hardly think you my master.
(II.1.16–30)
In Milan, Valentine has fallen in love with Silvia, the daughter of the Duke of Milan. The comic account by Speed, Valentine's servant, of his master's love-sickness presents all the stereotyped poses of the forlorn and melancholic lover. His speech is based on the notion of the metamorphosis of his master from a reasonable man into a lover. Speed's irony ultimately strengthens the romantic idealism of the plot by incorporating criticism of such untested idealism within the play.

7 Though the chameleon Love can feed on the air, I am one that am nourished by my victuals, and would fain have meat.
(II.1.163–5)
Speed, Valentine's servant, has just witnessed and satirized the romantic idealism of his master's meeting with Silvia, daughter of the Duke of Milan. Speed is characterized as a man of the senses, in love with food and his bed, in contrast to his master's aristocratic idealism. The notion that the chameleon lived on air alone was proverbial (compare *Hamlet* 119).

8 I have received my proportion, like the prodigious son, and am going with Sir Proteus to the Imperial's court. I think Crab my dog be the sourest-natured dog that lives. My

mother weeping, my father wailing, my sister crying, our maid howling, our cat wringing her hands, and all our house in a great perplexity; yet did not this cruel-hearted cur shed one tear.
(II.3.2–9)
The account of Launce, Proteus's servant, of his parting from his family, at which his dog (Crab) shed not a tear, parodies the parting of Proteus and Julia in the preceding scene. Launce's speech is a masterpiece of comic writing, a *lazzo* or comic interlude, which the actor may elaborate through the delivery of the malapropisms and by taking advantage of the cues for comic gesture.

9 Even as one heat another heat expels,
Or as one nail by strength drives out another,
So the remembrance of my former love
Is by a newer object quite forgotten.
(II.4.190–3)
Proteus, having arrived in Milan, has been reunited with Valentine and introduced to Valentine's love, Silvia. Valentine, from being love's opponent, has become its devotee and has boastfully praised Silvia above Julia, Proteus' own love. In this soliloquy at the end of the scene, Proteus is musing upon the strange effect by which Silvia's charms have replaced Julia's in his affections.

10 Except I be by Silvia in the night,
There is no music in the nightingale;
Unless I look on Silvia in the day,
There is no day for me to look upon.
(III.1.178–81)
Valentine's scheme to elope with Silvia from the tower in which she is kept has been detected by the Duke of Milan, her father. Valentine has been banished from the court of Milan and so from the company of Silvia. In this soliloquy he argues that death would be preferable to 'living torment' since, as Sylvia is himself, separation from her is a kind of death. The song of the nightingale is traditionally associated with lovers' complaints.

11 Much is the force of heaven-bred poesy.
(III.2.72)
The Duke of Milan, Thurio, and Proteus are plotting how Silvia's love may be won from Valentine, who has been banished, to Thurio. Proteus has spoken of the power of poetry and in this line the Duke agrees. Poetry, like love, was believed in the Renaissance to be a divine *furor.* It is agreed that Silvia shall be courted with music outside her chamber, ostensibly on Thurio's behalf; but, in fact, Proteus seeks Silvia for himself.

12 Who is Silvia? What is she,
That all our swains commend her?
Holy, fair, and wise is she;
The heaven such grace did lend her,
That she might admirèd be.
Is she kind as she is fair?
For beauty lives with kindness.
Love doth to her eyes repair,
To help him of his blindness;
And, being helped, inhabits there.
Then to Silvia let us sing
That Silvia is excelling;
She excels each mortal thing
Upon the dull earth dwelling.
To her let us garlands bring.

(IV.2.38–52)

This is the song dedicated to Silvia and sung before her chamber on behalf of Thurio. Although not made absolutely explicit in the text, the singer is presumably Proteus, since he is wooing Silvia on his own behalf under the pretext of aiding Thurio; this gives added pathos to the situation of Julia (Proteus' former love), who in the disguise of a page secretly witnesses the scene. The song is one of the most famous of all Shakespeare's songs from his plays and has been set by many musicians: the best-known setting is by Schubert.

13 How use doth breed a habit in a man!

(V.4. 1)

Valentine has taken up residence in the forest in the company of the outlaws. The themes of his soliloquy are praise of rural solitude in contrast to the corrupt society of men and the adaptability of men to circumstance. Unbeknown to Valentine, Sylvia has fled the court of Milan in the company of Sir Eglamour in order to join him in the forest.

14 JULIA
It is the lesser blot, modesty finds,
Women to change their shapes than men their minds.

PROTEUS
Than men their minds? 'Tis true. O heaven, were man
But constant, he were perfect!

(V.4.109–12)

At the dénouement of the play, Julia reveals herself to Proteus first by means of the ring he gave her in II.2 and then by disclosing her male disguise. The external metamorphosis is shown to be less grave than the transformation of men's minds by inconstancy. Julia's revelation has occurred when Proteus, having delivered Silvia from one risk in the forest, threatens her with his enforced love, only to be interrupted by Valentine. When Proteus begs forgiveness, Valentine renounces his claim on Silvia to his friend, so prompting Julia's revelation.

The Two Noble Kinsmen

1 Roses, their sharp spines being gone,
Not royal in their smells alone,
  But in their hue,
Maiden pinks, of odour faint,
Daisies smell-less, yet most quaint,
  And sweet thyme true,
Primrose, first-born child of Ver,
Merry springtime's harbinger,
  With harebells dim,
Oxlips, in their cradles growing,
Marigolds, on death-beds blowing,
  Lark's-heels trim,
All dear Nature's children sweet,
Lie 'fore bride and bridegroom's feet,
  Blessing their sense.
Not an angel of the air,
Bird melodious or bird fair,
  Is absent hence;
The crow, the slanderous cuckoo, nor
The boding raven nor chough hoar,
  Nor chattering pie,
May on our bridehouse perch or sing,
Or with them any discord bring,
  But from it fly.
(I.1.1–24)

At the end of his career Shakespeare wrote a number of plays in collaboration with his younger contemporary John Fletcher. Unlike *Henry VIII* and *Pericles*, *The Two Noble Kinsmen* has only recently been included in collected editions of Shakespeare's works. Quotations 1, 2, 3, and 6 are from parts of the play usually assigned to Shakespeare. *The Two Noble Kinsmen*, derived from Chaucer's *Knight's Tale*, has been very rarely staged, but Harley Granville Barker used this song, part of the celebration of the forthcoming marriage of Theseus and Hippolyta, as part of the blessing on the newly married couples in his famous 1914 production of *A Midsummer Night's Dream*. 'Quaint' means pretty; 'Ver' is the spring; 'dim' means pale; 'death-beds' are graves; 'Lark's-heels' are larkspurs. Cuckoos are slanderous because their song sounds like cuckold; 'boding' means ominous; the 'chough hoar' is the jackdaw; the 'pie' is the magpie.

2 O, my petition was
Set down in ice, which by hot grief uncandied
Melts into drops.
(I.1.105–7)

On their way to be married, Theseus and Hippolyta have been stopped by three queens in mourning who have asked Theseus to intervene to force the Thebans to permit them to bury their dead husbands. The Third Queen says to Emilia, Hippolyta's sister, that her first request was coldly formal but her grief has dissolved ('uncandied') into tears.

3 This world's a city full of straying streets,
And death's the market-place, where each one meets.
(I.5.15–16)

The Queens are burying their dead husbands after Theseus's defeat of the Thebans. The Third Queen ends their contribution to the play with this couplet.

4 It is the very emblem of a maid;
For when the west wind courts her gently,
How modestly she blows, and paints the sun
With her chaste blushes! When the north comes near her,
Rude and impatient, then, like chastity,
She locks her beauties in her bud again,
And leaves him to base briars.
(II.1.191–7)

Emilia, Hippolyta's sister, explains to her waiting-woman why a rose is an apt symbol for a maid. 'Blows' means blossoms; 'paints' means reflects; 'leaves him to base briars' means leaves him with just the thorns.

5 Once he kissed me;
I loved my lips the better ten days after.
(II.3.25–6)

Two Theban cousins, Palamon and Arcite, were captured in the battle between the Athenians and the Thebans and then gaoled. Here their gaoler's daughter soliloquizes about her love for Palamon.

6 We prevent
The loathsome misery of age, beguile

The gout and rheum, that in lag hours attend
For grey approachers; we come towards the gods
Young and unwappered, not halting under crimes
Many and stale; that sure shall please the gods.
(V.4.6–11)

Palamon and Arcite and their followers have fought a tournament to decide which of them may marry Emilia. The loser Palamon, about to be executed, encourages his companions with the thought that their early death will have its compensations. These include avoiding the illnesses which attend the last ('lag') hours of grey-haired old men ('grey approachers'). 'Unwappered' means not worn out.

The Winter's Tale

1 Nine changes of the watery star hath been
The shepherd's note since we have left our throne
Without a burden.
(I.2.1–3)

Polixenes, King of Bohemia, broaches the subject of ending his long stay with his childhood friend Leontes, King of Sicilia, and his queen Hermione. Although the lines are overtly no more than a statement that he has been away a long time, they convey some important information at a subliminal level and serve to establish the play's concern with the rhythms of nature: he has been away for nine months, which gives Leontes's suspicions that Polixenes is responsible for Hermione's advanced pregnancy a little plausibility; his country is associated with rural life from the beginning of the play; and there is a stress on the natural rhythms associated with the moon ('the watery star').

2 Two lads that thought there was no more behind
But such a day tomorrow as today,
And to be boy eternal.
(I.2.63–5)

Polixenes describes himself and Leontes as children to Hermione. 'Behind' means in the future.

3 We were as twinned lambs that did frisk i'th'sun,
And bleat the one at th'other. What we changed
Was innocence for innocence; we knew not
The doctrine of ill-doing, nor dreamed
That any did.
(I.2.67–71)

Polixenes develops his account of his and Leontes's childhood for Hermione. There is an ironic contrast being established between this childhood friendship and their estrangement after Leontes attempts to have Polixenes murdered for allegedly seducing Hermione. 'Changed' means exchanged.

4 Too hot, too hot!
To mingle friendship far is mingling bloods.
I have *tremor cordis* on me: my heart dances,
But not for joy, not joy. This entertainment
May a free face put on, derive a liberty
From heartiness, from bounty, fertile bosom,
And well become the agent – 't may, I grant.
But to be paddling palms and pinching fingers,
As now they are, and making practised smiles
As in a looking glass; and then to sigh, as 'twere
The mort o'th'deer – O, that is entertainment
My bosom likes not, nor my brows!
(I.2.108–19)

In a long aside, Leontes, who asked Hermione to persuade Polixenes to stay longer, reacts violently to her success in getting him to stay. '*Tremor cordis*' is Latin for palpitation of the heart; 'entertainment' refers to Hermione's behaviour with Polixenes; 'a free face put on' means may look innocent; 'heartiness' is cordiality; 'bounty' is generosity; 'fertile bosom' is abundant affection; 'And well become the agent' means and be a credit to the person who behaves in this way. 'Paddling palms' means fingering each other's hands, with definite sexual overtones. Leontes compares their sighing to the hunting horn announcing the death ('mort') of the deer – presumably the point of the comparison is that the sighing is long and obvious. When Leontes refers to his 'brows' not liking Hermione's behaviour, he is referring to the traditional belief that cuckolds grew horns on their foreheads which were an outward sign of their fate.

5 How like, methought, I then was to this kernel,
This squash, this gentleman.
(I.2.159–60)

In response to Polixenes's and Hermione's anxious questions about his health and state of mind, Leontes claims to have been comparing his young son Mamillius to himself as a child. 'Squash', meaning unripe peascod, is used here to mean youngster.

6 He makes a July's day short as December.
(I.2.169)

Polixenes is telling Leontes that his son (Florizel) is a constant delight. Although he is saying little more than time flies when you are having fun, there is an interesting undercurrent of summer being converted into winter which ties in with the play's general movement and development.

7 Inch-thick, knee-deep, o'er head and ears a forked one!
Go play, boy, play: thy mother plays, and I
Play too – but so disgraced a part, whose issue
Will hiss me to my grave. Contempt and clamour
Will be my knell. Go play, boy, play. There have been,
Or I am much deceived, cuckolds ere now;
And many a man there is, even at this present,
Now, while I speak this, holds his wife by th'arm,
That little thinks she has been sluiced in's absence,
And his pond fished by his next neighbour, by
Sir Smile, his neighbour. Nay, there's comfort in't
Whiles other men have gates, and those gates opened,
As mine, against their will. Should all despair
That have revolted wives, the tenth of mankind
Would hang themselves.
(I.2.186–200)

Having sent Polixenes and Hermione off, Leontes indulges his jealousy in the presence of Mamillius. Like the rest of the first line, 'forked one' may refer either to Hermione or Leontes: he may be saying that she is deceitful ('forked') and deeply involved in her affair, or he may be saying that he is already thoroughly cuckolded ('forked'). Leontes puns on various senses of 'play' in the following lines: Mamillius plays as a child; Hermione is playing around and is, therefore, playing the part of a dutiful wife when she no longer is one; Leontes is pretending to be polite to his wife and her supposed lover. 'Issue' means outcome, with a secondary reference to Hermione's expected child. The puns on 'play' lead Leontes to imagine an audience hissing him when they discover what part he is playing. 'Even at this present' means here and now, and also addresses the male members of the audience directly as men who are there at that moment. 'Sluiced in's absence', meaning seduced in his absence, introduces a series of basic sexual references that indicate the obsessive state of his mind. Leontes sees an imagined next-door neighbour ('next neighbour') smiling at the unsuspecting husband; 'gates' continues the sexual innuendos of 'sluiced', 'pond', and 'fished'; 'revolted' means unfaithful.

8 No barricado for a belly.
(I.2.204)

Leontes decides that there is no way of preventing a woman from seeking sexual satisfaction. 'Barricado' means barricade.

9 Is whispering nothing?
Is leaning cheek to cheek? Is meeting noses?
Kissing with inside lip? Stopping the career
Of laughter with a sigh? – a note infallible
Of breaking honesty. Horsing foot on foot?
Skulking in corners? Wishing clocks more swift?
Hours minutes? Noon midnight? and all eyes
Blind with the pin and web but theirs, theirs only,
That would unseen be wicked – is this nothing?
Why, then the world and all that's in't is nothing;
The covering sky is nothing; Bohemia nothing;
My wife is nothing; nor nothing have these nothings,
If this be nothing.

(I.2.284–96)

Leontes is attempting to persuade his faithful lord Camillo that Polixenes and Hermione have been having an affair; he gives an elaborate catalogue of their alleged misdeeds, characterized by an obsessive interest in the physical details and a stress on their misuse of time. 'Honesty' is chastity; 'Horsing foot on foot' means one person putting their foot on the other person's – it appears to be a unique Shakespearian usage; 'the pin and web' are cataracts. 'Nothing will come of nothing' is proverbial, but Leontes's use of 'gate' and 'pond' in sexual senses (see 7) suggests that the secondary sexual sense of 'vagina' may inform the uses of 'nothing' in this passage.

10 Make that thy question, and go rot!

(I.2.324)

Leontes reacts violently to Camillo's unwillingness to believe in Hermione's adultery. The phrase means: if you don't believe Hermione is guilty, go to hell.

11 A sad tale's best for winter. I have one
Of sprites and goblins.

(II.1.25–6)

Mamillius, playing with his mother Hermione and her Ladies, offers to tell her a 'winter's tale', the kind of tale traditionally told to while away a long winter evening. The play, as befits its title, is full of references to the seasons and re-enacts a seasonal myth with its tales of resurrection and the blossoming of children.

12 There may be in the cup
A spider steeped, and one may drink, depart,
And yet partake no venom, for his knowledge
Is not infected: but if one present
Th'abhorred ingredient to his eye, make known
How he hath drunk, he cracks his gorge, his sides,
With violent hefts. I have drunk, and seen the spider.
(II.1.39–45)
Leontes, who has arrived with Antigonus and other Lords to arrest Hermione, is congratulating himself in a perverse way for having discovered the truth about Hermione's supposed adultery. Here he refers to the belief that spiders (which were believed to be venomous) were only poisonous in food or drink if the person eating or drinking discovered their presence. 'Gorge' means throat or stomach; 'hefts' are retchings.

13 This child was prisoner to the womb, and is
By law and process of great Nature thence
Freed and enfranchised.
(II.2.59–61)
Paulina, Antigonus's wife, is persuading Hermione's gaoler to let her take Hermione's newly born daughter to Leontes. The legal imagery is appropriate to the context of gaols and trials, and the play is very much concerned throughout its length with the 'law and process of great Nature'.

14 A nest of traitors!
(II.3.81)
Leontes responds angrily to Paulina, who has brought his new-born daughter to see him, and to Antigonus, who cannot control her. His generalized anger probably includes everybody who is behaving rationally at this point in the play, though 'nest' is particularly appropriate to a family group.

15 It is an heretic that makes the fire,
Not she which burns in't.
(II.3.114–15)
Paulina disdains Leontes's threat to have her burnt. He is a heretic because he lacks faith in Hermione's innocence.

16 I am a feather for each wind that blows.
(II.3.153)
Leontes is besieged by his Lords pleading on behalf of the new-born child, and pushed in different directions by different impulses like a feather in the breeze.

17 My past life
Hath been as continent, as chaste, as true,
As I am now unhappy; which is more
Than history can pattern, though devised
And played to take spectators.
(III.2.32–6)

Hermione pleads her cause at her trial. As so often in Shakespeare, the reference to the theatre extends the range of the scene to include the audience's experience of watching the play. 'Take' means move.

18 My life stands in the level of your dreams.
(III.2.80)

Hermione addresses Leontes at her trial: her life is in danger because his fantasies have made it their target.

19 A thousand knees,
Ten thousand years together, naked, fasting,
Upon a barren mountain, and still winter
In storm perpetual, could not move the gods
To look that way thou wert.
(III.2.208–12)

After the supposed death of Hermione, Paulina takes charge of Leontes's repentance, initially claiming that his crimes are too great to be expiated in ten thousand years. In fact, as we discover only at the very end of the play, Hermione is still alive. The reference to perpetual winter ('still winter') shows how Leontes has destroyed the natural order and locked his world into apparently endless winter.

20 What's gone and what's past help
Should be past grief.
(III.2.220–1)

Paulina, moved by Leontes's grief, adopts a gentler approach, using proverbial wisdom.

21 Thou art perfect, then, our ship hath touched upon
The deserts of Bohemia?
(III.3.1–2)

Antigonus, sent by Leontes to expose Hermione's infant daughter in a wild place because he believes her to be a bastard, asks a sailor from his ship if he is sure ('art perfect') that they are in the wild places ('deserts') of Bohemia. Notoriously, as Ben Jonson pointed out in his conversations with William Drummond of Hawthornden in 1619 and as Laurence Sterne also noted in his eighteenth-century novel *Tristram Shandy*, Bohemia does not have a seacoast. Various attempts have been made to rescue Shakespeare from the charge of geographical ignorance including changing Bohemia to Bithynia, showing that Bohemia did in fact have a seacoast at various points in the thirteenth and sixteenth centuries, suggesting that Bohemia is another name for Apulia in Italy, and claiming that Bohemia was a stock joke like the Swiss Navy or Wigan Pier. Equally it has been suggested that no one would have known or cared much about central European geography in Renaissance England, although the fact that the play was performed as part of the celebrations of the marriage of Princess Elizabeth to Frederick of Bohemia in 1613 suggests some degree of knowledge of and interest in central Europe in court circles fairly soon after the accepted date of the play's composition, 1611. The whole argument is slightly ridiculous, since theatre audiences will be much more interested in the fate of Antigonus and the baby than in geography, but other aspects of the scene – such as its perfunctory storm and the notorious bear (see 22) – tend to support the view that Shakespeare is changing the play's mood through a series of distancing devices, one of which could be the reference to the non-existent seacoast.

22 The storm begins. Poor wretch,
That for thy mother's fault art thus exposed
To loss and what may follow! Weep I cannot,
But my heart bleeds; and most accursed am I
To be by oath enjoined to this. Farewell!
The day frowns more and more. Thou'rt like to have
A lullaby too rough: I never saw
The heavens so dim by day. – A savage clamour!
Well may I get aboard! This is the chase.
I am gone for ever! *Exit, pursued by a bear*
(III.3.48–57)

Antigonus abandons Perdita, Hermione's infant daughter ('Poor wretch'), believing that Hermione was guilty of adultery ('fault') with Polixenes. His rapid succession of comments on the storm reads like a set of stage directions and distances us from the horror of the moment by dividing the focus of our attention between Antigonus, the baby, the storm, and, latterly, the bear. Critics' ferocious arguments about the bear have been based on two main issues: the supposed crudity of Shakespeare's stagecraft and whether the bear was real or played by a man. Those who believe the stagecraft is crude tend to support the belief that the bear was real, a kind of imported guest attraction introduced to please the less intellectual members of the audience. There is no evidence that real bears were used in the Renaissance theatre, and commonsense suggests that an actor in a bearskin would be much more reliable than a real bear. In either case, the appearance of a 'bear' serves to further change the mood from the largely unrelieved gloom of the first part of the play to the more expansive comic mood of the second part by its introduction of a distancing element.

23 Though I am not bookish, yet I can read waiting gentlewoman in the scape: this has been some stair-work, some trunk-work, some behind-door-work. They were warmer that got this than the poor thing is here.
(III.3.70–4)
An old Shepherd has discovered the infant Perdita. Although, like Leontes, he jumps to conclusions about the child's parentage, his whole approach is refreshingly down-to-earth and compassionate after Leontes's jealous ravings. 'Scape' means escapade; 'stair-work', 'trunk-work', 'behind-door-work' refer to the places where the Shepherd imagines the clandestine sexual intercourse took place; 'got' means begot.

24 The men are not yet cold under water, nor the bear half dined on the gentleman; he's at it now.
(III.3.101–2)
The Clown (rustic) tells his father the old Shepherd that the ship which brought Antigonus has been sunk in the storm and the bear has killed and eaten Antigonus. The plot demands that there should be no trace of Perdita or Antigonus so that Leontes can make no attempt to find Perdita, but Shakespeare's treatment of the deaths ensures that our sympathies for Antigonus will be subordinated to other concerns.

25 Now bless thyself: thou met'st with things dying, I with things new-born.
(III.3.109–10)
The Shepherd tells his son that he has discovered the infant Perdita. There is a very strong sense here of the complementary nature of age and youth – the old man discovers the child, the young man sees death – which is reflected throughout the play in its emphasis on the rhythms of nature.

26 When daffodils begin to peer,
  With heigh, the doxy over the dale,
Why, then comes in the sweet o'the year,
  For the red blood reigns in the winter's pale.
The white sheet bleaching on the hedge,
  With heigh, the sweet birds O, how they sing!
Doth set my pugging tooth an edge,

For a quart of ale is a dish for a king.
The lark, that tirra-lyra chants,
With heigh, with heigh, the thrush and the jay,
Are summer songs for me and my aunts
While we lie tumbling in the hay.
(IV.3.1–12)

The atmosphere of the play continues to brighten with its first song, which is sung directly to the audience by Autolycus, a con-man and general rogue. The song's emphasis on the triumph of spring over winter sets a tone for subsequent scenes. A 'doxy' is a floozy; 'pale' means enclosure as well as paleness; 'Doth set my pugging tooth an edge' means whets my appetite for stealing; 'aunts' are whores.

27 My father named me Autolycus, who, being, as I am, littered under Mercury, was likewise a snapper-up of unconsidered trifles.
(IV.3.24–6)

Autolycus explains himself to the audience. The mythological Autolycus was the son of Mercury, the patron god of thieves; Shakespeare's Autolycus, born when the planet Mercury was in the ascendant ('littered under Mercury'), emulates his classical namesake.

28 For the life to come, I sleep out the thought of it.
(IV.3.29–30)

Autolycus ends his self-revelation to the audience, stating that he does not worry about the possibililty of retribution for his crimes in the afterlife or, possibly, that he lets the future take care of itself.

29 Out upon him! Prig, for my life, prig! He haunts wakes, fairs, and bear-baitings.
(IV.3.98–9)

Autolycus has pretended to the Clown that he is a traveller who has been attacked by Autolycus. Here the Clown reacts excitedly to the mention of Autolycus's name. 'Out upon him' means curse him; 'prig' means thief; 'wakes' are celebrations.

30 Jog on, jog on, the footpath way,
And merrily hent the stile-a:
A merry heart goes all the day,
Your sad tires in a mile-a.
(IV.3.121–4)

Having successfully picked the Clown's pocket, Autolycus concludes the scene with another song. 'Hent' means grasp (in order to pull oneself over the stile).

21 These your unusual weeds to each part of you
Does give a life: no shepherdess, but Flora
Peering in April's front. This your sheep-shearing
Is as a meeting of the petty gods,
And you the queen on't.
(IV.4.1–5)

Sixteen years have passed since the Shepherd found Perdita: Florizel, Polixenes's son, has fallen in love with her without his father's knowledge and consent. Here he addresses her at the beginning of the sheep-shearing festivity. She is dressed in special clothes ('unusual weeds') to preside over the festivities, and he compares her to the goddess of spring (Flora) appearing at the beginning of April ('Peering in April's front'); 'petty' means lesser; 'on't' means of it.

32 For you there's rosemary and rue; these keep
Seeming and savour all the winter long:
(IV.4.74–5)

Perdita greets Polixenes and Camillo, who have come to the sheep-shearing in disguise to check up on Florizel, with plants appropriate to old age symbolizing remembrance and sorrow. The flower symbolism extends throughout the following dialogue, reflecting the play's thematic concern with the seasons and natural processes. 'Seeming and savour' are appearance and scent.

33 The year growing ancient,
Not yet on summer's death nor on the birth
Of trembling winter, the fairest flowers o'th'season
Are our carnations and streaked gillyvors,
Which some call Nature's bastards.
(IV.4.79–83)

This description of the fairest flowers of the season is part of Perdita's explanation to the disguised Polixenes of her reasons for not cultivating them. Once again the idea of the complementary nature of the seasons is prominent as Perdita rejects hybrid flowers ('Nature's bastards') produced by cross-breeding different strains. 'Gillyvors' are pinks.

34 There is an art which in their piedness shares
With great creating Nature.
(IV.4.87–8)

Perdita explains her objections to the streaked (pied) gillyvors to the disguised Polixenes; she sees cultivation as a misguided attempt to improve on Nature.

35 I'll not put
The dibble in earth to set one slip of them:
No more than, were I painted, I would wish
This youth should say 'twere well, and only therefore
Desire to breed by me. Here's flowers for you:
Hot lavender, mints, savory, marjoram;
The marigold, that does to bed with' sun
And with him rises weeping; these are flowers
Of middle summer, and I think they are given
To men of middle age.
(IV.4.99–108)

Perdita continues to reject the disguised Polixenes's arguments in favour of cross-breeding, but now offers Polixenes and Camillo flowers more appropriate to their age. It is ironic that he is putting forward these arguments when he is about to try to prevent his son Florizel (referred to by Perdita as 'This youth') from marrying Perdita on the grounds that she is from a lower social class. 'Slip' means seedling; 'painted' means made up, linking with the argument on improving nature. The marigold closes its petals at sunset ('goes to bed with' sun') and opens them, wet with the dew, at sunrise ('with him rises weeping').

36 CAMILLO
I should leave grazing, were I of your flock,
And only live by gazing.
PERDITA Out, alas!
You'd be so lean that blasts of January
Would blow you through and through.
(IV.4.109–12)

The disguised Camillo expresses his admiration for Perdita in terms which allow Shakespeare to introduce the idea of winter again in connection with her attractiveness. Throughout the scene the audience are aware that Polixenes intends to prevent Perdita and Florizel's marriage, like a cold wind blowing through their happiness.

37 O Proserpina,
For the flowers now that, frighted, thou let'st fall
From Dis's wagon! Daffodils,
That come before the swallow dares, and take
The winds of March with beauty; violets, dim,
But sweeter than the lids of Juno's eyes

Or Cytherea's breath; pale primroses,
That die unmarried ere they can behold
Bright Phoebus in his strength – a malady
Most incident to maids; bold oxlips and
The crown imperial; lilies of all kinds,
The flower-de-luce being one: O, these I lack
To make you garlands of, and my sweet friend
To strew him o'er and o'er!

(IV.4.116–29)

Perdita wants Proserpina's flowers to make garlands for the country maidens ('you') and to cover Florizel ('my sweet friend') with. Her invocation of Proserpina is highly significant in terms of the play's concern with the rhythms of nature: in classical mythology Proserpina's mother Demeter was so distressed at her being carried off by Pluto (Dis) that she neglected to take care of the world; the other gods secured an arrangement whereby Proserpina spent part of every year with Pluto and part with Demeter. The story is a seasonal myth: when Proserpina is underground with Pluto Demeter is unhappy and we get winter, when she comes back we get spring and summer. 'Dis's wagon' is Pluto's chariot; 'take' means enchant; Cytherea is Venus; the primrose dies in early spring before the sun (Phoebus) is very strong.

38 PERDITA
Methinks I play as I have seen them do
In Whitsun pastorals: sure this robe of mine
Does change my disposition.
FLORIZEL What you do
Still betters what is done. When you speak, sweet,
I'd have you do it ever; when you sing,
I'd have you buy and sell so, so give alms,
Pray so, and, for the ord'ring your affairs,
To sing them too; when you do dance, I wish you
A wave o'th'sea, that you might ever do
Nothing but that – move still, still so,
And own no other function. Each your doing,
So singular in each particular,
Crowns what you are doing in the present deeds,
That all your acts are queens.

(IV.4.133–46)

Perdita and Florizel continue to express their feelings, oblivious to the other participants in the festivities. At Whitsun there were celebrations involving games and theatrical events (hence 'Whitsun pastorals') – Perdita may be referring specifically to Robin Hood plays, seeing herself as Maid Marian to Florizel's Robin Hood. At the end of Florizel's speech he picks up the theatrical theme with his use of 'acts' – her deeds appear regal because she plays her part so well, yet (as we know) she is *not* playing a part since she is actually a princess. 'Still betters what is done' means always seems better than what you have already done. 'Each your doing, / So singular in each particular' means everything you do, so outstanding in every respect; 'in the present deeds' means at the moment.

39 Good sooth, she is
The queen of curds and cream.
(IV.4.160–1)
Camillo, who has been watching Perdita and Florizel's courtship with Polixenes, responds to his praise of her as the 'prettiest low-born lass' with his own compliment. 'Good sooth' means truly; 'curds and cream' may refer to Perdita's complexion, and are perhaps more appropriate to dairy-farming; the idea of Perdita as the best of her kind is clear enough.

40 Lawn as white as driven snow;
Cypress black as e'er was crow.
(IV.4.220–1)
Autolycus makes his entry into the sheep-shearing festivities in the role of a pedlar, singing a song to draw a crowd. 'Lawn' and 'Cypress' are white and black cloths respectively.

41 Is there no manners left among maids? Will they wear their plackets where they should bear their faces?
(IV.4.242–3)
The Clown rebukes Mopsa and Dorcas, two country maids, who are rivals for his favours, for arguing about him in public. 'Plackets' were slits in petticoats, so the word came to be used with strong sexual overtones; the Clown does not want them washing their dirty linen in public.

42 I love a ballad in print a-life, for then we are sure they are true.
(IV.4.259–60)
Mopsa is asking the Clown to buy one of the ballads Autolycus is selling. 'A-life' means dearly.

43 I was not much afeard, for once or twice
I was about to speak and tell him plainly,
The selfsame sun that shines upon his court
Hides not his visage from our cottage, but
Looks on alike.
(IV.4.439–43)

Polixenes has left after revealing himself and forbidding Florizel to marry Perdita. Perdita responds to his diatribe by reminding herself and the rest of the company of Nature's indifference to human class distinctions.

44 This dream of mine –
Being now awake, I'll queen it no inch farther,
But milk my ewes, and weep.
(IV.4.453–7)

Perdita tells Florizel that after Polixenes's intervention she will no longer play the part of a queen – referring to her presiding over the sheep-shearing festivities and to her being Florizel's consort. Again there is irony for the audience, who are aware that she is a princess in reality.

45 Prosperity's the very bond of love,
Whose fresh complexion and whose heart together
Affliction alters.
(IV.4.570–2)

Camillo encourages Florizel to adopt his plan of going to Sicilia to avoid his father's wrath; Camillo suggests that Florizel's own plan is so hazardous it might affect Perdita's love for him.

46 Ha, ha, what a fool Honesty is! And Trust, his sworn brother, a very simple gentleman!
(IV.4.592–3)

Autolycus congratulates himself on having sold all his goods and robbed the credulous country folk.

47 If I thought it were a piece of honesty to acquaint the King withal, I would not do't. I hold it the more knavery to conceal it; and therein am I constant to my profession.
(IV.4.675–8)

Autolycus had been enlisted in Camillo's plans to help Perdita and Florizel to escape Polixenes's wrath. Here he confides to the audience his reasons for acquiescing in the plan.

48 Though I am not naturally honest, I am so sometimes by chance.
(IV.4.707–8)

Autolycus, fearing that the Clown and the Shepherd may hinder the escape of Florizel and Perdita by their plan to go to the King, tells the audience of his decision to intervene and excuses his apparently uncharacteristic behaviour.

49 I will but look upon the hedge, and follow you.
(IV.4.819–20)

Autolycus tells the Clown and the Shepherd that he needs to stop to urinate ('look upon the hedge'), which gives him an opportunity to stay behind and talk to the audience again.

50 Stars, stars,
And all eyes else dead coals!
(V.1.67–8)
In their discussion of why Leontes should not marry again, Paulina has reminded him of Hermione's eyes. This is his response.

51 Welcome hither
As is the spring to th'earth!
(V.1.150–1)
Leontes greets Camillo, who has arrived in Sicilia with Florizel and Perdita. Their arrival does indeed mark the beginning of renewal at the Sicilian Court.

52 Such a deal of wonder is broken out within this hour that ballad-makers cannot be able to express it ... This news, which is called true, is so like an old tale that the verity of it is in strong suspicion.
(V.2.23–5, 27–9)
The play has apparently been building up to a recognition scene in which Leontes and Perdita are reunited, but Shakespeare leaves it to three Gentlemen to narrate it at second hand. In fact Shakespeare has a bigger recognition scene between Leontes and Hermione in the next scene, which no one in the play except Paulina (and no one in the audience) anticipates because everyone believes Hermione is dead. This scene builds expectation and puzzlement in the audience by cheating them out of the expected scene: the Second Gentleman's lines stress the unlikelihood of the offstage events by stressing their resemblance to fiction – a modern equivalent would be saying something is incredible in order to demonstrate its reality.

53 Like an old tale still, which will have matter to rehearse, though credit be asleep and not an ear open.
(V.2.59–61)
The Third Gentleman replies to the Second Gentleman's question about Antigonus by comparing what happened to him to something in a fairy tale. 'Credit' is belief.

54 The fixure of her eye has motion in't
As we are mocked with art.
(V.3.67–8)

Leontes comments on the 'statue' of Hermione which Paulina is showing to him and the other members of the royal party. As the 'statue' is actually Hermione herself, Leontes is wrong in ascribing the motion of its eyes to art, other than that art which is part of 'great creating Nature' (see also 55).

55 Still methinks
There is an air comes from her. What fine chisel
Could ever yet cut breath?
(V.3.79–81)

Shakespeare continues to tantalize the audience by drawing attention to the statue's breathing. Obviously the person playing Hermione is likely to make small movements, but Shakespeare builds them into the fabric of the scene so that the audience may be partly convinced that they are looking at a statue and partly hoping that the statue is real – they would then get a recognition scene to replace the one of which they were cheated earlier (see 52).

56 PAULINA Music, awake her, strike!
'Tis time: descend; be stone no more; approach;
Strike all that look upon with marvel. Come,
I'll fill your grave up. Stir; nay, come away.
Bequeath to death your numbness, for from him
Dear life redeems you. You perceive she stirs.
Start not: her actions shall be holy as
You hear my spell is lawful. Do not shun her
Until you see her die again, for then
You kill her double. Nay, present your hand.
When she was young you wooed her: now, in age,
Is she become the suitor?
LEONTES O, she's warm!
If this be magic, let it be an art
Lawful as eating.
(V.3.98–111)

Paulina finally brings Hermione down from her pedestal and the products of Art and Nature are revealed as one and the same in the triumphant conclusion of a debate that has pervaded the whole play. The very heavy punctuation of the opening lines cf the speech in the Folio indicates the slow pace which builds up the tension until Hermione finally moves.

 Sonnets

1 TO THE ONLY BEGETTER OF
THESE ENSUING SONNETS
MR W. H. ALL HAPPINESS
AND THAT ETERNITY
PROMISED
BY
OUR EVER-LIVING POET
WISHETH
THE WELL-WISHING
ADVENTURER IN
SETTING
FORTH
T. T.

(Dedication)

Shakespeare's sonnets were published in 1609 by Thomas Thorpe, The 'T. T.' and assumed author of the dedication. The identity of 'Mr W. H.' as the 'only begetter' has given rise to much speculation. The first 126 of the 154 sonnets are addressed to a young man, the poet's friend. When the Friend is identified with 'Mr. W. H.' and 'only begetter' is taken to mean source of inspiration, one of two candidates is usually advanced: either William Herbert, Earl of Pembroke, who was one of the dedicatees of the First Folio, or Henry Wriothesley, Earl of Southampton, to whom *Venus and Adonis* and *The Rape of Lucrece* had been dedicated. It has been suggested that the dedication is a reference to Sir William Harvey, Southampton's stepfather, who may have commissioned the sonnets urging the young man to marry. The form of address as 'Mr' poses a problem in all three cases. It may be that the dedication is to a person unknown, who was the 'begetter' in the sense that he procured the sonnets for publication by Thorpe.

2 From fairest creatures we desire increase,
That thereby beauty's rose might never die.

(1, 1–2)

In the first seventeen sonnets (excluding 15), Shakespeare is urging a beautiful young man to marry in order to reproduce his beauty. The notion that virginity was reprehensible, because wasteful of nature's fertility, was an Elizabethan commonplace. The rose was a traditional symbol of beauty in the sonnet convention and in its precursors in Western European lyric poetry.

3 When forty winters shall besiege thy brow
And dig deep trenches in thy beauty's field.
(2, 1–2)

The poet urges the young man to marry, lest age should destroy his beauty before it has been reproduced in a son. Throughout the sequence, an analogy is pursued between the cycle of the seasons and the ages of man's life. Hence the approach of age is signalled by the passage of forty winters. The 'trenches' are the lines or wrinkles that forty years will produce in the young man's face and forehead.

4 Thou art thy mother's glass, and she in thee
Calls back the lovely April of her prime.
(3, 9–10)

Throughout the sonnets urging the young man to marry, there is an emphasis on succession and the defeat of time by passing the physical beauty of his line from one generation to the next. Here the young man's own beauty, which is described as having an almost feminine perfection, is seen as the 'glass' (mirror) or image of the beauty his mother possessed in her youth.

5 For never-resting Time leads summer on
To hideous winter and confounds him there.
(5, 5–6)

The young man is depicted as being in the summer, or perfection, of his beauty; but the sequence is permeated with a sense of the passage of time and of beauty's transience. Time, summer, and winter are all personified after the emblematic conventions of Elizabethan thought and literature. 'Confounds' means destroys. The underlying purpose of the image is to persuade the young man to marry and reproduce his beauty.

6 Is it for fear to wet a widow's eye
That thou consum'st thyself in single life?
(9, 1–2)

The poet is hypothesizing that the young man's refusal to marry is for fear of making a woman a widow. He argues that failure to reproduce himself in an heir will ultimately render the entire world his weeping widow, since there wili be no consolation for his loss.

7 When lofty trees I see barren of leaves,
Which erst from heat did canopy the herd,
And summer's green, all girded up in sheaves,
Borne on the bier with white bristly beard;
Then of thy beauty do I question make,

That thou among the wastes of time must go.
(12, 5–10)

The poet is exploiting visual images drawn from nature to create a vivid picture of time's destructive power. The 'beards' of the sheaves of corn being carried on carts from the field of harvest recall the white beards of aged men borne on their funeral bier. 'Erst' means before or formerly. The poet argues that only by reproduction of himself can the young man escape 'Time's scythe'.

8 If I could write the beauty of your eyes
And in fresh numbers number all your graces,
The age to come would say 'This poet lies;
Such heavenly touches ne'er touch'd earthly faces.'
(17, 5–8)

The poet is conflating an attack often made on poetry and a justification of it in order to persuade the young man to marry. The attack made is that poets exaggerate the beauties and virtues of their subjects. This idea is fused with the claims of poets, from antiquity onwards, to render their subjects immortal through their verse. By conflating the two ideas, he makes the reproduction of an heir the less contestable form of immortality. 'Numbers' (line 6) signifies metre or verses.

9 Shall I compare thee to a summer's day?
Thou art more lovely and more temperate:
Rough winds do shake the darling buds of May,
And summer's lease hath all too short a date:
Sometime too hot the eye of heaven shines,
And often is his gold complexion dimm'd;
And every fair from fair sometime declines,
By chance or nature's changing course untrimm'd;
But thy eternal summer shall not fade,
Nor lose possession of that fair thou owest;
Nor shall Death brag thou wander'st in his shade,
When in eternal lines to time thou grow'st:
  So long as men can breathe, or eyes can see,
  So long lives this, and this gives life to thee.
(18, 1–14)

Shakespeare extols the beauty of the young man as more perfect and more durable than that of summer. This notion is extended by the poet's claim to render the Friend's beauty eternal through his verse. This is a theme with an extremely eminent and lengthy pedigree in European lyric poetry. Ultimately, it may be traced back to Pindar's celebration of the victors of the Panhellenic Games in ancient Greece. More immediate models for Shakespeare are likely to have been Renaissance treatments of the theme deriving from the Roman poets, notably Ovid and Horace, and from the Italian fourteenth-century poet, Petrarch. Within the sonnet 'fair from fair ... declines' means beautiful object or being declines from beauty, and 'that fair thou owest' means the beauty you possess. 'Untrimmed' suggests stripped of ornament or beauty.

10 As an unperfect actor on the stage,
Who with his fear is put besides his part,
Or some fierce thing replete with too much rage,
Whose strength's abundance weakens his own heart;
So I, for fear of trust, forget to say
The perfect ceremony of love's rite.
(23, 1–6)

In this sonnet, the poet states that he expresses in his poetry the love he fears to declare directly in speech. Shakespeare's experience as a man of the theatre is evident in the image of the actor seized by stage-fright. 'For fear of trust' means that the poet fears to trust himself.

11 Let those who are in favour with their stars
Of public honour and proud titles boast.
(25, 1–2)

The sonnet argues that the poet's security in loving and receiving love eclipses all other forms of achievement and recognition. In the narrative that emerges from the sonnet sequence, but which is neither a prominent nor an important feature of its form, the security of the love which exists between the two men will be destroyed by the 'dark lady', who becomes the lover of both men. Far too much attention has been paid to attempts at recreating the narrative or identifying the persons involved. Neither is necessary for an appreciation of Shakespeare's Sonnets.

12 When, in disgrace with fortune and men's eyes,
I all alone beweep my outcast state,
And trouble deaf heaven with my bootless cries,
And look upon myself, and curse my fate,
Wishing me like to one more rich in hope,
Featured like him, like him with friends possess'd,
Desiring this man's art and that man's scope,
With what I most enjoy contented least;
Yet in these thoughts myself almost despising,
Haply I think on thee, and then my state,
Like to the lark at break of day arising
From sullen earth, sings hymns at heaven's gate;

For thy sweet love remember'd such wealth brings
That then I scorn to change my state with kings.

(29, 1–14)

This sonnet develops the theme that the young man's love compensates for the poet's lack of success and standing in the world. 'Fortune' in Renaissance thought was the power which governed men's material circumstances. The lark, because it sings at dawn when the sun arises in the east, was believed in the Christian tradition to sing at heaven's gate. 'Bootless' means vain or useless, 'art' skill, and 'scope' power of intellect. 'State' in the final line means status, rank, or position in the world; but, because in association with king 'state' can also mean majesty and power, the contrast of conditions is rendered more emphatic.

13 When to the sessions of sweet silent thought
I summon up remembrance of things past,
I sigh the lack of many a thing I sought,
And with old woes new wail my dear time's waste:
Then can I drown an eye, unused to flow,
For precious friends hid in death's dateless night,
And weep afresh love's long since cancell'd woe,
And moan the expense of many a vanish'd sight:
Then can I grieve at grievances foregone,
And heavily from woe to woe tell o'er
And sad account of fore-bemoaned moan,
Which I new pay as if not paid before.
But if the while I think on thee, dear friend,
All losses are restored and sorrows end.

(30, 1–14)

This sonnet is a companion piece to the preceding one (12 above). Whereas sonnet 29 treated the young man's love as compensation for lack of public standing, here it compensates for private griefs. The initial image is of the poet's thoughts holding council. 'My dear time's waste' suggests time's destruction of things dear or precious to me. 'Dateless night' is night without end. The metaphor of the final lines is based on commerce and accounting: 'cancell'd' means paid in full; 'expense' is loss; to 'tell' is to count up.

14 But since he died, and poets better prove,
Theirs for their style I'll read, his for his love.

(32, 13–14)

These lines constitute the concluding couplet of a sonnet in which Shakespeare imagines the reception of his poetry after his own death. It is a feature of the sonnet form and sonnet sequence that the poet projects himself into imaginary situations as a basis for exploration of his feelings. It is one reason why attempts to reconstruct a historical narrative 'behind' the Sonnets are fraught with danger. Here, Shakespeare deprecatingly suggests that his artistry may be surpassed but that he may be read for the quality of love expressed.

15 Full many a glorious morning have I seen
Flatter the mountain tops with sovereign eye,
Killing with golden face the meadows green,
Gilding pale streams with heavenly alchemy;...

But out alack, he was but one hour mine,
The region cloud hath masked him from me now.
  Yet him for this my love no whit disdaineth;
  Suns of the world may stain when heaven's sun
      staineth.
(33, 1–4, 11–14)

In the opening quatrain of this sonnet, Shakespeare is exploiting a convention of the sonnet tradition, that natural phenomena, here a sunrise, may prompt a recollection of or provide a comparison to the beloved. Here the beautiful sunrise deceives by being a prelude to an overcast day. On this basis, the poet justifies the Friend's conduct towards him. It is the first indication of a rupture in the relationship between the poet and the Friend.

16 Take all my loves, my love, yea, take them all;
What hast thou then more than thou hadst before?
No love, my love, that thou mayst true love call;
All mine was thine before thou hadst this more.
(40, 1–4)

The sonnet is a mixture of pain, caused by the Friend's betrayal, and love, which the poet continues to express for the young man. At a narrative level, the sonnet refers to the Friend's stealing a lover from the poet. The lover appears later to be identified with the 'dark lady'. Shakespeare contrasts this theft of sexual love with his generous and total gift of love to the Friend. The wordplay on 'love' and 'hast'/'hadst' and 'mine'/'thine', coupled with the rhetorical patterning in which it is cast, is a feature of the sonnet convention.

17 That thou hast her, it is not all my grief,
And yet it may be said I loved her dearly;
That she hath thee, is of my wailing chief,
A loss in love that touches me more nearly.
(42, 1–4)

The poet makes it explicit that his pain is not caused by the Friend's theft of his mistress so much as the mistress's possession of the Friend. The paradox is explained in the course of the sonnet sequence. Despite his betrayal of the poet, the Friend remains associated with beauty, virtue, and pure love, while the mistress is described in terms of sensuality bordering on ugliness, vice, and love so strongly sexual that it is hard to distinguish it from lust. The Friend's 'fair' qualities are opposed to the mistress's 'dark' ones.

18 If the dull substance of my flesh were thought,
Injurious distance should not stop my way.
(44, 1–2)
As a consequence of a temporary separation from his beloved, the Friend, the poet wishes that he could fly to him as quickly in the flesh as he can in thought. Renaissance thought, deriving ultimately from ancient Greek concepts, associated flesh with the elements of earth and water, but intellect with those of air and fire. Flesh is thus bound by earth and sea, but the mind/soul is untrammelled.

19 Mine eyes and heart are at a mortal war,
How to divide the conquest of thy sight.
(46, 1–2)
The strict discipline of the sonnet form lends itself to resolving conflicts or paradoxes. In this sonnet, the conventional conflict of heart and eye to possess the image of the beloved is resolved, equally conventionally, by attributing to the eye the outward right and to the heart the inner. The sonnet tradition, following Platonic thought, made sight the primary sense and ascribed to it great importance in transmitting experience to the mind/soul.

20 Against that time, if ever that time come,
When I shall see thee frown on my defects,
Whenas thy love hath cast his utmost sum,
Called to that audit by advised respects;
Against that time when thou shalt strangely pass,
And scarcely greet me with that sun, thine eye,
When love, converted from the thing it was,
Shall reasons find of settled gravity.
(49, 1–8)
The poet is mentally and emotionally preparing himself for the day of rejection by the Friend. The sonnet is an illustration of the sonnet form's tendency to exploit hypothetical situations in order to analyse the psychology of love. 'Against' means in preparation for, and 'whenas' simply when. The final lines quoted

contrast the rationalization of love's demise with an implicit assertion of the poet's constancy. 'Advised respects' are careful considerations, and 'settled gravity' signifies great weight or importance.

21 O, how much more doth beauty beauteous seem
By that sweet ornament which truth doth give!
(54, 1–2)

Sonnet 54 celebrates the beauty of the young man and the power of the poet's verse to distil the essence of that beauty. The beauty of the youth is likened to a rose which, when its beauty has passed, is distilled for perfume. So in the poet's verse, the beauty of the Friend exists in its purest form. 'Truth' in line 2 means loyalty or faithfulness.

22 Not marble, nor the gilded monuments
Of princes, shall outlive this powerful rhyme?
But you shall shine more bright in these contents
Than unswept stone, besmear'd with sluttish time.
When wasteful war shall statues overturn,
And broils root out the work of masonry,
Nor Mars his sword nor war's quick fire shall burn
The living record of your memory.
'Gainst death and all-oblivious enmity
Shall you pace forth; your praise shall still find room
Even in the eyes of all posterity
That wear this world out to the ending doom.
So, till the judgement that yourself arise,
You live in this, and dwell in lovers' eyes.
(55, 1–14)

Sonnet 55 is Shakespeare's most complete statement of the classical commonplace that poetry can secure everlasting fame both for its author and for the person celebrated. Although tracing Shakespeare's indebtedness to classical authors in the original tongue is a difficult business, here the formulation as well as the theme of the sonnet would seem to echo the Latin poet Horace's famous epilogue to his *Third Book of Odes*, which begins *Exegi monumentum aere perennius* (I have completed a monument more lasting than bronze). The theme has been assimilated to a Christian context, as the visual images of church monuments and the reference to the Day of Judgement indicate.

23 Being your slave, what should I do but tend
Upon the hours and times of your desire?
. . .
Nor dare I question with my jealous thought

Where you may be, or your affairs suppose,
But, like a sad slave, stay and think of nought
Save, where you are how happy you make those.
  So true a fool is love that in your will,
  Though you do any thing, he thinks no ill.
(57, 1–2, 9–14)

In this sonnet, the poet depicts himself in a state of total subservience to the Friend. The final couplet refuses to attribute blame to the beloved, even though it hints at betrayal. There is a pun on Shakespeare's name in the 'will' of the penultimate line. 'Tend' in the first line means wait.

24 Like as the waves make towards the pebbled shore,
So do our minutes hasten to their end;...

Time doth transfix the flourish set on youth
And delves the parallels in beauty's brow,
Feeds on the rarities of nature's truth,
And nothing stands but for his scythe to mow.
(60, 1–2, 9–12)

Sonnet 60 illustrates the classical theme of the power of the poet's verse to defeat the destructive force of time and to give the person celebrated in the poem eternal fame. The sonnet is marked by the striking, yet conventional, visual images which convey the passage of time. Line 12 alludes to the emblematic figure of Time with his scythe. 'Delves the parallels' means digs lines, and 'transfix' means remove.

25 Sins of self-love possesseth all mine eye
And all my soul and all my every part;
And for this sin there is no remedy,
It is so grounded inward in my heart.
(62, 1–4)

Sonnet 62 initially contrasts the poet's subjective esteem of self with the objective assessment he is forced to make when confronted by his image in a mirror. The poet then turns the argument on its head by suggesting that, since true lovers are one entity, what he loves in himself is the reflection of the beloved. Such turns or inversions of the argument are a feature of the sonnet's form.

26 When I have seen by Time's fell hand defaced
The rich proud cost of outworn buried age,
...
When I have seen the hungry ocean gain
Advantage on the kingdom of the shore,

And the firm soil win of the wat'ry main,
Increasing store with loss and loss with store;
When I have seen such interchange of state,
Or state itself confounded to decay,
Ruin hath taught me thus to ruminate,
That Time will come and take my love away.
(64, 1–2, 5–12)

The poet's meditation on the transience of all earthly power and pride prompts the recognition that eventually he must lose possession of the Friend. Fear of loss heightens the poet-lover's awareness of the value of his love. The sonnet is notable for the expression of the visual images which convey the destructive power of time. In the opening lines, 'fell' means cruel and 'cost' costly things. Line 8 expands the image of the sea gaining territory at the expense of the land, and the land at the expense of the sea. Lines 9 and 10 play on different meanings of 'state': condition or status in line 9 and pomp or greatness in line 10.

27 Since brass, nor stone, nor earth, nor boundless sea,
But sad mortality o'er-sways their power,
How with this rage shall beauty hold a plea
Whose action is no stronger than a flower?
(65, 1–4)

This celebration of the poet's power to evade the destructive force of time and give the Friend eternal fame has been seen to bear a relationship to the Latin poet Horace's treatment of the same theme. Indeed, the paired sonnets 64 and 65, have been compared with two consecutive odes of Horace, the Censorinus ode (4.8) and the Lollius ode (4.9). In this first quatrain, 'since' compresses since there is, while 'beauty' refers to the beauty of the Friend.

28 No longer mourn for me when I am dead
Than you shall hear the surly sullen bell
Give warning to the world that I am fled
From this vile world, with vilest worms to dwell:
Nay, if you read this line, remember not
The hand that writ it; for I love you so,
That I in your sweet thoughts would be forgot,
If thinking on me then should make you woe.
(71, 1–8)

The poet-lover projects his own death and urges the beloved not to mourn him. Ostensibly the poet's self-abnegation is such that he prefers to be forgotten rather than cause the Friend pain. In reality, the presentation of the hypothetical situation is so poignant that the poem acts as a safeguard against its becoming a reality.

29 That time of year thou mayst in me behold
When yellow leaves, or none, or few, do hang
Upon those boughs which shake against the cold,
Bare ruin'd choirs, where late the sweet birds sang.
In me thou see'st the twilight of such day
As after sunset fadeth in the west;
Which by and by black night doth take away,
Death's second self, that seals up all in rest.

This thou perceiv'st, which makes thy love more strong,
To love that well which thou must leave ere long.
(73, 1–8, 13–14)
The sonnet forms a compliment to the Friend's quality of love by denigrating the poet's age and lack of beauty. His age is portrayed through analogies to the natural world: to the cycle of the seasons and the structure of the day. The fall of leaves in autumn has even been related to hair-loss in middle-aged men, and seen as corroborated by the portrait of Shakespeare that has come down to us; but it is questionable how literally and autobiographically such images should be read. 'Death's second self' is sleep, which the Renaissance – like many other cultures – saw as an image of death.

30 Why is my verse so barren of new pride,
So far from variation or quick change?...

O, know, sweet love, I always write of you,
And you and love are still my argument;
So all my best is dressing old words new,
Spending again what is already spent.
(76, 1–2, 9–12)
The poet's apology for lack of invention in his verse is turned into a declaration of his constancy and fidelity in love. The act of poetic composition becomes an analogy for the activity of loving. In both, the poet-lover exhausts his resources.

31 Was it the proud full sail of his great verse,
Bound for the prize of all too precious you,
That did my ripe thoughts in my brain inhearse,
Making their tomb the womb wherein they grew?
Was it his spirit, by spirits taught to write
Above a mortal pitch, that struck me dead?
(86, 1–6)

Shakespeare attributes his loss of poetic inspiration to the rivalry of another poet who contends for the Friend's favours. The situation tends to confirm that the beloved, the Friend, is a patron of the arts. The rival poet has never been positively identified, but opinion inclines towards George Chapman (1559–1634). Chapman is best known for his translations of Homer – the *Iliad* appeared in 1611 and the *Odyssey* in 1614–15; but, by 1598, he had published *The Shadow of Night* and *Ovid's Banquet of Sense* and completed Marlowe's unfinished *Hero and Leander*. The ambition of his projects and style match the description in line 1 and could have made Shakespeare regard him as a potential rival in the late 1590s. Chapman was also a dramatist.

32 Farewell! thou art too dear for my possessing,
And like enough thou know'st thy estimate:
The charter of thy worth gives thee releasing;
My bonds in thee are all determinate.
For how do I hold thee but by thy granting?
And for that riches where is my deserving?
The cause of this fair gift in me is wanting,
And so my patent back again is swerving.
Thyself thou gavest, thy own worth then not knowing,
Or me, to whom thou gavest it, else mistaking;
So thy great gift, upon misprision growing,
Comes home again, on better judgement making.
  Thus have I had thee, as a dream doth flatter,
  In sleep a king, but waking no such matter.
(87, 1–14)

The poet takes leave of the Friend, acknowledging that he has no right to make any claim of love upon him. The legal and commercial imagery in which this recognition is couched not only conveys its bitterness and pain but also underlines that love must of its nature be a gift and not merited. The situation may be compounded by the beloved being of higher social rank, so emphasizing the poet's sense of undeserving. 'Charter' means right or privilege and 'determinate' expired. 'Upon misprision growing' means arising from a misunderstanding.

33 Some glory in their birth, some in their skill,
Some in their wealth, some in their body's force;
Some in their garments, though new-fangled ill;
Some in their hawks and hounds, some in their horse;...

Thy love is better than high birth to me,
Richer than wealth, prouder than garments' cost,
Of more delight than hawks or horses be;

And having thee, of all men's pride I boast.
(91, 1–4, 9–12)

The poet-lover elevates the love of the Friend above all things of which men boast. The energy of the listing is harnessed when it is argued that the Friend's love subsumes the delights of all other men. 'New-fangled ill' suggests that the garments represent an outrageous and extreme fashion.

34 They that have power to hurt and will do none,
That do not do the thing they most do show,
Who, moving others, are themselves as stone,
Unmoved, cold and to temptation slow;
They rightly do inherit heaven's graces
And husband nature's riches from expense;
They are the lords and owners of their faces,
Others but stewards of their excellence....

For sweetest things turn sourest by their deeds;
Lilies that fester smell far worse than weeds.
(94, 1–8, 13–14)

The first eight lines of the sonnet offer praise, perhaps ironic, of temperance. By contrast, the remaining six deal with the corruption of virtue from within, culminating in the final line – a proverbial tag. The entire sonnet is cryptic in expression and enigmatic. Its language is full of echoes of the teaching of Christ, from the Beatitudes and the parables. 'Husband' means manage wisely, and 'expense' means loss.

35 How like a winter hath my absence been
From thee, the pleasure of the fleeting year!
What freezings have I felt, what dark days seen!
(97, 1–3)

The poet's separation from the Friend is portrayed as a winter, because the Friend himself is depicted throughout the sequence as summer, 'the pleasure of the fleeting year', by virtue of the perfection of his beauty. The analogy to winter is employed to convey the poet's emotional deprivation in the absence of his beloved.

36 To me, fair friend, you never can be old,
For as you were when first your eye I eyed,
Such seems your beauty still. Three winters cold
Have from the forests shook three summers' pride,
Three beauteous springs to yellow autumn turn'd
In process of the seasons have I seen,
Three April perfumes in three hot Junes burn'd,

Since first I saw you fresh, which yet are green.
(104, 1–8)

The sonnet celebrates the third anniversary of the poet's love for the Friend. Though the cycle of the seasons has been performed three times, the beauty of the Friend, which is identified in the sequence with summer, appears undiminished. The sestet, which follows, qualifies the picture of the octave, for it argues that time must be effecting its work on the Friend's beauty, however imperceptibly. The sonnet concludes with the warning that summer, the archetype of the Friend's beauty, was dead before the Friend was born.

37 Let not my love be call'd idolatry,
Nor my beloved as an idol show.
(105, 1–2)

Despite the opening lines, the sonnet is a eulogy of the beloved's perfection. The Petrarchan sonnet tradition, like the lyric conventions from which it sprang, borrowed extensively from the language of divine love and elevated the beloved, conventionally though not exclusively a mistress, to a quasi-divine standing. Shakespeare is playing with the convention, in appearing to reject it, before continuing to create a trinity of adjectives, 'fair, kind, and true', with which he praises the Friend.

38 When in the chronicle of wasted time
I see descriptions of the fairest wights,
And beauty making beautiful old rhyme
In praise of ladies dead and lovely knights,...

For we, which now behold these present days,
Have eyes to wonder, but lack tongues to praise.
(106, 1–4, 13–14)

England's late literary Renaissance in the 1580s and 1590s nurtured, amongst many other strands of Renaissance culture, the interest that courtly humanism had shown for the etiquette and literature of chivalry. The sonnet, like other poetic forms, was influenced by this vogue and most Elizabethan sequences contain sonnets exploiting chivalric incidents or allusions. 'Wights', meaning people, is an archaism in keeping with the cult.

39 And thou in this shalt find thy monument,
When tyrants' crests and tombs of brass are spent.
(107, 13–14)

The final couplet of the sonnet sums its argument, which is another expression of the classical theme that poetry may immortalize its subject. Like Sonnet 55, the formulation here appears to owe a debt to the treatment of the theme deriving from the epilogue to the *Third Book of Odes* by the Latin poet, Horace: *Exegi monumentum aere perennius* (I have completed a monument more enduring than bronze).

40 O, never say that I was false of heart,
Though absence seem'd my flame to qualify.
(109, 1–2)
The poet-lover argues that physical separation is no evidence of any diminution in his love. 'Qualify' means moderate. The arguments that substantiate the poet's claim are that he cannot separate himself from the beloved who, like his own soul, resides eternally within him and that he would never abandon the Friend, who constitutes his 'all'.

41 Alas, 'tis true I have gone here and there,
And made myself a motley to the view,
Gored mine own thoughts, sold cheap what is most dear,
Made old offences of affections new;
Most true it is that I have look'd on truth
Askance and strangely.
(110, 1–6)
The sonnet constitutes a confession of infidelity by the poet-lover and a request for forgiveness. The poet presents himself as a ridiculous figure, a 'motley' or jester, who has harmed himself more than the Friend. Line 4 means that new passions have taken the form of old vices. 'Truth' is loyalty or fidelity, which has been given only a sideways and distant look.

42 My nature is subdued
To what it works in, like the dyer's hand.
(111, 1–7)
The poet is asserting that the Friend chides fortune for having allotted his lover, the poet himself, a humble condition and demeaning occupation in life. Playwriting and involvement in the public theatres was not considered a really respectable, let alone intellectual or elevated, activity within Shakespeare's lifetime. The poet suggests his vulgarity is the product of his environment, just as the dyer's hand absorbs the dye. The phrase 'the dyer's hand' gave the title to the well-known critical essay by W. H. Auden of 1963.

43 Since I left you mine eye is in my mind,
And that which governs me to go about
Doth part his function and is partly blind,

Seems seeing, but effectually is out.
(113, 1–4)

The poet describes the disorientation of his senses and emotions following his separation from the Friend. Lines 5–8 of the sonnet explicate line 3, since they explain, according to the principles of Elizabethan physiology, how the eyes fail to transmit images of the external world to the inner organs of apprehension. 'Seems seeing' means appears to see. The poet's mind's eye remains filled with the beloved, despite their separation, and this blocks out all other images.

44 But reckoning Time, whose million'd accidents
Creep in 'twixt vows, and change decrees of kings,
Tan sacred beauty, blunt the sharp'st intents,
Divert strong minds to the course of altering things.
(115, 5–8)

The theme of this sonnet is the unending growth of the poet's love for the Friend. Against this is set the poet's desire to make a statement of the fullness of his love. The conflict is resolved in the image of love as a babe, since the babe signifies the completion of the process of gestation and yet promises much growth. The second quatrain quoted above is an argument for making the declaration of love, which describes the power of time to change or cut off. The 'million'd accidents' are the innumerable events. 'Tan' means destroy or obscure by darkening.

45 Let me not to the marriage of true minds
Admit impediments. Love is not love
Which alters when it alteration finds,
Or bends with the remover to remove:
O, no! it is an ever-fixed mark,
That looks on tempests and is never shaken;
It is the star to every wandering bark,
Whose worth's unknown, although his height be taken.
Love's not Time's fool, though rosy lips and cheeks
Within his bending sickle's compass come;
Love alters not with his brief hours and weeks,
But bears it out even to the edge of doom.
If this be error and upon me proved,
I never writ, nor no man ever loved.
(116, 1–14)

The sonnet posits the complete and perfect union of two human beings. The union is based upon a fidelity and constancy strong enough to withstand the forces of time and circumstance. Although the union is presented as primarily intellectual and spiritual, not sexual, the opening lines echo the marriage service of the Book of Common Prayer. The 'mark' of line 5 is a sea-mark and the 'height' on line 8 the measured altitude of the star. Love becomes the point of reference to every 'bark' or individual in the storm of life. In the image of the third quatrain, love resists the power of time, represented emblematically with his sickle, and endures to the Day of Judgement and the verge of eternity.

46 In the old age black was not counted fair,
Or if it were, it bore not beauty's name;
But now is black beauty's successive heir,
And beauty slander'd with a bastard shame.
(127, 1–4)

The first quatrain of sonnet 127 asserts that brunettes have supplanted blondes as the ideal of beauty and introduces the poet's mistress, the 'dark lady', to whom the last 28 of the Sonnets are addressed. This feature alone suggests that the collection of the Sonnets, as we have it, does not constitute a chronological or narrative order. To attempt to re-order the Sonnets, by integrating those addressed to the 'dark lady' with those addressed to the Friend, in order to produce a plausible narrative, is a dangerous and futile exercise. There has been no positive identification of the 'dark lady', though several claimants have been advanced, most recently Emilia Lanier, a member of a musical family of French origin.

47 The expense of spirit in a waste of shame
Is lust in action; and till action, lust
Is perjured, murderous, bloody, full of blame,
Savage, extreme, rude, cruel, not to trust;
Enjoy'd no sooner but despised straight;
Past reason hunted; and no sooner had,
Past reason hated, as a swallowed bait,
On purpose laid to make the taker mad:
Mad in pursuit, and in possession so;
Had, having, and in quest to have, extreme;
A bliss in proof, and proved a very woe;
Before, a joy proposed; behind, a dream.
All this the world well knows; yet none knows well
To shun the heaven that leads men to this hell.
(129, 1–14)

Sonnet 129 comprises an analysis of the stages of male sexual desire unrivalled for its bitter accuracy of detail in the love poetry of its own and all other ages. The sonnet posits three stages of lust: before, during, and after the sexual act. In the opening line, in addition to the abstract characterization of lust, 'expense' signifies ejaculation or sexual expenditure and 'spirit' semen. 'In proof' (11) means experienced or while being experienced.

48 My mistress' eyes are nothing like the sun;
Coral is far more red than her lips' red:
If snow be white, why then her breasts are dun;
If hairs be wires, black wires grow on her head.
I have seen roses damask'd, red and white,
But no such roses see I in her cheeks;
And in some perfumes is there more delight
Than in the breath that from my mistress reeks.
I love to hear her speak, yet well I know
That music hath a far more pleasing sound:
I grant I never saw a goddess go,
My mistress, when she walks, treads on the ground:
  And yet, by heaven, I think my love as rare
  As any she belied with false compare.
(130, 1–14)

While the sonnet appears to be derogatory of the mistress's physical attributes, the entire poem conforms to an anti-Petrarchan convention which had developed within Petrarchism. The conventions of Petrarchan diction are subverted, only for the entire tradition to be inverted at the end of the poem in order to attest the poet's strength of love. The colours red and white conventionally stood for passion and purity. 'Reeks' means emanates or exhales, without any pejorative connotations.

49 In nothing art thou black save in thy deeds,
And thence this slander, as I think, proceeds.
(131, 13–14)

The stereotype of female beauty in the Petrarchan convention and in Elizabethan England was the fair mistress. The 'dark lady' so contravenes the rules of beauty that the poet-lover is only able to confess his love privately and not publicly. He is in agreement with the public opinion that sees her as 'black', and therefore associated with ugliness and evil, only on account of her conduct towards him.

50 Whoever hath her wish, thou hast thy 'Will',
And 'Will' to boot, and 'Will' in overplus;
More than enough am I that vex thee still,
To thy sweet will making addition thus.
(135, 1–4)

The sonnet is based on complex and multiple punning on the word 'will'. The term covers volition, passionate or wilful feeling, and sexual desire. It is also an auxiliary and modal verb and these uses are played upon within the sonnet. There is also a pun on Shakespeare's name and perhaps on the name of the Friend and/or the woman's husband (if she was married). In addition, 'will' could signify the sexual organ of either sex. 'To boot' means in addition and 'in overplus' in excess or in surplus.

51 When my love swears that she is made of truth,
I do believe her, though I know she lies.
(138, 1–2)
The poet portrays both the 'dark lady' and himself as untruthful: she lies to him and he knowingly tolerates her lies. The portrait of the 'dark lady' is far from flattering: she is sensual, deceitful, and mendacious. 'Made of truth' means faithful as well as truthful. In 'lies', there is a pun on the sense of lies with men or sleeps around, which is developed more fully later in the sonnet.

52 Two loves I have of comfort and despair,
Which like two spirits do suggest me still:
The better angel is a man right fair,
The worser spirit a woman colour'd ill.
(144, 1–4)
The first quatrain of sonnet 144 makes explicit several of the thematic contrasts exploited throughout the sequence. The fair young man is conceived as angelic, the dark woman diabolic. The love of the Friend, probably non-sexual despite its intimacy and passion, is seen as a source of comfort; the sexual desire for the woman brings only despair.

53 Poor soul, the centre of my sinful earth,
My sinful earth these rebel pow'rs that thee array,
Why dost thou pine within and suffer dearth,
Painting thy outward walls so costly gay?
Why so large cost, having so short a lease,
Dost thou upon thy fading mansion spend?
Shall worms, inheritors of this excess,
Eat up thy charge? Is this thy body's end?
So shalt thou feed on Death, that feeds on men,
And Death once dead, there's no more dying then.
(146, 1–8, 13–14)
The sonnet constitutes a meditation upon the relationship between the body and soul and the vanity of attending to the body at the expense of the soul. The 'sinful earth' of line 1 is the body. The repetition of the same phrase at the beginning of line 2 is a misprint of the 1609 edition. Several emendations have been proposed, of which the most favoured are: thrall to, fooled by and foiled by. The sonnet appears to bear only an indirect

relation to those that deal directly with the relationship with the 'dark lady', though they also contain self-reproach and disgust of the body's demands.

54 My love is as a fever, longing still
For that which longer nurseth the disease;
Feeding on that which doth preserve the ill,
The uncertain sickly appetite to please....

Past cure I am, now reason is past care,
And frantic-mad with evermore unrest;
My thoughts and my discourse as madmen's are,
At random from the truth vainly express'd;
For I have sworn thee fair, and thought thee bright,
Who art as black as hell, as dark as night.

(147, 1–4, 9–14)

The poet's desire for the 'dark lady' is portrayed in images of disease and appetite. In the sonnet tradition, the poet-lover's analysis of his own psychology often posits a conflict between reason and desire, but Shakespeare's characterization of his condition as crazed with lust for a woman he loathes and despises steps outside the bounds of the convention. The poet-lover's analysis fuses keen misogyny with contempt and recrimination of self.

55 Love is too young to know what conscience is;
Yet who knows not conscience is born of love?...

... I do betray
My nobler part to my gross body's treason;
My soul doth tell my body that he may
Triumph in love; flesh stays no farther reason,
But rising at thy name doth point out thee
As his triumphant prize. Proud of this pride,
He is contented thy poor drudge to be,
To stand in thy affairs, fall by thy side.

(151, 1–2, 5–12)

The sonnet depicts the conflict within the poet-lover between reason and desire. The betrayal of man's nobler part, his soul and reason, by the flesh is expressed according to the terms of Renaissance humanism. However, Shakespeare steps outside the conventions within which Petrarchism treated this topic by offering such an explicit analysis of the morality of the erect penis. 'Flesh', 'rising', 'point', 'stand', and 'fall' all carry sexual meanings.

Venus and Adonis

1 But if the first heir of my invention prove deformed, I shall be sorry it had so noble a god-father.
(Dedication, 5–6)
Shakespeare dedicated *Venus and Adonis* to Henry Wriothesley, Earl of Southampton. The work was published in 1593, when the Earl was only twenty years old, but Southampton was already a wealthy patron of the arts and destined to be one of the leading noblemen of the Elizabethan age. The work won Shakespeare immediate literary recognition.

2 Hunting he lov'd, but love he laugh'd to scorn.
(4)
The beautiful youth, Adonis, is dedicated to chastity and to hunting. His refusal to recognize the power of the goddess, Venus, and his rejection of her enticements cause her prophecy of his destruction by the boar while hunting. The myth is closely akin to the Hippolytus myth.

3 I will enchant thine ear,
Or, like a fairy, trip upon the green,
Or, like a nymph, with long dishevelled hair,
Dance on the sands, and yet no footing seen.
Love is a spirit all compact of fire,
Not gross to sink, but light, and will aspire.
(145–50)
Venus, who burns with desire for the beautiful youth, Adonis, has encountered him when he is out hunting and is importuning him to pass his time with her in amorous delights. The entertainments listed in the stanza above are the more innocent ones she proffers. The passion of love is associated with the element of fire. There is a pun on 'light', which also means wanton.

4 For looks kill love, and love by looks reviveth.
(464)
Shakespeare's narrative of *Venus and Adonis* is cast in the Ovidian style which was so popular in late Elizabethan England. Ovid (Publius Ovidius Naso, 43 BC–AD 17) was a poet of Augustan Rome. His poems, *Metamorphoses* and *The Art of Love* in particular, had a strong influence on the presentation of erotic themes in the Renaissance. In Elizabethan England, the style also shows a predilection for pithy maxims which encapsulate the action, psychology, or morality of the narrative.

5 Love surfeits not: Lust like a glutton dies.
Love is all truth: Lust full of forged lies.
(803–4)
Venus succeeds in enticing Adonis into some amatory foreplay, especially after Adonis's stallion breaks loose in hot pursuit of a jennet, leaving his master stranded in Venus's embraces. Eventually, however, Adonis extricates himself from the goddess's clutches in order to deliver her a lecture on the difference between love, in whose name Venus speaks, and lust which, according to Adonis, is her practice.

6 Sorrow on love hereafter shall attend.
(1136)
Adonis has been fatally gored while hunting the wild boar and has died of his wounds. The goddess, Venus, whose amatory advances Adonis had rejected and who had prophesied his death in this manner, has found the body of the lovely youth and lamented his death and her impetuous behaviour. She here prophesies that henceforth sorrow will be a concomitant of love.

The Rape of Lucrece

1 What I have done is yours; what I have to do is yours; being part in all I have, devoted yours.
(Dedication)
Shakespeare dedicated *The Rape of Lucrece* (1594) to Henry Wriothesley, Earl of Southampton, to whom he had dedicated *Venus and Adonis* the previous year. The young Earl, who came of age in 1594, was a wealthy patron of the arts and one of the leading noblemen of the Elizabethan age.

2 Birds never limed no secret bushes fear.
(88)
This proverbial saying is used to describe the unsuspecting virtue of Lucrece when she receives Tarquin at Collatium. He has left the siege of Ardea to practise his rape upon Lucrece. Bird-lime was a glutinous substance placed upon twigs in order to catch birds; 'secret bushes' are secluded bushes. In the First Quarto, this line was subject to gnomic pointing, the use of inverted commas at the beginning of a line particularly worthy of note as a maxim. *The Rape of Lucrece* is full of such maxims.

3 Who buys a minute's mirth to wail a week?
Or sells eternity to get a toy?

For one sweet grape who will the vine destroy?
(213–15)
Tarquin is debating with himself the moral cost to his honour of his intended rape of Lucrece. Although he rehearses many sound moral arguments, his lust carries the day. A 'toy' is a trifle.

4 All orators are dumb when beauty pleadeth.
(268)
The beauty of Lucrece is her undoing, for it was the cause of Tarquin's original incitement to rape, and it continues to prove a stronger argument than the moral precepts he rehearses.

5 Time's glory is to calm contending kings,
To unmask falsehood and bring truth to light.
(939–40)
These are the opening lines of a long passage on time, which emphasizes time's role as healer and revealer of truth as well as destroyer. The theme of time is appropriate to the Lucrece story, since the narrative unmasks the falsehood of Tarquin, vindicates the heroine's honour, and transforms disgrace into heroism.

6 And now this pale swan in her watery nest
Begins the sad dirge of her certain ending.
(1611–12)
Shakespeare's description of Lucrece, as she prepares to tell her husband and her kinsmen of her sad fate, likens her to the fabled swan that is said to sing immediately prior to death. Lucrece is resolved upon, and effects, suicide as the only remedy for her dishonour.

The Phoenix and the Turtle

1 Love and constancy is dead;
Phoenix and the turtle fled
In a mutual flame from hence.
(22–4)
The phoenix was a mythical bird of Arabia, said to arise from the ashes of its own conflagration, representing immortality, while the turtle-dove was a symbol of constancy. The poem celebrates a union in love so complete that it is consumed by its own fire. Such perfection seems unable to exist in this world. This enigmatic and metaphysical poem was published in a miscellany, *Loves Martyr*, in 1601.

The Passionate Pilgrim

1 Crabbed age and youth cannot live together:
Youth is full of pleasance, age is full of care;
. . .
Youth is wild, and age is tame.
Age, I do abhor thee; youth, I do adore thee.
(12, 1–2, 8–9)

The Passionate Pilgrim was an anthology of sonnets and lyrics published in 1599. This lyric, cast in a pastoral vein, presents the conventional opposition of age to youth.

2 Live with me, and be my love,
And we will all the pleasures prove
That hills and valleys, dales and fields,
And all the craggy mountains yields.
(19, 1–4)

The Passionate Pilgrim was an anthology of sonnets and lyrics published in 1599. This lyric offers a close version of Marlowe's famous pastoral lyric, *The Passionate Shepherd to his Love*, together with a quatrain of 'Love's Answer'. Sir Walter Ralegh also published a well-known answer to Marlowe's lyric in 1600.

Shakespeare's Will and Epitaph

THE EPITAPH
Good friend, for Jesus' sake forbear,
To dig the dust enclosed here!
Blest be the man that spares these stones
And curst be he that moves my bones.

These lines, which may be by Shakespeare, appear on his grave in the parish church at Stratford upon Avon. As the Gravediggers' scene in *Hamlet* demonstrates, it was common for graves to be reopened and reused but these lines and Shakespeare's reputation have, thus far, safeguarded his tomb.

THE WILL
Item, I give unto my wife my second best bed.

This is Shakespeare's only reference to his wife in his will. Since, however, it is possible that Shakespeare had provided for her already, and since she was entitled in law to one third of his estate, this apparent omission may well not be as significant as some people have believed it to be. Those who believe that Shakespeare and Anne were estranged view the gift of the second best bed as some kind of insult; others believe that the best bed was more likely to have been kept for visitors and that the second best bed was the marriage bed. The mere fact that there is no basis for speculation in either direction seems unlikely to stop an argument which has been continuing since the late eighteenth century.

Index

The key words–usually nouns–in each quotation form the headings of the index, where they are shown in their immediate context. Thus 'We are such stuff/As dreams are made on' appears in the index under both *Stuff* and *Dreams*. A swung dash (~) is used to represent the key word in its context, so that the entry at *Dreams* shows

such stuff As ~ are made on 493.*43*

Each index entry gives a reference to the page on which the quotation appears, and (in italic type) to the individual number of that quotation. Plurals of nouns and inflections of verbs are listed separately from their base form, but possessive forms (e.g. man's) are listed at the base form.

Overnight Use